INSIDE
CENTRAL
ASIA

Also by Dilip Hiro

NON-FICTION

Blood of the Earth: The Battle for the World's Vanishing Oil Resources (2007)

The Timeline History of India (2006)

The Iranian Labyrinth: Journeys through Theocratic Iran and Its Furies (2005)

Secrets and Lies: Operation "Iraqi Freedom" and After (2004)

The Essential Middle East: A Comprehensive Guide (2003)

Iraq: In the Eye of the Storm (2003)

War Without End: The Rise of Islamist Terrorism and Global Response (2002)

The Rough Guide History of India (2002)

Neighbors, Not Friends: Iraq and Iran after the Gulf Wars (2001)

Sharing the Promised Land: A Tale of Israelis and Palestinians (1998)

Dictionary of the Middle East (1996)

The Middle East (1996)

Between Marx and Muhammad: The Changing Face of Central Asia (1995)

Lebanon, Fire and Embers: A History of the Lebanese Civil War (1993)

Desert Shield to Desert Storm: The Second Gulf War (1992)

Black British, White British: A History of Race Relations in Britain (1991)

The Longest War: The Iran-Iraq Military Conflict (1991)

Holy Wars: The Rise of Islamic Fundamentalism (1989)

Iran: The Revolution Within (1988)

Iran under the Ayatollahs (1985)

Inside the Middle East (1982)

Inside India Today (1977)

The Untouchables of India (1975)

Black British, White British (1973)

The Indian Family in Britain (1969)

FICTION

Three Plays (1985)

Interior, Exchange, Exterior (Poems, 1980)

Apply, Apply, No Reply & A Clean Break (Two Plays, 1978)

To Anchor a Cloud (Play, 1972)

A Triangular View (Novel, 1969)

INSIDE CENTRAL ASIA

A Political and Cultural History of
Uzbekistan, Turkmenistan, Kazakhstan,
Kyrgyzstan, Tajikistan, Turkey, and Iran

DILIP HIRO

OVERLOOK DUCKWORTH
NEW YORK • LONDON

First published in hardcover in 2009 by
Overlook Duckworth, Peter Mayer Publishers, Inc.
New York & London

NEW YORK:
141 Wooster Street
New York, NY 10012
www.overlookpress.com

LONDON:
90-93 Cowcross Street
London EC1M 6BF
inquiries@duckworth-publishers.co.uk
www.ducknet.co.uk

Cataloging-in-Publication Data is available from the Library of Congress

Book design and type formatting by Bernard Schleifer
Printed in the United States of America
FIRST EDITION
1 3 5 7 9 8 6 4 2
ISBN 978-1-59020-221-0 US
ISBN 978-0-7156-3877-4 UK

CONTENTS

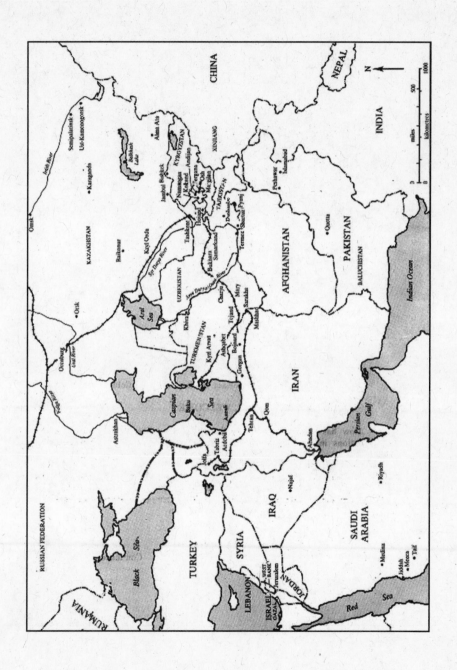

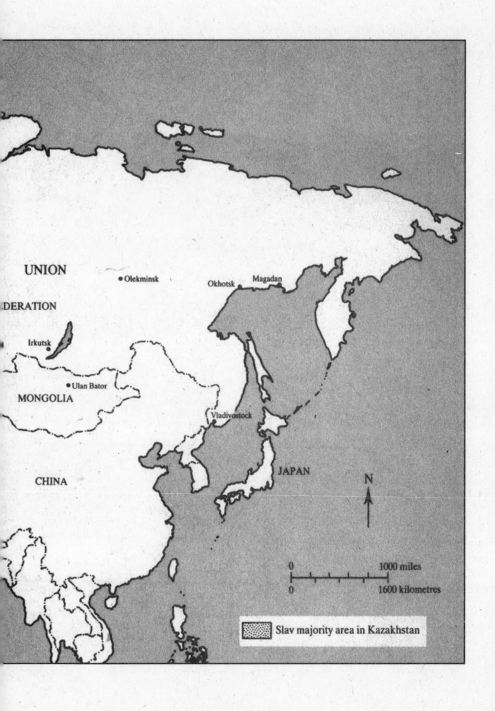

UNION

DERATION

Irkutsk

MONGOLIA

Ulan Bator

CHINA

Olekminsk

Okhotsk   Magadan

Vladivostock

JAPAN

N

0   1000 miles
0   1600 kilometres

Slav majority area in Kazakhstan

PREFACE

DURING THE SOVIET ERA AND ITS IMMEDIATE AFTERMATH, THE CENTRAL Asian region was officially known as "Middle Asia and Kazakhstan." In this book, however, the term "Central Asia" includes Kazakhstan. The names of the republics have undergone changes since the Bolshevik revolution of 1917, the latest version during the Soviet period being Uzbek Soviet Socialist Republic, Kazakh Soviet Socialist Republic, and so on. But once again, to simplify matters, I have used Kazakhstan, Turkmenistan, Uzbekistan, Tajikistan, and Kyrgyzstan (even though its 1993 constitution names it Kyrgyz Republic).

In the course of providing the political, economic, and military history of the five Central Asian republics, I have at the appropriate points sketched a cultural profile of the peoples living in these countries. I have described their evolution from the era of nomadic cattle-rearing to the modern era of launching spacecraft, thus highlighting what has changed in their day-to-day existence and what has remained largely unchanged at the core.

Every writer knows that to make sense of contemporary events one has to delve into the past. This is all the more so in the case of the Central Asian republics. They were delineated chiefly during the 1920s along ethnic lines, but containing some enclaves of those speaking a minority language, as a result of the policies devised mainly by Joseph V. Stalin (1878–1953). That is why this book's Introduction covers the period up to his death.

The breakup of the Soviet Union in 1991 signaled a new phase in the history of each of the Central Asian republics. Given the strategic location of Central Asia, its predominantly Muslim population, and its hydrocarbon and other valuable resources, the emergence of five independent states in 1991 opened up a fresh chapter in international relations—with the United States, China, Turkey, and Iran trying to fill the vacuum left by the collapse of Russia's nearly 150-year-old dominance. By the end of the first decade of the twenty-first century—following several ups and downs in the fortunes of the competing foreign powers—Russia had re-emerged as the Big Brother of Central Asians. As such, Russia's role is part of the main narrative of each of the five "–istans."

Among the region's other neighbors, I have chosen only two to discuss at length: Turkey and Iran. Historically, the Eurasian landmass was ruled first by the Persian tribes and then by the Turkic tribes. The fact that "istan" (a Persian marker for "place" or "land") appears as a suffix in the names of all Central Asian republics illustrates the importance of the Persian language and influence in the Eurasian landmass. Reflecting the distant past, in the immediate aftermath of the Soviet collapse, a debate raged whether the freshly independent Muslim-majority Central Asian states would follow the model of secular, pro-Western Turkey or the Islamic Republic of Iran.

I begin the main text with a history of Turkey. While concentrating on the dominant religious and secular aspects of its recent history, I briefly describe the country's religious and ethnic minorities as well as its outstanding architectural and literary heritage.

Due to the cultural and linguistic affinity between Turkey and Uzbekistan, my next chapter discusses Uzbekistan, focusing on the tension between its staunchly secular regime and Islamist forces. It is the most populous, complex, and strategic state in the region, with common borders with all the remaining Central Asian republics. Chapter 3 covers Turkmenistan to the southwest of Uzbekistan. While in recent times Turkmenistan has become intimately associated with its first president, Saparmurat Niyazov, a wildly eccentric dictator, its hydrocarbon reserves make it of key interest in the energy-hungry world of today.

Such is also the case with Kazakhstan, a colossal state, the subject of Chapter 4. It began its independent existence with almost as many Slav citizens, chiefly ethnic Russians, as Kazakh—a dodgy prospect for nation-building. Its leader, Nursultan Nazarbayev, helped by the slow exodus of Slavs and a high birthrate among Kazakhs, has managed the task adroitly by elevating the twelfth-century poet, Khwaja Ahmad Yasawi, to the status of the Father of the Nation. The construction of the new capital of Astana and a growing prosperity stemming from rising oil revenue have given Kazakh citizens confidence in their future that other Central Asians envy.

The early expectations that the tiny state of Kyrgyzstan would evolve into a properly democratic entity failed to materialize. On the other hand, Kyrgyzes could claim that they overthrew President Askar Akayev peacefully in 2005. Yet that event has failed to secure Western-style democracy in the republic. Paradoxically, political ferment in the country has persisted, along with the custom of "bride-stealing," a euphemism for abducting nubile women, dating back to the practice among rival tribes during the nomadic era.

Alone among the Central Asian republics, Tajikistan, the subject of Chapter 6, is culturally and historically close to Iran. Soon after its independence, it got mired in a civil war that lasted five years and devastated the country. The main factor that led to its end was the rise of the Taliban in the neighboring Afghanistan in 1996, and the danger it posed to Tajikistan and other Central Asian states. Since then the Islamist forces in Tajikistan have been in retreat while the secular regime of President Imamali Rahmanov has resorted to emphasizing the pre-Islamic origins of Tajiks dating back to Zoroaster, a prophet in antiquity.

As it is, the small Zoroastrian community is the longest-living group in contemporary Iran. After summarizing a history of Iran, the subject of Chapter 7, my narrative focuses on Islamization of the state and society after the 1979 revolution, and the geopolitics of its foreign policy as applied to Central Asia and Turkey. It also covers the changing roles of women, religious minorities, and the secular upper-middle and affluent classes in theocratic Iran. The book ends with a set of conclusions drawn heavily from the main text and, where necessary, from my earlier work, *Between Marx and Muhammad: The Changing Face of Central Asia*, published in 1994.

In the book, the term "Islamic" applies to Islam as a whole, whereas "Islamist" applies only to political Islam. Thus "Islamist terrorism" means terrorism perpetrated by those Muslims who stress Islam as a political ideology.

A foreign word, written in italics at the first mention, later appears in Roman.

The parenthetical dates appearing after the first mention of a monarch specify when he/she reigned. However, corresponding figures for non-hereditary figures indicate their years of birth and death.

To assist the English-speaking reader in grappling with a plethora of exotic names of people, places, and ethnic groups, it is necessary to set out some ground rules.

First, Turks and Turkic peoples. They can be broadly categorized as Western Turks and Eastern (or Central Asian) Turks. The term "Western Turks" applies to Turks of Turkey as well as Azeris and (linguistically, not geographically) Turkmens; "Central Asian Turks" applies to those inhabiting the Turkistan region under the Tsars. In between come Turko-Tatars or Tatars, the inhabitants of the Volga region in the Urals and parts of the Crimea.

"Turkish" means the language of the Turks of Turkey; and the term "Turkic" applies to a sub-family of Ural-Altaic languages as well as the peoples speaking these languages. In modern Turkish, written in the Roman alphabet, "c" corresponds to "j," "ç" to "ch," and "ş" to "sh." Wherever necessary, I provide the English pronunciation of a Turkish name in parenthesis the first time it appears: e.g. Celal (Jelal).

Second, the Russian language and Russification of Muslim names. Muslim names are almost always rooted in Arabic, the language of the Quran, or Persian, the language of many commentaries on it. Russian is written in the Cyrillic alphabet, which lacks "h," "j," "w," "x," etc.—their equivalents in Latin being respectively "kh" or "g," "dzh," "v," "ks," etc. Also, often the vowels "a" and "o," and "i" and "y" are interchangeable. So it is common to write Berdi or Berdy.

As a result, "Rahman" is Russified as "Rakhmon," "Tajikistan" as "Tadzhikistan," and "Heidar" as "Geidar/Kheydar." Sometimes the troublesome "h" disappears altogether, with "Mohammed" reduced to "Mamed," or even "Mama." Then there is the Russian custom of identifying a surname of a male with the suffix "ev," "yev," or "ov," which means "of." Russified female surnames end with "eva," "yeva," or "ova," meaning "of." So, "Kamalov" means "of Kamal" (male), and Kamalova means "of Kamal" (female). The metamorphosis of the original "Jehangir Muhammad" into "Dzhekhangir Mamedov" incorporates the above elements of Russification. To ease the non-Russian readers into the world of Russified names of Muslim people and places, wherever necessary I have provided the original Muslim name in parenthesis following the current Russified version. Thus, Yusupov (originally, Yusuf).

Since many of the personal names in the text are long and exotic, it should help to know the meanings of the most frequent suffixes: "al Din/ uddin/ iddin"(Arabic; "of faith"); "oglu" (Turkish; "son of"); "vich" (Russian; "son of"); "zade/zadeh"(Persian; "son of"). Also the following suffixes are used in the Turkic world to denote a person of high social status: "bai/bayev," "bay/bey," "manab/manap." The following Arabic, Persian, or Turkish words signify religious or secular titles: "ayatollah," "emir," "haji/hajji," "imam," "kazi," "mufti," "sayyid," "shah," "shaikh," "shaikh-al-Islam," and "sultan."

There is no standard way of transliterating Arabic and Persian names. In each case I have chosen one of most widely used spellings in the English-speaking world, and stuck to it, except when the spelling of another author is different from mine. There I have simply reproduced the published spelling in quoted material. While looking up the index, particular difficulty arises when different spellings of a proper noun or an object begin with a different letter, as in Koran/Quran. I have solved this problem by using one spelling in the text but including others as well in the index.

Some of the place names were changed following the Bolshevik revolution, and then again after the breakup of the Soviet Union. Wherever possible, at the first mention of a place name I provide the old version in brackets, or vice versa: thus, Leninabad (Khojand), Alma Ata (Verny), Volgograd (Stalingrad).

Finally, a key to understanding racial differences between various ethnic groups. The best way is to start with the "primary races" of the region—Mongols, Europeans, and Iranians—and then graduate to major combinations, or "secondary races": Mongols and Europeans yielding Turks/Turko-Tatars; and Mongols and Iranians producing Tajiks (meaning "crown-head" in Persian). Next come the most frequent combinations of primary and secondary races: Turks and Mongols resulting in Kazakhs/Kyrgyzes (meaning "wanderer"/ "forty tribes" in a Turkic language); and Turks and Iranians in Uzbeks (meaning "real man" in a Turkic language), the largest ethnic group in the region. In reality there are of course several more hybrids. But this fairly simplified formula should help the readers conjure up a mental image of a particular ethnic group.

During the Soviet era there were three centers of power at the republican and federal levels: the Central Committee of the Communist Party (headed by the first secretary); the Presidium of the Supreme Soviet (led by the chairman, the nominal head of the republic/Union), which dealt with legislation in between the infrequent and brief sessions of the Supreme Soviet; and the Council of Ministers, called People's Commissars during the first thirty years of the Bolshevik Revolution (led by the chairman, the head of the government). Changes in the Union constitution in early 1990 created the new office of the executive president, who became the head of the Union, superseding the chairman of the Presidium of the Supreme Soviet. This job went to Mikhail Gorbachev (1931-) in March 1990. Later, the constituent republics followed the same path.

The symbol used for Soviet/Russian rubles is R.

INTRODUCTION

I N TODAY'S WELL-DELINEATED WORLD, CENTRAL ASIA IS THE LAND MASS east of the Caspian Sea, framed by the frontiers of Iran and Afghanistan in the south, the Russian Siberia in the north, and the Xinjiang province of China to the east.

It was not always so. Yet the area straddling Asia and Europe—now called Eurasia or Central Asia—is so vast that only those warriors who captured it won a place in history as the preeminent empire-builders. Such was the case with Genghis Khan (aka Chingiz Khan).

Born to a Mongol couple of the Tengri Shaman cult, in 1162, he was named Temujin. He grew up to be a sturdy man of medium height, haughty, slit-eyed, with a scraggy, drooping beard and mustache—and a military genius of exceptional ability. At the age of forty-four, he displaced Ong Khan as the leader of the Mongol tribes and was crowned the Genghis Khan, or King of the Universe (in Persian). Though he soon extended his Great Khanate by acquiring Tibet and the Tarim Basin, it was only after he had marched westward and conquered Central Asia that he could rightfully call himself Genghis Khan. This immense region formed a major part of his 4.86-million-square-mile empire, a world record.

Another Mongol warrior entered history books as ruler of the world's second largest empire. This conqueror, who also prevailed by acquiring the vast and strategic expanse of Central Asia, was Timur Beg, better known as Tamerlane (1336–1405). Six centuries later, eager to establish a long-standing Uzbek identity, the post-Communist regime in Uzbekistan would zealously declare him the progenitor of the Uzbek nation, making his statues as ubiquitous as Lenin's had been during the Soviet era.

The third place in the league table of gigantic empires went to Alexander of Macedonia. During 329–327 BC, he seized present-day Uzbekistan,

Tajikistan, and Afghanistan from the Persians. He founded the modern Tajik town of Khojand, the site of his marriage to Roxanna, a local princess.

During the early Christian centuries, Central Asia became the stomping ground of the competing Huns, Persian Sassanians, Turks, and Chinese, whose emperors sought the unrivalled horses that the Fergana Valley had fostered.

Around 650 AD, a new force joined the Great Game for possession of the region. It originated in Arabia, the land of the freshly emergent Islam. Over the next century, the Arab armies conquered Samarkand and Bukhara, and turned them into bastions of Islam. This was particularly true of Bukhara—called Bukhara Sharif, Noble Bukhara—which became a leading center of Islamic learning. (Earlier, it had been a major center of Zoroastrian learning.) Its scholars competed with their counterparts from Baghdad and Shiraz in their contributions to astronomy, physics, chemistry, philosophy, literature, and music.

By inflicting a crushing defeat on the Chinese in 751 AD, the Arabs finally made Central Asia secure for Islam. The lasting legacy that the Chinese left behind was the silkworm agriculture in the Fergana Valley, which complemented the longer-established cotton crops.

In that environment arose Muslim principalities centered around oasis towns. Out of this grew the empire of the Persian Samanis, administered by the army and civil service, in the last quarter of the tenth century. It lasted until 1000 AD. Bukhara, its capital, became the preeminent city of the region. According to a popular adage, "The Sun does not shine on Bukhara, it is Bukhara that shines on the Sun." It thrived as a vibrant hub of culture, learning, and commerce along the famed Silk Road, the primary trade route between China, Central Asia, and Europe dating back to 100 BC. During the Samani reign, the Silk Road, the highway trunk nourished by a network of feeder roads, was much improved and made safe. It became the artery for the dissemination of the Persian culture and language, a 2,000-year-old written vernacular.

The Persian epic poet Abul Qasim Mansour, aka Firdausi, (circa 940–1020), a landowner who graced the Samani court, left a mark on the Persian language and culture that survives to this day. Among the other famous sons of Bukhara was the physician and philosopher Abu Ali ibn Sina, popularly known as Avicenna (980–1037). His medical encyclopedia, Qanun (Canon), translated into Latin, became a textbook for medical students in Europe.[1]

The Samani Empire gave way to the Turkic Ghaznavi and Qarakhani tribes, yet the rivalry between the Persians and the Turks would continue for half a millennium, and would revive briefly in the late twentieth century. The post-Soviet regime in Tajikistan, drawing on its heritage, named its currency "somani."

The Ghaznavis and Qarakhanis in turn were vanquished by fellow Turks called Seljuks. Having subjugated Central Asia and Turkey, the latest victors extended their rule southward, to Baghdad. Their writ ran all the way from the Chinese border to Iraq, with their empire including Central Asia, Persia, and some Arab lands. The transit fees they charged for the use of the Silk Road provided them with steady revenue and enabled them to maintain a large standing army.

Over time, the Seljuks became power-drunk and overconfident, which brought them into conflict with the Mongol tribes led by Genghis Khan. They aroused his wrath in 1218 when they executed his emissary and decapitated 450 tradesmen for continuing to trade with the Mongols. Within two years, Genghis Khan would march into Bukhara and avenge the killing of his envoy with a massacre of 30,000 people.

He extended his empire as far westward as Russia and part of Eastern Europe. Aware of the commercial value of the Silk Road, he turned it into a secure highway, built caravansaries, and introduced the world's first postal service.

Following his demise in 1227, Central Asia became the realm of his second son, Chaghatai Khan. During the subsequent generations, the region fractured into Transoxiana ("Land beyond the Oxus River") in the west and Turkistan ("Land of Turks") in the east. To the Chinese, all the nomadic tribes who threatened their empire were Turk or Turkic.

Over decades, rivalry arose between Turkistan and Transoxiana. Tension also developed between nomadic and sedentary populations, with nomads continuing their traditional pagan practices and settlers embracing Islam. In the armed confrontation that ensued, the sturdy, nomadic riders of the saddle gained the upper hand.

In Transoxiana, Emir Qaza Khan toppled the traditional Chaghatai ruler and ascended the throne in 1347. A decade later, he was assassinated by the Turkistani ruler's agents as a prelude to the latter's invasion of Transoxiana—starting with the Qashka River (aka Qashka Darya) valley, the home of the Barlas tribe.

Instead of fighting the invaders, the Barlas Turks' chief, Tamerlane, offered his loyalty to the Turkistani khan. By so doing, the twenty-four-year-old Tamerlane, noted for his malevolent eyes and knotted cheeks, con-

solidated his leadership of the Barlas tribe. He went on to capture
Samarkand in 1369, and gained the imperial Chaghatai crown. He expanded his empire beyond Central Asia into northern India, Persia, Arabia, and
segments of Russia. Populated by 150,000 people, his capital, Samarkand,
ranked among the largest cities of the time. He transformed it into an architectural wonder. A staunch Turk, he replaced Persian with Chaghatai
Turkish as the court language. By the time Tamerlane died in 1405, Turks
had been governing Central Asia for four centuries. Their stamp gave the
region a Turkic personality, which was at odds with the preceding Persian
domination and culture.

Many historians describe Tamerlane's domain as the last nomadic empire.
Not true. That distinction goes to a descendant of Genghis Khan's grandson,
Uzbek Khan, called Muhammad Shaibani Khan, the fourteenth-century
leader of the Mongol Golden Horde. Based initially in the region north of
the Aral Sea, he invaded Transoxiana in 1500. The following year, he
defeated Zahir Uddin Muhammad Babur, a descendant of Tamerlane, and
expelled him from Samarkand. He patronized Chaghatai Turkish, and it
was during his reign that poet Mir Alisher Navai (1441–1501) produced
the first Turkic script. Shaibani Khan's ascendancy, however, proved short-
lived. He was killed in 1510 during his battle with Persian Shah Ismail
Safavi near Merv (aka Mari, in modern Turkmenistan). This fateful event
highlighted the continuing Persian power and influence in Central Asia.

With the growing popularity of the recently opened sea routes from
Europe to Asia during the sixteenth century, the importance of the Silk
Road fell, and with it the need for establishing vast empires to assure its
safety. The Shaibani Empire split into fractious principalities. Over the next
two centuries, out of these squabbling entities emerged the khanates of
Khiva and Kokand, and the emirate of Bukhara, ruled respectively by the
Kungrad, Ming, and Manigit dynasties. The smallness and weakness of
these lands contrasted starkly with the immense, expanding empire of the
Russian Tsars. In their eastward march, the Russians had, by 1650, captured Siberia and arrived at the shores of the Pacific. Then they turned their
attention southward.

THE TSARIST EXPANSION

During the eighteenth and nineteenth centuries, the Tsars annexed
Central Asia in two stages: the capture of the Kazakh steppes from 1715 to
1854, and the conquest of the rest of the region from 1865 to 1881.

The Tsarist expansion in the Trans-Volga region in the early eighteenth century set the scene for Russian control over the Asian steppes. The steppes were used for grazing by Kazakhs (Kazak in Turkish means "free man" or "wanderer"), the largest of the nomadic cattle breeders. They were divided into three major groups, or Hordes, which were often at loggerheads with one another. The Small Horde was based between the Caspian Sea and the Aral Sea, the Middle Horde in the central Hungry Steppe, and the Great Horde in the Semirechie region stretching towards the Chinese border. Through trade and diplomacy, the Russians accentuated differences between the Hordes and weakened them, thus making them more vulnerable to attacks by the marauding Uzbeks.

Peter the Great (1682–1725) invaded the Kazakh steppe in 1715 and started constructing forts, the first at Omsk, to serve as garrisons. The Hordes sought and secured agreements with the Tsar—the Small Horde signed a treaty in 1731, followed by the Middle Horde a year later, and the Great Horde in 1742. However, the Russian-Kazakh relationship proved uneasy and led to periodic uprisings by Kazakhs, which invariably failed. Gradually tightening their grip over Kazakh land, Tsars Alexander I (1801–25) and Nicholas I (1825–55) deposed Kazakh rulers, starting with the khan of the Middle Horde in 1822 and ending with that of the Great Horde in 1848.

The vast open spaces of the Kazakh steppes appealed to many city-dwelling Russian intellectuals. Among them was Fyodor Dostoevsky. Journeying to the region in 1854, he announced his arrival at the Kazakh steppe with an enthusiasm rivaling that of a Christian sighting the New Jerusalem, marveling at the "open steppe . . . pure steppe!" Three years later, he found himself posted at Semipalatinsk (now Semey), twenty miles from the Siberian border, as a military officer. He lived there in a wooden house for the next five years.

In his classic novel, *Crime and Punishment*, Dostoevsky would exile the anti-hero, Rodion Romanovich Raskolnikov, to Semipalatinsk. "From the steep bank a wide stretch of the countryside opened up before Raskolnikov . . . There in the vast steppe, flooded with sunlight, he could see the black tents of the nomads, which appeared just like dots in the distance. There was freedom, where other people were living, people who were not a bit like the people he knew. There, time itself seemed to stand still as though the age of Abraham and his flocks had not passed."[2]

These "alien" people were the Kazakh and Kyrgyz nomads who herded sheep and cattle, moved from place to place on horseback, and kept cows for milk and other dairy products. Their temporary abode was a specially designed tent, or yurt, called *iuw* in the Kazakh language, which in Turkish becomes *ev*, meaning "house" or "home."[3] Over centuries, nomads had steadily improved the yurt to the point where it rivaled a brick house in protecting the occupiers from extreme weather conditions—from blazing heat to bitter cold, rain, snow, and gusty winds.

A yurt consisted of a cone sitting atop a circular wall, about six feet high, with a diameter of ten to twenty feet. Its felt cover was fastened to the latticed wooden framework of stripped willow saplings with leather stripes. The outside was covered with mats of cheegrass stalk, which protected the dwelling from wind and dust while allowing it to be aired. The structure was crowned with a tunduk, a wooden circle of wood with holes, which was held in place by one end of a bent pole while its other end fitted a hole in the upper part of the circular wall. The tunduk let the smoke out while allowing the daylight in. The moveable cover was opened or closed with the aid of lassos. The door frame, made of strong wood, was covered with felt or an embroidered curtain.

A yurt could be erected or dismantled in a few hours. The task was often performed by women, unveiled, who also worked alongside their men herding cattle. The interior walls of the yurt were insulated and decorated with a variety of ornamented items made of reeds, felt, and multicolored tassels and patterned braid, as well as colorful carpets—all made by the women of the family. The felt carpets and strips on the floor were covered with narrow quilts, also woven by the female members of the household. The quality and number of carpets reflected the economic and social standing of the occupier.

Over time, the right-hand side of the yurt became the quarter of the males of the family—a storage for their clothes, boots, and headgear. Men's dress consisted of an undershirt and pants, which in summer served as work clothes. Over the shirt, they wore long, quilted knee-length jackets with long sleeves, narrow at the waist but widening toward the bottom. Over the jacket they wore a belted robe with long sleeves and an open stand-up collar. In winter they wore jackets sown from the skins of sheep, lamb, ferret, or fox. The outer pants, made of animal skins, were embellished with ornamental embroidery. The high-heeled boots of tough animal skins were ideal for riding. A pointed fur cap with earflaps of lamb's wool and a felt base covered by heavy cloth completed the traditional male costume.

Kazakh and Kyrgyz women dressed almost like men. They wore a shirt and trousers as undergarments. Sometimes, however, the shirt was long and tunic-shaped and served as a dress. Fashioned out of cotton fabric, the shirt-dress was white, dark, or bright and variegated. Over the dress women wore sleeveless tunics extending down to the knees, with an open collar and a clasp at the belt. When venturing out of their yurts, women wore robes in summer and sheepskin overcoats in winter.

In the yurt, food was kept behind a screen. The minor pantry often consisted of a variety of cheeses and yogurts made from the milks of cows, mares, sheep, and camels, singly or jointly. Their smells, colors, and density varied wildly, from liquid yogurt to cheese as hard as a walnut shell. Some had medicinal applications, such as acting as laxatives. Besides yogurt, the most popular dairy product was *kumiss*, fermented mare's milk, mildly alcoholic with a sparkling taste. Kumiss was the first thing that a nomad offered his guest. Even today, kumiss flows freely at weddings in the countryside of Kazakhstan and Kyrgyzstan as well as elsewhere in the region.

The stove at the center of the yurt provided heat for cooking and warmth for its occupants. The horse harness was left near the door. The space farthest from the door was considered the most precious, where a row of trunks was covered with rarely used patterned carpets. It was also the spot reserved for the guest. This custom of seating guests farthest from the entrance to the room continues among urban Kazakhs and Kyrgyzes living in apartments and houses today.

The nomads' hospitality was legendary. They would not let a visitor leave the yurt unless he or she had eaten some flat bread, the centerpiece of their meal—another custom that continues among settled Kazakhs and Kyrgyzes as well as other Central Asians. (It is worth noting that those hawking bread in the urban neighborhoods always carry breadbaskets on their heads, and never on their backs or shoulders.)

Contemporary Kazakh cuisine is rooted in nomadic tradition overlaid with an Arab influence. Horse flesh and mutton are consumed daily. Rice, vegetables, and kebabs are cooked and seasoned in a Middle Eastern style. Yogurt is an essential part of a meal.

To honor a visiting guest, it is traditional to provide a minor feast, starting with such appetizers as smoked or boiled meat, pasta stuffed with carrots or pumpkin, and flat cakes. Then follow a rich broth and cooked vegetables. Then comes the boiled animal meat, often sheep, served on a platter with dough that has been boiled in broth.

Weddings, major birthdays, and religious and other festivals call for something grander. For the main dish, it is common to slaughter a sheep and boil its head. The eldest member of the family or the honored guest carves the head and distributes the different parts adroitly. The ears go to children, the message being that they should listen to their elders. The eye goes to one who is known to be deficient in wisdom. The tongue goes to an inarticulate individual, implying that he should cease to be tongue-tied.

SOUTHWARD MARCH

With the steppes under its firm control, Russia eyed the south. But Tsar Nicholas's attempt to capture the Khanate of Khiva in 1839 failed. This led to a revision of strategy. Instead of staging another lightning frontal attack on the enemy, he decided to surround him in a pincer movement carried out with due deliberation. Thus, in 1853 the Russians mounted a slow, two-prong attack, marching from the west up the Syr Darya (or Jaxartes) River, and from the east along the lower slopes of the Tien Shan (literally, "Heavenly Mountain") range. Although the march formally ended in 1864 during the rule of Tsar Alexander II (1855–81), it gained Kyzyl Orda ("Red Rock") and Almaty (then Verny) for Russia in the first two years.

The American Civil War of 1861 to 1865 resulted in the loss of cotton imports for the Russian textile factories. This gave urgency to Alexander II's military campaign in Central Asia because its soil was suitable for growing cotton. This was particularly true of the fertile Fergana Valley, which had been noted since antiquity for its cotton crops. Its high-quality cotton was exported as far as the Indian subcontinent. The Fergana Valley was also a center of the allied textile handicrafts. Indeed, its advanced handicraft industry processed not only cotton but also silk supplied by the silkworm agriculture of the region.

The yarn was woven in simple stripes or in arrow-shaped broad patterns of the rainbow called *abre*. The rainbow colors were obtained by using natural dyes, which over the past few millennia have been derived from leaves, flowers, and stems or roots of plants. Red came from the root of the madder plant and from St John's Wort; yellow from weld and yarrow, a Eurasian herb; and blue from indigo and woad.

Based in and around the Fergana Valley, the weavers devised geometric, vegetable, or flower motifs for decorative purposes—making sure to refrain from portraying people because Islam forbids representation of human beings, regarding it as the sole privilege of God. The weavers' output catered to all classes and tastes, from the indigent to the affluent, from bed clothes to decorative tapestries. From the mid-nineteenth century onward, their art and craft faced rising competition from machine-made textiles. Yet, in the 1870s, Tashkent (literally, "City of Stones") was home to more than fifteen hundred weavers, and the towns of the Fergana Valley hosted several hundred silk-weaving workshops.[4] Over the next few decades, cheap, mass-produced cotton, silk, and brocade textiles—looking flawless and carrying fake designs of oriental textiles using synthetic dyes—would undercut the traditional, handmade textiles of Uzbekistan.

Another major strategic reason for the Tsar's southward drive was to stop the advance of the British Empire in India. Over the past century, it had progressed from Bengal in the east toward Afghanistan. The Tsars were keen to prevent Afghanistan from turning into a British colony or protectorate. The resulting competition between Saint Petersburg (as the city was known from 1703 to 1914) and London for influence in Central Asia intensified to the extent that the term "The Great Game" was coined by British writer Rudyard Kipling to describe it. The Anglo-Russian rivalry led to the Anglo-Afghan War of 1839 to 1842, which resulted in the defeat of Britain. Later, British India managed to seize eastern Afghanistan, but Afghans resisted occupation and the situation remained unstable.

On June 27, 1865, under cover of darkness, 2,000 Russian troops led by Major General Mikhail Chernayev crossed the Anhar River and attacked the walled city of Tashkent, the richest and most populous in the Khanate of Kokand. After two days of intense combat, the Russians captured the city. To win instant popularity, Chernayev abrogated taxes for a year. The Tsar decorated him and his soldiers with medals, but rejected his idea of making Tashkent an independent khanate. Instead, in 1867, after subduing the rest of the Khanate of Kokand, he named Tashkent the capital of Turkistan, thus reviving a centuries-old name, to be administered by a governor general. He appointed General Konstantin von Kaufman to that post.

Beyond the walled city, across the Anhar River, the victors built a military cantonment with wide avenues and well-designed houses, shops, and offices. Russian settlers and merchants arrived in droves. (In 1871, Tashkent would acquire the first Russian Orthodox Church in Turkistan.) Tashkent emerged as the prime center of espionage in the Great Game as well as a leading military base where campaigns were mounted to conquer the rest of Central Asia. In 1868, the Tsar incorporated the Emirate of Bukhara into Turkistan as a protectorate. The same fate befell the Khanate of Khiva five years later. With the remaining area of Central Asia—known as Trans-Caspia, the land of Turkmen (meaning "me Turk" in a Turkic language) tribes—falling into Tsarist hands in 1881, Russia completed its control of the region.[5]

Having extended his empire to the northern border of Afghanistan, the Tsar was ready to bury the hatchet with Britain. London was in a similar mood, having suffered another humiliating defeat in the Second Anglo-Afghan War (1878–80). Together, they finalized the boundaries of Afghanistan, with the British insisting on attaching a tongue to eastern Afghanistan, called Wakhan, to provide a crucial wedge between Tsarist Russia and the British Empire in India. Tsar Nicholas II (1894–1917) agreed in 1895.[6] Thus the Great Game, which began with the two players 1,500 kilometers (930 miles) apart, ended with only 25 kilometers (15 miles) between them. Henceforth an independent Afghanistan was to be a buffer between the two empires.

Central Asia was populated mainly by races that were admixtures of Europeans, Mongols, and Iranians. European-Mongol interbreeding had created Turks andTatars; Iranian-Mongol interbreeding Tajiks. The admixture of Turks and Mongols resulted in Kazakhs/Kyrgyzes, and that of Turks and Iranians in Uzbeks. While the Kazakh, Kyrgyz, and Turkmen tribes were predominantly nomadic, others had a long history of sedentary life in the fertile valleys and oases. As in the earlier eras, the free-spirited nomadic tribes proved resistant to the new conquerors. Among the settled communities, the ones in the fertile Fergana Valley rebelled periodically, their resistance inspired and led by Islamic luminaries. These rebellions were crushed by the Russian troops stationed in the valley.

A call to jihad, holy war, by Muhammad Ali, head of a Sufi (i.e., mystical Islam) order in the Fergana Valley town of Andijan in May 1898 inspired a local militant, Ishan Madali, to lead a raiding party into the barracks and kill twenty-two Russian soldiers. The revolt spread to other towns in the valley. The governor general deployed troops to suppress the uprising. Severe retribution followed. Madali and seventeen of his collaborators were hanged in public. Over 300 participants in the jihad were banished to labor camps in Siberia, and their lands transferred to Russian settlers. Madali's village was demolished and a new Russian settlement built on its site.[7] More than a century later, Andijan would grab headlines in the international press for the massacre of 167 (the official figure) to 600 (the unofficial estimate) unarmed civilians by security forces following a jail break attributed to Islamic militants.[8]

The endless empty spaces of the steppes of Kazakhstan provided the Tsar with an opportunity to channel ethnic Russians and Cossacks to the area and encourage them to grow crops, particularly much-needed cotton. In 1891, more than a million newly arrived Russians and

Cossacks took to farming land in Kazakhstan adjoining Siberia.

To consolidate its newly acquired territories, the Russian government extended the Trans-Caspian railway to Samarkand and Tashkent from 1888 to 1889, and then to Andijan in the Fergana Valley a decade later. It was an engineering feat. Between the Fergana Valley and Tashkent lies a long mountainous ridge, red and full of minerals, with the town of Angren (from *ahangaran*, "iron workers") on the Tashkent side. Beyond Angren, the curvaceous rail track rose steadily up to the 7,000-foot-high (2,130 meters) Kamchik Pass, entered an open terrain, and sloped down to the valley's first town, Kokand, on its way to the easternmost city of Andijan, famed as the birthplace of Babur, who established the Mughal Empire in India in 1526.

By connecting Orenburg in the Volga region with Tashkent by railway in 1906, the government increased contacts between Central Asia and other parts of the empire. This contributed to the prosperity of Tashkent, which became the leading industrial, commercial, and administrative hub of Central Asia. Another contributory factor was the dramatic growth in cotton production. At Russia's insistence, almost half of the cultivated area in the former Khanate of Kokand was turned into cotton fields. Over time, the fertile Fergana Valley increased its contribution of raw cotton to the Russian factories from 20 to 90 percent, and Fergana became the foremost cotton center.

By the turn of the century, Tashkent, especially its Russian sector, basked in its affluence. In its thriving commercial district, rents shot up to the large sum of $5 US per square yard. It was a city with electricity, piped water, telephones, cinemas, and metaled roads bisected by tramlines. On public transport, an apartheid system existed, with the three front seats reserved for Russians who paid twice the normal fare.[9]

MUSLIM IDENTITY IN THE TSARIST EMPIRE

When the Russians arrived as conquerors, they found that Samarkand, Bukhara, Khiva, Kokand, Tashkent, and Mari (then Merv) possessed a rich heritage of historical monuments and functioned as eminent centers of Islamic learning. They refrained from interfering with the traditional way of life, which was in accordance with the requirements of Islamic law— *Sharia*, composed of the Quran and the sayings and deeds of Prophet Muhammad, called *Hadiths*—along with the decrees issued by the ruler in consultation with his cabinet.

After the ruler, called Emir or Khan, came the Prime Minister, followed by the Chief Judge or Minister of Justice, who formed the link between the royal court and the clergy-run madrassas, theological schools. The Emir ruled the provinces through local governors, called beks or begs. The word of these governors, generically called khans, was law. Recalling the old days, ninety-nine-year-old Qadir Baba, a resident of an Uzbek village, told Adiba Atayeva of the BBC Uzbek Service that "The khan would hang you or shoot you if your crime was big or beat you with a stick or imprison you or shackle your legs. I remember them binding three planks together to make a gallows, hoisting the criminal on a cart and taking him around the city for all to see before they hanged him. The bazaar was full of his officers, I remember. And, after he went, it did not change much. We were still afraid of the lord of the land."[10] A person found guilty of committing a serious felony had his face blackened and was forced to ride a donkey facing its tail as it meandered around lanes and pathways, with villagers jeering or merely staring, before being thrown into a prison cell.

Leaving aside nomads, most Central Asian Muslims were illiterate peasants. They lived in small communities in gated, single-story houses of stones or bricks, built on square plots with an internal courtyard garden of flowers and vegetables. A household often consisted of a father, one or more of his wives, and his married sons, with each family occupying rooms with verandas built along the perimeter, and sharing the garden vegetables and the milk of the cows and goats tethered in one or more rooms.[11]

Their peasant lives followed the cradle-to-grave cycle that had remained unchanged for many centuries. A baby born in such a household found itself swaddled and kept firmly in place in a cradle. Later the child would play in the family courtyard or village lane. Around the age of ten, a boy was circumcised during a ritual celebrated with a sumptuous party, and was decked with a glinting cardboard crown, marking his coming of age. He then began aiding his father on the farm. A girl of the same age plaited her hair and covered her head with a scarf in public, while at home she helped her mother with chores.

As the boy approached his late teens, his parents looked around for a potential wife for him, either directly or through intermediaries. The families of nubile daughters followed a similar approach. It was vital for both parties to ensure that the prospective groom or bride possessed unblemished character and that the young man had the wherewithal to support a family. In the case of a girl, virginity was a must. The next step was to determine the bride price to be paid in kind, often in the form of such domestic animals as goats, sheep, or cows. Alternatively, the young man's family offered a dozen or more dresses for the bride.

On the wedding day, a party led by the groom arrived at the bride's house where the marriage was solemnized by a cleric. The couple then left for the husband's parental home, the bride decked with a golden cap, in a procession led by trumpeters and drummers. A reception party attended by relatives and friends followed. The high point was the presentation of a mound of pilau, cooked in cottonseed oil in a cauldron over an open flame. Made of white, long-grain rice, with onions, apples, shredded carrots, and boiled or fried meat or chicken, pilau acquires its color by the addition of tomato purée, tomatoes, and prunes, and is topped with raisins, barberries, and boiled chickpeas. Placing the dish on the main table was a signal to the guests to dig into the conical heap and help themselves. Other tables were laid with almonds, dried apricots, grapes, mulberries, raisins, sultanas, and walnuts.

In her new abode, the young wife looked after her in-laws. Before leaving home on errands, she covered herself with a veil, as enjoined by the Muslim clergy, who cited the Quranic verse [24:31]: "And say to the believing women, that they cast down their eyes and guard their private parts . . . and let them cast their veils over their bosoms, and not reveal their adornment except to their husbands, or their fathers, or their husbands' fathers, or their sons, or their husbands' sons, or their brothers, or their brothers' sons, or their sisters' sons, or other women . . . or children who have not yet attained knowledge of women's private parts."[12] She typically gave birth to six children (half of whom died in infancy) and spent her time indoors raising them, weaving cotton, and making tallow candles.

When her husband began to grow bald, his hair turning gray, he took to wearing a turban and a long coat, which instantly won him the respect of the villagers. As the elder man in the family, he had the final say. In the local community, power rested with a body of elderly men with white beards. After death, the man's corpse was washed, covered in a white shroud, and taken to the graveyard to be buried with his grave marked by a thin strip of wood. Women of the household remained at home to mourn. A similar procedure was followed upon the death of the matron.

This pattern remained undisturbed by the arrival of the Tsarist rule. The Russian colonization centered around urban settlements, with the settlers including not merely civil servants, traders, and troops but also skilled and semi-skilled workers to operate the railways and industrial plants. Among local peoples, sedentary Uzbeks were foremost in supplying indigenous labor for railways and cotton-ginning factories.

Russian colonization imposed an alien layer on the traditional Muslim social order, noted for its close family and clan ties and strong religiosity. Indigenous society consisted chiefly of nomads and landless peasants who received their wages in kind from landlords or cattle owners living mainly in urban centers. Only a minority of peasants, tending cotton fields, received its remuneration in cash. Together, these peasants and nomads maintained not only landlords, craftsmen, civil servants, money-lenders, and soldiers, but also the religious hierarchy of prayer leaders, mullahs, and kazis (religious judges). Public service providers such as schools, hospitals, and post offices were either scanty or nonexistent.

Like the Muslims in Russia, their co-religionists in Central Asia stressed their Muslim identity. "The settled peoples of Central Asia regard themselves first as Muslims and then as inhabitants of any given town or region; ethnic concepts having virtually no significance in their eyes," noted Vasiliy V. Barthold, a leading Russian specialist on Islam.[13] They were also deeply religious. On the eve of World War I (1914–18), the Emirate of Bukhara, with a population of about 2.5 million Muslims, had 2,600 mosques.[14] Girls aged four or older had to wear a veil. The clergy were in cahoots with feudal lords and impressed on their impoverished congregations the value of a Spartan existence, a key to God's affection and entry into heaven. These other-worldly homilies had fostered fatalism and lassitude, contributing to the socio-economic backwardness of Muslims.

Noting the disparity between Russians and their community, Central Asian leaders argued that either Christian Russians had devised a system better than Islam or their community had failed to follow true Islam. To reverse the downward trend, one school, called Qadims ("Precursors"), much favored by the Islamic hierarchy, advocated strict application of the Sharia, while the other, Jadids ("Innovators"), proposed innovation in light of a fast-changing world, which they saw from a predominantly Westernized perspective.

Qadims wanted to change, but within the framework of Islamic tradition. Since their ranks consisted of guides of the Sufi orders and clerics scattered throughout the countryside, Qadims had a mass appeal. While opposed to the Russian rule, they refrained from confronting it, aware that the previous calls to jihad had not led to widespread uprisings.

While most Jadids were graduates of Quranic schools or Islamic colleges, they were also well-versed in one or more Western languages, an asset that gave them an understanding of Western political theory and practice. However, lacking access to the faithful, who were under the sway of predominantly Qadim clergy, they focused on socio-cultural reform. They established reformed schools, which offered Russian and modern sciences along with religious instruction, the standard fare at the traditional madrassas. They toyed with the ideas of adopting Western dress and changing the Arabic script of their languages to Latin. But because they accepted the Russian dominance as "a necessary evil," they failed to win popularity. A leading Jadid, Ismail Hasbarali (1851–1914)—better known by his Russified name, Ismail Gasprinsky—a Crimean Tatar aristocrat, encouraged the founding of reformed schools through his newspaper *Terjuman-Perevodchik* (Interpreter), established in 1893.[15]

Following the 1905 constitutional revolution in Russia, Jadid leader Abdul Rashid Ibrahimov convened a pan-Islamic conference. More than 120 Jadid delegates met aboard a yacht in Nizhniy Novgorod (later Gorkiy) 400 kilometers east of Moscow. They established the Alliance of Muslims, and demanded participation in politics under a constitutional monarch, freedom of expression for Muslims, and an end to the confiscation of Muslim land and its transfer to Russian and other Slav colonizers. There were two more such assemblies, the last one in August 1906, where the delegates decided to transform the Alliance of Muslims into a political organization, the Muslims Party, with its own election manifesto. Tatars from Volga dominated the party, accounting for eleven of the fifteen central committee members, while the only member from Turkistan was also an ethnic Tatar. Tatar intellectuals had a history of advocating pan-Turkism as an alternative to Westernization and pan-Islamism advocated by Qadims.

In 1910 the Emirate of Bukhara witnessed violence between Sunnis and Shiites, which weakened the hold of traditional Qadims. In contrast, Jadids widened their base, and founded the Association for the Education of Children. It expanded so quickly that, by 1914, it claimed the loyalty of most of the Muslim intelligentsia.

Between 1914 and 1925, Central Asia underwent turmoil of extraordinary severity: conventional warfare, revolution, civil strife, periodic shifting of the borders of its constituents, administrative reforms, founding of an all-powerful political party, the purging of chauvinist Russian settlers from the region, and sweeping land reform which uprooted centuries-old property relations.[16] No other region in the world had experienced such convulsions within the span of a decade.

On the eve of World War I, Jadid leaders allied with their Qadim counterparts and Każakh-Kyrgyz tribal chiefs on an anti-Russian platform. Together they convened a clandestine congress in Samarkand in June 1916.

It resolved to organize an armed insurrection against the Tsarist rule in Turkistan. Clerics urged a jihad against the Tsar.

Their calls fell on receptive ears. Responding to the pressures of World War I, which erupted on August 1, 1914, Tsar Nicholas II ordered the drafting of Turkistani Muslims, previously exempted from military service, into non-combatant army units. The authorities also requisitioned wheat from the region to feed the army. Both these decrees were deeply unpopular.

The Kazakh and Kyrgyz nomads rose up on July 13, 1916. The others in Central Asia followed. As in the past, the Russian troops took swift action, razing villages and slaughtering cattle, and crushed the jihad as well as the widespread insurrection.

THE FEBRUARY 1917 REVOLUTION

The protracted bloodiness of World War I led to a revolution in Russia on February 27, 1917. The abdication of Nicholas II on March 2 was followed by the official inauguration of the Provisional Government under Alexander Kerensky of the Social Revolutionary Party. Kerensky vowed to maintain Russia's territorial integrity.

Internally, the revolution produced favorable conditions for the rise of the Russian Social Democratic Labor Party (Bolshevik) under the leadership of Vladimir Ilich Lenin (1870–1924), then in exile.[17] At its Seventh Congress in April, the party reiterated its backing for the right of "all nations forming part of Russia" to "free separation and the right to form their own independent states." At the same time, in his report on the nationality question, Joseph Vissarionovich Stalin, the party's specialist on the subject since 1903, reaffirmed Lenin's position that recognizing this right did not mean the Bolsheviks would support every demand for separation.

As for Russia's Muslim citizens, their representatives met in Moscow under the aegis of the First All Muslim Conference to forge a common position. But they failed to do so. The delegates from Turkistan split along the Jadid-Qadim divide: the progressive Jadids forming the Islamic Council, and the conservative Qadims the Council of Ulema (Religious-legal Scholars). The Kazakh-Kyrgyz delegates kept out of the fray, and decided to establish Alash Orda (or Alash Group), a party named after the legendary ancestor of the Kazakh-Kyrgyz people, whose three sons founded the three Kazakh hordes (Small, Middle, and Great). Its main demand was that the Kazakh lands given to Slav colonizers be returned to their original owners. In contrast, the Islamic Council backed the slogans of

"Land to the Landless" and "Expropriate Feudalists and Capitalists" raised by the Bolsheviks. As expected, the Council of Ulema focused on religion, urging the Kerensky government to replace the Russian laws with the Sharia in Turkistan.

Following the revolution, Tashkent, the administrative headquarters of Turkistan, became the scene of two competing centers of power: the Provisional Government's Turkistan Committee and the Bolshevik-dominated Soviet (Council) of Workers' and Peasants' Deputies. Both were Russian in composition. The uneasy co-existence of the two bodies could not continue for long. In mid-September, 1917, the Bolsheviks staged strikes and demonstrations as a prelude to capturing power, but failed. In late September, the Second All Muslim Conference, led by intellectuals, met in Tashkent and demanded the formation of a Muslim government and autonomy for Turkistan in a federated Republic of Russia. But nothing came of it.

These events occurred against the backdrop of the war, which had led the Kerensky government to deploy half a million troops in the Caucasus to frustrate Ottoman Turkey's plans for an offensive. The war had created such acute political and economic crises that the Russian government had become weak and vulnerable. Sensing this, the Bolshevik leader, Lenin, thought the time had come to deliver a fatal blow to the system.

THE BOLSHEVIK REVOLUTION

According to the Julian calendar then in vogue in Russia, the Bolshevik revolution occurred on October 24 and 25, 1917, when Kerensky's Provisional Government was overthrown by the Bolshevik forces. But with the changeover to the Gregorian calendar on February 1, 1918, these dates became November 6 and 7.[18]

Power passed to the 650 delegates to the Second All-Russian Congress of the Soviets of Workers', Peasants', and Soldiers' Deputies, which assembled in St. Petersburg (known as Petrograd between 1914 and 24). They elected the Council of People's Commissars, the new Soviet government headed by Lenin. It signed a peace treaty with Germany at Brest-Litovsk in March 1918 and withdrew from the war. Domestically, the revolutionary regime resolved to decolonize the non-Russian areas of the Tsarist Empire, and allocate territories to individual non-Russian nationalities and nations—an ambitious task which would be accomplished in successive phases over two decades.

On October 25 (November 7) the Presidium of the Tashkent Soviet, which had secretly won over the loyalties of the Siberian Second Reserve Rifle Regiment (the local Russian military unit), resolved to stage an armed uprising. The commissar-general of the Provisional Government in Tashkent got wind of this. On October 27 (November 9), he declared martial law, and tried to disarm the soldiers suspected of disloyalty. Fighting broke out the next day with a workers' combat unit of 2,500 joining the mutinous troops against the Provisional Government's loyalist forces. The Bolsheviks won on November 1 (November 14).

The next day the Council of People's Commissars of the Russian Soviet Federated Socialist Republic (RSFSR) in St. Petersburg issued a Declaration of the Rights of the Peoples of Russia. It included equal sovereignty for all the nations of the former Tsarist Empire, the right to self-determination up to and including the right to secede and form independent states, an end to the privileges and limitations of a national or religious nature, and recognition for all national and ethnic minorities.

The Third Regional Congress of the Soviets of Workers', Peasants', and Soldiers' Deputies assembled in Tashkent on November 15 (November 28) and declared Soviet rule in Turkistan. Since soldiers and workers, overwhelmingly Russian, were the main engine of the revolution, ethnic Russians dominated the new governing bodies. The Regional Congress in Tashkent elected the regional Council of People's Commissars under the chairmanship of F. I. Kolesov. On November 19 (December 2), it decided by a large majority to give Muslims four places on the Regional Council, two on the Regional Executive Committee, but none on the Council of People's Commissars.[19]

Concurrently, the Third All-Muslim Congress gathered in another neighborhood of Tashkent. Reiterating its demand for autonomy for Turkistan, it demanded the immediate formation of a Muslim administration. It came out against the Bolshevik revolution. Later it would receive the support of clerics after their petition to the Tashkent Soviet to base its civil administration on the Sharia was rejected.

On November 25 (December 8), 197 delegates—three-quarters of them from the Fergana province, and the rest from the Syr Darya, Samarkand, and Bukhara provinces—assembled in Kokand under the auspices of the Fourth Extraordinary Regional Muslim Congress. Declaring Turkistan to be autonomous, they appointed a twelve-member Kokand Autonomous Government (KAG) under Mustafa Chokaloglu, an ethnic Kazakh, and elected a council of thirty-six Muslims and eighteen Russians.

The Muslim leadership saw a glimmer of hope on December 3 (December 16), 1917. On that day, the Council of People's Commissars of the RSFSR addressed an appeal, signed by V. I. Lenin, and J. V. Stalin, the commissar of nationalities, to "All Muslim Toilers of Russia and the East." It read:

Muslims of Russia! Tatars of the Volga and the Crimea! Kyrgyzes and Sarts[20] of Siberia and of Turkistan! Turks and Tatars of Trans-Caucasia! Chechens and mountain peoples of the Caucasus! All [of] you, whose mosques and prayer houses used to be destroyed, and whose beliefs and customs were trodden underfoot by the Tsars and oppressors of Russia! From today, your beliefs and customs, and your national and cultural constitutions, are free and inviolate. Organize your national life freely and without hindrance. You are entitled to this. Know that your rights, like the rights of Ali the peoples of Russia [i.e., RSFSR], are protected by the whole might of the Revolution and its agencies, the Soviets of workers', soldiers' and peasants' deputies. Support then this Revolution and its sovereign Government . . . Comrades! Brothers! Let us march towards an honest and democratic peace. On our banners is inscribed the freedom of all oppressed peoples.[21]

On December 13 (December 26), Prophet Muhammad's birthday, the Muslim leaders in Tashkent proclaimed Turkistan's autonomy. They backed it up by staging a big demonstration in the city, followed by a rally of Muslim workers and peasants in Kokand in early January 1918. On January 10 (January 23), 1918, the Kokand Autonomous Government urged the authorities in Tashkent to convene a Turkistan constituent assembly. The Tashkent Soviet's response was hostile.

In his speech to the Fourth Regional Congress of Soviets, Kolesov put the Kokand Autonomous Government in the same hostile column as the troops of General A. I. Dutov—a counterrevolutionary Cossack officer who cut communications between Central Russia and Turkistan—and vowed to quash the "counterfeit autonomy" of the Muslim nationalists. The reasoning behind his stance was that conflict between different nations had arisen on a class and not a national basis, and that self-determination for a nation meant self-determination for its toiling masses, not its bourgeoisie. The Bolsheviks argued furthermore that their proletarian revolution had destroyed Tsarist imperialism in order to end exploitation by all national bourgeoisies, and not to create opportunities for Turkistan's national bourgeoisie to exploit Turkistani workers and peasants.

This was the preamble to an armed confrontation between the Tashkent

Soviet and the Kokand Autonomous Government. Taking the initiative, some ministers of the Kokand Autonomous Government led an assault on the Kokand citadel holding the Russian troops. The Russians repulsed the attack, and called for reinforcements from other garrisons while engaging the enemy in truce negotiations. The military commissar of the Tashkent Soviet, leading a large Russian force, arrived from Tashkent on February 5 (according to the Gregorian calendar in use since February 1), followed by further reinforcements from the Orenburg front a week later. Backed by the local Russian Soviet detachments, the new arrivals encircled the Muslim Old City and breached its walls on February 18. For the next three days, the attackers went on a rampage, looting and massacring some 14,000 Muslims who had not managed to flee, and finally setting the Old City on fire.[22]

By then the Soviet authorities in the region had already solved another irredentist problem militarily. At the Third All-Kazakh National Congress sponsored by Alash Orda, meeting in Orenburg (then in counter-revolutionary hands) from December 5 to 13, 1917, the delegates declared the Kazakh-Kyrgyz region autonomous. They elected its government, called the Provisional People's Council of Alash Orda, headed by Muhammad Buyuki Khanev, a Kazakh chieftain. But the autonomy proved short-lived. On January 18 (January 31), the Bolshevik militia—Red Guards—from St. Petersburg, the Volga region, and Central Asia expelled the anti-Soviet forces from Orenburg and dispersed the Alash Orda government.

In contrast, the developments in Trans-Caspian/Turkmenistan Oblast (Province) went against the Bolsheviks, whose Congress of Soviets had established a Council of People's Commissars in Ashgabat (then Ashkhabad) on December 2 (December 15), 1917. A nationalist movement backed by local intellectuals and centered around Turkmen army officers emerged under the aegis of the Regional Turkmen Congress and its National Committee, headed by Colonel Oraz Sirdar. It assigned itself the task of helping famine victims, but overstepped its objective when one of its delegates joined the Kokand Autonomous Government.

In February 1918, to improve its military preparedness, the National Committee formed the Turkmen National Army, with the existing Turkmen Cavalry Squadron forming its core. In response, the Soviet regime set up a Turkmen section within its administration, convened an All-Turkmen Peasant Congress, and established the Turkmen Red Guards. It dispatched party cadres into the countryside to recruit partisans for a social revolution. The Soviet of Ashgabat, a Russian majority town, appealed to Kolesov in Tashkent for military assistance. At home, it ordered a census of all arms-bearing males in the town. On June 17, the scheduled date for the census, rioting broke out and continued for two days. A week later, an armed detachment under Commissar V. Frolov arrived from Tashkent and disarmed the Turkmen Cavalry Squadron.

But after Frolov had departed for Kyzl Arvat in early July to suppress an uprising there, a rebellion by an anti-Soviet alliance erupted in Ashgabat on July 11 and 12. It resulted in the overthrow of the local soviet and the emergence of a nationalist government. Frolov's attempt to pacify Kyzyl Arvat failed too.

The government in Tashkent—the capital of the Turkistan Autonomous Soviet Socialist Republic (ASSR), encompassing Trans-Caspian Oblast, established in April 1918—declared the nationalist Trans-Caspian government illegal. However, that made little difference. By July 1918, the nationalist government had secured the assistance of General Sir W. Malleson, the British commander posted in Mashad, Iran, to foil any Turkish-German designs to open a war front in the Middle East. In exchange for the rights to sabotage the Trans-Caspian railway and mine the Caspian port of Krasnovodsk (now Turkmenbashi) to spike the Central Powers' plan to mount an offensive, Malleson dispatched a detachment of Indian troops under his command to Ashgabat.

Civil War

By mid-1918, Russia was in the midst of a civil war, with the Bolsheviks facing opposition from regular and irregular armed men called the White Guards, local nationalist elements, and Russia's erstwhile allies in World War I, including Britain, France, America, and Japan. The future status of the non-Russian territories of the Tsarist Empire would become an important factor in determining the final outcome.

Prominent among White Guards leaders were Admiral Alexander V. Kolchak, General Anton I. Denikin, and General Dutov. After the Bolshevik revolution, Kolchak, who commanded the Russian Black Sea fleet in World War I, declared himself commander-in-chief of Russia, and was so recognized by the Allies. He took up arms against the Bolsheviks in Siberia and was joined by Dutov, whose forces conquered Orenburg.

In January 1919, the Rumanian troops captured Moldova (then Bessarabia). Two months later British, French, and American forces seized the port of Murmansk in northwest Russia, and established the Government of Northern Russia. Soon the Japanese occupied Vladivostok, and the Germans Kiev and Odessa.

To fight the Bolsheviks, France and Britain armed the Austro-Hungarian prisoners of war detained in Siberia, who seized Samara and Kazan. Along Russia's southern borders, Britain sent Cossack troops from Bojnurd (in northern Iran) to the Trans-Caspian Oblast and dispatched British (Indian) troops from Mashhad to Ashgabat in July 1918 to help the nationalist forces. General L. C. Dunsterville, the British commander of the Allied Supreme Command based in Iran, led an expeditionary force to Baku in August, claiming to safeguard oilfields owned partly by a British company.

In the spring and summer of 1918, most of the territory in the Kazakh-Kyrgyz region fell to the anti-Soviet alliance, resulting in the emergence of the Kazakh Autonomous Region based in Orenburg, controlled by Dutov. Thus, within a year of the October 1917 revolution, more than three-fifths of the territory under the Tsar was out of Bolshevik control.

Then the tide began turning against the anti-Soviet camp. After proclaiming himself the Supreme Regent of Russia in November 1918, Kolchak reiterated his vow to restore fully the Tsarist Empire. He ordered the abolition of the Kazakh Autonomous Region and put the Kazakh fighters under his command. This caused a split between Kazakhs nationalists and White Guards.

The repeated assertions by Kolchak and other counterrevolutionary leaders that they would recreate the old Tsarist Empire alienated Russia's Muslim citizens. Influential Muslim leaders, including Sultan Galiyev, allied with the Bolsheviks, since the latter had combined their promise of self-determination for all nationalities of the former empire with land to peasants and an end to the war. Soon Stalin, the head of the Commissariat of Nationalities,[23] appointed Galiyev to a high position in the Muslim section of the commissariat in Moscow—the national capital since March 1918—and instructed him to attract Muslims to the party. Reflecting the emerging trend, the Fifth Regional Congress of Soviets, meeting in Tashkent in April 1918, conducted its proceedings in Russian and Uzbek. After announcing the formation of the Turkistan ASSR within the RSFSR, it decided to nationalize land, water resources, railways, banks, and industrial enterprises.

Nationally, Galiyev was active. Starting with the founding of the Muslim Communist-Socialist Party independently of the Russian Communist Party (Bolshevik) (RCP)—the renamed Russian Social Democrat Labor Party (Bolshevik)—in March 1918, he transformed it into the Russian Party of Muslim Communists (RPMC). His move reflected the fracturing of the RCP into smaller units based on territorial, religious, or ethnic loyalties. This worried Stalin, who, in November 1918, attended the RPMC's First

Congress, held under the chairmanship of Galiyev, as a representative of the RCP. He rejected Galiyev's proposal for the RPMC's autonomy by stressing the need for "democratic centralism within a single united party capable of acting as the vanguard of the international proletarian revolution." Stalin won the debate. The delegates elected him as their representative in the Central Committee of the RCP.

Overall, in the continuing civil war, as the Red Army—created and led by Leon Trotsky nationally and by General Mikhail V. Frunze regionally—began gaining the upper hand, various Muslim groups abandoned the White Guards and joined the Reds. By late 1918, many Uzbek, Tajik, Kazakh-Kyrgyz, and Tatar units were fighting alongside Red Army contingents.

BOLSHEVIK SWAY IN CENTRAL ASIA

To tackle the nationality problem, Stalin created the Central Bureau of Muslim Organizations (CBMO) and put it in charge of the party organization in the Muslim areas of the RSFSR. In Turkistan ASSR, its task was to reshape the Russian-controlled party into a Muslim-dominated one. However, its fast progress in that direction would prove a mixed blessing for Stalin. At the First Conference of the Muslim Organizations in Tashkent in May 1919, organized by the CBMO, the representatives of 108 bodies demanded the establishment of the Soviet Republic of United Turkistan to include the Turks of Russia and the Caucasus. They thus revived the pan-Turkic scenario of the Muslim reformists of Central Asia before the Bolshevik revolution, of which Stalin disapproved.

By then the CBMO's program of indigenizing the regional Communist Party, founded in June 1918, had progressed so well that more than half of the 248 delegates to the Third Regional Congress of the party, held in Tashkent in June 1919, were natives. This boosted the confidence of Muslim Communists. At the Second Conference of the Muslim Organizations in Tashkent in September 1919, T. Ryskulov, a forceful Muslim leader, reiterated the First Conference's proposal for a United Turkistan. When Moscow failed to respond positively, the Third Conference, held a few months later, demanded the transformation of Turkistan into the Autonomous Turkish Republic, and proposed that the Turkistani Communist Party, affiliated to the RCP, be reconstituted as an independent Turkish Communist Party.

This angered Stalin, who promptly dissolved the CBMO. But the central leadership in Moscow had realized that there was an acute problem in the region which needed to be tackled. In early October, the RSFSR government and the RCP's Central Committee appointed a special Commission for Turkistan Affairs, consisting of six Russians, including General Frunze, to oversee the soviets in Turkistan. Its dual mandate was to rid the soviets of "nationalist deviants" and conciliate the Russian colonizers and Central Asians. This occurred soon after the units of the Turkistan front, led by Generals Frunze and V. V. Kuibyshev, had routed the White Guards in the northern and eastern parts of the Kazakh-Kyrgyz region, and linked up with the contingents of the Red Army of Turkistan ASSR at Muhajar (Mugodzhar).

By then, the nationalist Trans-Caspian government had alienated local peasants by forcefully requisitioning food grains in the midst of a famine. In urban areas the Bolsheviks had succeeded in establishing underground cells, facilitating the Red Army's capture of Mari in May 1919 and culminating in the expulsion of the anti-Soviet forces from Ashgabat in July, following the withdrawal of the British contingent a month earlier.

In the autumn of 1919, the Red Army prepared to regain the rest of the Kazakh-Kyrgyz region. In early November, Frunze declared an amnesty for those Alash Orda partisans who detached themselves from the White Guards and sympathized with the Kazakh-Kyrgyz aspiration for autonomy. His ploy worked. Most Alash Orda fighters switched from the White Guards to the Reds, poised to retake the western part of the Kazakh-Kyrgyz region. The Red Army completed its mission in early 1920, and crowned it with the recapture of the Semirechie region in March. In April, the RCP's Central Committee established the Kyrgyz[24] Regional Bureau of the Russian Communist Party, paving the way for the formation of the Kyrgyz Autonomous Soviet Socialist Republic within the RSFSR in August, with its capital in Orenburg.

However, despite its military victories, Moscow failed to dissuade Muslim Communists to abandon their Turkic aspirations. Indeed, heeding the call of Ryskulov, the delegates at the Fifth Regional Congress of the Turkistani Communist Party in January 1920 renamed their organization the Turkish Communist Party and called on the RCP to recognize it as such. Moscow was unbending. In its response on March 8, it declared that the only Communist Party in the area was that of Turkistan ASSR incorporated as a regional organization into the Russian Communist Party (Bolshevik).

By now, the Red Army had gained the decisive upper hand in the region's civil war. Responding to a petition from the Young Khiva Movement in January 1920, it marched into the Khanate of Khiva, enfeebled by inter-tribal violence. Out went the dynastic ruler, followed in April by the founding of the Khorezm People's Soviet Republic. Being less socialistic than a soviet socialist republic, it guaranteed private ownership of land.

In February, the Red Army expelled the anti-Soviet forces from Krasnovodsk, their last stronghold in Trans-Caspia. Two months later, it entered Baku, another important Caspian port. In August, responding to a call from the Young Bukhara Movement, the Fourth Army under Frunze attacked and conquered Bukhara, which had been much weakened by peasant revolts triggered by famine and repression. On September 2, Emir Said Alam Khan, the last ruler of the Mangit dynasty, fled to the eastern corner of the Emirate. His realm became the Bukhara People's Soviet Republic.

Communists had gained popularity by their actions as well, especially in rural areas where most Central Asian Muslims lived. Contrary to the Muslim clerics' dire warnings that the Bolsheviks would introduce wife-sharing and rape women in the countryside, they had concentrated on confiscating the lands of feudal lords and distributing them to landless and poor peasants, thus swiftly fulfilling their most far-reaching promise.

The Bolsheviks' military and political ascendancy encouraged the members of the major Muslim parties—the Himmat in Azerbaijan, Alash Orda in the Kazakh-Kyrgyz region, and the Young Bukhara Movement and Young Khiva Movement—to join the Communist Party.

THE BASMACHI RESISTANCE

The Communists' major problem now was how to counter the continuing nationalist Basmachi (meaning "bandit" in Uzbek) movement. It had emerged in the winter of 1919 to 1920 when, following a 62 percent drop in the cultivated area of Turkistan ASSR and the Russian government's policy of feeding the military at the expense of civilians, nearly half of the population had faced starvation. Many high officials of the former Kokand Autonomous Government got involved. The Basmachi partisans, operating from mountain bases, attacked Red Army supply convoys and outposts.

Since the Basmachi movement drew its ideological inspiration from Islam, it acquired popular backing in the Fergana Valley, a traditional bastion of Islam. The fugitive Emir Said Alam Khan, now based in the village of Dushanbe (Persian for day two, or Monday) in the mountainous, eastern part of his former emirate, joined the Basmachi movement. His two generals raised a militia of over 30,000 men.

The Soviet authorities combined their military campaign against the Basmachis with socio-economic reform to improve the condition of local peasants. A decree issued in March 1920 ordered the return to Central Asians of the agricultural land taken from them by the Russian settlers. Its enforcement was swift. In a little over a year, 280,000 hectares of land were handed over to Central Asian households.[25]

Moscow dispatched the powerful Commission for Turkistan Affairs to Tashkent with a mandate to tackle Russian chauvinism, which was vehemently denounced by Lenin. The Commission repatriated to Russia those Russians who were blatant chauvinists and exponents of the superiority of the Slavic race. It actively encouraged Central Asians to join the Communist Party and government organs. The revival of private trading as part of the New Economic Policy also helped to regain Muslim confidence, as commerce in the region was in the hands of Muslims. These measures diminished the appeal of the Basmachi movement, which had its own internal problems—the chief among them being the lack of a centralized political-military command, which enabled the Red Army to overpower the Basmachis.

But the arrival of General Enver Pasha, a former Turkish war minister, saved the resistance movement from extinction. An exile in Moscow after the end of World War I, he convinced the Soviet government that he could conciliate the warring parties in Turkistan. However, after his arrival in eastern Bukhara in the spring of 1921, he abandoned the task. Instead, he sought and forged an alliance of conservative and liberal Muslim leaders and mountain tribal chiefs under the twin slogans of pan-Turkism and pan-Islam, with the aim of creating a single Islamic state in the region.

In November 1921, Pasha succeeded in having the former ruler of Bukhara appoint him commander-in-chief of the Basmachis. He transformed the poorly led Basmachi groups into a professional army of 16,000 and launched a series of campaigns that brought a considerable part of the Bukhara People's Soviet Republic under Basmachi control by early 1922.

Little wonder that crushing the Basmachi rebellion was deemed the most pressing task of the local party and soviets by the Soviet government and the RCP's Central Committee. They sent Commander-in-Chief General S. S. Kamanev to Tashkent to oversee the anti-Basmachi campaign. Kamanev devised a dual-track strategy: political and economic reconciliation with the indigenous people, and the use of Muslim fighters to confront the Basmachi partisans. The New Economic Policy, launched in late 1921, signaled much-needed pragmatism and alleviated the material and political situation in the region. The government returned mosques and *waqf* (religious trust) properties to Islamic authorities, and allowed religious schools and Sharia courts to reopen, thus securing the neutrality of the clergy in its anti-Basmachi campaign. It also established a militia of indigent Muslim peasants, called the Red Sticks, and engaged them and regular Muslim soldiers to fight the Basmachis.

So, in May 1922, when Enver Pasha issued an ultimatum to Russia to withdraw from the region, Moscow was ready for a confrontation. In a battle at Kafrun, the Soviet units defeated the forces of Pasha, who retreated. During his flight to Afghanistan, he was killed on August 5 in an ambush near Khovaling in the Kulyab Valley of eastern Bukhara. This marked a virtual end to the Basmachi movement. Yet, seven decades later, this region would become the battleground between Communist and Islamist forces in the wake of the breakup of the Soviet Union.

In December 1922—when the government announced the founding of the Union of Soviet Socialist Republics (USSR)—there were only about 2,000 Basmachis left, mainly in the Fergana Valley. Within two years, the movement would become virtually extinct in Turkistan ASSR.

Addressing the Tenth All-Russian Congress of Soviets, Stalin, now the First Secretary of the RCP, pointed out that the independent soviet republics of Khorezm (previously Khiva) and Bukhara—being people's, but not socialist, republics—remained outside the framework of the USSR solely because they were not yet socialist. However, he added, "I have no doubt . . . that, in proportion to their internal development toward socialism, they [Khorezm and Bukhara] likewise will enter the structure of the Union state now being formed."[26]

"Internal development toward socialism" meant downgrading the "non-toiling" sections of society at the expense of workers and peasants. Much needed to be done in that direction. At the Fourth Conference of Responsible Workers of the National Republics and Regions in June 1923, Stalin noted that while Bukhara's Council of People's Commissars had eight merchants, two intellectuals, and one cleric, it had no peasants.

The Communist parties in Bukhara and Khorezm took heed. In September, the Third Congress of the Bukhara Communist Party disenfranchised the non-toiling citizens in its march towards socialism. A year later, the next congress transformed the Bukhara People's Soviet Republic into the Bukhara Soviet Socialist Republic (SSR). In early October 1924, the Fourth Congress of the Khorezm Communist Party followed suit by depriving its non-tolling members of voting rights. With this, Bukhara and Khorezm joined the family of soviet socialist republics. However, the union was short-lived.

On October 27, when part of the administrative reform coincided with the promulgation of the first USSR constitution, the multi-ethnic Khorezm and

Bukhara SSRs and Turkistan ASSR underwent territorial reorganization. None of them contained an ethnic group with a clear majority. In Bukhara, Uzbeks were 45 percent of the population; Tajiks, 40 percent; and Turkmen, 8 percent. In Turkistan, Uzbeks formed 41 percent of the total; Kazakhs, 19 percent; Kyrgyz, 11 percent; Russians, 10 percent; and Tajiks, 8 percent.

Contrary to the commonly held view, the following division of the region was not dictated by the central leadership in Moscow. "Rather, it involved a great deal of give and take between central Soviet authorities in Moscow and indigenous Communists in Central Asia," writes Adrienne Lynn Edgar, an American specialist on Central Asia. "At each stage of the delimitation, Moscow laid down general principles and asked local party organizations and specially designated committees in Central Asia to work out the details. Party leaders in Moscow, knowing relatively little about the national composition and popular mood of Turkistan, and even less about Bukhara and Khiva [later Khorezm], sought the opinions of Central Asian Communists before deciding the details of the delimitation. The precise location of borders was generally negotiated by indigenous Communists, with Moscow stepping in only in the case of intractable disputes."[27] In several cases, the hard bargaining between the contesting parties ended with small enclaves of one republic located inside the frontiers of another.

This was the case elsewhere as well. It was thus that Azerbajian ended up with the Armenian-speaking enclave of Nagorno Karabagh, which would lead to war between it and Armenia after the collapse of the Soviet Union in 1991. During the course of the war, Armenia would seize not only Nagorno Karabagh but also parts of the adjoining Azerbajian. Similarly, when the government of Georgia would attempt to regain the breakaway regions of South Ossetia and Abkhazia (whose mother tongues were different from the Georgian) in August 2008, the Kremlin would respond vigorously, its forces marching deep into Georgia. After the ceasefire and the Russian withdrawal from Georgia proper, Moscow would recognize South Ossetia and Abkhazia as independent states, thereby signaling to the world the arrival of a resurgent Russia.

STALIN'S THEORY OF NATIONALITIES

Following the Tsarist practice of calling Kazakhs Kyrgyzes, and Kyrgyzes Kara-Kyrgyzes, the Soviet authorities named the Kyrgyz-majority areas of Turkistan the Kara-Kyrgyz Autonomous Province (later, the Kyrgyz Autonomous Province, subsequently renamed Kyrgyz ASSR in February

1926), and retained it within the RSFSR. Its population was just under one million.

The Kazakh-majority provinces of Syr Darya and Semirechie of Turkistan were transferred to the existing Kyrgyz Autonomous Province. It was only in May 1925 that the central authorities gave it its historically correct name, Kazakh, upgraded it to an ASSR, and moved its capital from Orenburg to Kyzyl Orda (literally, "Red Rock"). It had nearly 6.5 million inhabitants.

The predominantly Turkmen areas of Trans-Caspia—the Ashgabat, Krasnovodsk, Tejand, and Mari districts—were coalesced with the Turkmen-majority districts of Khorezm and Bukhara to form the Turkmenia Soviet Socialist Republic. Its population was about 950,000.

The remainder of Turkistan and parts of Bukhara and Khorezm were reconstituted as the Uzbek Soviet Socialist Republic with a population of 5.2 million. It included the Tajik ASSR, consisting of the Tajik-majority areas—the Pamir (aka Badakhshan) mountainous region, eastern Bukhara, and parts of the Samarkand and Fergana provinces.[28] It had 0.75 million inhabitants.

Carving up the region into separate units broadly along ethnic-linguistic lines stemmed as much from administrative as political and ideological considerations. With Stalin ascendant, following the death of Lenin in January 1924, his theory on nationalities acquired an official stamp, and he began implementing it.

According to Lenin, nationalism (as a form of social relations) emerged during the early period of capitalism as a response to national-social oppression caused by capitalism. However, the later period of capitalist development, dominated by monopoly capital, spawned a trend towards internationalism. As late capitalism yields to socialism against the background of rising internationalism, he predicted, nationalism will wither and give way to class loyalties under socialism. As a practical politician, Lenin came to grips with specific nationalisms, which had emerged in response to Tsarist expansion, and backed the right to national self-determination vis-à-vis Great Russian imperialism, even extending its interpretation to mean "the right to free secession."[29] At the same time, he believed that the policies designed to build a socialist society would result in the dissipation of nationalisms and the rise of proletarian internationalism.

Stalin, born to Georgian and Ossetian parents in Gori, Georgia, accepted Lenin's thesis. Within its parameters he developed his own definition of nation (*natsiya*, in Russian), which, he argued, was different from people (*narod*, in Russian). He defined a nation as "a stable and historically developed community" based on four criteria: a common language, a united territory, a shared economic life, and a shared psychological outlook manifested in a common culture.[30] The national delimitation, carried out in 1924 to 1925, signified implementation of the policy of national self-determination in Stalinist terms, providing each of the major nations with "a united territory."

Stalin's linguistic policy was to give each delimited Union republic or Autonomous republic its own language. This led the policy makers in Moscow to exaggerate the differences between several Central Asian languages that were written in the Arabic script and rooted mainly in Turkic. Out of this arose a three-prong approach—enriching and completing a local language; replacing the Arabic and Persian loan words with Russian; and changing the Arabic script, written form right to left, to the Roman (on the ground that the Arabic script was difficult to learn) in 1929. The policy makers considered a switchover to the Cyrillic alphabet but rejected it. Such a move would have amounted to institutionalizing Russian supremacy, which was vehemently and repeatedly condemned by Lenin. Nonetheless, for the already literate Muslims, reversing the direction in which they wrote proved very exacting.

Often the Soviet regime acted as a catalyst for the creation of a nation out of a group of nomadic or semi-nomadic tribes. Of the Kyrgyz-Kazakh family of tribes, Kyrgyz, being almost universally nomadic, had proved immune to conscription. Therefore, Moscow quickened the process of separating them from Kazakhs, partly by providing them with a written, standardized language of their own. This occurred in 1922 when the Kyrgyz dialect, belonging to the Central Turkic group, was set down in the Arabic alphabet.

As for Turkmen, a largely dispersed and unassimilated ethnic group, in 1921 they forged a common written language (in the Arabic script) out of two tribal dialects belonging to the South Turkic group. In their case, the Soviet policy of nation-building coincided with the recently settled tribal society's aspiration to differentiate itself from the Azeri Turks to the west and the Iranian tribes to the south.

While policy makers in Moscow were quick to recognize Turkmen and Kazakh-Kyrgyz as the minorities which the ruling, martial Uzbeks held in contempt, they took several years to define correctly the relationship between the Uzbek majority and the Tajik minority. Thus, the Uzbek SSR came to accommodate sedentary and semi-nomadic Uzbek-speaking Uzbeks who belonged to the East Turkic group, and Tajiks who possessed a long settled history and spoke Tajik, a variant of Persian. This was because, until the 1917 revolution, Tajik had also been the cultural and political language of Uzbeks, which gave Tajik and Uzbek complementary roles.

However, since they had different roots, and since the Uzbek literary language had come into vogue by the mid-1920s, it dawned increasingly on the authorities in Moscow that the anomaly of the two nations with distinct languages living in a single Union republic needed to be resolved. Politically, too, the Tajik ASSR proved different from the rest of the Uzbek SSR. In early 1925, there was a revival of the Basmachi movement, whose activists managed to infiltrate the soviets in the countryside. The Red Army, assisted by the local auxiliary force, managed to suppress the movement, enabling the government to declare an official end to the civil war on August 14, 1926, after eight tumultuous years.

In December, the founding Congress of the Soviets of Tajik ASSR nationalized land, forests, and water resources. In the social sphere, it freed women from the restrictions imposed on them by the interpretation of the Sharia by male clerics. Women were encouraged to discard their veils, attend literacy classes, and go out to work. A ban on child marriage proved particularly beneficial to them. Progress towards socialism continued, as did the evolution of Tajik as a modern language containing many technical terms.

In the spring of 1929, when a railroad extension reached Dushanbe, Stalin concluded that the Tajik ASSR had progressed sufficiently along the socialist path to become a candidate for Union republic status. Lying on the southern slope of the Hissar Mountain in the picturesque and fertile Hissar Valley, Dushanbe, a marketplace since 1676, was situated at the confluence of the Varzob and Kofarnihan Rivers—the former running from north to south, and the latter from east to west—which enhanced its appeal.

Tajikistan possessed the geographic and ethnic requirements to secede from the Union as allowed by the 1924 constitution, being on the periphery of the Russian Federation and having its leading nationality, Tajiks, form a compact majority. What it lacked was the requisite population of one million. A solution lay in transferring the Uzbek SSR's Leninabad (later Khojand) Province to the Tajik ASSR on the dubious ground that its "primary population" was Tajik. In reality, it was a swap, with Uzbek SSR retaining the Tajik-majority cities of Samarkand and Bukhara while conceding the populous Khojand/Leninabad Province in the Fergana Valley to the new entity.

In foreign policy terms, Stalin considered it politically expedient to create a socialist republic "at the gates of Hindustan [India]" to provide a socialist model to the Eastern countries. In June 1929, therefore, the USSR's

Central Executive Committee decided to upgrade the Tajik ASSR to a Union republic, followed by the transfer of Leninabad to it. Finally, upon the endorsement by the Congress of the Soviets of Tajikistan, Tajikistan became a Union republic.

Kazakhs and Kyrgyzes, the two other nations of the region, however, had to wait until after the mass collectivization of cereal, cotton, and cattle-breeding farms had been virtually completed in their autonomous republics (within the RSFSR) in 1934 to see their territories upgraded to Union republics—Kazakh SSR and Kyrgyz SSR—by the new constitution of 1936. Their respective capitals were Alma Ata (Almaty, in the post-Soviet era) and Frunze (later called Bishkek).

For Moscow, the delimitation of the region along ethnic-linguistic lines had the additional merit of eroding any potential for the unification of Central Asia around the twin banners of pan-Turkism and pan-Islam, with Chaghatai (later called Uzbek), a Turkic language, as the cement. With this worrisome prospect out of the way, the planners in Moscow focused on the rapid socio-economic transformation of this predominantly rural region that was so heavily dependent on agriculture and cattle breeding.

The Soviet regime followed up its 1920 policy of distributing the lands of Russian colonizers to poor and landless Central Asian peasants with a program to redistribute the landholdings of local landlords and mullahs (managing religious trust lands) above a certain ceiling to poor peasants. This plan went into effect in 1925. By early 1926, all farms above fifty-five hectares (140 acres) in Uzbekistan had been confiscated and redistributed. The process continued elsewhere in the region until 1929.

The Communists' overall objective was to use the agrarian reform and the accompanying propaganda to emasculate landlords of their traditional political, economic, and social power, and free the peasantry from the deprivations of the past. The landless, poor, and middle-income peasants forming the bulk of the population benefited economically and politically. For instance, in the 1927 to 1928 elections to the Soviets in Tajikistan, the landless, poor, and middle-income peasants accounted for 87 percent of the deputies.[31] They (both men and women) were also the primary beneficiaries of the adult literacy campaigns mounted by Communists throughout the USSR.

ANTI-RELIGIOUS DRIVE & FARM COLLECTIVIZATION

The literacy drive was actually part of the Communists' larger campaign against religious superstitions and archaic customs through a planned reorganization of the socio-economic activities of the masses, socialist re-education of peasants and workers, expansion of educational facilities, and anti-religious propaganda. During the first decade of the Soviet rule, Communists directed their anti-religious drive chiefly at the European population. At the First All Union Conference of the Atheist Movement in 1926, of the 123 Slav and non-Slav nationalities in the USSR, the representatives of only 6 non-Slav nationalities were present.[32]

Communists conducted their anti-religious campaign cautiously in the Muslim-majority areas, partly because Muslim society was largely feudal, lacking a revolutionary industrial proletariat, and partly because of the all-pervasive nature of its faith. Islam impinged on every facet of life, individual and social; viewed the state and mosque as two sides of the same coin; and considered the right to private property sacrosanct.

Therefore anti-religious propaganda in Central Asia was limited to verbal attacks delivered in school classrooms, and at trade union and Komsomol (*Kommunisticheskiyo soyuz molodyezhy*, Communist Youth League) meetings. Those who devised the anti-Islamic argument took into account its doctrines and practices as well as its history in the region.

They argued that Islam was an alien faith, imposed on the local population by invading Arabs, Iranians, and Ottoman Turks. Since Islam discriminated against women, upheld the power of male elders, and encouraged intolerance and fanaticism, it was conservative, even reactionary. As it divided the world strictly into opposing believers and infidels, it was a barrier to fraternization among different peoples of the USSR. Such Islamic practices as circumcision, fasting during Ramadan, and self-flagellation (by Shiites during the Ashura ceremonies) were primitive, barbaric, or unhealthy. Islamic art, architecture, and literature had failed to evolve with the times and become static. The root cause of the malaise, according to Communist ideologues, was that Islam belonged to a feudal era and had not even caught up with the capitalist stage of human development, much less the socialist.

The overriding purpose of the anti-Islamic campaign was to engender a new Muslim "Soviet man" who, having released himself from the influences of the reactionary socio-religious traditions of Islam, was ideologically and culturally ready to join forces with his Russian counterpart. Thus both would be freed from their socio-religious traditions to construct a socialist order.

Given the paucity of literate adults and the sensitivity of the subject, Communists laid much stress on personal example. The party strategy was to convert a few inhabitants of a Muslim village to atheism, and let them quietly deflate the importance and relevance of Islam in modern times. While refraining from challenging Islam, these converts tried to explain natural phenomena and social problems in scientific terms with a view to undermining superstitious beliefs rooted in Islam.

Equally importantly, the state's takeover of religious trust properties initiated in 1925 began depriving mullahs of their income and starving mosques and theological schools (madrassas) of funds. This process was still in effect when the socialist family code, according equality to men and women, came into force in 1926 throughout the USSR. Among other things, it allowed daughters to inherit as much as sons, which ran counter to the Islamic practice of giving daughters only half as much as sons, and legalized civil marriage. This caused such an upheaval in Central Asia, Daghestan, and the Muslim areas of the Caucasus that Moscow exempted the Soviet Union's Muslim regions from the socialist family code. However, the governments at the republican level moved quickly to take up the slack.

Between 1926 and 1928, the authorities in the Muslim-majority Union and Autonomous Republics abolished the practices of polygamy, bride purchase, and wearing a veil, and closed down the Sharia and *Adat* (customary) courts. They also forbade religious propaganda in general and religious education to minors in groups of more than three. As a result, the last of the 8,000 Islamic schools that had been established in Turkistan Territory before the Bolshevik revolution closed. A ban on the Arabic script followed in 1929, striking at the root of Islamic scriptures and commentaries and making clerics wholly dependent on the religious material that the Soviet authorities passed for printing in the Cyrillic or Roman alphabet. Thus, in the late 1920s, the once powerful Islamic infrastructure, consisting of 26,000 mosques and 45,000 mullahs in the pre-revolutionary times, shrank to a fraction of its former self.[33]

During the First and Second Five-Year Plans (1929–38), Stalin focused on destroying this residual religious network by mounting campaigns to obliterate Islam—as well as Christianity and Judaism—and promote scientific atheism. What drove him was his obsession to vest all economic power in the state, and eliminate any creed capable of challenging Marxism-Leninism. A firm believer in historical materialism, he tackled the economic foundation of society first, before dealing with its religious-cultural superstructure.

In 1925, when Stalin had emerged as the leading light of the USSR, he argued that the peasantry provided the main fighting force to the national movements because the "peasant question" lay at the root of the "national question." Among peasants, he perceived kulaks (rich farmers) as prime adversaries of Marxist-Leninist internationalism since they were not only powerful economically, but were also the carriers of national consciousness.

To break the power of kulaks, Stalin initiated a drive for farm collectivization on a voluntary basis in 1927, mainly in the European sector of the Soviet Union. But he found progress patchy. Therefore, in December 1929, he introduced compulsory collectivization of farms, which he incorporated into the First Five-Year Plan (1929–33) that he had launched earlier in the year to replace Lenin's New Economic Policy.

His aim was to eliminate not only the power of kulaks (known in Central Asia as *bais*, *beks*, *begs*, or *manabs*, used as suffixes in names) but also the authority of tribal chiefs, clan heads, and village elders, to make the Soviet system the sole guiding force in the countryside, where a majority of citizens lived.

Stalin operated in an environment where the authority and size of the Communist Party were on the rise. The 1924 Soviet constitution, bearing his stamp, followed by the renaming of the Russian Communist Party (Bolshevik) as the All Union Communist Party (Bolshevik) (AUCP) a year later, had enabled the party to emerge as a powerful instrument of unity. Since the party functioned in all fields of activity open to citizens, it became all-pervasive. Its territorial organization ran parallel to the Soviet Union's administrative divisions, with a major exception: whereas each of the republics had its own Communist Party, the RSFSR had none.[34] The AUCP was also the party of the RSFSR. While each of the Union republics was nominally independent, with its own constitution and foreign minister, its Communist Party was not. A cross between a territorial body and an affiliate of the AUCP, a republican party was subservient to the AUCP— renamed the Communist Party of the Soviet Union (CPSU) in 1952—which was committed to cementing republican divisions into an ideologically and administratively centralized Soviet Union.

RESISTANCE TO COLLECTIVE FARMING

One of the side effects of the collectivization drive was to revive the Basmachi movement, with its self-exiled leaders returning from Afghanistan and Iran to Tajikistan and Turkmenistan. However, their renewed struggle proved short-lived. It collapsed in mid-1931 in the face of the offensives by the Red Army, assisted by the Russian-dominated militia and political police.

The same fate befell those who resisted farm collectivization. Some 2,100 kulak families from Turkmenistan were deported to Siberia. Turkmenistan was also the scene of two major anti-collectivization uprisings: in the Kara Kum (literally, "Black Sand") Desert in 1931 and near Yangi Tuar Oasis in 1932. In Tajikistan, there was resistance to collectivization even from within the Communist Party, which led to purges of the soviets in 1927 to 1928 and the party in 1929 to 1930. The collectivization went ahead nonetheless. After its completion in 1934, a major purge in the party reduced its membership of 14,329 by two-thirds in a year.[35]

The nomadic Kazakh and Kyrgyz tribes, who engaged chiefly in herding, suffered most. For them, the new state policy amounted to a double whammy. It meant an end to a centuries-old way of life that enabled them to feel free and live in tune with nature. To exchange their innovatively designed yurts for brick homes, and turn themselves into salaried workers on state farms, was too much to ask. Morever, they were being forced to pool their herds to create state-directed collectives. Some yielded, but many either slaughtered their herds or drove them into neighboring China.

During the First Five-Year Plan, Kazakhstan, Kyrgyzstan, and Uzbekistan experienced the loss of about half of their livestock, and migrations of whole clans to Iran, Afghanistan, or China. According to some specialists, between 15 and 20 percent of the Kazakh population of 4.5 million crossed over into the neighboring countries, and about the same number died due to collectivization and the ensuing famine in the mid-1930s.[36]

Moscow surmounted the resistance of local kulaks, peasants, and livestock breeders through force, mass deportations, propaganda, and the dispatch of Russian-dominated Communist Party brigades from the European part of the USSR to Central Asia to provide labor and technical and managerial skills for the newly established collective farms. These settlers were a sizeable part of the 1.7 million Russians who migrated from the European Russian Federation to Central Asia between 1926 and 1939.[37]

Agricultural collectivization led farmers to join a sovkhoz (state farm) or kolkhoz (collective farm). The government created sovkhozes by taking over large estates, and managed them through officially appointed directors who paid regular salaries to their workers. The capital investment for sovkhozes was part of the state budget, and their produce was purchased by the state. The Soviet authorities created kolkhozes by combining smaller individual farms. Members signed regular contracts with the elected management to lease land and equipment belonging to the collective, which also ran schools, clubs, libraries, cinemas, and agro-based industries. Though supervised by the local party's central committee, a collective farm had considerable freedom of maneuver. A typical collective farm in Central Asia evolved out of an existing village, attracting extended families and even whole clans. For instance, the Voroshilov kolkhoz in Kyrgyzstan, with 2,588 workers living in the villages of Darkhan and Chichkhan, possessed a flour mill, a club, a library, and schools.[38]

Thus feudal social relations were grafted onto a socialist system of production. Over decades this would create its own hierarchy and lead to strange distortions—especially in the cotton-growing areas of Uzbekistan, which became a major source of revenue to the state.

Towards the end of the First Plan, Stalin mounted a concerted five-year (1932–36) anti-religious campaign. The Soviet authorities placed the control of all places of worship into the hands of the Union of Atheists, which transformed them into museums, places of entertainment, or factories. They forbade the Muslim practice of going on pilgrimage to Mecca; the collection of a religious tax (*zakat*) to provide funds to the needy and for maintaining mosques and religious monuments; and the printing and distribution of the Quran.

The highly publicized burnings of some 3,500 books, banned on the ground of propagation of Islamic superstition, drove the message home. Muslim women were encouraged to burn their veils in public, and did so in the thousands. When the faithful, often led by clerics, took to the streets in protest, the authorities suppressed the marches and arrested the leaders.

SOCIAL REVOLUTION EMBEDDED, THEN PURGES

After the promulgation of the new Soviet constitution in December 1936, the Central Asian republics found it necessary to align their own constitutions with the Soviet Union's. They used this opportunity to consolidate socio-economic reforms. For instance, Article 109 of the new constitution of Tajikistan, promulgated in March 1937, explicitly forbade "giving minors in marriage, bride purchases, resisting women going to school or engaging in agricultural, industrial, state or other social or political activities."[39]

Within two decades of the Bolshevik revolution, the life of Central Asians underwent radical transformation in social, economic, political, cultural, and religious spheres. With the Soviet borders sealed from its southern neighbors, even the geographical perception of the region by its inhabitants changed. Instead of regarding themselves as the northeastern end of the Islamic world, as they had done since the eighth century, they now considered themselves citizens of the southern Soviet Union, which vigorously promoted scientific atheism. Their calendar changed from 1356 AH (After Hijra, Migration of Prophet Muhammad from Mecca to Medina) to 1937 AD. The local currencies disappeared and were replaced by the ruble and kopeks. Old weights and measures, centered around a dozen and a score, gave way to the metric system of kilogram and kilometer.

Villagers who had remained immune from the changes affecting urban centers lost their insularity. Traditionally, a Muslim man identified himself by stating his given name followed by his father's. Despite Lenin's decrying of Russian superiority, Russification crept into Muslim Central Asia. Sabir Kamal became Sabir Kamalov, and his sister Amina Kamalova (meaning, "of Kamal"). Muhammadjan Shukur in Bukhara turned into Mukhammadjan Shukurov. "I remember when passports came in, and all us children had to have identity papers," Shukurov told Monica Whitlock, the Central Asia correspondent of the BBC. "Of course, very few of us knew our birthdays, so there was a big commission sent to organize us. An official checked my teeth and felt my arms, and said my birthday was 30 October 1926. I said "No! I know I was born in 1925!" But he wrote it down, and there it was. They changed my surname at the same time. So, in five minutes I had a completely new identity."[40]

When, in 1936, Stalin initiated the Great Purge—called *Yezhovshchina* after N. I. Yezhov, the head of the Narodnyi Kommissariat Vnutrennikh Del (NKVD), People's Commissariat of Internal Affairs—Central Asia felt the impact. Directed against the "enemies of the people," the purge lasted for two years and was carried out in Central Asia to counter an alleged nationalist conspiracy in Uzbekistan involving the heads of two of the three centers of Soviet power. These were the Communist Party, headed by the First Secretary of the party's Central Committee; the government, led by the chairman of the Council of People's Commissars; and the state, headed by the chairman of the Presidium of the Supreme Soviet, which issued legislation between the (often brief) sessions of the Supreme Soviet.

Following an accusation that he had buried his brother according to the Islamic custom, Faizullah Khojayev, chairman of Uzbekistan's Council of People's Commissars, was dismissed by the Seventh Congress of the Communist Party of Uzbekistan (CPU) in June 1937. Three months later, a local newspaper accused Akmal Ikramov, the party's First Secretary, of being a nationalist. Both Khojayev and Ikramov were arrested. In March

1938, they were tried along with twenty-one other accused—including Nikolai Bukharin, a leading Russian Communist based in Moscow—as members of the "bloc of Rightists and Trotskyites," found guilty of various charges, and executed. Their jobs went respectively to Abdujabbar Abdurakhmanov (originally, Abdul Jabbar Abdul Rahman), aged thirty-one, and Usman Yusupov (Yusuf), aged thirty-eight. Molded by the Bolshevik regime, they represented the generation mobilized by the Soviet system in the earlier phase of its assault on traditional society.

A similar process was at work in Kazakhstan, the largest and the second most populous Soviet Socialist Republic in the region, and Kyrgyzstan. The party's membership campaigns in the 1920s had brought many young Kazakhs and Kyrgyzes into its fold, thus giving an increasing number of them a stake in the new system. The mortal blow that nationalization and collectivization of most rural property delivered to the power and prestige of traditional leaders opened up opportunities for young party cadres. They moved up steadily in the party and government hierarchy in a milieu where literacy campaigns, laced with ideological education and propaganda directed at adults, had a dramatic impact on predominantly nomadic and rural societies with literacy rates of below 5 percent.

In Tajikistan, the disgraced Tajik leaders included the chairmen of the Council of People's Commissars and the Presidium of the Supreme Soviet. Following their expulsion from the party in 1937, the job of the First Secretary of the Communist Party went to a Russian, Dmitri Z. Protopopov, who had earlier arrived in Dushanbe, the Tajik capital, as a representative of the AUCP's Central Committee. This illustrated the failure of Moscow to implement fully its earlier policy of indigenization.

Over the years, as Stalin became more and more obsessed with the idea of creating a highly centralized Union, the party and government authorities increasingly refused to make allowances for local traditions and interests. This led them to put a high premium on unquestioned loyalty from the capitals of the constituent republics. Consequently, Russian party members who were either domiciled in the region or sent from Moscow rose in the republican hierarchy. Lacking indigenous roots, they were immune to local lobbying and remained loyal to Moscow.

One of the major consequences of centralization was accelerated Russification of the non-Slavic parts of the USSR. In 1938, the central authorities made Russian compulsory in all non-Russian schools in the Union. Next, the script of Azeri was altered from Latin to Cyrillic. In 1940, Kazakh, Kyrgyz, Tajik, Turkmen, and Uzbek underwent the same change. The switchover to the Cyrillic alphabet made it easier for the indigenous pupils to learn Russian, particularly when the Russian grammatical forms and loan words had replaced the Arabic and Persian loan words in their languages, and had built up a fresh technical vocabulary. By depriving the regional people of their ability to read foreign publications published in the Roman alphabet, the authorities were able to control further their reading material.

The full impact of these changes could be gauged fully only against the backdrop of virtually universal illiteracy that prevailed. The literacy rate in Central Asia, as measured by the first post-revolution census in 1926, varied between 2.2 percent in Tajikistan and 7.1 percent in Kazakhstan, limited almost wholly to men. The census of 1939 showed the literacy rate jumping to 71.7 percent in Tajikistan, the most backward republic in the USSR.[41] This increased literacy applied as much to women as men, and had a dramatic impact on the lives of long-suffering Muslim women.

Freshly liberated girls discarded braids for short hair and de rigueur long trousers for knickers. Some of them left home to pursue higher education at colleges and universities, and took up jobs in towns and cities, instead of marrying in the late teens and bearing children. In an interview with the BBC's Central Asian service in the late 1990s, a secondary school teacher in Dushanbe recalled, "I felt I was the luckiest girl in the whole world. My great-grandmother was like a slave, shut up in her house. My mother was illiterate. She had thirteen children and looked old all her life. For me the past was dark and horrible, and whatever anyone says about the Soviet Union [now], that is how it was for me."[42] Unlike what happened to her mother and grandmother, under the Soviet system she got two years of maternity leave with a full salary, free health care for her baby, and a guaranteed place for the infant at a nursery.

Women came to have almost the same opportunities as men to develop their talents under a free educational system, which led to the opening of 1,600 public libraries in Tajikistan. It was also significant that the first grand public building to be constructed in Dushanbe in 1939 was the opera and ballet theater, which was open to both sexes. Three decades later, to the surprise and delight of most Tajiks and others, Malika Sobirova, an ethnic Tajik, would win a gold medal in an international ballet competition.

A similar improvement in the role of women in society occurred in Uzbekistan. Between 1925 and 1939, the proportion of women in the workforce rocketed from 9 percent to 39 percent. In addition to working in the civil service, women found jobs in such state-run institutions as schools, colleges, universities, hospitals, and laboratories.[43]

Overall, peasants and other villagers welcomed literacy drives. They had always envied those who were literate. In an interview with the visiting British writer Christopher Robbins in 2005, a former professor of philosophy in Almaty, born and raised in a small Kazakh settlement in a remote region of the steppe, said, "My father was very proud that I did well at school. All the old men in the village of his generation—all of them illiterate peasants—spent their money on their children's education. That was the point of their lives. One of the things you have to credit the Soviet system with is education. It was very good, and if you were bright, it helped you go all the way, even to Moscow University. And, even the small towns had good libraries. I began to read Russian classics, and grew to love and be influenced by [Anton] Checkov."[44]

Along with a dramatic rise in literacy came rapid growth in the mass media—including newspapers, periodicals, books, and radio broadcasts.

With the completion of the major road and rail projects in the region, as well as the massive Fergana Canal, Moscow tightened its grip over Central Asia while accelerating its socio-economic development. However, the eruption of World War II on September 1, 1939, gave an impetus to the Soviet conscription drive initiated a year earlier, and severely handicapped Moscow's plans for building socialism.

The Soviet Union, which had concluded a non-aggression pact with Nazi Germany under Adolf Hitler in August 1939, stayed neutral until June 1941 when Germany invaded it. For Soviets, this heralded the start of the Great Patriotic War in which they joined Britain and France to fight the alliance of Germany and Fascist Italy under Benito Mussolini.

THE GREAT PATRIOTIC WAR AND AFTER

Nazi Germany's invasion of the USSR on June 22, 1941, caused massive material damage to the country. At the same time it enabled the Soviet leadership to create a symbiotic relationship between patriotism and Marxist socialism. Thus the Bolshevik revolution got absorbed into the socio-psychological fabric of the Soviet public at large a generation after its launch in the midst of violence and chaos.

Accounting for nearly four-fifths of the Soviet Union's area and three-fifths of its population, the Russian Federation was the first among equals in the Union. Therefore, Stalin encouraged a revival of Russian nationalism to mobilize the populace to fight the powerful invader. Comparing the current German aggression to the 1812 invasion of Russia by France's

Napoleon Bonaparte, he described the latest armed conflict as "The Great Fatherland Patriotic War." Shortly after the celebrations of the Bolshevik revolution on November 7, Stalin revived the military titles used during Tsarist times. In order to placate traditional religious forces in the Soviet Union, he virtually deactivated the Union of Atheists. Ending his persecution of the Russian Orthodox Church, he co-opted it to raise patriotic feelings. In September 1943, he publicly received the Church hierarchy and allowed it to elect a new synod and patriarch.

Stalin executed a similar about-turn in his policy toward the Islamic hierarchy, which had felt aggrieved to see the number of the functioning mosques in the Soviet Union slashed by 95 percent of its pre-revolution total of over 26,000.[45] He combined an end to the persecution of Muslim clerics—often on charges of sabotage, spying for Germany or Japan, or counter-revolutionary activities—with the reopening of some major mosques. Then he permitted Muslim leaders to hold a pan-Islamic conference in Ufa, capital of the Bashkir Autonomous Region in the Russian Federation, in 1942. The conference urged Muslims at home and abroad to back the Allies (now including America, which joined the war in December 1941) and assist the Soviet Union defeat of Nazi Germany.

The next year Shaikh Abdul Rahman Rasulayev, the mufti of Ufa, reached an accord with Stalin similar to the one the latter had signed with the Patriarch Sergius for the Russian Orthodox Church. It marked the end of the anti-Islamic propaganda, and accorded a legal status to Islam along the lines followed by the Tsar in 1783. Stalin allowed the establishment of the Central Spiritual Muslim Directorate for European Russia and Siberia in Orenburg.

The Official Islamic Administration, established in October 1943, set up three Muslim Spiritual Directorates: in Ufa (Sunni sect) for the Muslims in the European sector of the USSR; in Tashkent (Sunni sect), for the Muslims of Middle Asia and Kazakhstan; and in Baku (Sunni and Shiite sects), for the Muslims of Trans-Caucasia. The overall function of these directorates was to manage that part of Islamic life that centered around working mosques and officially registered clerics and communities. In return, the leaders of the Official Islamic Administration saw to it that the mosque served the political interests of the Soviet regime at home and abroad. The concordat between mosque and state had a healing effect in the Muslim-majority region of Central Asia.

Hitler's invasion came at a time when Stalin had concluded that the basic economic objectives in Central Asia of increased output of cotton, cereals, fruit, and animal products could be achieved without further assaults on the traditional way of life. He therefore resigned himself to accepting what Donald S. Carlisle, an American specialist on Central Asia, calls "the continued co-existence of traditional and modern society with a semi-permeable wall separating and connecting the Central Asian and European worlds."[46] Actually, the pressures of war and conscription helped to erode the semi-permeable wall between the Asian and European sectors of the USSR. The full-blast Soviet propaganda succeeded in engendering a swell of anti-Nazi sentiment throughout the country.

The course of the war depended partly on the efficient maintenance of the Ashgabat railway and the Caspian port of Krasnovodsk (aka Turkmenbashi), Turkmenistan, which connected the southern fronts and the Trans-Caucasian republics with Central Russia, which had fallen into German hands. The uninterrupted use of this crucial transportation link during late 1941 and early 1942 enabled the Soviet forces to expel the German troops from the Volga region and the foothills of the Caucasus, and finally break the German siege of Volvograd (then Stalingrad). Little wonder that over 19,000 soldiers from Turkmenistan (with its population of roughly one million) received military honors.

The corresponding figure was 20,000 for Azerbaijan, a Muslim-majority republic which also helped the war efforts crucially by keeping open the rail link with Iran's Persian Gulf ports, where massive military supplies from the United States were unloaded for delivery to the Soviet Union. During the war, the Baku region produced 70 percent of the total Soviet oil output. [47]

Central Asia's industrialization received a boost due to the wartime policy of transferring factories from the frontline zones in the USSR to the peripheral regions. As a result, Kyrgyzstan gained more than thirty industrial enterprises, Kazakhstan 140; and Uzbekistan about 100, half of them belonging to heavy industry, including the manufacture of Ilyushin aircraft. In addition, Uzbekistan obtained dozens of military and civilian educational and scientific institutes and hospitals. During the war, Uzbekistan altogether acquired 238 new factories and seven hydro-electric plants.

Equally impressively, Uzbekistan, with a population of a just over 6 million, contributed about a million men and women to the military and its auxiliary units. In Kazakhstan, two-thirds of the members of the Communist Party (125,600) and Komsomol (347,000) joined the armed forces. Kazakhstan and Kyrgyzstan impinged far more on the Soviet psyche because their 316th Infantry Division commanded by I. V. Panfilov, participating in the combat near Moscow, fought bravely. Both the troops and civilians of Tajikistan also performed well, with more than 50,000 of them winning awards and medals. Kazakhstan received a million evacuees from the European USSR, as did Uzbekistan. The figure for the much smaller Kyrgyzstan was 139,000.[48]

The aggregate effect of these wartime developments was to unify the many nationalities living in the Union republics in several ways. In the process of working with Russian troops, the hundreds of thousands of indigenous Central Asians improved their Russian, which reinforced the political-economic unity of the USSR. It was in the military that Central Asian Muslims got their first taste of vodka and learned to drink it as Russians do—raising their glasses in a toast, and then emptying them wholesale in one gulp. The transfer of hundreds of factories from European Russia to Asia accelerated the region's industrialization. This, and the conscripting of the local labor, opened up unprecedented employment opportunities for women, furthering their emancipation.

Contrary to the popular perception in the West, what broke Nazi Germany's back was the combat on the eastern front with the Soviet Union. Hitler deployed three-quarters of his troops to fight the Soviets, with a battle at Kursk between 1.5 million German and Soviet soldiers. The scale of fighting on the Soviet front exceeded that of all other combats combined. The death toll of 30 million, including 22 million Soviet citizens, was staggering. However, victory in the Great Patriotic War, which ended in May 1945 with the Soviet troops capturing Berlin, was a great boost to the system. The warfare had created a more united Soviet Union, with its many nationalities sharing pride in their hard-earned victory.

After the war, Cenotaphs cropped up in all the capitals of the Union's republics, including Turkmenistan. In Ashgabat, at the Cenotaph arose a statue of motherhood towering opposite an eternal flame. Conducting the British writer Colin Thubron around the capital a few months after the collapse of the Soviet Union in December 1991, a nationalist Turkmen writer and poet Oraz Agabayev stopped at the Cenotaph and said, "This, at least we share with the Russians: the victory over Fascism."[49] Turkmenistan and all other Central Asian republics continue to celebrate May 9 as the Victory Day.

The task of constructing a new socialist order—through rapid development and cultural Sovietization—began in earnest, since the two preconditions for its success had now been satisfied. In the heat of the war, political education of the masses had reached its zenith. And the Communist Party had been fashioned as an effective ideological tool to unify the Russian core with the non-Slavic periphery—as well as perform managerial and executive jobs in the economic and administrative spheres. Indeed, a new generation of Soviet-educated, war-hardened party cadres, thoroughly loyal to the regime, had begun rising up the hierarchy in the Central Asian republics.

For the economic planners in Moscow, a special feature of Central Asia was its cotton, the leading raw material for clothing and a basic need of any society. No effort was spared to increase its output. In Uzbekistan and Tajikistan, irrigation and the switchover to cotton cultivation had emerged as complementary aspects of collectivization, an all-pervasive achievement of Communists in the countryside. The central government in Moscow had a special ministry for cotton. In 1950, Usman Yusupov, the erstwhile First Secretary of the Uzbek Communist Party, was promoted to run it. His colleague, Abdujabbar Abdurakhmanov (originally, Abdul Jabbar Abdul Rahman), was transferred to Moscow as well. Their jobs went to Amin Niyazov and Sharaf Rashidov, a former journalist, and the next year Nuritdin Mukhitdinov (originally, Nuruddin Muhyiddin) became chairman of the Council of People's Commissars. The latter two of these top three officials of the republic were in their early thirties.

This group of new regional leaders had to establish their credentials as party loyalists by carrying out purges, which occurred in 1951 to 1952. Though they were not of the same scale as those in the late 1930s, they were coordinated with similar moves by Moscow. The victims in Central Asia were party activists who allegedly had one or more of the failings of "local favoritism," "bourgeois nationalism," and "archaic customs" (meaning Islamic rituals or practices). The end to these intermittent purges came only when Stalin died on March 5, 1953.

Before his demise, Stalin had helped local Communists assume power in Albania, Bulgaria, Czechoslovakia, East Germany, Hungary, Poland, and Romania. These East European countries readily agreed to treat the Soviet Union as the first among equals in the Communist world. In 1949, the Soviet bloc found itself facing the formidable North Atlantic Treaty Organization (NATO), consisting of most of the North American and Western European states, led by the United States. NATO's European arm advanced further when its member states extended its membership to Greece and Turkey in 1952.

Turkey's membership of NATO was highly significant, as it was the only Muslim country in an alliance of Christian nations. What imparted it extraordinary strategic importance was its eastern border abutting the Soviet Union, a valuable asset to NATO, and almost touching the Nakhichevan enclave of Azerbaijan, the land of Azeri Turks.

CHAPTER 1

TURKEY:

From Militant Secularism to Grassroots Islam

HOME TO ONE OUT OF SIX TURKS, ISTANBUL, FORMERLY CONSTANtinople, is the prime metropolis of Turkey. It is the site of Aya Sofya (aka *Sancta Sophia* in Latin, and *Hagia Sofia* in Greek), Place of Divine Wisdom, and the Blue Mosque (aka Sultan Ahmet Camii)—the outstanding symbols and monuments, respectively, of Christianity and Islam, the two major religions that have largely shaped the histories of Europe and Asia. A city perched on seven adjacent hills, Istanbul is endowed with such a unique combination of air, water, and sunlight that over the centuries it has enchanted visitors from the four corners of the world.

One such visitor was Lord Kinross. "Istanbul is a classic example, unusual among cities, of a happy marriage between nature and man," he noted in *Europa Minor* in 1956. "Land and water are its elements: the land is resolved into architecture, the water forever girdling away from it, the two coalescing to create a city distinct with space and speed and a liquid cleansing light. Its rhythm is in the water, in the Bosphorus, racing like a deep salt river between Europe and Asia from a cold sea in the north to a warm sea in the south . . . It is a city of windows . . . their panes glinting gold as the sun dies away from it into the green hills of Europe beyond."[1]

Since then, Istanbul has expanded from an elegant Byzantine city into a sprawling megalopolis with suburbs of featureless concrete towers and bland apartment blocks. Behind their walls live Turks imbued with religiosity, their spiritual compass turned towards the local mosque, and their political loyalty to the Justice and Development Party (*Adalet ve Kalkınma Partisi*, in Turkish; AK Party) with its roots in Islamism. These suburbanites, who started arriving from the countryside in the 1960s, have little in common with the true natives of Istanbul, who tend to dominate the city center that teems with foreign tourists most of the year.

To witness the contrast between the secular elite and the religious masses, a visitor need not make a foray into the distant suburbs of Istanbul. A minor diversion from the beaten tourist path can be eye-opening. Near the covered bazaar of 4,000 shops in the Old City is the Beyazit Square (originating in 393 AD as the Forum of Theodosius), the main approach to the impressive portal of Istanbul University with its grand gate and a tall tower, sitting atop one of the seven hills. Throughout the day, with its open-air cafes and bars, patronized by Westernized Turks and foreign tourists, the plaza has a picnicking aura. Visitors might as well be in Athens or Rome.

Were they then to traverse the streets lying between Yenicheriler Caddesi at the bottom of Beyazit Square and Kennedy Caddesi along the sea front, they would encounter a different world altogether, one that has barely changed for the past few centuries. In this working-class district of higgledy-piggledy houses, they will find rubbish from small leather workshops strewn in the streets and women in black chadors gliding past like ghosts. In small, crowded teahouses, they will see a waiter pass the communal water pipe from customer to customer. Besides vans and cars parked bumper-to-bumper, the only other signs of modern life they will notice are hanging electric wires, TV antennas, and running water faucets. The universe of these Turks, living within spitting distance of smart cafes and bars, revolves around a different orbit from that of their affluent compatriots, who remain rigidly secular and determined to lead sensual, materially satisfying lives.

Overall, Istanbul is more renowned for its monuments catering to the spirit—world famous mosques and churches. The Old City, in its extraordinarily beautiful and dramatic setting, can seduce by its very appearance, while sharing the place of pride equally with the Blue Mosque and Aya Sofya. Built atop a hill in the early seventeenth century, the imposing mass of the Blue Mosque with its six minarets stands out for miles over water and land. Shaped like a four-leaf clover, with semi-domes ranked by smaller semi-domes on the four sides, it has a balcony on three sides, and a large central dome supported by massive pillars. Elegant, harmonious, and visually pleasing, it is popularly known as the Blue Mosque because of the predominantly blue color of its interior decoration—its arches and walls embellished with arabesque stenciling, and its windows of brightly colored Venetian glass.

Sultan Ahmet wanted his architect to surpass the marvel of Aya Sophia, built in the mid-sixth century, the largest church in Christendom for almost a thousand years, and the site for the crowning of Byzantine rulers.

The novelty of its thirty-meter dome, apparently unsupported by pillars, left the worshippers gasping with awe. Unseen to the naked eye, the massive dome is supported by forty massive ribs that rest on huge pillars in the interior walls.

The church fell to Mehmet II (1451–81), aka Muhammad the Conqueror, when he conquered Constantinople in 1453. He turned it into a mosque with a *mihrab* (prayer niche) pointing toward Mecca, and a *mimbar* (pulpit). In the mid-nineteenth century, calligrapher Mustafa Izzat Efendi inscribed the names of Allah, Muhammad, and the four rightly guided caliphs—Abu Bakr, Umar, Uthman, and Ali—in gilded Arabic letters on wooden medallions to embellish the central dome. When secular Turkish President Mustafa Kemal Ataturk proclaimed Aya Sophia a museum in 1935, he left the inscribed medallions in place.

The other church popular with the faithful was called St. Savior's Church in Chora (literally, "countryside"), located on the sixth hill. The original building, constructed in the late eleventh century, underwent remodeling a century later, and major refurbishing from 1315 to 1321. During the latter period it was embellished with frescoes and mosaics of extraordinary beauty. These images included the portraits of Christ's ancestors all the way back to Adam. This genealogy was the prelude to the pictorial narratives of the lives of Mary and Christ. The painting in the apse, depicting Christ— watched by the preeminent saints and kings—smashing the gates of Hell and raising Adam and Eve, completed the cycle.

St. Savior's functioned as a church until 1510 when Sultan Beyazit II (1481–1512) had it converted to a mosque called Kariya Camii. But, very wisely, he left the frescoes and mosaics untouched. During Kemal Ataturk's rule, the mosque became the Kariya Museum. In 1948, the Byzantine Institute of America embarked on restoring the unique collection of frescoes and mosaics—an enterprise that took a decade to finish and ultimately revived the most outstanding and important series of Byzantine paintings on earth.

Not surprisingly, it was an American organization which initiated and funded the restoration of the frescoes and mosaics—not the Greek Orthodox community of Turkey, which had shrunk dramatically since the founding of the Turkish Republic in 1923 when it and Greece signed the compulsory exchange of population agreement. Leaving aside the Turks of western Thrace in Greece, and the Greeks of Istanbul who were allowed to stay on, this pact led to the emigration of 1.3 million Greeks from Turkey and 0.5 million Turks from Greece.

The census of 1924 showed that of the 1.17 million residents of Istanbul, 61 percent were Muslim, 26 percent Greek, 7 percent Armenian, and 6 percent Jews.[2] The Armenians were preeminent in business, trade, and banking; and so were the Greeks. The Greek Orthodox Patriarchate in Istanbul dated back to 1454, and its St. George Church to 1720. The Turkish government's imposition of property tax on religious minorities in 1945 hurt many Greek and Armenian businesses, and led to an exodus of Greeks and Armenians from Istanbul. With the establishment of Israel in 1948, many Jews emigrated voluntarily to Israel. In 1954, the events in the British colony of Cyprus—four-fifths Greek, one-fifth Turkish—impacted the religious minorities in Turkey when the Greek government called for the union of Cyprus with Greece. On the night of September 6 to 7, 1955, the planned looting and burning of the houses and businesses of the Greek, Armenian, and Jewish communities ended up wrecking 3,000 buildings. As a result, many Greeks, Armenians, and Jews emigrated. The next wave of emigraton came in 1964, following the December 1963 massacre of Turkish Cypriots in independent Cyprus.

Today there are less than 5,000 Greek Orthodox left in Turkey, and they are mostly in Istanbul, where the Greek-language daily *Apoyevmatini* (circulation 1,200) is published. The number of Jews has remained static around 22,000, chiefly because about a quarter of them marry Turks, which requires conversion to Islam.[3] By contrast there are about 75,000 Armenians in Turkey, including some 30,000 from Armenia. Most of them live in Istanbul, which has twenty Armenian schools and thirty-five places of worship affiliated with the Armenian Orthodox Church, known also as the Armenian Apostolic Church. Splitting from the Eastern Orthodox Church in the fourth century, it adopted the Monophysite doctrine—the belief that Christ had a human and divine nature, united in one person—in 506.[4] Among the Armenian publications is the daily *Nor Marmara* (circulation 2,200). The controversy about the genocide of the Armenians during World War I, though not as fraught as it was a few decades ago, continues in a minor key. The assassination of Hrant Dink, an Armenian journalist, in 2007 caused deep distress among his co-religionists.

It is worth noting that since the founding of the Turkish Republic, only the religious minorities have been allowed to speak non-Turkish languages. That is how Ladino, the mother tongue of the Sephardic Jews from Spain, has remained a living language in Turkey. Also known as Judeo-Spanish, Ladino is written in Hebrew script, and its vocabulary consists of Hebrew words as well as Portuguese, Greek, and Turkish. The first book in Ladino, published in Istanbul, appeared in 1510.[5] That was eighteen years after Beyazit II—following the example of his father, Muhammad the Conqueror, who signed a decree offering the Jews safety upon capturing Constantinople—invited the Sephardic Jews expelled from Spain and Portugal during the Inquisition in 1492 to his empire. They settled in the empire's European as well as Asian parts.

Within five years of ascending the Ottoman throne, Beyazit II's son, Selim I (1512–20) defeated the Mamluke sultan, Touman Bey, near Cairo, the capital of the Islamic Empire of the Mamlukes. He proclaimed himself the Sultan-Caliph, the secular-religious ruler. With this, the Ottoman Turkish Empire became the center of the Islamic world.

TURKEY, HEART OF THE ISLAMIC WORLD

Today's Republic of Turkey, the successor to the Ottoman Turkish Empire, is populated by Osmanli (Ottoman) Turks. They and the Seljuks, the leading tribe of the Oghuz federation, have been the two Turkic groups found in West Asia and East Europe. Classified as Western Turks, they are distinct from Eastern/Central Asian Turks and Tatars/Turko-Tatars.

Turks were originally hunting people in the Altai Mountains of Western Mongolia at a time when the steppes supported Scythians, Huns, and other pastoral nomadic peoples, and the Mongolian plains the Kyrgyz/Kazakh people. As they moved westward, they adapted to pastoral nomadic life and occupied the steppes, reaching the shores of the Caspian Sea in the middle of the first millennium.

From the ninth to the eleventh centuries, Seljuks, the main players in the ethnogeny of Turkmens, followed them. In the tenth century, Mongols conquered Mongolia, displacing the Kyrgyz/Kazakh people and causing a migration of Turks and Turko-Mongols over the next several centuries. The Kyrgyz/ Kazakhs moved south to present-day Kyrgyzstan and into the Syr Darya region.

Of the various Turkish realms springing up in the region, the Ottoman principality—with its capital in Bursa, 100 kilometers (sixty-five miles) from Istanbul—emerged as the most powerful under Osman I (1259–1326), a leader of the Osmanli Turks, who had embraced Islam. It was from their base in Bursa that the Turks, led by Sultan Beyazit I, ventured to overpower the Byzantine Empire. Their success came with Muhammad the Conqueror.

Bursa is also famous for something more mundane, yet universal. It is the birthplace of the doner (derivative of *dönmek*, "to turn" in Turkish) kebab, invented by Iskander Usta in 1867. Roasted mutton and lamb, along with flat bread, have been the staples of the Turkish diet since the pastoral period of the Turkish tribes. During their nomadic phase, Turkish warriors skewered large portions of meat on their swords and roasted them over camp fires. Inevitably, the fat would melt and fall into the fire, causing flare-ups and burning the meat—an unsatisfactory phenomenon. There seemed to be no way to circumvent the problem—until Usta designed a vertical grill, filled it with red-hot coal, and placed the meat-holding sword on its point next to it. He thereby channeled the burning fat to baste the meat and was able to slice off the outer layer as soon as it was cooked. Then he placed the meat slices inside a flat bread, topped them with tomato juice and salt and pepper, and thus produced a delicious ready-to-eat meal. Though the doner kebab is now as universal as an Italian pizza, Bursa has retained as its claim as the city where the best doner kebabs are served.

The capital shifted to Istanbul—a corrupted Turkish derivative of Constantinople, or *eis tom polis*, meaning "to the city" in Greek. The Ottoman Empire expanded until the late seventeenth century, stretching from the Persian Gulf to Algeria, and from Sudan to southern Russia in the northeast, and just beyond Budapest to the northwest. Like its rivals, the Tsarist and Persian Empires, it had Muslim, Christian, and Jewish subjects. By the early nineteenth century, owing mainly to rapid advances made by European powers in technology and administration, the balance began to turn against the Ottomans. To reverse the trend, Sultan Mahmoud (1808–39) introduced administrative and military reforms along European lines under the title of Tanzimat (literally, "Reorganization") in 1827. European powers approved of Tanzimat, but that did not deter them from attacking the Ottoman Empire.

Tsarist Russia was the most aggressive empire, determined to act as the militant protector of 12 million Eastern Orthodox Christians under the Ottomans. At the same time, it was consolidating and expanding its territories in Central Asia, inhabited by Muslims. Taking their cue from the Russian aspirations toward the Christians of the Ottoman Empire, the leaders of Central Asian Muslims appealed to Sultan Abdul Aziz (1861–76) to become the guardian of the Muslims in Tsarist Russia. To them, the Ottoman Empire—containing the holy cities of Mecca, Medina, and Jerusalem, as well as the leading Islamic cultural centers of Cairo, Damascus, and Baghdad—was the prime embodiment of Islamic civilization and power.

But Abdul Aziz, heavily indebted to European powers, could do little. In the mid-1870s, at Russia's behest, Bulgaria, Bosnia, Serbia, and Montenegro rebelled against Istanbul. This paved the way for the overthrow of Abdul Aziz by Midhat Pasha, the leader of the Young Ottomans, a powerful group formed in 1859 with the aim of establishing an elected assembly of the believers. Midhat Pasha produced a constitution that formalized the religious status of the Ottoman sultan, and included a bill of rights and a provision for an elected chamber. Sultan Abdul Hamid II (1876–1909) promulgated it, reluctantly, in December 1876.

Five months later, the Russian army crossed the Ottoman borders with the objective of winning freedom for Slavs, and reached Istanbul. The sultan had to sign the humiliating Treaty of San Stefano in March 1878, revised in July in Berlin. The Treaty of Berlin required the sultan to hand over Cyprus to Britain and Tunis to France, and allow Russia to keep control of the districts of Kars, Batum, and Ardahan. The continued loss of territory, coupled with growing interference in the Ottoman Empire's internal affairs by the Europeans, convinced Abdul Hamid II that the fifty-year-old Tanzimat program had failed to reassure either European powers or his Christian subjects. He therefore changed direction.

In February 1878, he suspended the constitution and dissolved parliament. He arrested Midhat Pasha and banished the Young Ottomans to different parts of the empire. Repudiating Islamic modernism, he turned to traditional Islamic values and thought. He tried to regenerate cohesion in the Ottoman society by rallying the common folk on a religious platform around the Islamic banner. To succeed in the venture, he activated Sufi brotherhoods and used them as channels of communication to reach the masses. His strategy succeeded because there had long been a current of Islamic feeling among the humbler Muslim subjects of the Empire.

However, by the early twentieth century, Abdul Hamid II's populist approach to Islam at home and espousal of pan-Islamism abroad had proved inadequate to revitalize the disintegrating Ottoman Empire. In 1908, the army officers of the empire's European territories and a group of young intellectuals, later to be called the "Young Turks," compelled the sultan to reinstate the 1876 constitution. They stood not for pan-Turanism/pan-Turkism, the concept of uniting all Turks in Asia and Europe in one state; or pan-Islamism, the idea of uniting all Muslims in one state; but for pan-Ottomanism, the concept of forging a single Turkish-speaking nation out of the various peoples of the empire.

Soon after the 1908 coup, Crete announced its union with Greece, Bulgaria proclaimed its independence, and Austria annexed Bosnia and Herzegovina. In April 1909 came an unsuccessful attempt by the sultan to overthrow the Young Turks. They in turn deposed him, hoping that would stop the rot. They failed. The Balkan War of 1912 to 1913, which resulted in the Ottoman Empire's loss of its remaining European territories as well as Libya, underlined its continued weakness. The latest conflict destroyed the concept of pan-Ottomanism. At the same time, the shrinking of the empire made it religiously more homogeneous.

This encouraged the Young Turk triumvirate of Enver Pasha, Jamal Pasha, and Talat Bey—which assumed effective power in Istanbul in 1913—to highlight pan-Islamism and pan-Turkism. It was therefore receptive to the suggestion by the Kaiser of Germany in 1914 to liberate fellow Turks and fellow Muslims from Russian bondage in Central Asia, and thereby compensate the Ottomans' loss of empire in Europe and North Africa. To that end, Ottoman Turkey joined Germany in World War I in October 1914.

Encouraged by Enver Pasha, the Ottoman war minister Sultan-Caliph Mehmet VI (1909–23) urged Muslims worldwide to mount a jihad against their imperial masters—Britain, France, and Russia.[6] In March 1918, Bolshevik Russia concluded a peace treaty with Germany at Brest-Litovsk, which involved, inter alia, Russia returning to Ottoman Turkey the districts of Kars, Batum, and Ardahan it had appropriated forty years before.

Elsewhere, the Ottoman forces found themselves pounded by the Allies. The Young Turk ministers resigned, and the Sultan appointed a new cabinet. It signed an armistice with the victorious Allies on October 30, 1918, twelve days before the German surrender.

For the next several years, the situation in Turkey, the core of the old Ottoman realm, remained turbulent. Its new regime tried to break with its Islamic past and create a new nation-state after it had regained its full sovereignty from the occupying Allied forces. During this period, the unprecedented problems of the nature of sovereignty and the relationship between state and mosque engaged the minds of the new rulers.

BIRTH OF THE TURKISH NATION

In a duplicitous move, the Allies permitted Greek forces to occupy the Turkish port of Izmir on May 15, 1920. As the Greeks began marching east with the declared objective of annexing Western Anatolia to create a Greater Greece, the Muslims of Anatolia took up arms under the leadership of Mustafa Kemal Ataturk (1881–1938) to wage their War of Independence. This heightened hostility towards ethnic Greeks in Turkey, and would lead to a dramatic reduction in their numbers in Anatolia and Istanbul. Earlier, during World War I, a similar fate had befallen the Armenians, particularly in the area adjoining Tsarist Russia, a Christian nation, which opposed Ottoman Turkey on the battlefield.

Encouraged by the advance of the Russian troops into eastern Turkey, the Armenians in the Van area rebelled, killed local Turks, and captured the fort on April 20, 1915, until the arrival of the Russian troops. Four days later, the Ottoman authorities ordered the wholesale expulsion of the Armenians from the war zone to Greater Syria. The Ottoman troops butchered hundreds of thousands of Armenian men while marching their women and children across the Syrian border. In retaliation, the short-lived Russian-backed Republic of Armenia, covering the Kars and Ardahan districts, massacred the local Turks and Kurds—until the Ottoman forces reclaimed the Armenian area. Later Turkey claimed that up to 600,000 Turkish and Kurdish Muslims lost their lives, whereas the Armenians claimed that between 700,000 and 1.2 million Armenians perished between April 1915 and 1920. The controversy rages still today.

Mustafa Kemal was a tall, well-built man with a charismatic personality. With his fair skin and blue eyes, he looked more European than Turkish. As it was, he was born in a European city—Salonika (aka Thessaloniki)—in Greece, then part of the Ottoman Empire, to Ali Reza Effendi, a lumber merchant, and Zubeyde Hanum. His father died when he was seven, and his maternal uncle became his guardian. At the age of fifteen, he enrolled at a military school and graduated as a lieutenant six years later. After spending three years at the Military Academy in Istanbul, he acquired the rank of a major.

At the time of the deposition of Sultan Abdul Hamid II in 1909, he was the staff officer of the Special Forces of the Third Army, which arrived in Istanbul from its provincial garrison. During the 1912 to 1913 Balkan War, he led the units from Gallipoli and helped recapture Edirne (aka Adrianople). By the time World War I started in 1914, he had become a colonel and was in charge of the 19th division.

In March 1915, when the British and French navies' attempt to pass the Dardanelles Straits on their way to Istanbul led to heavy losses, the Allies decided to land troops on the Gallipoli Peninsula. When they tried to do so on April 25, Mustafa Kemal's forces slaughtered them. Their second attempt in August also failed. Kemal Ataturk proved to be an inspirational leader. Addressing his soldiers in the trenches, he said, "I am not ordering you to attack, I am ordering you to die." The resulting battlefield victories turned him into a war hero and won him promotion to general. By the time the war finished in 1918, he was the commander of the Seventh Army.

After the war, he took up the cause of a sovereign, independent Turkey. In February 1920, the Ottoman parliament adopted a nationalist manifesto, demanding self-determination for the (lost) Arab regions of the empire, but insisting that all other Muslim-majority areas should remain an undivided whole. The Allies disapproved, and showed it. On March 16, the British troops occupying Istanbul arrested 150 nationalists, including several parliamentarians. Sultan-Caliph Mehmet VI acquiesced in this.

Protesting the arrest of its members, the parliament prorogued itself indefinitely on March 18. The next day Mustafa Kemal ordered elections to a new emergency parliament, named the Grand National Assembly (GNA), to convene in Ankara, where the Turkish nationalists had established their head office. Aware that Istanbul was vulnerable to attack by gunboats, Kemal backed the idea of moving the capital to Ankara in the Anatolian plains. On April 11, Mehmet VI dissolved the parliament.

The collaboration of Mehmet VI with the occupying forces accelerated the transformation of Ottoman nationalism, the driving force of the Young Turks, into Turkish nationalism. The Grand National Assembly met in Ankara on April 23, 1920, under the chairmanship of Mustafa Kemal. The constitution it adopted read: "Sovereignty belongs unconditionally to the nation. The government is based on the principle of the people's direct rule over their own destiny"; and "the Grand National Assembly is the only representative of the people . . . the holder of both legislative and executive power."[7]

There was no apparent contradiction in being a nation-state and Islamic, maintaining the religious traditions of the Ottoman Empire. The parliament later appointed a clergy-dominated Sharia committee to vet all legislation for conformity with the Islamic law. Also, the earlier practice of having a minister for Sharia—a successor to the traditional office of the Shaikh-al-Islam, the Wise Man of Islam, the paramount religious official—continued.

Whereas Mehmet VI accepted the Treaty of Sevres in August 1920, which confirmed the dissolution of the Ottoman Empire, the Grand National Assembly rejected it. Kemal's prestige rose sharply when he secured a decisive victory over the Greeks at the Sakarya River in August 1921. This won him promotion to Field Marshall and Ghazi, an Islamic title accorded to those who defeat non-Muslim forces. By the following August, the Turks had formally won their War of Independence against the Greek army—an event that paved the way for Allied recognition of the sovereignty of Turkey under the Treaty of Lausanne of July 1923, which superseded the Treaty of Sevres.

World War I, the War of Independence, and the concomitant conscription, which extended to all able-bodied men fit to fight, affected the Turkish society deeply. The Grand National Assembly reflected the profound change. At Kemal's behest, it passed a law on November 1, 1922, that marked the formal end of Ottoman rule, depriving Sultan-Caliph Mehmet VI of all secular power in the new Turkish state, thus ending the ruling dynasty originating with Osman I in 1259.

But the new law left untouched the caliphate, a religious office now on a par with the Pope in the Catholic world. To justify his action, Kemal referred to the Abbasid period (750–1258) when the caliphs had lost all political authority and become symbolic figures of Islamic unity. Thus the GNA finally abrogated the principle of "sovereignty of an individual," which had been the foundation of Islamic empires. As for the caliphate, the GNA accepted the Ottoman dynasty's claim to it with the rider that it would choose as caliph "that member of the Ottoman house who was in learning and character most worthy and fitting." Since it did not consider the deposed Mehmet VI to be so qualified, he went into exile in 1923 after losing his office of sultan. The mantle of caliphate fell on his cousin, Abdul Majid.

Once Turkey, a nation of a mere 12 million people, had secured its sovereignty internationally through the Treaty of Lausanne, its Grand National Assembly amended the constitution on October 29, 1923, to describe the country's governmental form as "a republic," with the power to choose the republic's head resting with the Ankara-based GNA. It elected Mustafa Kemal president, a decision it would repeat every four years until his demise fifteen years later. With Caliph Abdul Majid based in Istanbul, the Turkish state had to define its relationship with Islam. Its constitution declared, "The religion of the Turkish state is Islam"; and the GNA continued to have its Sharia committee, and the cabinet its minister of Sharia.

However, having established a republic, a fledgling entity, Kemal resolved to strengthen it by eliminating the other center of power, the caliphate, which had the potential of rallying the opposition to the new order. Riding the surge of heady Turkish nationalism, Kemal decided to strike at the caliphate while it was recovering from the recent traumatic experiences.

Whether by design or chance, the struggle of Kemal Ataturk and his aides against the *ancien regime* came to include a campaign against religion and religious infrastructure, which the caliph's camp was bound to use to regain authority. Also, Islam, transcending national frontiers, was ideologically antithetical to the concept of a Turkish national identity, which Kemalist forces were striving to engender. Anticipating resistance and counter-attack by the caliph's followers, the new regime set up "independence tribunals" to try those attempting to restore the old system, and promulgated a stringent Law for the Maintenance of Order.

SECULARIZATION AND WESTERNIZATION

Addressing a new session of the GNA on March 1, 1924, Kemal Ataturk stressed the need to have "a unified system of education"—that is, to abolish religious schools and colleges—and to "cleanse and elevate the Islamic faith by rescuing it from the position of a political instrument to which it has been accustomed for centuries."[8] Two days later the 290-member GNA passed Kemal Ataturk's proposals, with only one voice dissenting.

This led to the deposition of Caliph Abdul Majid and the abolition of the caliphate, a 1,292-year-old office. Equally importantly, the Turkish government exiled all members of the Ottoman family, thus aborting any chance of them becoming a rallying force against the republic. At about the same time, the leading supporters of Kemal Ataturk established the Republican People's Party (RPP), a body that went on to claim the loyalties of all parliamentarians and most civil servants of various ranks. It adopted the following as its founding principles: statism, nationalism, populism, republicanism, secularism, and reformism. The amended constitution—guaranteeing equality before the law, and freedom of thought, speech, press, and association—was promulgated on April 20, 1924.

In May, in what proved to be the second phase of secularization, came a wholesale abolition of the religious infrastructure: the office of the Shaikh-al-Islam, the ministries of Sharia and *waqf* (religious endowments), the Sharia courts, religious schools, and Sufi lodges and hostels. The income from the religious trusts, now placed under the directorate-general of religious endowments, was transferred from the clergy to the public treasury. All Sharia judges were retired. The government retained control of mosques as well as the education, appointment, and salaries of the preachers (*khatibs*) and prayer-leaders (imams) through the newly created Directorate-General of Religious Affairs (DGRA) under the prime minister. It instructed the ministry of education to train a new generation of preachers and prayer-leaders, and the DGRA to organize the teaching of Quranic courses by schools.

Influenced by Europe's anti-religious movements of the late nineteenth and early twentieth centuries, Kemal and his close aides (later to be called the "White Turks") saw religion as a relic of the pre-modern epoch, and resolved to weaken and control it in order to advance modernization. Aware of the religiosity that prevailed among the masses, they adopted an authoritarian strategy which, thanks to the titanic prestige Kemal had acquired among Turks, they were able to implement. As a consequence, an authoritarian modernism rather than bourgeois, individual liberalism came to underpin public life, and the White Turks would define "secular republic" as the "republic of seculars," not the republic of all citizens.

Along with secularization came Westernization, at first in the form of dress. "Boots or shoes on our feet, trousers on our legs, shirt and jacket and waistcoat—and of course . . . [a] 'hat'," Mustafa Kemal stated in a speech in August 1925. His subsequent decree prescribed hats for all men, and made it a criminal offense to wear the traditional headgear. Interestingly, while describing the veil for women as "a ridiculous object," he refrained from banning it.

Another crucial step towards Westernization was the supplanting, in December 1925, of the Islamic calendar—beginning with the migration of Prophet Muhammad from Mecca to Medina—by the Gregorian calendar, beginning with the circumcision of Jesus Christ. Having curbed the orthodox Islamic infrastructure, Kemal focused on destroying the network of Sufi brotherhoods, which, he said, fostered superstition and retarded modernity and civilization. He disbanded them, outlawing their rituals and prayers, and confiscating their assets, including their lodges and convents.

Since this set of social reforms impinged directly on the everyday life of citizens, about 87 percent of whom were rural and conservative, it elicited more resistance than the earlier package, which had centered chiefly around Islamic institutions. The regime dealt with it by actively maintaining its instruments of coercion: the "independence tribunals" and the Law for the Maintenance of Order.

In 1926 came the final installment of reform—of the law. The existing combination of the Ottoman statutes and the Sharia gave way to the Swiss Civil Code, the German Commercial Code, and the Italian Penal Code. The Swiss Civil Code changed the legal position of women overnight, ending polygamy and the inequity suffered by women under the Islamic rules of inheritance, and legalized civil marriage. (However, women had to wait another eight years for the right to vote.)

Thus, between 1922 and 1926, using state authority, Kemal effected revolutionary changes at the macro- and micro-levels—from the abolition of the caliphate to the compulsory wearing of hats. Finally, in 1928, at his behest, the Grand National Assembly deleted the constitutional clause that described Islam as the state religion of Turkey.

In that year, the GNA also adopted a law to introduce a Latin-based alphabet to replace the Arabic script, which was banned. As in the Soviet republics of Central Asia and Azerbaijan, this had the immediate and dramatic effect of cutting off society from its literature, religious and secular. Kemal realized that the rising new generation would be unable to read the Quran or any version of Turkish history not vetted by him or his successors. Over time, the Roman script created an ever-widening gap between Turkey and other Muslim countries.

Secularization and Westernization continued until Kemal Ataturk's death in 1938, caused by the cirrhosis of his liver. Though he was familiar with beer, he preferred a limpid spirit distilled from aniseed and raisin, called raki, which turns milky when diluted with water. His addiction to drink was widely known. "I've got to drink," he explained. "My mind keeps on working hard and fast to the point of suffering. I have to slow it down and rest it at times . . . when I don't drink, I can't sleep, and the distress stupefies me."[9] Ironically, due to the insistence of his surviving sister, Kemal Ataturk's procession to a secular monument in Ankara was followed by the traditional Islamic rites at a mosque.

By the late 1930s, for all practical purposes, Kemalism had replaced Islam as the state religion, with the hard-drinking, chain-smoking Mustafa Kemal as its prophet. In the post-Kemal era, schoolchildren would be required to learn his sayings by heart. His image would become ubiquitous, appearing in all official and quasi-official institutions, in public squares, parks, and railroad stations, and on countless badges and posters, on postage stamps and bank notes, and even in a corner of television screens.

Educational reform made attendance at secular elementary schools compulsory in 1930 and downgraded Istanbul University's Faculty of Divinity to Institute of Islamic Research within the Faculty of Letters in 1933. Religious reform required that the call to Islamic prayer be given in Turkish, instead of Arabic, in 1932—a radical change in the most frequent ritual of Islam, which caused widespread resentment.

Further Westernization came with the replacement of Friday, the Islamic holy day, as the day of rest in public offices, with Sunday; and the introduction of surnames in the European style in 1935. Mustafa Kemal took Ataturk (literally, "father of Turks") as his surname, and his lieutenant, Ismet, chose Inonu, the name of the area where Mustafa Kemal stopped the advance of the Greek army during the War of Independence. More importantly, in 1937 the GNA inserted secularism or "laicism" as one of the fundamental principles of the state laid out in the constitution.

The strength of the Kemalist revolution was that it was thoroughgoing. Besides reforming or sapping Islamic institutions, it impinged on the daily existence of all citizens, urban and rural, in terms of dress, family relations, children's education, the alphabet, the weekly holiday, and so on. Its primary weakness was that it depended almost entirely on a single leader. The tremendous esteem and popularity that Kemal Ataturk won from his triumphs in the War of Independence helped him virtually to impose his will on the largely illiterate rural masses who lacked self-confidence. The active support for his modernizing ideas that came from military officers and liberal intellectuals concentrated in Istanbul was more effective than the opposition from religious and secular conservatives scattered all over the country.

Kemal Ataturk's major problem was the sheer inertia of traditional customs and patterns of thinking deeply embedded among the mainly rural masses. His strategy of relying on state coercion to suppress resistance was effective in curbing overt opposition by a literate minority, but it lacked an instrument to educate and inform the illiterate populace—something that the victorious Communists in Central Asia and Azerbaijan had done speedily and effectively. It was only in 1932 that Kemal Ataturk used his Republican People's Party to initiate a program of adult education. Lacking a full-fledged ideology beyond its commitment to Turkish nationalism and secularism, the RPP was a less powerful instrument of change than the Communist Party in the Muslim regions of Central Asia and Azerbaijan.

This deficiency was to become increasingly obvious in the years following Kemal Ataturk's death. To keep the republic on the narrow path of Kemalist secularism, the generals mounted four coups during the next half a century. They seized on that text of the constitution which charges the military with "the timely and correct identification of threats against the unity of the country and the nation," and requires it "to protect the territory against threats, which may necessitate the use of the Turkish armed force, within the framework of the Constitution and the law, against any overt or covert attempt to destroy the democratic parliamentary system . . . and the indivisible integrity of the Turkish nation."[10]

AFTER KEMAL ATATURK

Following the Kemalist dictum of "Peace at home, peace abroad," the Turkish government remained neutral in World War II—until January

1945, when it joined the Allies. But it could not insulate itself from the economic hardships caused by an armed conflict of such magnitude. The peasantry and the traditional middle classes—artisans, craftsmen, and petty traders—who had gained nothing, socially or economically, from the Kemalist revolution, became disenchanted, and remembered fondly the Islamic era of the Ottomans.

Sensing restiveness at large, President Ismet Inonu, the successor to Kemal Ataturk, allowed the formation of opposition parties. Among these, the Democratic Party (DP), consisting mainly of former RPP members and led by Celal (pronounced Jelal) Bayar and Adnan Menderes, the son of a wealthy landowner from Izmir, was the most important. While committing itself to upholding Kemalism, it called for less state intervention in the economy and religious affairs. The DP's demand that religious freedom be treated as "a sacred human right" proved popular. When, in 1950, the Bayar government offered an optional two-hour course on Islam on Saturday afternoons in schools, parents rushed to enroll their children. Attendance at mosques rose. In defiance of the law, Arabic inscriptions began appearing in shops, cafes, and taxis.

In the May 1950 election the DP won a landslide victory—408 seats to the RPP's 79—on a popular vote of 55 percent. The parliament elected Bayar president; and Menderes became the prime minister. With his round, steel-framed glasses, receding hair, and fleshy face, Menderes had the appearance of a professor. His government abrogated the penalty for reciting the Islamic prayer call in Arabic, a move that was widely welcomed.

In the next parliamentary poll in 1954, the DP's vote rose to 58.4 percent. The party made religious education compulsory at the primary level and optional at the secondary level, and recognized theological schools and colleges—called *imam-khatib* (prayer leader-preacher) institutions. The state-controlled radio began transmitting Quranic recitation and sermons, and new mosques sprang up at an annual rate of 200-plus. Such an environment proved conducive to the publication of the 130-volume *Risale-i Nur* (Treatise of Light), consisting of commentaries on the Quran by Badiuzzman Said Nursi (1873–1960). A native of south-eastern Turkey, and a one-time partisan of Kemal Ataturk in the War of Independence, Nursi turned against the war hero when the latter launched his secularization and Westernization campaign.

Nursi faced periodic imprisonment followed by exile to a small village in western Turkey where he wrote his Quranic commentaries in Turkish in a series of pamphlets, which became popular. "[H]e made Islamic theology accessible to the masses without robbing it of its mystic qualities; and his approval of technology and science as 'steeds that one should mount' and of progress as 'a train' that one should follow made his teachings attractive to many Turks . . . especially craftsmen, artisans and (rising) businessmen," noted Serif (pronounced Sherif) Mardin, a Turkish academic.[11] His followers, who included many former shaikhs of the (Sufi) Naqshbandi order, came to be known as Nurculuk (singular Nurcu/Nurju). Though prohibited under the law, the Democratic Party government tolerated the movement. In due course, commanding the loyalty of a quarter of a million members, the Nurculuk movement would edge its way into the political arena.

With a series of bumper harvests ending in 1954, the economic situation suddenly worsened. As food prices rose, annual inflation jumped to 14 percent. This hurt urban residents more than rural who grew their own food. Already, such influential segments of society as military officers, bureaucrats, and the urban middle class had become disaffected with Menderes, whom they saw favoring illiterate peasantry at the cost of urbanized, Westernized citizens.

The DP's share of the vote at the next general election in 1958 fell, but not enough to deprive it of power. This made the opposition restive. To counter the challenge, the Menderes government passed legislation that authorized it to retire judges and civil servants, and ban political gatherings and party coalitions. But since the root cause of its troubles—mismanagement of the economy—remained unresolved, the opposition refused to be cowed.

In April 1960, at the behest of Menderes, the parliament appointed a commission of inquiry to investigate "the opposition and a section of the press," and search and arrest suspects. The amalgamation of legislative and executive prerogatives violated the principle of the separation of powers specified in the constitution. There were protest meetings, which the government suppressed brutally. On May 27, 1960, the military, headed by General Celal Gursel, seized power to safeguard what it called "Kemalist values," arrested Menderes, and banned all political parties.

Following a long trial, Menderes was found guilty of violating the constitution and given capital punishment. Ignoring the calls for clemency by the heads of state of America, Britain, and France, the military junta went ahead with his hanging from the gallows on September 17, 1961.

In practice, restoring Kemalist values amounted to ending a governmental attempt to amalgamate legislative and executive powers, and at the same time stepping back from Kemalism's militantly secular phase to its religious reformist phase. Noting the religiosity of most Turks, the military leadership tried to refurbish the image and content of Islamic faith. "Islam is the most sacred, the most constructive, the most dynamic and powerful religion in the .world," Gursel said. "It demands of those who believe in this faith always to achieve progress and higher wisdom. But for centuries Islam has been explained to us negatively and incorrectly."[12]

THE 1961 CONSTITUTION

A National Unity Committee of thirty-eight military officers under General Gursel assumed the powers of the Grand National Assembly. In January 1961, as a freshly appointed Constituent Assembly began drafting a new constitution and electoral law, the military junta lifted the ban on political parties.

The preamble to the new constitution referred to Mustafa Kemal Ataturk as "the immortal leader and unrivalled hero." Article 2 specified that secularism was "the foundation stone" of the state. Article 19 read: "No individual can exploit religion with the aim of changing the social, economic, political or legal structure of the state so as to promote religious principle, neither can he use religion to promote his personal or political interests." Article 21 specified that religious education "should proceed in accordance with the foundations of modern science and education." Article 57 required political parties to conform to the principles of secularism. (Later, Article 163 of the criminal code would be used to prosecute individuals or groups "believed to endanger the principle of secularism.") At the same time, the constitution exempted the following laws from judicial review: unification of education, wearing of a hat, abolition of Sufi hostels and lodges, the civil code clause permitting civil marriage, and the Latin alphabet.

The constitution specified a two-chamber parliament, with one-third of the 150-member Senate resigning every two years, and the deputies of the 450-strong Grand National Assembly holding office for four years. The introduction of proportional representation made possible the rise of small parties, thus allowing the incipient leftist forces to participate in the electoral process.

In the October 1961 election, the RPP secured 36.7 percent of the vote, and the Justice Party (JP, the renamed Democratic Party), led by former General Ragip Gumuspala, 34.7 percent. Responding to Gursel's initiative, the Justice Party elected Suleyman Demirel (b. 1924) its chairman at its second conference in November 1964. Born in the village of Islamkoy, Demirel graduated as a civil engineer, and then pursued postgraduate studies in the

United States. On his return, he became director general of the State Hydraulic Works Department. After serving in the army, he taught hydraulic engineering at Middle East Technincal University in Ankara until his election as the Justice Party leader. For the next forty years, his bald pate, burly frame, and clean-shaven, sagging face became an integral part of Turkish politics.

At the military junta's insistence, the JP and the RPP formed a coalition government under Suat Hayri Urguplu in February 1965, with Demirel as deputy prime minister. In the next general election in October, the JP emerged as the clear winner, with 43 percent of the vote, and the RPP a loser at 20 percent. The Justice Party government extended religious education from the lower grades of secondary schools to the upper. To educate and train a new generation of orthodox clerics (*ulema*)—thus undoing an important element of Kemalist secularism—it set up higher Islamic institutes in Istanbul and Konya.

In the private sphere, charitable associations centered around mosque construction and Quranic schools, approved by the Directorate-General of Religious Affairs, became the chief instrument of Islamic revival. Between 1951 and 1967, the number of religious charities rose nearly eleven-fold, from 237 to 2510.[13] Most of these associations sprang up in provincial towns, where supporters of Islamic charities—craftsmen, petty traders, and middle-income peasants—found themselves exploited by big business, based chiefly in Istanbul and tied to Western capital.

However, their backing for the Justice Party waned, when at the insistence of its leader, Gumuspala, Turkey applied for and acquired associate membership of the European Economic Community (EEC) in 1963. The EEC was committed to the lowering of tariffs between its full and associate members. Since such an arrangement was bound to damage the material well-being of the traditional middle classes—artisans, craftsmen, and traders—the backbone of the JP, they felt betrayed and accused JP leaders of selling out to big business, the chief beneficiary of the EEC link. Their desertion of the JP led to the formation of several small parties—some, including the National Order Party (NOP) headed by Necmettin Erbakan (b. 1926), on the right; and others on the left, who were particularly active in cities.

THE RISE OF AN ISLAMIST PARTY

As a Justice Party parliamentarian, Necmettin Erbakan repeatedly attacked Demirel for being pro-American in foreign policy and pro-big business at the expense of small traders. This led to Erbakan's exclusion from the party list in the 1969 parliamentary election. He contested as an independent and won a seat from Konya, then a city of half a million souls and a bastion of piety, which had as many mosques as Istanbul.

Turkey was divided into eighty-five parliamentary constituencies, with each one allocated the number of seats proportional to its population. Political parties submitted lists to cover all the seats in a constituency, and won according to the percentage of popular vote, but only after crossing the legally specified threshold. The votes of those which failed the threshold test were divided proportionately among the winning parties. The threshold rule did not apply to independent candidates, who had to secure a minimum number of votes, depending on the size of the electorate, to get elected

Located in the midst of the windswept Anatolian plateau, Konya (aka *Iconium* in Latin, and *Ikonion* in Greek), is an ancient settlement with a history of four millennia, which, according to the Book of Acts, was visited by St. Paul. It developed as a way station for caravans during the Byzantine era, and was frequently targeted by the Arab armies. From 1097 to 1243, it was the capital of the Seljuk Sultanate of Rum, and acquired its present name in 1134. Today it is known as "the castle of Islam" due to its large number of mosques. Most women appear in public wearing headscarves, and boutiques specialize in stocking the latest in fashionable Islamic clothing for women.

Though, in keeping with its high Islamic standing, alcohol is not served in public in Konya, more raki is consumed here behind closed doors than in many other places. It is a thriving city of high-rise apartment and office blocks, with an honest, efficient local council elected on the ticket of an Islamist party bearing ever-changing names. Its local buses display the motto, "All of Turkey to be just like Konya."

Konya is the burial place of Jalaluddin Muhammad Rumi (1207–1273), bearing the honorific of *Mawlana* (derivative of *Mawla*, Arabic for "master" or "learned man"), a Sufi philosopher-poet, whose son Sultan Waalad organized Rumi's disciples into a Sufi fellowship, called the Order of the *Mawlawis* (followers of the *Mawlana*), popularly known as the Whirling Dervishes.

Jalaluddin was born to Bahauddin Waalad, a preacher, in Balkh, in today's Afghanistan. Anticipating a disaster, he convinced his father to leave Balkh—just before a marauding invasion by the Mongols. After the pilgrimage to Mecca, the family settled in Konya in 1228. After his father's death in 1232, Jalaluddin studied in Allepo and Damascus, returning to

Konya in 1840. Four years later, he came under the influence of peripatetic Sufi Muhammad Shams Tabrizi. After Tabrizi was murdered in 1247, the aggrieved Rumi withdrew from the world and meditated. His portraits show him as a wizened old man, with a white beard, his arms folded under a cloak, his face pensive and meditative, and his head covered with a long semi-conical cap held in place by a few turns of white cloth.

Out of his meditation emerged his magnum opus: *Masnavi-e Ma'navi* (subtitled, *The Spiritual Couplets of Maulana Jalaluddin Muhammed Rumi*) in Persian. Both *Masnavi-e Ma'navi* and the earlier *Diwan-e Kabir* (Persian for *Great Volume*), another masterpiece of Persian poetry, remain popular to this day. *Masnavi-e Ma'navi* is an epic poem of 50,000 lines, replete with metaphors not only of nature but also of sex and food. It is written in the *masnavi* (aka *mathnawi*; *mesnevi*) poetic form used in Persian and Ottoman literature, consisting of an indefinite number of couplets, with the rhyme scheme aa/bb/cc, and so forth. The epic narrative, consising of 424 stories that illustrate man's continuing search for mystic union with God, ranks as one of the most outstanding and influential works of Persian literature as well as Sufism. Here is an example:

> A true lover is proved such by his pain of heart;
> No sickness is there like sickness of heart.
> The lover's ailment is different from all ailments;
> Love is the astrolabe of God's mysteries.
> A lover may hanker after this love or that love,
> But at the last he is drawn to the king of love.
> However much we describe and explain love,
> When we fall in love we are ashamed of our words.
> Explanation by the tongue makes most things clear,
> But love unexplained is clearer.

Rumi's open-mindedness and liberal interpretation of Islam are well captured in "Take the road to rebirth, O hoja [religious teacher]! Leave what's old, / On your journey you'll find dull earth will turn to gold."[14] The great Sufi saint was against slavery and for monogamy and giving women a higher role in religion and public life. He called on his disciples to pursue all forms of truth and beauty, irrespective of their origins, and to be loving, tolerant, and charitable.

Rumi's bent of mind appealed to Kemal Ataturk, who particularly admired the following of Rumi's lines: "Locks bar all gates except Your own door, / So lovers of the mysteries lose their way no more." In his view, the Mawlawi approach to God broke loose from the straightjacket of the orthodox Arab tradition, and was thus illustrative of the "Turkish genius." But that did not stop him from confiscating the assets of the Order of the Mawlawis, and closing down their lodges in 1925 along with other Sufi orders.

It was only in 1957 that the government allowed the Mawlawis to function as "a cultural association to preserve a historical tradition." As a result, there is a weeklong festival of whirling dervishes in Konya in mid-December to celebrate the anniversary of Rumi's death. The whirling dance to the breathy music of *ney* (Turkish for "flute") is one of the physical methods the Mawlawis used to try to reach religious ecstasy and seek mystical union with God.

Islam had spread among those societies whose existing religious practice involved either idol or nature worship. So those who adopted Islam missed the psychic satisfaction they had derived from such worship since it was forbidden by the Quran. Strict obedience to Allah's commandments and meticulous observance of religious rituals left many believers spiritually and psychologically unfulfilled. They needed a humane, charismatic Islamic leader whose words and actions would impart warmth to their new faith.

Some Muslims sought solace in undertaking ascetic exercises and arduous spiritual practices, believing that such means would bring them closer to Allah. They were inspired by the example of Prophet Muhammad who used to withdraw into a cave and undertake nightly vigils. They came to believe that Allah, or the Ultimate Reality, could be apprehended only by direct personal experience, and therefore stressed meditation and contemplation of the Deity. Through their practices they injected warmth, piety, and altruistic love into Islam. They came to be known as Sufis—from the term *suf* (wool), linked to the woolen garments the pioneers among them wore as a sign of asceticism.

Whatever the reasons for the emergence of Sufis and Sufism, they had no place in the hearts and minds of orthodox Muslims who believed in strict adherence to the tenets of Islam. Among the orthodox Muslims in Turkey was Necmettin Erbakan. Born into a wealthy household in the Black Sea port of Sinop, Erbakan graduated with a mechanical engineering degree from Istanbul Technical University (ITU). He then received a doctorate from the RWTH Aachen University in West Germany. He thus acquired firsthand experience of Western life and found it incompatible with Islamic beliefs. On his return, he became a teacher at the ITU, rising up to a professor in 1965. Elected as an independent to parliament four years later, he gathered a few other likeminded members, and formed the National Order Party (NOP).

A member of the Naqshbandi order, Erbakan won the backing of the Nurcu movement. The first NOP congress opened in 1970 with the Islamic cry "Allahu Akbar (God is Great)," which had not been heard at political gatherings for almost half a century. In March 1971, the military mounted its second coup in a decade when it forced Prime Minister Demirel to resign, owing to his failure to contain the rise of the leftist tide in urban centers.[15] This facilitated the installation of a government "above parties" led by Nihat Erim, a former RPP deputy. It took Erbakan's NOP to the Constitutional Court, charging it with violating the constitution by using religion for political purposes. Upholding the charge, the court banned the party.

Undeterred, Erbakan formed the National Salvation Party (NSP) in October 1972 when another military-backed government led by Ferit Melen was in office. Erbakan argued against Turkey's membership of the EEC, "a product of a new Crusader mentality," because such a step would merely perpetuate Turkey's role as an economic underling of "Western-Christian capitalism." Instead, he advocated independent industrial development of Turkey as pursued by Japan. He attacked such aspects of the state-sponsored arts as Western dancing, ballet, and theater, which he said were alien to "real" Turks. Above all, he bemoaned the disintegration of the traditional Turkish family under Western influences in the mixing of sexes and disrespect for elders. He stressed "morality and spiritual values" as the nucleus around which Muslim society needed to be organized.

In the October 1973 general election, the NSP emerged as the third-largest party, winning nearly 12 percent of the vote and forty-nine seats, mainly in deprived rural areas and conservative neighborhoods of urban centers. It held the balance between the right-of-center JP and the left-of-center RPP, led by Bulent Ecevit (pronounced Ejevit; 1925–2006). Son of a medical professor in Ankara, Ecevit was more than a politician; he was also a writer, translator, and poet. After college graduation, he worked as a translator, and during his sojourn in the United States in the mid-1950s, he worked as a reporter for an American newspaper. A small, energetic man with a thick black mustache under his beaked nose, he entered politics in 1957 and became a fixture in the left-of-center political spectrum for the next half a century.

When Ecevit became the prime minister of a coalition government in early 1974, he appointed Erbakan as his deputy. When he was replaced by

Demirel as premier less than a year later, Erbakan retained his position in the new coalition government, which lasted until 1977. Thus, within a generation and a half of Kemal Ataturk's death, an Islamist party had emerged and grown to become a fixture in the politics of a country with a secular constitution. Defying the constitution, Erbakan propagated Islamic ideas, and called for the formation of an Islamic Common Market (ICM) consisting of Turkey and the Arab Middle East, buoyed freshly by the quadrupling of oil prices in 1973 and 1974. At the same time, like other political parties in power, the NSP ministers focused on appointing their nominees to posts in their ministries.

Though the NSP's vote declined to 8.6 percent in the 1977 election, Islamization of politics and education did not. An example was the government's decision to let a graduate of the imam-khatib colleges become a teacher of general subjects in primary schools, a virtual subversion of the Kemalist principle of "unification of education." Summing up the situation in April 1978, Turkey's interior minister said, "Politics had even entered the mosques and lower forms of secondary schools."[16]

By the late 1970s, the NSP had become the national voice of a sizeable section of the lower and middle classes. "In so doing, the NSP invested the Islamist movement with the legitimacy of a national party platform," noted Ronnie Margulies and Ergin Yildizoglu, coeditors of a Turkish newsletter. "The very existence of the NSP forced all major parties to take the existence of the 'Islamic' vote into account and court it more explicitly."[17]

A revived Islam began to compete with the ideologies of the secular right (fascism) and left (Marxism) as a savior of the disillusioned urban youths. Reflecting an accelerated emigration from the villages—with the urban population, up from 17 percent to 26 percent between 1935 and 1960, rising to 46 percent during the next generation—the number of youths in city slums grew sharply. Given the economic recession, caused by steep oil price hikes and the country's huge foreign debt, stemming from recklessly expansionist policies, joblessness shot up. Unemployed youths became ready recruits for extremist parties of the left and right, which resorted to violence for political purposes.

Kemalism had evidently failed. "Kemalism is dead," remarked columnist Mehmet Altan, "but nobody knows how to dispose of the corpse."[18] Unlike Marxism or liberal democracy, it was not an all-encompassing ideology that explained society and history at large and acted as a primary engine for progress. Nor was it a socio-ethical system in the form of a conventional religion. Kemalism's ascendancy over the past half-century had left the

Turkish society without moral-ethical moorings, provided in the past by Islam. Its main achievement had been to foster Turkish nationalism, but once nationalism had taken root, Kemalism lost most of its raison d'être. In the resulting moral-ideological vacuum, the parties of the militant left and right thrived—as did political violence.

As strife in urban areas spilled into villages, it rekindled old racial and sectarian hatreds—between Turks and Kurds, and Shiites and Sunnis. The underprivileged, pro-leftist Alevis (aka Alawis, a sub-sect within Shiite Islam), forming an estimated one-sixth of the population, became targets of ultra-nationalists organized under the banner of the National Action Party (NAP)—led by Alparslan Turkes (pronounced Turkesh), who allied with such militant Sunnis as Nurcus, who regarded Alawis as "worse than unbelievers."

The NAP had formed a youth wing with a very appealing name of the Gray Wolves. According to the pan-Turkic legend of *bozkurt* (steppe wolf, often called gray wolf), it was always a gray wolf who led their ancestors on their various migrations from their legendary place of origin, Turan, consisting of the Altai Mountains and the Gobi Desert. To catch up with its political rival, the NSP established its own youth wing, called Akincilar (pronounced Akinjilar). It resorted to attacking leftist students and teachers as well as Alevis. A three-day sectarian-political riot in the southeastern town of Kahramanmaras in December 1978 left 117 people dead, most of them Alevis. Premier Ecevit put twelve eastern provinces under martial law to reassure the Alevis. Despite his best efforts, overall, political violence did not subside during his premiership. Indeed, by the summer of 1980, when the coalition government was led by Demirel of the Justice Party, it claimed more than a hundred people a week.

On September 6, 1980, a rally in Konya by the World Assembly of Islamic Youth for the Liberation of Palestine, sponsored by the NSP and attended by delegates from twenty Arab countries, drew large crowds. Among other things, the rally called for the founding of an Islamic state in Turkey. This triggered a military coup six days later, on September 12, and the removal of the Demirel government. The communiqué issued by the military leaders, headed by General Kenan Evren (b. 1918), the chief of general staff, described their action as being against the followers of fascist and communist ideologies as well as religious "fanatics."[19]

The junta arrested Erbakan and other NSP leaders and prosecuted them under Article 163 of the penal code for attempting to change "the fundamental principles of the state" and organizing a demonstration against the secular laws of the country. It suspended all political parties, confiscating their assets and arresting their leaders—including Ecevit and Demirel. "You can take power with a bayonet but you can't sit on it," quipped Demirel.[20] The junta's iron hand also struck the leftist trade union movement, DISK (*Devrinci Isci Sendikalari Konfedasyony*, Confederation of Revolutionary Workers' Unions), which had broken away from the conservative Turk-Is trade union. The dissolution of the political parties would follow a year later.[21]

AFTER THE 1980 COUP

While the immediate aim of the military junta—constituted as the five-member National Security Council (NSC) led by General Evren—was to halt the slide towards a civil war, its medium-term objective was to rid society of Marxist ideology and parties. Therefore, seeing merit in encouraging Islamic ideas and education as an antidote to Marxism, the junta made the teaching of Islam compulsory in secondary schools, which had been optional since 1967.

During the three-year military rule, the number of Islamic faculties at universities rose from two to eight. The Higher Institute of Islamic Studies, established in 1959, was upgraded to the Faculty of Divinity of Marmara University in Istanbul, with a student body of 1,200—a blatant reversal of the policy followed by Kemal Ataturk. The state-run radio and television introduced Islamic programs.[22]

Repeating the view of Islam expressed earlier by General Gursel, leader of the 1960 coup, Evren said: "We interpret Westernization as setting our people on the road to becoming the most prosperous and civilized nation . . . In fact, the real nature of Islam is always open to science, civilization and development."[23] In early 1982, the National Security Council appointed a handpicked 160-member Constituent Assembly to draft a new constitution and electoral laws. With thirty-three lawyers, twenty-nine engineers, twenty-one retired military officers, nineteen academics, sixteen civil servants, and nine economists as its members, the assembly was widely regarded as unrepresentative and right-wing.

Little wonder that while retaining the preamble and many of the articles of the earlier constitution, the latest document whittled down certain basic freedoms. For example, it effectively emasculated trade unions, curbing collective bargaining and depriving them of any "political activity." It authorized the president to veto legislation and appoint judges to the

Constitutional Court, which among other things was required to pass judgments on political and human rights specified in the constitution. It also abolished the Senate.

After amending the draft constitution to its satisfaction, the NSC put it to vote in November 1982. The referendum, which also included the appointment of Kenan Evren, who resigned his military post, as president for a seven-year term, received massive support. Son of a prayer leader in the provincial town of Manisa, Kenan Evren went to a military high school and graduated in 1938. Later he qualified as staff officer after attending a military academy. He rose to the rank of a general in 1964. After serving as army chief of staff and commander of the counter-guerrilla branch, he achieved the highest military office, chief of general staff, in 1978. A balding, bespectacled, thick-jowled man of medium height, he evinced quiet authority.

Political life revived, but only the military-approved parties acquired the right to function. Among these was the right-of-center Motherland Party established by Turgut Ozal (1927–93), who had served as the economic overlord under the military junta. In 1977, he had unsuccessfully contested a parliamentary seat as an independent supported by the National Salvation Party.

By late 1982, while most of the leaders of the (pan-Islamic) NSP and the (pan-Turkic) National Action Party were released, the leading Marxist figures were in prison or exile. Therefore, the left ceased to exist as an opposition force. In contrast, members of the right wing opposition were allowed to secure jobs in those sections of the civil service and educational institutions where the left had been influential before the coup. Lacking legal political outlet, lower and middle cadres of the now-dissolved NSP and NAP joined the Motherland, thus turning the new organization more into a coalition than a unified party.

In the November 1983 parliamentary poll, held under an electoral law that discriminated against small parties by specifying a threshold of 7 percent, the Motherland won a slight majority in parliament. Ozal became the prime minister. In the local elections in March, the Motherland repeated its performance, securing 40 percent of the popular vote.

TURKEY UNDER TURGUT OZAL

Like Demirel, Ozal had a provincial background and a degree in engineering, electrical in his case, and pursued postgraduate studies in the United States in the early 1950s. After his return, he worked on electrification projects for the government and then moved to the State Planning Department. Later, again like Demirel, he lectured at the Middle East Technical University in Ankara. In 1979 Prime Minister Demirel appointed him his undersecretary. Small and portly, with a wide face and the trademark mustache of a Turkish male, he was a pious man, never without his prayer beads.

So the Islamic revival continued. In 1985, there were 72,000 mosques in Turkey, up from 20,000 in 1945, a three-and-a-half-fold increase compared to the two-and-a-half-fold growth in the population, from 18.7 million to 51.4 million. That is, whereas in 1945 there was one mosque for every 1,000 Turks, forty years later there was one mosque for every 700—an index of religious piety equaling that of the Emirate of Bukhara before the Bolshevik Revolution. A study by Professor Besir (pronounced Beshir) Atalay of Kirikalle, a town of 200,000 near Ankara, revealed a high degree of urban religiosity. It showed that 65.4 percent of the working-class men and 61 percent of the merchants prayed daily.[24] Unlike rural Turks, who were religious by tradition, urban Turks had been influenced by the mass media.

The adoption of Islamic dress by a growing number of women of all classes could be attributed partly to Islamic programs on television, especially a two-hour-long women's program every week. As Emile Serdengenchti, a sales assistant in Bursa, put it to me: "Women wear the veil voluntarily, out of fear of leading a sinful life. The idea of sin has come to them from the religious men who preach on the women's television program [begun under the military regime] every Thursday evening [which, to Muslims, is the beginning of Friday, since an Islamic day starts after sunset]."[25]

Ozal, a teetotaler and political conservative, was widely known to be sympathetic to Islamic elements, including Sufi brotherhoods. The orders of Naqshbandi, Nurcu, and Suleimanci (pronounced Suleimanji) became more visible and popular than before, with the *Islam*, a pro-Naqshbandi monthly, selling over 110,000 copies. The Quranic courses, specializing in the memorization of the Quran, offered by the Naqshbandi and Suleimanci orders, brought them young pupils. And their practice of providing free tuition and accommodation in their hostels to the students taking university entrance examinations helped them influence the educated generation of the future. The largest brotherhoods, the Naqshbandi, played an important role in electoral politics by offering or withdrawing its support to a leading political party.

Three of the country's twelve dailies were Islamic in outlook. The *Milli Gazete* (National Gazette) was the mouthpiece of the Welfare (*Refah*, in

Turkish) Party, the reincarnation of the National Salvation Party. Paralleling the rise of an Islamic press was the boom in Islamic publishing. According to Ahmet Kot, a Turkish researcher, at the height of Kemalism in 1934, religious books accounted for only 1.7 percent of the total published, whereas in 1985 the figure was 7 percent. In the latter year, 280,000 Turks went on *hajj*, the pilgrimage to Mecca—twice the figure for the Islamic Republic of Iran, which had about the same population.[26] This was as much a sign of growing religiosity as of rising living standards.

There was much ferment among Islamist intellectuals, who concentrated on producing journals and pamphlets, and convening small meetings. To them it seemed only a matter of time before those activities spilled over into the political arena. "Once Islamist intellectuals are integrated into the political thinking of Turkey, then the situation will change," Seyfettin Manisaligil, a sociologist at Istanbul University, told me in mid-1986.[27] This would prove to be a prophetic statement.

Buoyed by Turkey's healthy economic growth—caused by Ozal's introduction of export incentives and decriminalization of foreign exchange transactions—Ozal applied for full membership of the European Community (EC, which later became the European Economic Commission, and then the European Union) in April 1987. With political life returning to normal, except the continued exclusion of the Marxist left, competition for voter loyalty increased. Taking its cue from the Motherland Party, the parliament raised the threshold to 10 percent for a political group to gain seats in the chamber.

To meet this requirement, Erbakan's Welfare Party coalesced with Turkeys's Nationalist Labor Party (the renamed National Action Party) and another small group to fight the October 1987 election. Winning 10.9 percent of the ballots, including 7 percent for the Welfare Party, the alliance scraped through the barrier. Scoring 36 percent of the vote, the Motherland Party gained 64 percent of the seats. Then came the Social Democratic Popular Party (the successor to the Republican People's Party) led by Erdal Inonu, and the right-of-center True Path Party (the renamed Justice Party) headed by Demirel.

The governing coalition excluded the Welfare Party-dominated alliance, which helped the Welfare to widen its base as the leading opposition force. With the socio-economic conditions that spawned leftist politics in the 1970s persisting, and the left virtually outlawed, the role of opposition fell increasingly on the Welfare Party. The success of the Islamic forces in 1979—in Iran, where they toppled the powerful pro-Western monarch,

Muhammad Reza Pahlavi; and in Afghanistan, in securing the withdrawal of the Soviet troops a decade later—proved that Islam was capable of successfully confronting both Western capitalism-imperialism and Marxist socialism. It thus emerged as an indigenous third way, wedded to neither East nor West, a development which inspired the Welfare Party.

To widen the popular appeal of his party, Ozal continued to court the Islamic constituency. In July 1988, he went on a pilgrimage to Mecca, becoming the first eminent leader to do so since the founding of the republic sixty-five years earlier. In a sense, he was following a trend set by the military regime. Breaking with the country's precedent of sending its foreign minister to a summit meeting of the Islamic Conference Organization (ICO), established in 1969, the junta had dispatched the prime minister to such a gathering in Taif, Saudi Arabia, in 1981. Following the Islamic summit, it reduced its relations with Israel to the second-secretary level. Diplomatic recognition of Israel was the precondition that America had set for Turkey before letting it join NATO in 1952. But that did not inhibit Ozal's government from recognizing the Palestine Liberation Organization (PLO), and warmly receiving its leader, Yasser Arafat, in March 1986.

After Ozal's pilgrimage to Mecca, his government got embroiled in the controversy over the wearing of headscarves by women students on a university campus—an issue that would remain unresolved for two decades. When some female students arrived with their heads covered by scarves, the rector ordered the women to remove them or face expulsion.

Aware of the need to close the wide gap between secularism of state and religiosity of the people—the root cause of a series of political crises since Kemal Ataturk's death—Ozal intervened. He was aware, too, that pursuing this path would win more votes for his party (with local elections looming in March 1989). He had the parliament pass a bill legalizing the headscarf. But President Evren vetoed it, and asked the Constitutional Court to pass judgment. In February 1989, the court, dominated by hard-line secularists, overturned the bill on the ground that it contravened the secularist articles of the constitution.

Islamists mounted noisy countrywide demonstrations, which were broken up by the police. Iran joined the protest, with its Turkish language broadcasts attacking Evren as a blasphemer. The tension between the two neighbors reached a point where Turkey recalled its ambassador to Tehran in protest of Iran's meddling in its internal affairs.

In the municipal elections, the Welfare Party improved its vote from 7 to 10 percent, whereas the Motherland's vote nearly halved from the 40 percent it had gained five years before. In early 1990, the controversy over the headscarf and the turban (used to cover not only the head but also the ears and the neck) flared up again, when Islamic students staged a sit-in at Ankara's Middle Eastern Technical University to protest the ban. Seizing the opportunity to regain the lost electoral ground, the Ozal government issued a decree authorizing an individual university to decide whether to allow the (banned) headscarf or turban on the campus. Later that year, women students at a university that had banned the headscarf took their case to the local court. It repealed the ban on the ground that it infringed personal human rights. The subject became so charged that the students and teachers involved in the controversy resorted to boycotting classes. This time President Evren refrained from intervening.

In short, the secularist side found itself on the defensive as it attempted to reconcile Kemalist precepts with the right of religious freedom within a democratic context. Breaking with the Kemalist tradition, the Ozal government permitted Islamic finance houses, mostly controlled by the Naqshbandi order, to operate. This allowed the government to channel funds to support Islamic activists who now had jobs in all government departments, especially the secular educational system. The extent of Islamist infiltration of civil and military services became apparent when, in February 1990, the government sacked forty officials within the ministry of education for propagating Islamic fundamentalism, and dismissed fifteen air force officers for attempting to establish Islamic cells.

The expansion of the Suleimanci, an important Sufi order, could be gauged by the fact that it managed 1,900 Quranic schools, accounting for more than a third of 5,197 such schools with a student body of 290,000, run under the supervision of the official Directorate-General of Religious Affairs.[28] Reflecting the rise in popular interest in Islam, the staff of the DGRA grew 16 percent annually, from 47,000 in 1985 to 84,000 five years later, including 69,000 full-time clerics operating from mosques in Turkey, and 800 preachers and prayer-leaders attached to twenty-one Turkish embassies and consulates to serve Turkish expatriates abroad.[29]

By early 1990, Ozal had been elevated to the presidency, following the end of Evren's term in November 1989. The EC decided to defer, indefinitely, negotiations on Turkey's full membership. It justified its decision on economic and political grounds: the high price of integrating the Turkish economy into the EC, and Turkey's failure to bring its adherence to human rights up to European standards. But this explanation did not dispel the popular perception among Turks that their country was being excluded on religious grounds, a view strongly expressed by the pan-Islamic and pan-Turkic press.

Pan-Islamist and pan-Turkic elements in Turkey had begun looking east—towards Soviet Azerbaijan and Central Asia. Taking advantage of the liberalization of religious freedom and foreign travel in the Soviet Union between 1989 and 1991 (the latter part of perestroika), hundreds of Welfare and Nationalist Labor Party activists traveled to Muslim-majority Soviet republics to contact those interested in Islam and/or pan-Turkism, and help the people rediscover their Islamic and Turkish roots.

In Turkey, with the prospect of economic-political integration into Europe almost dead, and the Marxist forces in decline, the popular attraction of Islam as a viable social ideology increased. Islamic sentiment reached a peak on the eve of the Gulf War between Iraq and the U.S.-led forces in January 1991—due to Turkey's loss of trade with Iraq following the United Nations embargo against Baghdad in August 1990, and the presentation of the conflict as a struggle between believers and unbelievers by Iraq's president, Saddam Hussein.

Sensing the popular mood, the government revived the Higher Islamic Council (HIC), composed of senior clerics and theologians, which had been disbanded by the military in 1980. When the secular press described it as a precursor of the reformation of Islam along the lines of the earlier reformation of Christianity, which secularists have wanted since Kemal Ataturk's days, Hamdi Mert, deputy president of the DGRA, set the record straight. "Our religion is an unchanging system," he declared. "We believe it's the final revealed religion, so reform is out of the question."[30] The repeal of Article 163 of the penal code, dealing with those who challenged secularism, in April 1991, gave a further fillip to Islamist forces.[31] When the Iranian president, Ali Akbar Hashemi Rafsanjani, visited Turkey the following month, cheering crowds greeted him with shouts of "Allahu Akbar!" ("God is Great!"), an unprecedented spectacle in the history of the republic.

The unprecedented extension of access to information and personal mobility—television, telephones, and cars—to ordinary Turks during the decade of economic liberalization and prosperity under Ozal had by now irretrievably undermined the Kemalist heritage, which was currently upheld only by an elite of military officers, judges, and senior bureaucrats. The annual economic growth had averaged 7 percent.

With an equally rapid expansion of higher education during the earlier decades, the religious beliefs of a 99 percent Muslim society had permeated the top layers of a civil administration headed by popularly elected politicians since the return of democracy in 1983. The formation of an Islamic Human Rights Group by fifty-three intellectuals in Istanbul in the spring of 1991 was another indication of a new trend in Turkish life.

In other words, Islamic perceptions had been quietly gaining ground in popular thought and practice within the shell of secular law, largely avoiding a clash with the secular legal system or existing legal interpretations of a secular constitution. This paved the way for the religious revival in Turkey. In the October 1991 general election, the Welfare Party-led alliance won 17 percent of the vote, and sixty-two seats, forty of these going to the Welfare. The Motherland's strength shrank to 115 seats, losing power to the coalition of Demirel's right-of-center True Path Party (TPP), with a strong base in rural areas, and Erdal Inonu's Social Democratic Populist Party (SDPP). The new government headed by Demirel, and supported by 266 deputies in a house of 450, took office in November.

The Motherland's lackluster performance was due to poor economic growth—down from 9.2 percent in 1990 to 1.9 percent in 1991 (owing partly to the Gulf War)—and a lack of dynamic leadership, previously provided by Ozal, who, as president, had to stay away from party politics. With annual inflation running at 74 percent, interest rates exceeded 100 percent a year—a clear example of usury, forbidden by the Quran, said Welfare Party leaders. They called for an increase in the number and size of interest-free institutions, a popular demand.

As the inheritor of an economic mess, the new coalition government found itself unequal to the task. In this dark tunnel, suddenly a ray of light appeared: the breakup of the Soviet Union in December 1991 into fifteen independent states; the subsequent rise of Turkic nationalism in Azerbaijan and four of the five Central Asian republics; and the prospect of vast economic, diplomatic, and cultural possibilities for Turkey.

THE POST-SOVIET ERA

Turkey offered religious assistance to the former Soviet Union's Muslim-majority republics in the cultural field. Like Turks, Central Asian Muslims belonged to the Hanafi school, one of the four leading schools of Sunni Islam. Turkey's DGRA and its Religious Affairs Foundation provided voluntary aid in the form of shipments of the Quran and other religious books, dispatch of clerics, and scholarships to students from former Soviet republics to study Islam in Turkey.

With 50,000 students graduating annually from the religious vocational high schools in Turkey, staffed to provide vocational training for the clergy, there was no dearth of qualified Turkish clerics on foreign assignment. During the month of Ramadan (regarded holy because of its association with Prophet Muhammad receiving his first divine revelation) in March 1991, the DGRA sent 357 Turkish clergy to former Soviet republics and Outer Mongolia.

Yet in its public pronouncements, the Turkish government stressed its secular image, and projected itself as a rival to Iran, bent on exporting Islamic fundamentalism to these new Muslim-majority countries. Such a stance was at odds with the change that Turkey underwent in the aftermath of the Soviet Union's breakup. The euphoria created by the collapse of the barriers between Turkey and the Turkic populations of Central Asia and Azerbaijan lowered tension between secularist and Islamist Turks. "Secularists have stopped accusing Islamists of being funded by Iran and of having extra-territorial loyalties," said Fehmi Koru, the chief columnist of the *Zaman* (*Time*), an Islamist paper. "In any case there is not much hostility to Islamists from the government and the political establishment. After all, there is an Islamic faction within each of the two leading parties: the True Path and the Motherland. Strong opposition [to Islam] is now confined to diehard secularist intellectuals and military leaders."[32]

That, however, did not stop the Turkish government from devising its policy toward the former Muslim-majority Soviet republics in consultation with Washington, which was keen to impress upon these freshly independent countries the virtues of Turkey's secular constitution, free-market economy, and Islamic culture. As a republic with a well-developed industrial base and considerable commercial dealings with Europe and America, Turkey was capable of providing the newly arrived "Turkic" (the adjective routinely used by the Turkish media) states industrial know-how and managerial and commercial expertise—as well as practical advice on how to switch from a centralized, planned economy to a market economy.

In the cultural field, Turkey intervened in the debate about changing the alphabet for Azeri and Central Asian languages then in progress. It strongly advised a switchover from the Cyrillic script to the Roman—a step which, in time, was bound to wean the new states away from the Russian orbit toward Turkey and the West. As a gesture of practical help, Ankara shipped Turkish typewriters, dictionaries, and printing presses to these countries.

The presidents of Central Asia and Azerbaijan were quick to recognize the importance of Turkey. Within a month of their republics becoming independent in mid-December 1991, all of them, except the Tajik president, were invited to Ankara by President Ozal. The host appealed to their Turkic roots and proposed that they all issue a signed declaration of sharing "common Turkic purpose." Reflecting the view of the leaders of the former Soviet republics, Kazakh President Nursultan Nazarbayev said, "Mr. President, we just left the Russian Empire. We don't want to enter another empire now. Let's recall our culture, our history and our common blood, let's cooperate and trade with each other. . . . Assist us with your investments. "[33]

Ozal took the rebuff in stride and visited the Central Asian capitals soon after.

In February 1992, during his visit to Washington, Premier Demirel presented President George H. W. Bush with a thirteen-point program on Central Asia, topped by the proposal that all assistance to the region by America, other Western nations, and Turkey be coordinated through the recently formed Central Asian Trade Bank in Ankara. With the burgeoning federal deficit in the United States showing no sign of abating, however, President Bush could do little to help. In the political sphere, Demirel reassured Bush that by providing the Central Asian republics with a viable secular model, Ankara would assist Washington in its battle to keep Iran and its version of Islamic fundamentalism out of the region.

While projecting itself as a rival to Iran, Turkey had no option but to cooperate with it in economic matters. Along with Pakistan, they were both members of the Economic Cooperation Organization (ECO), originally established as the Regional Development Council (RDC) in 1967, when they were all firmly in the Western camp. Now, at Iran's initiative, ECO opened its doors to Azerbaijan and all Central Asian republics except Kazakhstan.

A summit of the expanded ECO took place in Tehran in February 1992. Much to Turkey's chagrin, Iranian president Rafsanjani portrayed the enlarged body as an Islamic Common Market of almost 300 million people. To the further embarrassment of Turkey, he announced that his initiative had led to the formation of a Caspian Sea Cooperation Council, composed of the littoral states of the Caspian—Azerbaijan, Russia, Kazakhstan, Turkmenistan, and Iran.

A month later came a boost for the Turkish side. All Central Asian states and Azerbaijan attended a meeting of the North Atlantic Cooperation Council, a body that included the sixteen members of NATO. Earlier, they had participated in a gathering of the Helsinki-based Conference on

Security and Cooperation in Europe (CSCE), later renamed Organization for Security and Cooperation in Europe (OSCE), which had accepted them as members. According to the Turkish media, both of these events were unmistakable signs that Central Asians and Azeris were going with Europe and Turkey, and not with Iran and the Muslim world. They also showed Turkey had taken under its wing countries that were untutored in the art and craft of diplomacy.

The predominantly secular Turkish media offered self-congratulatory reporting and analysis—"The Twenty-first century will be the Turkish century"; "We are the leaders of 200 million Turkic peoples extending from the Black Sea to China"; "We have won the race against a fundamentalist, obscurantist Iran"—along with jibes at Tehran as a loser in its competition with Ankara for influence in former Muslim-majority Soviet republics. Chauvinism in the media reached such a high pitch that even President Ozal, with his reputation for showmanship, found it excessive. "We have historic and cultural ties with them, and they want us as a model," he said. "But this is getting a bit exaggerated. This could induce over-optimism, and backfire against Turkey."[34]

However, Ozal's cautious approach did not percolate down. As it was, Turkey was the first country to sign treaties and trade agreements with the new Central Asian states. "We are the only ones who understand them, and therefore the only ones to offer aid without offending them," a senior Turkish diplomat told Tiziano Terzani, an Italian journalist, during their flight from Ankara to Ashgabat. "These states are counting heavily on the western world, on international aid, but they are already starting to realize that the system does not work [the way] they imagined." The Turkish diplomat had even worked out the future scenario for these states—the union of the five republics—with the Tajiks agreeing to be part of it as a minority. Azerbaijan would also join this union, he asserted. "In Baku they are already talking in terms of the formula 5+1."[35]

Moreover, while the Turkish media and government were attacking Iran's Islamic obscurantism, the official Directorate-General of Religious Affairs dispatched sixty-seven clerics to Central Asia during Ramadan (starting on March 5, 1992) to lead prayers in mosques and give sermons. It appealed to the Turkish faithful for funds to build a hundred mosques in the region. It disclosed that it was funding 197 scholarships to students from former Muslim-majority Soviet republics at Quranic schools in Istanbul, and that it had shipped more than 200,000 religious books to these countries.[36]

The Turks insisted on advising Central Asians on the alphabet. "On the language, as far as writing is concerned, we tell them they would be making a grave mistake by returning to Arabic script," the senior Turkish diplomat said. "That would isolate them and confine them to the Arab world."[37] Turkish universities went on to offer assistance to replace the Cyrillic script with the Latin as used in Turkey.[38]

Among many Turkish newspapers, only the *Zaman*, an Islamist daily, took immediate advantage of the new situation. Its management began publishing editions in Baku twice weekly and in Almaty twice a month, setting its pages in both Roman and Cyrillic scripts. Established in Ankara in October 1986 with a circulation of 10,000, the newspaper had seen its sales rise to 120,000 by the spring of 1992, most of the gains made during the previous three years.

On the official side, state-run Turkish television showed enterprise and speed. On the eve of Premier Demirel's tour of Central Asia and Azerbaijan in late April 1992, Turkish television's Avrasya (Eurasia) channel began beaming programs to Azerbaijan by transmitting television programs and popularizing the spoken Turkish of Turkey in Azerbaijan—and areas further east. Ankara claimed that in due course there would be two-way television traffic between Turkey and its eastern neighbors, but that seemed unlikely.

Despite repeated statements by Demirel that Turkey would not act as the Big Brother, senior civil servants and leading commentators in the media displayed a patronizing attitude. The remark by Kurtulus Tashkent, deputy director general of the Turkish foreign ministry's eastern section, was typical: "We feel moral and political responsibility toward Azerbaijan and other Turkic republics, and want to lead them in establishing a secular democratic system and free-market-oriented economy."[39] In any event, it was unrealistic to expect that any of these former Soviet republics, with populations ranging between 3.6 million and 21 million, could feel equal to Turkey with 57 million people.

During his visits to Azerbaijan, Turkmenistan, Uzbekistan, Kyrgyzstan, and Kazakhstan, Demirel stressed the historical link. "The star of history is shining for the Turkic people," he said. "We do not want any pan-Turkic aspirations. But this region is the land of our forefathers."[40] Among the many agreements he signed, there was a provision for 10,000 high school and university students from these republics to receive further education and professional training in Turkey. More importantly, he promised financial aid to these countries: $600 million in soft loans for buying Turkish wheat and sugar; and $600 million from the Turkish Eximbank for funding Turkish exports, construction, and investment.

While its cultural affinity and historic ties with Central Asia provided Turkey with strong cards, its geography weakened it. Turkey did not share frontiers with any of these states except a ten-kilometer (seven-mile) common border with the Nakhichevan enclave of Azerbaijan, separated from the mainland by a strip of Armenia. Continued instability in the Caucasian states of Azerbaijan, Armenia, and Georgia limited Turkey's overall geographical asset of being a bridge between East and West. Also, despite all the talk about getting together with long-lost Turkic cousins, private Turkish companies were more interested in such large markets as Russia and Ukraine than in sparsely populated Turkmenistan (3.6 million), Kyrgyzstan (4.5 million), or Tajikistan (5.2 million).

In the diplomatic field, Turkey's failure to aid Azerbaijan militarily in its battle with Armenia to recover its enclave of Nagorno-Karabakh (usurped by Armenia) dashed the high hopes of the Azeris. On the other hand, the election of Abulfaz Elchibey, a Turkic nationalist, in June 1992 was a plus for Ankara. He strengthened ties with Turkey. But he fared badly on the military front, losing a slice of Azerbaijan proper to Armenia in January 1993. Demirel resisted popular pressure to intervene militarily, aware that such a step would isolate Turkey in NATO, where it was the only Muslim member, and that public opinion in the West would swing towards Armenia and result in economic sanctions against Turkey.

Turkey's impotence in the face of Armenian aggression against a fellow-Turkic state was to hurt its future prospects in Central Asia. This perception struck many influential Turkish figures, including President Ozal, who happened to be in the midst of a tour of the Central Asian republics and Azerbaijan when the latest crisis erupted.

During his three-day visit to Baku in mid-April, Ozal offered Azerbaijan a defense pact, which was beyond his constitutional powers.[41] However, such a gesture was in tune with popular feelings in Turkey, so his public standing at home rose sharply. This was demonstrated by the huge crowd, which turned up at his funeral following his sudden death on April 17, 1993, due to heart failure. The funeral procession included tens of thousands of Welfare Party supporters, carrying green flags of Islam and placards paying homage to "Our Pious President." They shouted "Allahu Akbar!"—religious cries, which mingled strangely with the officially sanctified funereal music of Frederic Chopin.

Elchibey's failure on the military front in Azerbaijan undermined his position. He found his authority challenged by chairman of the parliament, Geidar (aka Haidar) Aliyev, a preeminent Azeri politician during the Soviet era. When, fearing for his safety, Elchibey fled Baku in the middle of the night for his birthplace in Nakhichevan, Turkey continued to recognize him as president, as did Washington. Therefore, when the Azeri parliament, acting within the constitution, passed presidential powers on to Aliyev, Ankara suffered a humiliating diplomatic defeat. By turning to Russia to mediate between Azerbaijan and Armenia, Aliyev downgraded further Turkey's diplomatic importance.

Turkey's Islamic opposition shed few tears for Elchibey, who had allied himself with America. At home, though, it received a jolt when Tansu Çiller (pronounced Chiller, b. 1946), an erstwhile minister of economy, became leader of the True Path Party, the senior partner in the coalition government, following the elevation of Demirel to the presidency in June.

Çiller not only became the first woman prime minister of Turkey, but did so within three years of joining a political party. Born into an affluent family in Istanbul, she graduated with an economics degree, and then earned a doctorate in the United States. After her post-doctoral studies at Yale University, she returned home and became a university teacher. Sporting short hair over a plump face and large, expressive eyes, she was highly Westernized and had a forceful personality. She joined the True Path Party in 1990 and won a seat in parliament next year.

With the Motherland Party weakened by the death of its charismatic founder, Ozal, and the True Path Party redefining its identity under a new, untested leader, Çiller, the Welfare Party gained further ground.

ISLAMISTS SHARE POWER

The Welfare Party vowed to work within the existing system to bring about "just order"—a vague reference to the Islamic system under the Ottomans, with Turkey leading the Middle East instead of chasing acceptance by the West. It had built up the most effective organization at the grassroots level. Despite running many town halls, the Welfare Party had remained unsoiled by corruption, which had tarnished the image of all major secular parties. Its leader, Erbakan, was an old-world, provincial notable, amusing and simplistic in equal measure, with a knack for disarming opposition—a valuable asset in a politician in a democratic system.

The March 1994 local elections, when a record 92 percent of 32 million voters went to the polls, shocked the secularist establishment. More than doubling its vote to 19 percent, the Welfare Party caught up with the secular True Path (21.5 percent) and Motherland (21 percent) parties. Besides capturing Turkey's most populous cities of Istanbul and Ankara, accounting for a quarter of the national population, it gained power in twenty-four other urban centers. Recep Tayyip Erdogan (b. 1955) and Meli Gokcek became the respective mayors of Istanbul and Ankara.

Erdogan stood out not only because he was a sharp-featured, tall, athletic former soccer player, but also because he was well trained in management, having served as an executive in the wholesale food business. He had entered politics as a committed Islamist, declaring that his political ideas centered around an Islamic state, and that "Sovereignty resides in God and that Islamic principles should replace Kemalism." He believed that the Western powers, being Christian, were bent on impeding the progress of the Muslim world.[42]

"At first we had a few local town halls in 1989; then they went up in 1992 and 1994," explained Abdullah Gül, a Welfare Party leader, in his parliamentary office in Ankara. "We had no corruption. We changed the top officials of the executive branches of municipalities, replacing them with apolitical experts, but not the small ones; and we rationalized the system. Therefore, revenue of the town halls went up and we could provide better services. Also we believe in implementing what we say." In sum, he said, "A new kind of force is unfolding. People are fed up with major parties due to their corruption."[43]

Welfare Party mayors loosened the public purse when it came to funding seminars and symposiums and tightened it in the case of Western classical music or the "decadent" art of ballet. On the other hand, their efforts to revive the traditional Turkish horseback sport of *cirit* (polo played with javelin—an exciting, spectacular game) received almost universal approval.

In general, the mayors of Turkey left the cultural life of the premier cities virtually untouched. There was, for instance, no change in the year-round festivals of art, music, jazz, theater, and film (screening everything from Islamist movies to erotica) in Istanbul. "The new [Welfare] municipality is almost better than previous ones," said Nilgun Mirze, an ardent secularist and a festival director. "They give us free billboards and venues and are very cooperative. We are not censored at all, and in fact we no longer rely very much on any public institutions. . . . We are all looking for a new synthesis, part of being a bridge between Europe and Asia."[44]

The secular parties' aggregate loss of 14 percent of the popular vote reflected electoral disenchantment due to the corruption associated with them. Following Ozal's death in 1993, corruption allegations against his family members gained such currency that his widow, Semra, and their elder businessman son Ahmet, went into self-imposed exile.[45] By contrast, the Welfare Party was perceived as not only honest, but also efficient. Since 1989, it had administered Konya, the ninth-biggest city, in an exemplary manner. Overall, the secular parties had failed to resolve a host of acute problems facing Turkey: rampant inflation, high interest rates, the declining value of the Turkish lira, bloody Kurdish insurgency, and rising rural migration to the cities.

The Welfare Party won strong backing from hundreds of thousands of poor migrants from the Anatolian hinterland who flooded into the shanty-towns (called *gecekondu*) of Istanbul, Ankara, and other major cities at the rate of half a million a year. A visitor arriving in Ankara by train would see squatter settlements cobbled together with corrugated iron posts, plastic sheets, and disused railroad sleepers. The new arrivals took advantage of an old Ottoman law that conferred legal ownership on whosoever could assemble a house in a night on a vacant plot.[46] Such owners then gradually upgraded their abodes into concrete apartment blocks. Over time, the original shanties became established, legitimate communities.

Appalled by the "decadent" ways of the Westernized middle and upper classes of large cities, these rural folk turned to the mosque and the Welfare Party, which promised to arrest this "moral decline." Many others, finding the country mired in worsening economic crisis and ethnic violence, sought solace and solutions in Islam.

Untutored in government administration, Çiller earned notoriety for making contradictory statements. Her notable achievement was to get half a dozen constitutional articles amended in August 1995 by securing the backing of more than two-thirds of the parliamentarians. The amended articles allowed civil associations, trade unions, and professional bodies to form links with political parties, and permitted teachers and professors to participate in politics. The voting age was lowered from 21 to 18, while the size of the parliament increased by 100 seats to 550.

The next month, a strike by more than 350,000 public sector workers for higher wages to compensate for the 85 percent inflation created a crisis for Çiller's coalition. Nearly twenty deputies left her True Path Party, jeopardizing the government's majority. Though the strike ended in late October after Çiller accepted the workers' demand, she found herself forced to call an early general election.

The Welfare Party fleshed out its "just order" slogan with a plan for new cultural and economic pacts with Muslim countries, and a revision of the laws to weed out "un-Islamic" legislation. Garnering 6 million votes, 21.4

percent of the total, and 158 seats, the Welfare emerged as the leading party in parliament, ahead of the True Path (135 seats), the Motherland, led by Mesut Yilmaz (131 seats), and the Democratic Left Party (*Democratik Sol Partisi*, DSP), led by Bulent Ecevit (76 seats).

For once, the two right-of-center secular parties—the True Path and the Motherland—coalesced to form the government, with Yilmaz as the prime minister and Çiller as his deputy, with the Democratic Left Party supporting it from outside. On March 12, 1996, the government secured a confidence vote of 257 to 206, with 80 abstentions. The Welfare Party challenged the result, arguing that with 543 deputies being present, the government needed 272 votes. The Constitutional Court upheld its argument on May 14 and declared the vote invalid.

Meanwhile, in parliament, the Welfare Party hounded Çiller on corruption charges. So, when the Yilmaz government collapsed, she considered coalescing with the Welfare to stop its pursuit of bribery charges against her. Politically, this was all the more stunning since during her election campaign she had pledged that, as a staunch secularist, she would treat Islamists as political pariahs. Now she devised a common program with Erbakan, focused on reducing 80 percent inflation and speeding up privatization. Erbakan was to be the prime minister for the first two years, followed by Çiller.

"Shock, anger, relief and celebration greeted the historic news on 28 June [1996] that for the first time [Welfare] an Islamist party was to head a government in secular Turkey, the crowning achievement of a long march to power by the new prime minister, 69-year-old Necmettin Erbakan," reported Hugh Pope in *Middle East International*.[47] In the end, relief prevailed as the public welcomed the end of an administrative vacuum that had lasted ten months. The Erbakan-Çiller coalition won a confidence vote of 278 to 265.

Among those who congratulated Erbakan was Iran's President Rafsanjani, who invited him to Tehran. On the other side of the spectrum, the latest twist in Turkish politics left Washington stunned and embarrassed. The United States ceased to urge Central Asian republics to follow the model of Turkey. For here was secular, pro-Western Turkey, where the democratic process had catapulted an Islamist party as the senior partner in a coalition government.

Domestically, the rise of the Welfare Party had occurred in an environment where the size of the peasantry had declined dramatically, the literacy rate had shot up to 85 percent, and the working and lower-middle classes had lost their traditional awe of the secular elite. Starting in the prosperous mid-1980s, an increasing number of ordinary Turks had come to possess cars, telephones, and televisions and learned to think for themselves. And a growing number of rural immigrants to cities came to realize the power of the ballot, and how the principle of "one person, one vote," if fully applied, could help to right socio-economic wrongs.

Thus, the rise of the Welfare as the senior partner in a governing coalition was a symptom of democracy striking firm roots in Turkey. As Abdullah Gül, then a Welfare Party parliamentarian, put it in the spring of 1992, "Democracy and party politics are creating an environment in which latent religious and native feelings of the voters are beginning to come to the surface."[48]

Yet Erbakan could never quite act like the man enjoying supreme authority. Constantly hounded by the predominantly secularist media and military, he retained his mentality as an opposition figure. His prime antagonist, the military leadership consisting of the five senior generals, also behaved in an unprecedented way. Erbakan's first act was to give a 50 percent pay raise to 7 million civil servants and pensioners, provide cheap loans to small businesses, and cancel farming interest debt.

Social-cultural life, however, remained unchanged. "There is general pragmatism among Turkish Muslims, which means that girls with their heads covered but wearing fashionable clothes can be seen walking hand in hand with their boyfriends, that a man sporting the long beard can sell mini-skirts on a market stall, or that an imam can gratefully accept a donation from a casino to have his mosque repaired," reported Hugh Pope from Istanbul.[49]

But Erbakan tried to set a different path for Turkey's external affairs. He traveled to Tehran to sign a $20 billion natural gas deal with Iran to run until 2020. This happened just a week after U.S. President Bill Clinton signed the Iran-Libya Sanctions Act (ILSA) on August 5, 1996. It authorized the American president to impose sanctions against any individual or company anywhere in the world that invested more than $40 million in the oil or gas industry of Iran or Libya.[50] The Clinton administration sent a delegation to Ankara to pressure the Turkish government to cancel its contract with Tehran. But Erbakan refused, arguing that he was implementing Turkey's long-established policy of diversifying its energy resources.[51] Such a public defiance of America by a Turkish leader was unprecedented.

Erbakan actively pursued the project of establishing an Islamic Common Market, an idea he had first broached, unsuccessfully, as deputy premier in 1974 with Turkey's Arab neighbors (several of whom found themselves fabulously rich due to the quadrupling of oil prices). During his two extensive foreign tours in summer—one eastward to Indonesia via Iran, Pakistan,

Bangladesh, and Malaysia, and the other westward to Nigeria via Egypt—he laid the groundwork for an Islamic Common Market, based on his doctrine that economic cooperation should be fostered among all Muslim states, irrespective of their governmental system or per capita income.

Erbakan excluded Azerbaijan and Central Asia from his itinerary, as their governments were unlikely to welcome a democratically elected Islamist prime minister. In any case, by now Central Asian leaders had realized that Ankara's international influence was limited. Also, the annual summits of Central Asian presidents that President Demirel used to hold ended in 1996. At the November 1996 Istanbul conference of 2,000 Muslim industrialists and government officials from twenty countries, Erbakan urged the Muslim states to aim to increase the level of mutual trade from the current 10 percent of exports to 90 percent.

In June 1997, Erbakan hosted the summit of eight Muslim states in Istanbul to establish an economic organization called the Developing Eight (D8), a secular mask for "Muslim Eight," meaning in reality an Islamic Common Market. A long-time proponent of such a grouping, as part of his vision of a Muslim world united by strong ties of trade and economic cooperation, he addressed the leaders of countries with a combined population of 760 million, including 640 million Muslims—nearly two-thirds of the global Muslim community. Following Erbakan's overthrow by the military, nothing came of his D8 initiative as his successor, Mesut Yilmaz, showed no interest in it.

While the senior generals chose to overlook Erbakan's foreign policy initiative as long as he went along, however reluctantly, with their strategy of forging military ties with Israel, they kept a watchful eye on his domestic policies. Indeed, they seriously considered overthrowing his government.

Erbakan versus the Generals

For once, the Turkish generals felt constrained. They had to take into account the drastically changed international scene following the Soviet Union's collapse. During the Cold War era, Washington had looked the other way when they sent tanks into city squares and arrested all politicians. Now, with NATO on the verge of opening its doors to Poland, Hungary, and the Czech Republic, the Clinton administration emphasized to the leaders of these countries the importance of unchallenged civilian control over the armed forces. A coup by the Turkish generals would have made a mockery of a cardinal principle of NATO.

Finding themselves restrained from mounting a coup, the Turkish generals encouraged a war of attrition against Erbakan on several fronts: the media, parliament, the National Security Council, and the courts. Devoting most of his time and energy to countering the military's attacks on him and his party, a substantial segment of parliament, and most of the media, Erbakan had little time or energy left to resolve the problems of high inflation and unemployment, the unwieldy, loss-making public sector, and the chronic Kurdish insurgency.

The roots of the Kurdish problem lay in Mustafa Kemal Ataturk's policies. Determined to forge a strong national Turkish identity, he outlawed the use of non-Turkish languages by the republic's Muslim citizens. That deprived ethnic Kurds—forming one-fifth of the population and concentrated in the southeast, adjacent to the Kurdish areas in Armenia, Iraq, and Iran—of their right to speak in their mother tongue in public. Unlike Turkish, the Kurdish language is part of the Indo-Iranian subfamily of the Eastern division of the Indo-European languages. It is written in Arabic script using the Persian alphabet.

Descendants of Indo-European tribes, Kurds appear in the history of the early empires of Mesopotamia, where they are described as *Kardouchoi*. They trace their distinct history as mountain people to the seventh century BC, and their presence in the Anatolian plateau precedes that of the Turkic tribes by thirteen centuries. When they embraced Islam in the seventh century, they retained their language as did the Persians.

During the Ottoman rule, there were periodic uprisings by Kurds against the central power. Kurdish nationalism manifested itself in the late nineteenth century, inter alia, in the publication of the first Kurdish-language periodical in 1897.[52]

None of this mattered to the government of Kemal Ataturk, which closed down all Kurdish schools and colleges, publications, and voluntary organizations. Its ban on the Kurdish language extended to the naming of babies. To obliterate their identity, the Turkish government prescribed certain surnames for them which were totally unrelated to their clannish or tribal origins. When the Kurds rebelled, the central authorities reacted with uncommon ferocity, and cut off the Kurdish region from the rest of the country.

The government's standard practice of describing Kurds as "mountain Turks" led to bizarre contortions of historical facts. For instance, Turkish history textbooks failed to mention that Salah al Din (aka Saladin) Ayubi, who regained Jerusalem from the Crusaders in 1187, was a Kurd. Instead, they said that he administered his realm according to the Turkish practices.

In today's Turkey, Kurds often stand out in cities where men appear in their traditional dress of baggy trousers, a long shirt tied with a cummerbund, and waist-length tunic, and women don long skirts of patterned cloth embellished with sequins, a silk headband, and a white scarf.

The central government's efforts to assimilate the Kurds had succeeded to the extent that by the late 1970s, only about a third of those who identified themselves as ethnic Kurds could speak Kurdish. What persistred, though, was their traditional celebration of *Nawruz* (also spelled Nauruz; literally, "New Day"), the New Year on the Spring Equinox, when, among other thngs, they light fires to symbolically destroy the impurities of the past year.

Following the coup in 1980, the repression unleashed by the military regime was most severe in the Kurdish region. Anticipating the worst, the leaders of the Partiya Karkaren-e Kurdistan (PKK)—the Kurdistan Workers Party, a leftist faction demanding an independent state—had fled Turkey on the eve of the coup. Yet jails in southeast Turkey overflowed with ethnic Kurds, and the authorities responded by intensifying the drive to root out the remnants of the Kurdish ethnicity.

As a result, on March 21, 1984, the PKK, led by Abdullah Ocalan (pronounced Ojalan) based in Syria, initiated an armed struggle—involving attacks on Turkish military and civilian targets from the party's mountain hideouts—to establish an independent Kurdistan. The central government reacted with force. During the next decade and a half nearly 40,000 civilian sand soldiers lost their lives.

The chaos that followed in the adjacent Iraqi Kurdistan after the first Gulf War in February 1991 enabled the PKK to shore up its arsenal of arms and ammunition. Faced with escalating violence, the civilian government in Ankara lifted the ban on the use of the Kurdish language. By then, many Kurds were watching the Kurdish-language satellite TV channels based in Europe. A Kurdish diaspora had emerged in Germany, France, Britain, and Sweden. Books and newspapers in Kurdish began appearing in these countries. Underground copies of these publications, as well as recordings of Kurdish music, were smuggled into Turkey. At home, in the course of rural emigration into cities, many Kurds left the southeast and settled in the large cities elsewhere. A survey in 1992 revealed that one-fifth of the residents of Istanbul were wholly or partly Kurdish.[53]

When a massive offensive against the PKK in 1995 proved inconclusive, the central government tried a soft approach. It belatedly, and very conveniently, realized that the Nawruz was also a Turkish festival. It then ordered the Turkish soldiers stationed in the southeast to light fires on the Nawruz and jump over them as the Kurds have been doing since ancient times. Having persecuted the Kurds for seven decades for clinging to their ethnic identity, the military leaders found the civilian government's decision on the Nawruz not to their taste. But having failed to quash the Kurdish insurgency with force, they temporized.

Then, with Erbakan as the prime minister, the generals found themselves having to deal with a pressing crisis. Erbakan let the generals pursue their own regional policy centered on forging a military alliance with Israel. Yet their relations with the Erbakan-led government deteriorated to the point where the defense establishment began giving briefings to the judiciary, the media, and businessmen on the evils of Islamic fundamentalism. By indulging in day-to-day politics—a messy, Byzantine affair in Turkey—the generals severely compromised the mystique that most Turks attach to their military. And by mounting an unremitting campaign against Erbakan, they accelerated the polarization of society.

Even otherwise, the gap between the secular and the pious had widened. This became particularly marked during the month of Ramadan when the faithful fasted between sunrise and sunset, breaking their fast after sunset, and eating a hearty meal before sunrise. By now it had become customary for the pious in an urban neighborhood to arouse the residents with drumbeats in the early hours of the day to remind them to have their meal before daybreak. This practice greatly annoyed secularists.

Though daily life changed little during Ramadan in popular tourist places and centers of major cities like Istanbul, Ankara, and Izmir, with restaurants and bars open during daylight, this was not the case in the metropolises where socially conservative people lived. Here, expecting no customers during daylight hours, many owners of eateries opened only after sunset to serve fast-breaking food like dates, bread, and yogurt. Such restauranteurs either did not serve alcohol or did so only in a particular section of the premise. Noting the prevalent religious atmosphere in the neighborhood, some secular residents fasted reluctantly, or feigned fasting. Many town halls, run by the Welfare (later Virtue) Party, offered free fast-breaking meals to the poor, or not so poor, gathered inside spacious tents. The accompanying small shows and other events with Islamic themes performed outside the tents created an atmosphere resembling that of an amusement park. In some cases, no lunches were served in municipal offices on the assumption that all the employees were fasting.

During Ramadan the use and sale of yogurt rose sharply, as it was customary to break the fast with yogurt and palm dates. As it is, "yogurt" or "yoghurt" is a derivative of the Turkish word "yoğurt." It has a long history as part of the Turkish diet, dating back to the nomadic period. Yogurt appears in Mahmoud Kashari's *Diwan Lughat al-Turk* (*Collection of Turkish Food*), written in the eleventh century, which mentions its medicinal use. In fact, that is how yogurt arrived in European kitchens in the first half of the sixteenth century. When the acute diarrhea of French king Francis I (1515–47) proved incurable at the hands of the local doctors, his ally Ottoman Sultan Suleiman the Magnificent (1520–66) volunteered to help by dispatching his physician. His prescription of yogurt cured the French monarch's malady.

Folowing the ways of their nomadic forebears, Turks consume yogurt with all other edibles, from rice and flatbread to kebabs and meatballs, from *meze* (Turkish for appetizer) to main dishes of fried spinach with minced meat, zucchini, or eggplant. Eggplant occupies a prime position among Turkish vegetables. No other nation knows as many ways of processing eggplant as Turkey. It appears invariably in *mezes*, side dishes, salads, moussaka, and main dishes—where it is served along with cheese, minced meat, or kebab, or wrapped up inside stuffed vine leaves. There is even an eggplant jam.

In the final analysis, present Turkish cuisine reflects the Ottoman Empire, being an amalgam of diets from Central Asia, the Balkans, and the Middle East—the home of Islam, which regards Ramadan, the tenth month of its lunar year, as holy. It was on the night of 26–27 Ramadan, *Lailat al Kadir* (Night of Power), that the first devine revelation was made to Prophet Muhammad.

Reflecting the rise of religious fervor among the believers during Ramadan, which started in early January 1997, Erbakan repeated his election pledges. He would lift the ban on headscarves in universities and places of public service, and build mosques in Istanbul's prestigious Taksim Square and Ankara's Çankaya district. Simmering tensions rose. While the generals approached President Demirel to act, trade unionists and feminists mounted protest demonstrations.

On the last Friday of Ramadan (January 31), celebrated in some Muslim countries as the Jerusalem Liberation Day, the Welfare mayor Ergin Yildiz of Sincan, an outer suburb of Ankara, organized the day with young actors dressed as Hamas militants. They threw imaginary stones at Israelis against the background of posters of Hizbullah (also spelled Hezbollah), a militant Lebanese organization. Addressing the gathering, the Iranian ambassador to Turkey said, "Do not be afraid to call yourself fundamentalists. God has promised them the final victory," and declared that "God will punish those who sign deals with America and Israel."[54]

On February 4, twenty tanks and fifteen armored personnel carriers paraded slowly through the streets of Sincan, ostensibly "on their way to a routine military exercise" in a rural area. The generals summoned Interior Minister Meral Akflener of the (secular) True Path Party. She instantly suspended Mayor Yildiz, then the State Security Court prosecutor ordered his arrest. On February 15, up to 10,000 women marched in Ankara to reassert their commitment to secularism.

At a heated, nine-hour meeting of the military-majority National Security Council on February 28, the generals submitted a list of eighteen demands to the civilian fellow members to curb the rise of political Islam. Erbakan refused to accept them, saying, "The National Security Council does not make the laws; the parliament makes the laws." He believed that being forced out of office by the military would help him at the polls. But his stance divided the True Path Party, threatening the fall of his coalition government with a slim parliamentary majority. Therefore, Erbakan finally came around to putting his signature on the document.[55]

One of the important demands of the military was to extend primary education from five to eight years. Currently twelve-year-olds had the option of attending middle schools leading to lycées, or vocational schools imparting technical training. The vocational category also included imam-khatib schools, established in the 1950s to train imams. Popular with religious conservatives, accounting for 500,000 students out of 20 million in all educational institutions, the imam-khatib schools had created an alternate network. Most Welfare leaders were graduates of these schools. Supervised by the Education Ministry, their curriculum was the same as that of other vocational schools, the only difference being Quranic studies and Arabic. By extending primary education by three years, the generals wanted to raise the entry age to vocational schools to fifteen in the belief that by then pupils would have been cast into a Kemalist mode and would be immune to Islamist ideas. They also wanted to restrict the imam-khatib graduates to theological studies at universities. Following the ousting of Erbakan in June, they would see this demand enforced, which would reduce the imam-khatib school enrollment to 71,000 in less than a decade.[56]

After the parliament had approved a free trade agreement with Israel, and Erbakan had received Israel's foreign minister, David Levy, in early April he set off for his twenty-fifth pilgrimage to Mecca along with his family and fifty Welfare Party parliamentarians as the official guests of King Fahd of

Saudi Arabia. By encouraging a growing body of Turks through personal example and governmental policy to strengthen their Islamic roots, Erbakan upset the most Europhile and secular section of the elite, the military leadership.

General Ismail Hakki Karadayi, chief of general staff, declared that given the violation of the principles of Ataturk's republic, no one could stay neutral. This was a clear hint the military was ready to strike. Indeed, it later transpired that, fearing a military coup, Erbakan had instructed the head of police intelligence to spy on the senior generals in order to "protect democracy."[57] Equally concerned about safeguarding democracy, following several private exhortations to Turkey's military hierarchy to stay its hand, U.S. Secretary of State Madeleine Albright publicly urged it on June 14 "not to exceed the armed forces' authority within the democratic system."[58]

The tense confrontation between Erbakan and the generals led to defection from the True Path Party, with its strength reduced to 102, thus depriving the Erbakan government of a majority. Erbakan resigned on June 18, 1997[59] President Demirel called on Mesut Yilmaz, leader of the second largest group, the Motherland, to appoint the next cabinet. Yilmaz formed a minority coalition government, including Ecevit's Democratic Left Party. The parliament passed the Education bill, as drafted by the military, by 277 to 242 votes, effectively closing down the imam-khatib schools.

In January 1998, the Constitutional Court ruled that the Welfare Party had acted against the secular principles of the state, and outlawed it. The Court also banned Erbakan from politics for five years.[60]

EXIT WELFARE, ENTER VIRTUE

Most Welfare leaders and ranks lost little time to reassemble under the umbrella of the Virtue Party (*Fadhila Partisi*, in Turkish). They held a public meeting in Ankara on May 14, 1998, to commemorate the date in 1950 when one party rule ended with Democratic Party leader Adnan Menderes assuming power.

Working behind the scenes, Erbakan managed to get his favorite Recai Kutan elected as the leader. Three of the Executive Committee members were women, two of whom did not wear the headscarf. Women accounted for a quarter of the party's membership. Abdullah Gül, the second most important Virtue Party leader, pointed out that, unlike the Welfare, the new party favored full integration with the West, which was the only way to ensure "full democracy and civilian rule" in Turkey.

Another rising star in the Virtue Party was Recep Tayyip Erdogan, elected mayor of Istanul as the Welfare's candidate. In December 1997, speaking in Siirt in the Kurdish region, he preached peace in the troubled area and stressed national unity. He cited a poem by Ziya Gökalp, a leading ideologue of Turkish nationalism, whose writings are taught in schools. Part of it read, "The mosques are our barracks / The domes our hamlets / The minarets our bayonets / And the faithful our soldiers." In April 1998, the State Security Court in Diyarbakir found him guilty under Article 312 of the penal code "provoking hatred by displaying racial and religious discrimination." In September, the Supreme Court upheld a ten-month prison sentence for him, with a minimum of four months to be served.

By all accounts, under Erdogan's mayoralty, Istanbul enjoyed better management than ever before. Its debts halved, and the city became greener following a tree-planting campaign, and cleaner due to the ban on the burning of obnoxious lignite coal and the introduction of compressed natural gas (CNG) buses as well as a subway and a tramline. Ergodan also subsidized bread, a boon to the poor. Despite their best efforts, the secular media had failed to discover serious corruption at the Town Hall. A charismatic, energetic man, Erdogan won plaudits for his integrity and good management and administration.

Little wonder that in the local elections held in April 1999, the Virtue Party retained the mayoralties of Istanbul and Ankara. These elections coincided with the parliamentary poll because of the fall of Yilmaz's coalition government due to the no-confidence motion passed by the parliament in December. Unlike its predecessor, the Welfare Party, the Virtue Party failed to lead in the national race, yielding that place to the Democratic Left Party (22 percent of the vote) of Ecevit. Still, its score of 15 percent (101 MPs) was a shade ahead of the Motherland and True Path parties.

When Virtue Party Deputy Merve Kavakci, a thirty-one-year-old computer engineer trained in Texas, entered the chamber wearing a navy blue scarf on May 2, the Democratic Left deputies banged their desks and shouted "Out, out!" She had to leave without taking her oath. She argued that nothing in the parliament's rules barred her from wearing a headscarf. As it was, the ban on the headscarf did not stem from a specific law, but was based on the Constitutional Court's interpretation of the principles of secularism. Some accused her of being an agent of Iran; others of links with Hamas, a Palestinian militant organization. It transpired that she had recently married a Jordanian-American and acquired American citizenship. Turkey allowed dual nationality, but a Turkish national was required to seek special permission from the authorities before running for an elective post. She had not done so. The government instantly stripped her of Turkish citizenship.[61]

In June 1999, Ecevit formed a coalition government of his leftist party, the National Action Party (*Milli Hareket Partisi*, in Turkish, MHP) of Devlet Bahçeli, and the Motherland, with the backing of 351 deputies. The veteran Republican People's Party was absent because it had failed to cross the 10 percent threshold.

Six months later, the European Union (EU) invited Turkey to become an official candidate for full membership, making it clear that the EU Accession Partnership document required Turkey to "align the constitutional role of the military-majority National Security Council as an advisory body to the government in accordance with the practice of EU states." In other words, Turkey had to downgrade the armed forces' role to fall in line with the rules of a democratic society.

Ankara got the EU invitation at a time when the Turkish economy was in the doldrums. 1999 ended with Turkey's GDP declining by 6.4 percent and inflation at 66 percent. The banking sector faced a severe crisis. During an escalating inflation, the eighty banks in the private sector grew rich by lending money to the government at exorbitant interest rates. They attracted deposits by offering ever higher interest rates to replenish the withdrawn sums while their top officials siphoned off funds through offshore accounts and front companies. Politicians in power were complicit in the scam. They misused many of the private banks by channeling subsidies and unsecured loans to their favored clients. Trouble ensued when inflation began to decline, and the banks could no longer offer rising interest rates to attract deposits. Thirteen of them went bankrupt.

The government took over another ten ailing private banks, which strained state finances. As a result, the three government-owned banks ended up covering half of the market, and losing $20 billion, which had been siphoned off through fraudulent means.[62]

Another major source of corruption was the large public sector and the politicians' reluctance to relinquish control of state enterprises. Most government contracts were subject to 15 percent "commission."

In May 2000, Ahmet Necdet Sezer, head of the Constitutional Court, won the presidency by 281 votes, a slim majority of five, by defeating two other candidates. Dour-looking and discreet, Sezer was appointed Constitutional Court chief in 1988 by President General Kenan Evren. A strong supporter of secularism and republicanism, he was backed by the military. As the commander-in-chief, he appointed the chief of general staff. He had the authority to appoint judges and university rectors, and approve or disapprove nominations to the cabinet. He could also veto legislation or government appointments whose secular credentials he suspected.

But Sezer was also a reformist who wanted to bring Turkish laws in line with universal standards of human rights and freedom of expression. "At the basis of all of Turkey's problems is the practice of not abiding by the rules and the lack of institutionalization," he said after his victory. "In society and in politics, democracy is not sufficiently developed. A tradition of democracy has not been established."[63]

Later Sezer came to agree with the assessment of Interior Minister Saadettin Tantan that "the corruption economy" was "the number one threat to Turkey's economic and political stability." At a National Security Council meeting in February 2001, Sezer criticized Prime Minister Ecevit for failing to act decisively against corruption. This incensed Ecevit. He walked out, complaining of the president's "ugly behavior," and won the backing of the government. The open split between the president and the cabinet led to a meltdown in the financial markets, and interest rates soared to 150 percent.

Recession, which had claimed 500,000 jobs in two months, deepened. To make matters worse, the government's anti-corruption drive fizzled out when Tantan was forced to resign by his party leader, Yilmaz. The economic meltdown and rampant corruption provided fodder for the Virtue Party. But just as it was capitalizing on the utter failure of the secular parties to manage the economy and run a clean administration, it received a fatal blow.

In June 2001, the Constitutional Court ruled by eight votes to three that the Virtue Party had become "a focal point of anti-secular activities," and ordered that all its assets be confiscated. However, the judges rejected the plea that the Virtue Party was a continuation of the old Welfare Party. Instead, they focused on the issue of the headscarves, and pinned their evidence on the actions of two Virtue Party deputies, Bekir Sobaci and Nazli Ilicak, a journalist. These women lawmakers had defended the action of Merve Kavakci when she appeared in parliament with a headscarf to take her oath of office.[64] The court deprived them of their parliamentary seats, and banned them from politics for five years.

The remaining ninety-nine Virtue Party deputies split into two factions. Forty-eight pro-Erbakan members formed Felicity Party (*Saadet Partisi*), and fifty-one founded the moderate Justice and Development Party (AKP) under Erdogan and Gul.

THE AK PARTY'S CLEAN SWEEP

After being elected chairman of AKP in August 2001, Erdogan said, "We see secularism as the guarantee of democracy. We are against the exploitation of religion, and we are also distorting secularism by misinterpreting it as animosity against religion." He added that since there were no dress code restrictions on AKP members, there was no need to expel AKP members wearing headscarves."[65]

Like the rest of the world, Turkey expressed shock at the terrorist attacks on New York and Washington, DC, and offered help. It granted access to its airspace and air bases to U.S. transport planes engaged in military campaign against the Taliban in Afghanistan. The post-9/11 international environment encouraged the military leaders to pursue, obsessively, the eradication of all signs of Islamism.

On the other hand, with the United States forging direct security links with Uzbekistan and Kyrgyzstan, the role of Turkey as a mediator between Central Asian republics and the West dwindled further.[66] And, to satisfy the EU's requirements, the parliament amended thirty-four articles of the Constitution, with more than two-thirds of the lawmakers voting for the changes. In January 2002, the parliament passed a new Civil Code of 1,030 articles to replace the one in force since 1926. It gave women equality with men in all spheres, and raised the legal age for marriage to eighteen for both sexes, from fifteen for girls and seventeen for boys.

But the chronic corruption continued to corrode the state and debase the secular political establishment. The local Show TV's sensational airing of the personnel director at the prime minister's office and another high official negotiating a fake businessman's bribe of $140,000 in applying for state funds to build a tourist resort highlighted the malaise. It compelled Premier Ecevit to admit that his anti-corruption drive had failed.

This scandal, and his failure to remedy the deep recession, which reduced the GDP by a whopping 9.4 percent in 2001, damaged the standing of all the constituent parties in his coalition government. Lacking any presence in the parliament, the Republican People's Party would escape blame for Turkey's woes. So, too, would the AKP, the child of the earlier corruption-free Islamist parties.

The AKP backed the second reform package to meet the EU's democratic standards presented to the parliament. The new law made it more difficult to close down political parties and stipulated withdrawing state funds from a party as a penalty. It also required torturers to pay compensation to their victims. The third package, adopted in August 2002 with the support of the AKP, would abolish the death penalty and grant education and broadcasting rights to minority Kurds.

Following Ecevit's illness and his sacking of the deputy premier in July, he saw his Democratic Left Party split, with half of the 128 deputies leaving to form the New Turkey Party. This paved the way for a general election.

To its disappointment, AK Party leadership found itself having to exclude Erdogan from its list of candidates because the Constitutional Court had earlier disqualified him from running for parliament for life.[67] During the campaign, party leaders repeatedly emphasized that they would not challenge the principles, foundations, or international alliances of the Kemalist state. On the other hand, the secular parties went all out to fan fears at home and abroad of the catastrophic result of a "fundamentalist" triumph.

Of the eighteen parties that entered the electoral arena on November 3, 2002, only two broke the 10 percent barrier: the Justice and Development Party (AKP, 34.3 percent); and the Republican People's Party (RPP, 19.4 percent). The votes for other groups were allocated to the AKP and the RPP proportionately, with the former gaining a total of 364 seats and the latter 178. The remaining nine seats went to independents. "The elections took place according to the rules," said General Hilmi Ozkok, the chief of general staff, adding that he will "respect the Turkish people's will."[68] An impressive 79 percent voter turnout left Ozkok with no other option.

The 2002 parliamentary poll caused a political earthquake. It consigned the traditional political class, corrupt and inept to the core, to the dustbin of history. It ended half a century of messy coalition governments and empowered an untainted, reformist party with Islamist roots.

Abdullah Gül became the prime minister. Under his guidance, the parliament passed a series of reforms, which nullified Erdogan's political disqualification. When the High Electoral Council invalidated the results of three parliamentary seats in Siirt province, Erdogan got his chance to get elected in March 2003, winning 84 percent of the ballots. Gul stepped down in his favor, and became foreign minister in the new cabinet.

TURKEY UNDER MODERATE ISLAMISTS

The first test of the Justice and Development Party government came in early 2003 as U.S. President George W. Bush tried to persuade allies to join

Washington in its plans to invade Iraq ruled by President Saddam Hussein.

The National Security Council meeting on January 31 urged the government to seek parliament's authorization for "military measures." It referred to Article 92 of the Constitution: "The power to authorize the declaration of a state of war, to send Turkish armed forces to foreign countries, and to allow foreign armed forces to be stationed in Turkey, is vested in the Turkish Grand National Assembly." The Constitution also specified international legitimacy for such an action. The Turkish government argued that the United Nations Security Council resolution 1441 of November 2002 did not grant automatic use of force.

Nonetheless, pressured by Washington and tempted by its offer of $6 billion in grants and another $20 billion in credit guarantees, the government introduced a motion to allow the stationing of 62,000 American troops in Turkey and send Turkish troops abroad (into northern Iraq). With nineteen deputies abstaining, the motion required 266 votes to pass. It received 264. The opposition RPP voted against the motion, and so did nearly 100 deputies of the ruling party. They were in tune with public opinion: 94 percent opposed the invasion of Iraq.[69] The Turkish parliament's vote forced the Pentagon to order its warships anchored off Turkey's coast to proceed to the Persian Gulf. In March, Prime Minister Erdogan asked the parliament to give the Pentagon access to Turkish air space—not its air bases—and its members obliged.

Soon after the Bush administration had toppled Saddam, its deputy defense secretary, Paul Wolfowitz, told CNN-Turk, "Let's have a Turkey that steps up and says, 'We made a mistake, we should have known how bad things were in Iraq, but we know now. Let's figure out how we can be as helpful as possible to the Americans.'" Erdogan was quick with his riposte. "Turkey, from the beginning, made no mistake and took all the necessary steps in all sincerity," he said. He got the backing of the opposition leader, Deniz Baykal, who reminded the Americans that the parliamentary decision was the result of a democratic vote.[70]

As promised in his party's platform, Erdogan pursued Turkey's endeavor to become a full member of the EU, an enterprise that senior generals backed. "The Turkish Armed Forces cannot oppose the European Union because the EU is a geopolitical and geo-strategic obligation laid out by Ataturk," said General Yashar Buyukanit, deputy chief of general staff.[71]

Responding to the sentiment prevalent among younger officers, General Huseyin Kivrikoglu, chief of general staff, avoided confrontation with the new government. Erdogan responded in kind. While introducing the sixth reform package to the parliament, he praised the military as "pioneer of Turkey's modernization process," and—contradicting historical evidence—described it as "the midwife of democracy." The new legislation removed the infamous Article 8 of the Anti-Terror Law used in the past to punish pro-Kurdish intellectuals.[72] It also granted cultural rights to Kurds, allowing parents to give their children Kurdish names, and permitting private radio and TV channels to air programs in Kurdish.

The next reform package passed in July 2003 was highly significant. It removed the executive powers of the NSC, with its military majority, thus turning it into a consultative body as required by the EU, and stipulated a civilian secretary-general to be nominated by the government and approved by the president.

At the end of one year in power, the Erdogan government could claim that while pushing a liberal agenda, it had avoided confrontation with the secular elite, and that it has started reducing the bloated bureaucracy—as well as reduced inflation to its lowest level in fifteen years. Voters approved. In the local elections in March 2004, they raised the Justice and Development Party's share of the vote from 34 percent in the parliamentary poll to 43 percent. It won fifty-seven of the eighty-one town halls.

President Sezer approved the package of constitutional reform, abolishing the State Security Court used by the military to prosecute political prisoners, and removing military representatives from the boards of higher education, as well as from radio and television.

For the first time since the founding of the fifty-seven-member Islamic Conference Organization in 1969, Turkey hosted its summit in Istanbul in June 2004. Its candidate, Ekmeleddin Ihsanoglu, a Turkish academic fluent in Arabic, became the secretary-general of the ICO. Addressing the gathering, Erdogan said that Muslims should not blame others for their problems. After declaring that "Democracy is a universal and a modern day requirement," he added a rider: "Changes should not be imposed from the outside"—an ill-disguised reference to the American occupation of Iraq. "The character and tradition of each country should be taken into consideration."[73]

Later that month at the NATO summit in Ankara, ignoring Erdogan's implied criticism of his foreign policy, President Bush praised Turkey for setting the example of "how to be a Muslim country and at the same time a country which embraces democracy and rule of law and freedom."[74]

The parliament amended the penal code containing 340 articles. Overall, it advanced freedom of expression,[75] requiring "stringent proof" that certain acts or statements presented danger to the state. (Yet, demanding the withdrawal of Turkish troops from northern Cyprus or supporting claims that massacres of Armenians from 1914 to 1916 amounted to genocide could land the speaker or writer in jail under Article 306.) More importantly, the new code signaled the end of Kemal Ataturk's statist approach, which viewed citizens as servants of the state, by limiting the government's power to interfere in citizens' private lives, and focused on their rights and responsibilities.

Reviewing Turkey's progress towards democratization and assuring human rights, the EU concluded that though "the government has increasingly asserted its control over the military" the army continued "to exercise influence through a series of informal mechanisms." While the independence of the judiciary had been strengthened, more work needed to be done. Article 301 of the Penal Code, criminalizing insult to "Turkishness," remained in force. It was invoked to prosecute Orhan Pamuk, the 2006 Nobel laureate, for saying in an interview with a Swiss magazine, "Thirty thousand Kurds and one million Armenians were killed in these lands and nobody dares talk about it."[76]

While the Turkish government focused on gaining full membership of the EU, its interest in Azerbaijan and Central Asia declined. Yet cultural and economic links continued to thrive. Turkey's investment in Central Asia's construction, consumer goods, and cotton sectors played an important role. There were more than 3,200 Turkish businesses in the region. Outside of construction, Turkish companies had invested over $5 billion. Construction contracts totaled $14 billion.[77]

Thanks to the strong, clean administration provided by the Erdogan government, Turkey's economy improved. Reversing the depressing trend of the recent past, Turkey ended 2004 with its GDP soaring by 10 percent, and inflation declining to 9.3 percent, the lowest in decades. This augured well for the Erdogan government's plan to introduce the New Turkish Lira (NTL) equal to 1 million old liras, at the exchange rate of NTL 1.35 = $1.00, on January 1, 2005.

With the economy booming and corruption down, and the reform progressing steadily in parliament, Erdogan turned his attention to the chronic problem of the Kurdish minority. Addressing a meeting in Diyarbakir, the virtual capital of the Kurdish region, in August, he publicly conceded that the Turkish government had made mistakes on the Kurdish issue, which was an unprecedented step. He asserted that the solution lay with "more democracy, more citizenship rights, and more prosperity." The rebellious

Kurdistan Workers Party—weakened by the arrest of its leader Abdullah Ocalan in 1999, followed by his sentence of life imprisonment—responded favorably and announced a one-month cease-fire.

With talks on Turkey's full membership of the EU commencing in October 2005, the progress in this field dominated news. The Turkish delegation was led by Foreign Minister Abdullah Gül, who would become president two years later. Born in Kayseri, Abdullah Gül—now a powerfully built, well-coiffed man, with a bristling mustache and expressive eyes—had come a long way. He was twenty-five when his mother chose a fourteen-year-old girl, named Hayrunisa, to be his bride. He waited until she reached the legal marriage age of fifteen. His further university studies took him to the London School of Economics where he got his doctorate. From 1983 to 1991, he worked in Saudi Arabia with the Islamic Development Bank. On his return home he was elected a Welfare Party parliamentarian. Belonging to the moderate wing of the Welfare Party, he allied with Erdogan to found the Justice and Development Party.

To maintain the momentum toward Turkey's full membership of the EU, Erdogan abandoned his election pledge to end the restrictions on women wearing headscarves in government offices, schools, universities, and hospitals. He also abandoned his pledge to allow the extension of alcohol-free zones—designated by some municipalities run by the Justice and Development Party—nationally. On the other hand, the party's policy of effecting changes quietly at the local level through an expanding network of pious teachers and civil servants recruited during its administration continued unabated. It focused on schools, teachers, and textbooks. By releasing them from strict centralized control, and empowering lower authorities to make important decisions, the party advanced its agenda.

For instance, in Denizli, a town near the Greek border run by the Justice and Development Party, while alcohol continued to be sold near mosques, pupils in primary schools were handed prayer books with the message, "Pray in the Muslim way. Get others to pray, too." The change pointed in a certain direction. "In a very quiet, deep way, you can sense an Islamization," said Bedrettin Usanmaz, a jeweler. "They're not after rapid change. They're investing for 50 years ahead."[78] As stated earlier, that was the way Islamists had been operating over the past quarter century.

The "softly, softly" approach did not preclude taking a bold step periodically. On April 27, 2007, Erdogan nominated Abdullah Gül to replace President Sezer, who was scheduled to step down on May 16. Gül vowed that he would defend the constitution and uphold its basic principles. But the opposition RPP, led by Baykal, boycotted the presidential poll and deprived the parliament of the required two-thirds quorum.

The military leadership was opposed to Gül, who had served as a minister in the Erbakan government in 1996 and 1997 and whose wife Hayrunisa wore a headscraf—as did nearly two-thirds of Turkish women, including Premier Erdogn's wife Emine. But, viewing the headscarf as a political symbol, secularists argued that if the president's wife donned one, the whole secular system would be threatened and all women would be required to wear one. Ultimatley the veil's political meaning was in the eye of the beholder. "Meaning is in our heads, not on our heads," wrote Jenny White, an anthropology professor, in a Turkish newspaper.[79]

On the night of April 27, 2007, describing themselves as "the absolute defenders of secularism," the generals, led by General Yashar Buyukanit, declared: "When necessary, we will demonstrate our attitudes. . . . Let no one doubt this." The EU's enlargement commissioner warned the military to stop meddling in the presidential poll.

Though Gül won the presidency later by securing two-thirds of those voting in parliament, the Constitutional Court, an integral part of the secular establishment, ruled that the election was invalid as the parliament was inquorate, with less than two-thirds of the total being present. Pointing out that previous presidents had been elected without the presence of the required number, Erdogan described the Court's decision as "a bullet fired at the heart of democracy."

The only way to end the impasse was to let voters decide by advancing the general election, due in November 2007, up to July 22.

THE END OF THE SECULARIST GRIP

The Justice and Development Party flaunted its achievement. Overcoming the financial meltdown it inherited in 2002, it achieved an average annual economic growth of 7 percent and nearly doubled the per capita income to $5,500.[80] It also expanded human, democratic, and minority rights by carrying out the most thoroughgoing reform of the laws and standards.

At the same time, the party continued to nurture the grassroots organization it had inherited from the Virtue/Welfare Party. It had stayed faithful to its strategy of working from the bottom up—a complete reversal of the way Kemalists had operated, from the top down. "You talk to the AK [Justice and Development] people and they try to sell to you, they try to persuade you," said Ali Caroglu, a professor of political science. "But the RPP is very

judgmental. They don't want to talk to the people they don't approve of."
Omar Karatas, leader of the AK party's youth branch in Istanbul, made the
same point more profoundly. "Before, you had a condescending approach
to citizenry,"he said. "The state was up here and the people down there.
Now, there's a harmonization between these two groups."[81] In other words,
the Justice and Development Party's rule had been the death knell of
Kemalist statism.

Ideologically, unlike in the 2002 poll, this electoral contest was a straight
fight between moderate Islam and secular fundamentalism, represented by
the Republican People's Party. Some moderate secularists switched sides.
On an 80 percent voter turnout, the Justice and Development Party won
46.7 percent of the ballots; the secular RPP, 20.9 percent; and the
Nationalist Action Party (MHP), 14 percent. The AK party's 12 percent
increase in its popular vote showed that the drive by its leaders to attract
young people of both sexes at ease with the modern world, and promote
women—with or without headscarves—to head the party at the district
level, had paid off.

Despite the rise in its vote, the seats won by the Justice and Development
Party declined slightly to 341 because this time a third party, MHP, crossed
the threshold of 10 percent and won 80 seats. Correspondingly, the RPP's
share fell to 103 seats.[82] Erdogan formed the next government.

"Voters rightly rejected the claim asserted by the traditional military-
secularist establishment that there is any fundamental incompatibility
between democracy and Islam," commented the *New York Times* editori-
ally on July 24, 2007. "The AK . . . has broadened its support by moving
away from its original, narrowly Islamic roots. It is still a visibly Muslim
party, but it is also a visibly democratic and tolerant party."

Ali Murat Yel, a sociology professor, illustrated the ruling party's tolerance by pointing out that nowadays AKP people "can sit at the same table
as some [other] people who drink alcohol while they drink their Coke," and
talk to them. Taking a long view, Suat Kinikli, a Canadian-educated secularist, said, "In fifty years, people will write that this [2007] was the time
when Turkey [as a state] started to come to terms with its own people."[83]

According to a survey in 2006 by the Turkish Economic and Social
Studies Foundation, a prestigious research organization, 59 percent of
Turks described themselves as "very religious" or "extremely religious,"
and two-thirds of the women said they covered their heads in some way
when they left home.[84]

But the military hierarchy had yet to come to terms with the new reality.

With all eyes now turned to the impending presidential poll, the hawkish General Buyukanit demanded that the president must be secular, not just in words but also in deeds. To pacify him, Gül, the ruling party's candidate, said, "Protection of secularism is one of my basic principles," and that "Impartiality will be my first and foremost principle." Yet Buyukanit was not satisfied. Premier Erdogan intervened: "Let us not mix the TSK [initials of Turkish armed forces] with politics. Let it stay in its place, because all our institutions conduct their duties in line with what is set out in the Constitution. If you draw them into politics, then why are we [politicians] in here?"[85]

On August 28, Gül won the presidency with a comfortable majority in parliament, finally breaking the secular establishment's eighty-four-year-old grip on power.

Little wonder that the generals boycotted Gül's swearing-in ceremony—but their sulk ended shortly. Two days later, General Buyukanit stood next to President Gül at the military parade to observe the eighty-fifth anniversary of the War of Independence.

Nonetheless, the tension between the generals and the ruling party had taken its toll. In its annual report, the EU reported that the Turkish government had done too little to eradicate corruption, modernize judiciary, reduce the military's power, and increase freedom of expression. The number of persons proecuted under Article 301 doubled from 2005 to 2006, and increased further in 2007. The promised amendment to the draconian Article 301 had yet to be passed by parliament.

On the other hand, the resolution of the long-running headscarf controversy for women at universities seemed imminent. Initiating the debate on the subject in parliament, Erdogan said, "Today, in a world where freedoms are debated, where everyone dresses up the way they want to everywhere they go, if Turkey still fails to resolve this issue, this is a serious problem in terms of freedoms." By 4 to 1, Turkish lawmakers voted in mid-February 2008 to lift the ban against women's headscarves at universities. The amendment in the constitution that followed said that "no one should be denied higher education because of his/her attire."[86] The secular opposition RPP called on the Constitutional Court to review the amendment to judge whether or not it contravenes the secular principles of the constitution.

Soon after, basing its case on the headscarf issue, Chief Abdurrahman Yalcinkaya, submitted a 162-page indictment of the AK Party to the Constitutional Court. "The AKP is founded by a group that drew lessons from the closure of earlier Islamic parties, and uses democracy to reach its goal, which is installing Sharia law in Turkey," read the charge sheet. "There is an attempt to expunge the secular principles of the constitution." The Constitutional Court decided unanimouly to hear the case calling for the closure of the Justice and Development Party, and the banning of seventy-one politicians including the prime minister and president from politics for five years, on the grounds that they were trying to impose the Sharia. The party had a month in which to respond.

Erdogan replied, "History will not forgive this. Those who couldn't fight the AKP democratically prefer to fight with undemocratic methods." The EU was equally critical in its response. "The prohibition or dissolution of political parties is a far-reaching measure which should be used with utmost restraint," said Olli Rehn, dealing with Turkey's bid to join the EU. "Such a measure can only be justified in the case of parties which advocate the use of violence or use violence as a political means to overthrow the democratic constitutional order."[87]

The uncertainity created by the case, which was expected to be last up to one year, had a negative impact on the economy and foreign investment. These events interested not just the leaders of the European Union, but also those of the Turkic countries east of Turkey—Azerbaijan and Central Asia. Though their interest in and fascination with Turkey no longer matched what they were in the immediate aftermath of the Soviet Union's collapse, these countries' leaders had maintained links with Turkey's military institutions, considering them, rightly, as the nearest they could get their officers to imbibing Western levels of efficiency and professionalism. So the program of Azeri and Central Asian cadets and officers receiving their training at the Turkish military academies and other institutions had continued uninterrupted. This was especially true of Uzbekistan's armed forces.

Within days of Turkey recognizing the Central Asian republics as independent countries "on an equal footing and on mutual respect for existing borders" on December 16, 1991, Uzbek President Islam Karimov flew to Ankara. In a dramatic gesture, he kissed the tarmac of Ankara's Esenboga Airport on his arrival there on December 20. "My country will go forward by the Turkish route," he declared. By then he had been in power for five years in the most strategic republic in the region, whose history was shaped by Joseph Stalin so long as he was alive.

CHAPTER 2

UZBEKISTAN:
THE COMPLEX HUB OF CENTRAL ASIA

FOLLOWING STALIN'S DEATH, THERE WAS MUCH JOSTLING FOR POWER AT the highest level of the Communist Party of the Soviet Union (CPSU), involving, inter alia, Nikita Khrushchev, Vice Premier Vyacheslav Molotov, and the head of the NKVD (forerunner of the KGB, *Komitet Gosudarstvennoy Bezopasnosti*, Committee for State Security), Lavrenti Beria.

It was not until the autumn of 1954 that Khrushchev—a small, portly, blunt-speaking fireball of peasant origins—emerged as the unbeatable front-runner. He initiated de-Stalinization, which affected all republics, including Uzbekistan. The high point was his revelation to the Twentieth Congress of the CPSU in 1956 that Stalin had grossly violated basic Leninist tenets about nationalities. This created a milieu which allowed some freedom to non-Russians to speak about their culture and identity without being denounced as "bourgeois nationalists."

The subsequent changes brought Sharaf Rashidov (1917–83)—a balding, smartly dressed, wounded war veteran—to the fore as the first secretary of the Communist Party of Uzbekistan (CPU) in 1959, a post he would keep until his death. Born into a poor peasant household in Jizak, he worked as a journalist in Samarkand before seeing combat on the German front where he was wounded in 1942. Soon after his election as the president of the Uzbekistan Writers Union, he became chairman of the republic's Supreme Soviet. Under his leadership the party demanded that the government give prominence to Uzbeks in administrative and social-cultural spheres. The first authorized history of the CPU, published in 1962, provided a long list of the Uzbek leaders executed during the 1937 to 1938 purges.

At the Twenty-Second CPSU Congress in October 1961, Khrushchev announced that the Soviet Union had entered "mature socialism," and that during this period the dialectics of national relations would follow the line of "blooming, rapprochement and amalgamation": the twin processes of blooming (fullest national self-realization of each Soviet nation) and rapprochement (coming together of nations, through mutual cross-fertilization, sharing a common socialist economy and social formations) resulting in rapid progress towards ultimate amalgamation. Later this assessment would prove too optimistic, and would be modified.

Khrushchev's fall from power three years later, leading to the elevation of Leonid Brezhnev (1906–82)—known for his rubbery face, double chin, and bushy eyebrows—as the first secretary of CPSU, slowed the de-Stalinization process but did not stop it.

Rashidov proved adroit enough to use Khrushchev's downfall to strengthen his power base in Uzbekistan, the most populous republic in the region, and the leading producer of cotton (*pakhta* in Uzbek) in the Soviet Union.

The earthquake of April 26, 1966, which razed almost half of Tashkent, changed the physical landscape as much as it did the political. Separated from the modern Russian settlement, the old walled city—a hodgepodge of uneven tarmac streets, leaning walls of clay, tunneled entrances, hidden courtyards, and flat roofs—survived the earthquake, as if to prove the adage, "Old is gold." Politically, the natural disaster brought the erstwhile adversaries together. This manifested itself in the way the government and the republic's Communist party praised Usman Yusupov, a staunch Stalinist predecessor of Rashidov, on his death in May, naming the Fergana Canal after him. In reality, such behavior had more to do with the excessive reverence a feudal society offers its "white beards" than with any ideological assessment or reassessment.

Honoring an old Stalinist did not result in any reversal of the asserting Uzbek nationalism, which thrived, at least partly, on resentment of Russian domination. Indeed, following further growth in the Russian population in Tashkent—due to Moscow's decision to give 20 percent of new apartments to the mainly Russian workers who had arrived to rebuild the shattered city,[1] a step that would make it two-fifths Russian—there was a spurt in anti-Russian feelings.

On the other hand, as a result of the mammoth reconstruction, Tashkent would emerge as the fourth most populous Soviet city, with vast spaces, broad six-lane avenues fringed by trolley buses and tramlines, and enormous parks sheltering statues of the good and the great. The Soviet architectural planning made the surviving old structures look puny by comparison. At the same time, it took into account Uzbeks' love of running water, with the populated parts of the republic dotted with fountains and artificial tanks, many of them old, and Uzbek families setting their beds next to canals and rivers in summer to escape the stifling heat. So, now, Soviet architects filled Tashkent's center with a battery of gushing fountains. Behind it, rose the largest bronze statue of Lenin yet forged on a fifty-foot plinth.

In a meaningful gesture to Uzbek nationalism, a museum dedicated to Ali Sher Navai (1440–1500), the most celebrated poet of the Turkic peoples, materialized. His statue—depicting the poet caressing his beard with one hand and holding an open book with the other—graced the nearby park.

A more significant sign of rising national consciousness came in late 1969, on the eve of the celebration of the Bolshevik revolution on November 7. Leading Russian-language newspapers in all Central Asian republics printed a joint issue commemorating the fiftieth anniversary of Lenin's letter to the special Commission for Turkistan Affairs, calling for the "elimination of the Great Russian chauvinism" in Soviet Turkistan.[2]

By then, a new generation of Uzbeks and other Central Asians had grown up, reared on Soviet education, possessing the confidence that had eluded their parents. Many young Uzbek intellectuals tried to rediscover their national and cultural roots; and because these were intertwined with Islamic heritage, their quest led them to Islam.

The rising interest in Islam could not be satisfied by the government-controlled Official Islamic Administration. Consequently, there was growth in "unofficial" or "parallel" Islam. By 1966, L. Klimovich, a party official active in anti-religious campaigns, acknowledged that the clergy of the "out of the mosque" (i.e., unofficial) trend in the Soviet Union were stronger than those of the "mosque" trend.[3]

Since Tashkent was the headquarters of the Spiritual Directorate of Central Asia and Kazakhstan, which supervised 230 mosques, nearly half of the Soviet Union's total, the city came to reflect emergent nationalist and religious consciousness among Uzbeks.

Brezhnev reassessed the national question and concluded that his predecessor's scenario of "mature socialism" would have to await the global triumph of socialism over capitalism. At the Twenty-Third CPSU Congress in March 1966, therefore, he declared that the party would continue to show "solicitude" for the interests and characteristics of each of the peoples constituting the Soviet Union.

Brezhnev ended the excesses of anti-religious propaganda initiated by Khrushchev and attempted to palliate the Official Islamic Administration by authorizing a program of restoration of religious monuments. In the earthquake-ravaged Tashkent, this administration capped its decision to rebuild all the destroyed mosques with a plan to construct more.

In 1968 the Muslim Spiritual Directorate in Tashkent started publishing *The Muslims of the Soviet Union* magazine in Uzbek, Arabic, Persian, English, and French. Its international department maintained contacts with Muslims abroad and made arrangements for Central Asian Muslims to make the hajj pilgrimage. Fifty Soviet Muslims won scholarships annually to study Islamic theology and law in Cairo and Damascus, the Arab capitals then allied with Moscow.

Encouraged by the state, and assisted by the Council of Ulema (religious-legal scholars), Shaikh Ziauddin Babakhan, the mufti of the Muslim Directorate of Central Asia, organized an international Islamic conference in Tashkent in 1970. It was the first such event in Russian or Soviet history: it signaled a concordat between state and mosque that had last been seen, briefly, during the Great Patriotic War. Islamic clerics rationalized their cooperation with the Soviet state on the ground that its ideology, Marxism-Leninism, was primarily focused on running the economy and government, whereas Islam was concerned with matters of spirit and ethical behavior. This perception helped to keep the relationship between official and parallel Islam almost trouble-free, since the latter also dealt with moral-ethical issues.

During the 1970s, the state and party did not have to worry too much about the rise of Islam, a phenomenon then affecting only a section of the intelligentsia. According to an official Soviet survey published in 1979, only 30 percent of "formerly Muslim peoples" described themselves as "believers"—the majority of them rural, old, and semi-literate—with 20 percent as "hesitant", and the remaining 50 percent as "unbelievers."[4]

But with an Islamic regime emerging in Iran in early 1979, and the Communist government in Afghanistan (originating in a military coup in April 1978) falling asunder to internal rivalries and inducing Soviet military intervention on December 1979, the situation began to change.

MOSCOW'S AFGHAN CAMPAIGN

The Kremlin claimed that it had been invited by the Kabul government to help foil conspiracies against it by the U.S. Central Intelligence Agency (CIA) and pro-American Pakistan, who were actively encouraging insurgency along Afghanistan's eastern and southern borders—as well as by Islamic Iran, who were backing subversion along Afghanistan's western frontier. The Soviet intervention led to the killing of the radical Afghan leader, President Hafizullah Amin, and the installation of Babrak Karmal, a moderate, as president.

Once the CPSU's Politburo had taken the decision to act militarily, the leaders of the Central Asian republics backed it. Tashkent, the regional military command-control-communications center of the Red Army, became a beehive of activity. Later the Soviet military high command would use the air bases in Uzbekistan to bomb targets in Afghanistan.

Termez is situated on the banks of the Oxus River amidst a sprawling, desolate desert, populated with small collective farms of three to four families cultivating fifteen to twenty hectares of land. This Uzbek city became the main entry point for the Soviet ground troops into Afghanistan for a simple reason. Termez was the site of the sole, sturdy iron bridge across the Oxus—delineating much of the Afghan-Soviet border—called the Friendship Bridge, capable of bearing the weight of the massive tank-trailers.

Given its vital importance, the bridge had always been well protected, with the guard post built solidly of brick and mortar surrounded by sandbags, and presided over by smartly dressed soldiers in polished boots and oversized bouffe hats of red and brown. These soldiers were equipped with field telephones and a robust metal barricade as wide as the tarmac road.

Addressing the Twenty-Sixth Congress of the CPSU in February 1981, Brezhnev explained that the Soviet Union's military intervention in Afghanistan had stemmed from "a direct threat to the security of . . . [its] southern border." With the Soviet military presence in Afghanistan increasing steadily from the initial 50,000 troops to 115,000 in the mid-1980s, the importance of the Central Asian republics in providing men, materials, and logistical back-up grew.

Intent on making the Soviet military presence appear racially as unobtrusive as possible, Moscow's armed forces high command decided to include a high proportion of Uzbek, Tajik, and Turkmen troops in the units that were dispatched to Afghanistan, a country whose citizens also belonged to these ethnic groups.

Following Moscow's intervention in Afghanistan, the administration of U.S. President James Carter intensified the anti-Soviet campaign. It relied heavily on Islam and Islamic forces, combining its material and military aid to the Islamic groups of Afghanistan with radio propaganda, aired by the U.S.-funded Radio Liberty and Radio Free Europe, against the Soviet system—directed specifically at the Muslim populations in Central Asia and Azerbaijan. Washington's lead was followed by Saudi Arabia, which combined propaganda broadcasts with courses on the Quran and Islamic law;

and later by Egypt, a close American ally since 1972, Kuwait, and Qatar.[5]

The Communist leaders of Muslim origin in Central Asia and elsewhere countered the Islamic onslaught by combining an ideological campaign with an intensified effort to root out underground Islamic organizations. In 1982, in a series of raids, the Uzbek KGB discovered four such groups, run either as study circles or Quranic schools, in Tashkent, and had their leaders—including Sayyid Karim Khojayev, author of *The Truth about Islam*—imprisoned.

As chairman of the Presidium of the Governing Councils of the Preservation of Monuments in Uzbekistan, Nuritdin Mukhitdinov (originally, Nuruddin Muhyiuddin), a former CPU first secretary, repeatedly attacked the reactionary role of Muslim clerics. Another Uzbek leader, Yadegar Nasruddinova, then chairwoman of the Union of Soviet Socialist Republics' Soviet of Nationalities, the second chamber of the USSR Supreme Soviet,[6] kept up her criticism of Islam for being discriminatory against women. On the political-diplomatic front, however, the Kremlin failed to win the backing of any of the heads of the Muslim Spiritual Directorates in Baku, Makhachkala, Tashkent, and Ufa on the Afghanistan issue.

ANTI-CORRUPTION DRIVE

In the mid-1980s, public attention in Central Asia, especially Uzbekistan, turned inceasingly to the prevalent corruption. Following the demise of Brezhnev in late 1982, his successor, sixty-eight-year-old Yuri Andropov, mounted a campaign to improve labor efficiency, which had declined during the Brezhnev era, and curtail corruption throughout the Soviet Union.

Uzbekistan figured prominently in this drive because it was here that, by chance, a Soviet reconnaissance satellite photographed fallow plots which were supposed to be cotton fields. Over the decades, the planners in Moscow and Tashkent had invested much capital to increase the acreage and productivity for cotton of the much desired American variety.

Being extraordinarily deep-rooted, cotton plants soak up immense quantities of water. To meet this demand, the authorities laid out 40,000 miles of irrigation channels. This, and the increased use of farm machinery, improved productivity by two-thirds, albeit at the expense of Uzbekistan draining half of the waters of the Oxus River and starving the landlocked Aral Sea, which began shrinking. In the absence of crop rotation, there was irreversible soil exhaustion. To counter it, collective farm managers used increasing amounts of chemical fertilizers, which caused severe pollution and became a health hazard to those picking cotton, a notoriously labor-intensive, backbreaking task. Recognizing this, the Soviet authorities introduced machinery to do the job and progressed until less than a third of the cotton was picked by hand.

In Central Asia, the anti-corruption drive was overseen by Geidar Aliyev, an Azeri member of the CPSU's Politburo and the first deputy chairman of the of Ministers of the Soviet Union. As head of the Azeri KGB from 1967 to 1969, Aliyev had supervised an anti-corruption campaign, and was therefore well qualified for the new task. Yet he failed to make much headway in Uzbekistan, principally because the party's first secretary there, Sharaf Rashidov, was far from cooperative.

It was only after Rashidov's death—either self-inflicted or due to a heart attack caused by unbearable KGB pressure—in October 1983 that Aliyev was able to investigate the allegations made against him and his aides. The charges included not only widespread bribery and nepotism, but also large-scale embezzlement of funds, arising from fraudulent cotton output statistics inflated by up to a quarter, and general economic mismanagement. Since Uzbekistan accounted for two-thirds of the Soviet Union's cotton production, which reached nearly eight million tons in the mid-1970s, this was a grave matter.

Inamjan Usmankhojayev (orginally, Usman Hoja), who succeeded Rashidov as the CPU's first secretary, pursued the anti-corruption drive while replacing his predecessor's appointees, and used every opportunity to highlight other failures of the Rashidov era.

THE GORBACHEV PERIOD

Usmankhojayev became bolder when Mikhail Gorbachev succeeded Konstantin Chernenko—who died, aged seventy-four, after a year long stint as the first secretary of the CPSU after Andropov—in March 1985. A balding, heavyset man with a chubby face and a vigorous handshake, Gorbachev was the youngest party official to assume the prime office. He gave early signs of reforming the CPSU and the government.

At the CPU Congress in January 1986, Usmankhojayev extended his criticism of Rashidov beyond bribery and falsifying cotton output by listing his other failings: "major miscalculations" in the selection, placement, and education of ideological cadres, neglect of anti-religious propaganda, and failure to combat vigorously "unofficial Islam."[7] Usmankhojayev's criticism was backed by Rafiq Nishanov, the new chairman of the Uzbek Supreme Soviet.

Of the twelve members of the CPU's Politburo, ten lost their positions. In the freshly reconstituted Politburo, ethnic Uzbeks, who formed two-thirds of the republic's population, lost their majority. This hurt Uzbek pride. Of the Central Committee's 177 members, all but 34 were replaced. Among them was Vahabjan Usmanov, minister of cotton-ginning, who was later arrested for inflating cotton production by up to 30 percent—which he had achieved by bribing officials all the way up to Yuri Churbanov, son-in-law of Brezhnev, and getting the producers paid by the central government. The kickbacks he received for his services were so abundant that he had thrown one envelope containing R40,000 into a corner of his office where police found it two years later. He was sentenced to death in August 1986.[8]

The anti-corruption investigation results, published in 1987, showed that during his twenty-four years as the party boss, Rashidov was at the center of a loss of $2 billion to the public treasury by securing payments for inflated cotton output figures. More than 2,600 officials in Moscow and Uzbekistan were arrested.[9]

The Moscow-based press, especially the *Komsomolskaya Pravda* (*Truth of the Komsomol*) and the *Moscow News*, played a crucial role. Taking advantage of glasnost (meaning transparency in official actions and policies), followed by the relaxation of press censorship in 1987, members of the press were in the forefront of exposing corruption in Central Asia, particularly Uzbekistan. Their reporting created a negative image of Uzbekistan and Uzbeks among Soviet citizens of European origin, who increasingly associated them with corruption and inefficiency. Extensive purges in the Uzbek party, government, and economic organizations before, during, and after the major investigation weakened the party and the administration.

Instead of restoring popular faith in the system that had flushed out corrupt elements, the scandal and purges left the populace, especially the Uzbek majority, confused and cynical, and less trusting of their political system than before. The leading role played by the Moscow-based media, and the speed with which officials and newspapers in the Soviet capital began using the terms "the Uzbek Affair" and "corruption" interchangeably—despite the fact that the bulk of the kickbacks had landed in Moscow—reinforced the affront that most Uzbeks felt in the wake of the exposed scam.

The initial hurt then transformed into a consensus to resist Moscow, which prepared the ground for the emergence of nationalist or religious opposition. "The crackdown they [Usmankhojayev and Nishanov] presided over—and the abrupt break with established ways under the guise of cleaning up local corruption—contributed to mounting local disorder and dissent," noted Donald S. Carlisle, an American specialist on Uzbekistan. "It stimulated resistance to Moscow, created grievances to be exploited by opposition forces within the Uzbek intelligentsia, and re-awakened restive religious feelings."[10]

Containing two-thirds of the 230 functioning mosques in Muslim Central Asia in the mid-1980s, Uzbekistan was the single most important Soviet republic in terms of Islam. At the Plenum of the CPU's Central Committee in October 1986, many speakers referred to the "complicated religious situation" in the republic. This was illustrated dramatically the next month when Sayid Taherov, a leading Communist and director of the telecommunications center in Tashkent, and Sabir Tarsuenov, leader of the local Communist Youth League, were caught conducting semi-clandestine Quranic studies at the center.[11]

The CPU's leadership tightened up the requirement of atheism for party members. In the first six months of 1987, it expelled fifty-three members from the party for organizing and participating in religious rituals—often those concerned with birth (circumcision for male children), marriage, and funerals.[12] The CPU's membership fell to 582,000 from 640,000 in January 1986.

However, as 1987 progressed, the anti-religious drive lost much of its force, partly because during the run-up to the millennium celebrations in 1988 the Russian Orthodox Church was accorded an honorable place in the Soviet Russian Federation. The Soviet media waxed eloquent on the inextricable bond between the Russian Church and culture, and the significance of religion in the history of Russia, applauding the glorification of the nine new saints of the Orthodox Church in the summer of 1988 in Zagorsk near Moscow.

Noting that while continuing to call Islam backward and reactionary, the Soviet press had taken to stressing the "progressive significance" of the adoption of Christianity in Russia a thousand years earlier, Amin Usmanov, an Uzbek writer, asked in June 1988: "Why have we not tired of looking into a one-sided manner at the dark aspects in Islam in our past culture? . . . Has not the time come to speak fairly of both the positive and negative aspects of religion?"[13] With the pace of political liberalization accelerating in the late 1980s during the latter part of perestroika, this sort of questioning of official policies became increasingly routine.

In the diplomatic field, in February 1988, Gorbachev agreed with Afghan Communist leader Muhammad Najibullah to start withdrawing 115,000 Soviet troops from Afghanistan from May onwards. This signified a politi-

cal-ideological setback for Moscow in the face of continuing armed struggle by Islamic guerrillas against the Kabul regime. So, once again, the Red
Army's tank-trailers, armored personnel carriers, and four-wheel-drive
vehicles rumbled across the Friendship Bridge, this time in the opposite
direction. By February 1989, Moscow had fully withdrawn its forces from
Afghanistan, leaving Najibullah in charge.

By then the CPU had undergone one more change at the top, with Nishanov
replacing Usmankhojayev as first secretary in January 1988. A veteran
Communist, Nishanov had been sidelined during the ascendancy of Rashidov
with a job as Soviet ambassador in the Middle East, to be recalled to
Uzbekistan after Rashidov's death.

Following his removal from the highest party post and then from the
party itself, Usmankhojayev was arrested on corruption charges, and found
guilty—an ironic development since he had made a career of condemning
Rashidov as a corrupt leader.

The continual purges, which reduced party membership by 58,000; the
relentless media publicity about the misdeeds of erstwhile respected figures;
and the convictions of many party and government officials on criminal
charges (resulting not only in long prison sentences, but also in executions)
devastated the party faithful. With one out of six households contributing
a member to the party, the recent events traumatized society at large. It
created an environment conducive to the rise of opposition groups—nationalist and Islamist—formally and informally.

Sickened by the stench of scandals, many Uzbeks took to religion. There
was a growing presence of men with beards and women with headscarves—
visual signs of rising Islamization. In 1987, the findings of a survey of
undergraduates with a Muslim background at Tashkent University jolted
the Communist leadership. It showed 60 percent describing themselves as
"Muslim," 33 percent as "hesitant," and only 7 percent as "atheist."[14]
Earlier surveys had shown religion to be strong only among older, rural
people. Now, many of the undergraduates declaring themselves to be
Muslim were also members of the Communist Youth League.

This religious revival in a republic of the Soviet Union which registered
doubling of the population between 1959 and 1979—from 16.4 million to
32.8 million—worried the party and government. The authorities activated
the houses of atheism and the scientific atheism departments in the philosophy faculties of universities. They sponsored lecture series and special days
of atheism. But these efforts were not as effective as they should have been
because those undertaking them were deficient in numbers and qualifica-

tions. Lacking a full grasp of Islam, a complex ideology, the atheist propagandists had failed to forge an appropriate tool to counter it. Also, unlike in the past, the general level of education of the new believers was high, and some of them were sophisticated thinkers.

Besides the young in general, another group that had come under rising Islamic faith was the old merchant class of the bazaar. Having been dormant for many decades, several merchant clans now showed signs of revival as traders when the state opened up opportunities for the cooperative sector—a euphemism for the private sector—in the economy. They had earlier carved out a niche in the "black" economy that had arisen during the latter part of Brezhnev's rule. Given the traditional link between the bazaar and the mosque, it was not long before religious charities, supported by traders, sprang up—following the passing of an all-Union law that permitted social and cultural organizations, including those engaged in repairing or constructing places of worship.

Such traders were in the vanguard when it came to staging a demonstration in January 1989 against the mufti of the Central Muslim Spiritual Directorate in Tashkent, Sharnsuddin Babakhan, son of the previous mufti, Ziauddin Babakhan, and a relic of the Brezhnev era. The protesters accused him of drinking alcohol and mixing with women who were not closely related to him, and therefore being unfit for the high religious office of mufti. Yielding to popular pressure, he resigned—an event that signaled a success for grassroots politics, applied in this case to a religious institution.

In March 1989, the delegates to the Fourth Congress of the Muslim Spiritual Directorate elected Shaikh Muhammad Sadiq Muhammad Yusuf as mufti. Soon after, he was elected to the Soviet Union Congress of People's Deputies, one of the seven deputies in a house of 2,250.

Earlier, in December 1988, a meeting called to honor the Uzbek language at Tashkent University turned into a spontaneous forum for Uzbek nationalism. Student spokesmen urged CPU leaders to declare Uzbek as the official language of the republic. Much to the unease of the local officials present, some students unfurled the green flag of Islam and recited the first verse of the Quran. This demonstrated bond between religion and a secular demand was an unorthodox development. It worried the government, which was aware of the disaffection among young people due to high unemployment, then affecting more than a million people in a country of about 4.2 million households.

The growing joblessness accentuated friction between majority Uzbeks and ethnic minorities, including Tatars (aka Meskhetian Turks) who, forming 4 percent of the total population, were concentrated in the Fergana Valley. In June 1989, Uzbek violance against the Meskhetian Turks resulted in 200 deaths, mostly Turks. More than 160,000 of them were rendered homeless. The unprecedented bloodshed shook the minorities, including Russians, who formed 11 percent of the republic's population.

Gorbachev decided to act swiftly. He eased Nishanov out of the top party position in Tashkent by offering him promotion to a job at the CPSU secretariat in Moscow. Going by the past pattern, Nishanov's position should have gone to M. Ibrahimov, chairman of the Uzbek Supreme Soviet, but it did not. The fact that Ibrahimov was part of the leadership during whose tenure severe rioting had occurred in the Fergana Valley went against him. The winner was a comparative outsider, Islam Abduganiyevich Karimov (b. 1938).

KARIMOV AT THE TOP

Islam Karimov was born in Samarkand of an Uzbek father and a Tajik mother into a poor family, which survived on bread and tea. A state scholarship enabled him to enroll at a boarding school. (In an official photograph of his class taken in 1947, he appears as one among many ill-clad pupils.) He graduated from the Tashkent Polytechnic Institute as an engineer in 1960. While working as a semi-skilled engineer at the Ilyushin aircraft factory in Tashkent, he simutaneously studied economics—a discipline which enabled a student to grasp the essentials of Marxism. A young, clean-shaven, energetic man of small stature, and a Communist with a belief in proletarian internationalism, he married a working-class Russian woman named Natalya Kuchmi. A botanist at the Institute of Botany of the Academy of Sciences of Uzbekistan, she was as impressed by his cleverness as by his eloquence in Russian.[15]

Karimov joined the finance ministry in 1966 and moved up the civil service ladder to become minister of finance seventeen years later. A long-time member of the CPU, he was elected a member of its Central Committee in January 1986, the year in which he was appointed chairman of Uzbekistan's Gosplan, the state planning department. Nishanov, the CPU's first secretary, demoted him and dispatched him to the distant province of Kashka Darya as party chief.

Karimov's brief career as a party functionary was enough to satisfy Gorbachev, who was looking for a youngish leader untarnished by scandals. Gorbachev was painfully aware that the opposition movement, Birlik

Halk Harakiti (Birlik Popular Front), founded in May 1989, was rapidly gaining the political ground lost by the CPU in the wake of continued scandals and the brutal violence against Meskhetian Turks. He expected his nominee to reverse the trend.

Karimov imposed an immediate ban on public meetings to cool tempers. "There could have been another six or seven Ferganas without firm action by the government," he explained later. "In Leningrad [St. Petersburg], Russia and the Baltic republics, you could have meetings which could go on for hours peacefully, but here people get easily excited. Once roused it would be easy enough for people to shout 'Kill the Koreans' or 'Kill the Russians.'"[16] In other words, to avert further outbreaks of inter-ethnic violence, it was essential to slow down the democratic process. This is the argument Karimov would advance for many years to come, substituting "inter-ethnic violence" with "anarchy."

Birlik had by now found a place in the political arena. An informally established public movement headed by intellectuals, it grew rapidly in 1988 on a program of democracy, nationalism, and economic liberalization. Its two prominent leaders were Abdurahim Pulatov (originally, Abdul Rahim Pulat), a cybernetics professor, and Muhammad Salih, a poet and a leading member of the Writers Union. Appropriating the student demand to make Uzbek the official language, Birlik set up an office at the Writers Union in Tashkent. The other issue that Birlik appropriated was the welfare of Uzbek draftees in the Soviet military. It alleged that most of them were assigned to the notorious construction battalions commanded mainly by officers suffering from alcoholism. Birlik staged demonstrations in Tashkent in October 1989.

Both were popular, emotional issues; and their vociferous espousal by Birlik helped the fledgling organization—which had already held a national congress as a recognized "public movement"[17]—to widen its appeal, especially among intellectuals and students. As an umbrella organization, which had appropriated such causes as a confederation of all Central Asian republics, propagation of Islam, and a wider use of the Arabic alphabet for Uzbek, Birlik had attracted not only Uzbek nationalists but also the adherents of pan-Turkism and Islamism.

With nationalist feelings rising sharply, Karimov considered it expedient to echo them. He was better equipped to do so than any of his predecessors. Being a comparatively new figure in the party hierarchy, he had escaped any categorization—"conservative," "radical," "pro-Moscow," or "pro-nationalist." He resorted to highlighting the plight of the republic's citizens, implicitly blaming the Kremlin for it. He pointed out that the average per capita income of 45 percent of the republic's population was below the official subsistence level of R78 a month, and that more than a million people were jobless.[18] To gain popularity in the countryside, which contained 60 percent of the population, Karimov issued and ensured a speedy implementation of a decree giving land for private homes and cattle-grazing to the members of cooperative farms.

Karimov found a common ground with Mufti Muhammad Yusuf in their distrust of "the elusive dimension of Islam," meaning the Sufi brotherhoods and Wahhabis, a Saudi Arabia-based puritanical sect within the Hanbali school of Sunni Islam, which they claimed endangered inter-faith and inter-ethnic harmony. The mufti was opposed to such groups on theological grounds, and the government on political grounds. There were other signs of rapprochement between the state and mosque. The media campaign initiated in Central Asia in early 1989 to repair some of the damage done by the biased presentations of Islam in the past gathered momentum as the year progressed.

The literary journal *Zvezda Vostoka* (*Star of the East*) printed a Russian translation of the Quran in installments. In its January, May, and June 1989 issues, the prestigious *Nauka i Religia* (*Science and Religion*) carried a series of articles on the life of Prophet Muhammad and the importance of the pilgrimage to Mecca. Later issues offered a Russian translation of numerous chapters of the Quran.

On the eve of the Uzbek Supreme Soviet elections in March 1990, the CPU stated its position on religion. "The republican Party organization is actively in *favor of freedom of religion and the legal rights of believers*, and for cooperation with religious organizations," its manifesto said. "Believers are entitled to all opportunities for participation in the public, political and cultural life of the Republic."[19]

Lacking status as a political party, Birlik could not contest a general election. Consequently, the CPU, often offering more than one candidate for a seat, emerged with a near monopoly in the chamber. It won 450 of 500 seats, with the remainder going to well-known members of the opposition and independents. Within Birlik, differences between the minority and majority factions, led respectively by Salih and Pulatov, reached a breaking point. For Salih, working for Uzbekistan's independence was the foremost priority, leaving democracy for later. In contrast, Pulatov stressed democracy—meaning toppling Karimov's regime—leaving independence for later.

In April 1990, Salih and two other leaders left Birlik to establish the Democratic Party of Erk (Freedom), which claimed the loyalty of thirteen Supreme Soviet deputies. They adopted the flag of the Kokand Autonomous Government, which had existed from November 1917 to February 1918, as their party banner in order to stress national independence.

Reflecting the rising tide of nationalism, at the CPU's Twentieth Congress in June 1990, Karimov aired the idea of Uzbekistan as a sovereign republic seeking local answers to its problems. The delegates demanded that Uzbek become the official language of Uzbekistan. Guided by Karimov, the Congress replaced all Politburo members except him, and three-quarters of the Central Committee members.

The re-branded party felt free to speak out. Uzbek leaders and journalists argued that fabrication of the cotton output figures stemmed from the pressure to meet ever-rising, unrealistic targets set by the central bureaucracy in Moscow. It had raised the Uzbek proportion of the total cotton area in the Soviet Union from 45 percent in 1940 to 60 percent in 1980. During that period, while the land under cotton in the Soviet Union had grown only by half—from 2 million to 3 million hectares—the yield had increased fourfold—from 2.24 million to 9.1 million · tons—with Uzbekistan contributing 59 percent of the total. However, decades of continued overuse of soil had led finally to depleted yields, so that at 4.9 million tons in 1987, Uzbekistan was 1.8 million tons behind the target of the latest Five-Year Plan.[20]

Secondly, according to the Uzbek argument, the corruption was sustained with the cooperation of high officials in Moscow, mostly Russian, who received the lion's share of the embezzled money. They were more responsible for the sorry state of affairs than Uzbeks. The arrest and conviction in 1987 of Yuri Churbanov on corruption charges provided convincing evidence. Beyond that, Uzbeks complained about the imposition of the cotton monoculture on their republic by the central planners, who had failed to expand Uzbekistan's textile industry. It processed only 15 percent of its own cotton.

Departing from the previous party line, Karimov counseled a balanced assessment of the late Rashidov, weighing both his flaws and his achievements. He thus indicated an end to the pattern of continuous purges that had bedeviled the party since 1984, and turned a new leaf in the organization's history. The Uzbek government's reassessment of Rashidov would lead to naming a street and a square in Tashkent after him and placing a statue of him in the city's main park.

With politics becoming more Uzbek-oriented, Birlik, invigorated by its second national congress in May 1990, was able to set the agenda. The status of Uzbek language and the treatment of Uzbek draftees were the two issues that it pushed to the fore through meetings, demonstrations, and newspaper articles. The government responded by issuing a decree stating that there would be a cut in the number of conscripts assigned to the construction battalions, which would be posted only within the Turkistan (i.e., Central Asian) Military District, with a corresponding rise in the number of draftees assigned to regular units.

The Supreme Soviet in Tashkent declared Uzbek as the state language, and appointed a commission to recommend the pace of implementation—from street names and public announcements to the broadcasting media and communications with official organizations. Zulfia Tukhthajayev Mansurova, an attractive, lively woman in her early forties who taught English at the Institute of Foreign Languages in Tashkent, amplified the Supreme Soviet's decision. "There is a seven-year transition period," she explained. "In the first two years it will appear on radio and TV, next two years all official work will be in Uzbek, and in the next three years there will be complete switchover from Russian to Uzbek." The official policy affected her family: "My husband Rahbar lost his job in the Russian section of the Uzbek TV when they abolished that section. He then got a job as a liaison officer for a Turkish consortium of 120 companies because he knows how the system works here."[21]

Profound changes were afoot in Moscow as well. In March 1990, Gorbachev got himself elected executive president of the Soviet Union. In June, under the chairmanship of Boris Yeltsin, still a member of the CPSU, the Russian parliament placed its legislation above that of the Soviet Union.

Taking his cue, Karimov had the Uzbek Supreme Soviet take similar steps. It declared its sovereignty in October 1990, which gave primacy to Uzbek laws over Soviet laws, and elected him executive president of Uzbekistan. The next fifteen months would prove uncommonly tumultuous as the newly independent republics tried to work out their relationships with each another. Events moved at a breakneck speed.

INDEPENDENT UZBEKISTAN

Karimov now felt freer to steal the nationalist clothing from the opposition. He blamed the central economic planning for turning Uzbekistan into "a raw materials base," and lambasted Moscow for offering "unjustly low prices" for Uzbek cotton.[22] He also continued to cooperate with Mufti Muhammad Yusuf, who gave media interviews, interpreting and analyzing the current affairs. Both leaders shared a common aim of marginalizing the militant Islamic tendency, be it in the form of Sufi brotherhoods, Wahhabis, or the newly arrived Islamic Renaissance Party (IRP).

The IRP, with its headquarters in Moscow, held its founding convention in June 1990 in Astrakhan, a Russian port on the Caspian Sea. An all-Union organization, it aimed primarily at obtaining concessions and religious freedoms equal to those granted to the Russian Orthodox Church under President Gorbachev, thus enabling Muslims to "live according to the Quran." It organized a demonstration in Moscow demanding a higher number of permits for the hajj pilgrimage—the figure in 1989 being only 1,300 for 53 million Soviet citizens with Muslim names. This led the KGB to inspire reports that the IRP was a fundamentalist body funded by Saudi Arabia.

The IRP's Uzbek branch, led by Abdullah Yusuf, declared itself ready to undertake political activity in order to "establish Islam as the Muslims' way of life in this republic." Karimov and Mufti Yusuf wanted to channel rising popular disaffection through such recognized forums as the official mosque and the refurbished CPU. The state-controlled broadcasting media also followed this policy. Yet public discontent was once again transmuted into inter-ethnic violence. In July 1991, the Tajik police in Samarkand city roughed up Uzbek revelers so badly that thirty of them had to be hospitalized. Any violence between Tajiks and Uzbeks in Uzbekistan had the potential of spreading to Tajikistan, with the Tajiks persecuting the Uzbek minority in their midst.

One way to dampen inter-ethnic tensions was to direct popular disaffection at Moscow for its past exploitative policies, ignoring the fact that central aid to Uzbekistan covered a third of its annual budget. Yet anti-Moscow feelings in Uzbekistan were not as sharp as in the Baltic states, Georgia, or Moldova—the republics which boycotted the referendum on a new Union Treaty in mid-March 1991. After the popular vote in the rest of the Soviet Union had favored overwhelmingly a renegotiated Union Treaty, Karimov and other Central Asian leaders pushed hard for republican control over local economic resources, foreign trade, and hard-currency earnings. Their apparent success in this matter was one of the main factors that led to a hard-line coup against Gorbachev in Moscow on August 19, 1991.

Karimov favored the coup partly because he had found Gorbachev lacking firm leadership during a rocky period. "Sometimes I cannot be sure that

Gorbachev is president," he told a press conference in Tashkent in mid-September.[23] However, once the coup had collapsed, he swiftly fell in line with the constitutionalists. Karimov announced that the Communist Party of Uzbekistan was breaking away from the CPSU because of the latter's "unprincipled and cowardly position during the coup." Following the lead of the three Baltic republics, which declared themselves independent and were so recognized by the West, the Uzbekistan Supreme Soviet passed the Act of Independence on August 31, 1991. It set out the constitutional law and basic principles of sovereignty, including the fundamental concepts of domestic and foreign policies centered around a multi-party system and the building of a market economy, which served as an interim constitution.

On September 2, 1991, Gorbachev and the presidents of the twelve constituent republics agreed to transform the Soviet Union into a confederation with a strong center. All Central Asian leaders, with the exception of President Askar Akayev of Kyrgyzstan, backed Gorbachev's idea of a strong center.

The Communist Party of Uzbekistan met in Tashkent on September 14, dissolved itself, and reemerged as the People's Democratic Party (PDP, *Xalq Demokratik Partiyasi*). It took over the assets of the Communist Party. (Later, after winning the Uzbek presidency, Karimov would base his secretariat in the former Communist Party headquarters in Tashkent standing on a hillock by the Anhar River, the strategic site selected by General Mikhail Chernayev for his artillery in 1865.) Now, as PDP chairman, Karimov announced that Uzbekistan would control recruitment for the Soviet military, and ensure joint control of Soviet military activities on Uzbek soil, thus ending a practice whereby Soviet generals had acted unilaterally in the past and done what they wished—such as bombing targets in Afghanistan from Uzbek airfields without the Uzbek government's prior approval.

Karimov's slogan of "discipline and order" was well received, especially by the intellectuals, an influential section of society. "The local intelligentsia are frightened that in Uzbekistan democracy will lead either to extreme nationalism or Islamic fundamentalism," said Albert Musin, a Birlik supporter.[24] Overall, the PDP government had actually benefited from ethnic divisions so far, projecting itself as the only authority that could prevent inter-ethnic violence. The secret hand of the republican KGB in instigating the inter-ethnic conflict in the Fergana Valley in June 1989 was widely alleged. Having gained from such violence, the Karimov administration, which came to office on the heels of the Fergana riots, was determined to control it lest it should lead to its downfall.

Intense negotiations continued in Moscow to settle the shape of the confederation to be forged out of the old Soviet Union, but showed little sign of success. Impatient with the slow progress, Russian President Yeltsin unfolded a radical economic and political program to the Russian Congress of People's Deputies on October 28. Two weeks later, he appointed three reformers as deputy prime ministers to accelerate the process of political-economic liberalization, thus setting the pace for the proposed new confederation which showed scant signs of emerging. On December 8, the presidents of two other Slav republics, Ukraine and Belarus, joined Yeltsin in a collective decision to form a Commonwealth of Independent States (CIS).

Feeling left out, the leaders of the Central Asian republics met in Ashgabat four days later, and resolved to join the CIS if they were listed as founder-members. Once this was agreed, the remaining republics, except Georgia, also decided to affiliate with the new body. This set the scene for the dissolution of the Soviet Union, which happened formally on the last day of 1991.

Two days before, Uzbekistan had held its presidential poll and a referendum on the constitutional law.

POST-SOVIET ERA

The quick dash that President Karimov made to Ankara on December 20, 1991, had as much to do with foreign affairs as domestic. On the eve of a presidential election and a referendum on the constitution on December 29, the candidate of the ruling PDP wanted to emphasize his pro-Turkic credentials to siphon off votes from his electoral rival, Muhammad Salih, whose Erk party was pan-Turkic.

Using subterfuge, Karimov's government had blocked the candidacy of Abdurahman Pulatov, the Birlik chief and a political heavyweight, for the presidency.[25] A comparative lightweight, Salih—a well-dressed man with crew cut and neatly trimmed beard—was allowed to run as a member of the officially recognized Writers Union, not as leader of the Erk party. The election campaign was heavily biased. The provincial governors, city mayors, and other PDP functionaries spent large sums to promote Karimov. The state-run television featured Karimov daily in its nationwide news bulletins. In contrast, Salih got a fifteen-minute slot on local television a week before polling day, with three minutes of his speech excised by the censors.[26]

Yet only 68 percent of the electors opted for Karimov. He did well among non-Uzbeks, forming 30 percent of the national population, who felt threatened by the strong Uzbek nationalist line taken by Erk (and Birlik). He also did well in rural areas, where his decree giving free land for private homes and cattle-grazing to cooperative farm members had benefited 2.5 million families.[27]

The full impact of the decree became apparent, for example, in September 1992 at Gulistan Cooperative Farm—covering 1,800 hectares and 22,000 people—twenty miles east of Fergana. The fertile land beside the tarred road was verdant with orchards of apricots and nectarines on one side and silkworm trees on the other. Sixty-three-year-old Musa Sharbitayev, with his graying, wispy beard and the traditional quilted gown and lacquered cap, had been the director of the cooperative farm for thirty years. He fondly recalled the trip the Indian ambassador in Moscow had made to his farm a quarter-century earlier, when the visiting dignitary had told him how much the long-stapled Uzbek cotton had been eagerly sought by the highly skilled weavers of the Indian city of Benares. The cotton was to be spun and woven into fine muslin used for the veils of the Uzbek women of high standing.

Then, turning to the present situation, Sharbitayev explained, "The land belongs to the collective, and it leases plots to families on an annual basis. We have 4,500 families. When a family grows, the young son gets land for his house, as decreed by President Karimov. That is how 200 hectares have been used for housing out of the original 2,000 hectares, leaving the rest for cultivation." The houses on collective farms were almost invariably two- to three-room bungalows, drab, lacking distinction, architectural or otherwise, and were barely furnished.

Two-thirds of the land was for cotton, called "white gold," and the rest for maize and vegetables. "We have only one harvest of cotton, with the seeds sown in April, and the crop ready in November," he continued. "The government gives us some fertilizer and irrigation water. With a good harvest, a man will pick 200 kilograms [440 pounds] of raw cotton, with seeds and stems, in eight hours, and with a bad one, about half as much. Depending on the circumstances, twenty hectares give thirty to thirty-five tons of cotton. Our farm has not used pesticide for ten years. The price of fertilizer is very high." The farm stored cotton in silos and sold the commodity directly to a textile factory at R25,000 a ton.[28]

A lifelong member of the Communist Party, Sharbitayev had switched to its successor, the People's Democratic Party, and won a seat in parliament. During the presidential election campaign, he had urged the collective's families to vote for Karimov—whom he called *padshah* (great king), the honorific used earlier for the Emir of Bukhara—dismissing airily the opposition claims that Salih had gained 46 percent of the vote, and not the 13 percent announced officially. Nonetheless, protest followed, and soon merged with something of daily concern: a price explosion.

For unfathomable reasons, CIS members unveiled the first day of the post-Soviet era, January 1, 1992, with a dramatic announcement: price decontrol. This would boost the price of the *Pravda Bostock* newspaper from 2 kopeks to 2 rubles, a hundred-fold increase. The cost of daily necessities rose overnight, gravely affecting those on fixed incomes—or grants, such as ones given to university students. As it was, these students and their teachers were already disoriented by the avalanche of changes of the past several months, which affected not just politics and administration, but also economics, culture, and education.

"The collapse of the Soviet Union has caused a crisis at our universities," said Zulfia Mansurova. "The teachers of history, political science, sociology, and philosophy find themselves in deep trouble. They had grown up citing Lenin every five minutes. Now they have lost the very center of their thinking. They don't know how to fill that big hole. On top of that, they have to lecture their students without proper books. There are no new textbooks, paper is expensive, and it takes time to produce new titles. The books they used to praise to the skies, now they criticize them. The academics too old to learn new ways quit, and took up other jobs in the government, or went off to live in the countryside and grow their own vegetables and fruit. Others retired and took their pensions."[29]

Finding the steep price hikes an urgent cause to rally around, students took to the streets on January 16 and continued for the next four days, demanding Karimov's resignation. Clashes between the protesters and security forces left two students dead.

Karimov ordered an inquiry into the shootings, and reinstated former prices for students. He treated these protesters with restraint, partly because he badly needed the United States to establish its embassy in Tashkent. Without that, Uzbekistan could not gain access to the International Monetary Fund (IMF) and the World Bank.

Washington had listed five conditions for establishing diplomatic links with CIS members: acceptance of all U.S.-Soviet Union agreements, respect for human rights, a free market, democratic elections, and a functioning multi-party political system. Later, the United States would moderate its policy, saying that it would be enough to show progress toward these objectives to win U.S. recognition.

In February 1992, the visiting U.S. Secretary of State, James Baker, stressed the need for Uzbekistan to demonstrate its advance toward democracy and a free market. To underline Washington's policy of staying in touch with local opposition, he visited Salih and Pulatov in their offices. Karimov therefore curbed his authoritarian tendency and liberalized his administration—at least until Uzbekistan secured admission to the United Nations and its allied organizations, Conference on Security and Cooperation in Europe, the IMF, and the World Bank.

OPPOSITION ON THE RISE

Taking advantage of the half-open window, Erk and Birlik sponsored the Congress of the Supporters of Turkistan in Tashkent on March 7, which attracted pan-Turkic delegates from other Central Asian republics. While sympathetic to pan-Turkism, especially in its cultural sense, Karimov disapproved of the event. It made his government appear lukewarm toward the idea of resurrecting historic Turkistan.

The religious opposition—now consisting of the IRP, led by Abdullah Utayev, and its breakaway faction called the Adalat (Justice), dominated by Wahhabis—also became more active, especially in the Fergana Valley, the traditional stronghold of Islam and home to nearly a third of the republic's 21 million people. These parties gained ground in the aftermath of a rift in the Official Islamic Administration. At the Fifth Congress of the Muslim Spiritual Directorate in Tashkent in February 1992, some delegates accused Mufti Muhammad Yusuf of cooperating with the KGB. Though he won reelection, the allegation tarnished his public image.

Based in Namangan, a city of 360,000 and a bastion of Islam, Adalat adopted a radical program while establishing mosques and madrassas in several Fergana Valley towns. Its leader, Imam Abdul Ahad, said, "The IRP . . . they want to be in parliament. We have no desire to be in parliament. We want an Islamic revolution here and now—we have no time for constitutional games."[30]

Even during the Soviet era, many local Muslims, including Communist Party members, in Namangan used to have Islamic ceremonies for marriage (nikah) and birthdays (sumat)—but in secret. Since the advent of perestroika in the mid-1980s, and especially after Uzbekistan's independence, there was a rapid revival of Islam in the Fergana Valley and elsewhere. The number of mosques in Namangan rose from 2 to 26. The region of Namangan (population 1.5 million) accounted for 130 mosques, more than half the total in all of Central Asia before perestroika—with another 470 in the rest of the republic. Until 1989, only four Muslims from this region received permission to undertake the hajj pilgrimage. Three years later, the figure soared to 1,500, accounting for nearly two-fifths of the republic's total.[31]

Unsurprisingly, it was in Namangan that Adalat formed vigilante groups to impose the veil on women and a ban on the sale of alcohol, and made citizen's arrests of suspected criminals. The Islamic judges often restricted themselves to sentencing the guilty to forced labor on the construction or repairs of local mosques, and transferred serious cases to the police.

Karimov's government let things be. Only after it had achieved its objectives of admissions to various international bodies—including the IMF and the Conference on Security and Cooperation in Europe (later renamed Organization for Security and Cooperation in Europe, OSCE)—and witnessed the opening of a spacious American embassy by early March 1992 (conspicuous by a gigantic satellite dish in its compound) did it act to curb the opposition. Aware of Washington's hostility toward Islamic fundamentalism, it targeted the IRP and Adalat first. On the eve of Karimov's visit to Namangan in mid-March, it arrested seventy leading IRP and Adalat members, and closed an Islamic center established in the premises of the former Communist Party.[32]

The government then repressed the secular opposition, focusing on Birlik, since it had the potential to pose a serious challenge to the PDP. As for Erk —a registered political group whose membership of 40,000 far exceeded the legal minimum required for official registration, and was therefore entitled it to publish its own journal, *Erk*—the government's censorship bureau did the job. For the April-May issue of its journal, the party could scarcely get one-fifth of its editorial material passed by it.[33]

Once independent Uzbekistan came into being, Birlik and Erk's old argument about prioritizing independence or democracy vanished. Pulatov and Salih began cooperating on a shared program of striving for a democratic state and society. When the two leaders came under official pressure to cancel a planned joint Birlik-Erk rally in Tashkent to demand fresh elections under a new electoral law, Pulatov refused. Four unknown assailants attacked him with an iron bar and broke his skull. A local hospital discharged him after three weeks even though he had not recovered fully. He went to Moscow for treatment, and from there to Istanbul to recuperate. He ended up in the United States.

Although Salih was the leader of a recognized opposition party, that did not exempt him from phone tapping and surveillance—a fate he shared with the leaders of Birlik and other minor opposition groups, and even Mufti Muhammad Yusuf. Indeed, anybody uttering dissident views was prone to having bugs installed in the walls of his home.

Karimov sponsored "loyal" opposition, which concentrated on fostering private property and enterprise. An example was the National Progress Party—led by Muhammad Azimov, who was close to Karimov—which won official recognition. It tried to attract property owners.

Karimov Consolidates Power

Externally, Karimov succeeded in making Uzbekistan an important player. At the CIS summit in Tashkent on May 15, 1992, he won the acceptance of his proposal for a mutual defense agreement. Nine of the CIS members—all Central Asian countries except Turkmenistan, Russia, Armenia, Azerbaijan, Belarus, and Georgia—formed the Tashkent Collective Security Agreement. Thus Karimov linked Russia with a Central Asian defense system, which gave the new treaty an impressive military muscle.

By the spring of 1992, Uzbekistan had signed a bilateral treaty with Russia on political, economic, cultural, and scientific relations. By virtue of the the Tashkent Collective Security Agreement, the 100,000 CIS troops stationed in Uzbekistan came under the control of the Uzbek authorities. As before, Tashkent continued to be a vital military command-control-communications center with facilities for training officers.

Moscow wanted the Uzbek government to be stable and strong to stave off any chance of anti-Russian pogroms in Uzbekistan or anywhere else in Central Asia. Uzbekistan's neighbors, too, wanted a powerful regime in Tashkent fully capable of preventing inter-ethnic tensions within its boundaries from escalating into violence and causing knock-on effects in their territories.

In August 1992, Karimov published a seventy-two-page pamphlet in Uzbek and Russian, *Uzbekistan: Its Own Road to Renewal and Progress*. It contained his assessment of the current situation and set out guidelines for the future. The publication enabled Karimov to give an ideological hue to the PDP, which would then call itself left-wing, dedicated to safeguarding the basic elements of a welfare state during the transition from a centralized command economy to a market economy, paying particular attention to the needy and socially vulnerable. The government-controlled media organized television readings of the text that were reprinted later in the press.

"Because of the perestroika experiment and decisions which were wrong, all former republics of the Soviet Union fell into long and deep economic crisis," Karimov wrote. "Due to inflation and the growing cost of living, social, economic and monetary systems are in a bad state." With agriculture producing 44 percent of the national income, he addressed the issue of land ownership: "If land is placed into private ownership, there will be price speculation and farmers will lose confidence. The main thing is to create a mechanism which gives potential to each farmer to be the owner of his labor's result."[34]

According to Uzbekistan's law on land ownership, a citizen could lease land from the government but could not sell or inherit it. The aim was to prevent speculation in land which could play havoc with prices and distort production. Also, if land were privatized, the government would not be able to ensure that a certain percentage would be used for growing cotton, and would thus lose its place as the world's fifth largest producer and second largest exporter of the commodity after the United States.

In sum, the PDP government would maintain the ownership of land by state and cooperative farms, a policy opposed by Birlik and Erk, among others. Karimov justified remaining in the CIS and the ruble zone. "If all [Soviet-era] connections are broken, it would damage and destabilize the region and the international arena," he observed. "The economy of the republics, their complete transport and energy systems were formed and developed within the borders of the old Union. Their accounting was done in rubles. Breaking off these relations can bring, and has already brought, a fall in production and made the economic situation worse and intensified social problems."[35]

High inflation in Uzbekistan and other CIS member states had reduced the value of the ruble from 60 American cents to one-third of a cent within six months of the Soviet breakup. The rise in wages had covered only a tiny fraction of the price explosion. Therefore, while reiterating his commitment to a "socially oriented market economy" (which, in reality, meant running a mixed economy with a strong public sector) and describing the market as a mechanism that makes "the producer responsive to the consumer," Karimov highlighted the problems of transition: "Due to the low living standard of the people in Uzbekistan, the tactic of shock therapy will not work. We should move to a market economy step by step, finding the right pace which is not too slow or too fast, to prepare the people for a market economy. . . . Before establishing a market mechanism we should provide strong social defense of the people."[36] He added that the domestic economic strategy should be "free from the influence of any political ideology."

Karimov's opposition to the state adopting an ideology did not inhibit him from stressing the importance of Islam in domestic and external spheres in a cultural and moral sense. "Consideration for religion and Islam plays an important part within our internal and international politics and conduct," he stated. "It manifests itself in the way of life of the people, their psychology and in the building of spiritual and moral values, and in enabling us to feel rapport with those who practice the same religion."[37]

Karimov reaffirmed the policy of closer ties with other Muslim countries, especially Pakistan, Iran, and Saudi Arabia—a country he had visited in May 1992 to perform an umra, a short pilgrimage to Mecca. He had then begun prefacing his public speeches with "*Bismallah al Rahman al Rahim*" ("In the name of God, the Merciful and the Compassionate").[38] To underline his own piety, he resorted to referring to his first name, Islam. He also allowed the state-run television channel to air a weekly program on Islam supervised by Mufti Muhammad Yusuf. And earlier, he had taken the oath of his presidential office on the Quran.

POLITICAL ISLAM, ENEMY NUMBER ONE

While Karimov and the PDP were prepared to treat Islam as an important part of Uzbek culture, they were determined to maintain a strict division between religion and government. In his pamphlet, Karimov acknowledged Turkish help in "our efforts to achieve good relations between the state and religion, conducted in the same ethnic-cultural conditions [as in Turkey]."[39] But political conditions in Uzbekistan and Turkey were different. After a decades-long battle by ballot, Islamists in Turkey had finally established themselves as a legitimate political force as the Welfare Party. In contrast, Uzbekistan outlawed and repressed political groups based on Islam.

Islamists resisted the state pressure. Following Karimov's visit to Namangan in March 1992, Islamists in the area responded to the arrests of their activists with protest demonstrations, thus challenging the government to escalate repression or discontinue it. It decided to back down, leaving the relations between the state and Islam unresolved.

But the events in neighboring Tajikistan pushed the issue to the fore. In September 1992, after months of armed agitation led mainly by Tajik Islamist forces—freshly inspired by the Islamic Mujahedin's overthrow of the pro-Communist regime of Muhammad Najibullah in Afghanistan five months earlier—Communist President Rahman Nabiyev was forced to resign. This led the Islamist-led alliance to become the dominant force in the government. The fighting in Tajikistan had created tens of thousands of refugees, with 40,000 seeking haven in Uzbekistan.

Karimov's government sealed its borders with Tajikistan and introduced internal visas for foreign visitors, putting the Fergana Valley (sharing borders with Tajikistan) off limits to non-citizens—especially Saudis, many of whom had become untraceable after their overstay in the republic. Security forces strictly controlled the entrance and exit to the valley.

The draconian measures were at variance with the natural beauty of the Fergana Valley, its thoroughfares bordered by dazzling flower beds in the midst of green shrubbery. A visitor to the valley would likely see children drying fresh cowpats for use as cooking fuel—an exotic sight that illustrated poverty. In the family of such children, the one who would labor most would be the young daughter-in-law. On arrival at her husband's abode, she would immediately relieve her mother-in-law of household chores. Her day would with start with milking the family cow, housecleaning, cooking breakfast, then weaving, followed by preparing a large dinner in the evening.

In the autumn of 1992, however, the authorities came to associate the Fergana Valley with Wahhabis, local and foreign, whose increasingly public activities contrasted sharply with their earlier clandestine ways. The origins of Wahhabis went as far back as the late 1970s, when Abdul Ahad joined the group secretly in Namangan. By 1989, local Wahhabis felt strong enough to stage a demonstration demanding a prime venue for their mosque. The city mayor conceded their demand in May 1991. The group, funded generously by the Saudi Arabia-based Ahle Sunna movement, used the same tactic to win important sites in Andijan, Kokand, and Margilan—as part of their plan to establish madrassas to teach 15,000 students. Their wide-ranging projects involved raising funds for new mosques in the countryside, and teaching the believers prayers and the performance of Islamic rites and instructing them in Sharia rules, interspersed with lectures on founding an Islamic republic after overthrowing "the Communist government in Tashkent."

While Uzbek officials claimed that militants were training a "secret army," Wahhabi preachers remained silent on the subject of "military training" for their students.[40] By striking roots in the Fergana Valley of Uzbekistan, Wahhabis were positioning themselves to spread quickly to the rest of the valley in Tajikistan and Kyrgyzstan.

The Official Islamic Administration (OIA) was as worried about the Wahhabi movement as the government because the movement was sectarian, rabidly anti-Sufi and anti-Shiite, and received funds from Saudi Arabia. But the OIA lacked the cash and imagination to compete successfully with it and siphon off a section of the thousands of young unemployed Uzbeks flocking to its congregations. Nor did the OIA fully share the government's insistence on division between the state and Islam. "Religion cannot be separate from life, and government is part of the citizen's life," said Haji Bilal Khan Rustamov, the young imam of the central mosque of Namangan. "It is therefore not possible to have the mosque and the government totally apart." Namangan had also spawned a large voluntary religious organization: the 30,000-strong Sawad Azam (Big Group). Based at Mullah Kyrgyz madrassa, it collected funds to construct and repair local mosques.[41] This was innocuous enough, yet the authorities felt that once such associations came into being—albeit for social or religious purposes—they could easily mutate into politically militant bodies.

Tashkent also faced the rising power of Islamists in Tajikistan. In October 1992, invoking Uzbekistan's membership of the Tashkent Collective Security Agreement, Karimov said, "Russia should take into consideration the powerful influence of pan-Islamic forces on the southern border [of the CIS]. Fundamentalism will not be limited to Tajikistan or even Central Asia. Russia, as a great powerful nation, should feel obliged to control to the fullest its interests in Central Asia as it has been doing for the past 100 years." He called for the continued presence of the Russian troops under the label of CIS forces in Tajikistan.[42]

Karimov provided covert backing for Nabiyev's Communist forces in their efforts to retake the Tajik capital, Dushanbe, from the Islamists. In a surprise attack on the night of October 23 to 24, pro-Nabiyev partisans captured the most important government buildings in central Dushanbe, but were unable to hold them in the face of a counterattack by the Islamist-led forces. Karimov then decided to intervene openly. His government trained a brigade of pro-Nabiyev loyalists. When they launched an attack on Dushanbe in December 1992, they were equipped with military hardware, including helicopter gun ships supplied by the Uzbek military. They expelled Islamists and their democratic allies from the capital, and later from the rest of the republic, except its Badakhshan region.[43] Karimov thus resolved a problem that had been threatening his republic's stability since the spring.

At home, Karimov went on to describe Birlik as a stalking horse for the members of the clandestine IRP, which became leaderless when Abdullah Utayev "disappeared" in December, an almost certain victim of the Uzbek KGB. The Uzbek parliament outlawed Birlik as a registered public movement by 383 votes to 7, thus reinforcing its rubber-stamp image. (Some of its members had taken to reciting poems honoring Karimov in the chamber.) Article 54 of the newly promulgated constitution banned political parties based on "nationalistic or religious principles."

A major incentive for the Uzbek government to conjure up the prospect of Islamists infiltrating Birlik was to win the approval of Washington[44] and Moscow, both of which were hostile to Islamic militancy and both of which realized that instability in Uzbekistan would destabilize the whole region. Above all, it was in Karimov's interests to exaggerate the threat of fundamentalism in order to encourage American diplomats to conclude that the only alternative to his regime was Islamist. He found it a winning strategy, and made it a cardinal principle of his foreign policy.

As for the PDP, Karimov had a firm grip on it. While it did not dominate all facets of public life and the economy like the Communist Party, it was the single most important political force in the republic. Within a year, it had acquired 550,000 members, more than four-fifths of the 664,520 that the CPU had in June 1990.[45] Since it had taken over CPU assets, including its multi-story offices in city centers, it had the same physical presence as its predecessor.

Yet it was plagued with a dilemma. Having lost its Marxist-Leninist moorings, the PDP was floundering, looking desperately for an ideology. Between Islam and Uzbek nationalism, it was resolutely against Islam as a socio-political philosophy. On Uzbek nationalism, as the party in power, it had to guard against alienating non-Uzbeks, who were crucial to the republic's economy. That allowed the opposition Birlik and Erk to outflank it on this emotionally charged front. Faced with an insoluble predicament, the PDP could do little to arrest the erosion of its power base, and became increasingly a vehicle for unprincipled opportunists.

NATION-BUILDING

On paper, the newly promulgated constitution specified a parliament, known as Oliy Majlis (Supreme Assembly), elected on a "multi-party basis" in an environment of "free mass media and no censorship." In practice, the Oliy Majlis met briefly twice a year while harassment of opposition, and censorship, continued.

Earlier, the government had banned the Moscow-based, pro-democracy newspaper, *Izvestia* (*News*), after censoring it regularly, and almost all other foreign publications. Censors checked all printed or broadcast words, imposing rigid control of news about neighboring Tajikistan, while Karimov's speeches and foreign jaunts formed the staple of electronic and print media. They closed down the only local independent publication, *Biznestnyen* (*Businessman*), after it had hinted that independent Uzbekistan was not unlike the old Soviet Union. After reprimanding the local editor in the president's office, the Uzbek officials told him, "In the old days you would have been shot, so you're getting off lightly with the closing down of the publication." Uzbek journalists writing for such liberal Moscow-based publications as the *Nezavisimaya Gazeta* faced perpetual harassment by the president's office.

The government was aware of the mounting criticism in the West. "Diplomats try to teach us lessons, but our traditions are different," said a senior Uzbek official in January 1993. "Uzbek people are very kind, but it is dangerous to give [them] things like democracy. We have to practice how to be a democratic state [first]."[46]

Unlike in adjoining Turkmenistan, where the government wanted a virtual embargo on opposition activities until the people had become prosperous, the stress in Uzbekistan was on nation-building. "We are telling the opposition, please wait some years," said Jamal Kamal, chairman of the Writers Union. "We have no proper army, no strong borders. We must strengthen national independence and secure our national borders first. Then we will go step by step towards democracy and human rights, which will take about ten years."[47]

History and historical narrative were important blocks in nation-building. Karimov would home in on Emir Timur Beg. The world-renowned general, whose writ ran from Mongolia to Anatolia and from Russia to northern India, was born in Khoja Ilgar near Shahr-e Sabz, south of Samarkand, a city he made his capital. This was enough for Karimov to elevate him as the Uzbek nation's founder, even though he was not an Uzbek. In those days, Uzbeks lived north of the Aral Sea under the tutelage of the Shaibani dynasty, which would later defeat the Timurids to control the land south of the sea, present-day Uzbekistan. The main thoroughfare in all major Uzbek cities acquired the name Emir Timur Beg. His statues cropped up where Lenin had stood before. Like the Soviet leader he replaced, Timur's graven image was true to life, thanks to the work of Mikhail Gerasimov, a Russian expert on forensic sculpture, in 1941.

Gerasimov opened the casket in Timur's domed burial place, the Gur Emir Mausoleum, in Samarkand to reconstruct his head meticulously. He found bits of skin and muscle clinging to his bones as well as remnants of his russet beard and mustache.[48] It was thus that Timur emerged with full lips, fierce eyes, and knotted cheeks. The Gur Emir Mausoleum was a striking monument. "The cincture of the dome was of marble set off with gold and azure," wrote Ahmad ibn Arabshah, a fifteenth century Syrian chronicler. "Within it was dug a vault in which to lay the emperor's body, and a charming garden was laid around it on the ruins of some houses."[49] The refurbishment of the mausoleum undertaken during Karimov's rule turned it into a dazzling cascade of gold.

Karimov also tried to revive a traditional way of life in order to preserve social and political stability. To that effect, he had the parliament pass a law to establish *mohalla* (literally, "locality") councils, governed by male elders called *aqsaqal* (literally, "white beards"). They were authorized to censure wayward ways of the young, grant or withhold permission for marriage by young couples, and keep a watchful eye on the comings and goings in the locality. The subsequent *mohalla* council network would become the bedrock of Karimov's electoral and referendum victories in the coming years. It would also help the political police to secure an informant in every apartment block or street.

Externally, the events in the United States, Afghanistan, and East Africa in 1993, 1996, 1998, and 2001 would provide Karimov with invaluable opportunities to reiterate his strong views on quashing Islamic militancy and striving for stability in the region. And the July-August 1998 financial crisis in Russia, which had embraced laissez faire capitalism with a vengeance, would vindicate his gradualist approach to economic liberalization.

The truck bombing in the basement of the World Trade Center in New York on February 26, 1993, which caused $500 million in damage and claimed six lives,[50] led Karimov to reiterate his viewpoint: "Stability is the basis for everything. If there were more Karimovs out here in this region—people whom [the Americans] call dictators but who are in fact the very bastions that stand in the way of fundamentalism—you would not have had that explosion in New York City at the World Trade Center [in 1993]."[51]

Nation-building depended on the state of the economy, which, as a professional economist, Karimov knew only too well. An industrious man, he was in the habit of familiarizing himself with the details of the problem at hand. Economic management and countering the Islamist challenge would become the predominant concerns of his government in the years to come. Karimov took cautious steps to move away from the centralized economy of yesteryears. In November 1993, he unveiled the Uzbek som, on a par with the Russian ruble, a measure which his government used to curtail the rate of inflation through its monetary policy. Seven months later, the Uzbek Central Bank fixed the exchange rate of seven new soms to one U.S. dollar.

As a result, branches of international supermarkets, often joint ventures, opened in Tashkent and other cities, with Turkish, Dutch, German, and Italian firms in the forefront. The wider choice and variety of their imported fare benefited customers, who happily carried their purchases in colorful plastic bags. But these supermarkets undermined the livelihood of traditional bazaar merchants. The arrival of fast food outlets with smartly clad waitresses cheerfully serving young customers with cash to spare in sparkling surroundings added a welcome dimension to city life. The contrast was even more striking when compared to the traditional behavior of the poorly paid staff at public offices and state-owned hotels, which ranged from bland indifference to outright insolence.

There were fewer ethnic Russians in the capital—home to two-fifths of the Russian population in the republic—than before. A new law stated that those who failed to adopt Uzbek citizenship by July 1, 1993, would be categorized as aliens and denied free education and health care. Among non-Uzbeks, the Russians had proved to be the most resistant to learning Uzbek, which was required of all civil servants. Only 5 percent of them had mastered Uzbek as a second language. When, in early 1994, Karimov rejected the idea of dual citizenship for Russians, the number of applications for the citizenship of Russia with the Russian embassy in Tashkent rose sharply, the total reaching 20,000 by July. Before the year-end, over 110,000 ethnic Russians received Russian citizenship in 1994, ten times the figure for 1993, and another 62,000 had left Uzbekistan for good.

Increasingly, those Russians who remained were the old pensioners. One such was Igor, a former water and irrigation engineer employed by a factory in Kokand. "I have worked in the factory for 48 years," he said. "Do I regret it [living in Uzbekistan]? I don't. There were my children. They're both in Moscow now, son and daughter. As for my wife, I buried her one and a half years ago. So, I've been alone since then. I was in Moscow, went to see the children in winter, but couldn't stand the climate. That's why I came back here. Maybe I have to return to Moscow. Who knows what the future holds? I can still cope with life, but that might as well change. There is no one here apart from me, neither brothers nor sisters, relatives, no one. I am all on my own."[52]

Police officers behaved the way they did before. They supplemented their meager salaries by pocketing petty summary fines on motorists, who often unwittingly violated some inconsequential rule, or sometimes got caught with tiny grains of hashish in the dashboard or a stray bullet in the upholstery planted by the policeman.

The gains made by Central Asian women, particularly in urban areas, during the Great Patriotic War were in place. Women continued to hold a wide spectrum of jobs, from shop assistants to brain surgeons. Yet in their social life, men kept them in the shadows. When Alisher Hashimov, a slim private car driver in his mid-twenties, invited me to tea, his wife, wearing the traditional flowered dress, velvet jacket, and a colorful headscarf, made the brew behind a closed door while he fetched a bowl of almonds, walnuts, and pistachios, along with crunchy samosas and sweet halva, to go with the tea.

There is a complex set of mores centered around preparing, offering, and drinking tea, which is played out when a group of adult men meet either at the home of one of their ilk, or at a tea shop, which is the equivalent of a British pub or a North American bar. On stifling summer afternoons and evenings, they sit on low, wooden tables placed in the midst of a small pool and drink green tea. In winter they switch to black tea, which they drink without sugar or milk. Hashimov relegating his wife to the kitchen away from the gaze of strangers did not surprise me. What astonished me was to see Tulanbai Kurbanov, professor of philosophy at Tashkent University, treat his wife, Galiya, an academic dressed in western clothes, in a similar fashion when I had dinner with him at his home.

Kurbanov demonstrated the ritual of the chief guest picking up a roundel of bread (called *obi nan*, in Uzbek), sprinkling it with salt, and passing it around the table for other guests to take a bite, thus gaining the loyalty of those present. According to the tradition in Central Asia, once you have eaten the salt of somebody, you must not betray him or her. The round nan, Kurbanov explained, had a history dating back five millennia to the days of Gilgamesh, the legendary Sumerian king of Uruk. The special clay oven, called tandoor, used to bake it is mentioned in *Eros about Gilgamesh*, one of the oldest written texts. The tandoor has been in vogue ever since. Archaeologists discovered tandoors while excavating a seventh century BC site near Samarkand, which established its use by the fire-worshipping Zoroastrians.

Kurbanov drew a sketch of a twenty-inch-long tapering cylinder with a strong base and small opening, a narrow spout, and two-inch-thick walls, which, he explained, should ideally be made from mountainous loess held together by sheep's hair. In the absence of loess, clay from an alluvial soil will suffice. This structure should then dry for a week in the sunshine. Next, the inner wall should be oiled to ensure that clay does not stick to the nan to be baked. Burning firewood or charcoal at the base provides the heat to make the interior of the tandoor red-hot. Before pasting the round, rolled dough against the wall of the tandoor for baking, the baker splashes the wall with salt water to prevent the dough from sticking to it. The appearance of a crunchy crust indicates that the nan has been cooked thoroughly. The baker then removes it from the oven with a scoop.

It was hard to imagine Kurbanov's fragile-looking wife acting as the traditional baker in their small kitchen. But, unknown to him, tandoori cooking had traveled from Central Asia to the Indian subcontinent with the armies of Emperor Babur, the founder of the Mughal Empire in the mid-sixteenth century. So, too, had the cooking of samosas. By the end of the twentieth century, Indian and Pakistani restaurateurs had popularized tandoori nans and chickens as well as samosas in Britain and America much as Italian chefs had done for pizza earlier.

In its original home of West and Central Asia, much praise has been lavished on the deliciously crunchy tandoori nan, which is also high in calories—a fact noted by Abu Ali ibn Sina (aka Avicenna). "After eating an obi nan in the morning with raisins, fried peas or walnut, one need not be thinking of food for a long time," he wrote. That Avicenna made his mark in philosophy and medicine while serving as a courtier in Bukhara, a city now located in Uzbekistan, was one of the several historical facts stressed by the Karimov regime to forge a strong Uzbek identity. This went hand in hand with shoring up the economy.

STRIVING FOR A SELF-RELIANT ECONOMY

On the macro scale in the Uzbek economy, the world's largest mining corporation, the U.S.-based Newmont, set up a joint venture with Kombinat—the state-owned conglomerate which mined Uzbek gold, uranium, copper, and other metals as well as phosphates—whose Murantau mine in the Qizil Qum desert yielded 1.5 metric tons of gold a week. Being the second largest hole on the planet, the Murantau mine was visible from space. Newmont's task was to reprocess the discarded mounds of ore considered rich enough in gold to justify the project.

British American Tobacco (BAT) set up a subsidiary UzBAT with an investment of $300 million—the largest foreign stake in the country so far—using Uzbek tobacco to produce cheap cigarettes near Tashkent for local consumption and export. Coca-Cola opened its bottling plant in the capital to satisfy the thirst of the region. It took the adroit step of giving the top job to Mansur Maqsudi, the rich, Uzbek-American husband of Gulnara Karimov, the Harvard-educated daughter of the Uzbek president.[53]

For the first time, the state-owned trading company started selling Uzbek cotton in the international market to the benefit of the public treasury. State control extended to fixing the price for the commodity, which was less than a quarter of the world market figure, and exercising export monopoly. The export of four-fifths of the cotton helped to shore up Uzbekistan's foreign currency reserves. The sale of 3 million metric tons of cotton abroad for $1.6 billion in 1997, for instance, contributed a third of Uzbekistan's total hard currency earnings.[54] The fate of cotton-pickers, however, remained pitiful: for seven hours of hard labor, they earned 300 new soms, $1.25 at the black market rate, or $3 at the official rate.

Overall, the Uzbek industry also began to register progress, with Kombinat leading the way. It refurbished the old gold foundry at Uchkuduk in the Kyzyl Kum (literally, "Red Sand") desert. Unveiling it, Karimov picked up the first gold brick. "Developed countries would be envious of our achievement," he declared. "Very few countries are so rich in minerals as we are. Soon we will be self-sufficient in oil and petrol, and in grain. We have secured our tomorrow."[55] Gold was also allegedly a source of high-level corruption.[56]

Those who shared Karimov's upbeat message could point out, rightly, that while neighboring Tajikistan, Azerbaijan, Georgia, and even Russia (in its region of Chechnya) were embroiled in war, Uzbekistan was so peaceful that a resident could walk the streets of its capital in safety even in the middle of the night. Tashkent's center had become a large construction site, with the age-old residential neighborhoods, called *mohalla*—consisting of single-story houses, square in design, with a large internal courtyard garden—razed to construct offices and apartment blocks. Elsewhere in the city and its suburbs, traditional single-story houses on square or rectangular plots with rooms built along the perimeter and the internal space cultivated as a vegetable garden remained the norm. Such indeed was the abode of Hashimov.

Though a class of new rich had emerged in Tashkent, it was neither as large nor as blatant as in Moscow, where the super-affluent thought nothing of paying an admission charge of $250 for a coveted nightclub. Unlike in Russia's capital city, the sight of a Mercedes-Benz or BMW was still so rare in Tashkent that people in the street stopped to gape. The freshly affluent were more interested in building luxury houses with swimming pools, and furnishing them with European articles imported through Dubai, which had emerged as a favorite holiday-cum-shopping destination, than in racing around in luxury cars.

On the other hand, Tashkent and Moscow had two things in common: beggars and changing thoroughfare names. Five years earlier begging had been a crime; no more. And now Pushkin Road had become Navai in Tashkent; Karl Marx Boulevard, Fergana; and Communist Avenue, Samarkand.

What had remained unchanged was the pride Tashkent residents took in their unique, earthquake-proof, underground railway resting on a vast bed of hard synthetic rubber, with aesthetically themed stations, which luckily had been completed on the eve of the collapse of the Soviet Union. To that outstanding achievement they now added the freshly unveiled Tashkentland amusement park, an Uzbek enterprise.

In retrospect, 1995 would appear as the year in which foreign direct investment (FDI) in Uzbekistan reached a peak, with the number of British businessmen rising to two hundred. With this, and the opening of more than thirty embassies in Tashkent, the demand for Uzbeks with knowledge of English rose to the point that even those with a smattering of English (like my young driver, Hashimov) earned more in a day in U.S. dollars than did a hotel receptionist at a monthly salary of thirty dollars.

A PHONY MULTI-PARTY SYSTEM

A referendum in 1995 extended Karimov's presidency to 2000. With that, he felt confident enough to re-brand Uzbekistan as an emerging democracy with a multi-party system. He surreptitiously sponsored loyalist opposition, choosing their names and programs. The result was the Justice Social Democratic Party (*Adalat Sotsial Demokratik Partiyasi*; claimed membership, 50,000) formed in February 1995; and the National Renaissance Democratic Party (*Milli Tiklanish Demokratik Partiyasi*; claimed membership, 50,000) formed in June 1995. Having established a "multi-party" system, Karimov would resign as leader of the People's Democratic Party in 1996 to show that as president he was above partisan politics.

The Justice Social Democratic Party, popularly known as Adalat, focused on trade unions and safeguarding working-class interests. The National Renaissance Party, popularly called Milli Tiklanish, on the other hand, came up with a program of reviving Uzbek culture at home, and promoting solidarity with fellow Central Asians with a view to establishing a Greater Turkistan homeland—thus vying with the outlawed Birlik. The farcical nature of the exercise became apparent when many of the delegates to the inaugural convention of Adalat were seen dozing off or sleeping.[57]

Karimov never took his eye off any Islamic personality with a high public profile. Abduvali Mirzayev (originally, Abdul Wali Mirza), the imam of the Friday mosque in Andijan, the biggest in the Fergana Valley, emerged as one. While refraining from speaking against Karimov, he also kept his mosque free of his portraits. On August 29, 1995, he and his assistant, Pamazanbek Matkarimov, left Andijan for Tashkent on their way to Moscow for a conference on religious affairs. They checked in at the Uzbek Airways counter for a flight to Moscow, but never arrived there.

A delegation of the Andijan faithful traveled to Tashkent to urge Karimov to find their missing imam. It was denied access to the president. Back in Andijan, tens of thousands of believers responded to the midday call to prayer in Andijan on the first Friday after the petitioners' arrival in Tashkent by walking to the Friday mosque, each holding a copy of the Quran. "There is one truth: it is unbreakable," said Mirzayev's deputy in his sermon. "The truth" in this instance was that Mirzayev and his assistant were the victims of the operatives of the SNB (*Slujba Natsionalnoy Bezopasnosti*, National Security Service), the successor to the KGB, who kidnapped and killed them. "The government says it is worried about what happened in Tajikistan, but I don't think the same would happen here," said a follower of Mirzayev. "It's more likely they [the authorities] are just afraid of anyone who is popular."[58]

As for Tajikistan, from its initial virulent state with a potential to destabilize the region, the long-running civil war between Islamists and former Communists there had settled down to a low-intensity conflict, which several foreign powers were trying to end.

What did shake up the region was the capture of Kabul in September 1996 by the newly emergent Taliban (literally, "religious students") movement in Afghanistan.

TALIBAN SENDS A TREMOR

On September 26, 1996, two mobile columns of the heavily armed Taliban militia, in loose pajamas and long shirts and donning the uniform of black turbans, packed into Toyota pickup trucks and converged on

Kabul from the east and the south as another column rushed north to cut off the Bagram military air base from the capital. At nightfall, the Taliban forces drove into the capital a few hours after their arch foe, Commander Ahmad Shah Massoud, had ordered an evacuation, taking most of the artillery and tanks with him to the north.

Fanatically puritan, the Taliban, led by Mullah Muhammad Omar, had imposed the Sharia edicts (as interpreted by them) in the seven-tenth of Afghanistan that they controlled—banning music, television, videos, and photography, and stipulating what women should wear and do outside the home, and what men, required to grow beards, should wear.

The lightning speed with which the Taliban captured Kabul dazed not just them and their domestic enemies but also the neighboring states, except Pakistan. It was the Pakistani government which had recruited students from the madrassas in the Afghan refugee camps in its territory, and trained and armed them to overpower the feuding Afghan ethnic groups engaged in a fifty-four-month-long civil war. For an organization that had barely registered on the political radar of Afghanistan two years earlier, the Taliban's victory was an astounding achievement. Nobody could have guessed then that history would repeat itself five years hence, with the Taliban withdrawing overnight from Kabul.

A week after the fall of Kabul, the leaders of Central Asian republics and Russia met in the Kazakh capital of Almaty. Karimov feared that the Taliban would advance in a pincer movement to overthrow the government of the Northern Alliance, led by General Abdul Rashid Dostum, which ruled six northwestern provinces of Afghanistan (out of a total of thirty-two) from its base in Mazar-e Sharif. Since the fall of President Najibullah in 1992, Dostum, an ethnic Uzbek and a former Communist, had been close to Karimov. Now, at the Almaty summit, Karimov urged fellow-presidents to bolster Dostum's government.

In theory, the leaders of Tajikistan and Turkmenistan, bordering Afghanistan, were in a position to enter the Afghan fray against the Taliban. But Tajikistan, mired in its own low-intensity civil conflict, was incapable of bolstering the anti-Taliban front. While recognizing the dangers of the Afghan civil war spilling over into the neighboring states, secular Turkmen President Saparmurat Niyazov was unwilling to back even covertly those battling the Taliban because he was confident that his country was immune to the Islamist contagion. That left Karimov as the sole Central Asian leader to channel military and economic aid to the anti-Taliban forces. In a way, it was a repeat of what the Kremlin did in the

Afghanistan of the 1980s—except that the current Uzbek economy was puny compared to the Soviet Union's in that decade.

In November, Karimov got an opportunity to show the world that his secular regime pursued a liberal policy toward its non-Muslim citizens. The occasion was the arrival in Tashkent of Patriarch Aleksei II, head of the Russian Orthodox Church, along with his entourage, to celebrate the 125th anniversary of the founding of eparchies of the Church in Tashkent.

An embroidered golden robe with an equally glowing turban topped by a neat golden cross invested the partiarch, a rotund figure with narrow eyes, a flowing white beard, and an aura of authority that secular leaders in their conventional business suits lacked. The purpose of his visit, the holy man anounced, was to offer spiritual and moral support to the Orthodox believers now living outside the Russian Federation. Karmov received him ceremoniously and informed him, with more than a hint of pride, that not only had the old St. Aleksei Church in Samarkand been renovated, but new churches had sprung up in Bukhara, Qashka Darya, and Syr Darya since independence. While this reassured the patriarch and ethnic Russians, the Uzbek Islamists saw it as further evidence of Karmiov's deviation from the faith.

WEATHERING THE 1998 RUBLE CRISIS

Disregarding the IMF's recommendation to throw open its markets to foreign capital and make its currency freely convertible, Karimov's government opened the Uzbek industry slowly and partially to foreign investors, controlled the outflow of capital, adopted an import-substitution policy in manufactured goods by encouraging production at home, and promised to make the som freely convertible after seven years. Its strict exchange controls permitted only a few foreign firms to repatriate their profits home. It allowed Uzbek citizens to open hard currency accounts only with the Foreign Economic Activity branch of the National Bank of Uzbekistan.

Yet, in 1996, Uzbekistan began losing foreign exchange rapidly. To stem the outflow, the government restricted imports, giving preference to capital goods over consumer articles, and required the licensed companies to purchase foreign currencies at the official, overvalued rates while others bought foreign currencies at the commercial rate. This disparity between the market and official rates grew to four-to-one.

The IMF disapproved of the artificially high exchange rate for the som. With Uzbekistan's reserves down to a meager $1 billion in September 1996, Karimov refused to devalue the som. The IMF suspended credits to

Uzbekistan in November, and closed its office in Tashkent. On the other hand, a study by the United Nations Commission for Europe, published in July 1998, showed a superior performance by Uzbekistan compared to Kazakhstan and Russia. Taking the 1989 figure as 100, the Russian GDP in 1996 was 57; the Kazakh GPD, 61; and the Uzbek GPD, 82.[59]

By happenstance, in that month a financial crisis hit Russia. The ruble collapsed. Russia under President Boris Yeltsin had lurched headlong into unfettered capitalism, giving free access to foreign companies, and selling natural resources and vast state enterprises to a few individuals at bargain-basement prices. Now, overwhelmed by foreign capital flight, Russia's Central Bank could not sustain the fixed rate of 7 rubles to the U.S. dollar. On August 17, it put a ninety-day moratorium on external debts, signaling a full-blown crisis. On September 2, the Central Bank decided to float the ruble. By September 21, the rate settled at 21 rubles to the U.S. dollar, a loss of two-thirds of its value.

The Moscow-based reporters of the state-run Uzbek television gleefully beamed images of panic from Russia, thus underlining the sagacity of Uzbekistan's gradualist policies. "If a country is not integrated into the world financial system, if there is no foreign exposure on the Uzbek treasury bills, foreign exchange or share markets, then obviously it will not be affected," said a Western economist based in Moscow. "The Uzbeks feel vindicated," said a Western investor in Tashkent. "The Russian collapse brings into question the whole argument for a market economy as the Uzbek government equates what has happened in Russia with market economy."[60]

While the meltdown in Moscow gripped the financial markets, a dramatic story from East Africa caught the attention of the political-diplomatic world.

EAST AFRICA BOMBINGS REVERBERATE

On August 7, 1998, a truck bomb near the U.S. embassy in Nairobi, Kenya, left 216 people dead. Eight minutes later, a truck bomb outside the American embassy in Dar es Salaam, Tanzania, killed 11 people. Following the confessions of the arrested bombers, the Bill Clinton administration blamed Osama bin Laden, the Al Qaeda leader then living in Afghanistan, where the Taliban had just captured Mazar-e Sharif and put Dostum to flight. Clinton ordered missile attacks on the Al Qaeda training camps in Afghanistan.

These events provided Karimov with further evidence that militant Islamists were a menace to stability, an assertion now endorsed by the American president. Clinton ordered the training of commandos for possible ground action against bin Laden, and he tapped into Uzbekistan and Tajikistan, which his administration had been cultivating since the mid-1990s. The Pentagon began admitting Uzbek officers to its military academies in 1995. Its troops participated in joint military exercises in Uzbekistan in August 1996. In order to kill or capture bin Laden, the Pentagon sent fifteen-member Green Beret teams—part of the Special Forces—to train Uzbek soldiers in marksmanship, map reading, and infantry patrolling. Soon, joint American-Uzbek squads began making periodic forays into northern Afghanistan in search of bin Laden.[61]

Military ties between Tashkent and Washington strengthened with the signing of two agreements in May 1999 in the wake of the bombings in Tashkent earlier that year. The provisions allowed the United States to deploy unmanned Predator drones equipped with missiles in Afghanistan in 2000 to try to kill bin Laden.[62] In addition, U.S. Special Forces conducted a training mission in Uzbekistan.

These activities went on against the background of the establishment of the Islamic Movement of Uzbekistan (IMU) in 1998 in Kabul. The IMU was enjoying the status of an official guest of the Taliban government. Its founders were Jumaboi Namangani (aka Jumaboi Khojayev; 1969–2001), a former Soviet paratrooper, and Tahir Yuldashev (b. 1967), an ideologue, both of them from the Fergana Valley. The IMU aimed to establish an Islamic state in Uzbekistan by waging a jihad against the regime of Karimov. In a rare interview with the *Voice of America* in 2000, Yuldeshev would explain the aims of the IMU as "fighting against oppression in our country, against bribery, against the inequities and also the freeing of our Muslim brothers from prison."[63]

Due to their traditional ties with the mosque, Islamists had managed to survive in Uzbekistan despite repression, which continued unabated. In September 1997, Nehmat Parpiyev, a former bodyguard of Abduvali Mirzayev, disappeared. In response, some masked men in Namangan decapitated a police officer notorious for his brutality. The subsequent police raid led to a gun battle, which claimed three more policemen and a suspect. The government imposed curfews in Namangan and other Fergana Valley cities, and arrested hundreds (thousands, by some accounts) of residents. Police officers, often drunk, carried out house-to-house searches at night, and arrested men who wore beards or had more than one wife. The state-run radio and television blacked out the wide-scale arrests.

Human rights activists, however, kept track of the events, as their subsequent reports would show. In its July 1998 report, the Brussels-based Human Rights Watch (HRW) said that "the government is painting with the same brush those who may have a criminal record and average Muslims who wear a beard or go the mosque" and "is subjecting Muslims on a mass scale to beatings, expulsions from universities and jobs, show trials and lengthy prison terms." Typically, police detain "suspects without an arrest warrant, plant small amounts of marijuana or several bullets, a handgun or grenade on their person in their car or in their home during a search and beat them until they confess to the crime." Such planting had become so common during the crackdown that men in the area resorted to wearing clothes without pockets. "By prominently denouncing Islamic extremism, the government of President Islam Karimov is trying to focus popular attention on supposed internal enemies to deflect social discontent," the HRW report concluded.[64]

During Ramadan (starting in late December 1997), the government banned the call to prayer from mosques by loudspeakers, a common practice in most Muslim countries. The sisters and wives of the arrested Islamists demanded the lifting of the ban in their demonstrations in Tashkent, where they arrived wearing an Islamic garb, covering their heads, arms, and legs. The authorities were doubly embarrassed: Uzbek women covered from head to toe was not the image they wanted the outside world to associate with Uzbekistan.

In April 1998, reversing its earlier policy of silence on the arrests of Islamists, the government began publicizing the trials of the suspected "Wahhabis." The first group of seventeen faced the charges of links with radical Islamists in Tajikistan and Pakistan, and plotting to install an Islamic regime. On the eve of the trial in May, Karimov addressed the parliament. He claimed that the fundamentalists' activities in the Fergana Valley included murdering government officials, and planning to blow up water reservoirs and power plants. Assuming a guilty verdict for the accused, he declared, "Such people must be shot in the head. If necessary, I will shoot them myself."[65]

The Uzbek parliament stiffened the 1991 Law on Freedom of Conscience and Religious Organizations. It stipulated that a religious group must have a minimum of a hundred members instead of the ten required earlier, and must register with the government. Unregistered religious associations became liable to criminal prosecution. The penalty for "extremist activity" was five to eight years in prison, and for wearing religious clothing (a *hijab*, headscarf, for women; and a turban for men) in public fifteen days in jail. The police acquired enhanced powers of detention. The existing mosques could function only after receiving state registration; and passing a state-sponsored test became the prerequisite for anybody to administer a mosque.

The Mufti's Office announced later that of the 5,000 mosques, 3,000 had "ambiguous status," and that "improper mosques" would become nurseries, shops, or sport centers.[66] At the same time, the government announced plans to open the Tashkent Islamic University in the spring of 1999. The university would conduct research on Islam as well as teach Islamic history and philosophy and the Sharia, thus providing an official institution for the young Uzbeks interested in delving deep into Islam.

The wide-scale crackdown that followed included the members of the Hizb ut-Tahrir al Islami (Islamic Liberation Party), a comparative newcomer, introduced into Uzbekistan in 1995 by a Jordanian named Salahuddin. The party made its presence known by scattering its leaflets overnight in bazaars. Its founder was Shaikh Taqiuddin al-Nabhani, a Palestinian Islamic judge, who lost his home in Palestine during the 1948 to 1949 Arab-Israeli War and settled in Jordan. He established the Hizb ut-Tahrir in 1953, and set out its rationale and objectives in a series of pamphlets and books. Emulating the life of Prophet Muhammad—who propagated Islam secretly, then openly, and went on to establish a state, and finally called for a jihad to expand the Islamic realm—Nabhani instructed Hizb members to follow a similar course. Just as Prophet Muhammad's earlier followers had suffered persecution, Hizb members should expect a similar fate. But they must remain steadfast and strive to achieve the party's ultimate aim of reviving the Caliphate that had existed until its abolition by Mustafa Kemal Ataturk in 1924. Nabhani envisaged Hizb achieving power in one or more Muslim countries, which would accelerate the process of co-opting the rest of the Muslim world to establish the Caliphate.

Initially Hizb gained supporters among Palestinian refugees living in camps in Jordan, Lebanon, Syria, and Iraq. It then extended its activities to Egypt—and Turkey, which was, after all, the core of the last Islamic empire under the Ottomans. Unlike the IMU and Al Qaeda, Hizb did not preach violence to overthrow the regimes in Muslim countries they did not consider Islamic. Rather, its strategy was to win popular support with the aim of staging massive yet peaceful demonstrations to topple the un-Islamic regimes in Central Asia.

The party functioned in cells of five to seven members, with only its leader aware of the next level in the hierarchy. The members, mostly young and male, gathered in each other's homes, had tea, prayed together, discussed some aspect of Islam, and received instructions from the leader to perform such tasks as distribute leaflets to houses or shops in the middle of the night or set up a new cell. Hizb leaders forbade alcohol and drugs, as well as dancing, and shunned attending ostentatious weddings as a sign of decadence. Most parents were relieved to see their sons combine piety with modesty. Unlike IMU members or Wahhabis, Hizb members did not use mosques, and their leaders were unknown even to the rank and file. But both IMU and Hizb members were incensed by the trip Karimov made to Israel in September 1998, when he signed the most-favored-nation trade pact with Israel. He was gratified to hear Israeli leaders declare Muslim fundamentalism as "the biggest threat to the free world after the failure of communism."[67]

As Hizb literature—books by Nabhani and his successor Shaikh Zalum, and the party magazine *Al Vai* (*The Consciousness*)—became available in Central Asian languages, the party's influence and membership grew significantly. According to a rumor circulating in Tashkent in 1999, Hizb members had distributed 200,000 leaflets in the region's bazaars in a single night.[68] Unlike the IMU and Al Qaeda, which appealed to rural Uzbeks, Hizb attracted young, urban, educated men. It made full use of the Internet, e-mail, and latest printing technology to spread its message.

The authorities tried to exploit the situation to their advantage. "Karimov needs a radical Islamic enemy he can point to [in order to] justify continued repression and to frighten people with the bogeyman of the Taliban-style government," noted Craig Murray, the British ambassador in Tashkent. "HuT [Hizb ut-Tahrir] fills this need and therefore HuT-style leaflets are routinely planted on political dissidents of all persuasion."[69]

The regime intensified its repression. As a result, it destroyed the moderate IRP, and drove the more committed Islamists to flee to Tajikistan, where the Islamist-led United Tajik Opposition started sharing power with former Communists from February 1998, or the Taliban-administered Afghanistan.

EXPLOSIONS IN TASHKENT

On February 16, 1999, five bombs rocked the Uzbek capital. The first exploded at 10:40 a.m. near the Interior Ministry in central Tashkent; the next two at the Independence Square near the ministerial cabinet building, where ministers had gathered for a meeting to be presided by Karimov who had yet to arrive; and the fourth outside the Foreign Economic Activity branch of the National Bank of Uzbekistan. The last bomb, which went off at noon on a quiet street called Glinka in south Tashkent, was so loud that many thought a plane had crashed. Although the death toll at sixteen was modest, the bombings shattered the image of Uzbekistan as a haven of stability.

Halting short of the Independence Square, Karimov's motorcade raced away. But, once the smoke had cleared, the president appeared at the bombed site at the Independence Square to deliver a television address. He claimed that he was the prime target of the bombers. "I am ready to rip off the heads of two hundred people, to sacrifice their lives, in order to save peace and calm in the republic," he declared.[70] The next day the Interior Ministry described the bombers as "Islamic extremists," which most people accepted as true.

Hundreds of arrests followed not only in Uzbekistan but also in Kyrgyzstan, Kazakhstan, Turkmenistan, Azerbaijan, Ukraine, and Turkey, with the suspects accused of being part of an international conspiracy. In the end, the prosecutor charged a group of twenty-two men, nearly two-thirds of them from the Fergana Valley, with attempting to assassinate Karimov and conspire to overthrow his regime to install an Islamic emirate. They had operated from a house on Glinka Street used as a bomb factory, which they blew up when their plan went awry.

The public trial, starting on June 2, became the talk of town. The accused, aged twenty-five to forty-four, sat on backless benches inside a cage of metal bars, each of them armed with a large orange folder containing their confessions of guilt recorded earlier during the investigation. When they glanced at the audience in the sweltering courtroom, they did not see their relatives, who remained barred. The trial, in essence, revolved around them confirming before the judge what they had already confessed. The legal system did not require corroborating testimony or forensic evidence. The Uzbek foreign minister explained the government's policy thus: "Under our system only the guilty are accused. You must allow us our own tradition."[71]

The Supreme Court judge listened or took notes as the chief prosecutor reeled out a list of charges, from armed robbery to Islamic militancy to plotting to overturn the nation's constitution. The demand for penalties varied from capital punishment for the ringleaders like Bahram Abdullayev (originally Abdullah)—a tall, thin, soft-spoken man in a well-pressed gray shirt—to fourteen to twenty years imprisonment for those who, as drivers or couriers like Delshad Kamalov, were accessories.

Yet, every night, television aired hours of court proceedings, jazzing up the images with ominous background music, and presenting the trial as a nail-biting detective tale. The confessions were surreal. "We were going to announce on television and radio that all Muslims should stay indoors," said Zainuddin Askarov, a slim man in his late twenties. "Then we were going to let off canisters of sleeping-gas all over Uzbekistan. Those in the streets would fall asleep for three to four hours. Then we would kill all the Russians and take power. We would release all the political prisoners, including the mullahs, and the government would go on trial according to the Sharia. Then we would declare an Islamic government." He ended by saying that he was not directly involved in the explosions: he was in Turkey on February 16.

Abdullayev outlined the conspiracy. During the previous two years, the plotters had met in Istanbul, Baku, and Kabul to devise a plan to assassinate Karimov. Those assigned to do the job received training in Afghanistan, Tajikistan, and Chechnya. The funding came from robberies in Andijan, and from Uzbek opposition leaders in exile, principally Muhammad Salih of the secular Erk party then based in Istanbul.[72]

The chaos resulting from Karimov's assassination would prepare the ground for the invasion by two "armies," about 5,000-strong, led by the IMU cofounders—one by Namangani, advancing over the mountains into Uzbekistan, and other by Yuldashev, crossing Afghanistan at Termez. In a pincer movement, they would advance on Tashkent, defeat the (50,000-strong) Uzbek army and air force, and declare Salih as president.[73]

However, Abdullayev did not participate in the bombings, for he had been behind bars since October 1998 after his arrest during a visit to Turkmenistan. Lacking his adroit leadership, the other conspirators apparently made a hash of the job. It would be incredible to think that his interrogators, well versed in torturing suspects, did not extract the vital intelligence regarding planned bombings from him during his four months in captivity before the explosions. It seems that their political bosses decided *not* to abort the plot. What gave credence to this theory were the following facts: four cars carrying explosives reached their important destinations without a hitch, and police officers failed to apprehend a single bomber as they leapt out of their vehicles and dashed off before the explosions.

"At times, the trial seemed preposterous, at times plausible, often within the course of a single session," observed Monica Whitlock, who covered it for the BBC. "A long confession could lull the listener into a sort of mesmerized acceptance: a sudden jab of the unbelievable jolted one awake. Sometimes it seemed as though at least some of the young men in the cages might be guilty—and at the same time their confessions [seemed to] be pure fabrication."[74]

Finding all of them guilty, the judge sentenced Abdullayev to death, four others to life imprisonment, and the rest to varying lengths of incarceration. During the second half of 1999, judges would hand down fifty-five death sentences, many of them against Hizb ut-Tahrir activists.[75]

The Kremlin expressed outrage at the bombings but considered the matter domestic and therefore outside the purview of the Tashkent Collective Security Agreement. Chaffing at this, Karimov withdrew Uzbekistan from the agreement at the next summit in May, which led to the renaming of the agreement as the Collective Security Treaty Organization (CSTO). For different reasons, Azerbaijan and Georgia did not join the CSTO, whose membership was reduced to six countries, with Russia as the nominal leader.

By contrast, the Clinton administration rushed Federal Bureau of Investigation (FBI) agents to Tashkent to assist in the investigation. To their disappointment, they found that the Uzbeks had filled up the bomb-craters, a vital forensic source. Three months later, the Pentagon inked two security agreements with Tashkent.

Also, in the aftermath of the bombings, Uzbekistan was invited to join the Shanghai Cooperation Organization (SCO) as an observer at its summit in August 1999 when it set up a joint anti-terrorism center in Bishkek. The SCO had originated three years earlier as the Shanghai Forum after China had hosted a meeting in Shanghai of the leaders of Russia, Kazakhstan, Kyrgyzstan, and Tajikistan—countries which shared common borders with China. They issued the Agreement on Confidence-Building in the Military Field along the Border Areas. This pertained to the lowering of tensions in the frontier areas.

The year-old National Democratic Party (*Fidokorlar Milli Demokratik Partiyasi*; claimed membership, 61,750), popularly called "Fidokorlar" (Self-Sacrificers), had formed with Karimov's blessing to encourage the nation's young elite who were interested in politics. In the December 1999 parliamentary poll, the party emerged as the second largest group (with 34 seats) after the long-established PDP (with 48 seats), in a house of 250 members, where 110 seats were held by local council nominees and were nonpartisan.

KARIMOV REELECTED

The threat of Islamist terrorism galvanized supporters of Karimov in his reelection bid for presidency in January 2000. He decided to break with the past, and entered the contest as the nominee of the National Democratic Party, Fidokorlar. His rival at the polls was Abdul Hafiz Jalalov, the fifty-three-year-old, spiky-haired head of the Philosophy Institute of the Uzbek Academy of Sciences, and a former Communist party official.

The bizarre nature of the ritual became obvious when Jalalov, after casting his ballot, announced that he had voted for Karimov. The universally expected result followed: the voter turnout was 95 percent, and 95 percent of the electorate opted for Karimov.[76]

Freshly reelected Karimov acted to liberalize the economy, somewhat, by devaluing the Uzbek currency by almost 50 percent in May, fixing the new rate at 231 soms to the U.S. dollar. Fulfilling an earlier promise, the Central Bank agreed to adjust the rate every week depending on demand and supply. Within three months, the official rate slipped to 280 soms, with the market rate of 675 soms to the U.S. dollar.

In the summer, the Uzbek government found itself facing its bête noire, the IMU. Having returned to his base in Tajikistan, along with a force of several hundred fighters—well armed, trained, and paid—Namangani carried out multi-prong incursions into neighboring Kyrgyzstan and Uzbekistan in July. His aim was to divert his enemy forces' attention while his men penetrated the Fergana Valley to supply IMU sleepers arms and ammunition.

A contingent of 170 IMU guerrillas built up such a fortified camp in Uzbekistan's Surkhan Darya province (capital Termez)—bordering Tajikistan, Afghanistan, and Turkmenistan—that it took the Uzbek troops one month and the deployment of helicopter gun ships, heavy artillery, and flame throwers to overrun the camp. The surviving few escaped. In late August, a small IMU unit of infiltrators killed two Uzbek soldiers and took another four hostage eighty miles north of Tashkent near a holiday resort. When besieged, the guerrillas kept firing until they ran out of ammunition, and were killed. "Tashkent's citizens could hear helicopter gun ships and fighter jets take off from Tashkent military airport for bombing and strafing runs every morning," reported Ahmed Rashid, a visiting Pakistani journalist. "Rumors filled the city."[77]

The episode made Uzbeks realize their vulnerability, and focused

Karimov's attention on the Taliban-administered Afghanistan. He stressed that it had become a sanctuary as well as a training center for Islamic fundamentalists, intent on committing terrorist acts throughout the world. Following the joint Uzbek-NATO military exercises in Uzbekistan in mid-2001, the Pentagon left its attack helicopter brigade behind at the Chirchik air base, one of the twenty-three air bases in the republic.

Karimov's warnings about Afghanistan proved prophetic with the terrorist strikes against the World Trade Center in New York and the Pentagon in Washington on September 11, 2001, which killed nearly 3,000 people. These attacks opened a new chapter in Uzbekistan's relationship with the United States.

STRATEGIC PARTNER OF AMERICA

Having formally recruited Pakistan into the coalition to wage his "war on terror," U.S. President George W. Bush turned to Central Asia, more specifically Uzbekistan and Tajikistan. Since the previous administration had already co-opted them into its plans to seize bin Laden, it was now a matter of broadening and deepening the earlier ties. Karimov particularly liked Bush's reference to the "war on terror" as a battle between barbarity and civilization, between good and evil—just the terms he had used earlier in his persecution of militant Islamists.

On September 18, two large U.S. Hercules transport planes, carrying 200 troops and loaded with surveillance equipment to be installed along the Uzbek-Afghan border, landed secretly at a military base near Tashkent. But it was not until October 1 that the government disclosed it would open its airspace to U.S. forces without mentioning that the Karshi base near Khanabad (aka K2)—one of the largest air bases of the Soviet era, 500 kilometers (310 miles) from Tashkent—was being made available to the Pentagon.

Since the American planes could not fly over Iran, they went through Turkmenistan's air space once its president had agreed. In a flurry of telephone conversations with Bush, Karimov and Tajik President Imamali Rahmanov struck deals to let the Pentagon use their air bases in return for increased financial aid and a freer hand to suppress their Islamists. Washington's annual grants to Uzbekistan were to rise threefold to $150 million, a very substantial amount for a country whose foreign reserves at one point had fallen to $1 billion.[78]

In early October, U.S. Defense Secretary Donald Rumsfeld arrived in

Tashkent with a letter from Bush to Karimov stressing the new relationship in view of the activities of the Islamic Movement of Uzbekistan. With 2,000 to 3,000 fighters, a training camp at a former Soviet base near Mazar-e Sharif, Afghanistan, and well equipped with weapons and surveillance equipment, the IMU had been conducting hit-and-run assaults on police and political targets in the Fergana Valley since mid-1999, with the aim of establishing an Islamic state in the valley.

Aware of the popular resentment that would result from bombing a Muslim country, however radical or terroristic, from the Uzbek soil, Karimov refused to let the Pentagon strike Afghanistan from K2 once the anti-Taliban military campaign—codenamed, Operation "Enduring Freedom"—got going on October 7.

Nonetheless, the presence of American troops at K2 rose to 5,000, with the base housing three squadrons of U.S. warplanes. The construction division of Halliburton, a large American corporation associated with Vice President Dick Cheney, would get the contract to improve facilities at the base to accommodate more warplanes.

Karimov's cooperation with Washington went beyond leasing an important base to the United States. His government was complicit in the Pentagon's notorious "extraordinary rendition" program, whereby "enemy suspects" were picked up in different countries by the CIA and then delivered to the regimes known to use torture. With its odious record of torturing suspects using stomach-turning methods, the Uzbek government was unsurprisingly at the top of the CIA's list. Karimov was only too eager to oblige. During his visit to Tashkent after the expulsion of the Taliban from Kabul on November 12, Rumsfeld was fulsome in his praise of Uzbekistan as a partner in the war on terror. Karimov, in turn, was pleased to hear of the death of Jumaboi Namangani in the Pentagon's air strike near Kunduz.

His reinforced ties with America emboldened Karimov to tighten further his grip on power. In January 2002 he held a referendum on the constitutional amendments, which extended his term of office by two years, and increased the presidential term of office to seven years. The referendum also changed a single-chamber legislative assembly of 250 members to a two-chamber parliament, with a lower house of 120 directly elected seats, and an upper chamber (the senate) of 100 seats, with each of the twelve regions getting 6 seats, and the rest to be nominated by the president. Over 91 percent of the voters approved the amendments.

Two months later, during Karimov's visit to Washington, he and Bush signed five agreements. The most significant was the Declaration on the

Strategic Partnership and Cooperation Framework. It covered political, security, economic, humanitarian, and legal cooperation, requiring Uzbekistan to implement democratic reform, and unveiled a new chapter in American-Uzbek relations. Washington reaffirmed its earlier pledge to assure Uzbekistan's security and territorial integrity, while Tashkent reiterated its wholehearted backing for the war on terror.[79] Uzbekistan also "reaffirmed its commitment to further intensify the democratic transformation of its society politically and economically . . . and to build in Uzbekistan a rule by law state and democratic society . . . to develop a law-based government system, [and] further reform the judicial system and enhance the legal culture."[80] The declaration received wide and glowing coverage in the Uzbek media, which described it as heralding a new era in the republic's international standing.

In a concession to Uzbek legislators, Karimov allowed the parliament to debate fully the bills and presidential decrees, instead of merely endorsing them during its two brief biannual sessions, and promised to let it draft legislation in the future. Assured of his close links with Washington, Karimov criticized Russia for failing to assist his government to quash Islamist terrorism in the late 1990s, and failing to use the Collective Security Treaty Organization to crush radical Islamists. "It was the United States and its coalition that destroyed terrorist bases in Afghanistan," he said in April 2002. "We should consider who played which part and who played the main role. I say that the United States played a decisive role [with] their determination, the exemplary professionalism of their soldiers and level of their armaments. Everybody [else] played secondary roles."[81] Six months later, addressing other Central Asian leaders, he said, "Americans should not leave our region until peace and stability is established in Central Asia . . . they should stay as long as needed."[82]

Stung by such remarks, two months later, the Kremlin set up an anti-terrorism rapid reaction force in Kant, Kyrgyzstan, barely 32 kilometers (20 miles) from Manas, where the Pentagon had freshly set up its base. Inaugurating the new force, Russian President Vladimir Putin stressed that the initiative was taken under the auspices of the multinational Collective Security Treaty Organization. But others were not convinced. Reflecting a general view prevalent in the region, the Kazakhstan-based *Kontinent* weekly remarked that Russia's decision to act was designed to counter the pervasive "American hegemony" in Central Asia.[83]

While Karimov basked in Washington's treatment of his government as a strategic ally, most American observers were disappointed to see no noticeable improvement in Uzbekistan's human rights or political liberalization, as mentioned in the March 2002 declaration. The Bush administration tried to fudge the issue by offering the typical argument along the lines of, on one hand, we see progress on political and economic reform as critical, and on the other, this kind of change takes time. The dichotomy continued, with the State Department refusing to certify that human rights were improving, while the CIA and the Pentagon flew suspect Islamist terrorists to Uzbekistan on their "renditions" to be tortured.

APPALLING HUMAN RIGHTS VIOLATIONS

While the State Department included Uzbekistan in its list of countries which violate human rights and religious freedom, the Pentagon continued to reinforce security ties with Tashkent. Aid to Uzbekistan shot up. Between the 2001 and 2002 fiscal years, the figure soared from $85 million to $300 million.[84]

To advance human rights and political reform, the State Department decided to open a branch of Freedom House[85] in Tashkent. U.S. Ambassador John Herbst invited his British counterpart, Craig Murray, to be the key speaker on its inauguration on October 17, 2002. A portly, bespectacled, middle-aged man with graying hair, given to wearing tartan kilts to highlight his Scottish origins, Murray was known to be a straight talker. "Uzbekistan is not a functioning democracy nor is it moving in that direction," Murray declared before TV cameras. "The major political parties [Birlik and Erk] are banned; parliament is not subject to democratic election; and checks and balances on the authority of the executive are lacking." He then referred to gross violations of human and civil rights. "World attention has recently focused on the prevalence of torture in Uzbek prisons," he continued. "The terrible cases of [Muzafar] Avazov and [Khusniddin] Alimov, apparently tortured to death by boiling water, has evoked great international concern. But all of us know that this is not an isolated incident. Brutality is inherent in a system where convictions habitually rely on signed confessions rather than on forensic or material evidence."[86]

Under such a judicial system, 220 Uzbeks faced the firing squad in 2002. There were others, whom police or other security forces killed during detention, besides those who "disappeared." According to independent human rights groups, there were over 600 politically motivated arrests a year, and an estiamted 6,500 political prisoners, most of them religious Muslims charged under Article 159 of the Criminal Code—conspiring to overthrow the government or constitution of Uzbekistan—with some tortured to death.[87]

The case of a Hizb ut-Tahrir suspect, Muzaffar Avazov, thirty-five-year-old father of four, tortured and killed in the Jasilk detention center in August 2002, caused international outrage, thanks to the initiative taken by his mother Fatima Mukahadirova. Following the official routine, the authorities delivered his corpse to his surviving parent in a sealed casket for burial the next day, and left a single Interior Ministry militiaman on the watch. In the middle of the night, finding the militiaman snoring, Mukahadirova got the casket pried open and the corpse placed on the kitchen table. Then she took photographs that showed signs of burns on the legs, buttocks, lower back, and arms, a large wound on the back of the head, bruises on the forehead, and hands with missing fingernails. These images ended up at the British embassy, where an examination by the Glasgow University's pathology department concluded that the victim had died "of immersion in a boiling liquid . . . because there was a clear tidemark around the upper torso and upper arms, with 100 percent scalding underneath."[88]

The Uzbek secret police, SNB, had devised extraordinarily gruesome ways of torturing and even killing suspects. Its favorite tactic to extract a "confession" was to put a gas mask on the face of the detainee, and then cut off the air supply by blocking the filters. Other methods included causing death by immersing the suspect into a drum of boiling water, and shackling normal, healthy suspects next to incurable tuberculosis patients in hospitals or prison cells.

Little wonder that, though the authorities let the United Nations special rapporteur on torture, Professor Theo van Boven, into Uzbekistan in December 2003 and allowed him to visit prisons, they barred him from the much-feared SNB detention center in Tashkent. Another place notorious for torture was Jasilk Detention Center in the desert near the Turkmen border. He concluded that torture of suspects was "routine" in Uzbekistan.

In his speech, Murray also alluded to a lack of freedom of expression: "Officially, censorship has recently been abolished. But you would not notice this by watching, listening to or reading the media which is patently under strict control and contains no significant volume of critical comment or analysis of central government policy." He referred to the closure of major bazaars in Tashkent and elsewhere, a government order that directly affected the livelihood of 50,000 people. Yet not a word about it appeared in the media.[89]

"The shock value of these statements [by Murray], as well as others discussing widespread torture in Uzbekistan and the government's refusal to convert its currency or foster cross-border trade, cannot be overstated," reported David Stern in the *Financial Times*.[90] The authorities controlled the media through a strict implementation of rules that required all publications and broadcasting outlets to register with the Interior Ministry and submit their annual plans, explaining how they collected and disseminated news. The reporters who overstepped the unstated "red lines" ended up being thrashed or detained, and charged with bringing the image of Uzbekistan into disrepute.

Only after making numerous attempts over the course of five years did the Independent Human Rights Organization of Uzbekistan (IHROU) obtain official recognition by the Ministry of Justice in March 2003. Human rights activists continued to be subject to surveillance. If they overstepped the official bounds, their organizations lost their registrations.

THE TAJIK FACTOR

To marginalize further the banned secular Birlik and Erk parties, Karimov vigorously pursued a policy of Uzbekization. Government employees had to pass a test in the Uzbek language, while public service jobs gradually became the preserve of native Uzbek speakers. All subjects at the university level were to be taught in Uzbek by 2005. This created a major problem. For three-fifths of university teachers, being Tajik or Russian, Uzbek was not their mother tongue.

Government pressure led to the closure of eighty of the ninety-two Tajik schools that existed at the time of independence. The authorities had also banned Tajik broadcasts. Many Tajik teaching staff at the universities of Samarkand and Tashkent lost their jobs. This was a bitter blow to Tajik identity. Tajiks had been the inhabitants of the region for millennia. They took particular pride in their predominant presence in the historic cities of Samarkand, renowned for its stunning monuments, and Bukhara, renowned as the center of religious learning, first Zoroastrian and then Islamic.

Bukhara (aka Bukhara Sharif, Noble Bukhara) is the site of the vast Kalon Mosque built in 795 to accommodate 12,000 worshippers. It is also the birthplace of Muhammad ibn Ismail al Bukhari (810–70; aka Imam al Bukhari)—the compiler of the most authoritative collection of Hadith, the Sayings and Doings of Prophet Muhmmad—and Muhammad Bahauddin

Naqshband (1318–89), the greatest Sufi leader of Central Asia. The city's importance as a leading trading post along the Silk Road was underlined by the construction of the 150-foot-high Kalon Tower in 1171—then the tallest structure to date—by Emir Abdullah to serve as both as a watchtower for soldiers and a lighthouse for traders. Its robust height so impressed Genghis Khan that he let it stand while razing the rest of the city. Since then it has become the hallmark of Bukhara worldwide.

Standing on an octagonal base, thirty feet across, the Kalon Tower tapers through ten bands of carved brick-and-tile work decorated with Kufic calligraphy. Its ornate rotunda gallery at the top, which has been lit at night ever since it was constructed, can be reached by ascending 109 dark, uneven steps. It was over these narrow steps that the hapless criminals sentenced to death by the Emir of Bukhara during the eighteenth and nineteenth centuries were dragged, screaming, by the soldiers to the top rotunda. There, each criminal was told his capital offense before being hurled down, much to the horror and fascination of the crowd watching from ground. Hence, the historic monument acquired the sobriquet, Tower of Death.

Overall, though, the Kalon complex—consisting of the Kalon Tower, the Kalon Mosque, with its turquoise dome and enormous courtyard, and the Mir-e-Arab Madrassa—is harmonious and graceful. The blue-domed Madrassa, dating back to 1535, was constructed from the profits of slave trade. Its central arched gateway is profusely embellished with glazed tiles arranged in eye-catching intricacy. Inside, the drums supporting the blue domes carry mosaics and Kufic calligraphy. Cloisters surround the courtyard in the back to accommodate the students. The Mir-e-Arab was one of the two madrassas in Central Asia that continued to function during the Soviet era, the other being the Imam al-Bukhari Madrassa in Tashkent. Since independence, the annual enrollment of Mir-e-Arab had doubled to eighty students. Students enroll at the age of eighteen for a five-year course to qualify as imams.

The twenty-one-foot-deep hole near the Kalon complex, called the Black Well, figures more prominently in British history books than the famed Kalon Tower.[91] In 1842, two Britons, Colonel Charles Stoddart and Captain Arthur Connolly of the Bengal Light Cavalry of the East India Company, were thrown into the vermin-infested well on the orders of Emir Nasrullah. They had arrived from India with the mission of coaxing the emir away from forging an alliance with Tsar Nicholas I as part of the early moves in the Great Game between British India and Tsarist Russia. However, the emir had felt insulted by the lack of response to his earlier letter to British

Queen Victoria. The fact that the two Britons claiming to be the envoys of their sovereign knew nothing of his missive convinced the emir that they were spies. That sealed their fate. He ordered them to be decapitated, and so they were.

In purely architectural terms, the Registan complex in Samarkand stands far above the Kalon complex in Bukhara. This architectural ensemble— three incredibly beautiful buildings, used as madrassas in the past (Ulug Bek, Sher Dar, and Tillah Kari)—blends grandeur with elegance. The proportions of the structures' heights, widths, and lengths are astonighingly exact, the minarets effortlessly tall, and the azure blue domes appear almost to be floating. As visitors enter the square, their eyes invariably turn upwards on the tympanums, the iwan, the top front of the buildings embellished with Arabic letters and floral motifs formed by tiles in sparkling blues, browns, greens, and yellows.

It was towards the end of the fourteenth century that Tuman Aka, a consort of Emir Timur Beg (aka Timurlane), set up a cupola-shaped trading mart, which would go through several phases to bloom into the Registan. In 1417, Ulug Bek (1394–1449), a grandson of Timur Beg, built a madrassa to teach astronomy, mathematics, and medicine along with Islam opposite Tuman Aka's trading post. He then had the trading post removed, using the vacated site to build a hospice with a spacious, high-ceilinged, domed hall. The construction in the 1430s of the large Kukuldash congregational mosque on the southern side completed the Registan complex. An oustanding mathematician and astronomer, Ulug Beg also left behind an observatory. The cultural flowering that occurred during his rule brought forth the genius of Avicenna, a pioneer in medicine, and Al Khorezm, the founder of algebra.

When the capital was moved from Samarkand to Bukhara in the sixteenth century, the Registan fell into disuse. During the first four decades of the seventeenth century, all its buildings, except the madrassa, were dismantled by the governor of Samarkand, Alchin Yalangtush Bahadur. Then, between 1645 and 1660, he built the Sherdar Madrassa and the Tilla-Kari Madrassa, which have remained intact ever since.

In this grand complex—full of abstract patterns, Arabesque lettering, and floral designs—visitors suddenly discover two drawings which stand out. At the top of the tympanums is a lion under a rising sun, sketched as the face of a plump, beneficent god in the image of the Buddha, with the sun related to the fire-worshipping Zoroastrians. Buddhism and Zoroastrianism were the two dominant religions along the Silk Road in ancient times. Those familiar with Islam find it jarring: Islam forbids representation of living beings. Although the drawing, captioned "Sher-wa-Khurshid" ("Lion and Sun," in Persian), was the emblem of Timur Beg and his successors, it came into existence during the Achaemenian era as a cylinder seal. Since the medieval times it has been adopted by many other ruling dynasties, including the Mughals in India and the Pahlavis in Iran.

On a more mundane level, Samarkand offers a winery—but that, too, comes with a historical allusion. It was in Samarkand that, having resisted the temptation to drink wine since the age of eleven, Prince Babur drank his first cup after he had captured the famed capital of Timur Beg (his great-great-great-grandfather), the second time at the age of twenty-nine.[92] In 1497, Babur wrote in his journal, "Grapes, melons, apples and pomegranates, all fruits indeed, are good in Samarkand. Two are famous, its apple and its grape called shahibi."[93]

The legend has it that when the Arab invaders attacked Samarkand and the countryside in the seventh century, trampling upon blossoming gardens, a magic vine with mysterious berries appeared, and the locals called it "Taifi," meaning "tribe." Since then, these pink, juicy grapes have proved to be an elixir for the people. These are the grapes which attracted an enterprising Russian, Dmitriy Filatov, who set up a winery selling "Samarkand wine of Filatov's gardens," which won several gold and silver awards. But it was only when Russian scientist, winemaker, and chemist Mikhail Khovrenko arrived in Uzbekistan in 1927 and designed modern methods of producing such vintage wines as Gulyakandoz, Shirin, Liquor Kaberne, Aleatiko, Uzbekistan, and Farkhod that the Filatov's business took off. This led to a winery library in Samarkand as well as the Museum of History of the Winery. Babur would have certainly approved.

Stressing these historical facts, Tajiks argued that Samarkand and Bukhara be included into the Tajikistan Soviet Socialist Republic when it was established in 1929. When this did not happen, relations between them and ethnic Uzbeks became strained. Six decades later, when the Soviet Union began to crack, the long-simmering tension between the two communities briefly boiled over into violence in Samarkand.

The 1989 census figures of about 100,000 Tajiks and 140,000 Uzbeks lacked credibility. Many Tajiks, conscious of their domicile in Uzbekistan, voluntarily registered themselves as Uzbeks to avoid any discrimination. With political liberalization, this attitude changed. Conscious of their historic dominance in Samarkand and Bukhara, Tajiks in these cities began to assert themselves and demanded incorporation into Tajikistan. When it received short shrift from Moscow—wary of opening a Pandora's box of claims and counterclaims in other constituent republics of the Soviet Union—some of them formed the Tajik Liberation Front in Samarkand. In the post-independence era, relations between the two communities were marred by ill will.

In early 2003, Tajiks found it particularly galling to see the rector of the University of Samarkand, an eminent Tajik figure, dismissed. When the students and staff staged a protest demonstration, many teachers and the parents of student leaders lost their government jobs. Among the active protestors was Jamal Mirsaidov, retired professor of Tajik literature at Samarkand University, who was a dissident during the Soviet era. In the changed environment, he was in touch with a new band of dissidents. During the visit of Ambassador Murray along with his superior from London, Simon Butt, to Samarkand in late March, Mirsaidov arranged a meeting of ten prominent Tajiks at his home. They briefed the British diplomats on the sorry state of the Tajik minority in Samarkand and elsewhere.

After their departure early in the evening, a grandson of the professor, Shukrat, left home at 8 p.m., never to return alive. Early the next morning, the family found his corpse, seemingly dumped from a truck, near its residence. Shukrat's arms and legs were broken, his right hand burnt, and his skull smashed with a fatal blow to the back of his head. Mirsaidov alleged that the secret police had murdered Shukrat in retaliation for the meeting he had organized with the British diplomats.[94] Incredibly, the government claimed that he had died of drug overdose. Shukrat's killing, abhorrent though it was, occurred against the backdrop of a momentous, international event: the Anglo-American invasion of Iraq.

KARIMOV'S DREAM SHATTERED

The Bush administration began beating war drums in early 2003, alleging that Iraqi president Saddam Hussein was engaged in producing weapons of mass destruction (WMDs), and that his links with Al Qaeda made it likely that such weapons would pass into the hands of Islamist terrorists, thus posing an imminent threat to America. In Bush's presentation of such an apocalyptic scenario, Karimov saw a further opportunity to ingratiate himself with Washington.

"We unambiguously support the position of the United States to resolve the Iraqi problem," he said on March 26. "If this genie is let out of the bottle, it won't be possible to put it back. It's necessary to take the most coordinated measures to make sure that the genie isn't out of the bottle. . . . I believe the U.S. has grounds for the stance it has assumed, and therefore radical measures need to be taken."[95]

Yet Karimov refrained from dispatching Uzbek soldiers to join the Anglo-American armies to invade Iraq on March 20. He was keenly aware that Putin opposed the Pentagon-led military campaign, a weighty factor he could not ignore. Then again, despite the full-throated support that the respective prime ministers of Spain and Italy, José Maria Aznar and Silvio Berlusconi, gave Bush, they did not dispatch their troops to the front lines either.

While the world watched the advance of the Anglo-American forces into Iraq, the toppling of Saddam's statue in Baghdad, and waited for the much-touted WMDs to turn up, the Uzbek media focused on the government's frantic preparations to host the annual general meeting of the London-based European Bank for Reconstruction and Development (EBRD) in Tashkent. The EBRD, captitalized by European nations as an intergovern-mental institution, lent funds to banks in former Soviet states for them to lend money to deserving small and medium enterprises (SMEs) to ease the transition of ex-Communist states to democracy and capitalism. Its direc-tors included Rustam Azimov, the Uzbek minister of economic affairs. Tashkent had emerged as the choice for the EBRD's annual general meeting some years earlier when a quicker transition to a market economy in Uzbekistan seemed likely.

Karimov saw a golden opportunity for Uzbekistan to gain a high profile on the world stage. Four new five-star hotels—Intercontinental, Meridien, Radisson, and Sheraton—sprang up. Half a dozen existing hotels under-went expensive refurbishing. The local muncipality erected fake shop fronts to conceal vacant properties and prettified the old Soviet-era concrete struc-tures by fronting them with Meccano-style frameworks and covering them with blue glass.

For the benefit of visiting EBRD delegates, the bazaars aquired the aura of vast movie sets, with fully stocked shops and stallholders wearing freshly laundered green gowns and surgical caps (never before seen in Central Asian bazaars), who were ordered to sell goods at a fraction of the actual price to those who appeared foreign. The generosity of the authori-ties would last only until the end of the EBRD gathering on May 5.

The EBRD headquarters had insisted that the inaugural session be held in the spacious Hall of the People's Friendship and aired live on all main Uzbek TV and radio channels. It would later appoint its own translators for the occasion. The session opened on May 4, with Karmiov sitting at the center of the top table, flanked by the presidents of Kazakhstan and Georgia on one side, and those of Kyrgyzstan and Tajikistan on the other. He expected to bask as a revered host of international stature. Instead, he heard Clare Short, British secretary of state for Overseas Development, and Jean Lemierre, French president of the EBRD, criticize his government on its economic strategy and its failure to ensure progress towards democracy and human rights.

"Clare Short's points were piled up relentlessly," noted Craig Murray. "Lemierre was sharp and expressive, his tone heavy with Gallic contempt. Karimov first went ashen-faced. Then he ostentatiously removed his earphone and tossed it away. Then he placed his head in his hands, covering his ears before slowly moving his hands round to close his eyes, then allowing his head to slump forward until it almost rested on the table. He remained in that extraordinary posture for ten minutes... All this was captured on Uzbek TV—and captured so well that the producer and director were sacked as soon as the conference delegates had left."[96] Thanks to the full-blast advance publicity by the state-run media, the TV audience for the inaugural session hit a record high.

What Karimov had envisioned as his moment of international glory turned out to be an instance of absymal humiliation in full view of the people he had governed for nearly fifteen years. The experience scarred him, and proved to be a turning point in his policies. Despite pleas from Washington to participate in normalizing the post-invasion situation in Iraq, Karimov did not contribute any peacekeeping troops. He started distancing himself from the Western nations, and turned more towards Russia and China.

He attended the summit of the Shanghai Cooperation Organization, where Uzbekistan's earlier observer status had been raised to full membership. The leaders adopted a new charter, which was not released immediately. Its later publication showed that it pledged "non-interference and non-alignment" in international affairs while aiming to create "a new international political and economic order"—implying thereby to end the role of the United States as the sole superpower.[97] To Karimov's delight, the summit also decided to move the SCO anti-terrorist center from Bishkek to Tashkent.

STRONGMAN STRIKES BACK

The first public sign of the shift in Uzbek foreign policy came in August 2003. Following his meeting with Putin in Moscow to strengthen commercial ties, Karimov described Russia as "a priority partner" in economic projects. As it was, Uzbekistan was the major source of cotton for Russia's textile factories. This was set to last as long as the state trading company in Uzbekistan had the monopoly in buying and selling cotton. It paid the Uzbek producers less than a quarter of the international market price of $1,500 per ton while ensuring to export four-fifths of the national output of 4 million tons of raw cotton ginned to 1.25 million tons of finished cotton. Due to the deteriorating maintenance of the vast national network of water drainage and irrigation—down from $120 a hectare during the Soviet era to $12—and the rising salinity of the land, output had declined from 4.5 tons of raw cotton per hectare during the Soviet era to 2.5 tons.[98]

Three months later, the Russian foreign ministry accredited Karimov's favorite daughter, Gulnara, as a counselor at the Uzbek embassy in Moscow. During his next meeting with Putin in June 2004, Karimov agreed to hold joint Uzbek-Russian special forces war games in the Uzbek mountains the following year.

While distancing himself from Western powers, Karimov stuck to his program of advancing his model of democracy—at his own pace. Noticing the absence of a center-right faction to balance the left-of-center People's Democratic Party, Karimov encouraged the founding of the Liberal Democratic Party (*Liberal Demokratik Partiyasi*). Standing solidly for private enterprise and initiative, market economy, and rule of law, the party attracted young, forward-looking Uzbeks whose outlook was modern and technocratic rather than traditional and ideological. Claiming an impressive membership of 141,818, it gained official registration in November 2003, a year before the next parliamentary poll. Earlier, Karimov had allowed the Erk party to hold a convention, followed by a meeting of its executive committee in January 2004. He also permitted the Independent Farmers Party (*Azad Dekhkanlar Partiyasi*) to hold its founding meeting in Tashkent.

Washington was unimpressed. In late 2003, the State Department said that the Karimov regime had failed to advance toward international standards on human rights and free access to information. It apparently chose to ignore the fact that Internet cafés had sprung up in all urban centers, albeit with access to "undesirable" websites blocked. Also, a substantial minority of homes in the capital had gained access to the satellite televison channels in Russian, Turkish, and English.[99]

On the other hand, military ties remained strong. During his visit to Tashkent in February 2004, Rumsfeld held talks with Karimov on making the K2 a permanent American base. At a press conference he described Uzbekistan as "a key member of the coalition's Global War on Terror," and expressed U.S. appreciation for its support in the "war on terror."[100] According to the report published by the *New York Times* in April, Tashkent's support involved cooperating with the United States as it sent "terror suspects to Uzbekistan for detention and interrogation" as part of the government's rendition program. However, a string of suicide bombs in Tashkent in late March compelled even the State Department to change its tone.

BOMBS LITE AND PARLIAMENTARY POLL

On March 29, 2004, between 8:20 and 9:30 a.m., while a suicide bomber successfully targeted a police facility in Tashkent, killing six officers, the authorities thwarted two other such attempts, with one aimed at the president's residence. The Uzbek government immediately claimed that the explosions were part of an insurrection planned by the Islamic Movement of Uzbekistan in alliance with Al Qaeda.

Accepting this account, U.S. Secretary of State Colin Powell telephoned his Uzbek counterpart, Sadik Safayev, offering American help to "contain the insurgency."

After visiting the sites of the explosions, however, British Ambassador Murray disputed the Uzbek version, and provided backup evidence for an alternative description of the episode to his government. Having examined evidence from varied sources, the Joint Terrorism Analysis Center in London concluded that the claims of IMU, Hizb ut-Tahrir, or Al Qaeda involvement could not be substantiated.[101]

Murray summarized his findings as follows: On the evening of March 28, when a middle-aged stallholder in Tashkent's Chorzu bazaar refusal to go to the police station to have his identity papers checked, he was beaten to death by policemen before a crowd. Later, unknown gunmen shot dead two police officers at separate checkpoints. The following morning, when policemen of the Chorzu district were gathered for the change of shift, an explosion allegedly killed half a dozen of them as well as an unknown female bomber. (Murray noticed no blast damage to windows, ground, or vegetation at the bomb site.) About an hour later, a young woman dashed out from the street beside the Children's World store, and ran between two buses. Shot by two cops, she collapsed to her knees, and a detonation occurred. It could not be determined whether she triggered a suicide bomb or bullets hit a hand grenade she was carrying. Just then, a driver failed to stop at a police checkpoint on the road going past the president's residence in the Durmen neighborhood. When the police opened machine-gun fire, the vehicle went up in flames. If it was a car bomb, it left no crater.[102]

The armed police raids that followed over the next two days in Tashkent claimed thirteen lives. The police arrested thousands. They resorted to harassing the affluent, extorting lucrative bribes to release them. Compared to the string of explosions in February 1999, this episode targeting ordinary policemen was poorly planned and executed. In contrast to the public outrage at the earlier bombings, the reaction of ordinary people—as far as it could be assessed from off-the-cuff remarks noted by a daring journalist—was muted. According to Bagila Bukharbayeva's Associated Press report, many Uzbeks showed an understanding, even sympathy, for those who felt alienated enough to kill themselves to express their hatred of an oppressive regime.[103]

Foreign powers reacted differently. After Karimov had hosted the annual Shanghai Cooperation Organizatoin summit in Tashkent in June, he and visiting Chinese President Hu Jintao issued a joint statement condemning "terrorism, separatism, and extremism" and agreed to further strengthen coordination and cooperation among relevant agencies of both countries.

As summer approached, attention turned to the parliamentary poll due in December. Mediation by a young American from the Washington-based International Republican Institute had led the divided opposition groups to consider forming a united front. In July, sixty delegates of the Erk, Birlik, Independent Farmers, and the Farmers and Entrepreneurs parties, as well as many NGOs, met in the large courtyard of a house in Kokand in the Fergana Valley. The presiding politician was Ismail Dadjanov, vice chairman of Birlik, conspicious by his clawed hands—the result of his attempt to save his wife and children from his house when it was set alight by unknown persons some years earlier.

After many speeches, including one by Ambassador Murray, the delegates signed the founding document of the Democratic Forum, pledging their parties to strive to achieve true freedom and democracy. But none of the attending organizations secured the official registration required to contest the upcoming poll. The government's motive for permitting the opposition's assembly was to improve the monitoring skills of its intelligence services. As for the recognized parties, though the election campaign officially began at the end of September for the general election on December 26, 2004, and January 9, 2005, potential voters had no information on the candidates or their platforms, or even how the new bicameral body would operate, according to Holly Cartner, executive director of the Europe and Central Asia division of Human Rights Watch.

All such parties expressed their loyalty to Karimov. Unexpectedly, the upstart Liberal Democratic Party won the highest percentage of the vote with 34 percent and 41 seats—well ahead of the longest established People's Democratic Party vote of 23 percent and 28 seats. Fidokorlar National Democratic won 18 percent, Milli Tiklanish National Renaissance Democratic 11 percent, and Adalat Social Democratic 10 percent.

While the participation of several parties in the elections seemed to indicate an evolving multi-party system, power remained concentrated in the political elite with Karimov at the apex. Inevitably, such a system could not keep running smoothly. Some internal cracks within the elite, stemming from personal jealousies and rivalries over how to distribute the material gains of political power, were bound to appear. Indeed, intense infighting within the regional government of Andijan in the Fergana Valley had started in the spring of 2004 and showed no sign of letting up.

THE ANDIJAN MASSACRE, A TURNING POINT

Encouraged by Karimov, the regional assembly of Andijan impeached Governor Kabiljan Ubidov in May 2004 for his involvement in several political-commercial scams, and replaced him with Saidulla Begaliyev, former minister of agriculture in Tashkent. Misusing the decree of 2002, which made a company changing its main line of activity since privatization liable to renationalization, Ubidov had done favors for his cronies and given them priority in opening new lucrative businesses.

In June, Begaliyev ordered the arrest of twenty-three businessmen who had thrived under Ubidov. To their horror, the detainees found themselves charged with membership of Akramiya, which was listed as a terrorist organization. It was named after Akram Yuldashev, a native of the Fergana Valley, who allegedly broke away from Hizb ut-Tahrir in 1996, arguing that establishing a pan-national caliphate was unrealistic and that the ultimate aim should be to set up an Islamic state locally.

As the trial of the businessmen neared its end in early May 2005, their relatives and friends started gathering outside the court. On May 11, nearly 4,000 demonstrators assembled to hear the verdict. The judge deferred the sentencing. The next day, the police arrested the ringleaders of the demonstration. On the night of May 12, a posse of armed men raided the jail where the accused were held. They killed several guards and released the businessmen as well as hundreds of other inmates. They seized the regional administrative office where they held hostage twenty government officials and called on Karimov to resign.

At daylight on May 13, thousands of people assembled in the central square (named after Mughal Emperor Babur, who was born in Andijan) to hear the articulate among them voice their rage at the deepening poverty and rising administrative and business corruption. The speakers knew first-hand why their country ranked 137th out of 159 countries on the Corruption Perceptions Index. The crowd remained in Babur Square even after some 12,000 troops from the military, the Interior Ministry, and the SNB had arrived by armored personnel carriers to close the passages to the prison and exchanged gunfire with some armed civilians. A rumor went around that Karimov would arrive to address the gathering, but by the end of the day there was still no sign of the Uzbek president. Instead, after closing off the exits from the square, troops fired live amunition from automatic rifles on unarmed civilians. According to some reports, soldiers killed at close range those who were injured in the intial shootings.

As a witness to "a mass of dead and wounded," Galima Bukharbayeva of the Institute of Peace and War Reporting said, "At first, one group of armored personnel carriers approached the [Babur] square, and then another group appeared. They opened fire without mercy on everyone indiscriminately, including women and children. The crowd began to run in all directions. We dived into a ditch and lay there for a while. I saw at least five bloody corpses next to me. The rebels who were holding the provincial administration [office] opened fire in response. They intended to stand to the end! When we got out of the ditch, we ran along the streets into the neighborhood. Then we looked for a place where there was no shooting. But shots could be heard everywhere."[104] Andijan's local radio station went off the air, and the authorities blocked all foreign TV channels.

The government claimed that the victims were all terrorists. The state-run Uzbek TV reported that "an armed group of criminals" had assaulted the security forces in Andijan, and that "the bandits seized dozens of weapons and moved on to attack a correctional colony, setting some convincts free." Karimov attributed the disturbance to "Islamic extremist groups." The estimated death toll varied between 187 (the official figure) and 400 to 600. The government removed corpses by air, with eighteen flights taking off from the Andijan airport on May 14. Scores of dead bodies were later located by gravediggers.

Thousands of people fled to neighboring Kyrgyzstan. In the frontier town of Qarasuv, they set alight police stations and cars, and then attacked the border guards. Army troops besieged the town. The Kyrgyz guards pushed back the refugees. In the Pakhatabad region, clashes between the soldiers and those attempting to cross the international border reportedly left 200 Uzbeks dead.

In its report, summarizing the testimonies of fifty victims and eyewitnesses, the New York-based Human Rights Watch concluded that the extensive and unjustified killing of unarmed civilians by the government troops amounted to a massacre. The NGOs and news organizations that reported the events objectively, or protested the excessive state violence, received orders to leave. They included the BBC World Service, Eurasia Foundation, Freedom House, Radio Free Europe/Radio Liberty, and the Uzbek branch of the UN High Commission for Refugees.

Though the Bush administration called for an international investigation into the episode, there were reports of a clash between the State and Defense departments, with the former advocating severing all links with Tashkent, and the latter arguing that the administration should examine separately each of the several programs funded by it before making a decision. Rumsfeld was keen to keep the U.S. troops and warplanes at the Karshi Khanabad base, but Karimov—angered by the vocal criticism by the American media, politicians, and NGOs—gave the Pentagon six months to quit the base. It did so in November 2005, marking the end of nearly a decade and a half of flirtation between Tashkent and Washington.

The demand for an international inquiry did not get far because Moscow and Beijing opposed it. The Shanghai Cooperaton Organization, to which both Russia and China belonged, accepted the official version of the events in Andijan and described them as "a terrorist plot." Indeed, the SCO called on other nations to deny asylum to the thousands of Uzbek refugees in Kyrgyzstan, who were being compelled to leave.

During his visit to Beijing in July 2006, the Chinese government greeted Karimov with a twenty-one-gun salute. He departed with a $600 million joint venture for oil.[105] In October, the European Union banned military sales to Uzbekistan, imposed sanctions, and put twelve top officials on the black list, denying them visas. Yet Karimov allowed Germany to keep a military base at Termez, and the German government allowed the Uzbek police chief into the country for medical treatment. At its behest, the EU removed four of the twelve names from the visa black list in May 2007.[106] Germany was keen to see that the EU did not antagonize irredeemably a country which possessed much-needed natural gas.

European energy corporations noted with envy Russia's Lukoil inauguration of the Khauzak gas field in Uzbekistan, with reserves of 400 billion cubic meters, amidst much fanfare on the eve of the presidential poll in December. Lukoil had sold the reserves in advance to Gazprom until 2040 when the prices of oil and natural gas had risen sharply.[107]

KARIMOV WANGLES A THIRD TERM

To project a different image, Karimov allowed the Liberal Democratic Party to nominate him as its presidential candidate. His critics pointed out that since Karimov had served two consecutive terms as president, he was constitutionally barred from contesting the poll due on December 23, 2007.[108] His supporters argued that Karimov's term of office had to be seen in the context of the amended constitution, which came into force in 2002.

As usual, there was a choice of candidates—in theory. In practice, they all praised Karimov, and failed to gain access to the media. Genuine opposition groups such as Birlik and Erk were barred from contesting. "Uzbekistan is like the Soviet Union, but the wrong way round," said Nigara Khidovatova, leader of the Independent Farmers Party. "Everything bad about the Soviet Union we still have. But everything that was good— like its welfare and education system—has disappeared."[109]

The election result was a foregone conclusion. Karimov won 91 percent of the vote, with the rest garnered by three nominal rivals. The only novelty about this poll was that a woman, Dilorom Toshmuhamedova, contested as the candidate of the Adalat Social Democratic Party. After being sworn in as president on January 16, 2008, Karimov promised to do his best to implement the goals set out in his election manifesto. These centered mainly on improving the economy, which now depended substantially on the remittances of nearly 1.5 million Uzbeks working abroad, chiefly in Kazakhstan and Russia.

The sharp rise in the prices of hydrocarbons and commodities in the early months of 2008 was welcome news for the Uzbek government. As an exporter of gold, Uzbekistan was set to improve its foreign earnings as the gold price exceeded $1,000 an ounce in mid-March. With cotton futures for March 2008 delivery rising to 64.55 U.S. cents at the Intercontinental Exchange in Atlanta, Uzbekistan stood to shore up its foreign reserves. With three-fifths of its raw cotton output of 3.63 million metric tons in 2007 being shipped abroad, it remained the second largest cotton exporter in the world.

CHAPTER 3

TURKMENISTAN:
MOLDED BY A MEGALOMANIAC DESPOT

C OTTON WAS VERY MUCH ON THE MIND OF NIKITA KHRUSHCHEV IN 1954 when he focused on raising the output of agricultural produce in the Soviet Union. This, and the general principle of division of labor among the union's constituents, intensified the effort to turn Turkmenistan into a cotton-producing republic.

As elsewhere in Central Asia, achieving this goal involved giving preference to suitably qualified ethnic Russians, born locally or brought in from Russia, for top jobs—a policy contested by Suhan Babayev, first secretary of the Communist Party of Turkmenistan (CPTu). He said that the Russians, forming only one-sixth of the republic's population, had a disproportionate share of senior positions. Soviet leaders in Moscow responded by replacing him with Balish Ovezov in 1959.

Since nearly 80 percent of Turkmenistan is part of the Kara Kum Desert, and cotton crops require a reliable source of water, something innovative had to be done. Out of this arose the idea of constructing, in stages, a tributary of the Oxus River (aka Amu Darya) flowing into the Aral Sea, to be named after Lenin and Kara Kum (Black Sand), the world's fourth largest desert.

Work on the Lenin Kara Kum Canal commenced in 1954 from the Oxus River end. By 1962, it was 850 kilometers (530 miles) long and reached the capital, Ashgabat (then spelled "Ashkhabad"), providing irrigation to an area extending fifteen to twenty kilometers (nine to thirteen miles) from each of its banks, and most of the drinking water to the capital. Since most of the canal was uncovered and unlined, it lost almost half of its water in transition. Yet its construction led to 62 percent growth in sown acreage, most of it for cotton. The rise in acreage and productivity, resulting in a 10 percent annual increase in agricultural produce from 1960 to 1965, was maintained during the following decade. Between 1940 and 1970, cotton output shot up from 211,000 to 920,000 tons.[1]

The early 1960s also witnessed the commercial extraction of natural gas. By 1971, the annual production in Turkmenistan rose to 17 billion cubic meters, with some of the exports being pumped to Western Europe. Oil output was up too, running at 310,000 barrels per day (bpd), the third highest in the Soviet Union, after Russia and Azerbaijan. In that year, Muhammad Nazar Gapusov (originally, Hafiz) became first secretary of the CPTu, whose membership had risen from 40,000 to about 66,000 within a decade.[2]

Like his fellow leaders in Central Asia, Gapusov tried to ingratiate himself with Leonid Brezhnev, first secretary of the Communist Party of the Soviet Union, by exceeding the economic targets set for his republic, especially in cotton. By the early 1980s, Turkmenistan's cotton output reached 1.4 million tons, second only to Uzbekistan's. As in Uzbekistan, there was some corrupt padding of production figures, but not to the same extent. However, that did not deter Mikhail Gorbachev from highlighting the issue when, in 1985, at his instigation, Gapusov was replaced by Saparmurat Atayevich Niyazov (1940–2006), who had been the first secretary of the Ashgabat City Communist Party since 1980. This deprived Gapusov of the ability to claim oversight of the extension of the Lenin Kara Kum Canal from Ashgabat to Krasnovodsk (later Turkmenbashi) in 1986, most of its new length being an enclosed aqueduct. Niyazov ended up celebrating the completion of the world's longest waterway.

Gorbachev wanted to stress that a new corruption-free era had begun. Following Gapusov's removal from the top party position, an inquiry into corrupt practices was instituted. Its report concluded that, during his leadership, party cadres were often promoted to important posts based on "personal loyalty, family ties or birth place."[3]

In the vital sector of cotton, there were other malpractices besides the doctoring of crop figures. Since cotton harvesting is labor-intensive, and the supply of mechanical harvesters was limited, directors of collective and state farms increasingly resorted to using child labor. The practice had become so entrenched that Gapusov's removal made little difference. A study in 1988 showed that rural children spent fifty-six to sixty-eight school days a year working in the fields.[4] As a former teacher in the provincial town of Merv (aka Mari; a six-hour train journey from Ashgabat), Akmurad Bahramovich Musayev, my translator in the post-Soviet era, was a witness to this practice.

FLAWS AND ACHIEVEMENTS

Such social malpractices aside, overall socio-economic progress under Gapusov was impressive, largely because of the sharp rise in gas output, which soared to 72 billion cubic meters in 1985, and which boosted the contribution of industry to the annual GDP to 47 percent—more than twice that of agriculture.

The universal literacy achieved in 1970 (from a base of 2.3 percent in 1926) had gone in tandem with the emancipation of women. Of the fourteen members of the Presidium of the Supreme Soviet, which passed laws between parliamentary sessions, five were women. Overall, women provided 45 percent of the membership of local soviets, and 42 percent of the workforce.[5] A case in point was Kumush Narziyeva, who worked as a trained accountant. Like all Turkmen women, she wore long velvet tunics of blue, brown, and red that extended to her feet, a jacket, and a flowered silk scarf over her glistening, black pigtails. Due to the housing shortage in the capital, she and her four children stayed in Merv—once the northeastern outpost of the Sassanian Empire, which became the eastern capital of the Abbasid Empire, only to be razed by the Mongol marauders. Under the Russians, its status did not rise above a garrison town.

An unveiled, emancipated woman, Kumush acquired a husband named Akmurad Musayev, a sturdy, muscular man of average height with large, expressive eyes and a well-formed mouth. He recalled the ecstatic moment in 1968 when Merv received the news that the Soviet engineers had struck natural gas at the nearby Shatlik site, which boosted his optimism in the Soviet educational system and reinforced his belief that socialism was creating the New Soviet Man. Musayev considered himself to be one, having served in the Red Army as a conscript. It was in the military that he learned how to gulp down several drinks of vodka in the traditional Soviet military style, which he demonstrated with flair. "The arm should be stiffened, with the elbow raised to the height of the mouth, so that the forearm becomes horizontal," Musayev explained, holding a vodka glass in his hand at Ashgabat Hotel. "Then turn your wrist, keeping the arm steady, to tip the drink into your mouth."

"I was posted in Hungary from 1973 to 1975 when the Soviet Union was a superpower," he continued. After the army, he enrolled at Ashgabat University, and majored in English in 1980, when he was twenty-six. Then he taught English at a school in Merv. Just as the Soviet Union started cracking up in 1991, the foreign ministry in Ashgabat sent word around encouraging English-language graduates to apply for jobs at the ministry. Musayev applied, and became a second secretary. After independence, his section in the ministry—consisting of one first secretary, four second secretaries, and four attachés—dealt with Asia. It was overseen by First Deputy Foreign Minister Boris Shikhmuradov, who would later become foreign minister and right-hand man of Niyazov from 1995 to 2000, and then turn against the president.

As elsewhere in Central Asia, knowledge of English suddenly became a valuable asset in the aftermath of the Soviet breakup. Even though Musayev's English was far from perfect ("We go by walk"; "Soup is absent"; "Much people were repressed during Stalin's days"), his services as a translator for visiting foreign journalists and writers, in exchange for much-coveted U.S. dollars, were in great demand. So he went to his office, signed the register, and moonlighted.

Musayev's grandfather, Musa Hakimov, was a cattle farmer. Sometime from 1937 to 1938, at the peak of Stalin's terror, thirty-five-year-old Musa was picked up by the secret police (because he was considered a "kulak"), never to be seen again. His stricken wife died two years later. "If two people said you were a spy, that was enough for you to be banished to Siberia," Musayev said. "People were afraid." At that time, Musayev's father was twelve, and his two sisters, eight and four. With both their parents dead, they were sent to an orphanage. "To this day we don't know where my grandfather was sent and when he died. This is a big hole in the family history. A year ago, they said that archives of such people were to be opened. My grandfather was a good man though he was not a member of the Communist Party," Musayev explained with sadness.

Musayev was honest enough to admit that though he taught English for many years, he did not practice it much himself. "We were told that the BBC was full of propaganda so we kept away from it," he recalled. "At the university we got Germans from GDR [German Democratic Republic] to visit us, and students practiced their German with them. But there were no British Communists arriving to converse with us." He added, "Sitting in this grand hotel's dining hall and talking to you in English, and overhearing Americans speaking English, such a scene was unthinkable—until a year ago." Then he downed another shot of vodka, in the Soviet military style. "I still don't believe it."

By now, Musayev was sufficiently inebriated to tell me something he would not have divulged in normal circumstances: the name of his tribe, Tekke.[6] Decades of Marxism-Leninism had muted, though not eradicated, the importance of tribalism, which had been the root cause of continual war-fare between the leading tribes—Tekke in the Ashgabat region, Yomut in the northern and western regions of the republic, Salori in the southeast, Sariki in the south, and Ersari in the east.[7] Each of the five major tribes had its own exclusive motif for the world-famous, handmade Turkmen carpets. These motifs now appear in a vertical strip on the hoist side of the national flag of independent Turkmenistan representing the republic's carpet heritage, which dates back to antiquity. Little wonder that the Turkmen National Carpet Museum in Ashgabat displays over 1,000 carpets and carpet products.

The Pazirik rug found in the Altai Mountains excavations of the fourth century BC is related to present-day Turkman carpets. In his travel account in the thirteenth century, Marco Polo noted that "the finest and the most beautiful carpets are made here [in the Turkmen region] and rich fabric of red and other colors are woven here."[8] A welcome contrast to the gray and sandy colors of the Kara Kum desert, the colorful Turkmen carpets, with their astonishing range of reds and other colors, became prized possessions during the Renaissance. Combining splendid designs and fine material, they represented the culmination of numerous generations of especially skilled, imaginative weavers. Along with an array of countless geometric patterns, their rhythmic carpet designs and composition reflected the flora and fauna around them—bushes, flowers, vegetation, irrigated fields, and animals—while refraining from representations of humans, as forbidden by the Quran.

The Turkmen and other nomadic and semi-nomadic peoples used carpets and carpet products in a variety of ways, including as rugs, wall decora-tions, doorways, and saddlebags. Turkmen women labored hard at the handloom to produce these long-lasting, valuable objects. "It is only when you have seen a Turkmen woman at her loom, watched her quick hands fly-ing like birds over the weaving of her carpet, witnessed the perseverance and energy she brings to her work and the dynamic strength of the whole process, only then can you understand how superb a worker the Turkmen carpet maker is—the uncrowned queen of Turkmen folk arts," noted V.G. Moshkova, a Russian anthropologist.[9] An unmarried young woman proved her worth by displaying how well she wove a carpet, much as a young man of the tribe showed off his riding skills.

While such social mores were of deep interest to Russian anthropologists like Moshkova, the Russian generals encouraged and accentuated the differ-ences between tribal identities in order to consolidate their control over the region. However, that changed with the 1917 Bolshevik Revolution, when Communists tried to detribalize Turkmen society. They also succeeded in almost completely eliminating the hold of Islam. Whereas in 1911 there were 481 mosques in Turkmenistan, relentless anti-religious propaganda and action reduced the number to 5 by 1941. The single mosque in Ashgabat was destroyed in the earthquake of October 6, 1948, and never rebuilt.

"The earthquake was really terrible, force 9 on the Richter scale," Musayev told me. "It killed 110,000 people. All the buildings fell to the ground. But not the monument to [Alexander] Pushkin and the statue of Lenin standing on a strong platform of stone and concrete."[10] We were standing in front of the statue of Lenin, built in 1927, with his trademark declamatory arm stabbing the air, at the center of a sprawling park. Lenin stood atop three receding plinths, each one carrying the dazzling motifs of the Turkmen carpets, inscribed with Lenin's promise of liberation to "the Peoples of the East."[11]

The destruction of Ashgabat in 1948 provided the central planners in Moscow an opportunity to rebuild the capital with a grid layout of bland avenues and streets, wide roads lined with trees, and vast parks sprinkled with the personalities of the past. Among the new statues that went up was one of Ali Sher Navai, an eminent Turkish-language poet. The Moscow planners would repeat the model in Tashkent on a larger scale after the earthquake of 1966.

In February 1979, there was another type of earthquake in the region: an Islamic revolution in Iran, which shared a border 1,500 kilometers (940 miles) long with Turkmenistan. Soon after, Radio Gorgan, operating 240 kilometers (150 miles) from Ashgabat, began beaming Islamic programs in Turkmen, and gradually built up an audience in the republic of 2.75 million people, 85 percent of whom had a Muslim background.

But it was not until several years later that the signs of rising interest in Islam became discernible. In 1986, due to the efforts of a young registered cleric, Annamuhammad Annaberdi, the historic Taltahana Baba mosque was renovated. Then, during the winter of 1987, clandestine Islamic activity came to light when the authorities uncovered two underground Islamic cells operating in Charju and Ashgabat—a city of some 450,000, three-quarters of whom bore Muslim names, but still lacked a mosque. Only in 1988 was a new mosque opened there.

NIYAZOV AT THE HELM

By then, Saparmurat Niyazov had consolidated his power base. He was born in 1940 in the household of Ataye Niyazov, a farm worker, and his wife Gurban Sultan Eje, in Gipjak, a village ten kilometers (six miles) from Ashgabat. Two years later, his father, who had been drafted into the army during the Great Patriotic War, died in combat. The family moved to the capital. His mother and two brothers perished in the earthquake of 1948, but he survived and grew up in an orphanage until the government found a distant relative who agreed to look after him.

A bright student, Niyazov became a power engineering graduate of St. Petersburg (then Leningrad) Polytechnical Institute in 1966, and worked at a generating station near Ashgabat. He joined the Communist Party in 1962, and married Muza Sokolova, a Russian with a Jewish background. His steady climb up the party's hierarchical ladder won him membership of the CPSU's Central Committee. In the mid-1970s, he received his political-ideological education at the Senior Party School of the Central Committee in Moscow. The fact that Niyazov belonged to the largest tribe, Tekke—estimated to claim the loyalties of two-fifths of Turkmens—helped him rise to the top, though not overtly.

However, he was unable to reverse the economic downturn. The basic problem was that in the Soviet Union's centralized economy Turkmenistan's natural gas was being sold to other republics at five kopeks (or three U.S. cents) a cubic meter, a paltry sum, especially by comparison to the price in the international market. There was therefore no improvement in the living standards of Turkmens. Half of the peasant households and two-fifths of the industrial worker households lived below the official poverty line. The annual subsidy of nearly R2 billion (or U.S. $1.2 billion at the official rate) that Moscow gave to Turkmenistan would have been unnecessary had the republic been paid a realistic price, if not the international one, for its gas. In agriculture, cotton output had fallen by 12 percent between 1980 and 1985, mainly due to the overuse of soil and chemical fertilizers. The modest growth in the economy was unable to keep pace with the annual 3.5 percent birthrate.

The disaffection caused by high unemployment among young people escalated into urban rioting in May 1989. But, unlike in other Central Asian republics, the disparate opposition forces failed to transform themselves into political groups. The republic's KGB (later renamed KNB, *Komitet Natsionalnoy Bezopasnosti*, Committee for National Security) was much too powerful, and Niyazov far too authoritarian to brook any opposition, however muted.

After the March 1990 elections to the 339-member Supreme Soviet, heavily dominated by the Communist Party, Niyazov became chairman of the

Supreme Soviet's Presidium. On August 22, following the example of the Russian Supreme Soviet, the Turkmen parliament declared its sovereignty, thus placing its laws above the Soviet Union's. Later, it took a lead in creating the new post of the directly elected executive president of the republic. Its example was followed by the Russian parliament, which resulted in the June 1991 election of Boris Yeltsin as president in a multi-candidate contest. His prestige as the first popularly elected president of Russia played a key role in frustrating the Communist hardliners' plot, led by Vladimir Kryuchkov, head of the KGB, to overthrow Soviet President Gorbachev two months later.

Niyazov stayed neutral during the coup. A few days after the failure of the coup, at his behest, the Supreme Soviet in Ashgabat declared Turkmenistan an independent sovereign state. This was ratified in a referendum on October 26, which coincided with the election for an executive president.[12] As the only candidate, Niyazov secured 98.3 percent of the vote. His autocratic rule from then until his death fifteen years later would be divided equally in two parts: until 1997, when, unknown to the world at large, he underwent quadruple-bypass heart surgery in Germany (an event treated as state secret in Turkmenistan, which became common knowledge elsewhere by 2003) followed by near-bankruptcy of the state treasury due to the stoppage of natural gas exports; and the post-1997 economic recovery in gas revenue, capped by him being proclaimed president for life.

Within a week of the decision of the Central Asian republics to join the newly formed Commonwealth of Independent States (CIS) on December 13, 1991, the Communist Party of Turkmenistan met to dissolve itself and re-emerged as the Democratic Party of Turkmenistan (DPT), with Niyazov as its chairman. (While his erstwhile Communist colleagues in other Central Asian republics chose to rename the Communist Party as the Socialist Party or the People's Democratic Party, he opted for the Democratic Party.)

Yet there were differences between the two organizations. Whereas the Communist Party was an integral part of the state, formed on the basis of the dictatorship of the proletariat, the Democratic Party was neither the sole functioning party nor was the state now expected to be based on the dictatorship of any class or nationality. With the dissolution of the Communist Party, its members became free to abstain from politics or join the Democratic Party or some other political group. More than half of 119,000 Communist Party members quit politics, so the Democratic Party gained only 50,000 former Communists. The party leaders pledged to work for inter-ethnic harmony, civic peace and stability, and nation-building.

POST-SOVIET TURKMENISTAN

Following the formal dissolution of the Soviet Union on December 31, 1991, President Niyazov decided to focus on developing bilateral relations with ex-Soviet republics and ensuring that the loose association implied in the CIS did not graduate into an active, multilateral relationship.

In February 1992, after listening politely to visiting U.S. Secretary of State James Baker wax eloquent on the evils of Islamic fundamentalism being exported by Tehran,[13] Niyazov let his official spokesman announce that Turkmenistan was ready to sell gas, oil, and electricity to Iran, and proposed a direct telephone connection with it. Work had already begun to link up the two countries by rail.[14] Turkmenistan then joined the Caspian Sea Cooperation Council, an economic organization proposed by Tehran.

As a balancing act, Niyazov cultivated Saudi Arabia, a powerful Islamic state and the custodian of Islam's two holiest shrines in Mecca and Medina, the respective birth- and burial-places of Prophet Muhammad. In April, accompanied by eighteen secular and religious aides, he flew to Saudi Arabia and undertook an umra, a short pilgrimage to Mecca. This paved the way for Turkmenistan's membership of the Jiddah-based Islamic Conference Organization (ICO).

The next month, back in Ashgabat, Niyazov welcomed the Turkish premier Suleiman Demirel, who offered $120 million in credits to Turkmenistan as well as 2,000 university places to Turkmen students. There were strong cultural and linguistic ties between the two countries: Seljuks (aka Oghuzes), who set up an empire in Turkey before the Osmanli Turks, came from Turkmenistan; and, being part of the South Turkic group of languages, Turkmen is nearer to the Turkish of Turkey than, say, Kyrgyz, which belongs to the Central Turkic group.

Niyazov was cautious about introducing economic reform, warning (like President Islam Karimov next-door in Uzbekistan) that speedy liberalization of prices and complete privatization would impoverish many people. He argued that the regime's indifference toward the suffering of a sizeable section of society for the sake of future prosperity smacked too much of the Bolshevik thinking, and proposed introducing a market economy gradually, starting with the privatization of small- and medium-sized enterprises.[15] The ratification of the draft constitution in a referendum on May 18, 1992, strengthened Niyazov's position. "Power is held by the president who is elected by the people," declared the constitution. The word "power" in this case meant absolute power.

Having been the first to create the office of the executive president in the Soviet Union, Turkmenistan now became the first Central Asian state to adopt a new constitution. It named the 2,507-member *Halk Maslahaty* (People's Council) as the highest representative body, partly elected and partly nominated by the president who was its chairman. The appointed members included cabinet ministers, regional, district, and city governors, parliamentary deputies, heads of the supreme and economic courts, as well as "people's representatives." Authorized to adopt constitutional amendments and international treaties, and hold referendums, it would meet only once a year. The legislative powers rested with the popularly elected fifty-member *Majlis* (Assembly) with a five-year tenure.

The Turkmen constitution's provisions would prove to be Orwellian. It guaranteed citizens' rights to private property, as well as freedom of religion with the proviso that "religion should not have influence on the government." Article 26 guaranteed citizens "freedom of expression except on revealing state secrets." But in reality, the broadcasting media was controlled by the government, and the newspapers and periodicals were almost wholly run by different official organizations or the ruling Democratic Party.

Article 28 gave citizens the right to form political parties except "those (a) which aim to change the constitutional system through force, (b) which oppose constitutional rights, (c) which propagate hatred against race, nationality or religious tolerance, or (d) which aim to set up military rule."[16] Yet no opposition group secured official registration. There was a well-known faction, functioning strictly within the constitutional limits: Agiz Birlik (Unity Party), led by Burburdi Nurmuhammadov (originally, Nur Muhammad). The Unity Party was a substantial entity, claiming a membership of 1,500—far above the minimum of 1,000—scattered over the republic, as required by the law on political parties. Originally registered by leading Turkmen intellectuals in Moscow in September 1989, its aim was to create a multi-party system as it existed in Turkey.

After the party was banned in Turkmenistan in January 1990, some of its founders established the Party for Democratic Development (PDD) with a narrow focus on political reform. It held its founding conference in the Russian capital on December 22, 1990, an event reported by the *Moscow News*. Yet not a word appeared in the Turkmen press. Soon the PDD, too, was outlawed. The only way to convey information about it was through the television, radio, or press of the neighboring countries, like Azerbaijan.

The Unity Party and the PDD jointly began publishing a journal, *Daianch* (*Support*), in Moscow in January 1992. When the publishers dispatched part of their print run of 30,000 from Moscow to Ashgabat, the shipment was tracked by the Turkmen authorities and confiscated. Nurmuhammadov was tried three times for insulting the president, a criminal offense, and spent some time in jail. He and other dissidents were prevented from attending a human rights conference convened by the Democratic Congress of Central Asia in Bishkek in December 1992. They were systematically harassed through "wire tapping, provocations, dismissals from jobs, all kinds of intrigues, telephone threats."[17]

"Since we don't have opposition papers in Turkmenistan, it is difficult to say that there is free press here," said Jeren Taimova, deputy editor-in-chief of *Ashgabat Vecherni* (*Ashgabat Evening*). "Journalists themselves are not active in either promoting free press or working for the opposition. If there is no free press and broadcast media, it is difficult to develop democracy."[18]

Government officials and others argued that the current stage in the country's political development required consolidation of independence and concentration on nation-building, not opposition politics. "At this time there is no need for a multi-party system," wrote Tagan Jumakov, a senior journalist for the *Ashgabat Vecherni*. "Many problems have to be solved, social problems, and we must raise living standards. When our living standards are high, and we are economically independent, then we can have a multi-party system. But if this happens now then there will be anarchy."[19] Addressing a meeting of the People's Council in December 1992, Niyazov estimated a period of ten years for Turkmenistan to achieve "economic prosperity." This aim would remain unachieved well past 2002.

The press functioned under the watchful eye of the regime. Briefly during perestroika, like other newspapers, the *Ashgabat Vecherni*, established in 1968 as the organ of the Ashgabat City Communist Party, acquired some independence. In mid-1990, when the Soviet law removed state or party control over the print media, it was sold to the city mayor's office, where the paper's ownership has since remained. Other prominent papers were sold to the parliament, the cabinet, and so on, and they continued to be owned by these institutions.

Following Turkmenistan's independence, censorship was formally abolished. That is, the KGB, which formerly acted as the censor, stopped performing this function. Its role was taken over by the all-powerful Presidential Council, the highest executive body (the members of the cabinet being mere departmental heads), and the State Security Committee, which set up the Department of Protection of State Secrets in the Media. "We have to keep well clear of about 200 points of censorship," a journalist in Ashgabat told me. "It is just not possible to publish straight criticism, and even indirect criticism is risky."[20]

"At the Presidential Council office, there is a Press Center," said Taimova. "It orders the press what to do and not to do. So the state is not using its strength like the Communist Party used to do in the past, but it acts through the Press Center which is supposed to try to persuade the newspaper editors." The "persuasion'" amounted to a simple phone call to the editor from the Press Center. Reporting on the conflict in Afghanistan and Tajikistan was banned on the ground that publishing these stories of violence and discussing them in the Turkmen press would create conflict in Turkmenistan. This argument ignored the fact that, of the television channels available in the republic, one was a Russian broadcast from Moscow that regularly carried news of strife in Afghanistan and Tajikistan.

Among the hot topics of the day, news of the president's activities in print and pictures was top priority. For weeks after the parliament gave Niyazov the Hero of the Turkmen People award in October 1992, local papers devoted most of their space to panegyric letters congratulating him on his accomplishments.

Such publications as *Today's Turkmenistan*—a weekly in Russian and Turkmen, registered in Moscow in June 1991 (with a circulation of 25,000), whose management remained outside the official institutions—had to submit all its material to the State Security Committee, which acted as censor. "It is not possible to publish straight criticism, and we don't want to do it," said Odek Odekov, chairman of the management board. "Then there is indirect criticism. For example, the gas pipeline going through Iran from Turkmenistan, that deal was done without consulting scientists, and they ignored the earthquake zone. Parliament is a closed institution, and it did not discuss this issue. I mentioned this on Radio Liberty."[21]

On June 21, 1992, came the presidential poll under the newly adopted constitution. Seven-eighths of the 1.86 million electors participated, with 99.5 percent voting for the sole candidate, Saparmurat Niyazov. He thus became the only Central Asian leader to continue to govern since achieving supreme power during the early days of the Gorbachev era. Now under the new constitution, his authority was all the more pervasive since the legislative and judicial bodies were subordinated to him as well. His executive powers entitled him to appoint not only the members of the People's Council and the cabinet, but also the governors of five regions and the administrative heads of forty counties.

Niyazov opted for meritocracy and consensus, and gave a stake in the system to all major tribes without saying so. Indeed, he resorted to stressing the "Turan" (the ancient Persian name for Central Asia) nation rather than any particular tribe. That is, instead of attacking tribalism, as Marxist-Leninists had done earlier, he tried to subsume tribalism into Turan-Turkic nationalism.

As early as May 1991, in Ashgabat, Niyazov had sponsored a convention of ethnic Turkmen from an area extending from Afghanistan and Uzbekistan to Iran, Iraq, and Turkey to renew a bond between the ethnic Turkmens and their native region. The resulting Association of Turkmens of the World elected Niyazov as its president. Out of that arose the honorific of Turkmenbashi (literally, "First among Turkmens"), which he popularized as Serdar Turkmenbashi, Great Leader of (all) Turkmen. He thus emulated Mustafa Kemal, who had acquired the honorific of Ataturk, Father of Turks.

THE RISE AND RISE OF TURKMENBASHI

Armed with the constitution he had drafted, Niyazov transformed the popularity he had acquired as a strong leader, who maintained stability during a period of rapid and cataclysmic change, into an iron grip on power. On major issues he consulted as many groups and individuals as possible, but once a decision was taken, he implemented it strictly. He revived the traditional Council of Elders (which each tribe used to have), and set up a forum to consult university students, ensuring that his consultations received maximum publicity in the state-run media.

Niyazov exceeded Joseph Stalin in fostering a personality cult. More than a temporal leader, he projected himself as Turkmenistan's spiritual master. Soon, an important thoroughfare in Ashgabat bearing Lenin's name was renamed after him, as were a collective farm near the capital and the Lenin Kara Kum Canal. It was the first time that a street or farm in a former Soviet republic was named after a living leader. "Some people make comparisons with Stalin, with his dictatorship and cult of personality," Niyazov told a press conference. "But Stalin achieved his personality cult through repressive measures whereas I achieved my popularity without conflicts."[22]

To meet the rising criticism in Russia and the West, Niyazov, like Karimov, came up with the idea of fostering "loyal" opposition in the form of the Young League of Turkmenistan and the Peasants' Justice Party in late 1993. Unlike in Uzbekistan and Tajikistan, there was no obvious sign of opposition from Islamic quarters, despite the fact that the size of the congregations and the number of mosques were growing dramatically. Between 1987 and 1992, the number of mosques in Turkmenistan jumped from 4 to 114, and that of the Ashgabat-based pilgrimages to Mecca from 10 to 141. As during the Communist rule, there was "official" Islam in the form of the Directorate of Religious Affairs. To meet the growing demand for clerics, the Directorate sent 116 religious students to Turkey for a four-year course in Islam, specifically the Hanafi School of the Sunni sect prevalent in Turkmenistan.[23] It was Turkey—and not Iran, a Shiite country—that was at the center of Islamization in Turkmenistan.

As was the case during the Soviet rule, opposition to official Islam was expressed intermittently. It came from Hazratkuli Khanov, the cleric in charge of the capital's largest mosque. Describing the current secular regime as an administration "run by the same old Communist functionaries whom the people did not trust," and criticizing the official Islamic leadership, headed by Kazi Nasrullah ibn Abdullah, as "weak and obedient," he predicted some sort of Islamic regime in all Central Asian republics.[24] But this was more an expression of wish fulfillment than a realistic assessment of the situation.

The threat to the determinedly secular, authoritarian regime of Niyazov from the opposition, secular or religious, was negligible. The reasons were cultural—due to the absence of political democratic tradition—and, more importantly, economic. The natural resources of the republic, with a population of a mere 3.7 million in the early 1990s, were stupendous. At the current global prices, its annual gas output of 82 billion cubic meters, the third highest in the world, was worth $6 billion. Of this, 72 billion cubic meters were available for export. Even under fairly unsettled economic conditions, Turkmenistan had met the International Monetary Fund's precondition for launching its own currency, the manat, on par with the U.S. dollar—foreign reserves of $300 million in hard currencies—within a year instead of the expected three. Inevitably, Niyazov's portrait appeared on manat banknotes.

Niyazov could afford to raise the salaries of public employees threefold in a year, continue hefty subsidies on food and other items as before, and provide free gas, electricity, and water to citizens from January 1993 onward. As Serdar Turkmenbashi, he took up residence in a palace in Arshabil with a helipad, 28 kilometers from the capital, and in due course he would turn his presidential Boeing 767 into a flying palace worth $130 million.[25]

Unlike all other Central Asian republics, Turkmenistan felt no need to approach the IMF or the World Bank for assistance, which would have required scrutiny of its financial affairs. So, the general management of the economy changed little from the Soviet era. Several hallmarks of the command economy remained intact: price controls, exchange rate restriction, loans by state-owned banks with minimal interest rates, and production and procurement quotas secured through state-run organizations.

The absence of any checks and balances at home or foreign export scrutiny enabled Niyazov to maintain a fiscal system that was opaque to outsiders. Official figures became unreliable. It was widely believed that much of the government's income and expenditure was processed through accounts that were not part of the official budget. The preeminent among them was Turkmenneftegaz State Trading Corporation, the government-owned company which dealt in oil and gas until its abolition in December 2005. Much of the foreign exchange was used to construct prestigious monuments and luxury hotels and apartment blocks, and not on improving the existing economic infrastructure or expanding it.

"[A]ccurate information about exports [of hydrocarbons and cotton] from Turkmenistan is impossible to obtain and is viewed by the Turkmen government as no one else's business," wrote Martha Brill Olcott, an American specialist on Central Asia. "Turkmen economists with access to information provided by foreign partners are sworn to secrecy and told that their well-being and that of their relatives is at risk if they divulge any of it. It is so widely rumored that trade in oil and gas directly benefits the president and his family that this supposition can virtually be treated as fact."[26]

In the first flush of independence, Niyazov tried to lure American corporations to invest in Turkmenistan. To that end, he hired Alexander Haig, former U.S. secretary of state, as a lobbyist in 1992. Haig arranged a private visit by Niyazov to Washington in 1993 to encourage American investment, but nothing came of it. (In the absence of an invitation to the White House, forged pictures of Niyazov and President Bill Clinton appeared in the Turkmen media.) The Haig-Niyazov effort failed for several reasons. Niyazov had not yet established a proper legal framework for large-scale foreign investments by reputable Western companies. Since the president was the sole authority to allow export of goods and allocate foreign currencies, a foreign investment required his approval. Lesser officials were afraid to take weighty decisions in the absence of a presidential order. This necessitated face-to-face meetings between the prospective foreign investor and Niyazov, when he reportedly demanded kickbacks of 33 percent of the deal.

Another major area of corruption was cotton. The difference between the price in the world market and the one paid to domestic cotton growers by the state trading companies provided officials and foreign intermediaries ample opportunities to enrich themselves in the course of exporting the commodity. Rumor had it that Niyazov and his family were among the beneficiaries of the export trade involving Turkish companies. Preeminent among these was Calik (pronounced Chalik) Holdings run by Ahmad Calik, a resident of Turkmenistan since 1994 who was granted Turkmen citizenship and was close to Niyazov. He was also active in the textile and construction industries, specializing in textile mills and upscale apartments.

"It is virtually impossible to know how serious a problem presidential corruption is in Turkmenistan because Niyazov exercises direct control over the country's Foreign Exchange Reserve Fund, through which the earnings of most foreign investments are managed," noted Olcott. "He also sets the priorities in how the foreign exchange is to be spent, which has gone disproportionately to large construction projects, rather than for investments in national infrastructure."[27] Unlike Karimov, Niyazov was not a trained economist; but like him, he was supremely self-confident and dogmatic.

The result was the demolition of traditional neighborhoods with character, and the construction of avenues lined on both sides with spanking new hotels. One road boasted as many as twenty-two five-star hotels, with the Grand Turkmen Hotel announcing its presence with the signs of a glamorous casino and gift-wrapped cars offered as prizes.

A foray by Darra Goldstein, a visiting American professor of Russian, into one of the newly built, marble-faced luxury apartment blocks revealed a marble-and-glass interior and sleek elevators. In an apartment where a young, unmarried professional lived with his mother, the hosts and guests sat down on the carpeted floor to consume food laid out on a brightly colored cloth—a continuation of a nomadic custom.

A dramatic contrast to the sanitized residences and hotels was provided by Ashgabat's public bakery seven days a week and the open-air market on Sundays. At the bakery, a visitor could witness a battery of tandoor ovens at work—heated not by the traditional firewood or charcoal, but by natural gas. The women bakers would brand the dough with geometric designs, paste the loaves against the inside walls of the tandoors to bake, and then lift them out with metal hooks while protecting themselves from the searing heat by wearing veils just under their eyes. The open air-market on Sundays was another lively diversion from the increasingly soulless city center. Here a visitor was free to elbow his or her way through the throngs of men, vehicles, and camels amidst dust and bin, and the aroma of fried food, to hunt for traditional oriental items—such as the little bells that Turkmen mothers attached to the clothes of their children to help locate them when they wandered off into a featureless desert.

On another occasion, Goldstein attended a post-wedding reception hosted by the groom's parents for the relatives of both parties in a newly built apartment. Though the bride had studied at an American university, as had the groom, she withdrew to a back room to be surrounded by the female members of her extended family. She wore the traditional Turkmen dress and, as behooves a newly married woman, was covered with heavy silver ornaments on her arms, neck, face, head, feet, and ankles under a hand-woven shawl. All she lacked was the pointed Mongol-style helmet that a Turkmen bride traditionally wears for her wedding. In stark contrast, the groom moved around in jeans and a T-shirt.

Later, the main reception room became the site where robust women from the two sides engaged in a symbolic wrestling match, with the groom's party mimicking wrenching the bride away from her family and adopting her into its own. The spectators watched merrily, cheering and clapping at the right moments of the make-believe struggle. It was a milder, more enter-taining version of the bride-stealing that is common in Kyrgyzstan and southern Uzbekistan.[28]

THE ECONOMY DIPS

Following Niyazov's sterile visit to the United States, his government fell victim to the economic woes of the countries which bought Turkmen gas through the Soviet-era pipeline network: Georgia, Ukraine, and Russia. Their foreign exchange earnings fell so steeply that they could not pay fully for the fuel they purchased from Turkmenneftegaz State Trading Corporation.

Responding to the partial payments, Turkmenneftegaz began reducing its exports and thus its output. The production fell by two-thirds to 30 billion cubic meters in 1994.[29] To dissipate the crisis, Niyazov devised a two-prong strategy. He ordered Turkmenneftegaz to form a consortium with the Russian company, Gazprom (given 44 percent of the equity), owner of the pipelines outside Turkmenistan, and the U.S.-based Itera International Energy Corporation (given 5 percent of the equity). And, to boost the local economy, he decided to furnish the main thoroughfares of the capital with luxury hotels and other upscale buildings.

The talks on pricing the Turkmen gas and transition fees became acrimo-nous and dragged on. But the construction boom—funded partly by the public exchequer, partly by kickbacks extorted from foreign investors, and partly by domestic dealers in drugs—got going. Preeminent among the government contracts given to foreigners was the one awarded in 1997 to the Israel-based Merhav Group—run by Yosef Maiman, who was personally close to Niyazov—to modernize the republic's largest refinery at Turkmenbashi (formerly Krasnovodsk) for $1.6 billion.[30]

"Modernizing" Ashgabat meant razing many central neighborhoods to create a network of boulevards with lavish palaces of white marble and green tinted glass, dotted with massive fountains and statues of Niyazov and his parents as well as historical Turkmen personalities, guarded by uniformed security men standing to attention. The city would become the site of the largest fountain in the world—a multi-storied shopping mall with water gushing out of the roof and pouring down in a ring of waterfalls. Its main avenue would end up with twenty-two five-star hotels, where foreign guests would be accommodated only in the rooms that were bugged. Many of the displaced families did not get alternative accommodation or compensation as they could not prove the ownership of their homes.

To sustain the economy, Turkmenistan's central bank resorted to printing money recklessly. This led to 3,000 percent inflation. The value of the manat, which had been launched on par with the American dollar, went into free fall, with its official rate reduced to 5,200 manats to one U.S. dollar, and the market rate nearly five times that figure. Moreover, after years of haggling, Gazprom made its final offer in the spring of 1997, and Niyazov found it unacceptable. In June he ordered Turkmenneftegaz to suspend the consortium and stop negotiating with Gazprom. By then, the arrears of the indebted nations had soared to a staggering $1.2 billion.[31]

This was a particularly difficult time for Niyazov personally. He learned that his arteries were hardening. He underwent major heart surgery in a German clinic, which remained a closely guarded secret until a month before his death nine years later when he revealed that he had a heart problem. He recovered from the surgery in Germany, but had to stop smoking. On his return home, he decreed that all cabinet ministers should give up smoking, and outlawed it in all public places. He would later extend the ban to lighting up in the street.

By 1998, the situation was dire on the natural gas front. The mounting arrears by its buyers led Turkmenneftegaz to cut off supplies. Its annual production plummeted to 13.3 billion cubic meters, with only 3 billion cubic meters available for export.

Throughout these vicissitudes in the Turkmen economy, Niyazov remained firmly committed to his policy of neutrality in external relations.

Years later, after Turkmenistan had formally joined the Non-Aligned Movement in 1995, his government would build the 170-foot-high Neutrality Arch at the center of downtown Ashgabat—an amalgam of a tripod Eiffel Tower and a marble-covered space rocket—by far the capital's tallest and largest structure. It would be crowned with a twenty-foot-tall, gold-plated statue of Niyazov in a Superman cloak, his arms raised aloft, set to rotate 360 degrees every twenty-four hours to face the sun and reflect light on the city—and be visible from the international airport, named after him, many miles away. Even the official daily newspaper was titled the *Neitralny Turkmenistan* (Neutral Turkmenistan).

Two years later, Niyazov would replace the earlier national anthem, "Turkmenistan" by Veli Mukhatov and Aman Kekilov, with a new one titled "Independent, Neutral, Turkmenistan State Anthem," for which he would provide both words and music.

STRICTLY NEUTRAL

Niyazov's first priority in foreign policy was linkage with Russia and the newly formed Commonwealth of Independent States, followed by relations with neighboring Iran and Afghanistan, then Turkey, and then the United States.

Relations with Moscow were tied to the fate of ethnic Russians in Turkmenistan and the future of Russian in the republic. The constitution tackled the ticklish language problem by specifying Turkmen as the official language and adding that "all citizens are guaranteed to use their own language," a statement intended to reassure Russian settlers. Unlike elsewhere in the region, Turkmenistan allowed dual citizenship—a provision much valued by the small (less than 10 percent) but highly skilled Russian minority. Providing them with a device guaranteeing their return to the motherland as full citizens reassured them as individuals while ensuring that Turkmenistan continued to use their much-needed services during its hazardous transition to a market economy. The attitude shown towards ethnic Russians stemmed as much from pragmatism as from the fact that Niyazov had a Russian wife, Muza Sokolova, with whom he had a son, Murat, and a daughter, Irina. Several of his senior advisers were also Russian. In 1993, Turkmenistan signed a ten-year treaty on dual citizenship with Moscow.

However, the pro-Russian bias did not prevail when it came to choosing the script for Turkmen. The government decided to discard the present Cyrillic script. Murad Annapesov, vice-president of the Academy of

Sciences, summed up the debate on the choice of the Arabic or Latin alphabet thus: "If we switch over from the Cyrillic to the Arabic script, then we would be integrated only with Iran and the Arab world. But if we adopt the Latin alphabet then we would get closer to Turkey and Europe."[32] So the parliament opted for a Latin script to be used from January 1, 1995.

Confident of its economic future underwritten by ample hydrocarbon resources, Turkmenistan drifted away from the CIS. Niyazov had visualized the CIS as a political club, a consultative body, lacking any central coordinating mechanisms. When the summit at Bishkek in October 1992 included in its agenda the signing of a CIS charter, Niyazov developed a "diplomatic illness" and stayed away. The document failed to materialize. Finally, when the CIS charter was presented for signature at the next CIS summit in Minsk in January 1993, Niyazov abstained. The presidents of Ukraine and Moldova did the same, but they as well as the remaining seven leaders of CIS member states signed a more generally worded document. This enabled Turkmenistan to stay in the CIS while it considered its long-term position.

In line with Niyazov's policy of steering clear of multinational treaties, Turkmenistan did not join the Tashkent Collective Security Agreement in May 1992. Equally, in line with its policy of developing bilateral relations, it concluded a three-year military cooperation agreement with Russia in June. The signatories agreed that while Turkmenistan would form its own military on the basis of former Soviet Union army units in the republic, then 120,000 strong, it would submit such forces to the joint control of Moscow and Ashgabat. As for the air force and air defense units, these were to remain under Russian command. The cost of maintaining the troops was to be shared by the two states.[33] The signing of such a pact during the run-up to the presidential election under the new constitution raised further Niyazov's already high prestige at home: it showed Turkmenistan dealing with Russia, the erstwhile Big Brother, on an equal basis. It also endeared Niyazov to Moscow.

Yet, in May 1994, Turkmenistan became the first Central Asian republic to be accepted by NATO in its Partnership for Peace program. Three months later, much to the annoyance of Washington and Ankara, Niyazov visited Tehran, his third such trip during 1994, to further strengthen economic and cultural relations with Iran. In May 1996, Niyazov and his Iranian counterpart, Ali Akbar Hashemi Rafsanjani, inaugurated the rail link between Tejand, Turkmenistan, and Sarkhas, Iran. With this, Turkmenistan as well as the other four Central Asian republics gained access to Iran's ports in the Persian Gulf, which were open throughout the year, unlike those in the Baltic which froze in winter. Niyazov viewed increasing economic ties with Iran as one way to reduce dependence on Russia, whose gas behemoth, Gazprom, had the monopoly over the pipelines carrying Turkmen gas to foreign destinations.

None of this affected Niyazov's continued cultivation of strong diplomatic, economic, and cultural ties with Turkey, even when Islamist leader Necmettin Erbakan became the prime minister in mid-1996, and Washington stopped holding up Turkey as the role model for the Central Asian republics. Indeed, in May 1997, Niyazov signed a memorandum of understanding with Rafsanjani *and* Erbakan at the summit of the ten-member Economic Conference Organization in Ashgabat for a pipeline to carry annually 30 billion cubic meters of Turkmen gas at the cost of $7 billion, with Iran paying half of it.[34]

In December, Niyazov and Iranian President Muhammad Khatami inaugurated the 200-kilometer pipeline from Korpeje, Turkmenistan, to Kord-Kui, Iran, to carry 2 billion cubic meters of Turkmen gas annually, rising to 4 billion cubic meters by 1999. It was to be the first phase of a project that would ultimately take Turkmen gas to Turkey and destinations farther west without touching any part of Russia. Since neither Tehran nor Ashgabat approached such international financial institutions as the World Bank and the IMF—dominated by the United States—for loans to finance the project, Washington never got a chance to veto it. Also, plans were afoot to supply a refinery in Tehran with 280,000 barrels per day of Turkmen oil through a pipeline from the Iranian port of Neka on the Caspian, with Iran exporting that amount of crude to Turkmenistan's foreign customers.

Alone among his Central Asian colleagues, Niyazov was blasé about the rise of the Taliban militia as the predominant force in Afghanistan after its capture of Kabul in September 1996. Keen to export Turkmen gas to Pakistan via Afghanistan, Niyazov figured, rightly, that the Taliban had the best chance of pacifying Afghanistan then in the throes of a civil war, and that, anticipating lucrative transit fees, it was unlikely to destabilize Turkmenistan by aiding Islamist forces there. He therefore stayed away from the Central Asian summit in April 1997 called to strengthen the anti-Taliban front, and sent his deputy instead.[35]

During the run-up to the celebration of Turkmenistan's National Independence Day on October 25, the BBC reported that a high-level, helicopter-borne Taliban delegation, led by Maulavi Ahmadjan, minister for energy and mining, had arrived in Ashgabat secretly to meet Foreign Minister Boris Shikhmuradov regarding a plan to erect a gas pipeline through

Afghanistan.[36] The cordial talks with the Taliban minister led Niyazov to dispatch Shikhmuradov to Washington to press the Clinton administration to recognize the Taliban regime. He failed.

On Independence Day, Niyazov announced the signing of a $2 billion protocol between his government and Centgas, a consortium of seven companies led by Unocal, an American corporation, for the erection of 1,400-kilometer pipeline from Daulatabad, Turkmenistan, to Multan, Pakistan, to carry 20 billion cubic meters of gas annually.[37] Awarding the lucrative contract to an American-led consortium which faced stiff competition from Bridas, an Argentinean corporation, created goodwill for Niyazov at the White House.

It was not enough, however, to soften the State Department's annual report on human rights, published in January 1998, which noted that Turkmenistan had made little progress in switching from the Soviet-style political system toward democracy. The Clinton administration asked Niyazov for a gesture toward democratization as a precondition for an invitation to the White House. In February, Niyazov aired the idea of curtailing his powers by amending the constitution, and promised to hold a meeting of high officials in May to discuss giving more authority to the parliament at the expense of the presidency. But once he had obtained the coveted invitation, he changed his tune. Addressing the parliament on March 26, he announced that there would be amendments to the constitution only after the parliamentary poll in December 1999, implying that such reform would be suitable only for the next century.

A month later, Niyazov started his week-long tour of the United States with a lunch at the White House after several hours of talks with Clinton and Vice President Al Gore. However, there was no joint press conference to round off the high-level meetings. In his press briefing, the White House spokesman explained that, just as in the case of China, the U.S. national economic interest outweighed the administration's concern over Niyazov's dismal record on post-Soviet reform.

When questioned on the issues of civil liberties and multi-party democracy at such forums as the Council on Foreign Relations in New York, Niyazov repeated the argument that political liberalization would follow only after independence and stability had been consolidated. His statement that no one had been arrested in Turkmenistan for political reasons flew in the face of the conclusion of the recent U.S. State Department's human rights report on Turkmenistan that the opposition was repressed, with leading dissidents either imprisoned or committed to psychiatric hospitals.

Regarding the establishment of legitimate opposition parties, Niyazov promised that future law would allow it, but only if the groups had "certain programs." He omitted to mention that, to meet the criticism in Russia and the West, he had permitted the formation in January 1994 of the Peasants' Party (as loyal opposition) even though it lacked the legal requirement of having 1,000 members spread throughout the republic. But as the economy nose-dived, with hyperinflation impoverishing the populace and providing the new party a chance to gain genuine popularity at the expense of the governing Democratic Party, Niyazov ensured that the Peasants' Party remained stillborn. By 1997, though, inflation had been curtailed to a manageable 60 percent.

On the eve of Niyazov's departure for America in the spring of 1998, the state-guided Turkmen media hailed the White House gesture as a promising omen for tackling the formidable task of exporting Turkmen gas to the markets outside former Soviet republics. The only result was that the Trade and Development Agency in Washington agreed to contribute a paltry $750,000 to finance a feasibility study of a gas pipeline running underneath the Caspian Sea to Azerbaijan, giving Turkmenistan access to Turkey without involving Iran or Russia. But this gesture was enough to cause consternation in Moscow. Gazprom eased up in its negotiations with Turkmenneftegaz on the price and transit cost of Turkmen gas brought to the Russian border, which satisfied Niyazov and led to an agreement. The gas output would rise by 71 percent to 21.3 billion cubic meters in 1999.

On the political front, too, Clinton had to be satisfied with "jam tomorrow"—a joint communiqué that referred to the prospect of "free and fair elections for parliament and president as planned for 1999 and 2002 respectively." This was billed as part of "progressive engagement" with Turkmenistan, a term used by Gore. But things soon went awry. The Pentagon's missile attacks on the Taliban training camps in Afghanistan on August 20, 1998, in retaliation for the bombings of the U.S. embassies in East Africa, rearranged the pieces on the Central Asian chess board. They fatally damaged incipient ties between Central Asia and Pakistan through Afghanistan, and encouraged alternative links between Central Asia and China to grow and prosper.

During his visit to China soon after, Niyazov signed several cooperation agreements with his counterpart, President Jiang Zemin, including economy, air traffic, tourism, and education agreements. In the economic sphere, by far the most important was the project to ship Turkmen natural gas to China and Japan by a pipeline. In contrast, Unocal put its pipeline project through

Afghanistan on ice, and a further setback for the Clinton White House was in store: the Turkmen People's Council would declare Niyazov president for life.

PRESIDENT FOR LIFE

According to the official claim, a record 98.9 percent of voters turned out to participate in the general election on December 12, 1999, to choose amongst 104 candidates contesting fifty seats, all of them members of the Democratic Party of Turkmenistan. The Organization for Security and Cooperation in Europe (OSCE) did not dispatch its observers due to the absence of opposition parties and the president's control over selection of the contestants. The new parliament reelected Sahat Muradov as speaker.

On December 28, DPT delegates decided to appoint Niyazov president for life, and the People's Council unanimously passed a constitutional law conferring this office on him. Addressing the new legislature in January 2000, Niyazov announced that there would be amendments to the constitution and the introduction of a new civil code, giving increased civil rights to citizens as they entered the twenty-first century. In true Orwellian fashion, his first major move to widen civil rights was to withdraw all Internet licenses except for the state-owned Turkmen Telecom in May.[38]

His life presidency assured, Niyazov went into overdrive to indulge his megalomania and narcissism. His confidence grew when, with rising prices of gas and oil, Turkmenistan's current trade account changed from deficit to surplus in 2000. At that point, Niyazov took on the role of the spiritual-cultural commissar of the Turkmen nation. After banning ballet and opera, which he considered alien to Turkmen culture, he closed down all cinemas and replaced them with a giant puppet theater in Ashgabat.

With the publication of his 400-page book, *Ruhnama* (*Journal of the Soul*), in 2001, he claimed to offer cultural and spiritual guidance to Turkmens. *Ruhnama* was a hodgepodge of revisionist history, pedantic moralizing, petty philosophizing, and unsubstantiated claims. Its style was a blend of sermonizing and a call to exploration.

A typical passage reads:

> Come and visit us! Come and travel in the lands of Oghuz Khan, Gorkut Ata, Seljuk Khan, Alp Arslan, Melik Shah [son of Alp Arslan], Sultan Sanjar, Gorogly Beg, and Magtymguly Feraghy.
>
> My fellow countrymen, though you are not travelers, you visit this territory; touch the soil on which many valued people, rulers and your ancestors lived.

This land is a sacred and miraculous land.

Ruhnama is a visit to this land. *Ruhnama* is a visit to the past of this territory and a visit to the future of this territory. *Ruhnama* is the visit made to the heart of the Turkmen. *Ruhnama* is a sweet spiritual fruit grown in this territory. No human being who has not experienced what I lived through can understand me.

As a narrative, *Ruhnama* can be described as a book of discovery, oscillating between now and the Middle Ages. It revolves around an orphan named Saparmurat Niyazov whose temporal arrival is ordained by God. In his quest, full of adventure and discovery, the orphan comes to grip with his parentage and the glorious history of Turkmens.[39]

While incorporating recorded history in his volume, Niyazov indulged in exaggeration and distortion to underscore the vital role played by the Turkmen tribes. This was quite unnecessary, as the bare facts were quite complimentary to Turkmens. After all, it was they who initiated the westward migration of the Turkic peoples in the late tenth century. And it was the Oghuz federation of twenty-three Turkmen tribes who then turned south under the leadership of the Seljuk tribe and overthrew the Arab Buyid dynasty in Baghdad in 1055. The Turkmen Seljuks, led by Sultan Alp Arslan (literally, "Brave Lion"), then attacked the Byzantine Empire at Manzikert (aka Malazgirt) in 1071. Their victory in that battle paved the way for the settlement of the Turkic people in Anatolia, who established control over large parts of contemporary Turkey, Central Asia, and Iran. The forward march of Genghis Khan's army in the thirteenth century from Mongolia drove eastern Turks into Anatolia. When Genghis Khan overpowered the Seljuks, the leadership of the Oghuz federation passed on to the Ottomans.

Niyazov erected a commemorative complex in his home village of Gipjak, conceived as a symbol of the rebirth of the Turkmen nation, which included a mosque whose walls carry quotations from the Quran as well as the *Ruhnama*. The Turkmen government ordered a prominent display of the *Ruhnama* not only in bookshops and official buildings, but also in mosques and churches, sharing its place with the Quran or the Bible. A colossal pink statue of the *Ruhnama* in Ashgabat was too conspicuous to be missed. Another decree extended the book's presence to libraries and schools, and made it part of the curriculum. To be able to recite passages of the book became a badge of honor. Next, civil servants, teachers, and doctors were required to pass a test on its teachings. Then, this requirement also became part of the driving test. The *Ruhnama* was lauded in songs, and the state-run media regularly broadcast or printed excerpts from it. Criticizing the book, even in private, was tantamount to criticizing Niyazov, an offense punishable with a five-year jail sentence.

Niyazov redesigned the educational system, reducing the compulsory schooling by two years to nine, and higher education by three years down to a mere two. Inexplicably, he reduced the college and university enrollments to 10 percent of the then current figure. He banned the teaching of foreign languages, and decreed that the exceptional history and culture of Turkmen must be stressed, with his *Ruhnama* to act as the lodestar.

Niyazov's increasing obsession to promote Turkmen culture and history put him at odds with his foreign minister, Boris Shikhmuradov, son of a Turkmen father and an Armenian mother. He was demoted to the president's special adviser on the Caspian region in July 2000 and supplanted by Ahmad Calik, who became the president's senior adviser on the economy and the energy sector. Shikhmuradov was then shunted off to Beijing as Turkmenistan's ambassador.

In the region, despite the rising hostility between Washington and the Taliban in the wake of the August 1998 bombings at the U.S. embassies in East Africa, Niyazov had maintained normal relations with the Taliban. This changed abruptly after September 11, 2001.

THE POST-9/11 ERA: NARCISSISM UNBOUND

Within a week of the 9/11 attacks, Niyazov turned against the Taliban and helped the Pentagon's anti-Taliban buildup in the region. Barred from flying over Iran, two large U.S. Hercules transport planes, destined for a military base in Uzbekistan, went through Turkmenistan's air space on September 18. Niyazov gave the permisison on the condition that it be kept secret.

As elsewhere in Central Asia, further cooperation was on offer to Washington—at a price. During the Clinton administration, the military aid to Ashgabat had amounted to a derisory $600,000 a year, spent on the purchase of U.S.-made weapons and the training of local officers to use them. After Niyazov had allowed the United States overflight rights through the Turkmen air space, limited landing rights, and the use of transit routes for food and other goods to help post-Taliban Afghanistan, the military aid to Turkmenistan soared thirty-two-fold to $19.2 million in 2003.[40] By then, two-fifths of the food aid provided by the World Food Program, funded mostly by Washington, entered Afghaninstan through Turkmenistan.

Like his fellow dictator Karimov, Niyazov used the security alliance with Washington to crush any sign of serious dissent. But unlike in Uzbekistan, there was no political opposition in Turkmenistan. The only threat to Niyazov's monopoly over power lay with a top official defecting and becoming the nucleus for an opposition group. His nightmare materialized when Boris Shikhmuradov resigned as ambassador to China in October 2001 and immediately condemned his regime. The following day, the Turkmen prosecutor general charged that Shikhmuradov had embezzled $30 million through illicit weapons sales in 1994 when, as deputy prime minister, he supervised defense and security agencies.[41] He denied the allegation, and revealed that Niyazov had rigged elections, ordered deaths of important political prisoners, and diverted vast amounts of funds from the public exchequer to his own accounts.

For the next twelve months, Shikhmuradov worked relentlessly to bring about the downfall of Niyazov's regime. He founded the People's Democratic Movement of Turkmenistan (PDMT) under his leadership, and set up its website, Gündogar. In January 2002, he urged the Organization for Security and Cooperation in Europe to consider suspending Turkmenistan's membership because its regime had unleashed "a new wave of terror and cruelty against its citizens."[42] "It is impossible to hide any more of Niyazov's pure hypocrisy, the absence of elementary norms of political and diplomatic behavior, the insidiousness and cruelty in relations to the people, and the spreading of an atmosphere of fear," Shikhmuradov said.[43]

He traveled widely, from Russia to America to Turkey and Uzbekistan, spending most of his exile in Russia or Uzbekistan where he had forged high-level contacts as the Turkmen foreign minister. Angered by the Niyazov government's mistreatment of the Uzbek minority in Turkmenistan, and nursing the long-running tension over sharing the waters of the Oxus, heightened by the building of a colossal reservoir called the Grand Turkmen Lake in eastern Turkmenistan, Uzbek officials lent a sympathetic ear to Shikhmuradov's plans.

Niyazov was rattled. He resorted to sacking top officials summarily, a tactic he had used before, but sparingly. On January 5, 2002, he dismissed Hudaiberdy Orazov, deputy prime minister and chairman of the Central Bank, accusing him of "shortcomings in his work and immodesty in his personal life." With Orazov's dismissal, Niyazov became the sole arbiter of the republic's foreign exchange. Orazov went into self-exile in Moscow.

The next month, Niyazov sacked the commander of border guards, Major-General Tirkish Termyev. He accused KNB officials of bribery, detaining citizens illegally, and forging evidence by planting drugs, torturing suspects, and trafficking drugs. Once the prosecutor general had laid out the charges in detail, Niyazov downgraded the KNB chief, General Muhammad Nazarov, from a four-star to a three-star general and dismissed him as the coordinator of defense and law enforcement agencies. Soon after, the prosecutor general accused Nazarov of premeditated murder; printing and selling counterfeit documents, seals, stamps, and bank forms; embezzlement; receiving bribes; and procuring prostitutes.[44] Thus, exceeding his normal practice of periodically humiliating cabinet ministers and top civil servants by rebuking them on television, Niyazov demoralized the political-bureaucratic elite.

In April, while Shikhmuradov visited Washington to deliver a paper titled "Turkmenistan's Political Crisis: Inside Niyazov's Regime" at a prestigious think tank, and to brief human rights organizations on the brutality and corruption of the Turkmen despot's government, U.S. Defense Secretary Donald Rumsfeld called on Niyazov in Ashgabat. "As you know Turkmenistan is a member of NATO's Partnership for Peace and the United States has had a relationship with it for some time," Rumsfeld told a press conference. "We also thanked the President for the overflight rights with respect to the global war on terrorism which has been a big help to the United States. . . . His country has been cooperative with respect to the global war on terrorism, for which we are grateful and appreciative."[45]

In August, Niyazov welcomed the visiting combatant commander of U.S. Central Command (CENTCOM), General Tommy Franks, who promised further military cooperation between the two countries due to the enhanced strategic signficance of Turkmenistan. Meanwhile, on the other side, during his visits to Washington, Moscow, Tashkent, and Ankara (where Nur Muhammad Khanamov, the Turkmen ambassador to Turkey, had defected), Shikhmuradov solicited support for his plan to overthrow the Niyazov regime through a civil disobedience movement.

Having seemingly tackled the unexpected threat from Shikhmuradov, Niyazov returned to the pursuit of his eccentric ideas. At the annual session of the People's Council in August 2002, he declared his wish to rename the months of the year to commemorate legendary Turkmen heroes and Turkmenistan's outstanding national symbols and principles. January, was renamed *Turkmenbashi*, being the first month of the year; February became *Baidag*, meaning flag, marking the month when the Turkmen emblem was designed; March became *Nawruz*, which is the traditional Turkmen New Year, starting on the spring equinox; April became *Gurbansoltan Eje*, after Niyazov's mother, because the month signified growth; May became *Magtymguly*, after a renowned Turkmen poet; June became *Oguz Khan*, after the legendary progenitor of Turkmens; July became *Gorkut*, after the hero of the Gorkut-Ata epic; August became *Alp Arslan*, after the sultan who defeated the Byzantine emperor in 1071; September became *Ruhnama*, the month when Niyazov finishing writing his magnum opus; October became *Garashsizlik*, meaning independence in Turkmen; November became *Sanjar*, after the last ruler of the Seljuk Empire; and December became *Bitaraplyk*, meaning neutrality, as it was on December 12 that the Turkmen ambassador declared his country to be neutral in his speech at the United Nations General Assembly.[46]

A similar treatment was given to the days of the week. Monday became *Bash Gun*, Beginning Day; Tuesday, *Yash Gun*, Young Day; Wednesday, *Hosh Gun*, Good Day; Thursday, *Sogap Gun*, Blessed Day; Friday, *Anna Gun*, Mother Day; Saturday, *Ruh Gun*, Soul Day (signifying the day to read the *Ruhnama*); and Sunday, *Dynch Gun*, Recovery Day.

These measures required endorsement by the People's Council and the parliament, which followed instantly. In another example of Niyazov turning a mere whim into a decree, when he found that traffic policemen were harassing drivers and extorting petty bribes, he sacked them all and deployed army recruits to do the job.

While running the day-to-day administration, Niyazov allowed himself to ponder higher thoughts. Inspired by what he believed to be a semi-divine revelation, he decreed that the life of a Turkmen consisted of nine stages of twelve years each: starting with childhood, and progressing through adolescence, youth, maturity, the prophetic stage, the inspirational stage (61 to 72 years, Niyazov's age bracket in 2002), wisdom, old age, and finally the Oguz Khan stage, ending at the incredible age of 109.

While indulging his fancies, neither he nor his secret police, the KNB, got a clue that his bête noire, Shikhmuradov, had slipped back into Turkmenistan in September 2002 and secured refuge in Ashgabat.

A FAILED COUP ATTEMPT AND ITS AFTERMATH

At 7 a.m. on November 25, 2002, a car and two trucks attempted to ambush Niyazov's motorcade in downtown Ashgabat as it was proceeding to the golden-domed presidential office, with the president riding in an armored Mercedes. In the following shoot-out involving machine-gun fire, several assailants and four policemen were injured, and one person was killed. Niyazov was unhurt.

In his television speech, Niyazov described the incident as an attempt to assassinate him. Among the alleged conspirators, he singled out Boris Shikhmuradov, Hudaiberdy Orazov, and Nur Muhammad Khanamov. His government described the attack as "an act of international terrorism" carried out by former high officials with the aid of "foreign mercenaries." It confiscated the properties belonging to them and their close relatives in accordance with the articles of the Betrayers of the Motherland Decree. Orazov and Khanamov, who were living in exile, denied any involvement. From his hideout, Shikhmuradov said on his website, Gündogar, that any number of people could have wanted Niyazov dead: "Niyazov deserves as many deadly gunshots as the lives and destinies he has ruined."[47]

The wide-ranging arrests that followed covered not only the suspected conspirators, which included Batir Berdyev, who succeeded Shikhmuradov as foreign minister, but also their close relatives, totalling over a hundred.[48] The manhunt slowed down only after Shikhmuradov surfaced on December 25. Before surrendering to the authorities from his hideout in the Uzbek embassy in Ashgabat, he explained on his website that he was doing so to spare his relatives further torture and see an end to further detentions.[49]

Four days later, the authorities aired a confession by Shikhmuradov on the state-run television, excerpts of which appeared on Russian TV1. He said he had devised the plan to assassinate Niyazov while under the influence of drugs, and that he and his co-plotters intended to overthrow the constitutional order in Turkmenistan. He thanked Niyazov for his forgiveness, and praised his spiritual guidance in the matter. "Among us there is not one normal person," he concluded. "We are all nobodies. I am not a person capable of running a country. I am a criminal, able only to destroy it."[50] Within days, the Supreme Court tried him, found him guilty of treason, and sentenced him to twenty-five years in prison, the maximum statutory penalty. But when his filmed confession was shown to the People's Council, it retrospectively raised the legal penalty for treason to life imprisonment.

Appearing on television, Niyazov revealed that he had rejected calls for Shikhmuradov's execution. "We sentence him to life imprisonment," he said. "We will put aside the word—death. Only Allah decides that." On January 25, 2003, he announced that forty-six people had been convicted of attempting to assassinate him, without providing the details, and said the trial was over.[51] He promoted the ministers of interior and state security to major-generals, and awarded a special prize to the prosecutor general. He ordered the publication of a book to record the conspiracy. Western observers condemned the trial by confessions and the mass arrests of suspects' families, as well as the state-controlled media's treatment of the defendants.

Given the dictatorial nature of the regime, much credence was given to the theory that the authorities had stage-managed the assassination attempt to provide Niyazov with a rationale to quash the opposition even further. However, in his interview with the Berlin-based *Der Spiegel*, in June 2003, Hudaiberdy Orazov disclosed that he and Shikhmuradov had planned to abduct Niyazov, take him to the parliament chamber, and compel him to resign. The plan went awry when the assailants failed to intercept the presidential motorcade at its head, letting Niyazov's armored Mercedes pass,[52] before firing their weapons. This version was confirmed by Leonid Komarovsky, a naturalized U.S. citizen of Russian origin and a business associate of Shikhmuradov, who was arrested as a suspect but freed in May 2003 following pressure by Washington.[53] Komarovsky had been given to understand that no weapons would be used in the ambush. This sensational information, given voluntarily, provided a radically different perspective on the ambush of November 25, 2002.

The bloody shoot-out in downtown Ashgabat was the first and most serious challenge to his authority that Niyazov faced since his rise to power in 1985. It left him shaken. He curtailed his highly publicized tours of the provinces. To his disappointment, he found that his label of the attack on his motorcade as "an act of international terrorism" did not resonate in Western capitals. Distraught, Niyazov concluded, reluctantly, that he needed a Big Brother after all, and that role could be performed only by Russia.

Internally, he exploited the episode to the hilt. The incarceration of his leading adversaries put to rest any plans the PDMT had to stage nonviolent, anti-Niyazov acts. But, leaving nothing to chance, he locked up several hundred citizens suspected of possible ties with the opposition. To ratchet up pressure on dissidents, present or potential, he revived exit visas, having abrogated them only a year earlier. He ordered secret services and law enforcement bodies to monitor conversations conducted in public places. He called on citizens to report any "anti-national" talk they overheard to the police. His subsequent ban on listening to car radios was meant to eliminate the background speech or music used by those indulging in subversive conversation.

Niyazov imposed further restrictions on the nongovernmental organizations (NGOs), limiting their activities and narrowing their access to funds from abroad. Even before the latest crackdown, foreign diplomats complained that at their meeting with Turkmen officials they found their interlocutors tongue-tied since "everything was bugged as far as they know." A Western businessman told a visiting American journalist that his office was stacked with Turkmen informants from the local intelligence agency.[54]

When the OSCE's Office for Democratic Institutions and Human Rights (ODIHR) insisted on its right to send a representative to investigate human rights in Turkmenistan, Niyazov's government refused to give a visa to its rapporteur, Professor Emmanuel Decaux. It also denied OSCE access to political prisoners.

At Niyazov's behest, the People's Council, freshly elected in April 2003, with all its members belonging to the Democratic Party of Turkmenistan and chaired by Ovezgeldi Atayev, changed the constitution to make itself the prime legislative body at the expense of the parliament, which lost its power to amend the constitution or call referendums. The Council acquired the authority to dissolve parliament and order fresh elections, and it empowered the president to participate in the parliamentary proceedings as its supreme leader. With the power to appoint Supreme Court judges already conferred upon him, Niyazov became the absolute ruler of Turkmenistan, constitutionally.

In the parliamentary poll that followed in December 2004, all 130 candidates who were allowed to contest the fifty seats were members of the Democratic Party of Turkmenistan, and were vetted by Niyazov. Officials reported the turnout to be 77 percent, down from the incredible 99 percent in the previous poll. More importantly, veering from past practice, all the contestants were ethnic Turkmen, a further sign of Turkmenization initiated by Niyazov. This left the non-Turkmens, forming one-seventh of the population, unrepresented, which was a matter of concern to Uzbekistan and Russia (ethnic Uzbeks making up 5 percent of the total; and ethnic Russians 4 percent).

RELATIONS WITH TASHKENT AND MOSCOW

With the Uzbek government's complicity in the failed coup attempt now proven, Niyazov intensified official discrimination against ethnic Uzbeks. He ordered further curtailment of the Uzbek-language media and education. Uzbek clerics, who had traditionally run Turkmenistan's Official

Islamic Administration, found themselves replaced by their Turkmen counterparts. The reintroduction of exit visas severely affected ethnic Uzbeks, concentrated as they were in the Turkmen-Uzbek border region. The already strained relations between Ashgabat and Tashkent worsened. It would take two years before Niyazov would agree to meet Karimov to discuss water sharing and drug trafficking, which had increased with the big jump in poppy production in post-Taliban Afghanistan, which became the source of 90 percent of the global supplies of heroin.

Russian complicity, if any, in the failed coup attempt had been passive. Ever since the breakup of the Soviet Union, Moscow had emerged as the city to which the dissidents from Central Asia gravitated. The anti-Niyazov dissidents had found refuge there under the provisions of the dual citizenship treaty between Turkmenistan and Russia. Despite repeated requests for the extradition of Turkmen opposition leaders, the Kremlin had refused to comply. This cooled Niyazov's attitude toward local Russians and the Russian language. With the introduction of the *Ruhnama* signalling a concerted drive to Turkmenize society at large, Niyazov drastically curtailed the use of Russian in education and official communication.

In response, the Kremlin refrained from condemning the assassination attempt on Niyazov. Only after a successful meeting between Niyazov and a Russian delegation led by Vladimir Rushailo, the national Security Council chief, in Ashgabat in January 2003, did Rushailo describe the ambush as a "manifestation of terrorism." The two sides initialed protocols on mutual cooperation in arresting and extraditing "suspected criminals" and in the sale of Turkmen gas for the next twenty-five years. Three months later, presidents Vladimir Putin and Niyazov signed the two agreements in Moscow.

But that was not enough of an incentive for Niyazov to extend the dual citizenship treaty with Moscow, which was about to expire. Those ethnic Russians who failed to acquire Turkmen citizenship by late June faced expulsion. Those wishing to remain Russian citizens had to fly to Moscow to complete their documentation, but needed exit visas to leave—trapping them in a Kafkaesque situation. Their failure to do so resulted in the confiscation of their property. The plight of several thousand ethnic Russians in Turkmenistan stirred parliamentarians and the press in Moscow, but had no impact on Putin's government.

Once Niyazov had fully recovered from the trauma of the assassination attempt, and noticed that the price of natural gas had more than doubled in five years, he demanded that Russia's Gazprom should renegotiate the terms for the Turkmen gas. When that did not happen, he shut off the supplies in December 2004, and relented only after Gazprom agreed to substitute partial payment in technical equipment with cash four months later.

The big spurt in the opium poppy crops in Afghanistan from 2003 to 2004, resulting in soaring exports of opium and heroin, provided Niyazov with a legitimate ground to tighten Turkmenistan's security cooperation with Washington. In 2004, he used the annual visits by the combatant commander of CENTCOM, General John Abizaid, and his deputy, Lt. General Lance Smith, to strengthen the ongoing military-technical cooperation with the Pentagon.

Taking Niyazov's word at face value that he would enter into a "human rights dialogue" with the European Union, the European Commission and the international trade committee of the European Parliament voted to grant Turkmenistan "most favored nation" trading status with the EU. These concessions were motivated by the energy-hungry EU's interest in Turkmen natural gas.

With relations with Washington on an even keel, a long-term gas contract with Moscow firmly in place, and gas output running at 55 billion cubic meters a year in an international market of sharply rising fossil fuel prices, Niyazov was in a buoyant mood. Surrounded by sycophants, he implemented his ideas—often absurd, sometimes eccentric—with unrestrained aplomb.

NIYAZOV'S DECREES: ECCENTRIC, ABSURD, INTRUSIVE

According to Shikhmuradov, fanciful ideas typically struck Niyazov over the weekend, on *Ruh Gun* (Saturday, the day to read the *Ruhnama*) and *Dynch Gun* (Sunday, Recovery Day). It was his onerous task to dissuade the president from transforming his whims into decrees. Following Shikhmuradov's departure for Beijing, Niyazov reached his decisions after perfunctory consultations with his advisers.

Niyazov's orders required that entrance to universities be contingent on applicants passing a test on the *Ruhnama*, and that prisoners be denied release until and unless they had taken an oath on it. When he decreed the use of *Ruhnama* in mosques in 2004, Mufti Nasrullah ibn Ibadullah protested. He lost his position and found himself behind bars, accused of treason as a co-conspirator in the attempted coup of November 2002.

During one of his tours of villages in 2004, Niyazov noticed that local libraries were deserted, so he issued a decree that *all* rural libraries must be closed. Later, in order to economize, he would order the closure of all hospitals outside the capital and major cities.

When a string of weather forecasts proved wrong, he dismissed the lead weatherman. He banned makeup for the television news reporters, male and female, because it masked their natural wheatish color, making them look white, and masked the difference between the appearances of men and women.

In February 2004, he instructed his cabinet to increase video surveillance of all official buildings and important economic facilities. As it was, intelligence agencies had already ensured that all restaurants were bugged. Though Niyazov tolerated satellite dishes, common in the capital, cable TV remained outlawed. Turkmen Telecom, the sole Internet service provider, charged excessive subscription fees, monitored e-mails, and increased the number of websites that it blocked.

Later that month, during a TV interview, he instructed the Education Ministry to monitor the students' hairstyles, taking state intervention in private life to a new record. He declared that young men would not be allowed to wear long hair or beards, implying that the ban did not apply to old men. As goatees were common among young and middle-aged men in Ashgabat, they were the ones to get the chop.[55] Niyazov also ruled that all licensed drivers must pass a morality test or forfeit their license.

In the course of cutting the health care budget as part of restructuring and privatizing the health service, he ordered the dismissal of 15,000 health visitors, nurses, midwives, and orderlies—apparently without consulting the health ministry or hospital managements. The sacked employees' jobs were to be performed by untrained army conscripts.

Sitting on a podium alongside the rector of Agricultural University and other dignitaries in Ashgabat on April 5, Niyazov gave a vintage performance after he had noticed the gold teeth of a female speaker named Selbijan:

Selbijan, don't be offended. Your golden teeth are beautiful but you, the youth, are even more beautiful when you have your own white teeth. I am not saying this to you [students] only but also to the entire Turkmen youth . . . We have the minister of health [Gurbanguly Berdymukhammedov, deputy chairman of the cabinet, who would later succeed him] sitting here and he is a dentist himself. Selbijan, he will fix you such good teeth . . . Please agree to this. And don't take this to heart, and say *I am getting involved in everything*. I have a dentist from Germany taking care of my teeth. That poor man says that they made a mistake in Europe by trying to save teeth by eating mincemeat, mashed vegetables or apples, or drinking juice made from them. If teeth are not used to chew solids, they grow weak . . . He says that our [Turkmen] people gnaw bones—chicken bones and sheep bones . . . The harder the substance you chew, the stronger your teeth will become . . . This is my advice.[56]

Later that month, Niyazov banned importing foreign print media, thus depriving rural citizens of news of events even in the neighboring states. The only foreign journalist with accreditation in Turkmenistan was a correspondent for the Moscow-based Itar-Tass news agency.

In his unending crusade to safeguard and promote pristine Turkmen culture, in August 2005 he outlawed sound recordings "at musical performances on state holidays, in broadcasts by Turkmen television channels, at all cultural events organized by the state . . . in places of mass assembly and at weddings and celebrations organized by the public." He did this to protect the musical and singing traditions of the Turkmen people.

Turkmenistan has a long-established musical culture. Magtymguly Feraghy (1733–1800), its preeminent poet, composed lyrics—four-line poems with a distinctive rhyming scheme—which more recently came to form the core of Turkmen folk music. They have become the staple of most folk singers who play the two-stringed *dutar* (literally, "two strings"). Dutar and similar plucked musical instruments have a very long history in the region, as revealed by archaeological finds in Merv (aka Mari) dating back to the third century.[57] Deploring the sight of "old voiceless singers lip-synching their old songs" on television, Niyazov called for creating "our new culture."[58]

In February 2006, a third of the republic's elderly stopped receiving their pensions, while an additional 200,000 received smaller amounts. Furthermore, pensions received during the previous two years had to be returned to the state. This had to do with Niyazov's declaration in 2004 about the nine stages of a Turkmen's life, each spanning twelve years, with old age starting at eighty-five. However, the real reason for this cruel diktat was the deficit in the state pension fund, which had compelled the government to draw on the currency reserves to pay state benefits. Niyazov's order had also terminated state maternity and sick leave payments.

Next, Niyazov banished dogs from Ashgabat because of their "unappealing odor." This was a bizarre turn, after having said in his April 2004 address to university students, "When I was young, I used to look after a dog. . . . Dogs chew bones not out of hunger but because they contain calcium and fluorine, and that is natural."

The one area in which Niyazov was always consistent was his megalomania. In late 2005, he decreed that instead of taking the universal Hippocratic oath, physicians in Turkmenistan should swear an oath to him. Almost a year later, the Education Ministry ruled that those teachers who failed to publish praise of Niyazov would face dismissal or a lower salary. The only way newspaper editors could cope with teachers' frantic efforts to publish was to give each of them only a couple of short paragraphs.

In 2006, Niyazov declared the first Saturday (*Ruh Gun*) in November as Health Day. He ordered his cabinet ministers to undertake an eight-kilometer (five-mile) walk, starting at the Turkmenbashi Eternally Great Park on the outskirts of Ashgabat, up the concrete path built into the mountains to the top, where they would be greeted by Niyazov (arriving there by a helicopter) before TV cameras. He rebuked those ministers who took longer than 120 minutes to complete the task. Given his heart problems over the past decade, he should have been the one to undertake the "health walk."

As fate would have it, seven and a half weeks later, on December 21, 2006, Sapramurat Niyazov, bearing the recently enhanced honorifics of the Great Leader of Turkmens (*Beyik Turkmenbashi*) and God's Prophet on Earth, died of heart failure. The Turkmen despot left behind a republic where the average monthly income was $60. Yet most people managed to get by on the generous state subsidies for housing and basic foods, and free electricity, water, and gas. "We are not free but we are not hungry," an unnamed Turkmen told visiting *New York Times* correspondent C. J. Chivers, who noted that food was inexpensive, gasoline sold for 4 U.S. cents per American gallon, and the bazaars were full with Chinese goods.[59]

Niyazov's legacy was a Turkmenistan where it was impossible to escape his image. A serious-looking Niyazov stared out of every banknote, coin, and postage stamp. His grinning face embellished not just crockery, yogurt containers, vodka bottles, posters, plaques, and hoardings, but also passenger train coaches and the national airline's aircraft cabins. A miniature of his gold-plated face crowning the Neutrality Arch lit up a corner of TV screens. Large portraits of him hung all over the republic, particularly on major roads and public buildings. When it came to statues of Niyazov, even the desolate Kara Kum Desert boasted one.

The Turkmen dictator left behind Ashgabat, a settlement of 600,000 which had expanded well into the Kara Kum Desert and bore no relationship to the city in which he had grown up. Most of the five-star hotels remained almost empty, as did the high-rise blocks which, priced at a staggering $25,000 each, were too expensive to rent or purchase.

"There is, indeed, a touch of Istanbul about the place, crossed with Stalin's Moscow, and dipped in the moods of the Taj Mahal," wrote Waldemar Januszczak, a visiting British journalist in 2006. "Every new building erected since independence has been clad in identical white marble tiles that are exactly 80 cms long and 40 cms wide. Wherever possible, this marble gets topped off with gold, notably in the President's Palace [built to comemmorate Niyazov's rule], an enlarged Parthenon upon which sits the world's biggest nugget, a particularly huge golden dome."[60]

The next occupant of the Presidential Palace would be Gurbanguly Berdymukhammedov.

CONTINUITY WITH SOME CHANGE

The transfer of power was surprisingly smooth. Under the constitution, acting presidency should have gone to Ovezgeldi Atayev, chairman of the People's Council. But it was revealed that, following a criminal investigation into his activities, he had lost his office. So the choice fell to the cabinet's deputy chairman, Berdymukhammedov. The People's Council met to amend the constitution to permit the acting president to contest the supreme office along with five other candidates on February 11, 2007. The contestants did not include the dead president's son, Murat, partly because he was only half-Turkmen, and partly because of his reputation as a playboy.

Like Niyazov, Berdymukhammedov had a humble background. Born in 1957 in a peasant household in Baba Arap village, he graduated as a dentist at the age of twenty-two from the Turkmen State Medical Institute in Ashgabat. After several years of working as a dentist, he pursued higher studies in Moscow, where he received a Ph.D. in medical sciences. There was no record of him joining the Communist Party, which probably worked in his favor in independent Turkmenistan. In 1995, he headed the dentistry section of the Health Ministry while also serving as dean of the dentistry faculty of the Turkmen State Medical Institute.

Berdymukhammedov's star rose when Niyazov selected him as his personal dentist. He became health minister in 1997, and four years later Niyazov promoted him to deputy chairman of the Council of Ministers. It fell upon him to implement the near-abrogation of the free health care system of the Soviet era.

A stocky man with a pudgy face and thick, black hair, he looked so much like a younger, albeit taller, Niyazov that word went around that he was an illegitimate child of the Turkmenbashi—a rumor which seemed to improve his already very high chances of electoral success. For the sake of continuity and stability, he promised to follow in the footsteps of Niyazov, his mentor. He he won 89 percent of the vote, according to official sources, who also claimed an unrealistic turnout of 98.7 percent. What followed was continuity with some change. Large portraits of Berdymukhammedov began appearing on public buildings and major intersections.

On the other hand, some of Niyazov's decrees were so blatantly unjust, insanely megalomaniac, or downright silly, that his successor lost little time reversing them. He extended compulsory education to the original eleven years and reintroduced the teaching of foreign languages in schools. He issued a new Code of Social Guarantees, which restored pensions and state maternity benefits, and raised monthly the pension for war veterans' families to one million manat (U.S. $40), the minimum pension being 300,000 manat.

In theory, he authorized licensing of new Internet cafes. In practice, some state-run Internet cafes opened in Ashgabat, each charging $4 an hour, the equivalent of two days' average salary in the city, with the sole Internet service provider blocking access to critical websites in Russian.

Berdymukhammedov emulated his predecessor's style of rebuking ministers and state officials on TV, and even dismissing them instantly. He sacked the top law enforcement officer thus: "I have a whole file of evidence against you, and I could dishonor you like a dog."[61] On the other hand, the golden profile of Niyazov disappeared from the right-hand corner of state-run TV channels on July 8. Also, his name was excised from the country's patriotic oath, as was his portrait from most banknotes. Yet, fear persisted. The mere mention of the new leader's name in public made locals twitch, flinch, whisper, fall silent, or look the other way.

On the eve of his fiftieth birthday in July 2007, Berdymukhammedov called on the people and officials not to turn the occasion into an "ostentatious national festival," and ordered that he not be greeted by singing school children, dancers, or public oaths of loyalty. Yet, on the fateful day, he awarded himself a huge gold-and-diamond pendant and issued silver and gold coins with his portrait.

Contradicting Niyazov's declarations, Berdymukhammedov admitted that a drug problem exised in Turkmenistan. He put an end to the erratic payment of salaries to the employees of collective farms, which had become endemic under Niyazov, and resumed regular payments. He released thousands of prisoners, including some government officials jailed by Niyazov.

He countermanded Niyazov's ban on the opera and the circus.[62] However, he also overturned his predecessor's tolerant attitude toward satellite dishes in the capital, decreeing their removal because they were "ugly."

Overall, there were early signs that citizens were slowly losing their fear of speaking out. On the eve of the December 9 elections to the People's Council, whose members were still required to belong to the Democratic Party of Turkmensitan, some voters expressed their views to the correspondents of Radio Free Europe/Radio Liberty (RFE/RL). "Frankly speaking, at this moment I know nothing about candidates for the Halk Maslahaty [People's Council] because we were not invited to the meetings with them," said Tejen Aga, a seventy-year-old pensioner in Ashgabat. "And there is not enough information in the media about their programs." He also exposed, albeit inadvertently, an electoral malpratice, by stating that he had received just one ballot for a family of ten. "I was told I could vote with all passports of my family members older than eighteen." This was an outright negation of the basic democratic principle of one person, one vote.

"Some members of the Halk Maslahaty live in our village, but we don't see any results from their work," said Rozy Allakov, a farmer in the Lebap region. "There is no telephone connection in our village. Only the village governor has one. . . . Many villages in the region have no natural gas. Turkmen gas is used in Europe but not in our village. The members of the Halk Maslahaty should take care of the peoples' needs [but they don't]."

Such grievances were not limited to distant villages. "We don't know the results of directives related to the agricultural sector of the country that were adopted at the 20th Halk Maslahaty session," said Azgeldi Hommadov, a thirty-four-year-old civil engineer in Ashgabat. "Neither do I know about measures taken by Halk Maslahaty members against corruption, which is a serious issue in all regions. At the meetings with their voters, the candidates are afraid to raise such criticism." Nor did the media deal with those issues, he added. "They cover only success stories. Only one side of life is shown."

Besides Niyazov and his family, at the core of high-level corruption were other favored families to whom the government had allocated quotas for growing cotton and selling it privately outside the state trading system. Such families were thus making fortunes due to the vast disparity beween the local cost of production and the price in the international market.

Though none of these complaints had become part of the public discourse, murmurs could be heard. Among those who noticed the change was the eighty-year-old writer, Rahim Esenov. The Niyazov government had banned his book, *The Crowned Wanderer*, and put him under house arrest in 2004. That won him the PEN Freedom to Write Award two years later. He compared the post-Niyazov thaw in Turkmenistan to the thaw that ensued when Khrushev succeeded Stalin in Moscow.

"A huge billboard appeared near my home," he said. "It contains candidates' photos and biographies in both Turkmen and Russian. I have to admit that I was happy to see it. There wasn't such a [practice] before. Only newspapers used to publish information [about candidates] that was only in the Turkmen language. Now, there are also pictures. It was such a big surprise that I even stopped walking [when I saw it first]. Other people also stopped walking and read it. I guess it is not enough but they are the sprouts of the new and the good." In short, there was change, however incipient, in the air. It remained to be seen whether the newly elected People's Council would reflect the evolving mood of the nation, or block it.

In foreign affairs, though, Berdymukhammedov continued Niyazov's policy of fortifying the already strong economic ties with Moscow. Gazprom purchased 50 billion cubic meters of Turkmen gas annually out of its total output of 62 billion cubic meters. During a conference call with Berdymukhammedov from the Kremlin in December 2007, Putin signed a tripartite deal with Kazakh President Nursultan Nazarbayev to build a pipeline along the eastern rim of the Caspian northwards to Russia to carry 10 billion cubic meters a year. The pipeline, said Putin, would "become a new, important contirbution of our nations into strengthening the European energy security."[63]

Washington had different priorities. "What we want is for this system to change where Gazprom can practically dictate the price of gas on the Turkmen end, and sell it for nearly three times that amount in Europe," said an unnamed U.S. official. Actually, Gazprom bought Turkmen gas at $100 per 1,000 cubic meters, and sold it to Western Europe at $250 after transporting it for thousands of kilometers, thus raising its value. The delivery price of gas varies with the distance it travels to reach its destination. Gazprom agreed to pay $130 per 1,000 cubic meters of Turkmen gas from January 1, 2008, and $150 six months later.[64]

To the further disappointment of the United States and the EU, a Chinese company signed up to develop a gas field along the eastern side of the Oxus River, and agreed to buy 30 billion cubic meters of gas annually for thirty years, with a plan to build a 7,000-kilometer pipeline, operational from 2009.[65]

On the other hand, continuing Niyazov's annual ritual of receiving the Combatant Commander of CENTCOM, Berdymukhammedov reviewed the security relations between the two countries. He also emulated his predecessor's interest in the underwater gas pipeline in the Caspian to be extended to Turkey, as favored by Washington, while pointing out the lack of border demarcation in the Caspian between the five littoral states.

For its part, the State Department continued to hold the Turkmen government in low esteem. The $16 million in annual aid to Turkmenistan, including grants to NGOs, was derisory. Washington dramatized its disapproval of the despotic regime when it sent an assistant secretary of state, Richard Boucher, to attend Niyazov's funeral.

In stark contrast, three regional presidents turned up for the occasion. Among them was Nazarbayev—a country which loomed large in the mind of Nikita Khrushchev as he contemplated a huge increase in the agricultural produce of the Soviet Union.

CHAPTER 4

KAZAKHSTAN:

RISING OIL STATE COURTED BY BIG POWERS

KAZAKHSTAN, ALONG WITH SOUTHERN SIBERIA, BECAME THE CENTER-piece OF Nikita Khrushchev's virgin land plan in late 1953 to trans-form its vast, underused territory into fertile agricultural land to give the Soviet Union self-sufficiency in food and meat within three decades.

The Central Committee of the Communist Party of Kazakhstan (CPK) quickly fell in line. At its meeting in February 1954, it replaced the first and second secretaries respectively with P. K. Ponomarenko and Leonid Brezhnev, a Moscow-based, part-Ukrainian, part-Russian protégé of Khrushchev. They resolved to transform 3.5 million hectares of grazing land into 300 state farms within a year as the first step toward turning 16 million hectares of steppe into agricultural fields. To achieve this, they needed to attract volunteers from outside Kazakhstan, a proposition opposed by native Kazakhs. They had seen their proportion in the population decline by nearly half from 57 percent in 1926 (a census year), with the share of European settlers—Russians, Ukrainians, and Germans—rising by about half from 34 percent.[1] When Ponomarenko failed to overcome Kazakh resistance to the virgin land plan, he was replaced by Brezhnev in July 1955.

Brezhnev adroitly used the stick-and-carrot approach to dissipate Kazakh opposition, an achievement that accelerated his rise in the Communist Party of the Soviet Union. He in turn quickly promoted those who were energetic and enthusiastic, and expanded a network of cadres, both Slav and Kazakh, personally loyal to him. He initiated a program of transforming collective farms into state-run enterprises, thus placing Kazakh farmers unfamiliar with modern agricultural and livestock breeding practices under the super-vision of well-trained Slav cadres, and improving output as well as integrat-ing the new agricultural lands into the Soviet economy.

In March 1956, Brezhnev returned to Moscow to take up a better party job, but maintained contacts with his loyalists in Kazakhstan. Following a rapid turnover of the first secretaries during the next few years, a Kazakh protégé of Brezhnev, Dinmuhammad Kunayev (1912–93), came to the fore in January 1960. A graduate of the Moscow Institute of Nonferrous Metals and Gold, Kunayev started his working life as a machinist at a copper-smelting plant and rose to become the administrative director of a mine. He joined the Communist Party in 1939, and within three years became vice-chairman of the Council of Ministers (i.e., deputy prime minister), with the special task of overseeing the republic's industry during the Great Patriotic War. After a decade in that post, he became president of the Academy of Sciences of Kazakhstan, and in 1955 chairman of the Council of Ministers (i.e., prime minister). As the CPK's first secretary, he concentrated on improving the productivity of land under cereals, which had shot up from 7 million hectares in 1953 to 23 million hectares in 1960.[2] Kunayev proved unequal to the monumental task, and was reverted to his earlier post of chairman of the Council of Ministers in 1963.

However, the rise of Brezhnev as the supreme leader in October 1964 paved the way for Kunayev's reemergence as the party chief in Kazakhstan. He now ruled over a republic of some 11 million, which had during the past decade absorbed a Slav workforce of nearly a million. He now stressed scientific management of agriculture, and steered the state farm sector, consisting of 1,500 units, away from acquiring gigantic fields. This raised productivity, with 2,059 state farms providing two-thirds of the republic's agricultural produce by 1970.[3] Elected as a candidate member of the CPSU's Politburo in 1966, Kunayev was elevated to full membership in 1971—an unparalleled honor for a Central Asian with a Muslim name.

The arrival of hundreds of thousands of young, politically conscious Russian and Ukrainian volunteers during the decade of 1954 to 1963 raised the CPK's membership by nearly two-thirds to 317,700.[4] It strengthened the Slavs' hold over the party, which upset most Kazakhs.

In the countryside, the Russian and Kazakh agricultural cooperatives and state farms remained apart, physically and culturally. For instance, a casual visit to these establishments showed that Kazkahs had larger families than Russians. But even in cities, there was little social intercourse between the two communites. The Russians living in the republic stuck to their culture and dietary habits, and the native Kazakhs stuck to theirs.

In Russian homes, after the hors d'oeuvre of smoked fish or pâté came borscht, beet soup, followed by meat or fish served with potatoes, bread, or dumplings, and vegetables. By contrast, the Kazakh diet, reflecting the nomadic legacy, centered around horse meat and mutton processed into sausages or boiled in cooking oil and served with onion and pepper. Round, flat loaves of bread, often baked in tandoor ovens, were de rigueur. Eating with hands was common practice. Indeed, the pride of the Kazakh cuisine— boiled horse meat on the bone and noodles covered in a meat broth—was called *beshbarmak*, meaning five fingers. And kumiss, the mildly alcoholic mare's milk, long regarded as therapeutic by Central Asians, remained a very Kazakh drink.

What Kazakhs and Russians shared was their love for vodka and black tea. Vodka had penetrated the Kazakh life as thoroughly as had whiskey among Native Americans. It had become the standard beverage at all important meals and functions, Kazakh or Russian, with a toast preceding each round. As for the commonly shared nonalcoholic beverage, Russians drank tea from cups filled to the brim whereas Kazakhs did so in small, half-filled, wide-mouthed saucers.

Undeterred by such differences between the two dominant ethnic groups, Kunayev reactivated traditional Kazakh-dominated networks consisting of extended families. The existence of such networks went back to the era of the Small, Middle and Great Hordes, when it was customary to pinpoint a person by his or her kin group by identifying the individual's family and its home base. This tradition continued during the Soviet period, and Kunayev tapped into it. His approach went down well with Kazakhs who joined the Communist Party in large numbers. Also his elevation to the position of party chief reassured Kazakhs that the hijacking of their republic by Slavs had virtually ended.

While remaining loyal to Brezhnev, Kunayev consolidated his power base by rewarding those he thought were serving the party and state well, making no distinction between Kazakh and Slav. By so doing, Kunayev, married to a Russian, healed the breach that had developed between Kazakhs and Slavs, and created an ethnically mixed team of senior cadres committed to developing Kazakhstan along socialist lines.

By the late 1970s, the republic met its targets for food production, measured by four-year running averages, with its contribution to the central pool varying widely, from 5 million tons in 1975 to 20 million tons in 1976. With three-quarters of the workforce engaged in agriculture, this achievement was a matter of republican pride.

Industrialization progressed as well. By the early 1980s, Kazakhstan with 6 percent of the Soviet population produced 10 percent of Soviet coal and

5 percent of Soviet oil. Kazakhstan had also acquired a massive space complex at the Baikonur Cosmodrome 300 kilometers (188 miles) away. Unrelated to the Baikonur village, the facility's misleading name was chosen by the government as a decoy for the secret site. It was here that the Soviet spacecraft, Sputnik, was launched in 1957.

Alone among the Central Asian republics, starting in 1949 Kazakhstan provided 18,500 square kilometers (7,140 square miles) of steppe and low hills—centered around Polygon, 160 kilometers (100 miles) east of Semipalatinsk (now Semey)—for nuclear arms testing under Igor Vasilyevich Kurchatov, the chief scientist in charge of the program since 1943.

During the next four decades, 753 nuclear explosions would take place there—27 in the atmosphere, 78 on the ground, and the rest underground. These tests left 300,000 square kilometers (115,800 square miles), inhabited by 2 million people, contaminated with radioactive material, resulting in many cases of birth defects and mental illness.[5] Given the vast size of Kazakhstan, the Kremlin decided to station strategic and tactical nuclear arms on its soil.

SOCIAL CHANGE

Mirroring the modernization of agriculture and industry, the social mores of Kazakhs underwent a sea change. Gone were the feudal ways dominated by *bais*, village notables, and *aksakals*, clan or tribal leaders. Instead, socioeconomic prestige came to rest chiefly with the party leaders, or sometimes with the directors of collective farms if they had a *bai* or *aksakal* background.

Gone too were the practices of the past, when the majority of Kazakhs, being semi-nomadic, maintained separate winter and summer dwellings. To withstand severe cold, they insulated their winter homes by furnishing them with wooden outbuildings. Since their summer migrations with their herds took them south in search of pasture land, they needed separate summer dwellings. Recognizing that grassland was limited, and that perpetual inter-tribal violence was harmful to all, different tribes and clans had over centuries demarcated their turfs and stuck to them. The collectivization of agriculture and animal husbandry in the 1930s ended a way of life originating in pre-medieval times.

An important aspect of the Kazakh traditional life was that they should be able to name seven ancestors—an essential requirement in a community which forbade marriage between relations over so many generations. In the absence of literacy, this could only be done by Kazakh parents and grand-parents spinning yarns about their antecedents to their progeny.

Settlement on collective and state farms, accompanied by literacy in Russian and Kazakh, caused most traditional customs to become extinct. But some persisted. For instance, only family members had the privilege of viewing and admiring a newborn baby in the first forty days. Likewise, the mourning period for a dead person was kept to forty days, as required by Islam. Harking back to their nomadic past, when their ancestors rode horses under clear skies, Kazakhs continued to revere the sun, the moon, and the stars. Even today, most ethnic Kazakhs do not dare point at these celestial objects. And, as a community whose break from pastoral and feu-dal life extends only a few generations, Kazkahs revere old people and refrain from speaking ill of women in public.

On the other hand, the influence of mullahs and Islam—always peripher-al among Kazakhs—withered. The anti-religious drives conducted during the 1930s and again during the Khrushchev era led to large-scale closures of the places of worship and religious schools, reducing the number of mosques in the capital, Almaty, from sixty-three during the pre-revolution days to one. The total number in the republic now was a mere thirty, based mainly in the south, where Kazakhs outnumbered Slavs, and where the mausoleum of the much-revered Khwaja Ahmad Yasawi (d. 1120) near the historic town of Turkestan was located.

Before the Bolshevik revolution, Kazakh intellectuals were engaged in a debate about the relationship between Islam and Kazakh culture, and between the Sharia and the Adat, customary law, which had evolved over centuries among Kazakhs. Many intellectuals argued that Islamic practices should follow the cultural needs of Kazakhs, rather than precede them—showing their conversion to Islam to be superficial, as was the case with the community at large. After formally embracing Islam, Kazakhs had main-tained strong pagan beliefs and practices and, being nomadic, failed to pray regularly at mosques, which were sparse in the steppes.

The conversion of the Kazakh majority in the early nineteenth century occurred due to two distinct reasons. One was the influence of wandering Tatar clerics, often of the Sufi ilk, originating outside the Kazakh territory. The other was the pressure of colonizing Russians, who perceived Islam (already prevalent among settled Kazakhs) as a cement for the disparate nomadic tribes that would make them easy to control.

Those Kazakh intellectuals who wanted Islamic practices to reflect Kazakh culture preferred the Adat to the Sharia in Kazakh courts. They included Ali Khan Bukeikhanov, head of Alash Orda, the leading Kazakh nationalist party. "Kazakhs are non-Muslims or at very most half-Muslims," he said. "The preservation of customs and traditions is useful to Kazakhs. The Sharia is harmful to Kazakhs."

Both Kazakh and non-Kazakh intellectuals maintained that language was an essential part of Kazakh identity. This was as true of the pre-Bolshevik era as of the revolutionary period. But as Russian influence increased in all facets of Kazakh life, especially after the compulsory collectivization and rapid settlement of nomads during the 1930s, Kazakhs who became universally literate by the late 1960s reacted to Russification.[6]

To preserve and strengthen a separate cultural identity, a minority among Kazakh intellectuals began stressing the significance of Islam in Kazakh history and culture, aware that Islam was alien to Russians. This view was articulated by N. Ashirov, a Kazakh academic, in his book *Islam i Natsiya* (*Islam and Nation*), published in 1975. Stating that "some intellectuals and party elite of Central Asia have tacitly accepted Islam as an important component of their national history and cultural heritage," he argued that "Islam is therefore worth preserving or at least [worth] special treatment by the regime."[7]

That Islamic customs remained a significant factor in Kazakh culture was confirmed by the findings of a survey by T. Saidbayev, a Kazakh researcher, in 1978. The survey showed that 50 percent of the respondents observed Muslim rituals, whereas only 10 percent had any grasp of the Islamic doctrine. It also revealed that most Kazakhs feasted on major Muslim religious days, gave at least "ceremonial importance" to religion to commemorate birth, marriage, and death, and that circumcision of male children was virtually universal.[8] The persistence of Islamic traditions in personal life, especially among the old, was widely known. What the 1978 survey disclosed was that a growing number of young Kazakhs were turning to Islam to fill the moral-ethical vacuum left by the erosion of morality among the party cadres, a characteristic of the latter years of Brezhnev's rule.

Increasingly, the party hierarchy, arrogating ever greater powers to itself, was losing touch with the people. Many farm and factory workers were losing motivation, and attitudes towards public property were deteriorating, as widespread pilfering, bribery, and nepotism gave rise to a parallel economy. The fact that during his final years Brezhnev was too ill to know what was really going on, and was therefore open to manipulation by his close aides, was another negative factor.

Saidbayev's findings captured the symptoms of rising public unease at the way the country was being run, but the party leadership failed to examine the cause of the deepening malaise in order to remedy it, focusing instead on decrying the effect. In early 1981, Kunayev addressed the subject of religion at the CPK's 16th Congress. He regretted that Islam was gaining acceptance even among party members, some of whom were encouraging others to observe Islamic customs and rituals. He urged a reversal of this trend. The party militants and the Communist Youth League (CYL, Komsomol) took up his call, and resorted to highlighting the failure of the party cadres in this sphere.

But there was an important, extraneous element working against them: foreign radio broadcasts. From the late 1970s onward, Islamic broadcasting programs beamed at the Central Asian Soviet republics were launched by Iran, the anti-Communist resistance in Afghanistan, the Persian Gulf monarchies, especially Saudi Arabia, and the Washington-funded Radio Liberty and Radio Free Europe. Despite the jamming ordered by Moscow, some of these transmissions were received and recorded. Many of the commentators tried to combine religion with nationalism, a potent mixture.

By the mid-1980s, on the eve of perestroika, Kazakh mullahs and secular intellectuals, both demanding greater cultural autonomy, recognized Islam as an important part of Kazakh identity. Beyond that, the two groups diverged. Clerics saw no role for Marxism-Leninism in society. In contrast, secular intellectuals wished to adapt this doctrine to Kazakh cultural values, which, they concurred, were formed partly by the moral-ethical values of Islam.

The situation had parallels with what prevailed, politically, in the early twenties, when a special body of Muslim Communists was established in Soviet Russia. The difference this time was that the new intelligentsia was well-versed in Russian, the common language of most Soviet citizens, and was therefore able to address a large body of Muslims and others who were also literate in Russian. Now, as then, the party elite in Moscow was adamant about being the sole decider of doctrinal purity, be it in economic management, nationality relations, or culture.

These developments occurred against the background of Kunayev's diminishing power, which, starting with Brezhnev's demise in 1982, went into a tailspin with the rise of Mikhail Gorbachev as the supreme authority three years later. Kunayev managed to get reelected as the CPK's first secretary in February 1986, but failed to prevent the removal of his half-brother, Askar, from the chairmanship of the Kazakh Gosplan (State Plan).

Although later that month, at the CPSU's 27th Congress, Kunayev retained his Politburo seat, he was so much at odds with Gorbachev's policies that a denouement was inevitable. Weakening party discipline emboldened Nursultan Nazarbayev (b. 1940), chairman of the Kazakh Council of Ministers (i.e., prime minister) since 1984, to criticize Kunayev and his record. This happened on December 17, 1986.

BIRTH PANGS OF KAZAKH NATIONALISM

On that day, the state-run media announced that, following the resignation of Kunayev as the CPK's first secretary due to "poor health and old age," the CPK's Central Committee had chosen Gennadi Kolbin, the then first secretary of the Communist Party of his birthplace, Ulyanovsk, 300 miles east of Moscow, to succeed him.

Kolbin's sudden promotion to the highest party job in the Soviet Union's second largest republic at a time when Kazakhs had reached demographic parity with Russians sent shock waves throughout the republic. The appointment of Zakash Kamalidenov, a Kazakh, as second secretary failed to pacify the popular anger. Kazakhs were unprepared to accept the reversal of primacy given to them for the past twenty-two years. Replacing Kunayev with Kolbin sharpened the contradiction that had existed between the center, Moscow, and the periphery, Almaty, strengthening Kazakh nationalism even within the Kazakh ranks of the CPK.

The next day there was a demonstration by about 10,000 people—mainly students, including ethnic Kazakh and Russian members of the CYL—in Almaty. Their placards read, "We are for Kazakhstan" and "Where is Kunayev?" Some of them shouted "Kazakhstan for Kazakhs!" When the armed guards ordered them to disperse, they refused. Communist Party leaders organized a counter-demonstration by workers, who came armed with metal bars and cables and attacked the student demonstrators. In the subsequent melee, which involved firing by the guards, between 2 and 20 people lost their lives, and between 763 and 1,137 were injured. More than 2,200 demonstrators were arrested.[9]

In twelve of the republic's twenty regions, attempts were made to mount pro-Kunayev demonstrations, and thousands of protesting pamphlets were distributed. The Kremlin rushed a team of CPSU bureaucrats under M. S. Solomentsev to calm the situation. On arrival in Almaty, being patrolled by soldiers wearing bullet-proof vests, Solomentsev deplored the rising popularity of "extremism." The authorities hinted that Kunayev had been behind the disturbances. Actually, Kunayev wanted to pacify the rioters, but Kolbin prevented him.[10] It was not until mid-1988, when Kunayev had been out of the CPSU Politburo for a year, and when glasnost had advanced further in the Soviet Union, that the *Izvestia* (*News*) organ of the Soviet government conceded that Kunayev's removal was seen "by certain young people" as "a blow against national esteem and pride, as the eclipse of their hopes."[11]

The watershed event would later be portrayed, rightly, as the first spontaneous "democratic uprising" involving Kazakhs and Russians. Indeed, one of the three leaders—Andrei Statetin, M. Akuyev, and D. Kunayev—convicted for the rioting was a Russian. He received the harshest punishment, eight years' hard labor for "stealing public property," and expulsion from the party. Despite this, the episode came through as basically anti-Russian or at least as a rebellion by young Soviet-educated Kazakhs against the Russian "elder brother." The presence of many people from the countryside led Yegor Beliayev, a Soviet expert on Islam and the Muslim world, to see the hand of Sufi brotherhoods.[12]

Kolbin reacted sharply, singling out the CYL for a severe purge, insisting that it was not aimed solely at the Kazakh members—a claim received skeptically by Kazakhs. He also acted against those who were found participating in religious ceremonies or rituals. Said Aqa Ziayev, the party head in the Jambul region, was sacked for a "public show of respect for religious rites." Later another official was accused of diverting public finances for the construction of an unauthorized mosque.[13] Both these cases were widely publicized, thus further inflaming Kazakh passions.

The Kremlin realized the highly explosive nature of the nationalities problem throughout the Soviet Union and the inadequacy of its means to tackle it. Therefore compromise became its watchword, and Kolbin fell in line. 1988 started with a multi-candidate election for the leadership of CYL organizations in Almaty, followed by an official decision to widen the use of Kazakh in the social-cultural life of Kazakhstan. Action against Islam was limited to rooting out underground Islamic organizations.

As Moscow lifted central trade monopolies in May 1988, the constituent republics set up their own trade organizations, with Kazakhstan and Kyrgyzstan establishing commercial links with neighboring China. While this and other economic liberalization measures gave greater powers to the republics and large enterprises, these changes in the highly centralized economic system caused a drop in output, inducing recession and increasing unemployment.

In spring 1989, word spread in the cities of western Kazakhstan that the refugees from Armenia, which had suffered a devastating earthquake in

December, were being offered scarce housing. This triggered riots, which were quickly suppressed. The event, symptomatic of rising frustration especially among unemployed young men, provided Gorbachev with a rationale to return the top republican party job to a Kazakh. He chose Nazarbayev, who had been the prime minister for five years.

In that job, Nazarbayev had lent his support to a rising campaign against nuclear testing, initiated by Olzhas Suleimanov, an eminent poet. It took the form of protest demonstrations and a mass petition signed by one million citizens.[14]

NAZARBAYEV TAKES THE REINS

In June 1989, Nursultan Nazarbayev—a tall, robust man with Mongoloid features, a receding hairline, and a taste for well-tailored business suits— was elected the CPK's first secretary, a promotion which cooled Kazakh passions but did not guarantee peace.

Nursultan Abishevich Nazarbayev was born into the household of a shepherd, descended from the nomads of the Great Horde, in Chemolgan in the Almaty region—a village without a school. At the boarding school he attended, he accepted an invitation to join the CYL. After he had failed to gain entrance to the Kazakh State University's chemistry faculty, he got a job as a trainee smelter at the Temirtau steel plant then under construction.

Decades later, in his interview with Christopher Robbins, a Russian-speaking British writer, he would describe his life as a steelworker being harsher than that on a collective farm, where he had grown up. He would refer to the nearby town of Karaganda, then a gulag[15] center, harboring violent criminal gangs that terrorized locals. For training he was sent to a steel plant in Ukraine for a year. "The plant made a terrible impression," Nazarbayev said. "The noise was unnerving. Sparks flew like snowflakes in a blizzard, and molten cast iron ran like a spring torrent. Few of us had been raised in a city and we had only a vague idea about the conditions in which Soviet industrial workers had to live and work. Life had been hard for us [on the collective farm]—but this was terrible."[16]

Back at the Temirtau steel plant, twenty-year-old Nursultan worked in front of a blast furnace, amidst hot air filled with gas and dust. "During a shift we had to drink half a bucket of water to replace what we had lost in sweat," he recalled. "After work we needed half an hour in a cold shower to recover." Though his salary of R450 a month (half of which he sent home) was generous, he earned every single kopek of it. "A steel plant runs twenty-four hours, seven days a week," he said. "It is a tough environment in every way. Temperatures of 2,000°C, pressure as high as six times the atmospheric average—if you make a mistake, things explode and people around you die. You have to be sharp and concentrate every second. You cannot shift responsibility on to the shoulders of your neighbor or you lose the respect of your team."[17] What distinguished him from his coworkers was that, like Islam Karimov, he simultaneously took a correspondence course in economics.

Having joined the Communist Party at twenty-two, he became a full-time party official seven years later. Under Kunayev's patronage, he rose steadily from being secretary of the CPK's Central Committee in 1980 to chairman of the Council of Ministers four years later. As he developed a rapport with Gorbachev in Moscow, he began to drift away from Kunayev. His relations with his erstwhile mentor worsened after the latter lost his prime position in the party, and became tense after Nazarbayev stepped into his shoes in mid-1989.[18]

Unable to secure economic independence for his republic, Nazarbayev found other ways of asserting Kazakh autonomy in order to defuse rising grassroots pressure. He protested Moscow's continued use of Kazakh territory for nuclear testing and the creation of environmental pollution. At the same time, he allowed social and political liberalization to proceed.

Among the various political groups that emerged was one focused on rehabilitating the leading protesters in December 1986. Out of this arose the Kazakh National Democratic Party, popularly known as Jeltoksan, the Decembrists. In early 1990, its supporters—mainly Kazakhs with a sprinkling of Russians—condemned Kolbin, Kamalidenov, and Solomentsev, and upheld the "December Glasnost Rehabilitation."

Feeling freer to function as an independent body than before, the 360-member Supreme Soviet, elected in March 1990 with 338 Communist deputies, appointed a committee to investigate the events of December 1986. Its report, published six months later, was a political bombshell:

The demonstration was not nationalistic but part of perestroika. It was not against law and order. It was protest by youth, and it occurred because the Communist Party and its leaders had neglected the consciousness of the people. It was a spontaneous demonstration by the working and university youth. The assessment by the Central Committee of the Communist Party [that it was an extremist outrage] was an insult to the nation. Since the leaders of the demonstration challenged the legitimacy of the [armed] forces of the republic's new party leader [Kolbin], they freed themselves from accepting the decisions of the local governors as well as other high executive organs. A narrow circle of leaders decided to send troops [from their regions] to Almaty to suppress the demonstration.[19]

Accepting the report's findings, the Supreme Soviet ordered an appropriate tablet to be placed at a corner of the Square of the Republic, formerly Brezhnev Square.[20]

The report was applauded outside the chamber, especially by the Jeltoksan, Alash Orda, and the Azat (Free) Movement, which combined Kazakh nationalism with pan-Turkism. Alash, led by Aron Atabek Nutushyev, revived in late 1989. It offered a three-plank platform of pan-Turkism, Islam, and democracy. Its vehement criticism of the government and Russian citizens, and its call for a revolt against "Russian colonial policy," made it a target of official harassment. Its meetings were broken up by security forces. Nutushyev fled to Moscow in February 1990 and went underground. Although less strident, the Azat Movement was equally committed to pan-Turkism, which it tried to popularize through such Turkic symbols as a grey wolf and the crescent and star. It had grown sufficiently by October 1990 to start its own journal, *Azat*, in Almaty.[21] The rising demand for schooling in Kazakh and the continued housing shortage in cities helped the opposition to grow.

To meet the pressing demand for autonomy, the Kazakh Supreme Soviet followed the lead of its Russian counterpart, and on September 28, 1990, declared the primacy of Kazakh legislation over Soviet laws. To underscore the point, Nazarbayev signed a decree outlawing nuclear tests. With ethnic Kazakhs forming an absolute, albeit slim, majority in the parliament, and ethnic Russians reduced to less than a third, the chamber made Kazakh the official language, limited certain civil service posts to Kazakh speakers, and specified 1993 as the date for the full implementation of the policy, giving the Slav-majority areas a two-year extension.

The new law proved popular with Kazakhs, as more new members, almost entirely Kazakh, enrolled in the CPK than the year before, bringing the total to nearly 800,000 in mid-1990.[22] However, as expected, many Slav (Russian and Ukrainian) citizens disapproved of the linguistic law. Some among them advocated the establishment of a Slav autonomous region in the north. Settled primarily on cooperative or state farms and cattle-breeding centers, Slavs formed 60 percent of the population of seven northern regions, five of them abutting the Russian Federation.

As leader of the second-largest republic, rich in resources and home to nearly two-thirds of the 11 million Russians settled in Central Asia,

Nazarbayev occupied a special place in the Soviet hierarchy. So Gorbachev paid attention to his ideas on forming a new association of sovereign states before and after the referendum on the subject in March 1991. Like his Central Asian colleagues, Nazarbayev was for political autonomy rather than outright independence. He advocated an inter-republican concord that would maintain economic union of the integrated Soviet system while a constituent republic controlled its resources as well as its foreign trade and currencies. He acted as a successful mediator between the conflicting views of Presidents Gorbachev and Boris Yeltsin on the formation of a new association. This led to the signing of an interim agreement between nine Soviet republics and the Kremlin on the structure of the new union in April.

The hard-line centralists in the Kremlin felt that too much was being conceded to the republics by the new union treaty to be signed on August 20, so they mounted a coup against Gorbachev. Unlike most Central Asian leaders, Nazarbayev opposed the coup. The anti-coup protests in Almaty condemned it as anti-democratic, so the coup's failure was received as enthusiastically there—where there were nearly five ethnic Russians to two Kazakhs—as it was in Moscow. The three Baltic republics seceded from the Soviet Union and won international recognition as sovereign independent states, reducing the constituent Soviet republics to twelve.

Nazarbayev resigned as the CPK's first secretary, saying the party had "discredited itself in the eyes of the people." Later he advised the party leaders to dissolve it. The CPK's Central Committee, meeting in October, did so by 586 votes to 4. Efforts were then made, successfully, to reconstitute the old organization as the Socialist Party of Kazakhstan. It won official recognition under the Law on Public Associations, which came into effect on September 1. But the Jeltoksan and Alash Orda refused to register, even though they had more than the requisite 3,000 members. They protested at the provisions requiring the party leadership to submit a list of members with addresses, phone numbers, and signatures to the Ministry of Justice, suspicious that the intelligence and security departments would use the information to harass them.

Nazarbayev participated actively in the discussions to finalize a union treaty. He hosted a meeting of the leaders of twelve republics in Almaty on October 2 where the participants initialed an agreement that laid the ground for a union-wide economic structure. On October 18, eight republics signed the document in Moscow, with Azerbaijan, Georgia, Moldova, and Ukraine abstaining. The new agreement was to be a precursor to a similar setup in the political arena, together producing the Union of Sovereign States to replace the Union of Soviet Socialist Republics. But it was superseded by one initiated by Yeltsin.

At home, to implement more effectively the forthcoming reform in Kazakhstan, Nazarbayev decided to hold a ballot for the presidency. Considering success by a wide margin as insufficient, he resolved to achieve an absolute victory. "Now, when transitions to unpopular measures are beginning, only a politician backed by all the people can be sure of himself," he said.[23]

At his behest, the Supreme Soviet had passed an electoral law that required a presidential candidate to produce signatures of 100,000 supporters in eight weeks. But the electoral commission gave the candidates only nine days' notice to do so. Despite this, Hasan Kojahmedov, leader of the Jeltoksan—capitalizing on the 22 percent economic downturn during the year and 155 percent inflation—made sufficient progress to unnerve Nazarbayev. Two days before the deadline, government militiamen attacked Kojahmedov in the street and snatched the list of signatures from him. Thus, on December 1, the polling day, there was only one candidate: Nazarbayev. Of the nearly 10 million electors, 92 percent reportedly turned out, with 89 percent voting for Nazarbayev as president for four years.

On that day, 90 percent of the voters in Ukraine opted for independence. A week later, the presidents of the three Slav republics of Russia, Ukraine, and Belarus, meeting in Minsk, announced the creation of a Commonwealth of Independent States (CIS). This upset Gorbachev's plan, which had aimed to form a multinational Union of Sovereign States on the Soviet territory around the axis of the Slav heartland.

A statement in the Minsk Declaration that "The state-members of the Commonwealth intend to . . . guarantee unified control of nuclear weapons and their non-proliferation" provided Nazarbayev with a bargaining chip. His republic had nuclear arms on its soil, and unified control over the nuclear arsenal of the "state-members of the Commonwealth" could not be complete without Kazakhstan's inclusion in the new political entity. He also noticed the Minsk Declaration stated that the new agreement was open to all members of the Soviet Union that shared "the goals and principles of its founders." These provisions made Nazarbayev a key player in reshaping inter-republican relationships.

After consulting Yeltsin, Nazarbayev telephoned other Central Asian leaders. They met in Ashgabat on December 12 and decided to join the CIS, but only on equal terms with its founders, which necessitated minor rewriting of the Minsk Declaration. The Slav countries agreed.

By aborting the prospect of the Soviet Union splitting into Slav-centric and Turko-centric segments, the latest decisions brought much relief to Almaty and Moscow. It reassured the Slavs of Kazakhstan, forming 43 percent of the population, that they would not be left out of a Slav-centric grouping of former Soviet republics. And, aware of the susceptibilities of the 18 percent mainly Asian and Muslim minorities in the Russian Federation, many Russian citizens were relieved not to belong to an exclusively European union.

On December 16, the Kazakh Supreme Soviet became the last parliament in the region to declare its republic an independent sovereign state. Once the treaty encompassing all the constituents of the Soviet Union, except Georgia, was signed in Tashkent on December 21, 1991, to form the Commonwealth of Independent States, the stage was set for a formal dissolution of the Soviet Union.

AFTER SOVIET DISINTEGRATION

Given Kazakhstan's 48 percent European (i.e., Slav and German) population, the highest proportion in the Muslim-majority republics, Nazarbayev visualized Kazakhstan as a bridge between Russia and Central Asia. He realized that if any Central Asian republic came under the sway of Islamic militancy, it would make his self-appointed task extremely difficult. During his first visit to a European country, Austria, in February 1992, he declared that his country had "a special responsibility," along with Russia, to steer other Central Asian states away from Islamic fundamentalism and Iranian influence.

For the present, though, Kazakhstan's possession of nuclear arms engaged the attention of its leaders and Western powers, especially America, which wanted proper controls maintained over the nuclear arsenals outside Russia. During his visit to Almaty in mid-December 1991, U.S. Secretary of State James Baker reportedly expressed concerns about nuclear weapons in the republic.[24] In late February 1992, Nazarbayev promised to transfer Kazakhstan's 650 tactical nuclear arms to Russia, but insisted on keeping the strategic nuclear weapons, with the proviso of destroying them only if the United States, China, Russia, Ukraine, and Belarus did the same. Along with its 104 SS-18 intercontinental ballistic missiles (ICBM), each with ten independently targeted nuclear warheads, Kazakhstan possessed the fourth-largest nuclear arsenal in the world.[25]

Western capitals feared that Pakistan and Iran, intent on advancing their nuclear ambitions, would prevail upon Kazakhstan, a fellow-Muslim state, to sell them nuclear arms and/or technology for hard currency. The reports in the Western media—based on information provided by an Iranian resistance organization in March, later proved to be baseless—that Almaty had sold three tactical nuclear weapons to Tehran added to Western apprehension. Washington pressured Kazakhstan to give up all its nuclear arms.

Nazarbayev explained that he could not do so because some Russian politicians were claiming Kazakh territory, and textbooks in China continued to show parts of Kazakhstan as Chinese territory. The other factors that worried him were the uncertain future of the CIS and the current Russian leadership.

The Kazakh leader also had to cope with rising domestic challenges. Kazakhstan started its life as an independent state against the background of a strike by workers in ten state-owned coal mines of Karaganda, demanding fulfillment of the government's promises to improve wages during the past two years. In February, there was a mutiny against poor working conditions by the troops of the construction battalion at a base near the Baikonur space center, which had fallen into disuse, causing much economic suffering in the area. The suppression of the mutiny led to the deaths of three soldiers. After dismissing many officers, the authorities promised to improve conditions.

Political opposition, especially pro-Turkic, became active. A Jeltoksan delegation, led by Hasan Kojahmedov (originally, Hoja Ahmad), participated in the Congress of the Supporters of Turkistan in Tashkent in March. The assembly decided to work for the unification of the Central Asian republics into a supra-state to be called Turkistan—an unpalatable prospect for the Slav settlers in Kazakhstan.

Not to be outflanked by the Jeltoksan on the pan-Turkic front, Alash Orda leaders had combined pan-Turkism with Islam in a powerful program of Islamic pan-Turkism. They believed in Islamic revival since Islam upheld the ethics they wished to revive. They were also committed to reviving the old Turkistan as a first step towards creating Turanistan, stretching from Turkey to the Chinese border, a dream of the early proponents of pan-Turkism. But these aims were not to be achieved at the expense of democracy, which they perceived as essential for maintaining harmony in a multi-ethnic country like Kazakhstan.[26]

The foreswearing of violence by Alash leaders did not apply to some of their followers. On December 13, 1991, five young Alash activists assaulted and injured Haji Radbek Nisanbayev, head of the Muslim Spiritual

Directorate of Kazakhstan. Accusing him of being insufficiently nationalist in his public statements and dealings with the government "run by former Communists," they forced him to sign a letter of resignation.

In his defense, Nisanbayev could claim that due to his effort, the authorities had introduced an hour-long television program on Islam on Fridays, including a sermon by him, not to mention two to five religious radio programs a week. During his two years as the mufti of Kazakhstan, each week had seen the opening of a new mosque or the reopening of an old one, raising the total number of mosques to 140. At his central mosque, the average size of the congregation for Friday prayers had grown from about 500 mainly elderly men before perestroika to 3,000 to 4,000 believers of all ages. On his relationship with the regime, he could rightly say, "The government respects us, and we respect it. At the same time we are separate from the state."[27]

His assailants were arrested. They and other Alash militants were tried in the spring of 1992 for insulting the president, organizing unauthorized rallies, and attacking Nisanbayev, and given prison sentences of varying lengths. However, their trials did little to subdue the registered opposition, which gained support as the economy shrank in the wake of the Soviet collapse. To provide relief to the people, Nazarbayev signed a decree in mid-1992, giving ex gratia ownership of the house to the occupying family. Its implementation in the capital began in September 1992. Earlier in the year, privatization had started there with the sale of rows of state-owned shops.

Unlike the domestic measures which, though important, were hardly dramatic, Nazarbayev scored notable successes in foreign affairs. At the CIS summit in Tashkent in mid-May 1992, he announced a fifty-year Kazakh-Russian agreement on the joint use of the Baikonur and Plesetsk space facilities, with the Kremlin paying an annual rent of $120 million.[28] He was a signatory to the Tashkent Collective Security Agreement, which included Russia. Referring to this agreement as "the guarantee Kazakhstan had sought for its security," Nazarbayev announced on the eve of his visit to America three days later that Kazakhstan would sign the nuclear Non-Proliferation Treaty (NPT), which Washington had urged it to do.

An agreement between America, Russia, Ukraine, Belarus, and Kazakhstan stipulated the destruction of all strategic nuclear weapons by former Soviet republics, except Russia. Later, Nazarbayev, along with the presidents of Ukraine and Belarus, agreed to transfer all tactical nuclear arms to Russia for demolition, with Washington paying the cost and granting Almaty $150 million in aid. A seven-year security cooperation agreement between Almaty and

Washington, signed in December 1993, covered the earlier arrangement and added the destruction of 147 ICBM silos in Kazakhstan.[29]

These acts of Nazarbayev engendered goodwill for him and Kazakhstan, and encourged American and other Western oil companies to invest in the republic's hydrocarbon industry. Even otherwise, with his background as a successful oilman from Texas, U.S. President George H. W. Bush was keenly aware of the opportunities that the Kazakh oil and gas reserves held for American corporations.

Soon after his return from Washington, Nazarbayev flew to Moscow to sign a bilateral treaty of friendship, cooperation, and mutual aid between Kazakhstan and Russia. It committed the two sides to establish joint military areas with common use of military installations—and, more importantly, it recognized the inviolability of each other's borders. That set to rest ethnic Kazakhs' fears about future Russian claims on their republic's territory.

Meanwhile, the rising tide of Kazakh nationalism left ethnic Slavs apprehensive of the future. Within a decade and a half, their percentage in the population would fall from 48 to 30 due to emigration.

KAZAKH-SLAV TENSIONS

Slavs found much to fret about when the Supreme Soviet—now called the Supreme Kenges (Assembly)—published the 148-article draft constitution on June 2, 1992, for public discussion. The draft described Kazakhstan as "the national state of Kazakhs." (In reality, Kazakhstan was then a binational state, with six Russians to every seven Kazakhs.) It retained Kazakh as the state language, but guaranteed free development for all others, making Russian in practice the language of interethnic communication.

One of the fundamental rights guaranteed "political parties and public organizations . . . equal opportunities," and added that "the ideology of political parties and other public organizations, including religious organizations, may not be established as state ideology." This foreclosed the possibility of pan-Turkism or Islam being adopted as the state ideology if Alash Orda or Jeltoksan won power singly or jointly through constitutional means. One of the provisions for "the registered public associations" required them to open their membership to all Kazakh citizens irrespective of nationality (i.e., ethnic origin), sex, language, social origin, domicile, or attitude towards religion. So, to obtain official registration, Alash Orda would have to open its membership to Europeans. Equally, Slavic- or other European-dominated political parties would have to be open to all citizens.[30]

The registered pan-Turkic parties—Azat Movement, Republican Party, and Jeltoksan—joined the debate. They rejected the draft constitution's articles on the language and political associations, demanding that Kazakh be made the sole language of the republic, and that the registration requirements for a political group be made far less stringent. This, and their general disaffection with the government, led them to call a protest demonstration on June 17. Appealing to all those "who consider themselves Kazakh," the sponsoring parties said: "Until now yesterday's Communists have been ruling us. The Communists do not take into account the opinion of the nation. The government lurched into the market economy without any preparation. Speculation is rife." They demanded a coalition government involving all registered parties, including the governing Socialist Party. It should divide the assets of the former Communist Party among the registered parties, and dismiss the officials responsible for selling land to the Russians as well as those responsible for selling public property cheaply to bogus foreign companies during the recent privatization program.

They called on the parliament to appoint commissions on (a) repatriation (of European settlers), (b) the language issue, (c) freedom of the press, (d) rescinding the treaty with the United States on nuclear weapons, and (e) abrogation of Kazakhstan's recent defense and security agreement with Moscow since it legitimized the stationing of the 40th Russian Army in Kazakhstan in the guise of CIS forces.[31] Their strongly Kazakh nationalist demands were designed to establish Kazakh hegemony in the republic.

Some 5,000 opposition supporters gathered in Almaty and demanded a meeting with Nazarbayev. He refused, accusing them of "generating instability." So they mounted pickets outside the parliament, which went on for two weeks. Finally, the security forces removed them forcibly in the middle of the night.

As Kazakh nationalists were flexing their muscles at the expense of Slavs, martial Cossacks in Northern Kazakhstan and their kinsmen in the adjoining Southern Siberia became restive. On July 1, a meeting of the "Large Cossack Circle of Siberia and the former Steppe Krai [Northern Kazakhstan]" in Omsk, Russia, just north of the Kazakh border, protested against the violation of the rights of Russians in Kazakhstan. Condemning the renaming of Russian settlements and the destruction of Russian monuments in Kazakhstan, it called on the Supreme Soviets and presidents of Kazakhstan and Russia to protect the rights of Russians in Kazakhstan, and allow them dual citizenship. It reiterated its right to defend "its [Russian] brothers [in Kazakhstan] by all available means."

During its meeting with Nazarbayev in Almaty, a delegation of the Russian settlers in Northern Kazakhstan urged amending the draft constitution to prohibit discrimination against non-Kazakh speakers and postpone the switchover to Kazakh for official business.[32] Given the large size of the Russian population in his republic, and a virtually unguarded land frontier of 4,000 kilometers (2,500 miles) between Kazakhstan and Russia, Nazarbayev had no choice but to listen patiently.

To withstand the mounting pressure from the militant Kazakh and Slav lobbies, the government needed to activate the political organization which had the backing of nearly 80 percent of the parliamentarians—the Socialist Party. Whereas Nazarbayev, intent on being president of all citizens, had refrained from joining any grouping, his premier, Sergel Tereshchenko, had enrolled in the Socialist Party. But, with only 60,000 full members, the Socialist Party was a poor successor to the CPK with its 866,262 full and candidate members.[33] Therefore, political life came to revolve around the words and deeds of Nazarbayev.

His aides advised him that one way to contain the tide of Kazakh nationalism was to direct it into non-threatening cultural channels, so he sponsored a World Congress of Kazakhs in Almaty in October. Attended by 750 delegates from abroad, including Turkey, Russia, Uzbekistan, Afghanistan, Egypt, and Germany, its proceedings were televised to popular acclaim among Kazakhs. Nazarbayev combined his appeal to the diasporic Kazakhs to return to the motherland with an offer of instant citizenship—a step intended to increase the Kazakh proportion in the population.

Such assemblies failed to mask the grim fact of falling living standards due to a steep drop in the GDP. The drop stemmed from the closure of many factories, especially in the defense sector, partly due to the lack of demand following the end of the Cold War, and partly due to the lack of raw or semifinished materials and the shortage of hard currencies. Joblessness was rising. High inflation made a mockery of assessing correctly the value of industrial assets as a prelude to privatization.

Yet denationalization plans were more advanced in Kazakhstan than anywhere else in Central Asia. This was so because Nazarbayev had a good grasp of economics, and because he had taken on board Grigory Yavlinsky, one of Gorbachev's radical economists, who had parted with the Soviet leader in 1990. Also, given Kazakhstan's vast resources—not only in copper, zinc, lead, titanium, gold, and silver, but also in oil, natural gas, and coal—Western companies showed great interest in investing, making Kazakhstan the third most favored ex-Soviet republic, after Russia and

Ukraine. However, prosperity ensuing from such investments lay in the future.

In desperation, Nazarbayev took to criticizing his own government for blindly following Russia's economic reform model, which, in his view, was going nowhere. Yeltsin's administration had opted for a headlong rush into free-for-all capitalism, along with uncontrolled access to Western companies and the disposal of natural resources and large public sector enterprises to a few favorites at nominal prices. Nazarbayev asked parliament for additional powers to administer a strong anti-crisis medicine, meaning greater government intervention. Despite this, his popular standing fell ten points in a month, to 59 percent in October 1992.[34] Tereshchenko halted further privatization due to high inflation.

As if this were not enough, in early December some 15,000 Russian protesters gathered in Ust-Kamenogorsk, the capital of East Kazakhstan Province, to call for an equal status for Russian along with Kazakh as a state language, a law allowing dual nationality, and self-determination in culture and natural resources for their region. Such a large demonstration revived Nazarbayev's fear of irredentist agitation by ethnic Russians encouraging Russia to claim a part of Kazakhstan.

To stem the tide, Nazarbayev and a large majority of parliamentarians finalizing the constitution decided to make concessions. The final document, adopted by 309 deputies on January 28, 1993, accorded Kazakh the status of the official language while recognizing Russian as the lingua franca, and required merely that the republic's president should "speak Kazakh fluently," thus making a Kazakh-speaking Slav eligible for the highest office. It authorized the president to appoint regional governors, who were empowered to appoint local administrators.

But the failure to grant dual citizenship for ethnic Russians displeased the Kremlin, which had succeeded in securing this provision in Turkmenistan. Moscow used its economic levers. It imposed such strict conditions for the continued membership of the ruble zone that Kazakhstan had no option but to launch its own currency, tenge, in November at the official rate of 4.5 tenges to one U.S. dollar. In less than a year, due to high inflation and a shrinking economy, the tenge would lose nine-tenths of its value, making life for ordinary Kazakhs more miserable than before.

Although Kazakhstan was believed to be rich in oil, its proven recoverable reserves (according to the BP Statistical Review of World Energy, 1994) were only 5.2 billion barrels—mostly attributed to the Tengiz oil field covering 2,500 square miles (6,475 square kilometers) along the scraggly northeast shore of the Caspian—out of the global total of 1,009 billion barrels.

The first major contract to develop the Tengiz field was won by a consortium named TengizChevroil, led by Chevron (with 50 percent of the equity) and Exxon Mobil (20 percent), with the rest owned mostly by KazMunayGaz, the republic's state-owned oil and gas conglomerate. The total cost to develop it was put at $20 billion.[35] As elsewhere in Central Asia, foreign companies, dealing with the government and local contractors, had to pay bribes or protection moneys for the successful conduct of their business.

Once oil production started in 1993, TengizChevroil encountered a problem in exporting it due to Moscow's obstructionist attitude. Russia owned the oil pipeline leading to the Black Sea port of Novorossiysk. Frowning upon the Nazarbayev government's contract with TengizChevroil, Moscow demanded 20 percent of Kazakhstan's takings from that deal. It also wanted priority for Russian petroleum companies in oil and gas exploration and their entry into the Chevron-led consortium. In May 1994, it cut off almost all of the Kazakh oil exports by blocking its only pipeline.[36] Therefore, in that year, Kazakhstan's petroleum output fell to 430,000 barrels per day (bpd), one-third below the figure for 1991.

The Krelmin's hard line was part of its Greater Russia policy, which included classifying former Soviet republics as "Near Abroad," and which the Yeltsin government had adopted following the electoral success in December 1993 of the ultranationalist Liberal Democratic Party (LDP), led by Vladimir Zhirinovsky. Winning 25 percent of the popular vote, the LDP emerged as the largest single group in parliament. The LDP called for bringing back into Russia's orbit the republics in Central Asia, the Caucasus, and the Baltics. It also demanded the protection of diasporic Russians living outside Russia.[37]

This encouraged the Russian settlers to protest against the Kazakhization that had been in progress since 1989: the growing role of the Kazakh language; increasing domination of Kazakhs in the political, economic, and administrative spheres; and pauperization of the Slavic-controlled enterprises and collective farms in the north to facilitate their privatization by Kazakhs. On top of that came the manipulation of the general election in March 1994.

The respective ethnic breakdown of the new parliament and the national population was: Kazakh, 60 percent and 43 percent; and Russian-Ukrainian, 34 percent and 42 percent. Because of the high proportion of children and adolescents among Kazakhs, their percentage among the voters was only about 30. In other words, they had managed to secure twice as many parliamentary seats as their proportion among electors warranted. Such a feat became possible due to the electoral decree that Nazarbayev issued after dissolving the parliament in December 1993. Of the 176 seats, he allocated only 75 to public associations (i.e., political parties and mass movements), dividing the rest into the "state list" of 42, nominated by him, and the "general list" of 59, open to the electors contesting as individuals.

In the last category, the local election commissions, composed of government officials, tried to dissuade the president's opponents from running. When this failed, they disqualified the undesirable candidates arbitrarily. There were also instances where the male head of a household was allowed to vote for the whole family. The parties and individuals backing Nazarbayev were given maximum coverage by the state-run radio and television.[38] Thus, the pro-Nazarbayev parties, the Society for National Unity of Kazakhstan and the People's Congress Party, won more than two-thirds of the seats on the party list.

The Azat Movement and Republican Party together secured only four seats—as few as the Republican Slavic Movement (RSM), which demanded dual nationality for the Slav settlers and protested against increasing anti-Slav discrimination in housing, education, and government jobs. Though the parties at the core of the Kazakh-Slav tension were virtually excluded from the parliament, relations between the two groups remained fraught. Indeed, the stereotypical nicknames—"Potato Noses" for Russians, and "Black Arses" for Kazakhs—that were whispered in Soviet times were now openly and frequently uttered.

The Kremlin kept pressuring Nazarbayev to grant dual nationality to the Slav settlers. He resisted, arguing that such a step would divide the population between "us" and "them." At the same time, to ease the handicap of Slav citizens who were unfamiliar with Kazakh, he called on the newly elected parliament to loosen up the language law.

To reassure his Kazakh constituency that no territorial compromise was in the offing, Nazarbayev had the parliament pass a law in July 1994 to transfer the capital, over the next six years, from Almaty in the extreme southeast to the north-central city of Akmola (literally, "white grave," because of the color of the earth)—1,200 kilometers (750 miles) to its northwest along the Irtysh River. By immediately moving his office to Akmola (renamed Astana, meaning Capital), with its 58 percent Slav population, he underlined his resolve to retain the Slav-majority northern provinces inside Kazakhstan.

Then Nazarbayev suffered a setback. Accepting the opposition's arguments, the Constitutional Court declared the parliamentary poll unfair. But he managed to exploit the verdict to his advantage.

NAZARBAYEV'S SLEIGHT OF HAND

After dissolving parliament, Nazarbayev, assisted by the newly appointed prime minister, Akezhan Kazhegeldin, resorted to governing by decree. This gave him unrestrained power to advance the economic reform the way he saw fit. He exercised this privilege until the convening of the new bicameral legislature (with a partly nominated upper chamber), elected in December 1995 with a large pro-Nazarbayev majority against the background of fresh discoveries of oil and gas reserves.

By then, having established his Kazakh nationalist credentials, he had taken to displaying his attachment to Kazakh traditions to improve his popularity. When he went on to provide historical ballast to Kazakhs' national identity, the personality of Khwaja Ahmad Yasawi (1106–66) proved valuable to him. An outstanding Sufi poet, Yasawi was credited with bringing Islam to Turkistan, present-day Southern Kazakhstan. Since he composed his poems in Turkish—and not in Persian, the language of literature in the region—his message reached the ordinary, illiterate Kazakhs. He thus provided a bridge between the pantheism of Kazakh nomads and the strict edicts of orthodox Islam. His Sufi order of Yasawiya proved popular and continues to this day. And other poets, religious and secular, followed his lead in composing poems in Turkish.

Ahmad Yasawi's father died when he was a boy of seven, and the family moved from his birthplace of Sairam to Yasi, now called Turkestan, where he became a student of Arslan Baba. After Baba's death, he migrated to Bukhara, where he became a student of Yusuf Hamadani. After Hamadani's demise in 1140, Yasawi returned to Turkestan, and turned it into a place of Islamic learning.[39] After his retirement, he meditated in a bunker until his death. His portrait shows him as a man with a contemplative face, a small mouth, an aquiline nose, a well-trimmed beard and mustache, and an onion-shaped white turban which would later become the headgear of Ottoman sultans.

His modest shrine was upgraded into a mausoleum by Timur Beg. Further work was done on it in late sixteenth century by Shaibani ruler Abdullah Khan Shaibani. In the nineteenth century, the ruler of Kokand built a wall around the mausoleum, transforming it into a fortress.

Therefore, during the Tsarist period, the site was used as a military depot. The eight-year-long restoration work, undertaken by the Nazarbayev government in 1992, raised the status of the mausoleum to the point where it got included in the World Heritage List.

The portal is guarded by imposing, round towers. The main aquamarine dome in the back shields a smaller dome over the burial chamber embellished with glazed blue-and-white tiles. Reflecting Yasawi's openmindedness, a verse from his poetry inscribed on the wall of the main chamber reads:

> When one day you meet a stranger,
> Do not do him harm.
> God does not love people with cruel hearts.[40]

Nazarbayev went on to impress the Yasawi mausoleum's image on the republic's banknotes. He did so in an environment where the Islamic phrases "Inshallah" ("God willing") and "Mashallah" ("This is from God") had become common currency among Kazakhs.

In line with the revival of traditional Kazakh behavior, Nazarbayev would spot the oldest person in any gathering to be addressed, and seek his or her blessing as a preamble before speaking. For a community which over three generations had known nothing but fear or debilitating respect for the man with supreme power, the sight of the republic's president seeking some sort of favor from an ordinary citizen, however elderly, raised his popular standing.

Such heartwarming gestures, however, had no impact on the shrinking economy, with agricultural output falling, and the cattle population reduced by half since pre-independence to 4.3 million.[41] The decline in the GDP—down to 17 percent in 1993—continued unabated while inflation at 75 percent remained high. The national currency had plummeted, with 58 tenges trading for one U.S. dollar, down from the original 4.5 tenges to the dollar.

Since the economy had deteriorated in stages, it could only improve gradually. The newly born private sector needed five to ten years to show positive results. Meanwhile, given the comparative freedom that the print media enjoyed, the opposition had a credible chance of successfully challenging Nazarbayev's leadership. To eliminate that possibility, he devised a dual-track policy: one track to be implemented immediately, and the other over the next few years, along with the opening up of the broadcasting media to private companies dominated by his family members.

Instead of holding the presidential poll on time in 1995, Nazarbayev emulated Saparmurat Niyazov, who in late 1994 had used a referendum to have his tenure extended, as had Islam Karimov. But whereas Niyazov and Karimov had opted for a single-point referendum, Nazarbayev came up with a multi-point one. Besides mentioning the postponement of the presidential election to mid-2000, the ballot included the right to private property, the character of statehood, and the official language—requiring a single yes or no.

When the European Union and the United States argued that a referendum fell well short of a proper presidential contest with a multiple choice, Nazarbayev ignored the criticism. "Due to the difficulties Kazakhstan is experiencing, the leadership struggle of any kind is not in the country's best interests," he said.[42] So the embassies of the EU and the U.S. declined his invitation to monitor the referendum on April 30. The referendum produced the anticipated result. Almost 90 percent of the 10 million voters went to the polling stations, and 95 percent said yes. When Western embassies cast doubts on the veracity of the exercise, Nazarbayev retorted, "After seventy years of authoritarian rule [in Kazakhstan], transition to democracy will be difficult. Western views of democracy have to be modified in the specific context of Asia."[43]

Contrary to the predictions of Nazarbayev's critics that he would find life intolerable in Astana and would rush back to Almaty, he stayed put in the capital-in-the-making. However, the commercial dominance of Almaty, a city of 1.2 million, remained undiminished.

HISTORIC ALMATY, UPSTART ASTANA

Almaty has a long recorded history. In 1493, in his journal, the *Babur Nama*, Emperor Babur noted, "In the earlier period, there must have been towns such as Alma Ligh and Alma Atu. Both owed their names to the apple (*alma*)." His later entry read, "Kabul was peaceful when Sultan Said Khan arrived to seek his cousin's protection after his defeat by his brother Mansour Khan at Almaty followed by his escape."[44]

Part of the Silk Road, Almaty entered history books in the thirteenth century. Later it became known as the site of an official mint. The region around it fostered the evolution of Kazakh identity. The war between the Kazakh and Dzungar tribes in the Anrakhai Mountains 70 kilometers (45 miles) northwest of Almaty in 1730 established the supremacy of Kazakhs in the region.

When the Tsarist army built a fort called Verny in 1854 near the historic site, Cossak and Russian peasants and Tartar traders settled around it. Like

Ashgabat and Tashkent, the new settlement was prone to earthquakes (as well as mudslides). The one in 1887 destroyed most of Verny, and another one in 1911 played havoc with the rebuilt town. A decade later, under the Bolshevik rule, the local authorities restored the town's historic name of Alma Ata—its Kazakh version being Almaty.

Some years later, Almaty was recognized officially as the site of the apple's origin. The world-renowed Soviet botanist, Nikolai Vavilov, credited with identifying the birthplace of more plants than any other botanist before or since, arrived in the area on horseback, leading a mule train carrying his equipment. "All around the city one could see a vast expanse of wild apples [of different varieties] covering the foothills which formed forests," he noted. "In contrast to very small wild apples in the Caucasian mountains, the Kazakh wild apples have very big fruit, and they don't vary from cultivated varieties. On the first of September, the time that the apples were almost ripe, one could see with one's own eyes that this beautiful site was the origin of the cultivated apple."[45] Today, an aerial cable car connects downtown Almaty with the Blue Hill, a mountain to the southeast.

During the Great Patriotic War, the city benefited from the Kremlin's program of shifting factories from the European region to Central Asia, and became a center of the defense industry. It developed as the most striking Kazakh city, with wide, tree-lined streets, parks, and orchards against the dramatic backdrop of snow-covered mountains. It became a city of enormous plazas and parks.

Once Soviet engineers and architects had perfected a system of designing and erecting earthquake-proof buildings in the mid-1960s, and deployed it first in Tashkent in 1966, and then in Almaty, a construction boom ensued in the Kazakh capital. Nearly 300,000 square meters of housing became available annually. In the mad rush, quality was sacrificed for the sake of quantity, and the result was a plethora of grim, featureless structures. "In the past we had a centralized system from Moscow and built these huge matchboxes," explained Anet Bektemisov, chairman of the parliament's Architecture and Construction Committee, in 1992. "We started to build private houses only in 1989."[46]

Given the central command economy during the Soviet era, the government offices, schools, hospitals, banks, post offices, and telephone exchanges rose all over the Soviet Union in a standardized fashion—in terms of size, shape, color, and building materials, limited mainly to bricks and concrete. Residential quarters consisted of five- or six-story buildings, each floor containing three to four apartments of one to three bedrooms.

To keep out the cold, architects provided a typical apartment in Almaty with double front doors, and a sturdy outer door followed by a generously padded inner one. The narrow corridor, with a bathroom to the left and a large bedroom to the right, led to the kitchen. The sitting room, with its back door opening to a small, enclosed balcony, was where an enterprising occupant might furnish it tastefully, albeit in the traditional heavy style favored by Russians. Even though streets were no longer unpaved and city dwellers did not work the fields, Kazakhs and Slavs continued to remove their shoes and put on clean slippers on entering their homes.

With burgeoning oil and gas income and foreign investments, both Almaty and Astana changed. Five-star hotels, fast food restaurants, American steak houses, and casinos started to spring up, and the nouveau riche began building multistory houses with two-car garages and gated compounds.

Released from the dominance of the Russian Big Brother, Kazakhs were expected to follow a different path in public architecture and private housing as they built their new capital, Astana. As it was, there was more to the transfer of the republic's capital to Astana than consolidating Kazakh authority over the Slav-majority in the north or strengthening national security by depriving Almaty, located near the border of China, of its capital status. "I have taken a lot of risks in my life but Astana was the biggest gamble of all," Nazabayev said. "I put everything on it. . . . The decision was to expand the idea of private property where *everything* [before] was owned by the state. And I knew that if I got it wrong, and it proved a terrible mistake, that would be the end of my political career as a leader of the country."[47]

Actually, Kazakhs had taken to private enterprise with the gusto of late converts. In the tower block where Anet Bektemisova's cousin lived in 1992, practically every other apartment on the ground floor had been turned into a shop that sold clothes, shoes, and electrical goods. At one of these shops, goods were displayed on hangers and scattered all over the rooms, with chewing gum, sweets, candies, and cigarette lighters on sale along with shoes and transistor radios, most of them imported from China.[48]

It was run by a female gynecologist named Nina Nurjanova.

While Nurjanova was engaged in a legal commercial activity, that was not the case with Batirkhan Umatayev. A dark-complexioned young man with curly hair who was a familiar sight at the cafetaria of the twenty-six-story Kazakhstan Hotel, Umatayev called himself a currency speculator. Soon after he had finished his two-year draft in the army with a posting in a hellish place in Eastern Siberia, where most soldiers were hooked on morphine injections, he borrowed some money from relatives. "I started out in the commercial sector by selling personal computers [PCs] and videos which I bought in Singapore," he said. "I told my agent there to get PCs with Latin and Cyrillic alphabets." After a few years in that business, he switched to currency speculation. "The only way I can make money is by illegal means," he added, disarmingly. "If you stay fully legal you cannot make money. One of my friends who is only in his mid-twenties has made $10 million in six months in currency speculation. I am not in that league."

To remain in the business of buying and selling dollars for rubles, he had to bribe the police, the KGB, the tax authorities, and the bank manager. "One day a man in the police department told me that my transactions were not above board and that he would report me to the tax authorities. So I paid him 20,000 rubles. If I had been taken to court I would have been fined 100,000 rubles. When I buy dollars from a bank there is 20 percent service charge. So I pay 2 percent to the bank manager. There are about a dozen banks in Almaty now."[49]

It was not long before such corrupt practices spread to legitimate commerce. Foreign firms wishing to invest in Kazakhstan discovered that it was virtually impossible to do business without bribing government officials or private contractors. Yet the building of a new capital in Astana, including the presidential palace, ministries, office towers, apartment blocks, shopping malls, mosques, and churches held a rosy promise for experienced foreign construction corporations, in which Turkish enterprises had become preeminent in Central Asia.

Within a decade, and at the expense of more than $10 billion, Astana had reinvented itself into a thriving city of 0.75 million. With the introduction of special high-speed trains between Almaty and Astana, the journey time from the old capital to the new one was cut by two-thirds, from twenty-eight hours to nine. Traveling by train instead of air allowed passengers to get a true measure of the massive expanse of the republic—the size of Western Europe—which was in stark contrast to the paucity of its people.

Given the unbearably harsh winters of Astana, with temperatures falling to minus 30 degrees Celsius amidst the freezing gales from the surrounding steppe, the pace of building was astonishing. It was the result chiefly of the joint innovation of the architects and the Turkish construction companies. During winter, the Turks fabricated building components at home, then their employees in Astana assembled them in summer and autumn.

Just as in the Turkmen capital, in Astana every public building was personally approved by the president. The old neighborhoods of two- or three-story buildings with ungainly heating pipes on unasphalted streets disappeared under the combined assault of bulldozers and demolition balls as fast as they did in Ashgabat. The cranes filled the skyline while work continued day and night.

And just as the Neutrality Tower in Ashgabat symbolized the new Turkmenistan, a ninety-seven-meter-tall (the height determined by the year 1997) skeletal steel observation tower, named after the mythical tree Baiterek, did the same for Kazakhstan. Unlike Niyazov, though, Nazarbayev did not place his statue at the top, an omission noticed by many of his acolytes. "Some people approached me saying they would like to raise a monument to me like they do in Turkmenistan for Turkmenbashi," he told Hugh Pope, the visiting *Wall Street Journal* correspondent. "I asked, What for? Astana is my memorial."[50]

Instead, Nazarbayev capped the tower with an aluminum-and-glass sphere, painted in gold, representing the golden egg laid by the mythical bird Samruk. According to a Kazakh legend, the Samruk laid an egg bright as the sun at the top of the Baiterek, but at night an evil dragon gobbled it up. When the patience of local Kazakhs ran out, they killed the dragon, allowing the sun-like egg to brighten up the world. While observing the new capital from the top of its highest tower, an unsuspecting visitor might touch the upturned palm of a golden hand on the raised podium at the center of the golden egg, and thus trigger the recorded voice of a choir, backed by an orchestra, singing the national anthem.

The tower stood at the center of an axis linking the ostentatious presidential palace to a giant, transparent, 150-meter-high pyramid called the Palace of Peace and Harmony, designed as a meeting place for the leaders of the planet's religions.

Unlike in Ashgabat, the locals of Astana felt sufficiently bold to nickname some buildings—calling a yellow skyscraper the Banana Building, three cylindrical structures the Beer Cans, and a quasi-Soviet, semicircular headquarters of the state energy company KazMunaiGaz, "the Cigarette Lighter," before it went up in smoke in May 2006.

HYDROCARBON RESERVES

Nazarbayev's calculation that the benefits of privatization would start accruing from the mid-1990s proved correct. And the foreign companies' successful exploration for oil and gas raised the republic's proven petro-leum reserves by half to 8 billion barrels, and its natural gas deposits to 1.84 billion cubic meters, in 1995.

It is a common practice for governments of oil-bearing countries to exaggerate the reserves. But, in the aftermath of the Soviet disintegration, U.S. administrations resorted to hyping the size of the hydrocrabon reserves in the Caspian Basin. By the late 1980s, America had become increasingly dependent on petroleum from a perennially unstable region of the Persian Gulf, and this worried the policymakers in Washington. But they were unwilling to broadcast their unease for fear of accentuating the problem by turning it into a topic of popular discourse. Instead, they and oil executives clutched at any straw that held up the prospect of oil supplies from a region that was not Arab or Iranian. Azerbaijan and Kazakhstan fitted the bill. Also, creating a hoopla about the incoming oil bonanza in the Caspian Basin made the oil-rich Arab states nervous and kept their oil prices subdued.

On July 21, 1997, referring to the energy and investment flows in the southern republics of the former Soviet Union, U.S. Deputy Secretary of State Strobe Talbott stated that "it would matter profoundly to the U.S. if failure of political and economic reform were to happen in an area that sits on as much as 200 billion barrels of oil."[51]

Talbott had been appointed head of the special task force to oversee American interests in the region by President Bill Clinton. It included offi-cials not only from the Energy and Commerce Departments, but also from the National Security Council (NSC) and the Central Intelligence Agency (CIA). Its first important decision was to direct the American corporations not to allow under any circumstances the erection of an oil pipeline passing through Iran on its way to a maritime outlet. This was an order, not advice. "Usually the American oil companies find other countries are way ahead in using political influence," said Robert Ebel, director of the energy and national security program at the Center for Strategic and International Studies of Georgetown University in Washington. "Not this time. And then the oil companies always knew that this would end up being a political decision. The stakes are just so high."[52]

Such statements by top U.S. officials and oil experts boosted the already inflated ego of Nazarbayev. In November 1997, three years ahead of sched-ule, he made Astana the official capital of Kazakhstan. To celebrate the occa-sion, he built a ninety-seven-meter-tall column crowned with an aluminum-and-glass cap. Like the Eiffel Tower in Paris, it provided a bird's eye view of the republic's capital. While he spared no expense to erect a grossly spectacular presidential palace for himself, complete with an arrary of domes and pillars and an interior rivalling a city plaza, he also decreed a meticulous restoration of the mausoleum of the twelfth-century Sufi poet, Khwaja Ahmad Yasawi, near the town of Turkestan, revered among others by Tamerlane, who had renovated and improved the original site.[53] He also ordered that this historic monument be printed on all Kazhak banknotes.

None of this, nor the shaping of the finance ministry building in the form of a dollar sign, could mask the continued weakness of the economy. According to the United Nations Commission for Europe, taking the UN Commission 1989 figure as 100, Kazakhstan's GDP in 1996 at 61 was marginally better than Russia's GDP at 57.[54] With Russia as its number one trading partner, Kazakhstan could not insulate itself from the meltdown of the ruble in August 1998. The subsequent rise in the cost of borrowing on capital markets for the emerging economies forced Kazakhstan to cancel its plans to issue up to $450 million in Eurobonds. "The Russian financial crisis represents a serious threat to the welfare of our state," said Akezhan Kazhegeldin, who, after resigning as the prime minister in October 1997 for "health reasons," had been elected president of the Union of Industrialists and Entrepreneurs of Kazakhstan.[55]

In this gray Kazakh sky, a ray of hope appeared—from the East. The American missile attacks on the Taliban training camps in Afghanistan on August 20, 1998, severely damaged the ties being forged between Central Asia and Pakistan through Afghanistan, and boosted the chances of strenghening links between Central Asia and China. This revived interest in a plan first conceived in 1995 by the China National Petroleum Company (CPNC), Exxon, and the Japanese Mitsubishi Corporation, to build an oil and gas pipeline network to carry Central Asian oil and gas from Turkmenistan through Uzbekistan and Kazhakstan to China and onward to Japan.

The fast-industrializing, oil-thirsty mega-nation of China noticed that Kazakhstan's oil output at 535,000 barrels per day in 1997 was up by a quarter from the record low in 1994, and that the annual natural gas output had doubled in three years to a record 8.2 billion cubic meters. Hence, the Chinese energy companies became the latest suitors of the Nazarbayev government.

As it was, China had taken a diplomatic initiative in the region earlier. In April 1996, it hosted a summit in Shanghai of the leaders of Russia, Kazakhstan, Kyrgyzstan, and Tajikistan—countries that together shared a total of 7,000 kilometers (4,380 miles) of common frontiers with China—to settle border disputes dating back to 1963, which were not fully resolved by the time of the Soviet demise in 1991. Following the meeting, the Shanghai Forum issued an "Agreement on Confidence-Building in the Military Field along the Border Areas." It involved creating demilitarized zones, twenty to one hundred kilometers wide, and placing caps on the stationing of troops and deployment of soldiers and weaponry during military exercises in the area. The agreement became effective a year later.

COURTED BY EAST AND WEST

In September 1997, the CNPC inked a $9 billion contract with Kazakhstan to develop oil and gas fields in the northwestern Aktyubinsk and Uzen regions, involving oilfields east of the Caspian Sea, and to build a 3,000-kilometer oil pipeline between Kazakhstan and the Alashenko terminal in the Xinjiang province of China. After Nazarbayev and the visiting Chinese Prime Minister Li Peng signed the deal, both sides described it as "the deal of the century," with the CPNC paying $4.7 billion and pledging to invest another $10 billion in the infrastructures.[56]

This was Kazakhstan's attempt to balance its pro-Western tilt while loosening its traditionally tight links with Russia. As part of the Soviet Union, which was hostile to Communist China from 1960 onward, contemporary Kazakhs had grown up thinking of China as an exotic and threatening country. However, by signing the latest economic agreement with it, Kazakh officials recognized that China was a source of enormous economic opportunity. In a larger context, they concluded that while the East—China, Japan, and South Korea, in particular—had both money and technology, it was desperately short of energy, a firm basis for strong, mutual commercial ties.

By tapping into the oilfields of a neighboring country, and bringing the commodity to its own border province of Xinjiang, China wished to solve the economic and political problems of both itself and Kazakhstan. Of the three economic segments of China—the comparatively well-off east, the middle-income center, and the poor west—Xinjiang was in the last category. Whereas the annual per capita GDP in the Shanghai province was $2,440, in Xinjiang it was $715. Xinjiang's drive for industrialization had faltered due to lack of energy and foreign investment, which at $4 per capita was minuscule compared to $278 in Shanghai.[57] Over the long run, the Chinese leaders visualized their investment in Kazakhstan as a means to expanding China's influence there.

By shipping Kazakh oil to Xinjiang by a pipeline,[58] the CNPC planned to boost the industrialization of the underdeveloped province. Moreover, oil imported overland from Kazakhstan cost China far less than having it shipped from the Persian Gulf region. Also, raising the living standards of Xinjiang's population was expected to help Beijing contain the growing discontent among the native Muslim Uighurs. For many years, militant Uighurs, forming nearly half of the province's population, had been agitating to reestablish the sovereign state of East Turkistan, which existed in 1933 and again from 1944 to 1950. Some of them went as far as exploding bombs in Beijing. Astana-Beijing relations warmed further in July 1998 with the formal demarcation of nearly 1,000 square kilometers of disputed frontier territory, with Kazakhstan retaining three-fifths of it.

The meltdown of the Russian ruble in August 1998 made Nazarbayev receptive to Washington's pet project to build a long pipeline from Baku to the Turkish port of Çeyhan (pronounced Cheyhan) via Tbilisi (Baku-Tbilisi-Cayman, BTC) at a cost of $4 billion, chiefly because it circumvented both Russia and Iran. In October, Nazarbayev—along with the presidents of Azerbajian, Georgia, and Turkey—endorsed the project since the plan was to feed Kazakh oil into that pipeline at a later date to make it economical. Later, he would balance this decision by cooperating with Moscow and Beijing in the construction of the Aktau-Novorossisk and the Kazakhstan-China pipelines. The Aktau-Novorossisk pipeline would become the first to be finished, in March 2001, four years before the BTC pipeline.

With his prestige running high abroad, Nazarbayev directed the parliament to amend the constitution to extend the presidential tenure from five years to seven, and remove the age limit of sixty-five years for the president and the requirement of 50 percent turnout for a valid presidential poll. The parliament did so, and then called an election for president in early January 1999, nearly two years ahead of schedule. This severely curtailed the time for the opposition candidates to collect 170,000 signatures from at least two-thirds of the republic's twenty regions.

When opposition leaders formed the Movement for Honest Elections and held a public meeting, which was addressed among others by Akezhan Kazhegeldin, the authorities charged the main speakers with sponsoring a gathering of an unregistered organization. The resulting three days' administrative detention, ordered by the Supreme Court (at Nazarbayev's behest), disqualified Kazhegeldin, the preeminent opposition leader, from challenging Nazarbayev. Kazhegeldin would later become the president's nemesis.

What alarmed Nazarbayev was the popularity that Kazhegeldin started gaining against the background of the administration's gross maldistribution of wealth, which left a majority of Kazakhs living below the poverty line. The swirling tales of underhanded kickbacks from contracts in the hydrocarbon and other industries to top officials, including oil and gas minister Nurlan Balgimbayev, had driven the uncorrupt Kazhegeldin to resign as prime minister, to be succeeded by Balgimbayev.

In the run-up to the poll, Nazarbayev made a virtue of his many years in office; the vast election billboards declared, "We know Nazarbayev, we believe in him." He also highlighted his success in attracting billions of dollars of Western and Chinese investment in the country's oil, natural gas, and metal sectors, ignoring the fact that the accruing benefits had yet to reach ordinary citizens.

Washington concurred with the Organization for Security and Cooperation in Europe (OSCE) that the electoral process in Kazakhstan fell short of international standards for open, free, and fair elections. The candidates received unequal access to the media, and there were numerous instances of voter and opposition intimidation. The OSCE also objected to the president's practice of stipulating the electoral process.

Election officials claimed 86 percent turnout, with 80 percent voting for Nazarbayev, and his nearest rival, Serikbolsin Abdildin, a Communist, garnering 13 percent. "Given the existing [low] level of political activity and the rudimentary state of the infrastructure in Kazakhstan, who could believe that nearly nine out of ten people found their polling stations and voted?" asked Abdildin.

On the other hand, Nazarbayev's reelection, and his subsequent sponsorship of the Nur Otan (Light of Fatherland) party, reassured Western energy corporations, and encouraged Washington to press on with its overarching policy of isolating Iran and reducing Moscow's influence in the region while increasing its own. President Bill Clinton extended the U.S. Central Command's area of responsibility to the littoral states of the Caspian Sea, except Russia. This was a preamble to promoting an underwater pipeline to transport Kazakh and Turkmen hydrocarbons westwards and cultivating military links with Azerbaijan, Georgia, and Kazakhstan.

1999 witnessed the establishment of the Offshore Kazakhstan International Operating Company (OKIOC), a consortium of nine companies—including (Italian) ENI, Exxon, Royal Dutch Shell, and BP Amoco—to explore and exploit the Kashagan oilfield, named after the nineteenth-century Kazakh poet. The OKIOC started drilling in the shallow waters of the northern Caspian near Atyrau to reach 4,270 meters (14,000 feet) below the seabed. Its $600 million investment in an exploratory well was the biggest of its kind. It went on to spend close to $1 billion on a seismic survey of the entire Kazakh sector of the Caspian and drilling two exploratory wells at the opposite ends of the Kashagan's oil-soaked limestone structure. Measuring 85 by 25 kilometers (53 by 16 miles), the Kashagan field was a 350 million-year-old coral reef buried 5 kilometers (3 miles) beneath the shallows, about 50 kilometers (30 miles) south of the Caspian's northern coast. During the Soviet era, the authorities had been aware of this field's high potential since the 1970s, but lacked the technology to develop it, so they had opted for the easier sites in Azerbaijan and Western Siberia.

In July 2000, Kashagan's first exploratory well yielded high-quality light crude. In March 2001, the consortium announced that it had struck oil at 4,982 meters (16,340 feet), just 200 meters (670 feet) deeper than the first well located 40 kilometers (25 miles) away. This confirmed the initial belief that the Kashagan was similar in structure to the richly endowed Tengiz field. However, early declarations that Kashagan was "the largest field ever found"[59] proved to be over-optimistic; it turned out to be the tenth largest oilfield, yielding 13 billion barrels, albeit mixed with high proportions of poisonous hydrogen sulfide gas.

Prominent among those who got carried away by the Kashagan euphoria was Nazarbayev. He confidently forecast that by 2015, when Kashagan, Tengiz, and a number of lesser fields would reach maturity, Kazakhstan would be producing 8 million bpd a year, up from the current 750,000 bpd—and on a par with the current world leader, Saudi Arabia. Robert Ebel of the Center for Strategic and International Studies in Washington described Nazarbayev as "too optimistic by half" and added: "I understand he wants the income, but I wouldn't anticipate any significant production before 2008. And I know the companies are in no great hurry."[60]

By 2002, the CPNC-led consortium boosted the production from these onshore oilfields to 550,000 bpd, amounting to half of the total national figure. The CPNC shipped some of its Kazakh oil by tankers in the Caspian to refineries in northern Iran. In return, the National Iranian Oil Company (NIOC) dispatched an equivalent amount to China by sea, thus giving China, Kazakhstan, and Iran a common economic interest—a throwback to the Silk Road of ancient times.

By 2002, independent Kazakhstan had been a recipient of more than $14 billion in foreign direct investment (FDI), chiefly in its hydrocarbon industry.[61] And long-whispered allegations about Nazarbayev, his family, and other top officials receiving huge sums in bribes had found their way into print in Kazakhstan.

"KAZAKHGATE" AND THE U.S. LINK

To prosecute Akezhan Kazhegeldin, who set up the opposition Republican People's Party before going into exile in late 1998, the Kazakh government approached the Swiss authorities to check his secret bank accounts. Their inquiries unearthed secret accounts "nominally owned by offshore companies but beneficially owned, directly or indirectly, by Nurlan Balgimbayev [then the oil and gas minister] and Nursultan Nazarbayev . . . into which Mr. [James] Giffen had made tens of millions of dollars in unlawful payments."

When the allegations were first aired outside Kazakhstan, they embarrassed the Nazarbayev government. It spent large sums in the West on a public relations campaign to counter the charges, apparently to little effect. A meticulous investigation ending in 2003 brought to light a labyrinthine arrangement of money transfers to the accounts held in Switzerland and the British Virgin Islands—allegedly originating with Mobil (later ExxonMobil), Texaco (later Chevron), Phillips Petroleum (later ConocoPhillips), and Amoco (later acquired by BP), and pertaining to assorted "fees" for obtaining hydrocarbon rights in Kazakhstan in the 1990s. Numerous payments added up to $78 million.

At the center of these transactions was James Giffen, a clean-shaven, middle-aged American merchant banker, who headed Mercator Corporation. The company acted as an oil and gas consultant to the Nazarbayev government. It was alleged that Mercator Corporation had transferred part of the brokerage fees it received from the oil companies to the secret accounts of the president and the then oil and gas minister. Besides cash transactions, Giffen had allegedly bought an assortment of luxury goods such as expensive jewelry and fur coats for Nazarbayev's wife, Sara Alpysovna, and her daughter by an earlier marriage, Dariga; and paid $45,000 in tuition fees for the youngest daughter, Aliya, at an exclusive Swiss high school. Giffen had also purchased an $80,000 Donzi speedboat and two American snowmobiles for Nazarbayev and his wife. Among the top Kazakh officials who resented Giffen's influence over Nazarbayev was Kazhegeldin. "The biggest problem with Giffen was that he was trying to create an instrument of government that would keep himself and the president in power [for ever]," the former prime minister would later tell the *New York Times*. "He never dreamed he'd be so close to power."[62]

In spring 2003, as Giffen, accompanied by his lawyer William Schwartz, was preparing to fly to Paris from New York's JFK airport, U.S. agents arrested him for violating the 1974 Foreign Corrupt Practices Act, which outlaws U.S. citizens or corporations paying bribes to foreign officials to secure business. They found that he was carrying a Kazakh diplomatic passport even though there was no dual nationality agreement between the United States and Kazakhstan. Later he had to surrender his American passport as a condition for bail. In April 2004, a grand jury in New York City upheld the charges against Giffen.

"Beyond the large amounts of cash involved and the top-flight access that such sums often secure, the case against Giffen has opened a window onto the high-stakes intercontinental maneuvering that occurs when Big Oil and political access overlap, a juncture marked by intense and expensive lobbying, deal-making and the intersection of money, business and geopolitics," reported Ron Stodghill in the *New York Times*.[63] "The case also illustrates the U.S. government's struggle to reconcile its short-term energy interests with its longer-term political goal of encouraging democracy in countries the international community has deemed corrupt."

While admitting that Giffen moved moneys from one secret bank account to another, his lawyers claimed that he did not act alone. In the words of Schwartz, he was working with "the knowledge of our government," and his access in Kazakhstan was "a function of a bizarre historical time."

In June 2004, Giffen's attorneys filed a motion with Judge William Pauley III of Federal District Court in New York seeking access to classified government documents. In their submission, they said that senior officials at the CIA, State Department, and White House encouraged Giffen to use his close connections with Kazakh leaders to collect top class intelligence for the United States. (When this information was made public, the names, titles, and government affiliations of individuals mentioned in the lawyers' document were blacked out.[64]) They argued that much of the evidence necessary to clear him rested with various officials and agencies that helped him conduct business in Kazakhstan. Without such witnesses, it would be difficult for them to prove that their client was simply performing his duties as an American patriot. Judge Pauley backed the lawyers' motion, but the U.S. attorney's office appealed it, arguing that giving access to the requested documents to Giffen's lawyers would undermine national security. In any event, since Giffen acted as an official adviser, and as he routinely debriefed senior U.S. officials on the inner workings of the Kazakh government, he could not be found guilty of bribing a foreign government, his lawyers argued.

Whereas the stories about the kickbacks on Kazakhstan's hydrocarbon contracts—labeled "Kazakhgate"—received wide coverage in the American print media from 2000 onwards, Kazakh newspapers ignored them. It was not until Giffen's arrest in 2003 that the news found an outlet in a minority of Kazakh publications. As for the privately owned electronic media, the family members of Nazarbayev had scooped most of them up and censored this vital news. Nazarbayev dismissed "Kazakh-gate"as a political ploy by the opposition and rarely answered the charges in detail for years.

However, on the eve of the court hearings of the Giffen case in early 2004, Nazarbayev answered a question about the subject on a popular call-in television program: "[This trial] is precisely against Giffen because he is a citizen of the U.S., and he is liable to that country's jurisdiction. Therefore, I don't find it necessary to follow this process or comment on it, because from a political side, [or a] diplomatic side, a politician shouldn't comment on a trial in a foreign country." He assured his audience that the contracts that Giffen facilitated for U.S. oil companies were done in the interest of the Kazakh people: "Today our oilmen say those contracts were executed on a high level; they completely met the interests of Kazakhstan. The oilmen are grateful to him [Giffen]."[65] And yet there was another scandal centered around petroleum.

CORRUPT TO THE CORE

At the turn of the century, word went around that President Nazarbayev had salted away $1 billion in hydrocarbon income in his personal, secret Swiss bank accounts. The sources of this ill-gotten fortune were one-off commissions for awarding contracts for oil and gas exploration, and an ongoing arrangement related to the quantity of oil produced and sold.

In the latter case, there was ample opportunity for illicit gains, particularly when there was a wide difference between the prices being paid locally and internationally. Since crude oil must end up at a refinery for distillation into different petroleum products, the number of intermediaries between the spigot at the oil field and the refinery can vary from one to several—each making a neat profit by adding a few dollars to the price of an oil barrel. Or there could be just one intermediary operating behind several front companies. This has long been a common source of corruption among the royal families in the oil-rich states in the Persian Gulf.

Such became the case in Kazakhstan as well. That explained why a perusal of the Economist Intelligence Unit's report on Kazakhstan, published in August 2003, showed that in 2002 the tiny Caribbean island of Bermuda was Kazakhstan's second largest trading partner, after Russia, purchasing one-fifth of all its exports—almost exclusively crude oil. (In practice, most of the Kazakh oil may not have been shipped to Bermuda for re-export, but sent directly to a different destination.) "We've known about Nazarbayev's corruption for at least fifteen years because our own intelligence agencies have told us," said Jonathan Winer, a former deputy assistant secretary of state during the Clinton administration.

According to the World Bank's 2005 Worldwide Governance Indicators, Kazakhstan was as corrupt as Angola, Bolivia, Kenya, Libya, and Pakistan.[66] Transparency International defines corruption as "abuse of public office for private gain" and includes "misappropriation of public assets, the dispensing of state benefits, influence peddling, bribes, and extortion." According to the World Bank, "high corruption"—graft and state capture by state officials—and "petty corruption"—solicitation of bribes and extortion by civil servants—are rampant in the seven poorest CIS countries, including Kazakhstan.

Such large-scale pilfering of state funds could not remain hidden from the public for long. But when the *Respublika* (*Republic*) newspaper bravely reported in late March 2002 the allegations that Nazarbayev had deposited $1 billion of state oil funds in his secret Swiss bank accounts, anonymous threats and warnings followed. These were capped by an overnight display of a dog's head outside the newspaper office bearing a note, "There will be no next time"—a scene reminiscent of the horse's head laid next to the targeted man's pillow in the movie *The Godfather*. Lesser warnings took the form of inexplicable overnight fires at dissident newspaper and magazine offices.

Yet the curiosity of the public and politicians persisted. The rise of the nouveau riche—a term that got transmuted into "New Kazakh" or "New Russian"—was more pronounced in Kazakhstan than anywhere else in Central Asia due to its rising output of oil and gas. Members of this new class had no compunction about flaunting their affluence. They rode expensive, chauffeur-driven automobiles, donned designer clothes and expensive jewelry, frequented exclusive clubs, and threw lavish parties while most people drove old Soviet cars or rode buses, donned cheap clothes made in

Turkey or China, and scrimped for months to save enough for a birthday party. For a people whose basic needs had been met by the state for three generations in return for making a contribution to the GDP, this emerging social system appeared increasingly inauspicious.

The freshly appointed prime minister, Imangaliy Tasmagambetov, tried to dampen down popular unease by informing the parliament on April 4, 2002, that a secret foreign bank account was opened in 1996 to deposit nearly $1 billion that the Kazakh government had received by selling one-fifth of the Tengiz oil field. Subsequently, the money was used to wipe out the pension arrears and to cover deficits in national budgets, and a balance of $213 million was deposited in Kazakhstan's National Fund, a savings account for oil income, set up in 2001.[67] In the absence of opinion surveys, it was hard to tell whether Tasmagambetov's statement satisfied the opposition politicians or the public, but it was not likely.

As for Nazarbayev, he was as intolerant of criticism as his Uzbek counterpart, Karimov. In the absence of censorship in the republic, he resorted to harassing and persecuting journalists in the print media (since most of the electronic media was controlled by his family members or sympathetic oligarchs). The longstanding provision that criminalized harming the president's "honor and dignity" also came in handy. And in an example of a blatantly political charge, Sergei Duvanov, who reported the grand jury proceedings in the Giffen case in the United States in 2003, was convicted of committing rape. Widespread protest from outside Kazakhstan brought about his transfer from a prison cell to house arrest. And, as in Uzbekistan, there were numerous cases of independent-minded reporters being beaten up by intelligence agents.

Alarmingly, contrary to his promises, the improved economy due to greater finds of hydrocarbons in a world market of rising prices did not lead Nazarbayev to advance political reform. Instead, he took steps not only to perpetuate his office for life, but also to set up a dynastic rule.

LIFE PRESIDENCY THROUGH THE BACKDOOR

During the decade of 1993 to 2002, Kazakhstan's proven reserves rose steadily from 5.2 billion barrels to 9 billion. Then came an eye-popping surprise: the new findings in 2003 amounted to three times the previous total, pushing the new aggregate to 36 billion barrels!

However, the consequent euphoria was deflated by the adverse news that commercial production of the Kashagan oilfield would start in 2008 instead of 2005, with the modest target of 450,000 bpd by 2010. The delay led two of the consortium's constituents to sell their stakes. The shares of the reconstituted entity, with ENI as the operating company, were: ENI, ExxonMobil, Royal Dutch Shell, and Total, 18.5 percent each; ConocoPhillips, 9.33 percent; (Japanese) Impex, 8.33 percent; and KazMunayGaz, 8.33 percent.

This was the background to the parliamentary poll in September 2004, to be contested only by the parties that met the provisons of a strict law enforced in July 2002, which required all the existing political parties to reapply. Several, including the Communist Party, failed to win registration. The newly formed Democratic Party of Kazakhstan Ak Zhol (Bright Path)—led by Kazakh oligarchs with political ambitions, and committed to keeping the economic and political reform on track—hoped to make a mark. But whereas the exit polls showed Ak Zhol garnering 23 percent of the vote, it actually secured only one seat! In protest, Ak Zhol refused to claim it. Even Asar (All Together)—set up by Nazarbayev's eldest daughter Dariga to encourage young people to participate in politics by highlighting grievances at the local level—officially received half as many votes as the exit polls indicated.

On the other hand, the entry of Dariga Nazarbayeva, a professional opera singer, into politics highlighted the fact that the gains women had made during the Soviet period had persisted after 1991. Women accounted for half the workforce in the republic, often taking jobs as bank managers, headmistresses, accountants, and police officers. They were often better students and better qualified for the jobs they performed than their male counterparts. Indeed, given the rising alcoholism among men and their continued underperformance in educational institutions, women were set to become more important contributors to the GDP than men.

Filial relations did not stop Nazarbayev from making an angry telephone call to Dariga to rebuke her for describing the apparatchiks of Nur Otan as "hollow yes-men" while campaigning for her party during the run-up to the election.[68] Unsurprisingly, according to the Election Commission, Nur Otan, which scored less than twice the figure for Ak Zhol in the exit polls, won 60 percent of the popular vote, and forty-two seats out of seventy-seven, with Dariga's Asar getting a mere four seats. Calling the election "a farce," Zharmakhan Tuyakbai, a Nur Otan leader and speaker of the outgoing parliament, resigned. Nazarbayev's message to his daughter was, "Keep away from attacking the leaders of my party"; and to the Kazakh oligarchs, "Stay out of politics."

The disenchanted Ak Zhol leaders co-opted Tuyakbai and Zamanbek Nurkadilov, the former cabinet minister and Almaty mayor who had split with Nazarbayev earlier, to call for a referendum to annul the election result. Nothing came of it. In the aftermath of the peaceful overthrow of President Leonid Kuchma in Ukraine, most of the political opposition groups in Kazakhstan formed a bloc called For a Just Kazakhstan, which adopted Tuyakbai as its presidential candidate at a convention in Almaty in March 2005. Ak Zhol stayed out of this bloc and fielded its own candidate, Alikhan Baimenov.

In foreign affairs, as the long-standing leader of a vital geo-strategic country being courted by three great powers, Nazarbayev had the privilege of balancing one with the others. Just as the much-heralded BTC pipeline was commisisoned in May 2005, he unveiled plans to link the Kazakh oil port of Aktau to the BTC by a pipeline under the Caspian, thus making one of the George W. Bush administration's pipe dreams come true. This won him much acclaim in Washington. Two months later, his government signed an agreement with China to develop strategic partnership. It set the scene for the CPNC's acquisition of Canadian-registered PetroKazakhstan, owning oil fields in southern Kazakhstan, for $4.2 billion.[69]

These developments added to Nazarbayev's stature at home. He had every reason to be confident of winning the presidential poll on December 4, 2005, by a thumping majority. Yet, during the run-up to the election, there were arrests of opposition leaders, break-ins at political offices, and muzzling of the independent media. Three weeks before the polling day, Nurkadilov, who focussed on rampant corruption, was found dead of gunshot wounds at his home.[70]

According to the Election Commission, 77 percent of the eligible electors cast their ballots, with 91 percent favoring Nazarbayev, and less than 7 percent Tuyakbai.

"Regrettably, despite some efforts which were undertaken to improve the process, the authorities did not exhibit sufficient political will to hold a genuinely good election," said Bruce George, leader of OSCE monitors. The OSCE report referred to "Unauthorized persons interfering in polling stations, cases of multiple voting, ballot box stuffing and pressure on students to vote were observed during voting and during the count; and tampering with result protocols and a wide range of procedural violations."[71] Yet Washington did nothing more than issue a muted protest.

Persecution of opposition leaders continued. In February, Altinbek Sarsenbayev, a former minister and ambassador and confidant of Nazarbayev until 2003, was murdered and his body found on a road near Almaty along with his driver and bodyguard. This led to the arrest of five "rogue" members of the elite combat unit of the Kazakh National Security Committee as suspects.[72] None of that mattered to the Bush White House, which rolled out the red carpet for Nazarbayev when he arrived at Andrews Air Force Base in Maryland in his private Boeing 767 in September 2006. In the course of a busy schedule, the Kazakh leader spent time at the Bushes' family retreat in Kennebunkport, Maine, with former President George H. W. Bush.

Such bonhomie did not deflect Nazarbayev from following his policy of strengthening Kazakhstan's links with Russia and China. The Shanghai Cooperation Organization had proved to be an apt platform to do so after it had adopted a new charter in May 2003, which aimed to bring about a "new" international political and economic order—meaning one in which the United States was not the sole superpower. Four years later, the SCO conducted its first joint military exercises, codenamed Peace Mission 2007, in the Russian Ural region of Chelyabinsk, with the forces of all Central Asian member states participating.

The rising profile of Kazakhstan in the world rubbed off on Nazarbayev at home. In May 2007, Nazarbayev had the pliant parliament amend the constitution to exempt him from the two-term limitation for presidency and allow him to seek reelection as many times as he liked. He thus achieved his aim of presidency for life, which he shared with his blatantly despotic neighbors in Uzbekistan and Turkmenistan. However, the size and strategic location of the republic, and its hydrocarbon riches, afforded him to be less authoritarian than Karimov or Niyazov. As a result, unlike in Uzbekistan and Turkmenistan, ordinary people did not feel that the KNB would haul them to the nearest police station if they criticized Nazarbayev or his family in private.

The soaring hydrocarbon prices in 2007 and 2008, with the price of an oil barrel fluctuating around $100, raised the confidence of both Nazarbayev and his government. So they were in no mood to hear more bad news from the Kashagan oilfield front, yet that is what they got in the autumn of 2007. The start-up expenses had shot up from $57 billion to $137 billion, and the date for its on-stream operation, which had earlier been pushed back to 2008, was then delayed further to 2011, with the modest target of 450,000 bpd to be achieved three years later. That meant the Kazakh government would have to defer its own development projects and plans to expand its energy sector.

It pressured the Western-dominated consortium to make concessions. The consortium resisted, but facing the prospect of the cancellation of the contract altogether, it agreed a deal in January 2008. It let KazMunayGaz double its share to 16.8 percent of the equity at the below-market price of $1.5 billion, with the top four Western companies reducing theirs from 18.5 to 16.8 percent each, and shelling out a bonus of $4.5 billion. The government announced that it would spend the funds on education, health care, and infrastructure.[73]

The health care infrastructure had deteriorated considerably in the post-Soviet period. Most hospitals were staffed by under-qualified and over-worked physicians, surgeons, and nurses. Doctors were trained under the old system of specialization, with only few graduating as general practitioners. In the absence of up-to-date testing devices, the doctors relied almost solely on symptomatic diagnosis. Even simple blood tests were hard to come by. As a result, both Kazakhs and Russians turned increasingly to home remedies of honey, steaming tea, vodka—and even an ultra-hot version of a sauna, called *banya*, meant to sweat out bodily impurities and diseases.[74]

Nazarbayev had another priority as well. Assured of a lifetime presidency, he moved to get rid of the pretender to his throne: forty-five-year-old Rakhat Aliyev, married to the president's eldest daughter, Dariga, for twenty-three years, and serving as Kazakhstan's ambassador to Austria since February 2007.

SPLIT IN THE FIRST FAMILY

The day after signing the constitutional changes on May 25, 2007, Nazarbayev sacked Aliyev as the Kazakh ambassador in Vienna. Accusing Aliyev of kidnappings, involvement in organized crime, and money laundering in Austria, the interior ministry issued an international arrest order for him. More specifically, he was charged with having the chairman and deputy chairman of Nurbank, the seventh largest bank in the republic, kidnapped and forcing them to sign over their families' interest in the bank to benefit him.

A stocky man who looked older than his years, Aliyev had a glittering career. Son of a former minister of health, at the age of twenty-two he married Dariga. The young couple had two sons and a daughter. During the regime of his father-in-law, he initially made a career in banking. Then he went into real estate, sugar and alcohol processing, mass media (including KTK TV channel), while serving as the deputy chief of the secret police,

KNB, in charge of the anti-corruption campaign, along with assuming a high-ranking post in the tax police. He curbed incipient political opposition by arresting its leaders on the charge of abuse of office and securing their convictions.

But when a rival TV company transmitted evidence showing Aliyev misusing his position for personal gain in 2002, he lost credibility. To repair the damage, Nazarbayev shunted him off to Vienna as Kazakhstan's ambassador. After he had cooled his heels in Vienna for a year, he was recalled to Astana, and appointed the first deputy foreign minister while he managed his sprawling business interests. He served in Astana until his second ambassadorial posting in Vienna.

Now, armed with an international arrest warrant against him, the Austrian police detained him in Vienna. In the absence of an extradition treaty between Austria and Kazakhstan, the court decided to release him on a hefty bail of €1 million ($1.36 million). He was given police protection while his case was under consideration. According to the interview he gave to the Vienna-based *Profil* magazine (published on June 1, 2007, before his arrest), his problems started when he expressed hopes of running for president in 2012. He argued that while a strong hand was needed to rule Kazakhstan soon after the Soviet collapse, now it was time for a separation of powers and an independent judiciary. "A younger, more open generation should come to power," he said. "Otherwise they all sit either in jail or abroad."

He criticized the constitutional amendment conferring life presidency on Nazarbayev. The dramatic action against him, which sent shock waves throughout Kazakhstan, was a dire warning to the Kazakh elite to abide by Nazarbayev or face ruin. Aliyev claimed that Kazakh secret agents had attempted, unsuccessfully, to abduct him and take him back to Kazakhstan, and that his wife, Dariga, and their seven-year-old daughter were being held captives in Astana.[75] Aliyev debunked the charge of arranging the kidnap of Nurbank's top officials by claiming that they were engaged in illegal banking practices.

To Aliyev's dismay, Dariga soon divorced him without his consent, following the president's successful pressure on courts to approve the divorce without the proper legal process. "They stuck a fax through the fence at my home at quarter past midnight [in Vienna]," Aliyev told *The Times* (of London). "They even falsified my signature on the document. I spoke to my wife on the telephone and she said, 'My father pressured me very much,' and she could not do anything."[76]

Finding himself an outcast from the portals of power, Aliyev spilled the beans on the inner workings of Nazarbayev's regime, confirming all that its critics had been saying for years. He disclosed that when he ran KTK TV channel and showed a video of anti-government demonstrations in Georgia in 2003 (a peaceful revolution which toppled the post-Soviet old guard), he was severely reprimanded by Nazarbayev for doing so. Aliyev detailed how Nazarbayev suppressed potential rivals through "media control, police action and rigged elections."

In his interview with the *New York Times*, Aliyev produced a thick stack of electoral ballots which, he said, were used by the government to create an extra set of documents to change the poll results it did not like. In the 91 percent vote for Nazarbayev in December 2005, at least 20 percent were fake ballots, he asserted. "The head of the administration of the president is the real chief of the Central Election commission," he continued. "These crazy leaders in the regions [of Kazakhstan], they put them [fake ballots] in. It is like a competition: who can get the most votes for the president?"[77]

Aliyev further revealed that the KNB ran its own jails, and that he would be thrown into one if he returned home. He also confirmed that several opposition leaders had been murdered or had died mysteriously.

The speculation that, following her divorce, Dariga Nazarbayeva would emerge as the political favorite of the president died down when Nazarbayev blocked her move to seek reelection to parliament on the Nur Otan party ticket after abandoning her Asar party. That raised the chances of Nazarbayev's second son-in-law, forty-year-old Timur Kulibayev, married to Dinara (a younger sister of Dariga), rising to the top. Son of a former regional communist leader from western Kazakhstan, who would later become construction minister, Kulibayev was for many years the first vice president of the state-owned oil and gas conglomerate KazMunayGaz. Then he was appointed the first deputy chairman of Samruk, a holding company which managed several state-owned corporations.

There was also Aliya, the youngest of the three sisters, a successful businesswoman in her own right. Now into her second marriage to Daniyar Khassenov, a Kazakh businessman, she had made regional headlines with her first marriage to Aidar Akayev, son of Askar Akayev, the then president of Kyrgyzstan. Aliya and Aidar had met as students at an American university.

CHAPTER 5

KYRGYZSTAN:
The Tulip Revolution, A False Dawn

WHILE BEING ONLY ONE-THIRTEENTH THE SIZE OF KAZAKHSTAN, Kyrgyzstan shared two elements with it in the 1950s: it was part of the Kremlin's Virgin Land project, and it had a similar ethnic composition. At 40 percent of the republic's population, native Kyrgyzes were only as numerous as European settlers—Russians, Ukrainians, and Germans.[1] Yet the reasons for the parity between the indigenous people and recent settlers were different in the two cases.

"Before coming to Bishkek, I thought I would see the Russians in managerial positions and as professionals with the Kyrgyz doing the menial jobs, cleaning streets, waitressing, and so on," said U.S. Ambassador Edward Hurwitz. "But it is not like that at all. When Russians colonized Bishkek, they brought everything and everybody from Russia, including house servants, mechanics and skilled workers. So today you see that most taxi drivers are Russian, and also car mechanics as well as chambermaids and waitresses in hotels and restaurants. The Kyrgyz lived mostly in the mountains, and tended sheep and cattle. Now in Bishkek, Russians are about 55 percent of the population."[2] Overall, though, according to the 1989 census, due to their higher birth rate, the Kyrgyz formed a slim majority in the republic named after them.

With mountains covering three-quarters of its territory, Kyrgyzstan is rich in minerals. It emerged as the leading source of mercury and antimony in the Soviet Union, and one of the main producers of Soviet coal and uranium. Since, in the early 1950s, it also had a potential for developing further its agriculture and animal husbandry, Moscow included it in its Virgin Land project. The Congress of the Communist Party of Kyrgyzstan (CPKz), meeting in February 1954 in Bishkek (then Frunze, named after the Red Army General Mikhail Frunze, who was born there), duly committed itself to advance the scheme.

Six years later, when Kyrgyzstan failed to meet its targets under this program, the Moscow leadership installed a comparatively young party member, Turdahun Usubaliyev (originally, Yusuf Ali) as the CPKz's first secretary. He had graduated from the Senior Party School of the CPSU's Central Committee, and then become an instructor in Communist ideology at the institute. That brought him close to the rising stars in the party's central bureaucracy.

Therefore, Khrushchev's replacement by Leonid Brezhnev in October 1964 did not affect Usubaliyev's fortunes. He rapidly ingratiated himself with Brezhnev, during whose rule the party became even more powerful and more distant from the people than before. "We were a highly centralized party, which did not ask the people what they wanted," said Kybanychbek Idinov, chairman of the Kyrgyzstan Supreme Soviet Commission on Inter-Parliamentarian Relations, who joined the Communist Party in 1972. "We considered ourselves the embodiment of the nation, and that was it."[3]

On the ground, an unrelenting obsession with meeting economic targets—despite mounting problems of red tape, unethical behavior among managers, and low morale among workers—engendered corruption and nepotism in the economy and government administration. As the quality of leadership in Moscow deteriorated, Republican Party bosses like Usubaliyev found greater chances to strengthen their grip over local networks. Intoxicated with power, and running a distant republic at the back of beyond, Usubaliyev fostered a personality cult which was in full bloom when Brezhnev died in 1982.

It was not until Mikhail Gorbachev became the CPSU's first secretary in March 1985 that the future of Usubaliyev, now sixty-six, was threatened. The axe fell on him in November, and he was replaced by Absamat Musaliyev (originally, Musa Ali), the erstwhile mayor of Bishkek. A mining graduate of Moscow University, Musaliyev had worked in mines in Kyrgyzstan before being transferred to the party organization.

The following year another Kyrgyz with an engineering science background traduced a similar path, moving from a technological-scientific job to a position in the party bureaucracy at the CPKz's Central Committee secretariat. His name was Askar Akayev. Born in 1944 to a farm worker and his wife in the village of Kyzyl Bairak in Northern Kyrgyzstan, Akayev graduated from St. Petersburg (then Leningrad) Institute of Exact Mechanics and Optics as an award-winning nuclear physicist.

Musaliyev set out to reform the party and the social system, which had become atrophied under Usubaliyev, but proved unequal to the daunting task. He was therefore shunted sideways to chair the Presidium of the Supreme Soviet, with Jumagalbek Amanbayev becoming first secretary of the CPKz. Rivaling him was the up-and-coming Akayev. Elected a deputy to the Soviet Union's Congress of People's Deputies (CPD) in the March 1989 elections, he became vice-chairman of the Commission on Foreign Affairs of the Supreme Soviet, the super-parliament whose 460 members were drawn from the larger CPD. At Gorbachev's recommendation, he was elected to the CPSU's Central Committee at its congress in July 1990.

INTERETHNIC TENSIONS

As elsewhere in the Soviet Union, perestroika and glasnost brought to the fore interethnic tensions, which were all the stronger in Kyrgyzstan, where the Kyrgyz had just inched up to 52.4 percent of the total population. Ethnic Russians were down to 22 percent, and Uzbeks held steady at 13 percent.[4]

Most Uzbeks lived in the southern region of Osh, containing part of the fertile Fergana Valley. It became customary to think of the republic as composed of the North, dominated by the Kyrgyz, and the South, with a heavy presence of ethnic Uzbeks. Since two-thirds of the population lived in rural valleys or on the steppes of the western ranges of the Tien Shan, inhabited largely by Kyrgyzes or Uzbeks, Russians and other Slavs were to be found mainly in cities like Bishkek.

Located at the foot of the Tien Shan range, and surrounded by permanent snow-capped mountains, Bishkek acquired the status of an important city only after World War II. It was a place of enormous parks and plazas (one of which harbored a vast yurt), impressive public buildings, educational and cultural institutions, and bustling bazaars, as well as major industrial plants. Bishkek remains spruce and unhurried; many people walk or bike to work. Its concession to the hurly-burly of the post-Soviet life has been the introduction of the privately run *marshrutka*, mini-buses, blaring Kyrgyz music, to ferry people around. Its countless trees, painted white at the bottom of the trunk, are fed by the melting snows of the surrounding mountains through a system of irrigation channels. These features made it particularly attractive to ethnic Russians during the Soviet era.

However, as elsewhere in Central Asia, social intercourse between Russians and Kyrgyzes was minimal here. Unlike the other non-Kyrgyz groups in the republic, Russians did not learn the Kyrgyz language, and Russian-Kyrgyz marriages were rare.

Since many of the Kyrgyz inhabitants of Bishkek and other urban centers were less than three generations removed from their nomadic forebears, they were still influenced by their ancestoral mores. They respected elders as well as authority figures, addressing males as *aga* or *baikay* (older brother) and females as *eje* (older sister). Men and women sat on the opposite sides of a table, while the most venerable person occupied the seat farthest from the entrance. The Kyrgyz families erected yurts to celebrate weddings and important birthdays.

A Kyrgyz wedding, which involves the groom paying the bride price in cash and kind, is an elaborate three-day affair. First, the bride, wearing a Western-style wedding dress, and the groom, sprucely attired, obtain a marriage license in the presence of friends. Then the newlyweds part. The following day, each side celebrates the occasion separately with food (where the popular dish of *lagman*, hand-rolled noodles in a broth of meat and vegetables, dominates), drink (vodka for men and kumiss for women), and dancing. On the last day, the bride is taken to the groom's residence where, faced with the prospect of leaving her parental home, she cries. This is a prelude to the exchange of gifts by the two sides, followed by food and drinks. The groom's parents choose two female relatives to stay on until the next morning to bear witness that the marriage was consummated overnight and that the bride was a virgin, the evidence to be found in the blood stains on the bedsheet.

Kyrgyz families erected yurts also for funerals when, following the nomadic tradition, a male corpse was laid out on the left side of the yurt, and a female on the right. Only women were allowed into the yurt to grieve while men stayed outside. Then, for the next forty days, every Friday evening (i.e., Thursday evening in Christian calendar) the deceased's family sacrificed a sheep in remembrance.

Despite several decades of habitation in towns and cities, the Kyrgyz had not developed the habit of standing in a queue in an orderly fashion at public places like bus stops, booking offices at cinemas, or railway stations—a drawback which ethnic Russians would readily point out to visiting foreigners. But far more scandalous to Russians was the Kyrgyz practice of wife-stealing—a euphemism for kidnapping a nubile woman. The practice was centuries old, when men from one nomadic tribe stole women from an enemy tribe to weaken its rival. Among settled Kyrgyzes, the abducted girl would share the bed with her prospective husband, who would then present her to his mother. The older woman would then tie a white scarf around her head to indicate that she was married. In Soviet times and later, the abducted woman had the option to flee and sue her kidnapper, but that never happened, for such a step would have brought shame to her family and make her unmarriageable.

In recent times, a milder version of wife-stealing has emerged. The case of twenty-eight-year-old Ainur Tairova and Melis Aliyev of Bishkek was illustrative of about a third of Kyrgyz marriages. After three months of dating, when Aliyev proposed, Tairova demurred. So one day Aliyev and his friends tricked her into entering their car. Aliyev then kept her in his house while his relatives tried to tie a white scarf on her, signaling her acquiescence. She resisted for two days, then gave in when her own parents described bride-stealing as part of the Kyrgyz way of life.

Some Kyrgyz NGOs have toured the rural areas and tried to convey the message that bride abduction is a crime, but such efforts have failed. "We get a lot of resistance," said Elmira Shishkarayeva of Winrock International. "People say, 'We live in a patriarchal society, and this is the only way. Our young people do not have opportunities to meet or date each other. If you say this is such a bad tradition, suggest something new.'"[5]

Reflecting the rising tide of ethnic nationalism, the Supreme Soviet declared Kyrgyz the official language in November 1989, and specified an eight-year period for a complete changeover from the current practice of treating Kyrgyz and Russian equally. This proved popular with the Kyrgyz, and helped the CPKz to gain over 85 percent of the 350 seats in the Soviet in the multi-candidate election in March 1990, with the remaining seats going to independents propounding nationalism and/or democracy. But the republic's new linguistic policy upset ethnic Russians and Uzbeks.

Relations between Uzbeks and the Kyrgyz had been strained over a long period. Ethnic differences were accentuated by the dearth of arable land in the predominantly mountainous republic, resulting in frequent disputes between the two groups over land and supplies of irrigation water from the large Fergana Canal. The authorities in Bishkek alleged that the Uzbek population of the Osh region was being encouraged by the clandestine Birlik Popular Front (of Uzbekistan) to agitate for autonomy as a step towards secession to join Uzbekistan. In many urban centers of the province, minority Uzbeks monopolized commerce and trade, which made them unpopular with the Kyrgyz. With unemployment among the Kyrgyz, especially young men, rising sharply, tension between the two communities rose.

It exploded in Kyrgyz-Uzbek rioting in the Osh region in June 1990. The trigger was the forcible takeover of a large plot of land belonging to an Uzbek-dominated collective farm by the local Kyrgyzes in the Kyrgyzstan-

Uzbekistan border area, accompanied by much violence and arson in which Uzbeks were the victims. The evicted Uzbeks sought and received assistance from fellow-Uzbeks across the border. The subsequent fighting ceased only after a large-scale intervention by Kyrgyzstan's Interior Ministry forces under the command of forty-two-year-old Felix Kulov. Trained as a policeman, he had risen through the ranks partly because he belonged to the Salto clan whose members had traditionally been army and police officers. Salto was one of the seven important clans, the others being Adigina, Bugu (literally, "Red Deer"), Ich Kilik, Ong, Sari Bagish, and Sol. An individual's clan affiliation mattered as much socially as it did in business and politics.

The estimate of 300 dead in three days of violence, which spread to Osh city and Jalalabad, was considered low by many observers.[6] One side blamed Birlik supporters among Uzbeks for instigating the bloodshed, while the other side accused leaders of a newly established group known simply as "Kyrgyzstan" backed by local CPKz figures intent on underscoring their nationalist credentials. The Uzbeks' open demand for autonomy, once they had recovered from the shock, intensified ethno-centric sentiment among the Kyrgyz, who complained bitterly of housing shortages and joblessness.

Matters came to a head in November when about 1,000 Kyrgyz protesters, led by the Unit of Builders, a grassroots organization focusing on unemployment and homelessness among the Kyrgyz, undertook a hunger strike in the administrative center of Bishkek. To divert the rising public protest, and following the lead of the Supreme Soviet in Moscow, Musaliyev persuaded the republic's Supreme Soviet to create the new post of executive president. According to the precedent set by Moscow, this job should have gone to Musaliyev. But with the street protest in full swing in Bishkek, Gorbachev thought it prudent to give Supreme Soviet deputies a free hand to settle the matter on November 22. He delegated Vladimir Kryuchkov, a CPSU Politburo member, to oversee the election.

Eleven aspirants, including Musaliyev, came forward, but none of them got the absolute majority required. A stalemate ensued. Prodded by Gorbachev and Kryuchkov, Akayev arrived in Bishkek from Moscow and offered himself as a presidential candidate. He won. Though an ethnic Kyrgyz, this small, compact, prematurely bald man with a ready smile was an outsider in the republic's politics. That proved to be his political asset. To placate Musaliyev, the Kremlin offered him the post of the CPKz's first secretary.

Since a majority of the economic enterprises in Kyrgyzstan were controlled by Moscow and their directors appointed by it, they employed the

Kyrgyz chiefly in manual and semi-skilled jobs, thus alienating the Kyrgyz youth. In 1988 and 1989, socially conscious Kyrgyzes started forming Youth Democratic Forums. Ulan Orazaliyev (originally, Araz Ali), a heavily built man from Bishkek, with the full moon face of a Mongol and a wispy beard, recalled the ferment in the late 1980s. He joined the Communist Party in 1977 after graduating from Moscow University in philosophy at the age of twenty-two, and taught the subject in Moscow schools for nine years. On his return to Bishkek in 1986, he got involved in publishing the journal of the Academy of Sciences. Responding to the rise of the Youth Democratic Forums, the government appointed him director of publishing for a youth journal with a mandate to provide the young generation with an ideology. It proved to be a thankless task.[7]

Encouraged by the success they had in frustrating Musaliyev's ambition to become the republic's president, the disaffected elements—consisting largely of Kyrgyz writers, journalists, and university teachers and students—formed the Democratic Kyrgyzstan Movement (DKM) in Bishkek in May 1990. This was a perfectly legal move since a republican law now allowed the formation of political parties so long as they were not based on religion, race, or ethnicity. Though the DKM was open to all, there was little support for it among ethnic Russians, who did not encounter unemployment and homelessness like their Kyrgyz fellow citizens. Thus the democratic stream in Kyrgyzstan came to be virtually monopolized by Kyrgyz nationalists.

Even though the parliamentary poll had given the Russian minority a share of seats commensurate with their proportion of the population, about 20 percent, they were increasingly apprehensive of their future. They noticed Kyrgyz nationalism growing at the expense of the Russian language and hegemony that had been an integral part of the Bolshevik Revolution in the region.

By the autumn of 1991, more than 8 percent of the 920,000 Russians in Kyrgyzstan had left.[8] Since most of them possessed high technical, scientific, or managerial skills, they were confident of thriving elsewhere in Russia. This created a serious problem for the Kyrgyz industry. Others with lesser skills stayed on because food and housing in Kyrgyzstan were better than in the Russian Federation, and there were ample supplies of vegetables and fruit.

Another positive factor from the Russian perspective was the weakness of the Islamist movement. The Kyrgyz came under the influence of Islam late—largely as subjects of the Khanate of Kokand in the 1820s. They often converted to the mystical Sufi school of Islam whose propagators incorporated the Kyrgyzes' shamanistic practices in their teachings to soften their switch. It was Kokand's ruler who fortified a rest stop along one of the feeder routes to the ancient Silk Road through the Tien Shan Mountains in 1825 with a mud tower. It fell to the Tsarist army in 1862, and emerged as the garrison town of Pishkek in 1877, with its surroundings to be settled by imported Russian peasants.

The freshly converted Kyrgyzes were set in their nomadic ways, and failed to develop the Islamic practice of praying at a mosque on Fridays. Their women continued to work unveiled alongside men. As pagans of long standing, they found it hard to adjust to the straightjacket of monotheism. "Given our style of life and our cattle-breeding economy, we still have a pantheistic outlook," said Orazaliyev. "We were children of nature, our God. We worshipped the wind, sun, fire and sky before embracing Islam."[9]

The early Turkic tribes believed in shamanism, a primitive faith in which the metaphysical world of gods, demons, and ancestral spirits could be accessed only through shamans—priests, magicians, and healers, all rolled in one. They led the communal worship of the elements such as the sky, earth, air, sun, water, and fire, and natural objects like rocks and trees, by chanting pleas and praises to their spirits. To scatter evil spirits, shamans lit a fire and sprinkled incense over it and chanted verses.

The preeminent position of fire in nature's pantheon was recognized by Zoroaster (circa 628–551 BC), the founder of the first organized religion in the region. He made it a central tenet of Zoroastrianism, with a Zoroastrian temple maintaining an eternal flame within its premises. "The Turks venerate fire to an extraordinary point, and honor air and water," noted a Byzantine envoy in the sixth century. "They address praises to the ground, but prostrate themselves only in front of him who created the sky and the earth, and call him God. They sacrifice horses and sheep to him."[10] Among the Turkic tribes, the Kyrgyzes stuck to the shamanistic traditions until the early nineteenth century.

In the Soviet era, religion was suppressed to the extent that only twenty-five mosques were allowed to function in Kyrgyzstan, most of them in the Osh region, where Uzbeks and Tajiks with long histories of settlement were more drawn to the mosque than the Kyrgyz. Yet, during the Soviet era, the Islamic customs regarding birth, male circumcision, marriage, and death persisted. Despite the official ban, almost all Kyrgyz Muslim funerals were conducted according to the Islamic tradition.[11]

With the onset of glasnost and perestroika, more people began attending

the mosque or church, and the quality of clerics, graduating from the officially run theological colleges, had improved. Commenting on this change,
Moldo Kasimov, a Kyrgyz researcher, wrote in the *Leninchil Zhash*
(Leninist Youth) of August 6, 1987: "In the past they lectured on atheism,
but now they wear turbans and have become mullahs."[112]

There was a growth in secular organizations too, since perestroika
allowed the formation of voluntary social and cultural groups. The Unit of
Builders, claiming a membership of 20,000 in the late 1980s, was the best
known example. This gave a general impetus to the democratic movement
in the republic.

A DEMOCRATIC NICHE, BY DEFAULT

Since Musaliyev had contested the republic's presidency and failed, he did
not take kindly to President Akayev. In return, Akayev cold-shouldered the
power base of Musaliyev, the Communist Party, and turned a benign eye on
the emergent democratic opposition. While other Central Asian republics
followed Moscow's lead in having the top party leader also assume the
republic's executive presidency, Kyrgyzstan emerged as an exception—a
democratic niche.

It began attracting democrats from elsewhere in the region. Assembling in
the Kyrgyz capital in May 1991, they formed the Democratic Congress of
Central Asia and Kazakhstan as a discussion forum and a coordinating body
with its headquarters in Bishkek. Its first conference concentrated on ethnic
issues, and concluded that "any reconsideration of [current inter-republican]
borders could cause inter-ethnic conflict that could become international,"
and should be avoided.[13] The founding of this organization boosted the
morale of the democratic forces in Kyrgyzstan, and thus of Akayev.

Unlike most other Central Asian presidents, Akayev publicly and strongly
opposed the hard-liners' coup in Moscow in August 1991. This angered the
local military and KGB bosses (since their superiors in Moscow were
among the coup leaders). Following the lead of Kryuchkov—the KGB chief
of the Soviet Union and one of the main plotters—his deputy in Bishkek
arrived at the presidential administrative building to arrest Akayev. The
move boomeranged, and he found himself arrested by the security men
guarding the president. Akayev dispatched loyal troops to surround the
headquarters of the Communist Party, a rival center of power. He also
ordered television and radio stations to broadcast Russian President Boris
Yeltsin's appeal for resistance to the coup.

Following the collapse of the coup, Akayev resigned from the Communist Party and emulated Yeltsin by suspending the party and confiscating its properties. The party in Kyrgyzstan, with 154,650 full and candidate members on its rolls,[14] had reportedly acquired substantial funds through the underhanded economic activity of its apparatchiks. As the founders and managers of many cooperatives, chiefly in small enterprises from 1986 onwards, several of them had become involved in shady dealings, including the laundering of black money, which had started to grow during the latter part of the Brezhnev era.[15]

With the Communist Party extinct, most of its top bureaucrats fled Kyrgyzstan, heading mainly for Moscow. The parliamentarians elected on the party ticket ceased to belong to any recognized organization, and became independent. They unanimously supported the Supreme Soviet motion on August 30 declaring Kyrgyzstan an independent, sovereign state. The government came to rely on the rising popularity of Akayev, who refused to join any party. Focusing on establishing democracy in Kyrgyzstan, Akayev declined Gorbachev's offer of vice-presidency of the proposed Union of Sovereign States.[16] He made it part of his weekly agenda to consult the leaders of all political hues inside and outside parliament on important matters.

Yet when it came to contesting the presidency of independent Kyrgyzstan in October 1991, Akayev temporized. Expecting to be opposed by Jumagalbek Amanbayev, a former first secretary of the CPKz, Akayev spiked his guns by getting parliament to pass a law that required a presidential candidate to secure 25,000 signatures within two weeks.[17] This was an impossible condition for an opposition leader to meet in the absence of an established network. Thus Akayev, the sole candidate, secured 95 percent of the vote on a reported turnout of 90 percent.[18]

THE POST-SOVIET INDEPENDENCE

The collapse of the Soviet Union, causing the immediate loss of Moscow's subsidies amounting to 75 percent of Kyrgyzstan's budget, played havoc with the local economy. Yeltsin came to Akayev's rescue by offering subsidies from the Russian treasury. In return, Akayev followed Yeltsin's example in January 1992 and removed price controls on basic and other goods. This led to high inflation.

One way to divert public attention away from the economic downturn was to focus on nation-building. A prerequisite for it was to come up with the founder of the nation. In Uzbekistan, the government lost little time to invest Emir Timur Beg with that role. Here, in Kyrgyzstan, that honor went to a legendary hero called Manas. Since he had unified the forty Kyrgyz tribes by waving a red emblem, the color of the national flag was settled instantly. The symbol that uniquely represented the Kyrgyz nation became the round tunduk of a yurt, turned into the sun radiatating forty rays, each ray signifying a tribe that had followed the lead of Manas to defeat the nation's enemies. To round off the exercise, the term "kyrgyz" was offcially descibed as the compound of "kyrk" (forty) and "uuz" (tribes).

With powerful China and unstable Tajikistan as its neighbors, Kyrgyzstan needed to have Russian-dominated Commonwealth of Independent States troops on its soil, but lacked funds to maintain them even partially. Once again, Russia came to its rescue. In return, Kyrgyzstan promised to honor its commitment to provide recruits to CIS forces, its annual supply of conscripts being 21,000. It also joined the Tashkent Collective Security Agreement in May 1992.

While Kyrgyzstan's links with China had strengthened, especially in the economic field, following the establishment of republic-level trading organizations after spring 1988, its relations with Tajikistan had deteriorated. The Tajik government had rejected Akayev's demand for a readjustment of borders. Matters grew worse when civil war erupted between Tajik Communists and the opposition composed of democrats and Islamists. Akayev was anxious to see an end to the turmoil in Tajikistan, whose Islamist elements raised Islamist feelings among ethnic Uzbeks in Kyrgyzstan. As the host of the CIS summit in October 1992 in Bishkek, he won the backing of his colleagues to dispatch a peacemaking mission in Tajikistan under the leadership of his vice-president, Felix Kulov.

But when it was announced that Kyrgyzstan would send a contingent of 450 troops to Tajikistan for peacekeeping, the proposal was received coolly by the public. The mothers of the Kyrgyz soldiers likely to be sent to Tajikistan mounted a picket outside the Defense Ministry. Many parliamentarians argued that if a CIS peacekeeping force had to be dispatched to Tajikistan, it must be composed of all the remaining signatories to the Tashkent Collective Security Agreement, and not only Kyrgyzstan. The Supreme Soviet rejected the proposal for a peacekeeping mission—a triumph for grassroots politics in the region.

Against the background of a declining economy and tense interethnic relations, Akayev admitted that law-enforcement agencies were failing to apprehend "armed bands" smuggling weapons and narcotics from

Tajikistan and Afghanistan, with many Tajik refugees in Kyrgyzstan acting as conduits. He resorted to appointing local governors and abolishing the local soviets which had exercised that authority before.

In January 1993, eleven opposition groups—including the Democratic Kyrgyzstan Movement, Democratic Party of Erkin (Free) Kyrgyzstan, and Party of National Unity—issued a joint warning against the return of dictatorship. They argued that since Akayev found it easier to get along with technocrats than democrats, his circle of close advisers was bereft of members of the democratic parties.

Though Bishkek continued to be the freest capital in the region, providing once again the venue for the Second Conference of the Democratic Congress of Central Asia and Kazakhstan in December 1992, all local opposition groups were kept under surveillance. Phone-tapping was the most common technique used. Although Orazaliyev was a small fry in the opposition camp, the KGB did not overlook him. With most Kyrgyz political groups being sympathetic to pan-Turkism, and looking up to the democratic order in Turkey, they had developed cordial relations with the Turkish embassy. "During his visit to Bishkek, the vice-premier of Turkey gave me a device to jam the bug," Orazaliyev said. "I use it sometimes, not always, because if I did it all the time, the [local] KGB would get suspicious."[19]

Within months of Kyrgyz independence, Turkey had emerged as an important foreign player in Bishkek. During his visit to the Kyrgyz capital in May 1992, Premier Suleyman Demirel had offered $75 million in credits to Kyrgyzstan, as well as training for its university students in Turkey. Earlier, Ankara had reiterated Turkic fraternity with Kyrgyzstan, stressing common linguistic and cultural origins, to such an extent that rhetoric had overwhelmed reality. As a member of the Central Turkic group, Kyrgyz is not as close to the Turkish of Turkey as Azeri. This became obvious when, during their tour of Central Asia in April and May 1992, Demirel and his party had to engage interpreters everywhere.

Later, television programs in Turkish beamed at Kyrgyzstan failed to gain much of an audience. "The programs are of low quality, they have lots of song and dance, and very little serious information about Turkey's problems," said Orazaliyev. "I understand only about 60 percent of it." This was because, in his drive to create a homogenous Turkish nation, Mustafa Kemal Ataturk had purged Persian and Arabic loan words from the Ottoman Turkish, thus distancing the new version from its root which the languages of Central Asia shared.

Language figured prominently in the Supreme Soviet debate on the draft constitution which started in April 1993. Much to the disappointment of the ethnic Russian and Uzbek citizens, it rejected the clause describing Russian as the language of interethnic communication. It also turned down the provision for dual citizenship, which had been demanded by the Russian and Uzbek minorities. But it approved the change in its own name—to *Zhogorku Kenesh* (Supreme Council)—and that of the country, to Kyrgyz Republic. Yet the earlier name, Kyrgyzstan has remained in vogue. The draft constitution was unanimously adopted by the Supreme Soviet on May 5, and promulgated on the same day.

Soon thereafter, Kyrgyzstan launched its own currency, the som, with the backing of the International Monetary Fund, which encouraged Akayev to accelerate the transition from a command economy to a market economy. The central bank's strict monetary policy that followed reduced the annual inflation from 40 percent to 5 percent in a year. This pleased the Bill Clinton administration in Washington, as did Kyrgyzstan's decision to join NATO's Partnership for Peace Project (PFP) in June 1994.

The country's most valuable resource was gold, with the Kumtor mine alone believed to contain deposits of nearly 700 tons, or 22.4 million ounces—along with 100 tons of platinum, 250 tons of palladium, and 400 tons of silver.[20] (Due to the high cost of extraction, which involves the use of deadly sodium cyanide, the industry becomes profitable only if the price exceeds $300 an ounce.) Such a bounty attracted Cameco, a Canadian corporation. In 1992, it set up a joint venture with the state-owned gold company Kyrgyzaltyn—headed by Dastan Sarigulov, a cousin of the president's wife, Mairam Akayeva—on very favorable terms, including the right to operate the mine. The resulting Kumtor Gold Company would produce its first ingot five years later, and in 2001 raise its annual output to 20 tons, or 640,000 ounces, worth about $200 million.[21] Other gold mines remained in the public sector.

As in the case of Kazakh oil, the production and sale of gold, handled by Kyrgyzaltyn, became a major source of corruption. Allegations that the authorities were clandestinely transferring gold bars to Swiss banks, which first appeared in the opposition newspaper *Respublika* (Republic) edited by Zamira Sydykova, were taken up by parliamentarians, and reached such a pitch that the prime minister was forced to resign.[22]

As elsewhere in the developing world, having to follow the IMF's strict prescriptions created much popular resentment. This resulted in the lawmakers' disenchantment with Akayev, which led him to dismiss two successive cabinets in the first nine months of 1994. To tame the parliament, he called a referendum in October to reduce its power by having a bicameral chamber (the lower house being a 35-member Legislative Assembly and the upper house a 70-member People's Representatives Assembly) with reduced authority and a corresponding increase in the presidential power.

Although a dozen parties contested in the general election to bicameral parliament held between February and April 1995, most of the elected legislators were pro-Akayev independents.

FORTIFYING KYRGYZ IDENTITY

The millennium anniversary of Manas in August 1995 provided Akayev a golden opportunity to underscore Kyrgyz national identity. Instead of meeting the wages bill of its employees, his cash-strapped government diverted $5 million to fund the weeklong Manas 1000 International Festival at the Manas Village, an encampment of yurts on the outskirts of Bishkek, where sidewalks were paved to represent popular Kyrgyz weavings.

The festival's aim was to highlight the historical importance of the endeavors of Manas and his forty warrior companions in unifying all Kyrgyz tribes and preserving the Kyrgyz culture. It aspired to establish Manas as a Kyrgyz superhero, born in the Talas River Valley in northwestern Kyrgyzstan, where hundreds of costumed actors reenacted *The Epic of Manas*, ending with the climactic victory of Manas over the forces of evil. Though the performance was impressive in its scope, it was questionable whether the authorities succeeded in turning Manas into a historical personality by observing his birthday on August 28, 995, and placing a statue of him astride a horse on a high column in front of the Kyrgyz State Philharmonic

The legend of Manas—a composite heroic figure credited with fighting valiantly from the age of twelve to end the oppression of Kyrgyzes and succeeding to establish their homeland—rendered as an epic poem provided a perfect foundation for nation-building. Such was the physical strength of Manas that he hurled boulders from the cliffs of the Tien Shan Mountains at his enemies. Sadly, though, he became a victim of treachery, which led to his death and the burial of his corpse at a secret location. Efforts throughout the past centuries to reach his grave have failed; the moment a seeker gets close to it, a sudden storm strikes and does not subside until somebody recites the epic poem. What some claim to be the mausoleum of Manas in the Talas River Valley carries an inscription dedicating the carved-stone tomb to a Chagatai Turkish princess of the early fourteenth century.

Manas is the protagonist of the world's longest piece of oral poetry, *The Epic of Manas*. At 500,000 lines of verse, it is two and a half times the length of the *Mahabharata*, which is twelve times as long as *The Odyssey*. "The epic text is as stirring as the *Iliad*, and as episodic as *Don Quixote*, and as rich in moral guidance as the Gospels," noted Stephen Kinzer of the *New York Times* after discussing the epic with Akayev.[23] *The Epic of Manas* is the only piece of literature to have survived for nine centuries in an oral form.

Generations of *Manaschis*, professional recounters—wearing the traditional dress of trousers, a shirt under a knee-length coat with a stand-up collar and tied at the waist with a colorful kerchief/cummerbund, and a white-and-black embroidered felt hat—chanted the epic poem at festivals and other assemblies, reciting it for hours, even days, on end, lapsing into a trance. The aural tradition continued for centuries until the mid-nineteenth century. The *Manas* was then transcribed piecemeal. Its translation into Russian provided a tool for the Bolsheviks to propound the cause of Kyrgyz self-determination, leading to the formation of the Kyrgyz Autonomous Soviet Socialist Republic in 1920.

By now there are more than sixty recorded versions of the epic. Though scholars say unanimously that the epic is a mélange of fact and legend, they disagree on when it was composed and which of the events in the narrative are factual. Most scholars see it as a three-layered historical narrative—the earliest layer reflecting the traditions of the ninth and tenth centuries in the aftermath of the overthrow of the Uighur state; the next representing the fifteenth to seventeenth centuries, dominated by the fighting between the Kyrgyz tribes and the Mongol Kalmyks; and the last rooted in the nineteenth century. On the other hand, a minority of scholars argues that since the word Manas is akin to Manu, the name of the first human being in the Indo-Aryan myth, the epic's origins lie in the first millennium BC.

Records show that the contemporary Kyrgyz clans moved into present-day Kyrgyzstan in the ninth century. "The feats performed then may have been the basis of some episodes [in the *Manas*]," reported Kinzer. "The next 300 years proved to be a rich period for Kyrgyz life and culture. Along with the *Manas* a dozen other epics emerged."

Little wonder, then, that in his inaugural speech, Akayev described the epic as "our historical chronicle, spiritual foundation, and cultural reality," and that "Every one of us carries a piece of it in his or her heart." In his interview with Kinzer in January 2000, Akayev recalled that he first heard the *Manas* recited when he was four or five. "For the Kyrgyz people, the *Manas* is more than an epic," he said. "It is what the Bible is to Christians.

It inspired people in their hard times. Thanks to the *Manas*, this small nation preserved its traditions and history, and survived to become a country in Central Asia."

While Kyrgyzes grow up thinking of *The Epic of Manas* as a tale of love of the Kyrgyz land, tribal unity, and independence, scholars regard it as an encyclopedia of the steppe, describing the traditions, mores, facts, and fancies of the region that bridges the civilizations of China and the Mediterranean. The Kyrgyz government encouraged schools to offer courses on *The Epic of Manas*. Some students of the epic become apprentices to practicing *Manaschis*, observing their mentors, memorizing their favorite passages (especially the spectacular episodes), and imitating their expressions and narrating styles. Then they started performing at weddings, birthday parties, and other gatherings.

Enthused by the heady atmosphere created by the Manas 1000 Festival, many pro-Akayev lawmakers proposed extending his term of office through a referendum.

Akayev liked the idea. But the Bill Clinton administration told him that he would first have to hold a multi-candidate presidential poll if he wished to continue getting generous financial aid from the IMF.

So, in the December 1995 election for president, Akayev faced three rivals, including Jumagalbek Amanbayev, then deputy prime minister. Akayev got 72 percent of the vote from a turnout of 86 percent. Thus offering a credible alternative to the incumbent in the presidential palace, and reporting the true outcome in the official results, made Kyrgyzstan exceptional in Central Asia. But then Akayev had, in a moment of uncommon candor, once conceded, "I am not a professional politician. I am a technocrat who, thanks to the collapse of the Soviet Union, moved from physics to politics."[24]

Akayev got his payoff in the form of more bountiful aid from the IMF for Kyrgyzstan.

AKAYEV CHANGES TACK

Assured of enhanced authority for five more years, and the IMF's largesse, Akayev changed tack: he joined the ranks of his Central Asian counterparts, noted for monopolizing power, enriching themselves and their families, and suppressing opposition. In his case, the alleged beneficiaries of corrupt practices, besides him, were his wife Mairam, their eldest son Aidar (married at that time to Aliya, the youngest daughter of Kazakh President

Nursultan Nazarbayev), and their daughter Bermet, married to Adil Toigonbayev, an ethnic Kazakh.

Aidar Akayev and Adil Toigonbayev were rumored to hold monopolies in running casinos and cabarets, distributing alcohol and fuel oil, and operating real estate agencies where they compelled those with up-market properties to sell their assets below the market value.[25] Only a president with overarching powers could give protection to those indulging in such malpractices. Akayev achieved this through a referendum in 1996, which approved the constitutional amendment allocating more power to the presidency at the expense of the legislature.

Independent journalism became hazardous as the Akayev government began to harass those who investigated and reported corruption and nepotism at high places, and prosecuted them under the criminal charge of insulting the president. The best known case was that of Zamira Sydykova, editor of *Res Publika*, whose relentless campaign against corruption in the gold industry, centered around Dastan Sarigulov, landed her in jail for a year in 1997. She was found guilty of libeling Sarigulov. But that did not end either the embezzlement of public funds or the unease it aroused among the public and politicians.

In March 1998, dreading the grilling by parliamentarians on a scandal involving the sale of gold abroad, Prime Minister Apas (originally Abbas) Jumagalov resigned, referring to his age (sixty-four) as the reason for stepping down. This latest scandal concerned a local company which a year earlier had been given the sole right to purchase the gold extracted by a large state-owned gold company for sale abroad. Public furor ensued when it was discovered that this firm was exempted from paying taxes on its profits, which were large enough to cover the nation's annual budget deficit.[26]

Appointing Kubanichbek Jumaliyev as the new prime minister, Akayev said, "Over the next two to three years I want to breathe new life into reforms." In practice that meant instituting the right to purchase and sell agricultural land; more privatizing in mining, energy, and telecommunications; and introducing privatization in pension and insurance schemes.

The IMF and the World Bank judged that Kyrgyzstan's progress toward a market economy had been satisfactory. So they awarded the tiny nation of 4.5 million with over U.S. $1 billion in international credits. This would prove to be an albatross in the near future.

Like his counterparts in the region, Akayev turned his attention to circumventing the constitutional limit of two consecutive terms for the president. His supporters approached the constitutional court. It ruled in July

1998 that since the two-term limit was specified by the 1993 constitution, it could not be applied to the period that Akayev had served before 1993. Therefore he was entitled to contest the next presidential election. That put his mind at rest.

But then, a year later, his government found itself in the eye of a radical Islamist storm—a sudden and unprecedented challenge.

RADICAL ISLAMISTS STRIKE

In early August 1999, a unit of the armed Islamic Movement of Uzbekistan, based in Tajikistan and the Taliban-controlled Afghanistan, abducted three village officials near Osh, and demanded $1 million ransom and a flight to Afghanistan by a helicopter. Taken by surprise, the Akayev government capitulated within days and negotiated a deal. It surreptitiously paid the IMU unit $50,000 and provided it safe passage to Tajikistan, from where it would be easy to slip into neighboring Afghanistan.

Later that month, while Akayev hosted a summit of the Shanghai Forum, the precursor to the Shanghai Cooperation Organization, in Bishkek, more IMU units moved into the area around Batken in the Osh region. They abducted eight hostages, including four Japanese geologists working for a mining company. An international crisis ensued. Kyrgyz troops and Russian advisers arrived in the area while the number of hostages rose to twenty.

IMU leader Juma Namangani had focused on the Batken territory due to its grinding poverty and 60 to 80 percent unemployment. "Batken's rich soil has turned to salt because of over-irrigation during the Soviet period and the closing of canals at the Uzbekistan border," noted Ahmed Rashid, a Pakistani specialist on Central Asia. "Rusting factories have been shut down, electricity is available for only four hours a day, and there are no jobs. The milk plant, the oil mill, and a wine-making factory have been shut since 1991, and the government has made no attempt to revive them."[27] The absence of young men in the surrounding villages was explained to him by Gulmira Dovutoka, a social worker. "Either they have gone to Russia to look for work or they join [IMU leader] Namangani because at least he pays them and there is so much poverty here." The IMU was believed to be paying guerrillas monthly salaries of $100 to $500 in dollar bills. Its leaders raised money by robbing banks and abducting foreigners or local officials for ransom.

Pressurized by a Kyrgyz military offensive, the IMU units released all the captives except the Japanese. Their demand for ransom and the release of thousands of IMU prisoners in Uzbekistan were rejected by the Akayev government. Responding to Bishkek's request, Uzbek warplanes bombed IMU-controlled villages around Batken and Osh while the Kyrgyz ground troops separated the IMU units and pushed them back into Tajikistan. Meanwhile, as a result of behind-the-scenes contacts between Kyrgyz officials and senior IMU commanders, between $2 million and $6 million, paid by the Tokyo government, changed hands, and the Japanese geologists became free on October 25.[28]

Once the crisis was over, public attention turned to the parliamentary poll due in February 2000. Although the number of political parties and blocs participating in the general election had risen to thirty, the pro-Akayev Central Election Commission found a way of disqualifying the long-established Democratic Movement of Kyrgyzstan. And the prosecutor general started action against several political parties and prominent candidates—including Felix Kulov, the most prominent opposition figure, who led the newly formed Ar-Namys (Honor) party. A retired general with cropped white hair capping his clean-shaven Mongoloid face, Kulov had impressive credentials. During the Kyrgyz-Uzbek riots in 1990, his Interior Ministry soldiers had acted forcefully to suppress the interethnic violence. Later he became the first vice-president of the republic, and then served as national security minister. Later he was elected mayor of Bishkek. He resigned that post to found the Ar-Namys party.

Kulov's illustrious background did not impress the Central Election Commission. In the first round, he gained 36 percent of the ballots in the Kara-Buura district, and his leading rival, Alimbai Sultanov, 18 percent. In the second round on March 12, incredibly, Sultanov more than tripled his vote to 56 percent, whereas Kulov inched up to 40 percent. Kulov protested. (The OSCE mission noted that there was a significant increase in the number of advance voters and pressure on the electorate in the Kara-Buura constituency. There was something so wrong about the episode that on March 17 the Kara-Buura district election commission chairman Rasul Aitmambetov hanged himself.) On March 22, Kulov was arrested on the charges of forgery and abuse of power as he lay on a hospital bed undergoing treatment for a heart ailment. The Clinton administration described the elections as a setback in the democratization process. While popular protest at the electoral malpractices fizzled out, the military court, trying Kulov, found him innocent and released him in August 2000.

By then, rumor and official news had gripped Kyrgyz public interest in the drama unfolding in the rugged mountains of the Batken region. Namangani's forces, more numerous and better equipped than before, returned, targeting Kyrgyzstan as well as Uzbekistan. Once again, they caught the Kyrgyz military napping as they sneaked in from Tajikistan.

The skirmishes between IMU guerrillas and Kyrgyz troops left twenty-five dead on each side. In a single ambush, IMU insurgents killed twenty-two soldiers, and then separately abducted twelve foreign mountain climbers and four Americans for ransom. While the climbers managed to escape, or were left alone, the Americans were held hostage by a senior IMU commander. It was not until late September that Kyrgyzstan's Special Forces managed to encircle the insurgents and their quarry, and then kill or capture IMU guerrillas.[29] In early October, the Kyrgyz Security Council finally announced the end of the violence, exaggerating the number of Islamist militants killed and minimizing the death toll of soldiers. As a victim of Islamist terrorism, Kyrgyzstan would loom large on the U.S. radar after 9/11. But for now, the violent drama enacted in the rugged mountains highlighted a severe threat to national security and thus favored the incumbent, Akayev, in the presidential poll due on October 29, 2000.

For a voter to qualify as a candidate for president, he or she had to pass the Kyrgyz language test behind closed doors. This was part of the official effort to fortify Kyrgyz nationalism. Akayev passed, but did poorly on spelling. Kulov, his most eminent rival for the presidency, failed.

With three political ciphers challenging him, Akayev won 75 percent of the vote in the October presidential election in which 75 percent of the electorate participated. Both the OCSE and the United States asserted that the poll did not conform to international standards. While the Kyrgyz Central Election Commission chairman admitted "some voting irregularities," the freshly elected Akayev agreed that the international criticism of the election was "justified" and that the situation needed to be rectified for the future.

The economic scene continued to be dire. Agriculture was languishing, and the populaton of cattle had shrunk to a fraction of what it had been in the pre-independence era. By mid-2001, the country's foreign debt at $2 billion was a third higher than its annual GDP![30] However, when the 9/11 attacks turned the world's attention to security, concern about the still faltering economy of Kyrgyzstan receded among the policymakers in Washington.

9/11 FUELS AKAYEV'S AMBITION

Shortly after 9/11, Russian President Vladimir Putin offered full cooperation to Bush in his "war on terror" and acquiesced to the Pentagon's use of former Soviet bases in Central Asia.

Within weeks of the U.S.-led war against Taliban-controlled Afghanistan in early October, Akayev agreed to let the Pentagon use the recently modernized Manas International Airport, twenty kilometers (twelve miles) from Bishkek, for military purposes for the duration of the war. He settled for a nominal rent of $2 million a year. The first warplanes arrived on December 16, 2001.

Kyrgyzstan thus became the only Central Asian republic to give U.S.-led coalition forces unrestricted overflight rights for combat and humanitarian and search-and-rescue missions. Uzbekistan did not allow bombing raids from its soil, and Turkmenistan only permitted overflights and limited landing rights. By March 2002, Manas had become a refueling hub for transport planes, where the fuel was supplied by a company owned by Akayev's son-in-law, Adil Toigonbayev,[31] This cozy arrangement made the Bush administration part of the corrupt Akayev regime.

Soon the number of U.S. and allied armed personnel would reach 2,000. Compared to the dusty and desert-like temperatures at the tent city at Karshi-Khanabad (or K2, in the lexicon of the Pentagon) in Uzbekistan, Manas was almost like a resort. (By mid-2004, the tents at Manas would be replaced by solid structures.)

Having received the Pentagon's soldiers with open arms, Akayev turned to Moscow to tighten up domestic security—a balancing act. Finding the American version of democracy too cumbersome and unpredictable, he cast a benign eye at Putin's way of forging a Russian version of popular participation in politics, combining commitment to regular elections with circumventing and suppressing opposition skillfully without resort to strong-arm tactics. Putin obliged by lending him some high-level Russian internal security officials.

Ironically, it was an external subject—demarcation of Kyrgyzstan's border with China—which created a serious internal challenge for Akayev. The long and complicated negotiations with China, which entered an intense phase after Akayev's trip to Beijing in 1998, ended in late 2001, with Kyrgyzstan agreeing to part with 1,250 square kilometers of the disputed territory. Objecting to the deal, Azimbek Beknazarov, chairman of the parliamentary committee on legal affairs, demanded Akayev's impeachment. This led to Beknazarov's arrest in January 2002 on charges pertaining to an action dating seven years back. Hundreds of his followers in his hometown of Aksi in the southern Kyrgyz region of Jalalabad mounted pickets outside the court house. Some went on a hunger strike. When one of them died, the protest grew.

In mid-March, police fired on the protesters, killing five. This shocked the nation and united the opposition as never before. As protesters began marching from regional centers to Bishkek, demanding Akayev's resignation, his advisers panicked. When the protest did not end with Akayev ordering an inquiry into the police firing, he found a scapegoat in Prime Minister Kurmanbek Bakiyev. He dismissed the Bakiyev government in May, and named an ethnic Russian, Nikolai Tanayev, as his successor.

This was an uncommon event. While the Kyrgyz government's efforts to reassure the Russians had succeeded in stemming their emigration, and had even led to the opening of new Russian Orthodox churches in the north, ethnic Russians had largely stayed out of politics. They stuck to their traditional areas of service and manufacturing industries, just as ethnic Uzbeks had maintained their dominance in petty trade and commerce. Ironically, while the primacy of the Kyrgyz language was secure under law, the republic's citizens placed those who spoke Russian fluently and dressed in a Western style higher in the social order than those who did not. Indeed, these two attributes—buttressed by the possession of a two-story residence with a BMW or Mercedes in the driveway—came to define the upper class in post-Soviet Kyrgyzstan.

When it came to molding popular opinion, the Russian-language publications and TV channels mattered more than their Kyrgyz counterparts, which were in the minority. In politically significant Bishkek, home to one-fifth of the national population of five million, the residents had access to a dozen Russian-language TV channels, the most popular being the Kremlin-run ORT and RTR, reporting foreign events at length. So the Kyrgyz majority's views on international and other affairs often coincided with its Russian counterpart.[32]

Akayev placated the parliament and sacked police commanders in Jalalabad. But it was not until June, when Beknazarov was freed, that the street protest ended.

Responding to the public mood, Akayev initiated a debate on amending the constitution to curtail presidential authority, enhance the prime minister's powers, and revert to a single-chamber parliament. The final version of the amendments, however, was biased in favor of the president. When it was put to referendum in February 2003, it was endorsed by a large majority. So, finally, Akayev got what he wanted, but lost the trust of most politicians.

On the other hand, this sleight of hand won Akayev quiet plaudits from Putin. The Russian president's acquiescence to Washington on military bases in Central Asia had gone down badly with the hawks among his close aides. They regarded the region as Russia's "near abroad." To pacify them, and to show Russian voters during the run-up to the parliamentary poll in December 2003 his staunch commitment to advance national interests, Putin signed a bilateral agreement with Akayev in September, which allowed the Kremlin to set up a military base in Kyrgyzstan.

To stress the importance of establishing Russia's first foreign military base, Putin made a point of inaugurating it at Kant (meaning "Sugar" in Kyrgyz), 20 kilometers (12 miles) east of Bishkek. The facility used to be home to a major Soviet military pilot training school. "By building up an aviation shield in Kyrgyzstan, we aim to strengthen the security of this region, whose stability is an increasingly significant factor," Putin declared. Describing the new base as "a deterrent for terrorists and extremists of all kinds," Putin added, "It will be possible to reach the hideouts of criminal groups and international drug traffickers in mountain areas." These objectives, he implied, were different from those being pursued at the Manas Air Base by the United States. "The American base, the base of the international coalition, was set up for a concrete task—to last during the operation in Afghanistan."[33]

But Islamist radicals in Kyrgyzstan evidently did not share Putin's view on the subject. To them, the continued presence of the American troops long after the Taliban had been overthrown in Afghanistan in December 2001 was unacceptable. Little wonder that, in July 2004, U.S. Air Force Colonel Steven Kelly, commander of the Manas Air Base, revealed that Kyrgyz security services had aborted three planned terrorist attacks on the American facility.

In its annual report of 2003, the U.S. State Department noted deterioration in human rights in Kyrgyzstan, noting particularly the executive authority's ongoing domination of the judiciary, including interference in the verdicts involving opposition leaders. The case of Felix Kulov remained in the public eye, with periodic demonstrations for his release. After his re-arrest in January 2001 on charges of involvement in illegal arms sales, he was given a seven-year jail sentence, his property was confiscated, and he was divested of his military rank.

The merger of the Democratic Movement of Kyrgyzstan and seven other parties into the People's Movement of Kyrgyzstan (PMK) under the leadership of former Prime Minister Kurmanbek Bakiyev in November to contest the upcoming parliamentary poll alarmed Akayev.

The Kyrgyz leader was equally alarmed by the Rose Revolution in Georgia in November 2003, which installed the American-educated

Mikheil Saakashvili in the presidential palace, and the ongoing Orange Revolution in Ukraine to replace Leonid Kuchma, where widespread peaceful protest had led to the annulment of a rigged election for president with fresh polling on December 26, 2004.[34]

In his interview on Christmas on the state-run TV channel, Akayev warned against a repeat of the Rose and Orange revolutions: "We should remain a country of stable development, which makes us fend off all forces whose goal is to repeat these Georgian- and Ukrainian-style revolutions using Western financial organizations' money."[35]

THE TULIP REVOLUTION

During the run-up to the general election in late February 2005, the opposition PMK candidates highlighted the heavy burden of external debt of $2.5 billion that Kyrgyzstan had acquired under the Akayev regime. The decision of the Paris Club of creditors in mid-March to write off $555 million in the republic's foreign borrowings, though welcomed, still left Bishkek heavily indebted. The anti-Akayev candidates also pointed out how the continued weakness in the local economy had driven tens of thousands of Kyrgyz nationals to work abroad, chiefly in Russia, to support their families, and that the remittances of expatriates had soared to a quarter of the GDP.[36] However, it was hard to tax such income in Kyrgyzstan where it had become a common practice for residents to hide income to avoid taxation by trading in cash rather than through checks or credit cards.

Yet, due to widespread electoral malpractices, opposition candidates suffered heavily at the hands of their pro-Akayev rivals in the first round of the general election on February 27. The winners included Akayev's son Aidar and daughter Bermet, leader of the Alga ("Forward" in Kyrgyz) Kyrgyzstan party. That led to widespared suspicion that Akayev intended to retain power by getting Aidar or Bermet elected president or by getting a pliant parliament to abrogate the two-term limit on the presidency.

The prospect enraged the anti-Akayev camp. Demonstrators demanded cancelation of the fraudulent electoral results and Akayev's resignation. The government responded by suppressing several newspapers while state-financed mass media gave wide coverage to pro-government candidates. On the eve of the second round on March 13, twenty-three opposition parliamentarians issued a symbolic vote of no confidence in the president and the Central Election Commission.

The turnout of 51 percent in the second round was lower than in the first. A coalition of three NGOs, For Democracy and Civil Society, reported electoral malpractices in many precincts. The People's Movement of Kyrgyzstan led protests, with its leader Bakiyev demanding an early presidential poll. It had strong support in the south, with demonstrators occupying seven regional government offices as well as the Osh airport. Other protesters marched northwards, to Bishkek.

On March 19, security forces blocked 3,000 protesters from entering the capital, while as many as 50,000 assembled in Jalalabad. The next day, the authorities ordered Interior Ministry troops to disperse the demonstrators in Jalalabad and Osh. They succeeded only to find the protesters regrouping in the suburbs of Jalalabad. On March 21, the government lost control of the cities in the south. Akayev refused to resign, but promised to refrain from using force to end the protest—which, in his view, was instigated by foreign interests wishing to provoke a violent state response.

Addressing the newly elected parliament (boycotted by ten anti-Akayev members) on March 22, Akayev rejected calls for negotiations with the opposition. Russia, America, and Kazakhstan urged a peaceful solution to the crisis. The following day, the opposition claimed control of two-thirds of Kyrgyzstan. Akayev dismissed the interior minister for failing to defuse the escalating protest.

The denouement came on March 24. Up to 20,000 protestors assembled in the central square of Bishkek, demanded Akayev's resignation, and began marching toward the presidential administration building. They overpowered the contingent of riot police posted along the perimeter of the building, and seized the seat of supreme power. Journalists of the state-run mass media switched sides and began broadcasting live anti-Akayev opinions. Widespread looting and arson ensued, causing $100 million in damage. Akayev and his family escaped, first to Kazakhstan, and then to Moscow, where they sought and secured political asylum. The peaceful overthrow of the Akayev government acquired the name "The Tulip Revolution" because of the onset of the spring in Kyrgyzstan, which is marked by the blooming of tulips.

In his hasty flight from the presidential residence, Akayev left behind his secret diaries, which fell into the hands of the succeeding government and provided scandalous details of the corruption of the first family.[37] Other incriminating documents included records of government jobs for sale and the bribe rates, varying from $30,000 for a parliamentary candidacy to $200,000 to serve as a top civil servant or an ambassador to an important capital.[38]

These disclosures confirmed the popular perception that political or top bureaucratic power was linked to wealth, and that most politicians were more interested in lining their pockets than working for the welfare of the public at large. Given the underfunding of the law enforcement agencies, drug trafficking and organized crime thrived. The poorly paid police officers were open to bribes. Corruption and nepotism were widespread. Little wonder that in Transparency International's Corruption Perceptions Index, released in October 2004, Kyrgyzstan ranked 122nd among 146 countries.

On March 25, the day after Akayev fled Bishkek, opposition leaders formed an interim government under Bakiyev as acting president and prime minister. It was recognized by both Moscow and Washington. The interim government immediately released Felix Kulov, and recognized the freshly elected parliament as legitimate. In turn, the parliament appointed a commission to investigate the assets of Akayev and his family. It dispatched a delegation to Moscow to meet Akayev. On April 3, he submitted his resignation.

In his interviews with the foreign media, Akayev claimed that he had been violently forced out of Kyrgyzstan following a coup d'etat. (Later he would become a math professor at Moscow State University.) In Kyrgyzstan, the AKIpress news agency disclosed a list of forty-two companies controlled wholly or partly by Aidar Akayev and Adil Toigonbayev, the former president's respective son and son-in-law. The list included Kumtor gold mine, Bitel GSM mobile phone operator, banks, the leading fuel distribution companies, cement works, and mass media, with profits running into hundreds of million dollars.[39] Further revelations produced a "shame list" topped by Ulan Sarbanov, head of the National Bank, who allegedly transferred $480 million to Akayev's account illegally in 1999. He denied the charge, asserting that Akayev should be held responsible for the money transfer.

In his interview with the Associated Press in Moscow on June 30, Akayev accused the Bush administration of funding the Kyrgyz opposition and bringing about his downfall since it was opposed to his increasingly close relations with the Kremlin. He singled out western NGOs, particularly Freedom House, for introducing the concept and practice of democracy in Kyrgyzstan without taking into account the republic's history and culture.

His remarks reflected more than the pique of a leader forced to flee like a thief at night. In Kyrgyzstan, the Washington-based Freedom House had gone beyond propagating democracy. Starting in November 2003, it operated a printing press in Bishkek, financed by the State Department, to provide Kyrgyz newspaper and magazine editors an alternative outlet to print their publications. Until then, they had been captives to the government's monopolistic hold over the printing and distribution of newspapers. Aware of the impact that the nongovernmental arrangement was having on the 2005 poll, the authorities cut off power to the printing plant after the first round of the general election. The U.S. embassy intervened and procured portable generators to run the presses. Among its beneficiaries was the opposition daily, *Moya Stolitsa Novosti* (*My Capital News*), which managed to print 200,000 copies of its special issue.[40]

During the turmoil of the Tulip Revolution, it was business as usual at the American base at Manas. During his meeting with visiting U.S. Secretary of Defense Donald Rumsfeld in mid-April, Bakiyev reassured him of the continuation of the lease on Manas. Equally, Bakiyev declared that Russia remained "our best friend, and friends must not be changed." He also expressed a need for increased cooperation with the Shanghai Cooperation Organization.[41]

Domestically, Bakiyev and Kulov considered it wise not to compete against each other in the race for president. In mid-May, they formed an alliance, with Kulov agreeing to become prime minister if Bakiyev won the presidential poll on July 10.

On the eve of the election, at the Shanghai Cooperation Organization summit in Astana, Kyrgyzstan backed the decision calling for a deadline for the Pentagon to close its bases in Central Asia. But, when Rumsfeld visited Bishkek later that month, the freshly elected President Bakiyev declared that the American base at Manas was needed to counter terrorism and improve bilateral relations. This would not be the only subject on which Bakiyev would do an about-face.

BAKIYEV AS PRESIDENT

During the election campaign, Bakiyev vowed to reform the constitution, including curtailing presidential authority, and eradicate corruption. In the poll, he won 89 percent of the vote. The voter turnout was officially reported to be 53 percent, a refreshingly accurate figure.

Thus, fifty-six-year-old Kurmanbek Saliyevich Bakiyev—a cheerful-looking, moon-faced, portly man with a receding hairline—achieved his life's ambition. Like all Central Asian leaders, his background was in engineering (electrical, in his case) and science. He worked as deputy chief engineer at a factory in Jalalabad, and rose to become its director. In 1990, he switched to politics. Five years later, he became the governor of the

Jalalabad region, and then governor of the Chui region in the north. He served as prime minister for a year and a half before being sacked in May 2002. He then became a leading opposition figure.

After occupying the Kyrgyz presidential palace, Bakiyev forgot his promises of constitutional reform and eradication of corruption. Instead, he tried to divert popular attention away by threatening in April 2006 to expel the American troops if the Pentagon did not increase its rent for the Manas Air Base by June 1. When the Pentagon failed to oblige, he withdrew his threat. This encouraged the opposition to call his bluff on constitutional reform. In a repeat of the pre-Tulip Revolution scenario, the opposition rallied its ranks in November, encamped in central Bishkek, and demanded Bakiyev's resignation. He capitulated and agreed, reluctantly, to amendments that trimmed presidential authority. This would to prove to be a rerun of a tug-of-war between the parliament and president which had dogged Kyrgyzstan during Akayev's rule.

When differences over the interpretation of the constitutional changes arose between Bakiyev and the opposition, he amended the document in his favor in December, soon after Kulov had resigned as the prime minister in protest and joined the opposition.

Nine months later, when the Constitutional Court ruled that the parliament could not change the 2003 constitution without consulting the voters, Bakiyev ordered a referendum on the amended constitution and electoral law on October 21. The constitutional amendments established some sort of balance between the executive and legislative branches by empowering the majority party in parliament to nominate the prime minister, which had been the prerogative of the president. The new electoral law discarded the old system of single-member constituencies. Instead, based on proportional representation, it turned all of Kyrgyzstan into one constituency in which a political party must reach a threshold of 5 percent to gain seats in parliament.

Bakiyev founded his own party, Ak Zhol ("Bright Path" in Kyrgyz). But, just a week before the referendum, he introduced an amendment to the election code stipulating that, to qualify for parliamentary seats, a party must secure 0.5 percent of the vote in each region besides meeting the overall 5 percent threshold nationally. After the referendum won 76 percent of the vote, there were allegations of ballot boxes being stuffed with fake votes. But before the opposition could protest, Bakiyev struck. Promulgating the amended constitution on the day after the referendum, he dissolved the parliament, accusing—ironically—its members of plotting "a parliamentary coup" against his power.

In the subsequent parliamentary poll in December 2007, only three of the twelve parties satisfied both the national and the regional thresholds. Bakiyev's Ak Zhol won 48 percent of the vote and 71 of the 90 seats, while the opposition Communist Party and Social Democratic Party each won just over 5 percent of the vote and shared the rest of the seats. The OSCE noted that the election failed to meet a number of OSCE requirements, particularly in the transparency of counting and tabulation.

With the parliament dominated by his own party, Bakiyev added legislative power to his executive authority. It remained to be seen whether Bakiyev would deploy his enhanced power to tackle the chronic weakness of the economy, persistent corruption, and the unstoppable rise of a black economy. It was estimated that as much as 52 percent of the Kyrgyz economy was black or related to smuggling.[42] Another problem was the growing influence of organized crime related mainly to the smuggling of drugs from Afghanistan via Tajikistan.

CHAPTER 6

TAJIKISTAN:
THE RISE AND FALL OF POLITICAL ISLAM

SOVIET AUTHORITIES SUPPRESSED THE EXPRESSION OF HISTORICAL ANIMOSITIES between different nationalities in ethnic or racial terms, so such sentiments sometimes got transmuted into competition in the economic sphere. Tajik-Uzbek relations were a case in point. Being superior fighters, Uzbeks had historically dominated Tajiks, a sedentary community of Persian ancestry. Now, with the prevalence of cotton in both Tajikistan and Uzbekistan, its yields became a yardstick by which the two republics measured their worth. After an indeterminate race for several years following the Great Patriotic War, Tajiks finally established their lead over Uzbeks in 1953 with an average yield of 2,810 kilograms of cotton per hectare. Indeed, they set an all-Soviet record.

Moscow's policy of devoting a greater proportion of sown area to cotton got a boost when Nikita Khrushchev launched his policy of increasing the output of food grains, tea, tobacco, and cotton. By 1956, cotton crops in Tajikistan took up a third of the cultivated area in collective farms, up from one-fifth in 1940.[1] Part of the increase in this predominantly mountainous republic—with only 7 percent of its land being arable—resulted from encouraging mountain Tajiks, particularly those in the Karategin region, to grow cotton in warm valleys.

Also, by then, the younger Tajiks had acquired a cultural consciousness quite apart from Uzbeks', thanks largely to Moscow's policy of developing Tajik historiography. At the same time, because of the introduction of compulsory Russian in 1938, a switchover to the Cyrillic alphabet for Tajik, and a big jump in literacy, Russian had emerged as the interethnic language in Tajikistan.

As for the Russian settlers, their political power outstripped their size. Though accounting for only 13 percent of the population (versus the Tajiks'

53 percent) in the 1950s, they provided 40 percent of the membership of the Communist Party of Tajikistan (CPT). Culturally, ethnic Russians remained as far apart from the predominantly rural Tajiks as they did from Kyrgyzes or Kazakhs. A rural Tajik man wore a traditional knee-long jacket secured at the waist with a colorful kerchief, baggy trousers, and a skull cap with a paisley design. His female counterpart covered herself with a long jacket of colorful, bright silk, baggy trousers with embroidered cuffs, and a hat embroidered with precious stones under an eye-catching scarf. Village elders wore long cloaks and turbans, and sported beards, thus earning them the generic honorific of *aksakals*, "white beards" in Tajik.

There was nothing in common between the Tajik and Russian diets. Like its Persian counterpart, the Tajik cuisine centered around pilau, mutton, and flat bread called nan. Tajiks'respect for flat bread is legendary. It must not be thrown on the ground, and if it falls by mistake, it must be retrieved and placed on a high ledge for birds. And according to a widely held belief, it must not be placed upside down, as that would bring bad luck.

Tajiks also differed from Russians, and indeed other Central Asians, in that they started their meals with tea, green in summer and black in winter. Then they would serve a tray with sweets and fruit, followed by the main dish of a pilau along with a soup and a vegetable salad. No reception or even informal meeting with friends was complete without tea. Outside the home, a tea-shop was to Tajiks what a pub is to Britons.

Large tea shops in cities often played music. Throughout most of the Soviet era, traditional and classical Tajik music, drawing heavily on lyrics by poets like Jalaluddin Rumi and Shamsuddin Hafiz-e Shirazi, popularly known as Hafiz, remained in vogue. Also, the legendary epic, *Guriguli*, maintained its venerated place in Tajikistan's musical ensemble. The music of southern Tajikistan remained close to that of Iran; and its version of folk music, called *falak*, was often an indispensable part of celebratory occasions like important birthdays and weddings. By comparison, the music in northern Tajikistan, being part of the Fergana Valley, was akin to that of Uzbekistan.

Forming a quarter of the republic's population with ethnic Uzbeks, Tajiks had a clear majority in the CPT. The policy of having a non-Slav as the CPT's first secretary and a Russian as the second secretary, introduced in 1946, had put Babajan Gafurov (originally, Ghafur) in the top position. When Gafurov was replaced in 1956 in the aftermath of Khrushchev's anti-Stalinist speech, his job went to Tursunbai Ulaajabayev (originally, Ula Ajab), the erstwhile chairman of the Council of Ministers. The political change was reflected in the name of the Tajik capital. Having been renamed Stalinabad in 1932, it now reverted to its original name, Dushanbe, and was now a city of striking, elegantly painted, neoclassical buildings, including an Orthodox church, standing against a mountainous backdrop.

Reflecting the mood in Moscow, the CPT—led since its 1961 Congress by Jabar Rasulov, a Tajik—became self-critical, especially of its performance among rural Tajiks, who formed four-fifths of the ethnic Tajik population. Its Congress in March 1966 singled out the party's poor accomplishment in political education and propaganda, particularly in the mountainous areas, and its failure to eradicate medieval practices and traditions, feudal attitudes towards women, and clan loyalties amongst Tajiks in the countryside. Village Tajiks, organized in collective or state farms, had adopted the socialist mode and tools of production and were achieving their economic targets, but they clung to feudal values and practices in their social-political behavior (perpetuated through family and informal social circles) and resisted Marxist-Leninist education imparted by the mass media and the CPT.

In contrast, the urban-based Tajik intelligentsia had developed a commitment to the socialist system and imbibed its social-political values. They were concentrated in Dushanbe and the Khojand (then Leninabad) region. While accounting for only a third of the republic's population, the Khojand region produced nearly two-thirds of Tajikistan's industrial output. Dushanbe was a predominantly Tajik city, having absorbed large numbers of Tajik émigrés from Bukhara and Samarkand after it became the republic's capital in 1929. Khojand city and region were also home to many Uzbeks, which led to a high degree of bilingualism and some intermarriage. Such a state of affairs was anathema to the Tajiks of Samarkand and Bukhara now settled in Dushanbe, who considered their Persian origins to be superior to the Uzbeks' Turkic ancestry.

Unsurprisingly, by the mid-1960s, cleavages based on geographical and clan loyalties had developed within the CPT and consolidated themselves. The major factions were the Khojandis in the north, the Badakhshanis (or Pamiris) from the Pamir Mountains to the east, the Kulyabis to the southeast, and the Kurgan-Tyubis to the southwest. The river valleys of Kulyab and Garm had been rivals for centuries. Since the Kulyab Valley was developed under the Soviet rule as a cotton-growing area with many collective farms, its population rose sharply and it became a CPT stronghold. On the other hand, Kurgan-Tyube, another traditional rival of Kulyab, fell behind economically. It also lost its clan homogeneity with the influx of government-encouraged immigration from the small, narrow Garm Valley, which has a history of exporting manpower

Generally, party and government cadres from Moscow and Russian settlers in Tajikistan got along well with urbanized Tajiks and Uzbeks in the Khojand area. Thus, the Khojand and Kulyab regions, containing three-fifths of the republic's population of 2.5 million, monopolized political and economic power. That alienated the rest of the republic. The anti-Khojand feeling was all the stronger because the region was isolated from the rest of the country by the formidable Hissar (spelled "Gissar" in Russian) Mountain, linked only by a tenuous road and a railway track over the 3,370-meter (10,500-foot) pass at Anzab.

Among Khojand's politicians, who achieved prominence in the early 1970s, was Rahman (aka Rakhman) Nabiyev (1930–93), a native of the village of Shal Burhan in the Khojand region. A graduate of the Tashkent Institute of Irrigation and Agricultural Mechanization, he joined the CPT in 1960. A few years later, he started working at the secretariat of the CPT's Central Committee, and rose up the bureaucratic ladder to become minister of agriculture in 1971. Two years later, he became chairman of the Council of Ministers. Due to his successful drive to expand cotton-growing areas, this stocky, chain-smoking man with prematurely white hair became a favorite of Leonid Brezhnev. He expanded his power base through patronage with the aim of becoming the CPT's first secretary.

Because of the blood ties between Tajiks in Tajikistan and those who had migrated to Afghanistan during the 1918 to 1926 civil war in Soviet Tajikistan, and because of the affinity of Tajik with Persian, the events in Afghanistan (where Persian was the official language) and Iran impacted Tajikistan more than any other Central Asian republic.

THE AFGHAN FACTOR

Following the overthrow of King Muhammad Zahir Shah by his cousin Muhammad Daoud Khan in July 1973, and the declaration of a republic, the new ruler curbed Islamist opposition, driving its leaders—Gulbuddin Hikmatyar and Borhanuddin Rabbani, an ethnic Tajik—to Pakistan. Their clandestine followers in Tajikistan established the Islamic Renaissance Party (IRP) in 1976. Most of its backing came from the economically backward Kurgan-Tyube (aka Kurgan Teppa) region, bordering Afghanistan. Among its young activists was Muhammad Sharif Himmatzade (b. 1951), a mechanic who would later emerge as its official leader.

The situation in Afghanistan grew increasingly unstable, with Daoud Khan persecuting not only Islamists but also leftists functioning as the People's Democratic Party of Afghanistan (PDPA). Matters came to a head in mid-April 1978 with the assassination of a leftist trade union leader. It triggered a series of events, which culminated in a coup on April 27 by military officers belonging to the PDPA and the assassination of Daoud Khan. Nur Muhammad Taraki, the party chief, succeeded Khan as president and prime minister. This marked the beginning of Moscow's overt involvement in Afghan politics. The Kremlin loaned the Marxist regime in Kabul several hundred Central Asian—chiefly Uzbek and Tajik—administrative and technical personnel, who shared their ethnicity with a third of Afghanistan's population.

The victory of Islamists in Iran in February 1979 gave a boost to religious forces in the neighboring areas. The new regime's Tajik-language broadcasts beamed at Tajikistan helped to foster clandestine Islamic groups. And the events in Afghanistan provided increased exposure to the Afghan people and politics. As internecine fighting within the ruling PDPA grew bloodier, resulting in debilitating purges and increased resistance by Islamic partisans, Moscow started posting its troops in Afghanistan. In October, Soviet Central Asian contingents began taking over guard duties from Afghan troops to free the latter to fight the rebels. By the time the Kremlin decided to move into Afghanistan in force on December 27, 1979, there were already 8,000 Soviet troops and 4,000 military advisers there.[2]

The Kremlin brought its army divisions to full strength by drafting the reserves living in Central Asia before dispatching them to Afghanistan via Termez (in Uzbekistan) to overthrow the government of Hafizullah Amin, a Communist hardliner who had alienated large sections of Afghan society, and install a moderate PDPA leader, Babrak Karmal. It also airlifted military construction units, manned by Central Asian conscripts, to Afghanistan to construct camps and repair air bases. Altogether, about 50,000 regular troops and 15,000 construction troops were involved.[3]

The regular units contained 15,000–20,000 Central Asians, mainly Tajik and Uzbek. This ethnic mix and the frequent parading of Central Asian troops in Kabul were meant to illustrate that the Soviet military intervention in Afghanistan was a good, neighborly act. As the Kremlin was amassing freshly mobilized troops along the Afghan borders with Tajikistan, Uzbekistan, and Turkmenistan, popular awareness of Moscow's involvement in Afghanistan increased. The Soviet media explained that it was the duty of the Soviet Union, according to the Friendship and Cooperation

Treaty it had concluded with Afghanistan in December 1978, to assist that country in its hour of need against imperialist powers.

ISLAMIC REVIVAL

Sharing a 1,200-kilometer (750-mile) frontier with Afghanistan, Tajikistan was more exposed to developments in Afghanistan than Uzbekistan or Turkmenistan, which had much shorter common borders. The Soviet media rehashed the history of the Basmachi movement of the 1920s on television and in learned articles, and drew parallels with the current situation in Afghanistan, explaining that the neo-Basmachis were being assisted by foreign imperialist powers, reactionary mullahs, and Sufi brotherhoods. But, drawing succor from the past, the authors of these articles and documentaries assured their readers and viewers that the Soviet regime would eliminate the new danger.

At the same time, the Tajik government became more vigilant, with the KGB smoking out clandestine Islamic groups. These groups gained ground as Soviet troops in Afghanistan failed to win a quick, decisive victory against Islamist resistance, which was being directed by the leaders of six Islamic parties based in Peshawar, Pakistan. The armed cadres of these parties numbered 73,000 (versus the Afghan army's 80,000 troops), with the three fundamentalist parties accounting for two-thirds of the total.[4]

Prominent among those arrested by the KGB in 1980 was Abdullah Nuri (b. 1947)—later known as Said Abdullah Nuri—a young, charismatic cleric, with a beard and long hair under a flowered skull cap, in Kurgan-Tyube. At seven, he began reading the Quran with the help of his pious father, Nurridun, who retired as a state farm director to become a self-appointed mullah. Abdullah pursued his interest in Islam by traveling to Dushanbe to study under an old cleric who had trained abroad. He was Muhammad Rustamov Hindustani.

Born in the Chahar Bagh village on the outskirts of Kokand in 1892, Hindustani was almost a century old when he died in Dushanbe. His life and times rivaled those of the hero of Francois Voltaire's *Candide*. After his preliminary studies in Islam, Muhammad enrolled at the famed Mir-e Arab madrassa in Bukhara. When he returned home after graduation in 1916, he got wind that the Tsarist authorities were drafting men to fight in World War I. So he fled, and ended up in the holy city of Mazar-e Sharif in Afghanistan, where he stayed to study linguistics, logic, and commentaries on the Quran for four years. On his tutor's advice, he journeyed to British

India (aka Hindustan) and enrolled at a madrassa in Ajmer in Rajasthan. Besides following an Islamic curriculum, he mastered herbal medicine.

In 1927, at the age of thirty-five, he undertook a pilgrimage to Mecca. By the time he returned home to Kokand, he was a sturdy man with a trimmed mustache and a resolute look. Fluent in not only Tajik, Uzbek, and Arabic, but also Persian, Turkish, Urdu, and Hindi, he became known as Hindustani, "of Hindustan." He took charge of the Kizil Mahnad Mosque in Kokand.

During the anti-religious campaign in the early 1930s, he was jailed briefly. On his release, he took his family to the mining town of Angren. After a peripatetic life, he settled for a job as a cashier at a collective farm. In the course of another anti-religious campaign, he was jailed in 1937 for four years. He spent part of his incarceration at a labor camp, which many younger and hardier prisoners did not survive.

Hindustani was drafted during the Great Patriotic War in 1943, and sent to Semipalatinsk, Kazakhstan, to work in a labor camp. His exposure to combat came during the battle to regain Minsk from the Germans, when he was wounded in the arm. After he had recovered in a Moscow hospital, he was shipped to Kemerovo, an intensive labor camp in the Far East. His task was to tend a herd of five hundred sheep. "I used to take them [the sheep] into the woods, and while they grazed I would recite the Quran to myself, all the way through every three days," he recalled later. "Of course, I had no books at Kemerovo, and I was all alone, but I knew the scriptures by heart."[5] On demobilization in 1946, he was sent to Dushanbe and given charge of the only mosque. In yet another anti-religious drive, he was arrested in 1952, and shipped to Karaganda, Kazakhstan. His release came in the amnesty that followed Khrushchev's anti-Stalinist speech in 1956.

Now aged sixty-four, he was ready for retirement. But instead of resting, he started teaching, discreetly, the old Islamic syllabus he had learned in Mazar-e Sharif. His students included Abdullah Nuri and Hajji Akbar Turajanzade (b. 1953), both of whom would emerge as Islamic leaders. In 1967, at seventy-five, he started translating the Quran in Uzbek and wrote a series of commentaries on it.

It was not until 1982 that Hindustani's clandestine classes in Islam were discovered by the KGB and closed down. In that same year, the KGB arrested Imaduddin Ahmedov, a young engineer who headed an Islamic group in Dushanbe. He received a nine-year jail sentence.[6] However, the more important Himmatzade of the IRP eluded the KGB and crossed into Afghanistan, where he trained with the Islamic

Mujahedin ("holy warriors") whose struggle with the Soviet-backed regime in Kabul had intensified.

It was in 1982 that Rahman Nabiyev finally achieved his ambition of becoming the first secretary of the CPT. After Mikhail Gorbachev's ascendancy in the Communist Party of the Soviet Union in March 1985, Nabiyev's position became insecure. He lost it to Kakhar Mahkamov before the year ended, during the CPT's most turbulent period.

Mahkamov's first task was to tackle the rising influence of Islam among Tajiks. He was deeply embarrassed when Abdullah Nuri submitted a much-publicized petition to the CPSU Congress in February 1986 to establish an Islamic state in Tajikistan.

Cemeteries, situated far from normal venues for socio-political activities, had emerged as centers for Muslim festivals and celebrations. They offered a freer environment than did the officially managed mosques. Also, by now, unregistered mullahs were much younger and better educated than their predecessors. Most of those arrested in the mid-1980s for illegal Islamic activities were born in the 1950s to parents raised under the Soviet system—a matter of concern to the government.

Addressing the party's ideological cadres in August 1986, Mahkamov revealed that some graduates of the Faculty of Oriental Languages in Dushanbe University had become (self-appointed) clerics, and urged intensification of atheist propaganda. Party discipline remained intact, as any member found practicing Islamic rituals was punished with expulsion—meaning the loss of all party membership privileges. But later that month, when Abdullah Nuri was arrested in Kurgan-Tyube, mass protest ensued and turned violent.

A survey published in the *Leninchil Zhash* in August 1987 showed that 45 percent of the respondents in Tajikistan declared themselves "believers," the highest figure in the post-war Soviet Union. This meant that a substantial proportion of party members were observing Islamic rituals. It was also noticed that during the month of Ramadan, when believers fast between sunrise and sunset, sales in cafeterias and restaurants fell perceptibly. Other signs of growing religiosity, to which Mahkamov alluded in the spring of 1988, were the wearing of Islamic symbols and amulets and the decoration of car interiors with Quranic verses. Noting that a growing number of parents were giving their babies names with Islamic connotations, Mahkamov proposed that a panel of philologists and historians should produce a list of "patriotic non-religious names."[7]

Running in parallel were the waning fortunes of the Soviet troops in

Afghanistan and the pro-Moscow regime of President Muhammad Najibullah, who had diluted the Marxist-Leninist content of the ruling PDPA's program. Addressing the party conference on April 27, 1988, the tenth anniversary of the Saur (April) Revolution, he urged the delegates not to underestimate the role of Islam and the prestige of clerics.[8] A joint communiqué by Najibullah and Gorbachev in February 1988 stated that Soviet troops would start pulling out from Afghanistan in May and complete the exercise in ten months. This signified Moscow's failure.

Long beforehand, the ethnic Russians in Tajikistan concentrated in Khojand and Dushanbe had sensed danger in the ongoing Marxist-Islamist battle in Afghanistan, and begun emigrating. Between 1979 (a census year) and 1988, some 120,000 Russians left. Owing to this and a high birthrate among Tajiks, the percentage of Russians in Tajikistan fell from 10.4 to 7.

As elsewhere in Central Asia, the declining power of the republic's Communist Party led to the emergence of nationalist and Islamist opposition, which gathered momentum during the latter period of perestroika. CPT leaders therefore stopped disciplining party members who openly practiced religious rituals.

Responding to the growing nationalist fervor, the Tajik government tried to persuade Moscow to award Samarkand and Bukhara to Tajikistan. Knowing that a transfer of territory from one republic to another in this or any other case would unleash an unmanageable list of disputes, the Kremlin rejected Dushanbe's request. This provided a palpable motive for Tajik nationalists to rally around the newly formed Rastakhiz (Resurgence) People's Organization, led by Tahir Abdujabarov (originally, Abdul Jabar) and Davlat Khudanazarov, a filmmaker. The party pinpointed two trends threatening Tajik identity and culture: mixed-nationality marriages, which—having risen from 16.7 percent to 22.3 percent in the urban areas between 1959 and 1970[9]—had continued to grow; and bilingualism, which was rampant in the Khojand region, where a majority of the 1.4 million Uzbeks lived.

Also, the Islamic Renaissance Party, which had existed clandestinely, started showing its colors gingerly. However, the IRP was just one, albeit the most politicized, element in the Islamist spectrum. The others were the traditional, rural (unregistered) Muslim clerics and the branch of the Muslim Spiritual Directorate of Central Asia in Dushanbe, headed by Hajji Akbar Turajanzade, a young kazi (religious judge) trained in Tashkent and Amman, Jordan.

At the CPT Congress in January 1990, party luminaries aired concern about the growth of mosques and Islamic publications, and the increasing participation of mullahs in the political process. To counter this trend, they urged the cadres to explain the party's program of economic development and social progress in a secular environment to religious leaders, and to emphasize that the republic's 1978 constitution gave citizens freedom of conscience.

But the socio-economic development in the milieu of glasnost and perestroika was following uncharted territory, creating intractable problems for the authorities. Given the freedom to express their grievances in a contracting economy, ethnic Tajiks, forming 60 percent of the population in the poorest republic in the union, became restive. Believing the rumors that the government was going to give scarce apartments to Armenian refugees from the January 1990 anti-Armenian riots in Baku, while denying them to locals, Tajiks protested in Dushanbe from February 12 to 14.

Some of the demonstrators started assaulting Armenians, and then Russians and other Slavs. The protest escalated to rioting. Among the more popular slogans shouted was "Long live the Islamic Republic of Tajikistan!" This signified the blending of Tajik nationalism with Islam, which had occurred earlier in Afghanistan. The riots were so serious that the media in Moscow described them as "round the clock clashes." The Kremlin dispatched its Special Purpose Militia Units, known by their Russian acronym OMON, to restore order. By the time they had done so, 23 people were dead and another 110 wounded. The local reporters would later erect a memorial slab with the names of the fallen, and rename the square, where the pinkish-gray Presidential Palace stood, "Shahidan (Martyrs) Square."

After the removal of state and party control over the press in mid-1990, it became easier for the opposition to propagate its ideas and programs. IRP supporters called a meeting in late 1990 in Dushanbe to establish the party officially. The Supreme Soviet tried to prevent it. When it failed, it passed a law banning the IRP, and then adopted another which outlawed any "religious political party."[10] This alienated the head of official Islam, Turajanzade. He distanced himself from the authorities, and began acting as a mediator between traditional, rural mullahs, the clandestine IRP, and the underground Sufi brotherhoods. That raised his popular standing.

As a member of both the central Supreme Soviet, and the Central Committee of the Soviet Union's Communist Party, Khudanazarov was in Moscow during the anti-Gorbachev coup from August 19 to 21, 1991. He took a strong line against the plotters. On August 27, he claimed to have received documents showing Mahkamov supporting the coup.[11] Two days later, he revealed his papers on the floor of the Supreme Soviet in Moscow. Mahkamov disputed the claim. His denial carried much weight in Tajikistan, as his prestige had risen sharply when, three days earlier, at his behest, the Supreme Soviet in Dushanbe had declared Tajikistan's independence.

INDEPENDENT TAJIKISTAN

The revulsion against the CPSU in Moscow in the wake of the failed coup found its echo in Dushanbe. It became transmuted into a growing demand to rename the capital's main thoroughfare called Lenin Avenue, and to remove Lenin's towering statue on a marble plinth in the capital's administrative-political center.

Soon Lenin Avenue gave way to Abdullah Jaafar Muhammad, popularly known as Abdullah Rudaki (858–941), after his native village of Rudak (now Panjakent) in Tajikistan. From an early age, Rudaki began composing poems, which he wrote in the freshly fashioned Persian alphabet, a transcription of the ancient Pahlavi language using Arabic letters. His wide-ranging poetry covered all existing genres—odes, quatrains, *ghazals* (rhyming couplets and a refrain), and *masnavi* (couplets with the rhyme scheme of aa/bb/cc, etc.)—and totaled more than 100,000 lines. Though simple and free of religious references, his poems were profound and had the spellbinding quality of pre-Islamic poetic compositions of Persia. They appealed as much to the common folk as they did to scholars and aristocrats. He became the royal poet in the court of Emir Nasr Samani of Bukhara, and lived to the ripe age of eight-three. The United Nations Educational, Scientific and Cultural Organization (UNESCO) portrait of Rudaki presents him in profile with a flowing, snow-white beard and deep-set eyes, wearing a white turban over a red skull cap.

Like poet laureates of modern times, Rudaki sometimes composed poems with a particular aim. For instance, when required to persuade the emir to end his overlong vacation in the salubrious city of Herat and return to Bukhara, Rudaki wrote:

> The fragrance of River Muliyan overwhlems me.
> It brings sweet memories of my beloved.
> The roughness of the river's gravel
> Like silk under my feet . . .
> Emir the moon, Bukhara the sky;

The moon is rising in the sky.
Emir the tall cypress, Bukhara the garden;
The cypress is coming to the garden.[12]

But the fate of Lenin's statue remained unresolved. Sensing the direction
in which popular mood was moving, Kadriddin Aslonov, chairman of the
Council of Ministers, urged the Supreme Soviet to ban the CPT. With 288
of the 310 deputies elected in March 1990 on the CPT ticket, the Supreme
Soviet refused. When Aslonov persisted, the Supreme Soviet dismissed him,
and replaced him with Rahman Nabiyev, then in retirement.

Nabiyev allowed the IRP to register as a political party provided it agreed
to stay within the law. When the IRP stated that it would employ "exclu-
sively democratic means in pursuit of its ultimate objective: a state based on
the Sharia, Islamic law," it won registration in September. But Nabiyev
nursed an ulterior motive. He estimated that the IRP, headed by
Himmatzade, would grow at the expense of support for Turajanzade, who
was fast emerging as the leading star in the growing opposition camp.
Turajanzade had already established a working alliance between his directorate, the IRP, and the Sufi brotherhoods—a considerable achievement.

Among those who had joined the opposition was Maksud Ikramov,
mayor of Dushanbe. He allowed the gigantic statue of Lenin to be removed
on September 21, which created a crisis. The next day, the Supreme Soviet
declared a state of emergency in Dushanbe. Nabiyev capped it with martial
law, and posted Interior Ministry troops to guard all the remaining statues
of Lenin.

Having watched the Supreme Soviet proceedings on television, many rural
citizens began marching to Dushanbe in protest. In the capital, the
Communist deputies' action brought together all opposition leaders. They
resolved to get the CPT banned and have a special commission investigate
links between top party leaders and the failed coup in Moscow. With rural
protesters arriving daily in Dushanbe by the hundreds, their spirits rose. It
was their first taste of grassroots politics, and they felt heady with confidence.

The opposition leaders saw the first sign of success when Interior Minister
Mamadayaz Navjavanov (originally, Muhammad Ayaz Navjavan), who
hailed from the impoverished Badakhshan mountainous region, refused to
break up an opposition demonstration when ordered to do so by the party
leaders. The Soviet army and special Interior Ministry units posted in
Tajikistan declared their neutrality in domestic politics.

The split in the republic's administration, coupled with a public withdrawal of the center's backing for it, signaled that the days of a monolithic party exercising total power under the direction of Moscow were over.

Realizing this, and finding martial law being flouted since September 23 by a round-the-clock sit-in by thousands of protesters gathered in tents in Azadi (Freedom) Square outside the Supreme Soviet, Nabiyev lifted martial law on October 6. And, yielding to popular pressure, the Supreme Soviet endorsed Aslonov's earlier order banning the CPT. It amended the constitution to create the office of a directly elected executive president, and fixed October 27 as the polling date. Opposition leaders felt satisfied, except they felt election day was much too soon. They convinced the Supreme Soviet, which moved the date to November 24.

Taking its lead from the Communist Party of Uzbekistan, a hurriedly called congress of the CPT dissolved the organization, and re-emerged as the Socialist Party of Tajikistan—but with Mahkamov replaced by Shudi Shahabdulov (originally, Shah Abdul) as its head, and with only a fraction of the CPT's original membership of 130,000. The Socialist Party adopted Nabiyev as its presidential candidate. He resigned his chairmanship of the Supreme Soviet, which went to Akbarsha Iskanderov (originally, Akbarshah Iskander).

The dissolution of the CPT, which had dominated state and society for seventy years, created a favorable climate for the opposition. Its ranks were bolstered by the establishment of the Democratic Party, a secular body popular with younger, urban Tajik intellectuals, led by Khudanazarov. It advocated free media, an equitable political system, and industrialization. "For seventy years gold from Tajik mountains and cotton from Tajik fields had gone to Moscow," said a party activist. "We should have been rich, not the poorest part of the Soviet Union."[13] The Democratic Party and other opposition factions adopted Khudanazarov, a magnetic personality, as their candidate.

The opposition was also aided by a dramatic move by the activists of the Rastakhiz People's Organization. On the plinth vacated by Lenin's statue, they erected the statue of the famous Persian poet, Abul Qasim Mansour, popularly known as Firdausi (940–1020). He composed the *Shahnama* (*Journal of Kings*)—an epic poem of 60,000 rhymed couplets, narrating the chronicle of the Persian-speaking region from the beginning of time to the Arab conquest in the seventh century. Oddly enough, the *Shahnama* was commissioned by Sultan Mahmoud Ghaznavi, a ruler of Turkic pedigree. According to his statue, he was a man of medium height with a high brow, a small nose, a neatly trimmed beard and mustache, and deep-set eyes beneath a turban.

Under popular pressure, the authorities allowed debates and roundtable discussions on radio and television, thus raising the political consciousness of the electorate. As an eminent political figure of long standing, Nabiyev received the most exposure on television. Unable to gain access to Tajik television as a sole speaker, Khudanazarov, a well-established national film director, tried to tap the central television network directed from Moscow. He succeeded in getting three-minute slots, which were balanced by an equal time allotted to Nabiyev. Five independent newspapers sprang up, providing an unprecedented variety of political opinion and comment. Campaigning for Khudanazarov, Turajanzade expressed his preference for a parliamentary, secular state with a free-market economy. "Religion must be separated from the state so no one will ascribe the sins of society to Islam as happened with communism," he said.[14]

On the polling day, 86 percent of the 2.5 million electors voted. Nabiyev won 57 percent and Khudanazarov 34 percent, with the remaining six candidates getting the rest. Khudanazarov immediately challenged the result, alleging voting irregularities. As a result, the election commission cancelled 3 percent of the vote, but that did not alter the final result.

Nabiyev did well in the traditional strongholds of the CPT—Khojand and Kulyab—which accounted for over three-fifths of the electorate. The deprived areas of the thinly populated Badakhshan region, the pro-Islamic Garm Valley, and Kurgan-Tyube supported Khudanazarov. Ethnically, Nabiyev outperformed Khudanazarov among Uzbeks (23 percent of the population), Slavs and Germans (9 percent), and other non-Tajik minorities. Perceiving Khudanazarov as a Tajik nationalist backed by Islamists, most of the 40 percent non-Tajik voters backed Nabiyev, whereas the remaining ethnic Tajik voters split almost evenly between the two leading candidates. At the age of sixty-one, Nabiyev's many years of administrative experience and authoritative style of leadership were broadly considered essential to steer Tajikistan through the painful transition to a market economy.

Nabiyev's victory was received rapturously by old party stalwarts. Now that their leader was backed by a popular mandate, they felt they would be able to cling to their power and privilege for another five years. In this they would not be disappointed. Nabiyev selected a cabinet that was dominated, as in the past, by the old nomenklatura from Khojand and Kulyab. This, and the reiteration of his commitment to the current five-year economic plan, showed that Nabiyev was too set in the old ways. He summed up his program thus: "My aim is to create a multi-party system. But before I do that I have to put food into the shops."[15] In other words, economic aims had to be achieved before any meaningful progress towards political liberalization—a refrain that would be heard elsewhere in Central Asia.

When Nabiyev attended the summit of Central Asian leaders in Ashgabat on December 12 to 13, 1991, he could rightly claim that alone among them he had won executive presidency in a multi-candidate contest. As leader of the poorest republic, heavily dependent on subsidies from Moscow, Nabiyev favored a continuing association of the Soviet Union's current constituents. To withstand the pressures from Afghanistan—in the throes of a civil war nearly three years after the departure of Soviet troops, with 90 percent of the Tajik-Afghan border in the hands of the Afghan Islamists—he wanted his republic to join a loose federation called the Commonwealth of Independent States.

AFTER THE SOVIET BREAK-UP

Alone among former Soviet republics, Tajikistan presented the founding of the Commonwealth of Independent States as "a revival of the Soviet Union." This was not the only unique feature of independent Tajikistan, the smallest Central Asian republic. It became a cauldron of traditional and contemporary conflicts in its domestic affairs, and a cockpit where a multitude of foreign powers competed for a domineering position. The end result was a civil war that raged for five years, and left the state and society devastated.

The delegates to the Congress of the Socialist Party of Tajikistan in January 1992, led by Shudi Shahabdulov, believed so strongly that the CIS was a reincarnation of the Soviet Union that they reverted to calling their party Communist. The speakers at the gathering argued that since the present organization had a different constitution from the old Communist Party, and was not an integral part of a supra-republican entity like the Communist Party of the Soviet Union, it was quite distinct from its old namesake.

When the renamed Communist deputies attended the next session of the Supreme Soviet, they passed laws curtailing media freedom and the right to hold marches and rallies. The government used the new legislation to settle scores with the organizers of grassroots demonstrations and sit-ins in September 1991. In March, it arrested Maksud Ikramov and charged him with corruption in his dealings with Iran. It leveled similar charges against Mamadayaz Navjavanov—the interior minister who had refused to break up opposition demonstrations—and dismissed him.

This onslaught brought about an alliance of the main opposition group-ings—the IRP, the Democratic Party, Rastakhiz, and the Muslim Spiritual Directorate—named the National Salvation Front (NSF). Its protest rallies around the administrative center of Dushanbe demanded the reinstatement of Ikramov and Navjavanov, as well as a new constitution, dissolution of the Supreme Soviet, and fresh elections. Nabiyev's supporters argued that nobody had the legal power to disband the Supreme Soviet before its term expired in 1994, and only courts had the authority to settle Ikramov's guilt or innocence. Nabiyev did agree to reinstate Navjavanov, but this did not pacify NSF leaders. Their meeting with him in mid-April 1992 ended in a deadlock.

Just then the news came that, following the downfall of pro-Communist Najibullah in Afghanistan, the victorious Islamic Mujahedin had arrived in Kabul. This raised the spirits of the Tajik opposition, especially its religious constituents, while the morale of the Communist government fell. Reflecting the precipitous change in Afghanistan, the Supreme Soviet con-ceded the demands for a new constitution and fresh elections, but in exchange for a three-week moratorium on demonstrations. The anti-Communist camp rejected the deal. It set the deadline of April 23 for the resignation of the hard-line chairman of the Supreme Soviet, Safarali Kenjayev, a former KGB deputy chief.

PREAMBLE TO CIVIL CONFLICT

The mounting pressure split the government. A large section of the Tajik Interior Ministry troops—mostly Badakhshanis supporting the Democratic Party or Lal-e Badakhshan, a regional body—had defected to the opposi-tion NSF. They did so after the Supreme Soviet of Gorno-Badakhshan Autonomous Region, covering nearly half of Tajikistan, declared the terri-tory as Pamir-Badakhshan Autonomous Republic on April 11, and endorsed the NSF's demands, particularly for closer ties with Afghanistan and Iran.[16]

Backed by Interior Ministry troops, the protesters took several parlia-mentary deputies hostage on April 21. The next day, Kenjayev resigned. The hostages were freed. The Supreme Soviet abolished censorship, and fixed a date for promulgating a new constitution. Nabiyev ordered amnesty for all protesters.

Just as opposition leaders were discussing their next move on April 26, thousands of pro-government supporters from the Kulyab region who were loyal to Kenjayev, a fellow Kulyabi, arrived in Dushanbe. They converged on Martyrs Square opposite the Supreme Soviet. The interjection of these demonstrators, some of them armed, radicalized the opposition, which until then had been peaceful and good-natured.

The opposition gathered at Freedom Square, less than a kilometer away along Rudaki Avenue. Indeed, this long avenue, which connected the rail-road station in the south to the bus station in the north—the arrival points of the out-of-town demonstrators, and also the main axis along which stood most of the leading administrative and cultural buildings—became the epicenter of the struggle between the opposing camps. Its reverberations would spread throughout the republic.

Nabiyev declared presidential rule, which heightened tension further. The size of the pro- and anti-government rallies grew to some 100,000 partici-pants each. Nabiyev ordered the formation of a National Guard under his own command. This allowed him to arm the pro-government militias from the Kulyab and Hissar Valleys with Kalashnikov assault rifles. In response, the opposition established its own armed militia, called the People's Volunteer Corps (PVC), and equipped them with weapons stolen or bought from the CIS forces stationed in the republic.

Emboldened by the emergence of the National Guard—2,000 to 4,000 strong—the Supreme Soviet reinstated Kenjayev as its chairman on May 3, thereby aborting the meeting that NSF leaders were scheduled to have with Nabiyev later that day. The Supreme Soviet's decision triggered a civil war, even though Kenjayev failed to turn up to resume his post. (Seven years later, he would be shot dead by an unknown gunman outside his home in Dushanbe.)

CIVIL WAR: PHASE I

On May 4, 1992, the simmering tension boiled over. Clashes broke out between the armed men of rival camps. The next day, the PVC captured the sole state-owned television station, which started transmitting the opposi-tion's statements. Nabiyev declared a state of emergency and curfew, but both sides ignored them.

The anti-government NSF speakers declared solidarity with the victorious Afghan Mujahedin, who, they claimed, had sent messages promising help. The ambience at the opposition camp at Freedom Square became predom-inantly Islamic—embellished with Islamic placards and slogans, many of them copied from Iran. Bearded men and veiled women declared their readiness to be martyred for Islam. Their leaders demanded Nabiyev's resignation and fresh elections, alleging that the result of the earlier poll had been rigged.

On May 6 the PVC seized most of Dushanbe, including the presidential palace, abandoned by Nabiyev—leaving only the Supreme Soviet building, the KGB (now renamed KNB) headquarters (where Nabiyev was rumored to have taken refuge), and the radio station held by pro-Nabiyev forces. The death toll in the fighting reached sixty.

The next day, Nabiyev withdrew his decrees concerning state of emergency and the establishment of the National Guard, thus showing his willingness to compromise. But his bargaining power weakened when his forces lost the radio station to the opposition, who announced the formation of a Revolutionary Council to rule Tajikistan.

The Council proved stillborn as both camps split between moderates and hardliners. Finally, the constitutional line advocated by Khudanazarov in the NSF prevailed. "It is up to the Supreme Soviet and a national referendum to decide if the republic needs a new president, and if they do, which one," he said. "But these matters must not be decided by clans and street rallies."[17] Throughout the mayhem, the commander of the CIS forces in Tajikistan repeated that his troops had kept out of the local conflict.

On May 11, fifty-one days after the protest started and 150 people had died, it was announced that the opposition NSF had agreed to let Nabiyev continue as president, and that it would get a third of the seats in a twenty-four-member cabinet, corresponding to Khudanazarov's proportion of the popular vote, headed by Prime Minister Akbar Mirzayev. This allowed Nabiyev to attend the CIS summit in Tashkent a few days later and join the Tashkent Collective Security Agreement.

Once it was decided that the heads of the opposition parties would stay out of the government, ministerial posts went to their deputies, with Davlat Usman of the IRP becoming vice-premier, overseeing security forces. Rejecting the prospect of disarming, the pro-Nabiyev militias from Kulyab and Hissar had left the capital two days earlier. And, fearing for his life, Kenjayev had escaped inside a tank of the CIS 201st motorized division.

The installation of a new cabinet bearing the title of "national reconciliation government" did not end the conflict, based as it was on deeply rooted clan and regional loyalties. Nonetheless, it published a draft constitution to be debated by the Supreme Soviet. It described the president as the head of state and the National Assembly (*Milli Majlis* in Tajik) as the highest legislative body. It confirmed the 1991 law on Tajik, which specified a switchover from the Cyrillic script to Persian over five years, and limited the use of Russian. It ruled out dual citizenship, thus dimming the future prospects of Russian settlers, who often possessed much-needed skills. Fearing the worst, they had started leaving in droves.

The top officials in the Khojand and Kulyab regions defied the central authority, refusing to pay their budget contributions; and so did those in pro-Islamic Kurgan-Tyube. The Kenjayev loyalists, calling themselves the Popular Front and led by Sangak Safarov, took over the city of Kulyab, and began settling scores with their traditional adversaries, the inhabitants of the Kurgan-Tyube region. The fighting between the two sides—equipped with arms smuggled from Afghanistan or bought from CIS forces with much-coveted U.S. dollars—left forty-two dead in June.

There was a cease-fire on July 7, which lasted only a few weeks. When the fighting resumed, Nabiyev faced strong criticism. The republic's economy suffered, with cotton output down by half from the peak of 900,000 tons in 1987. Because of the demonstrations in Dushanbe from April to May, the Turkish premier, Suleiman Demirel, skipped the city during his tour of Central Asia, and failed to offer Tajikistan much-needed aid and trade. A budget deficit amounting to 40 percent of the GDP fuelled inflation and depressed already low living standards.

Partly to escape from domestic pressures, and partly to placate the Islamists within his coalition government, Nabiyev flew to Tehran. He signed a treaty of friendship and cooperation with Iran, covering culture, trade, banking, and science. Pleased with Tajikistan's decision to adopt the Persian alphabet for Tajik—also known as Tajiki Persian, being a dialect of modern Persian—Tehran helped Tajik linguistic experts to modify the alphabet that they had prepared for their language. Some weeks later, Iran offered Tajikistan 300,000 tons of free oil to alleviate its energy crisis, which had brought public transport in Dushanbe to a virtual halt.[18]

Nabiyev's domestic woes persisted. During the Supreme Soviet session starting on August 12, chaired by Akbarsha Iskanderov, a Badakhshani politician, Turajanzade demanded the president's resignation for failing to stop Tajikistan's political and economic disintegration. Tension rose further when the chief prosecutor was murdered in Dushanbe, and the KNB chief accused Hikmatyar, an Afghan Islamic leader, of training Tajik Islamists to overthrow the Nabiyev regime.

Nabiyev decided to act. He signed an agreement with the CIS secretariat in Moscow allowing the arrival of CIS military units in Tajikistan for peace-keeping. Since he acted without consulting the opposition cabinet ministers, they criticized him. Prime Minister Mirzayev resigned on August 30, citing severe limitations on the "political freedoms" of Nabiyev.

PRESIDENT HELD HOSTAGE

The rift within the cabinet emboldened militant anti-Nabiyev elements. On August 31, between fifty and a hundred armed opposition demonstrators occupied the ground floor of the presidential palace and took thirty-five hostages, including ministers. During the mayhem, Nabiyev escaped and took refuge at the CIS headquarters.

Urgent talks between the hostage-takers and senior government officials followed. The former issued a statement on September 2: "We consider that President Nabiyev has been removed from power because of his failure to end the crisis threatening the future of the country." Iskanderov called on the Supreme Soviet to meet two days later to decide inter alia the fate of Nabiyev.

This alarmed the capitals of Central Asia and Russia. The presidents of Uzbekistan, Kazakhstan, Kyrgyzstan, and Russia issued a communiqué warning Tajikistan's government and politicians of severe consequences of continued conflict—described as "a danger to the CIS"—and declaring that they would intervene to stop the bloodshed. Alluding to the large-scale smuggling of arms and narcotics from Tajikistan's "southern neighbors," which threatened the republic's sovereignty and its continued CIS membership, they announced the dispatch of additional border troops to the Tajik-Afghan frontier.[19]

In Dushanbe, the scheduled Supreme Soviet session on September 4 failed to materialize because only 80 deputies, about half of the quorum of 156, turned up. The following day, bitter fighting between the pro- and anti-Nabiyev camps in Kurgan-Tyube led to the deaths of several hundred people. Nabiyev, operating from the CIS headquarters in Dushanbe, declared a state of emergency in the region.

On September 7, Nabiyev intended to fly secretly to his home base of Khojand to confer with its Communist leaders. According to one version, opposition leaders were tipped off, and confronted him at Dushanbe airport's VIP lounge. After several hours of talks, he resigned under duress, possibly at gunpoint, and handed his powers over to Iskanderov. In a second version, Nabiyev was lured from the CIS headquarters to Dushanbe airport's VIP lounge by some of the men occupying the presidential palace. Then, members of the Tajikistan Youth—a pro-Islamic militia led by Juma

Khan—encircled the lounge with tanks and armored personnel carriers, and threatened to fire unless Nabiyev resigned, which he did.[20] A third version, a blend of the above two, had Nabiyev kidnapped by an armed opposition group at the Dushanbe airport as he was escaping to Khojand.[21]

What followed is also disputed. According to one account, Nabiyev flew to Khojand unharmed. Another version reported guns blazing all over the airport, with Nabiyev being whisked back to the CIS garrison, and later at night leaving clandestinely by road, hidden in the trunk of his car, for Khojand.[22]

ISKANDEROV HOLDS THE RING

Iskanderov became acting president. Attempts to convene the Supreme Soviet to confirm him in his new post failed due to the lack of a quorum. To preempt Nabiyev's next move, he ordered the blowing up of a major bridge connecting Dushanbe with the north to "prevent military movement"—that is, to prevent armed forces from Khojand traveling south to overthrow his government in Dushanbe or aid pro-Nabiyev fighters farther south. But the destruction of the bridge between the industrial north and the rest of the country curtailed transport facilities and made fuel scarce. Lack of public funds and the breakdown of communications and road systems badly affected the economy and public morale.

By the end of September 1992, fatalities in the civil war exceeded 2,000. In the anti-Nabiyev camp, most of the fighting was done by the militias loyal to the IRP. Its membership of 30,000 extended to village level, and was aided by the vastly increased number of mosques, which was many times the pre-perestroika figure of seventeen. (However, the figure of 2,870 published by the *Far Eastern Economic Review* in January 1992 included tea houses and private halls used for prayers. Dushanbe, for example, had only five proper mosques.) IRP militiamen had marginalized secular, nationalist forces within the anti-Communist camp. They were equipped with weapons from Afghanistan supplied either by Hikmatyar or Ahmed Shah Masoud, an ethnic Tajik.

The pro-Nabiyev forces were armed mainly with weapons bought or stolen from the CIS depots, or supplied by the Uzbek government.[23] The posting of an extra 1,000 border troops from Russia, Uzbekistan, Kazakhstan, and Kyrgyzstan along the Tajik-Afghan border made little difference, since the largely mountainous frontier was difficult to seal, and fighters on both sides of the international line had become adept in moving men and materials across it.

Trying to maintain a semblance of neutrality between the opposing forces, Iskanderov appointed an ethnic Uzbek from Khojand, Abdumalik Abdullajanov (originally, Abdul Malik Abdullah Jan)—an ex-Communist economist-turned-businessman—acting prime minister on September 21, thus meeting one of the demands of the pro-Nabiyev partisans from Kulyab. He set September 24 as the deadline for an end to the hostilities in Kurgan-Tyube and Kulyab. Nothing came of it.

His request for the purchase of heavy weapons from Russia fell flat as well. The Kremlin regarded his government as illegitimate since it had failed to win a vote of confidence from the Supreme Soviet, though it refrained from saying so publicly. Also, the Kremlin was unwilling to sell weapons for anything but hard currency, which the Iskanderov government lacked.[24] Beyond that, while loudly claiming its neutrality in the Tajik civil war and refusing to allow the Russian-dominated CIS units to be used in any role other than assisting the local Interior Ministry troops to guard important installations, Moscow pursued its undeclared policy of helping the pro-Nabiyev forces through illicit sales of locally stored weapons and ammunition.

Russia was against Tajik Islamists for practical, ideological, and strategic reasons. Victory for Islamic forces would have resulted in a large-scale exodus of the remaining 300,000 ethnic Russians to a Russia with an acute shortage of housing and jobs, thus inflaming opinion in parliament and on the streets. This would have added to the headaches of President Boris Yeltsin, who was already burdened with other, almost intractable problems. It would have exposed him to a damaging charge from the conservative-nationalists that he was unable to protect the Russians living abroad.

Moreover, a successful expulsion of ethnic Russians from Tajikistan was bound to whet the appetite of pan-Turkic nationalists in the rest of Central Asia, thus compounding Moscow's problem and creating a backlash among Russians at home with calls for expelling the Central Asians living in Russia.

Thirdly, as the leading secular democracy in the CIS, Russia was loath to see a religious state within the CIS. Finally, the emergence of an Islamic regime in Tajikistan would destabilize the neighboring republics, especially Uzbekistan, the most strategically important Central Asian state. Indeed, Uzbek President Islam Karimov had taken secretly to aiding and training pro-Nabiyev partisans in Kulyab, using the border town of Termez to channel arms and ammunition to them.

During the third week of September, freshly equipped with four tanks and six armored personnel carriers secured from the CIS 201st motorized division, the Kulyabi forces mounted devastating raids on villages and towns in

Kurgan-Tyube, killing hundreds and displacing tens of thousands. Kurgan-Tyube's mayor accused CIS troops of assisting the invaders before losing his city to them. When Iskanderov protested to Moscow about the use of Russian tanks by the pro-Nabiyev forces against unarmed civilians, the CIS command replied that an armed militia had "stolen" these tanks after "besieging" a CIS unit near Kurgan-Tyube.[25]

With thousands of refugees from Kurgan-Tyube pouring into the capital, and many people demonstrating daily before the Russian embassy demanding an end to Moscow's military aid to the pro-Nabiyev camp, Iskanderov appealed to the CIS and the United Nations to help stop the armed conflict. Meanwhile, he allowed CIS troops to guard the Dushanbe airport.

On the eve of the CIS summit in Bishkek on October 8 to 9, 1992, leaving aside the thinly populated autonomous Badakhshan region, Tajikistan was politically divided into four parts: the pro-Nabiyev Khojand (aka Leninabad) region in the north; Dushanbe and its environs, dominated by the anti-Nabiyev Democrat-Islamic alliance; the pro-Nabiyev Kulyab region in the southeast; and the pro-Islamic Kurgan-Tyube in the southwest.

CIS leaders declared that, due to the threats to "the external borders" of the CIS, they would send a CIS peacekeeping force as soon as "the legitimate authority" in Tajikistan requested it; and that the present CIS troops should not be withdrawn from Tajikistan until the situation had improved. Later, though, Kyrgyz President Askar Akayev's plan to dispatch 450 Kyrgyz troops to Tajikistan as peacekeepers was overruled by the Supreme Soviet, which opted for non-interference in the internal affairs of a neighboring state.[26] However, in Bishkek, Karimov and Yeltsin privately reaffirmed their undeclared policy of expelling the anti-Nabiyev forces from the seats of power they had managed to acquire in Dushanbe. This meant that Uzbekistan would continue to arm and train pro-Nabiyev fighters.

When a cease-fire agreed in mid-October failed to hold, a desperate Iskanderov established a National Security Council made up of leading members of the Supreme Soviet and the cabinet, and appointed Khudanazarov, a fellow Badakhshani, his chief adviser. Khudanazarov flew to Moscow. In his meeting with Russian Foreign Minister Andrei Kozyrev, he sought the Kremlin's help to end the civil conflict. Kozyrev declined, saying Russia could not interfere in Tajikistan's domestic affairs. The Kremlin did not want to help Iskanderov, who was dependent for his political survival on Islamists, to consolidate his power.

For their part, Muslim leaders, especially Turajanzade, had started reiterating that the aim of establishing an Islamic state could only be realized through law, and that such an outcome would require the support of a substantial majority of Muslims, but that given the current trends such a change could not be envisaged during the lifetime of the present generation of voters.

In any case, Turajanzade stressed, an Islamic republic in "this ethnically mixed, Soviet-educated population of 5 million people in Tajikistan" was unlikely to be in "the rigid Iranian mold," with women wearing veils. He also made a distinction between the predominantly Sunni Tajiks and overwhelmingly Shiite Iranians. "The Sunni tradition never had a place for a single authoritarian religious figure like [Ayatollah] Khomeini," he explained. "Besides, over the past 70 years [under Communism] we have simply acquired a different view of the world."[27]

Claiming that Russia was assisting the pro-Nabiyev camp, Turajanzade said that it could end the civil war "in two days" if it wanted to. But that would have necessitated a large-scale military intervention, which would have required parliamentary approval. That was most unlikely in view of the Soviet debacle in Afghanistan in the 1980s.

Meanwhile, Karimov pursued his plan to topple the Iskanderov government. The military planners' task was facilitated by the fact that the Tajik government had lost effective control over its frontier with Uzbekistan, and renegade Safarali Kenjayev had sheltered in Uzbekistan. They acted on the night of October 23. Kenjayev led a column of forty buses and trucks, assembled earlier in Tursunzade (aka Regar) in the Hissar Valley, twenty-five miles west of Dushanbe, near the Uzbek border. His men, including many ethnic Uzbeks, were equipped with weapons supplied by the Uzbek garrison commander in Termez.[28]

In their surprise attack on Dushanbe in the dark, the invaders met little resistance in capturing the presidential palace, the Supreme Soviet building, and the radio station. In his broadcast, Kenjayev accused the Iskanderov coalition of establishing a fundamentalist Islamic state. Following this, he had visualized a popular uprising against the Iskanderov government, but nothing of the sort happened.

Having recovered from the shock, the much larger militias of the IRP and Turajanzade mounted a spirited counter-offensive. Two days of heavy fighting, resulting in death or injury to three of the attackers' commanders, showed that the invaders' position was untenable, particularly when the expected reinforcements from Kulyab failed to arrive due to unexpected last-minute hitches. Therefore, the aggressors used the CIS commander as an intermediary to negotiate a cease-fire and evacuation. Escorted by CIS units, they left, claiming that their action had put the question of the Iskanderov government's legitimacy on the national agenda. The episode left 60 to 150 people dead.

However, compared to the carnage in the south, which had, according to the Tajikistan Radio, claimed 18,500 lives so far, the loss of life in Dushanbe was insignificant.[29] The political advantage that Iskanderov's government extracted from the latest episode did not alter its inherently weak position. The external forces backing the pro-Nabiyev side— Uzbekistan actively and Russia tacitly—were far more powerful than a fractured Afghanistan and distant Iran, which Iskanderov could have hoped to achieve.

On November 4, 1992, the summit of the Tashkent Collective Security Agreement members, except Tajikistan, in Almaty more or less decided the future of the troubled republic. Its joint communiqué stated that (a) the (nominally CIS) Russian 201st division should continue its "peacekeeping" role until a proper CIS peacekeeping force had been constituted to replace it; (b) a State Council, consisting of all factions in Tajikistan, should be formed; and (c) a committee of representatives of the presidents of Uzbekistan, Kyrgyzstan, Kazakhstan, and Russia (henceforth the Almaty Committee) is being mandated to bring about peace in Tajikistan.

By the time the Almaty Committee arrived in Dushanbe on November 7, the pro-Nabiyev force under Safarov of the Popular Front was well on its way to controlling all of the Kurgan-Tyube province after largely depopulating it and creating hundreds of thousands of refugees. (By now, the civil conflict had displaced 430,000 people, with 55,000 seeking shelter in Dushanbe.) Safarov therefore rejected the invitation to meet Iskanderov in Dushanbe as a prelude to conferring with the Almaty Committee to name a State Council composed of all Tajik factions. Instead, Safarov demanded a ban on all opposition factions.

The cabinet members submitted their resignations to Iskanderov to let the special session of the Supreme Soviet summoned in Khojand on November 16 make a fresh start. Khojand was selected as the venue for the session because repeated attempts to hold one in Dushanbe had failed due to the deputies' fears that, as in the past, they would be pressured by well-orchestrated crowds to vote in a certain way. At the Almaty Committee's initiative, all sides agreed to abide by the decisions of the Supreme Soviet, which was expected inter alia to discuss the legality of Nabiyev's resignation.

Deprived of the crucial supplies from Khojand—due to the only surviving link of a railroad having been blown up at several places, blocking nearly

500 wagons of badly needed food and fuel from the south—the economic situation worsened in Dushanbe.

When the Supreme Soviet met in Khojand under the chairmanship of Iskanderov, nearly 200 deputies attended, virtually all of them Communist. By 140 to 54 votes, it accepted the resignation of Iskanderov as chairman of the Supreme Soviet and acting president of the republic. Then, by 186 to 11 votes, it elected forty-year-old Imamali Sharifovich Rahmanov—the erstwhile Communist governor of Kulyab—chairman of the Supreme Soviet, thus making him the effective head of state. Rahmanov publicly acknowledged his debt to Safarov for achieving high office, thus recognizing him as leading powerbroker. By naming Abdumalik Abdullajanov as his prime minister, Rahmanov satisfied Communist deputies while maintaining a link with the immediate past.

Then the Supreme Soviet decided that Nabiyev's resignation was invalid because it had been offered under duress. Having thus retrieved his honor, Nabiyev resigned voluntarily, and a majority of deputies accepted it. This ended the most fractious political episode in the brief history of independent Tajikistan. His exit satisfied those Communist deputies who considered him a weak leader. It also mollified the opposition which, having contested the fairness of the November 1991 poll, had never reconciled itself to his presidency.[30]

The thorny questions of who should follow Nabiyev as the republic's president and how were resolved on November 27, when the Supreme Soviet amended the 1978 constitution to "abolish presidential rule" and declare Tajikistan a "parliamentary republic." It thus reverted to the old Soviet practice of conferring the title of the head of state on its Supreme Soviet's chairman, Rahmanov.

ENTER IMAMALI RAHMANOV

Born in the Kulyabi village of Dangara, Imamali Rahmanov finished his compulsory army service in 1974, and worked as an electrician in an edible oil factory for a couple of years. He then served as secretary to the board of directors of a collective farm for twelve years, with a break to study economics at the Tajikistan State University, where he graduated in 1982. In 1988, he was appointed director of the state-owned farm, Lenin Sovkhoz, in Dangara. Married to Azizmo Asadullayeva, he would father nine children.

Having overseen the installation of a legitimate government in Tajikistan, the Almaty Committee focused on achieving a cease-fire between the warring parties as a preamble to the Supreme Soviet's acceptance of a CIS peacekeeping force. Safarov was in a hawkish mood. But the anti-Communist alliance, aware of its comparative weakness, was willing to cease fire in exchange for the lifting of the blockade of Dushanbe from the north. This was done, and a truce was signed on November 25, but it proved short-lived.

With their political supremacy underwritten by the Supreme Soviet, the Tajik Communist forces coordinated their military plans with the Uzbek military high command to regain Dushanbe. They got their go-ahead when, meeting in Termez, the defense ministers of Russia, Kazakhstan, Kyrgyzstan, and Uzbekistan and the supreme commander of the CIS military, Marshal Yevgeny Shaposhnikov, endorsed the plan for a CIS peacekeeping force on November 30.

That day, Premier Abdullajanov's presentation of a cabinet, dominated by Kulyabis and Khojandis, to the Supreme Soviet made the anti-Communist alliance realize that politically it was back to the period before the populist uprising of May 1992. Its administrative authority was now reduced to Dushanbe and its environs, overwhelmed by the flow of refugees, estimated at 120,000 in a city of 540,000, due to the ongoing military successes of its adversaries. Its militias, now collectively called the Popular Democratic Army (PDA), were badly armed, poorly trained, and lacked central command. Nonetheless, they were in high spirits.

On December 4, the Communist forces—led by the new Tajik interior minister, Yakub Salimov, and equipped with machine-guns, artillery, tanks, and armored personnel carriers supplied largely by Uzbekistan—used Hissar as their staging post to enter Dushanbe from the west. They met stiff resistance on the outskirts of the capital. On December 8, the authorities in Dushanbe handed out arms to the people to fight the attackers. Bitter combat ensued.

Two days later, the battle took a decisive turn. The Popular Front reinforcements from Kulyab attempted to penetrate the capital from the south in a column of tanks, while Uzbekistan's fighter aircraft and helicopter gunships targeted the anti-Communist defenders. According to local CIS sources, there were "hundreds of burnt corpses" in the streets.[31] The next day, Salimov entered the city to negotiate the surrender of the anti-Communist PDA, which did not materialize. Talks and fighting continued over the weekend of December 12 and 13.

Having lost most of Dushanbe, anti-Communist partisans, especially Islamists, totaling 5,500, fanned out to the surrounding villages, with some of them regrouping in Kofarnihan, the home base of Turajanzade twelve miles east of Dushanbe. But they were chased by Communist troops, and forced to retreat farther into the Pamir Mountains of Badakhshan after the fall of Kofarnihan on December 21. A similar fate was to befall the Islamist fighters in the Kurgan-Tyube region.

For all practical purposes, the civil war was over by the end of December 1992, with neo-Communists almost fully back in power and their opponents on the run. The only difference was that the present party membership of 25,000 was a fraction of the pre-independence figure of 130,000.

While democratic and Islamist forces had enough popular support to make them, singly or jointly, an effective opposition in a democratic system, they faced insurmountable difficulties in winning and keeping power, or even sharing it with Communists. They had to operate within the republican constitution of 1978, which, like its predecessors, was based on the Leninist principle of "All power to the Soviets." The provision of an executive president, inserted as an amendment by a Communist-dominated Supreme Soviet, never really took root, primarily because the presidential election in November 1991 threw up a viable alternative to the Communist candidate, something Communist deputies had not foreseen. Whatever concessions the anti-Communist alliance won through grassroots politics—be it a share of cabinet posts or the appointment of Iskanderov as the acting president—had to be sanctified ultimately by the Supreme Soviet, which was firmly in neo-Communist hands.

Had the anti-Communists overcome this hurdle by gaining majority support in the Supreme Soviet, they would have faced the problem of maintaining the territorial integrity of Tajikistan. For, as threatened, the authorities in Khojand would have seceded, and then either declared the province independent or unified with Uzbekistan, thus intensifying the civil war and turning it into an international crisis. The loss of a third of the republic's population and over three-fifths of its industrial production would have played havoc with the economy of the rest of Tajikistan. Any effort by the government in Dushanbe to regain Khojand by force would have made matters worse.

In short, the anti-Communist alliance was in a no-win situation. The economy was reeling from the impact of the civil war. The death toll varied from "at least 20,000" to 30,000. The estimated cost of damage was R90 billion. In a country already short of housing, 600,000 square meters of living space were lost. The economy was damaged further by the emergence of an army of 537,000 refugees, one-tenth of the national population.[32]

Industrial output shrank by 23 percent, and the national GDP by 13 percent; and rural unemployment soared to about 70 percent.

VENDETTA

Instead of pursuing reconciliation, the Rahmanov government opted for vengeance. It combined this policy with a search for a non-Communist ideology that could trump Islamism. The answer lay with ethnic nationalism. The most effective way to popularize it was to personify it in a towering historical figure—as, for instance, Karimov had done in the case of Emir Timur Beg.

The Tajik government conferred the honorific of the Father of the Nation on Emir Ismail Samani (d. 907), the founder of the Persian dynasty regarded as the original Tajik state. To imprint the idea on the popular psyche, Rahmanov ordered that the statue of Firdausi in central Dushanbe give way to that of Ismail Samani. Unsurprisingly, the designers of Samani's statue opted for a masculine figure with an almost clean-shaven face, raising his right arm in the style that Lenin had perfected.

To implement the second part of the twin-headed policy, the Rahmanov government mounted a campaign against opposition leaders who had either fled or gone into hiding: Shodmon Yusuf of the Democratic Party; Muhammad Himmatzade and Davlat Usman of the IRP; and Turajanzade, now the founder-leader of the Islamic Nationalist Movement of Tajikistan. They were accused of conspiring to overthrow the government. The secular leaders secured refuge in Moscow, whereas the Islamists headed for Afghanistan and Iran, with Abdullah Nuri operating from Kabul, and Turajanzade from Tehran.

The government banned foreign financing of madrassas. It curtailed press freedom, leading to the immediate closure of two independent newspapers. It threatened dissident journalists, who left the capital for the provinces. A far worse fate awaited those residents of Dushanbe who were born in the areas that backed the opposition: Garm and Karategin Valleys, and Badakhshan Autonomous Region. Those from Badakhshan, popularly known as Pamiris, were easy to spot. Their dialect is different from Tajiks', and they were Ismailis, a subsect within Shiite Islam. Starting in Dushanbe, death squads operating with official approval or complicity carried out assassinations. By spring of 1993, there were estimated to be between 300 and 1,500 killings.

The bloody vendetta in Dushanbe and the south caused an exodus of nearly 200,000 Pamiris and other persecuted groups to the Badakhshan

Autonomous Region, which, being largely inaccessible, continued to resist central control from Dushanbe. An opposition leader in the regional capital, Khorog, claimed that there were 15,000 anti-Communist fighters in the area. Since the government's efforts to recover unregistered arms had failed, between 18,000 and 35,000 weapons were in circulation.[33]

Russia and the remaining Central Asian countries welcomed the restoration of a legitimate government in Dushanbe. The CIS summit in Minsk on January 22 to 23, 1993, decided to increase the CIS peacekeeping force by four motorized infantry battalions. Kazakhstan promised Tajikistan 400,000 tons of food grains, and Russia pledged food, fuel, and medicines. They encouraged Tajikistan to continue the economic reform initiated by Nabiyev, which included removing price controls, enacting new banking and tax laws, encouraging private enterprise, giving concessions to foreign investors, and implementing privatization. Tajikistan went on to sign a wide-ranging treaty with Russia on political, military, security, economic, and cultural cooperation. It required Russia to safeguard Tajikistan's external and internal security.

Having pacified all the areas of civil conflict by March 1993, the Rahmanov government turned its attention to Badakhshan, which shared a border with the Badakhshan region of northern Afghanistan. Since the only access to Badakhshan was through two mountain passes, it was comparatively easy for the regional government to block the arrival of Tajik ground forces. Yet it compromised. Its parliament recognized the supremacy of the Dushanbe government in exchange for the latter's promise not to attack the autonomous region.[34] This reassured not only the pre-civil war population of 200,000, but also the 200,000 Badakhshani refugees from the rest of the republic, and an additional 100,000 Tajik opponents of the central government.

The Islamist and secular opposition parties formed an alliance called the United Tajik Opposition (UTO), with Abdullah Nuri as its leader, and Turajanzade as his deputy. Because of Badakhshan's long border with Afghanistan, much of it inaccessible, IRP activists set up camps in Afghanistan and strengthened their ties with Iran. The UTO set up its headquarters in Taloqan in northern Afghanistan.

CIVIL WAR: PHASE II

With the ban on the Democratic Party, IRP, Lal-e Badakhshan, and Rastakhiz from engaging in violent anti-state activities, imposed in March 1993 and confirmed by the Supreme Court, there was scant chance of rapprochement between the opposing camps. Indeed, the Tajik Islamist rebels, now concentrated in Badakhshan, strengthened their links with Islamists in Afghanistan led by Ahmad Shah Masoud and Gulbuddin Hikmatyar, who aided them with arms, cash, and guerrilla warfare experts.

On the other side, Tajikistan and its CIS allies reinforced the guard along the Tajik-Afghan border. The Islamist government in Kabul took umbrage at the presence of Russian forces along its frontier. With tens of thousands of Tajiks crossing the Oxus River frontier into northern Afghanistan, relations between Dushanbe and Kabul deteriorated sharply, with each side accusing the other of violations of its border and air space.

In July, in a major attack on Border Post 14, Tajik Islamists operating from Afghanistan killed twenty-five Russian border guards and lost scores of their fighters. The Russians bombed Afghan villages, killing more than a hundred civilians. Yelstin was enraged: "Why did we not have a plan to protect this border, which everyone must understand is effectively Russia's, not Tajikistan's, border?"[35] He reinforced the border guards force, and pressured Central Asian states to do the same.

The importance of this mission was underlined by Russian Security Minister Viktor Barranikov thus: "By guarding the Tajik section of [CIS] border we defend the strategic backbone of Russia. If we lost our [Central Asian] allies there, we will have to defend a [Russian] border, which is far longer and absolutely transparent."[36] Tajik officials chimed in. "Tajikistan is the crossroads of Asia, the crossroads with the Indian subcontinent, China and Iran," said Gennady Bilinov, Tajik deputy interior minister and an ethnic Russian. "Russia has very serious geopolitical interests here."[37]

Internally, too, peace failed to strike roots. The Badakshan regional authorities let the UTO use its territory as a major conduit for arms and narcotics from the Islamic State of Afghanistan, and harass the Rahmanov administration. Gun and drug running were interlinked businesses. The funding for arms came partly from the trade in narcotics—hashish as well as opium and heroin, derived from Afghan poppies, destined for Russian cities.

After the fall of the Najibullah regime and the onset of civil war in Afghanistan, trading of illegal weapons and drugs thrived. The seizure of opium by the Tajik authorities jumped from half a metric ton in 1994 to more than 1,000 metric tons in 1995![38] The highly lucrative business of transporting soft and hard drugs to Russian cities corrupted the Russian border guards along the Tajik-Afghan frontier, making them complicit in the outlawed trade.

It had a debilitating impact on the Tajik economy. "[T]he narcotics trade
. . . throughout the 1990s was presumed to have been equal to 50 to 100
percent of Tajikistan's GDP, depending on the size of each year's Afghan
poppy harvest," noted Martha Brill Olcott. "Tajikistan's drug trade was in
part fueled by the economic desperation of its people."[39] Illicit cash generated from the drugs business fueled corruption, which in turn retarded
much-needed economic reform.

This led Rahmanov to turn increasingly towards Moscow for its security
and economic survival. While the population of ethnic Slavs dwindled to
100,000, the number of Russian troops in Tajikistan rose to 25,000.[40] Of
these, 15,000 were deployed along the Tajik-Afghan frontier. The Kremlin
bore the expense, and also provided cash to Dushanbe to enable it to meet
some of its basic obligations, such as paying the salaries of civil servants.

With the violence in Tajikistan impacting on several countries, the United
Nations got invited to help pacify the country. The remaining Central Asian
republics, Russia, Iran, and Pakistan endorsed the UN-sponsored peace
negotiations between the warring parties. Aware of the cultural ties between
Tajikistan and Iran, a stable state, Yeltsin saw merit in securing Tehran's
active assistance to restore law and order in the troubled republic. With the
help of the UN, peace talks started in Moscow in April 1994.

Nudged by Russia to replace the old Soviet constitution, the Tajik government published a draft constitution. It specified executive presidency,
which had been abolished in November 1992. This set the scene for a meeting between the warring camps in Tehran, the base of Turajanzade, in June.
The talks were also attended by the representatives of Russia, Iran, and
Pakistan. The Tajik government agreed to a four-month timetable to release
political prisoners and grant amnesty for oppositon leaders as a prelude to
the presidential election.

It then reneged, and announced September 25 as the polling date. In
response, the opposition escalated its insurgency. In late July, there were
large-scale clashes between the government and rebels near Tavil Dara, east
of Dushanbe, and in Garm Valley, reviving memories of the earlier bloody
battles. The central government retaliated by invading Badakhshan in
August. It managed to acquire nominal control over Khorog, but the rest of
this inaccessible, mountainous region remained beyond its pale.

In another round of talks in Tehran in mid-September, the Tajik government postponed the presidential poll to November 6. The deal was signed
by Tajikistan's deputy speaker, Abdul Majid Dostiyev, and Turajanzade,
specifying "temporary cease-fire" until the holding of a simultaneous refer-

endum on the new constitution and a presidential poll, with the truce to be supervised by UN observers. However, the Islamists found the six-week extension insufficient to choose their candidate and campaign properly, so they boycotted the poll.

The government's claim of 95 percent voter turnout was suspect. The suspicion rubbed off on the official claim that Rahmanov's secular rival, Abdulmalik Abdullajanov—Tajikistan's ambassador to Moscow and a former prime minister—won 35 percent of the vote, whereas Rahmanov received 60 percent. A similar figure was attributed to the constitution. Abdullajanov alleged widespread electoral malpractices, but to no avail.[41]

For the Kremlin, however, it was enough that its favorite, Rahmanov, had legitimized his power through an election held under a post-Soviet constitution, and that parliamentary elections had followed in February 1995, with Communists winning 60 seats (out of 181) and emerging as the largest group. These elections, Russian policymakers concluded, would enable Rahmanov to consolidate his position and redouble his efforts, with their backing, to squash his Islamist opponents.

This was not to be. With the spring thaw in 1995 ending the immobility imposed by winter snows in Tajikistan and Afghanistan, the insurgents reactivated the crisis by launching fresh assaults along the Tajik-Afghan frontier. In April, they attacked a Russian military post near Khorog. Yeltsin retaliated by providing the Moscow-based border guard chief, General Andrei Nikolayev, with more Russian troops and aircraft to decimate the Tajik rebels. They failed to do so.[42]

At home, Russia's military began battling highly motivated Islamist insurgents in the Russian Federation's mountainous Chechnya region in December with no quick victory in sight. This led Yeltsin to rethink his policy of helping the Rahmanov government to crush Islamist rebels in Tajikistan, 1,500 kilometers (900 miles) from the Russian border. So Yeltsin pressured Rahmanov to soften his stance and establish lines of communication with his chief adversary, Said Abdullah Nuri, leader of the United Tajik Opposition. Rahmanov made a dramatic offer to meet Nuri in Kabul, and Nuri agreed. Meeting in mid-May, they hammered out a memorandum of understanding, which mentioned discussing amendments to the constitution.

During 1996, while low-level civil war continued in Tajikistan, with the Islamists recapturing some towns in the south, the government and the UTO conducted a series of meetings in different capitals to work out a comprehensive peace plan centered around the creation of a national reconciliation council. These talks acquired urgency in September when the Taliban,

made up of ethnic Pashtuns, captured Kabul, defeating the incumbent government led by President Burhanuddin Rabbani, an ethnic Tajik and leader
of the Northern Alliance, a coalition of the anti-Taliban groups.

Flushed by their most notable military victory, several Taliban field com-
manders talked openly of extending their jihad to the countries in Central
Asia, which they believed were still ruled by Communists. This made
Central Asian leaders edgy. It also led Rahmanov and Nuri to meet in Khos
Deh in the Tajik-dominated region of northern Afghanistan, in December.
They concurred on a cease-fire and specified July 1, 1997, as the deadline
for an agreement on a permanent peace settlement.

By now it had dawned upon Rahmanov that his ultimate power base,
Kulyab, was much too narrow for him to rule the republic effectively.
Concerned primarily with the future of the IRP, the backbone of the UTO,
Nuri noted the resolve of Presidents Yeltsin and Karimov to marginalize the
Islamist organization by any means, including impoverishing the popula-
tion in the process.

The interests of each of the important foreign players now converged on
ending the conflict in Tajikistan. Karimov concluded that, lacking cohesion,
committed leadership, and broad popular support, the Rahmanov government was incapable of bringing all of Tajikistan under its control. Focused
on blocking the Taliban's further rise in Afghanistan, Iran was keen to have
a peaceful Tajikistan so it could continue arming the anti-Taliban militia
loyal to Masoud in northern Afghanistan. The Kremlin shared Tehran's aim
of saving the Tajik- and Uzbek-dominated northern and northwestern
Afghanistan from being captured by the Taliban. It also wanted to curtail
its commitments to safeguarding its eastern and southern frontiers in order
to focus more on its western border—due to the Western nations' resolve to
extend their sixteen-member North Atlantic Treaty Organization eastward
in Europe.

Meeting in the eastern Iranian city of Mashhad in February 1997, the
warring Tajik sides signed an agreement on the composition of the National
Reconciliation Commission (NRC), which would have an equal number of
representatives of the government and the UTO, and Nuri as its chairman.
This was to be the first move in giving the UTO 30 percent of the posts in
the cabinet and the top civil bureaucracy. Then came an accord on merging
the regular army and the UTO's 5,500-strong Islamic Movement Army.

On May 17, 1997, Rahmanov and Nuri finally signed a document in
Bishkek that formally ended the five-year-old civil war in Tajikistan.[43] On
balance, more concessions came from the governmental side than from the

opposition. The accord paved the way for the legalization of the opposition parties, and a revival of the multi-party democracy that Tajikistan had enjoyed between the springs of 1990 and 1992, by September. Presidential and parliamentary elections were to be held in 1998 under an amended constitution to be ratified in a referendum. For his part, Nuri had stressed a moderate face of Islamism, reiterating that the IRP was wedded to democratic means to bring about an Islamic state. The UN appointed an independent International Contact Group to oversee the implementation of the peace accord.

All told, the five-year civil war consumed an estimated 60,000 to 100,000 lives, and displaced 730,000 people. And the Tajik government suffered a staggering loss of $7 billion.[44]

TAJIKISTAN TURNS THE PAGE

Once the Tajik parliament had passed the amnesty law for the UTO in August 1997, Nuri returned to Dushanbe and chaired the first session of the twenty-six-member National Reconciliation Commission, charged with monitoring the enforcement of the peace accord.

Contrary to the peace accord, Rahmanov failed to release all political prisoners and allow all UTO exiles in Afghanistan and Iran to return home. He showed no sign of integrating the Islamic Movement Army into the regular military, nor did he form a transitional national unity government including the UTO.

It was only when UTO members boycotted the NRC in January 1998 and the Russian, Iranian, and UN envoys pressured Rahmanov that he relented. He started appointing UTO leaders as cabinet ministers, and permitted Turajanzade to return from Tehran, and named him first deputy premier in charge of relations with CIS members. Turajanzade narrowed his agenda to seeking permission for religious groups to function as political parties if they agreed to promote their Islamist cause through legal means.

Putting the experiment in peaceful coexistence between secular socialist forces and Islamists to the test caused much nervousness in Dushanbe and neighboring capitals, particularly Tashkent. Karimov, who had declared that an Islamic government in Tajikistan would pose a threat to Uzbekistan, was not reassured by Turajanzade's reiterated commitment to democratic, peaceful means to establish such an entity.[45]

Karimov's fears were inflamed when, in its latest offensive, the Taliban—already controlling four-fifths of Afghanistan—extended its rule to the borders of Turkmenistan in July. Early next month, it seized Mazar-e Sharif in the Uzbek-dominated region, and the border town of Hairatan, facing Termez across the Oxus. The Northern Alliance's loss of an additional three provinces left Tajikistan, Uzbekistan, Russia, and Iran dazed. They had no coherent plan, individually or collectively, to meet the Taliban threat.

Internationally, the situation changed after the bombings of the American embassies in East Africa in August. Besides striking the military training camps in Afghanistan, Washington decided to undermine the Taliban regime by aiding the Northern Alliance. That led to the dispatch of National Security Agency (NSA) technicians (for intercepting all telephone calls in Afghanistan) and CIA agents, first to the Northern Alliance-controlled northern Afghanistan, and then to Tajikistan.

Regionally, the Taliban's dazzling march compelled Rahmanov to strengthen his national unity government by almost doubling the UTO's share of posts in his cabinet to eleven. He realized that only a genuinely bipartisan government in Dushanbe would be able to withstand Taliban pressure. Such a development would also provide succor to the Northern Alliance, which was weakening.

With more and more Islamic Movement Army ranks taking the oath of allegiance to the national unity government, their integration into the regular military was complete before September 26. On that day, amendments to the constitution, including allowing political parties with a religious orientation to register, were put to plebiscite. For once, the result—68 percent for; and 25 percent against—was credible. And the 92 percent voter turnout was impressive. It signified that most people in Tajikistan were ready to put the civil war behind them.

Yet, soon after, Rahmanov faced a challenge from an unexpected quarter. In early November, Mahmoud Khodabardiyev, a former Tajik army colonel, and Abdumalik Abdullajanov, a former Tajik premier—both ethnic Uzbeks—captured Khojand and its airport with the help of some 1,000 insurgents. They demanded that their "Third Force" party be given 40 percent of the seats in a provisional council to act as the ruling body before free and fair elections were held. The term "Third Force" was a code word for the ethnic Uzbeks of Tajikistan, who formed a quarter of the national population, and who had stayed out of the civil war. Rahmanov rushed reinforcements from Dushanbe to the north. More than 300 former Islamic Movement Army fighters joined the battle against the rebels, with another 800 ready to go. After six days of fighting, which claimed over 300 lives, the central forces, aided by the Russian air support, won. Khodabardiyev and Abdullajanov fled to Uzbekistan.

The Karimov government denied involvement. But, addressing the parliament on November 12, Rahmanov said, "The military coup in the north of Tajikistan was a thoroughly planned military aggression and a rough intrusion in the internal affairs of sovereign Tajikistan by Uzbekistan. We have proof that Uzbek President Islam Karimov completely supports the organizer of the Tajik mutiny, former Prime Minster Abdumalik Abdullajanov."[46]

Reflecting the new mood of national unity, the Tajik parliament legalized the Islamic Renaissance Party in line with the recently amended constitution. This provided the IRP an opportunity to challenge the recently established People's Democratic Party of Tajikistan (PDPT), led by Rahmanov, in the presidential election a year later. But, surprisingly, Turajanzade opposed the idea of the IRP challenging Rahmanov at the polls. This split the IRP, with the hardliners defecting to the Islamic Movement of Uzbekistan, which maintained a base in the Tavil Dara Valley and had its headquarters in Mazar-e Sharif, Afghanistan. Moreover, short of money due to the prevailing poverty, IRP activists could no longer run the madrassas they had opened earlier, often with foreign funds. So they lost an important source of strength in rural areas.

"As I traveled through the Karategin and Tavil Dara [once the headquarters for the IRP military] Valleys . . . there were few active madrassas or overt attempts at Islamic education in the valleys, and local mullahs had gone back to their mosques and farms," reported Ahmed Rashid. "Young people stopped attending prayers at mosques, which were now filled only with old men, as they had been during the Soviet era. The young had left home to look for work or spent their free time learning martial arts or watching videos. Education was once again secular rather than Islamic."[47]

Recovering from the disastrous impact of the civil war, citizens were more inclined to revert to the lifestyle they had known during the stable years of the Soviet rule. The drive for a radical departure from the earlier era was practically gone. Sensing a change in popular mood, Rahmanov tried to advance the Tajik nationalist theme by stressing the Zoroastrian heritage of the Tajik people. He claimed that Zoroaster, born in the Balkh region of ancient Bactria in the thirteenth century BC, was an ethnic Tajik. By thus linking Zoroastrianism—the faith of Achaemenid royals, and later the state religion of the Sassanids of Persia until their overthrow by the Arabs in 637—with Tajikistan, Rahmanov aimed to weaken further the IRP's appeal.

As it was, the electoral chances of the IRP rival, Davlat Usman, were none too bright. Yet, Usman's derisory 2 percent of the vote, compared with Rahmanov's 97 percent, in the November 1999 poll beggared belief. Equally incredible was the official claim of a 96 percent voter turnout. Noting the heavily pro-government bias in the media during the run-up to the election, the Organization for Security and Cooperation in Europe did not send observers to Tajikistan. The Eureopean Union described the election as incompatible with democratic principles and values. And the New York-based Human Rights Watch accused the Tajik authorities of "extensive and egregious violations" during the campaign.

The Rahmanov government ignored such criticism. It gave a repeat performance at the February to March 2002 elections for the bicameral parliament: the popularly elected sixty-three-member Assembly of Representatives, and the indirectly elected thirty-three-member National Council. The local councils were authorized to nominate candidates to the National Council, with the five regions electing five members each to the national body. The remaining eight seats were to be nominated.

The Central Election Commission's statement that 87.3 percent of 2.8 million voters had cast their ballots by 6 p.m. on February 27, 2000, aroused widespread suspicion of fraud. Abdullah Nuri charged that CEC officials allowed ballot-box stuffing, interference from PDPT leaders, and non-transparent tabulation of the ballots. "This was a clear violation of the protocol on parliamentary elections that President Rahmanov co-signed with me last November," he added.[48]

The final results after the second round in March showed the IRP securing only two seats in the Assembly of Representatives, with the Communist Party gaining thirteen, and the PDPT thirty. The IRP's dismal electoral performance encouraged its radical defectors in the IMU to intensify their destablizing activities in the spring and summer, with the IMU's military leader striking targets in Kyrgyzstan and Uzbekistan.[49] They were also heartened to hear that Taloqan, the headquarters of Masoud, fell to the Taliban in September. On the other side, following their meeting in Dushanbe, Rahmanov, Russia's Defense Minister Igor Sergeyev, and Iran's Foreign Minister Kamal Kharrazi together pledged enhanced backing to Masoud.

In Washington, the incoming George W. Bush administration decided to ratchet up pressure on the Taliban. During his first visit to Dushanbe in May 2001, General Tommy Franks, combatant commander of CENTCOM, described Tajikistan as "a strategically significant country," which needed to be strengthened. He promised U.S. military aid against the backdrop of the plans being forged in Washington to bring about the downfall of the Taliban regime.

The United States already had its military, CIA, and NSA personnel in Tajikistan, where they had been aiding Masoud's Northern Alliance now operating from Dushanbe.[50] By July, Washington's plan to move against the Taliban was almost ready, and a warning was issued to Pakistan to curb the Taliban—which had been created by Islamabad six years earlier, and which had provided haven to Al Qaeda's leader, Osama bin Laden.

THE POST-9/11 PERIOD

Having decided to mount a war on terror after the 9/11 attacks, Bush acted swiftly to co-opt Russian President Vladimir Putin, and fortify the security and intelligence links that Washington had established earlier with Uzbekistan and Tajikistan, which had special relationships with Russia. The Kremlin, which had upgraded its surveillance equipment along the Tajik-Afghan border, offered to sell the Pentagon its intelligence gathered at its fiber-optic spy station. Russia's Defense Minister Sergei Ivanov held out the prospect of the United States using Dushanbe airport, guarded by Russian-dominated CIS troops.

Once Putin had given his clearance on direct contacts between Washington and Central Asian capitals, there was a flurry of telephone conversations between Bush and Rahmanov. On September 22, Rahmanov offered Bush his government's assistance in the latter's war on terror. But it was only after the Pentagon had mounted its campaign against the Taliban on October 7 that the Tajik government confirmed it had allowed the U.S. passage through its airspace and use of its airbases. What it did not say was that, in return, it had gained increased financial aid from the White House. The upgrading of the Dushanbe and Kulyab airfields by the Pentagon followed.

This smoothed the way for Tajikistan to sign NATO's Partnership for Peace (PFP) program in February 2002. It was the last Central Asian state to do so. Washington's aid to Dushanbe shot up to $141 million, amounting to more than a third of its national budget. Both the United States and the International Monetary Fund had approved of the introduction of the local currency, the somoni—named after Ismail Samani (spelled Ismoil Somoni)—in October 2000, with the official exchange rate being 2.2 sominis to 1 U.S. dollar. It heralded the beginning of private banking in Tajikistan.[51]

By then, the Pentagon had two hundred uniformed personnel operating from the Kulyab airbase.

Soon after the first anniversary of the fall of the Taliban on December 8, 2001, Rahmanov appeared at the White House, and became the last Central Asian leader to do so. The joint statement by him and Bush promised reinforcement of strategic ties. This involved maintaining military cooperation, which included, among other things, the Pentagon training the Tajik security forces in counterterrorism.

The installation of the Tajik-dominated Northern Alliance in Kabul eased the onerous task of guarding the Tajik-Afghan border, and improved the prospect of the Russian forces handing the job over to the Tajik troops. And with Rahmanov firmly on the same side as Karimov in the U.S.-led war on terror, the tense relations between Tajikistan and Uzbekistan eased.

At home, emulating Karimov, Rahmanov took advantage of the heightened apprehension and distrust caused by 9/11 to suppress legal opposition, particularly of the Islamist hue. His government began hinting of links between the IRP, the IMU, and Hizb ut-Tahrir without offering any evidence. In the spring and summer of 2003, it arrested several leading IRP members, including the party's deputy chairman, Shamsuddin Shamsuddinov, and charged them with offenses ranging from murder and crossing the Tajik border illegally to polygamy and raping underage girls. IRP leaders saw this as a deliberate ploy of the authorities to discredit them as a group and reduce their popular appeal. As a native of the Khojand region, Shamsuddinov was particularly valuable to the southern-dominated IRP. So his conviction and jail sentence of fifteen years was a blow to the party.[52]

Rahmanov coupled his strategy of smothering the Islamic opposition with moves to (a) stress the pre-Islamic history of Tajikistan, and (b) to perpetuate his rule through legal means. To carry out the former, he announced in September 2003 that his government would celebrate 2006—Tajikistan's fifteenth year of independence, and the 2,700th year of the founding of Kulyab—as the "Year of the Aryans." This was in line with the state's overarching policy of emphasizing the pre-Islamic identity of Tajiks, as it had earlier linked Tajiks with Zoroaster. Little wonder that the government named its online news agency, unveiled in March 2004, as Avesta News Agency. Written in the ancient Persian language called Pahlavi, the Avesta is the scripture of Zoroastrianism that flourished in the region then populated by the Aryan tribes.

One of the fifty-six changes in the constitution passed by the parliament allowed the president two consecutive seven-year terms in office "as determined by the government." It then decided to cancel Rahmanov's previous terms of office on the ground that they pertained to the earlier versions of the constitution, and permitted him to contest two seven-year terms beginning 2006.

In the referendum on the amended constitution, held in June 2003, a reported 93 percent, of a turnout of 96 percent, endorsed it. The result was unbelievable because the amendments included the deeply unpopular dele-tion of the state's guarantee of free education and healthcare—a hallmark inherited from the Soviet era—which would result in falling literacy rates and lifespans of citizens. Mahmudruzi Iskandarov—leader of the Demo-cratic Party, former head of the state-owned oil and gas company, Tojikgaz, and constitutional adviser to the president—described the results as "false," saying that no more than 20 percent of eligible voters cast ballots. "The unusually high turnout of 96 percent raises concerns regarding the accura-cy of the reporting of results," said the OSCE.[53]

A year later, ignoring the objections of the opposition parties, the PDPT-dominated parliament amended the electoral law, introducing a $500 fee: "The entry fee [of $500] for a candidate equals 200 times the minimum wage, and bars 80 percent of the population from exercising their right to be elected," said the IRP.[54]

While OSCE and human rights organizations in the West deplored Rahmanov's underhanded methods of undermining democracy, Moscow was far more interested in stability. During his visit to Dushanbe in October 2004, Putin signed an agreement with Rahmanov to set up a Russian mili-tary base in Tajikistan on a forty-nine-year lease. He referred to the Kremlin's "comprehensive approach" in its relations with post-Soviet republics, covering military security and economic aspects. Announcing plans by the Russian state and private companies to invest more than $2 bil-lion in Tajikistan during the next five years, he said, "No one has invested such money in Tajikistan." Rahmanov pointed out that the Russian military in Tajikistan employed thousands of local people.[55]

In the course of a subsequent trip to Dushanbe in July 2005, Putin wrote off a $350 million loan given to the Tajik government in lieu of the control of a satellite surveillance complex in Nurek, and an earlier agreement to grant Russia a permanent military base. The accompanying officials of the conglomerate Russian Aluminum, RUSAL, announced an investment of over $1 billion in aluminum and hydroelectric projects.[56]

THE ECONOMY PERKS UP

After a decade of catastrophic economic downturn in the 1990s, which resulted in the reduction of the GDP by 64 percent, the economy began to grow appreciably from 2000, which registered 8.3 percent expansion. Between 1999 and 2003, the families living below the official poverty line fell from 83 to 68 percent.[57]

The widescale impoverishment had affected women more than men. Their chances of obtaining gainful employment almost evaporated, and they were underpaid for the jobs they held. Their educational opportunities declined as well, as many indigent families in villages sent only their sons to school. The one-to-one ratio of female to male students in colleges during the Soviet times had declined to one-to-three. The practice of polygamy and arranged marriages of underage girls had risen sharply. So, too, had domestic violence. The common, albeit illegal, practice of the father voting for all family members in rural and poor urban areas effectively disenfranchised women. Little wonder that women had less than one-fifth of the seats in the popularly elected lower house of the parliament in 2005.[58]

What aided Tajikistan enormously was the concession it won from Moscow in 2000 for visa-free travel between the two countries. The improvement in the Russian economy due to rising oil and gas prices increased the demand for Central Asian labor. These two factors increased opportunities for Tajiks, who were almost universally literate in Russian, to work (legally and illegally) in Russia. Within a few years, according to unofficial estimates, more than one million Tajiks became migrant workers, obtaining seasonal employment mostly in Russia and earning higher wages than they did at home. Their remittances of $800 million a year were twice the state's annual expenditure.

The overthrow of the Taliban in Afghanistan in late 2001 improved the political-economic climate in the region. More specifically, the Taliban had banned poppy growing in 2000, because drugs are unIslamic, but once the ban was lifted, poppy production rose sharply in Afghanistan, and the narcotics trade, whatever its moral and health hazards, benefited Tajikistan. "Even Tajik officials privately admit that much of Tajikistan's commercial revival is linked to the drug trade, especially in the capital city of Dushanbe," wrote Martha Brill Olcott.[59]

Most of the drugs arriving in Tajikistan were destined for Russia and beyond. The Dushanbe-Moscow train proved to be the easiest and cheapest way to transport the contraband. Soon, the Russian security forces cottoned on to the racket, and the Dushanbe-Moscow train—nicknamed Heroin Express and Narcoechelon—became the prime target of the border control and customs officials. They took to harassing all those who were traveling with a Tajik passport. And the Russian railway authorities often refused to let the Dushanbe-Moscow trains into the Russian Federation on the ground that they were dirty and unsanitary.

In Tajikistan, there was a turnaround in industry as well. The output of TadAZ, the state-owned aluminum factory in Tursunzade—and the third largest in the world, with a production capacity of 517,000 metric tons a year—almost tripled its production to 309,000 metric tons in 2002 from 2001. Accounting for almost half of the country's export income, it employed 13,000 people and supported a community of 100,000.[60]

A majority of Tajiks attributed the economic upturn to Rahmanov, who, in their opinion, had stabilized Tajikistan after a decade of turmoil. Nearly three out of five respondents in a survey by the U.S.-funded International Federation for Electoral Systems (IFES) in 2004 considered him as the most trusted public figure. They found the opposition factions to be deficient in alternative policies, and more interested in attacking one another than in forging an alliance to confront, peacefully, the president and his PDPT.[61]

Despite this, Rahmanov did not slacken his policy of harassing high-profile dissenters, shutting down major opposition publications, and arresting their leading critics. In 2004, the National Association of Mass Media in Tajikistan registered 204 instances of violations of journalists' and media rights.[62]

THE TULIP REVOLUTION REBUFFED

By happenstance, Tajikistan's parliamentary poll took place on the same day—February 27, 2005—as the one in Kyrgyzstan. The well-practiced trickery of vote-rigging enabled election officials to claim 93 percent voter turnout, with the governing PDPT beating its previous record by securing 38 of the 41 constituency seats, and another 17 on the basis of proportional representation. This reduced the shares of the two parties that cleared the 5 percent threshold—the Communists and the IRP—to 4 and 2, respectively.

As before, Western observers described the election as anything but free or fair. The opposition politicians agreed, warning of street protests if their complaints were ignored as before. They took to heart what happened in Kyrgyzstan, where popular protest led to the overthrow of the Akayev government. Rahmanov, meanwhile, was rattled by the Tulip Revolution next door.

Instead of admitting to flaws in the election and seeking compromise with his opponents, Rahmanov used his state of the nation speech on April 16 to reject their complaints. Instead, he focused on the alleged compact between opposition leaders and Western embassies that, he believed, had brought about the peaceful revolutions in Kyrgyzstan, Ukraine, and Georgia. He reiterated the Foreign Ministry's order—issued to block "propaganda"—that foreign diplomats and international organizations' representatives must give it prior notice of contacts with Tajik citizens affiliated with political parties, NGOs, and the press.

Rahmanov's hand was strengthened when state-run newspapers gave front-page prominence to a document showing that the United States provided funds to Akayev's adversaries before the Tulip Revolution on March 24. The two TV channels, both controlled by the government, followed the print media's lead.

In its statement on April 20, the U.S. embassy in Dushanbe described the document as a "crude fabrication," and added, "Such irresponsible 'journalism' is not conducive to promoting regional stability and to building the strong bilateral U.S.-Tajikistan relations that both President Bush and President Rahmanov have called for."[63] By the time the document was proved to be fake, the damage to Tajik-American relations had been done.

To reiterate its hard-line policy, the Tajik government revealed on April 27 that Mahmudruzi Iskandarov, leader of the Democratic Party, was being detained in Dushanbe, charged with engaging in subversive activities. So, for most people, it was business as unusual—top politicians, government bureaucrats, and managers of state-owned enterprises all bent on lining their pockets, engaged in a game of snakes and ladders. The people merely shrugged their shoulders and carried on their daily business, if they had any.

Had the official statement referred to the arrest of some high-ranking police officer or director of a large public-sector factory, charged with corruption, the popular response would have been different.

THE SCOURGE OF CORRUPTION

An IFES poll in 2004 showed that 56 percent of Tajiks regarded the government's anti-corruption measures "most unsatisfactory." Corruption was so endemic that Tajikistan ranked 142nd out of 163 countries in Transparency International's 2006 Corruption Perceptions Index with a score of 2.2 on a scale from 0 ("highly corrupt") to 10 ("highly clean")—on a par with war-torn Somalia and Sudan.[64]

Since civil servants were grossly underpaid, they were tempted to demand and accept graft. It became common practice to bribe hospital staff to get a bed, teachers to get a pass on an examination, and police to be spared a trial or a penalty. And politicians in power sold important administrative jobs to the highest bidder. According to a 2004 survey, 98 percent of Tajik businessmen claimed to have bribed state officials. "Those engaged in construction, the service industry, and retail trade generally keep two sets of books to hide employees and revenues from government inspectors," observed Martha Brill Olcott. "Because of its civil war, the Tajik government has been more vulnerable to the pressures of patronage than elsewhere, making officials very wary of privatization."[65]

Allegation of large-scale embezzlement of public funds pertained to exports of aluminum and cotton, accounting for four-fifths of all exports. During 2005, aluminum brought in revenues of over $600 million and cotton fiber nearly $160 million. After dismissing TadAZ's director, Abduqodir Ermatov, in December 2004, the government revealed that the aluminum factory had incurred $160 million in debt in a decade, and that Ermatov had been charged with embezzlement of funds, and ordered not to leave the country. Yet he managed to escape to Britain.[66]

In 2005, more than three-quarters of the global supply of heroin originated in Afghanistan, where 4,000 tons of opium poppies were grown. The takeover of the guard duties along the Tajik-Afghan border by Tajiks from Russians had left 50 kilometers (30 miles) on the Tajik side and 100 kilometers (60 miles) on the Afghan side unguarded. The poorly paid Tajik guards were tempted to take bribes. So the narcotics business thrived, and with it corruption.

In a major speech in December 2004, Rahmanov himself listed corruption as a major domestic threat, along with Islamic extremism, organized crime, and the narcotics trade. Yet, to the discredit of his government, an anti-corruption law passed in 1999 had remained largely unimplemented. Every so often, a case against a highly corrupt official was given much publicity to reassure the increasingly cynical public.

Since drug trafficking was of grave concern to the European Union and the United States, they provided technical and financial aid to Tajikistan to help guard its southern border. At the same time, the Pentagon was keen to maintain its facilities at the Kulyab airport. The subject came up in July 2005, when the Shanghai Cooperation Organization summit concluded that, due to the improved socio-political environment in Afghanistan, there was no need for the United States to keep support bases in Uzbekistan and Kyrgyzstan. Although the SCO did not mention Tajikistan in its statement, U.S. Defense Secretary Donald Rumsfeld visited Dushanbe in late July and declared America and Tajikistan as "solid partners in the global struggle against extremism." Sharing the sentiment, Rahmanov said that the Pentagon could maintain bases in Tajikistan as long as it needed to.[67]

RAHMANOV REBRANDS TAJIKISTAN

During the run-up to the presidential poll in early November 2006, the week-long celebrations in September, to mark the country's fifteenth independence anniversary and 2,700th year of the founding of Kulyab as part of the Year of the Aryans, favored Rahmaonv's candidacy. IRP leaders saw this as a ploy to boost Rahmanov's electoral chances, but could do nothing but wring their hands.

The celebrations opened on September 7 with a military march at the Samani Square, which was dominated by the towering statue of Ismail Samani, the founder of the ninth-century Samani kingdom of Bukhara, on a vast, terraced plinth and framed by a gigantic arch of pink-and-white stone. The several cultural programs that followed alluded to the pre-Islamic civilization of the Tajiks and their Aryan antecedents. It was pointed out that their territory—known in ancient times as Sogd (or Sogdiana) and Tukhara (or Tukharistan), including Bactria—was the homeland of the ancient race of Aryans, and that from there the Aryans tribes fanned out to several regions of Eurasia, stretching from Germany to the Indian subcontinent.

The immediate political impact of revisiting this ancient history was to de-emphasize the importance of Islam and the Islamic Renaissance Party in the upcoming election. As it was, Rahmanov had ensured that any serious challenger to his bid for the presidency was either in jail or exile. In protest, the IRP and the Democratic Party boycotted the poll, arguing that the election was invalid because the electoral law was passed before the adoption of the amended constitution in November 1994.

With five other candidates in the race, who received scant exposure in the state-run media, Rahmanov could claim it was a multi-candidate contest. Each of them had to produce signatures of at least 5 percent of the eligible voters to be allowed to run. The electoral officials' claim that they had jointly secured 1.5 million signatures (three times the minimum required), nearly half of the total electorate, stretched credulity. By late morning on November 6, election day, 70 to 90 percent had voted at many polling stations in the capital. Rahmanov rode to victory with 79 percent of the vote, while his nearest rival scored only 6 percent. Having thus consolidated his political-administrative power, Rahmanov followed the footsteps of Niyazov, and refurbished the ethnic identity of Tajiks.

On March 21, 2007, marking the first day of spring and Nowruz, the New Year of Tajik-Persian-Kurdish speakers, the president announced the change of his surname change to "Rahman" (literally, "Merciful"). "We should return to our cultural roots and use our national naming systems," he said to a group of intellectuals during a televised meeting. He then ordered "appropriate authorities" to introduce "a Tajik pattern of naming newborn children."[68]

To reduce social tensions created by a widening gap between the tiny, rich minority and the overwhelming, poor majority, which would likely bolster opposition, he banned students from arriving at school by car, using mobile phones at school, and throwing lavish graduation parties. "We want to comprehensively support and revive our national traditions from the scientific and historical points of view," Rahmanov said. "We should refuse all those customs . . . that harm the development level of the state and [hinder] the improvement of people's living standards and their welfare."

In an anti-Islamic campaign, modeled along Karimov's in Uzbekistan, his government banned headscarves in schools, imposed official examinations on clerics, and closed hundreds of "unauthorized" mosques. Within two summer months of 2007, the authorities in Dushanbe—its population being nearly 600,000—shut 300 mosques, leaving only 57 intact, with the sites of the closed places of worship transformed into beauty salons, public baths, community centers, or police stations. This was a repeat of the pattern set in Soviet times.[69]

Only registered mosques were to be allowed to function. But before applying for registration, the cleric had to get permission from twelve different agencies, ranging from the police to the fire department to environmental authorities. "People in those agencies get suspicious and nervous as soon as you mention 'mosque registration,'" said Kalandar Sadriddinov, a cleric in Kurgan-Tyube. It took him more than seven months to register his mosque.[70]

From 2005 onward, an average of one bomb a month blast racked Dushanbe, causing far more structural damage than bodily harm. No organization claimed responsibility. And by calling the perpetrators either hooligans or members of the banned IMU or Hizb ur-Tahrir, without producing any evidence, the authorities left the field open to speculation—which ranged widely to include Islamist extremists, drugs lords, disenchanted oppositionists, and "rogue" government officials.

"As a possible scenario, one can assume that some Islam-related members of the opposition, wanting to demonstrate that they are still alive, are behind this [the bombing]," said Alexei Malashenko of the Carnegie Center in Moscow, commenting on the bomb blast in November 2007 near the presidential palace in Dushanbe. "On the other hand, any authoritarian ruler needs an external threat. It's always nice when there is an insidious enemy from without."[71] In other words, it was an effective way to keep the people in a state of fear and suspicion, and it enabled the government to slow down an advance toward democracy and human rights.

For diverse reasons, the Bush administration had come to widen its focus on the region, treating democratization and respect for human rights on a par with such other objectives as broadening cooperation on military affairs, combating terrorism and the drug trade, expanding commercial links, upgrading the transportation system in the region—and, of course, gaining access to hydrocarbons.

As it happened, the United States' major rival, Iran, had all along shunned ideological approaches to Central Asian republics, concentrating on strengthening economic and cultural ties. From that perspective, Tajikistan had emerged as the most suitable candidate to be cultivated by Tehran.

CHAPTER 7

IRAN:
The Geopolitics of the Islamic Revolution

I RAN, HISTORIC OR CONTEMPORARY, IS UNIQUE. IT WAS ONE OF THE TWO Muslim countries that was not colonized by a European power, the other being Afghanistan. In more recent times, the Iranian regime has provided a template of how to transform a secular state into a religious one. Another distinguishing feature is that nearly 90 percent of Iran's 72 million citizens are Shiite, the highest figure among the four Shiite-majority countries, the others being Azerbaijan, Bahrain, and Iraq. But it was not always so.

Before the Safavid rule (1501–1722), Iran was a largely Sunni society. The founder of that dynasty, Shah Ismail, born in the Azeri-speaking part of present-day Iran, adopted Twelver Shiite doctrine as the state religion to differentiate his realm and subjects from the competing Sunni Ottoman Turks, who were intent on incorporating Iran into their empire. Keen to spread his sect, Shah Ismail ordered all preachers to lead Friday prayers in the name of the Twelve Imams of Shiite Islam,[1] and curse the first three Sunni caliphs—Abu Bakr, Umar ibn Khattab, and Uthman ibn Affan—for usurping the rightful place of Imam Ali ibn Abi Talib, a son-in-law of Prophet Muhammad. The resulting theological affirmation and sharpening of his confrontation with the Sunni Ottomans helped Shah Ismail to consolidate his realm.

To reduce the intersectarian gap, Nadir Shah Afshar (1736–47) banned public cursing of the first three caliphs. He renamed Shiite Islam as the Jaafari school after Imam Jaafar al Sadiq, the sixth imam and the main codifier of the Shiite jurisprudence. But his steps proved inadequate to blur the acute sectarian divide. The differences spanned doctrine, ritual, law, theology, and religious organization.

Unlike Shiites, Sunnis regard caliphs as fallible interpreters of the Quran and the Hadiths (Sayings and Deeds of Prophet Muhammad), collectively called the Sharia, as Islamic law. Shiites insist that the ruler must be just and refer to the appropriate verses in the Quran. Conversely, say Shiite clerics, if the ruler is unjust, he must be overthrown. They argue that the Quran bears a pledge of sovereignty of the earth to the oppressed. Rooted in this promise are the concepts of the return of the (Twelfth) Hidden Imam—the arrival of the Mahdi (the Messiah)—and the rehabilitation of society. In short, according to Shiites, Islamic history is moving toward a fixed goal— against the forces of injustice. This belief acts as a spur towards radical activism. In contrast, Sunnis view Islamic history essentially as a drift away from the ideal *umma* (Islamic community), which existed under the rule of the four Rightly Guided Caliphs, including Caliph Imam Ali.

Sunnis and Shiites differ on how to organize religion and religious activities. Sunnis regard religious activities as the exclusive domain of the (Muslim) state. When clerics act as judges, preachers, or educators, they do so under the aegis of the state. There is no role for Sunni clerics to organize religion on their own—even in present-day Turkey under its secular constitution. This is not the case among Shiites, as a study of Iran amply shows. Also, the Shiite religious establishment is hierarchical, starting with the *mullah* (a learned man), and rising to *thiqatalislam* (trust of Islam), *hojatalislam* (proof of Islam), *ayatollah* (sign of Allah), *ayatollah ozma* (grand sign of Allah), and *marja-e taqlid* (source of emulation).[2]

During the rule of the Qajars (1790–1921), clerics administered vast religious endowments, *waqfs*, and received 10 percent of the income as commission. Since they were regarded as trustees of the Hidden Imam, they also collected Islamic taxes—*khums* and zakat. Though *khums* ("one-fifth" in Arabic) was originally one-fifth of the booty that the believers took from the conquered nonbelievers, to be handed over to the ruler of the Islamic umma, Shiites interpreted it as a general income tax to be paid to clerics. The clergy used these funds to run educational, social, and charitable institutions. They conducted Sharia courts, which dealt with personal and family matters. To enforce court decisions, they resorted to deploying private armies composed of their religious students and the fugitives they had sheltered. The clergy enjoyed higher esteem among believers than the local Friday prayer-leaders or judges appointed by the monarch to deal with crimes according to the customary law.

Moreover, the clergy felt uniquely independent since their superiors, living in the holy cities of Najaf and Karbala in Iraq, were outside the jurisdiction of the Qajars. Parallel to this ran the concept of religious sanctuary, *bast*. Since the clergy claimed that mosques, religious shrines, and their homes were in principle territories of the Hidden Imam, the Qajar government had no right to enter them. So, these places came to provide sanctuary to all sorts of fugitives. More importantly, this tradition turned mosques into centers of opposition to unjust Iranian monarchs.

During the Qajar period, the *mujtahids* (senior clerics who practice interpretative reasoning in applying the Sharia) took to naming the most revered colleague as the *marja-e mutalaq* (absolute source), whose guidance they agreed to accept. Overall, these developments gave the clergy much muscle—political, spiritual, and ideological—and helped to make their teachings coherent and spawn unity among them. Curiously, the practice of choosing the *marja-e mutalaq* without the interference of the state, and the presence of senior clerical leadership outside Iran, led the Iranian society to develop a mosque-state divide along the lines seen earlier in Christian Europe. This was unlike the situation in Sunni countries.

An independent socio-economic base gave mullahs the potential for independent action. They protested against the erosion of Islamic tradition in society and the economic penetration of Iran by European powers, particularly Britain and Tsarist Russia. The 1892 Tobacco Protest was a good example. The clergy allied with secular intellectuals and nationalists to protest against the concession given to Britain by Nasiruddin Shah (1848–96) for a monopoly over the production and sale of tobacco. Facing popular pressure, the Shah withdrew the concession. This episode was a forerunner of something bigger: the Constitutional Revolution.

THE CONSTITUTIONAL REVOLUTION, 1907–11

The constitutional movement was backed by the propertied classes as well as religious and intellectual leaders. The former, consisting of landowners, administrators, merchants, and artisans, wanted Iran to be free of European domination, to develop their own potential, unfettered by the Shah's practice of giving economic concessions to Europeans. Religious luminaries felt, rightly, that a reduction in the royal authority would increase their power in manipulating tribal chiefs, feudal aristocrats, and mullahs.

Though the clergy formed a majority in the assembly convened in October 1906 to produce a constitution, they failed to act as a bloc. Untrained in political theory, they did not have a constitutional model in mind. On the crucial question of sovereignty, radical clerics argued that since it had been delegated by Allah to the Hidden Imam, and then on to mujtahids, it did not rest with the people. Their view was opposed by moderate clerics and secular constitutionalists, who won. "Sovereignty is a trust confided (as a Divine gift) by the People to the person of the King," stated Article 55. The final document, Fundamental Laws, modeled on the Belgian constitution, was a compromise between the moderate and radical camps. With certain modifications, this constitution remained in force until the 1979 revolution.

It was framed within an Islamic context. Article 1 declared Jaafari or Twelver Shiite Islam to be the state religion. Only a Jaafari Shiite could become the king, a minister, or a judge. Article 27 confirmed the right of Sharia courts to exist. Article 39 enjoined upon the monarch to "promote the Jaafari doctrine" and "to seek the help of the holy spirits of the Saints of Islam to render service to the advancement of Iran."

In practice, neither the Qajars nor the succeeding Pahlavis implemented this article. Indeed, the last Pahlavi ruler, Muhammad Reza Shah (1941–79), had become so secular that in his vast palace in Tehran there was not a single image of Islam such as the Kaaba, the holiest shrine of Islam in Mecca, or even the sign of "Allah" in Arabic or Persian.

In 1907 came the longer Supplementary Fundamental Laws, which specified a bill of rights for citizens and a parliamentary form of government in which power was concentrated in the legislature at the expense of the executive. Significantly, Article 2 specified that no bill passed by the Majlis (parliament) was valid until a committee of five mujtahids—elected by the Majlis from a list of twenty submitted by the clergy—had judged it to be in conformity with Islam. That is, while the mujtahids' committee possessed veto power, it was not a creative body in its own right as the radical clergy had wanted. In practice, however, this article was never implemented. The Qajars ignored it, and so did their successors, the Pahlavis.

In 1909, Muhammad Ali Shah mounted a royalist counterrevolution against the 1906–7 constitution. This was foiled, and the ruler was forced to abdicate in favor of his twelve-year-old son, Ahmed. But in order to forestall the occupation of Tehran by Russian troops at the behest of the Tsar, who wanted the constitution abrogated, the regent dissolved the Majlis in November 1911. This marked the end of clerical involvement in politics and the Constitutional Revolution, but not of the constitution itself.

THE PAHLAVIS' MODERNITY DRIVE

Disregarding Tehran's neutrality in World War I, the forces of Tsarist Russia and Britain invaded and occupied Iran. After the Bolshevik

Revolution in Russia in October 1917, the Russians withdrew. The revolution deprived the Iranian ruler of his major foreign patron, the tsar. Two years later, Britain foisted a treaty on the Iranian regime which reduced Iran to a virtual protectorate of London. But, reflecting the popular mood, the Majlis refused to ratify it.

Iran was by now an important oil-producing state, with British capital and expertise playing a leading role. Britain thought it essential to have a strong administration in Iran to facilitate oil extraction. It instigated Colonel Reza Khan of the Cossack Brigade (originally established by the Russian High Command as the palace guard for the Shah) to depose the current government and install himself as war minister. Having done so in February 1921, Reza Khan consolidated his position by suppressing internal rebellions. He cultivated the clerical leadership, which supported his deposition of the Qajar ruler, Ahmad Shah, in December 1925. Four months later, he crowned himself king. Later, he acquired the surname Pahlavi, after the ancient Iranian language.

After ascending the throne and consolidating his power as head of the military, a secular power center, Reza Pahlavi Shah started curtailing clerical authority. He brought the Sharia courts under government control, and then reduced their powers. Emulating the dress code decreed by Mustafa Kemal Ataturk in Turkey in 1925, he required—by a law passed in 1928—all males to wear Western-style dress and a round, peaked cap. The 1934 Law of Religious Endowments increased the power of the endowments department of the education ministry at the expense of the clergy. In 1935, he surpassed Kemal Ataturk by outlawing the veil—particularly the chador, an all-embracing shroud commonly worn by Iranian women. The clergy opposed this vehemently since the veil, to them, is sanctified by the Quran, but Reza Shah ignored their protest. He then passed a decree requiring all men to replace round, peaked caps with European felt hats. He also rigged parliamentary elections, creating a dramatic result: whereas in the Sixth Majlis (1926–8) 40 percent of the deputies were clerics, in the Eleventh Majlis (1936–8) there was not a single well-known mullah.

The cumulative effect of these changes was to divide society between the religious masses and the secular elite. "The upper and new middle classes became increasingly Westernized and scarcely understood the traditional or religious culture of their patriots," noted Nikki R. Keddie, an American specialist on Iran. "On the other hand, peasants and urban bazaar classes continued to follow the ulema [clergy], however politically cowed the ulema were. These classes associated 'the way things should be' more with Islam than with the West."[3]

When Reza Shah was forced by the British and Soviet forces to abdicate in favor of his twenty-three-year-old son, Muhammad Reza, in September 1941, the clergy were among those who celebrated his departure. They had endured fifteen years of relentless pressure from the Shah, who had considerably reduced their power and prestige.

Muhammad Reza Pahlavi Shah was too young and inexperienced to rule autocratically even if he wanted to. His kingdom was occupied by the Soviet Union and Britain, and his government beset with acute problems stemming from World War II. He therefore tried to win the sympathy of clerics, who were in daily touch with the masses.

So long as Ayatollah Muhammad Hussein Borujerdi—a moderate who urged clerics to keep away from politics—was the country's most senior mullah, the Shah had little problem with the mosque. But, in the leadership vacuum that followed Borujerdi's death in 1960, a comparatively junior cleric, Ruhollah Khomeini, a radical who considered religion and politics as two sides of the same coin, came to the fore. He publicly challenged the Shah in June 1963, and was exiled.

THE RISE OF THE AYATOLLAH

After spending a year in Bursa, an Islamic center in western Turkey, Khomeini moved to Najaf, Iraq, the burial place of Imam Ali and a center of Shiite learning, which was visited by thousands of Shiite Iranian pilgrims. He stoked an anti-Shah movement which grew slowly and culminated in a tidal wave. The revolutionary process passed through several steadily rising stages over a two-year period, from February 1977 to February 11, 1979, which marked the end of the Pahlavi era.

Khomeini had the shrewdness and charisma to unite disparate forces in the revolutionary movement behind the most radical demand: abolition of the monarchy. He kept the alliance together during a highly turbulent period by championing the cause of each of the groups in the anti-Shah coalition; and by maintaining a studied silence on such controversial issues as democracy, agrarian reform, the clergy's role in the future republic, and the status of women.

He aroused hopes of deliverance and improvement in different strata of society. The traditional middle class of artisans, merchants, and better-off farmers saw in Khomeini an upholder of private property, a partisan of the bazaar, and a believer in Islamic values. The modern middle class of professionals, businessmen, and industrialists regarded him as a radical nationalist wedded to the program of ending royal dictatorship and foreign influence in Iran. The urban working class backed Khomeini because of his repeated commitment to social justice, which, it felt, could be achieved only by transferring power and wealth from the affluent to the needy. Finally, the rural poor saw the Ayatollah as their savior: the one to provide them with arable land, irrigation facilities, roads, schools, and electricity.

Unlike the earlier secular revolutions—from the French Revolution in 1789 to the Russia Revolution in 1917—the popular upsurge in Iran was rooted in religion, more specifically in Shiite Islam. Aware of the deep religiosity of the Iranian public, Khomeini turned religion into an instrument of revolution, a novel strategy which succeeded. For instance, he made use of the Islamic custom of mourning the dead for forty days, with a remembrance ceremony on the last day. In defiance of the ban on public gatherings, he called for demonstrations on the fortieth day following the anniversaries of the deaths of those killed by the Shah's security forces on earlier occasions. With this, each successive demonstration became larger than the one before, and boosted the anti-Shah movement.

The month of Ramadan, when religious fervor runs high even in normal times, raised the tempo of the revolutionary crusade, when activists met in mosques to break the fast after sunset and plan further actions. Khomeini succeeded in transforming the traditional Ashura (10th of Muharram, the day Imam Hussein was killed) processions, the high point of the Shiite calendar, into demonstrations for the revolution. Aided by the reenactment of the passion plays of the early days of Islam, he created a revolutionary play of modern times.

Khomeini's other remarkable contribution was to devise and implement an original strategy to neutralize the Shah's 440,000-strong military. He pioneered the concept of a "moral attack" on the army. "We must fight from within the soldiers' hearts," he said. "Face the soldier with a flower. Fight through martyrdom, because the martyr is the essence of history. Let the army kill as many as it wants until the soldiers are shaken to their hearts by the massacres they have committed. Then the army will collapse, and you will have disarmed the army."[4] His advice chimed with the martyr complex that is embedded in the psyche of Shiite Iranians. At the same time Khomeini tried to dissuade soldiers from firing by warning them that shooting their brothers and sisters "is just as though you are firing at the Quran." Since these words came from a grand ayatollah, a *marja-e taqlid* (source of emulation), and since most of the troops were Shiite, they were effective.

In short, since Khomeini devised a revolutionary strategy that stemmed from Shiite Iran's specific religious-cultural ambience, most Iranians adopted it willingly and used it effectively. Of course, the mosque played a crucial role in the revolution, both as an institution and as a place of prayer and congregation. Its inviolability by the government made it uniquely qualified as the operating venue of the revolutionaries. Khomeini knew this and made maximum use of it. Operating now from a Paris suburb, he urged the clergy to base local Revolutionary Komitehs (Committees) in mosques. He thus spawned an institution that proved invaluable during the last, critical months of the revolutionary movement.

Of all the revolutionary bodies that sprouted during the final stages of the anti-Shah movement, the Revolutionary Komitehs proved to be the most broad-based and effective. They took over administrative and police powers when the Shah departed on January 16, 1979, and consolidated their hold once Khomeini had overthrown the Shah's appointee, Prime Minister Shahpour Bakhtiar, on February 11.

ISLAMIZATION OF STATE AND SOCIETY

On his return home from exile, Khomeini lost no time in dismantling the secular state he had inherited, and installing an Islamic one. He drew his own authority from the seventeen-point charter adopted by acclamation by the two-million-strong rally in Tehran on Ashura, December 11, 1978, which called for an end to monarchy, acceptance of Khomeini as the leader, and the establishment of an Islamic government.

A popular referendum in March, based on universal adult franchise, opted overwhelmingly for an Islamic republic. In early August, voters were given the opportunity to elect a seventy-three member Assembly of Experts, including three representatives of religious minorities—Christians, Jews, and Zoroastrians. The recognized communities were allowed to follow their religious laws regarding marriage, divorce, and inheritance—and drinking alcohol, as long as it was done inside their homes.

Zoroastrians were the longest-lasting religious group in Iran, with a history dating back to the early thirteenth century BC. Patronized by the Achaemenid dynasty of Persia, Zoroastrianism became the state religion under the Sassanians (224–637). Following the Arab overthrow of the Sassanians, most Zoroastrians either converted to Islam or migrated to faraway places like the western coast of India. Yet the Zoroastrian legacy continues in Iran, and is reflected in the grand scale on which Iranians celebrate Nawruz, the New Year staring on the Spring Equinox, a ten-day holiday. In the late 1970s, the Zoroastrian community was about 40,000 strong, concentrated mainly in Tehran and the central Iranian city of Yazd, which boasted a finely built fire temple fronted by an elliptical pool of water in a marble-lined tank.

With an estimated size of a quarter million, the Armenian community was the largest religious minority. Intermarriage between Armenians and Persians went back to antiquity when they shared Zoroastrianism as their religion. It was only when Armenians embraced Christianity in 301 that relations soured. And the conversion of Persians to Islam in the seventh century increased the divide between the two communities. The Seljuk conquest of Armenia in the eleventh century led to the migration of Armenians to northwest Iran where they made their living as traders or artisans. In the late sixteenth century, Shah Abbas relocated many of the Armenian artisans to help him build up Isfahan as the new capital. When the Qajars moved the capital to Tehran in 1790, many Armenians followed. Today, their marble-faced St. Sarkis Church in central Tehran stands out.

Armenians were one part of the Christian community, the other being Assyrians, also called Assyro-Chaldeans. Like Armenians, Assyrians were initially concentrated in the northwest. Later, some of them moved to Tehran. Though their number is now down to 20,000, they are, like the much larger Armenian community, entitled to one seat in the Majlis.

That was also the case for the Jews, who traced their Iranian heritage to their exile from Babylon in the late sixth century BC. In the Book of Ezra, the Persian emperors—Cyrus, Darius, and Artaxerxes—are mentioned as the ones who allowed the Jews to return to Jerusalem and reconstruct their Temple (Ezra 6:14). Over the centuries, the Persian Jews settled in Central Asia and northwestern India. Among the prominent Jewish monuments in Iran are the shrines of Esther and her cousin Mordecai, and Habakkuk in Hamadan—as well as the mausoleum of Daniel in Susa, in southwestern Iran. Regarded as one of the prophets of monotheism—starting with Adam and ending with Muhammad—Daniel is revered by Muslims, who make a pilgrimage to his tomb in the thousands.

In latter-day Iran, Jews settled in Shiraz, Isfahan, and Tehran, the capitals of the country at different times. In the mid-twentieth century, there were 150,000 Jews in the country. Due to emigration to Israel and North America, their size declined to about 80,000 in the late 1970s. Within a few months of the Islamic revolution in 1979, that number shrank to about 20,000, even though, on his return to Tehran from a long exile, Khomeini issued a fatwa (religious decree) saying that the Jews must be protected.[5]

Those who remained became more observant than before, eating only kosher food, refraining from driving on Shabbat, and attending one of the twenty-five synagogues in the country—almost half of them in Tehran, and many of them running Hebrew schools.

Active in trade, business, and banking, the religious minorities were financially and socially well off. It is not known how active their members were in the revolutionary movement of the late 1970s, if at all. Nonetheless, the intense turmoil caused by the popular surge against the Shah led to a large-scale emigration of these minorities, mainly to North America, West Europe, and Israel. Those who remained behind backed the new regime. For instance, they participated fully in the referendum on the new constitution held in December, when it was approved with near unanimity.

Significantly, the Assembly of Experts conceded the demand of the predominantly Sunni Kurds, Baluchs, Turkmens, and Arabs that the Sunni schools of Islam—Hanafi, Hanbali, Maliki, and Shafii—be recognized on a par with the Twelver Shiite Islam. Article 5 was based on the Shiite doctrine of the missing Twelfth Imam, Muhammad al Muntazar (aka Muhammad al Qasim). The article stated that, owing to his occultation, "the governance and leadership of the nation devolve upon the just and pious *faqih* [jurisprudent] who is acquainted with the circumstances of his age; courageous, resourceful, and possessed of administrative ability; and recognized and accepted as Leader by the majority of the people." The Leader (*Rahbar*, in Persian), who combined the role of head of state and chief justice, was Ayatollah Khomeini. He was to be succeeded by a Leader, or Leadership Council of three or five, to be appointed by a popularly elected Assembly of Experts.[6]

Sovereignty rested with the people. The official title of the Islam Republic (*not* State) of Iran was illustrative. "The affairs of the country must be administered on the basis of public opinion expressed by means of elections of the president of the republic, the representatives of the National Consultative Council [Majlis] and the members of councils, or by means of referendums in matters specified in the articles of the constitution," stated Article 6.[7]

To ensure that parliament's decisions did not contradict "the ordinances of Islam and the constitution," Article 91 specified the establishment of a twelve-member Council of Guardians, with six Islamic jurists selected by the Leader or Leadership Council, and six lawyers to be elected by the Majlis from a list submitted by the Supreme Judicial Council. The Islamic jurist, acting as the Leader, was required to be fully conversant with "the issues of the day . . . the circumstances of his age." That is, he must know how to apply and interpret basic Islamic precepts in the conditions prevalent in the late twentieth Christian century or early fifteenth Islamic century.[8]

Iran's 1979 constitution was a pioneering document. While it drew its inspiration from Islamic precepts, it was designed to serve the needs of a community in modern times. It incorporated such concepts as the separation of legislative, executive, and judicial powers, and based the authority of the Leader and the president on popular will—expressed either directly, as in the president's case, or indirectly, through the popularly elected Assembly of Experts empowered to select the successor(s) to Khomeini.

Khomeini was the final arbiter of who or what was Islamic or not. He decided that all non-Islamic elements had to be expunged from the government administration, the military, the judiciary, public and private enterprises, and educational institutions. This was to be achieved by official decisions and popular actions.

The other major task was to purify society, which had been corrupted by alien influences over the past few centuries, and Islamize it. Alcohol and gambling were banned immediately, and so were nightclubs, pornographic films, and mixed bathing. Society was Islamized in a positive sense as well. Friday noon prayers and sermons were made the focal point of the week, and were used to inform and educate the faithful. All Friday prayer-leaders were appointed by Khomeini, and reported to him.

Those who resisted the Islamic government were to be punished along the guidelines in the Sharia. Raising arms against the Islamic state or spreading corruption in society were declared capital offenses. This was the ideological framework which Khomeini laid out, and within which he operated during the various phases of the Islamic revolution.

With the takeover of the U.S. embassy in Tehran by militant students on November 4, 1979, the Islamic revolution entered a virulently anti-American phase. The regime's focus turned to expelling the remaining vestiges of American influence, which had dominated Iran since the CIA-backed coup in August 1953 restored the Shah to the throne he had lost briefly to the democratically elected prime minister, Muhammad Mussadiq. When this led to economic sanctions against Iran by the United States and Western Europe, the Soviet Union stepped in to aid Iran. But cordial feelings withered when Soviet troops marched into Afghanistan in late December 1979.

Iraq's invasion of Iran on September 22, 1980, heralded the next phase of the revolution in which patriotism and Islam became inseparable.

Traditional rivalry between Iraq and Iran worsened when, following the Islamic revolution, Khomeini started appealing to the faithful in Iraq to overthrow the secular regime of President Saddam Hussein. In return, Hussein encouraged Iranian Arabs in the oil-rich province of Khuzistan to rebel against Khomeini's government. Prompted by reports of low morale in Iran's military and internecine fighting among its leaders, Saddam invaded the Islamic Republic.

In the spring of 1982, the tide began to turn in Iran's favor. In a major offensive in May, the Iranians recaptured most of the territory they had lost to Iraq at the beginning of the conflict. In June, Tehran rejected the Iraqi offer of an immediate cease-fire, and repeated its call for the overthrow of Saddam, the "corrupt infidel" whom it held responsible for aggression against Iran. In early July, the Iranian government threatened that if Saddam were not punished for invading Iran, and $100 billion not paid to it as war damages, it would carry the war into Iraq. Four days later, Iran did so with a view to capturing Basra. It failed. Nonetheless, these events demonstrated that the armed conflict had entered a phase where the initiative lay with Tehran.

At home, the Iranian government kept up its Islamization drive. On May 30, 1982, the cabinet approved comprehensive plans to bring the existing penal and legal codes, civil law, trade law, and the registration of documents and land in line with the Sharia. Khomeini issued a decree on Islamization of the judiciary. The parliament passed a law on moral offenses. Adherence to Islamic dress for women, mandated by law in 1981 and applicable to all women irrespective of their nationality or religious affiliation, was enforced strictly.

This fiat of the regime met with resistance at first. Soon after the revolution, when Khomeini ruled that women employees in government ministries must dress "according to Islamic standards"—that is, wear a veil—protest ensued. Day after day, thousands of women marched through the streets of Tehran. Responding to this as well as private pleas, Khomeini's spokesman announced that the Ayatollah had said that a chador was a desirable, not compulsory, form of dress for women. This would prove to be a temporary retreat, however.

During Ramdan in July 1980, an official order stated that all women in government offices and publicly-owned enteprises must wear a hijab (veil). The hijab traditionally worn by Muslim women in public always covers the head, but not necessarily the face. The half a million urban women above the age of twelve who had such jobs, and those who labored in workshops and factories, were 9 percent of the female population. A large majority of them worked in small, all-female workshops or sections of factories. So, overall, the government order affected about 3 percent of the urban female population aged twelve or older.

Due to this, and the mass media's frequent reiteration that prescribing a proper dress for women had the sanction of the Quran, resistance to the official fiat collapsed. The appropriate verse in the Quran (24:30–31) states: "And say to the believing women that they cast down their eyes, and guard their private parts . . . and let them cast their veils over their bosoms, and reveal not their adornment (*zinah*) save to their husbands, or their fathers, or their husbands' fathers, or their sons, or their husbands' sons, or their brothers, or their brothers' sons, or their sisters' sons, or their women . . . or children who have not yet attained knowledge of women's private parts."[9] The intention is to avoid arousing sexual passion between men and women who are not present or potential partners, and thereby protect the sanctity of the family, which is portrayed as the bedrock of an Islamic way of life.

A year later, in 1981, the Majlis passed the Islamic Dress Law, which applied to all women in Iran, irrespective of their religion or nationality. The maximum penalty for violating the law was a jail sentence of a year. The law remains in force and is applied with varying degrees of severity.

Actually, the custom of veiling women existed in pre-Islamic times and non-Muslim societies, during the Sassanian and Byzantine Empires, and in the European Mediterranean and India. Within Islam, peasant and nomadic Muslim women seldom accepted the veil. Indeed, when the semi-nomadic Seljuk, Mongol, and Timurid dynasties ruled Iran from 1037 to 1500, the unveiling of women spread among the local elite and lower ranks. It was only later that veiling and secluding women became the ideal for those who did not labor in fields or elsewhere.

The single most blatant sign of the Islamic revolution was the presence of women in black chadors shuffling through the streets like ghosts, which became the iconic image of theocratic Iran. Every so often, pictures of women in black veils, bearing machine guns and marching in the streets of Tehran, clashed with the sterotypical view of Iranian women. In every day life, however, behind the veil, women continued to work as shop assistants, bank clerks, immigration officers, factory workers, journalists, news readers, and academics. With the eight-year-long war against Iraq drawing much manpower, job opportunities for women improved, as did their proportion in universities and colleges.

By early 1983, Islamic revolutionary organizations, which had sprung up in the wake of the Shah's downfall, covered all spheres of life: political, military, security, judicial, economic, social, cultural, and religious. Some of these bodies functioned independently; others in tandem with government ministries. These organizations were so preponderant that one-sixth of all Iranians above fifteen years of age belonged to one or more of them.[10]

When the Marxist Tudeh (Masses) Party was banned in May 1983, all prerevolution, clandestine parties—except the liberal Liberation Movement headed by Mahdi Bazargan, the Islamic regime's first prime minister—were outlawed. Political life thus became the near monopoly of the official Islamic Republican Party and its smaller allies.

In the military, the erstwhile bedrock of the Pahlavi monarchy, a series of purges resulted in the dismissal or retirement of all but a thousand officers of the prerevolution period. The regime took steps to inculcate Islamic values and ideas among armed forces. A political-ideological department was instituted in the military, and was often manned by young clerics fiercely loyal to the Islamic Republic. They educated officers and ranks in Islamic history and ideology. The information and guidance department performed the general task of creating and sustaining support for the government's actions and policies, and the particular job of keeping an eye on potential dissidents or deviants.

Then there were the Islamic Associations among military personnel— voluntary bodies that aimed to raise the Islamic consciousness of their members and guard the security of their units. Earlier, the Islamic Revolutionary Guards Corps (IRGC) was created as a counterforce to the army commanded by officers of dubious loyalty to the new regime. Recruitment to the IRGC was strictly controlled, requiring knowledge of the Quran, *Naha al Balaghe* (Fountain of Eloquence) by Imam Ali, and *Hukumat-e Islami* (Islamic Government) by Khomeini.

Schools also underwent Islamization. New Islamic teaching materials were made available to primary schools within six months of the revolution. Similar speed was shown in furnishing secondary schools with Islamic textbooks. Special emphasis was put on the teaching of Arabic, the language of the Quran, with lessons in Arabic being offered on television. Universities and colleges were closed for two and a half years while new or modified textbooks were produced. Within three years of the revolution, all coeducational schools had been transformed into single-sex schools, and about 40,000 teachers purged.[11]

These efforts went hand in hand with tackling specific moral ills such as prostitution and drugs. The Family Protection Law of 1967 and 1975, restricting polygamy and giving women the right to initiate divorce proceedings, was first suspended and then abolished. However, in late 1983, a woman's right to divorce her husband was restored. Contraceptives, considered un-Islamic, were banned. There were hundreds of public floggings or executions for adultery. There were also capital and other punishments for homosexuality. These originated in the Quranic verses, which describe allowable sexual relations and punishments for transgressing them.

Islamic principles were also applied increasingly to the economy. The Majlis passed the interest-free banking bill in June 1983. During the eighteen-month transition period, depositors were required to split their investments between their bank's two sections: interest-free and term deposit. Then the bank's interest-free section began lending funds to needy customers without interest, while the term deposit section advanced funds to commercial customers according to Islamic contracts. The profits earned or losses incurred by the loans were then shared by the depositors proportionately. Thus, the idea of a fixed interest rate was replaced by variable profit or loss margins by treating depositors as business partners.

All along, efforts were being made to create an Islamic ambience in the street, in the media, and on the war front. One method was to paint slogans and images on street walls. The mass media contributed by covering the proliferation of Islamic events throughout the year, not to mention the daily prayers which were broadcast on radio and television. Besides the holy month of Ramadan, there were the ten days of Muharrarn culminating in Ashura, the six-day-long hajj pilgrimage to Mecca, the birthdays of Prophet Muhammad and twelve Shiite Imams, and the two joyous *eids* (religious festivals). In addition were the highlights of Iran's revolutionary Islam: ten days celebrating the revolution, a week commemorating the war with Iraq, and the founding days of the Islamic Republic, the IRGC, the Reconstruction Crusade, and so on.

Believers had an opportunity to involve themselves in the Islamic process by joining the Islamic Association at work or in the neighborhood. These associations performed many functions, including identifying un-Islamic elements in society, aiding the war effort, strengthening Islamic culture, and encouraging voter participation in elections and referendums. In all such activities, clerics were in the forefront. They were now more numerous than before. Estimates of qualified clerics varied from 90,000 to 120,000. In addition, there were an unknown number of unqualified village preachers, prayer-leaders, theological school teachers, and procession organizers. The number of theology students rose to 30,000, tripling from the prerevolution figure of 10,000.[12]

Within two years of the revolution, the number of mosques reached 22,000, with urban mosques doubling their prerevolution total of 5,600.[13] Besides being the place for religious activities, larger mosques became centers for food and fuel-rationing systems, consumer cooperative stores, recruitment for the IRGC and its auxiliary, the Baseej (*Niruyeh Muqawamatt Baseej*, Mobilization of Resistance Force), collections for the war effort, the teaching of Arabic, and offering interest-free loans to those in dire need. On election days, mosques were often used as polling stations.

The Islamization process and the rise of revolutionary organizations affected the lives of all Iranians. Most of them either backed the change or went along with it, sometimes reluctantly. As for the large majority of Iranians, the onset of Islamization made little difference to their everyday lives. Untouched by westernization in their personal or social lives, they had been religious before the revolution. The only difference now was that Shiite Islam, to which they had been affiliated for centuries, had now been adopted and codified by the state, which became the official sponsor of all Shiite festivals and such Islamic dates in the calendar as the birthday of Prophet Muhammad. Womenfolk had no problem donning the hijab or even the chador, as this is what they had done during the rule of the secular Shahs.

By contrast, the onset of Islamic values and behavior, mandated by the theocratic regime, made life difficult for the westernized upper-middle and upper classes in Tehran and other large cities. The revolution had disempowered all those among them who had wielded political power in the past. They were replaced by the mullahs, who largely came from lower-middle class or poor families, untouched by westernization. In Tehran, this secular, westernized minority mostly lived north of the east-west thoroughfare bisecting the metropolis, on the upscale, salubrious slopes of El Borz mountain.

With the outlawing of alcohol for Muslims and the closing of all alcoholic outlets, the price of spirits and wine shot up. But they were available as contraband, particularly when non-Muslim minorities like Christians, Jews, and Zoroastrians were allowed to drink, as drinking did not violate their religion, and most of their members lived in north Tehran. (However, there was no way of circumventing the ban on importing foreign movies.)

The inhabitants of the upscale neighborhoods of Tehran were almost invariably related to the 1.5 million Iranian exiles settled in North America and Western Europe. They had stayed behind not because they sympathized with the Islamic revolution, but because they wanted to safeguard their valuable properties. As long as there was a brother or sister, or a son or daughter, present in Iran, the properties of the whole family were safe from the threat of confiscation. As it was, the Islamic regime upheld the right to property as inviolable, a policy rooted in the Sharia.

In political science, revolution is defined by Webster's dictionary as "the overthrow or renunciation of one government or ruler, and the substitution of another, by the governed." The depth of revolution is determined by the degree to which the ruling elite of the ancien régime has been displaced from power, whether society has undergone a fundamental change in its perception of itself, and whether the revolution is inspired by an overarching ideology.

By these criteria, the February 1979 revolution in Iran was profound. It was inspired, in the main, by Islam, a faith seen as sanctifying ending oppression and instituting social justice nationally and internationally. The ruling elite of the monarchical regime was replaced totally. In the immediate aftermath of the revolution, most Iranians came to regard themselves more as part of a religious community, Islamic umma, than a nation-state. But that changed with the war with Iraq, when nationalism became as important as Islam.

REVOLUTIONARY ISLAMIC FOREIGN POLICY

Iran's constitution laid out the guidelines for its foreign policy. "In accordance with the [Quranic] verse 'This your nation is a single nation, and I am your Lord, so worship Me,' all Muslims form a single nation," read Article 10. "The government of the Islamic Republic of Iran has the duty of formulating its general policies with a view to the merging and union of all Muslim peoples, and it must constantly strive to bring about political, economic and cultural unity of the Islamic world."[14]

More specifically, Article 152 stated that the Republic's foreign policy is based inter alia on "the defense of the rights of all Muslims" and "nonalignment with respect to the hegemonic superpowers." These superpowers were the United States and the Soviet Union. Article 154 implicitly sanctified exporting revolution. "The Islamic Republic of Iran considers the attainment of independence, freedom and just government to be the right of all peoples in the world . . . [It] therefore protects the just struggles of the oppressed and deprived in every corner of the globe."

Several months before the promulgation of the constitution, Khomeini's regime declared it to be its "Islamic duty" to support the national liberation movements of the "deprived peoples" of the world. Later, several attempts by its internal and external enemies to overthrow it led the regime to conclude to that the argument for exporting the revolution was not merely ideological, but also pragmatic: an effective way to defend the revolution was to try to extend its influence abroad. As President Ali Khamanei put it in November 1983, "If the revolution is kept within Iranian borders, it would become vulnerable."[15]

But following this path had its downside. Tehran's attempts to bolster a revolutionary organization in a foreign country soured intergovernmental relations, and increased its isolation in the international community. This policy therefore proved unpopular with many officials of the Foreign Ministry headed by a comparative moderate, Ali Akbar Velayati, from late 1980 onward. Velayati resolved the conflict by establishing a separate department in the ministry to deal with national liberation movements. Later, its functions were transferred to an independent body, the World Organization of Islamic Liberation Movements, led by Ayatollah Hussein Ali Montazeri, based in the holy city of Qom. Prominent among the affiliates of this organization were the Islamic Daawa party in Iraq and Kuwait; the Hizbollah in Lebanon; and small groups in Afghanistan, later amalgamated into the Hizb-e Wahdat-e Islami.

The Soviet military presence in Afghanistan continued to cast a shadow over friendly ties between Tehran and Moscow. In the early days of the Iranian revolution, the Kremlin thought that, with Iran quitting the Western-dominated Central Treaty Organization and joining the Non-Aligned Movement, relations between it and Iran would blossom. However, on the eve of the Iranian New Year in 1980, Khomeini stated, "We are the enemies of international Communism in the same way we are against the world predators of the West, headed by the United States."[16]

IRAN AND SOVIET CENTRAL ASIA

Within a couple of months of the revolution, Tehran started beaming radio broadcasts at the Soviet Central Asian republics in Tajik, Uzbek, and Turkmen to revive religious feeling among the Muslim citizens of the region. This did not affect the economic links that the Kremlin had forged with Iran during the Shah's regime. These ties covered 140 industrial and other projects, accounting for 90 percent of Iran's coal output, 87 percent of its iron ore production, and 70 percent of its steel output.[17]

In his survey of world developments before the Twenty-Sixth Congress of the Communist Party of the Soviet Union in February 1981, Leonid Brezhnev referred to the Iranian revolution as "a major event in the international scene in recent years." He added, "However complex and contradictory, it is essentially an anti-imperialist revolution, though reaction at home and abroad is seeking to change this feature."[18] In other words, the Kremlin wanted to continue forging its policy towards Iran on the basis of the latter's actions rather than its slogans.

So, when Iran refused to accept a cease-fire in its war with Iraq in June 1982, and tried to seize Iraqi territory, the Soviet Union reversed its earlier decision to stop supplying arms and spares to Iraq, its long-term ally, when it invaded Iran in September 1980 and earned the opprobrium of the Kremlin. This soured relations between Moscow and Tehran. A year later, when Iraq began using the newly supplied Soviet weapons, especially Scud ground-to-ground missiles, Khomeini responded by banning the Tudeh Party and launching a campaign on behalf of "the oppressed Muslims of the Soviet Union." Propaganda posters depicted the Kremlin as the capital of the devil.

The move was directed towards sharply rekindling interest in Islam among the Muslims of the southern republics of the Soviet Union. The efforts of Iran and other Muslim states began to bear fruit. One manifestation of this was the rise in the number of unofficial clerics. In late 1983, Turkmenistan, with a population of 2.8 million, was reported to have 300 such clerics. With their language being a variant of Persian, Tajiks had always been close to Iranians culturally. In Tajikistan and other Central Asian republics, there was a growing demand for mosques and religious schools, and more and more women were adopting Islamic dress. These developments, disapproved by the Soviet authorities, created ill will towards Iran in the Kremlin.

Moscow blamed Tehran for its refusal to end the armed conflict with Iraq. In April 1984, following a meeting between Soviet Premier Nikolai Tikhonov and Iraqi Vice President Taha Yassin Ramadan in Moscow, a joint communiqué publicly blamed Iran for not ending the hostilities.[19] It was not until two years later that, owing to the steep fall in oil prices caused by the deliberate flooding of the oil market by Saudi Arabia and Kuwait, Iran's financial capacity to wage war was irrevocably damaged. But it took two more years for Iran to reach a point where it realized the futility of further fighting. The result was a cease-fire in August 1988 under United Nations auspices.

By then, the Kremlin, run by Mikhail Gorbachev, had withdrawn half of its 115,000 troops from Afghanistan, thus considerably easing the strain on its relations with Tehran. Gorbachev's move was noted with approval by Khomeini. This augured well for the visit of Alexander Besvernikh, first deputy foreign minister of the Soviet Union, to Tehran in November 1988 to strengthen bilateral ties.

With the hurdles of Iran's war with Iraq and the Soviet military presence in Afghanistan removed, Khomeini took the initiative of addressing a long epistle to Gorbachev in January 1989, advising him, among other things, to study Islam. In his letter of reply, Gorbachev referred to the Soviet Union's "conviction that conditions are ripe for relations between our two countries to enter a qualitatively new stage of cooperation in all fields." This was welcomed by Khomeini, who had in his letter emphasized the importance of "expanding strong ties in various fields so as to confront the devilish acts of the West."[20]

Before he died on June 3, 1989, Khomeini was said to have offered his aides last-minute advice to improve relations with the "Northern neighbor," meaning the Soviet Union. Within three weeks of Khomeini's death, Ali Akbar Hashemi Rafsanjani, the powerful speaker of parliament, flew to Moscow. Here he had a series of meetings with Gorbachev. The two leaders signed diplomatic, economic, and military protocols, and topped them with a Good Neighborly and Cooperation Agreement. Referring to "the new thinking in the Soviet Union on one hand and the victory of the Islamic revolution on the other," the agreement specifically called for "more contacts and exchanges between Iranian and Soviet religious leaders." The military cooperation between the two countries led to Iran's purchase of Soviet weapons worth $10 billion between then and 1993.[21]

From the standpoint of Gorbachev's government, the wide-ranging agreements with Iran were useful in demonstrating to the world that its policy was now pragmatic, not ideological, and that it was able to have cordial relations with regimes of any political color. In any case, the Soviet Union was eager for rapprochement with a country with which it shared its second longest border (2,000 kilometers; 1,200 miles) after China, and whose revolution a decade earlier had removed a pro-American monarch.

THE POST-SOVIET ERA

Following the unraveling of the Soviet Union, Tehran devised an overall policy towards the Central Asian republics as well as the Caucasian republics of Azerbaijan and Armenia. Of these seven states, it decided to focus on those with which it had common land frontiers—Azerbaijan, Armenia, and Turkmenistan—as well as Tajikistan, because of the affinity of Tajik with Persian and the common cultural heritage that Tajiks and Iranians shared.[22]

"Given the role of the Islamic Republic in the region, our responsibilities are manifold," said Iran's foreign minister, Velayati, after his tour of all the Central Asian republics in November 1991. "Iran shares the Islamic heritage with its neighboring countries and in view of the recent urge for independence in Central Asia, it has to fill the existing cultural and economic vacuum. Hence all countries that seek Iran's assistance in these realms [of culture and economics] will be welcomed."[23]

So, contrary to the claims of America and, to a lesser extent, Turkey that Tehran had a political agenda for Central Asia, Iran's focus was limited to culture and economics, and fell short of exporting Islamic revolution to this region. Iran realized that, with the possible exception of Tajikistan, conditions for such a revolution did not exist. Since Muslims in Central Asia had been deprived of religion and religious education for more than three generations, they needed at least a decade to learn the basics of Islam and its rituals. They also needed to build up a sufficient body of clerics to provide religious education and guidance before any serious attempt could be made to create a Sharia-based social order. The obstacles that Islamists in the region faced were summed up aptly by a Western diplomat in Ashgabat thus: "Being nomads and semi-nomads, the Turkmen were never strong Muslims to start with, and 70 years of communism turned them into secularists and vodka-addicts. Turkmen women never wore a veil."[24]

Given the diverse ways Shiite and Sunni sects are organized religiously, and the preponderance of the Sunni sect's Hanafi school in the region, Iran's contribution to training clerics in these countries was miniscule. The bulk of this task fell to the Sunni religious establishment in Turkey, which was Hanafi, and to a lesser extent on the Islamic institutions of Egypt and Saudi Arabia. The dramatic increase in the number of mosques in Turkmenistan, for instance, was financed by foreign money that came largely from the Mecca-based World Muslim League, funded by Saudi Arabia, not Iran.

Among Turkmen officials and intellectuals, there was no fear of contact with Iran and Iranians. Besides their affiliation to different sects of Islam, their languages belonged to different families. "We have lived with the Iranians for the past two thousand years without being dominated by them," said Jeren Taimova, deputy editor of *Evening Ashgabat*. "We can live with them much longer and maintain our identity."[25]

Had she been familiar with the *Shahnama*, and its author, Firdausi, a native of Tus in eastern Iran near the border of today's Turkmenistan, she would have alluded to the slave-hunting Turkmen warriors' practice of keeping the captured Shiite Iranians in perpetual bondage.

IRAN'S GEOSTRATEGIC STRENGTH

Iran's strong geostrategic position stood out. All Central Asian republics as well as Azerbaijan and Armenia were landlocked, whereas Iran's shoreline covered not only the full 1,450-kilometer (900-mile) length of the Persian Gulf, but also 480 kilometers (300 miles) of the Arabian Sea. Iran held the key to providing access to warm-weather seaports to these landlocked countries.

Iran wanted to assist them partly out of a feeling of Islamic solidarity, and partly to frustrate what it perceived as the avaricious ambitions of Western multinational companies to exploit their natural resources while denying them advanced technology. "Azerbaijan and Central Asia could be turned into a raw materials store for the West," said Rafsanjani, addressing the seventeenth session of the Islamic Development Bank in Tehran. "To enable these countries to avoid this trap they need to be given large-scale economic aid."[26]

The Rafsanjani government adopted this policy in the post-Soviet era. In February 1992, at its behest, the long-established Economic Cooperation Organization (ECO), consisting of Pakistan, Iran, and Turkey, was expanded to admit Azerbaijan and all Central Asian republics, except Kazakhstan, which was given observer status. The first summit of the expanded ECO was held in Tehran. Turkey and Iran viewed the new body differently. Turkish President Turgut Ozal hoped ECO would emerge like the European Community, whereas Rafsanjani hailed the enlarged body as "one great Muslim family of 300 million."[27]

Next month, Tehran offered $50 million to Turkmenistan to enable it to buy Iranian food, and promised assistance in the construction of a gas pipeline to carry Turkmen gas to Turkey and Western Europe through Iran, thus bypassing other CIS members. The idea of such a pipeline, costing $3 billion, upset Washington, which tried to sabotage it. Its economic muscle proved effective. In July, it was announced that the plan was being held in abeyance since international bankers were unwilling to finance a project involving Iran, which could, for political reasons, turn off energy supplies to Turkey and Europe.

But the one project where neither Iran nor Turkmenistan was dependent on Western funds or expertise was the 150-kilometer (90-mile) rail link between the eastern Iranian city of Mashhad and the border town of Sarakhs to link up with the Central Asian rail network at Tejand, Turkmenistan, costing $210 million. Work started in June 1992.

Border restrictions between the two neighbors were eased, allowing increased trade and human contact—a stark contrast from the Cold War era, when a high double-barbed-wire fence with watchtowers along the entire 1,000-kilometer (620-mile) frontier was still in place.

In August, Turkmen President Saparmurat Niyazov visited Tehran, where he signed economic, technical, cultural, and scientific agreements. Later that year, Iran staged its second trade fair in Ashgabat, which attracted representatives from other Central Asian republics. Announcing a two-and-a-half-fold increase in trade with Iran in 1992, Niyazov said, "All possible measures will be taken to expand and consolidate ties with Iran."[28]

With the anti-Communist movement rising in Tajikistan in late 1991 and early 1992, Iran's interest in the republic rose. Tehran approved the Tajik Supreme Soviet's decision to change the Cyrillic script of the Tajik language to Persian. It was heartened to note that many Tajik intellectuals favored learning to write Persian, which they considered an integral part of the Tajik culture.

Iran's government predicted the victory of the Afghan Mujahedin in Afghanistan in April 1992, which fueled Islamic feeling in Tajikistan. Its media gave wide coverage to the popular protest in Dushanbe, in which Islamic elements played a leading role. Commenting on the decision of President Rahman Nabiyev in May to include members of the opposition, secular and religious, in his administration, Radio Tehran hailed it as a triumph of "the Muslim people of Tajikistan" who were engaged most importantly in renovating their "Islamic, national identity."[29]

As described in the previous chapter, having incorporated Islamist forces into the government, Nabiyev flew to Tehran in July, where he signed a treaty of friendship and cooperation covering culture, trade, science, and banking. Soon after, Iran began beaming television programs in Persian to Tajikistan. It helped the Tajik authorities to rehabilitate Persian culture and language by supplying them with Persian-language school textbooks.

To help Tajikistan overcome the setback to its economy, Tehran offered it oil worth $40 million as grant aid, a gesture particularly welcomed by the mayor of Dushanbe, who was thus able to keep public transport running.

Following Nabiyev's forced resignation, Velayati told the visiting Tajik culture minister, Zakirian Vazirov, that Iran was ready to help devise a peaceful settlement to the civil war. But Tajikistan ignored this offer because Iran was not regarded as truly neutral. Indeed, there were reports in the early autumn that Iran had supplied arms to the Islamic Renaissance Party in southern Tajikistan, and that the Russian Foreign Ministry had admitted that its relations with Iran were undergoing "some problems at present."[30]

However, given the logistical hurdles faced by Iran, the absence of Shiite Tajiks, and the comparative ease with which the Afghan Mujahedin, bristling with weapons, could and did arm Tajikistan's Islamic fighters to a far greater extent, the impact of any weapons supplied by Tehran was marginal. Both Moscow and Washington had their own reasons for exaggerating the Iranian contribution to the Tajik civil war. Russia did so to justify its supply of arms and ammunition to the pro-Nabiyev forces, and the United States was only too willing to paint its long-term adversary as hell-bent on destabilizing the Muslim world, starting with its Muslim neighbors.

In the end, when Islamist partisans in Tajikistan were defeated and butchered by pro-Nabiyev forces in December 1992, there was very little Iran did, or could, do.

Equally, on the American-Turkish side, there was a limit to what Washington could do to discourage Central Asian republics from having cordial relations with Tehran. Whatever else diplomatic and economic power can do, it cannot suppress the imperatives of geopolitics for long.

Even Kazakh President Nursultan Nazarbayev, who had declared in early 1992 that Kazakhstan and Russia had a "special responsibility" to steer Central Asia away from Islamic fundamentalism and Iranian influence, concluded that there was no alternative to having normal, friendly relations with Iran. Thus, he visited Tehran in November, and signed protocols of mutual cooperation. Before then, his government had invited Iran's oil minister, Ghulam Aqazadeh, to Almaty to discuss the idea of Kazakhstan supplying its oil to north Iran through a short pipeline, with Tehran exporting an equivalent amount of Iranian crude through its Gulf ports. The proposal underlined the role Iran could play in helping Central Asian republics to integrate themselves into the world economy.

Last but not least, Uzbek President Islam Karimov, an ardent enemy of Islamic radicalism, made his peace with Iran. Though the Islamic Republic recognized independent Uzbekistan swiftly, it was not allowed to open its embassy in Tashkent until October 1992. A month later, Karimov made a surprise decision to visit Tehran to meet Rafsanjani. They discussed the rail link between Tejand and Mashhad, which would provide the shortest route for Uzbekistan's trade with the world outside former Soviet republics. The two leaders signed a series of economic and cultural agreements, areas that Iran had earmarked for cooperation.

1996, A CRITICAL YEAR

The inauguration of the rail link between Sarakhs (in Iran) and Tejand (in Turkmenistan) in May 1996 was a milestone in regional history. It was attended by twelve prime ministers and presidents from five Central Asian republics, Iran, Turkey, Azerbaijan, Armenia, Georgia, Pakistan, and Afghanistan. With this, the old Soviet rail system, covering all eight land-locked republics of the southern tier of the former Soviet Union—Kazakh-stan, Kyrgyzstan, Tajikistan, Turkmenistan, and Uzbekistan of Central Asia and Azerbaijan, Armenia, and Georgia of the Caucasus—linked up with Iran's railway network.

This provided the landlocked Central Asian states with access to the warm-water ports of Iran in the Gulf and the Arabian Sea, and thus released them from their dependence on Russia. Instead of selling their cotton exclu-sively to Russia, Uzbekistan and Turkmenistan could now explore world markets and deliver the commodity without the involvement of Moscow in any form. Indeed, Uzbekistan ended up selling some of its cotton to Iran. The new link was expected to move 2 million tonnes of cargo and half a million passengers annually between Tejan and Mashhad.[31] While the regional leaders welcomed the options that the new rail link offered their countries, the administration of U.S. President Bill Clinton viewed it as a setback to its policy of isolating Iran economically, codified in its Iran-Libya Sanctions Act (ILSA) of August 1995.

A year later, another reversal for America occurred when, during his visit to Tehran, Turkish Prime Minister Necmettin Erbakan signed a $20 billion natural gas deal with Iran, scheduled to run for twenty-five years. A pipeline was to be laid to carry initially 3 billion cubic meters of Iranian gas annually, rising to 10 billion cubic meters in 2005. Trade between the two neighbors was expected to double to $2 billion in two years.

In the region, Iran suffered a setback when the anti-Shiite Taliban, backed by Saudi Arabia and Pakistan, captured Kabul in September. As radical Sunnis, the Taliban shared the view of the Islamic Movement of Uzbekistan and Hizb-ut Tahrir that the Shiite doctrine was not a legitimate branch of Islam. Iran's feeling of despondency was shared by the Kremlin. Both gov-ernments visualized the ultra-radical leadership of the Taliban extending its influence in the region by stoking Islamist militancy, with Tajikistan as its prime target. So they pushed hard to conciliate the warring sides in Tajikistan, and end the civil war with a peace deal. They succeeded in the spring of 1997.

Both governments also aimed to prevent U.S. oil corporations from carving up a major role for themselves in the region's oil and gas industry. Equally, Washington was intent on keeping Iran and Russia out of the hydrocarbon industry of Central Asia and Azerbaijan. Confident of their oil and gas wealth, Turkmenistan and Kazakhstan continued to defy Washington's policy of economic boycott of Iran. As discussed in Chapter 3, in December 1997, Iran's President Muhammad Khatami and Niyazov inaugurated a pipeline to carry natural gas from Turkmenistan's Korpeje gas field to Kord-Kui in northeast Iran.

In June 1998, the National Iranian Oil Company invited bids for a $400 million contract for a 400-kilometer (250-mile) pipeline between the Caspian port of Babol Sar and Tehran, to carry oil supplied by tanker to Kazakhstan and Turkmenistan. The pipeline was designed to handle 200,000 bpd, with Iran exporting the same amount from its Gulf ports to the customers of Kazakhstan and Turkmenistan.[32]

Iran's chances of forging strong commercial links with Uzbekistan were limited since they did not share a common border; and, unlike Kazakhstan and Turkmenistan, Uzbekistan lacked abundant hydrocarbon reserves. (This was also true of Kyrgyzstan.) Then there was Karimov's hostility towards anything that smacked of political Islam. So he maintained a policy of minimal ties with Tehran, and Iran reciprocated. However, while generally refraining from interfering in Uzbekistan's domestic affairs, Iran did not shy away from speaking up when it felt that Karimov was being excessively repressive towards pious Muslims. When the trials of Uzbek Islamists got going in April 1998, the state-run Iran Radio criticized Karimov for "suppressing Muslims," arguing that he did not differentiate between "Islamic extremists" and "Islamic reformists"[33]—a viewpoint it shared with Western human rights organizations.

All along, Iran kept a wary eye on the Taliban. It esclated its arms shipments to the anti-Taliban camp in Afghanistan as the Taliban steadily brought more territory under its control. Its capture of Mazar-e Sharif, the base of General Abdul Rashid Dostum, an ethnic Uzbek and an ex-Communist, in May 1997—which led Pakistan, Saudi Arabia, and the United Arab Emirates to recognize the Taliban administration as Afghanistan's legitimate government—made Karimov rethink his policy toward Tehran. Overcoming his antipathy toward Iran, Karimov allowed it—along with Russia and Turkey—to use the Uzbek territory to increase its weapons supplies to the forces of Dostum. Thus fortified, Dostum regained Mazar-e Sharif. His National Islamic Movement combined with the Northern Alliance to form the United National Islamic Front.

But, the Taliban, now openly backed by Pakistan and Saudi Arabia, mounted a series of offensives in the spring and summer of 1998. Its forces recaptured Mazar-e Sharif in early August, leaving only four of the thirty-two provinces unconquered. Dostum fled to Turkey, and the United National Islamic Front reverted to being the Tajik-dominated Northern Alliance.

PRE- AND POST-9/11

Following the Taliban's seizure of Mazar-e Sharif, ten diplomats and one journalist at the Iranian consulate "disappeared." The Taliban claimed that these individuals had been involved in weapons supplies to their enemies and fled the city when they captured it. Tehran alleged that they had been taken to Kandahar, the headquarters of the Taliban's spiritual leader, Mullah Muhammad Omar.

Tempers rose sharply in Iran. "We are opposed to the Taliban's vision of Islam," Rafsanjani told the Friday prayer congregation in Tehran. "We are opposed to their ideology and their war mongering." Tehran announced military exercises 40 kilometers (25 miles) from the Afghan frontier. "These exercises are not without links to the new situation in Afghanistan," said Major General Yahya Safavi, commander of the Islamic Revolutionary Guard Corps, charged with protecting the country's borders.[34] On September 1, 1998, the IRGC started its annual exercises, involving 70,000 troops, near the Afghan border.

Having earlier suffered U.S. missile strikes on their training camps in Afghanistan on August 20, the Taliban leaders could not withstand pressure from Tehran. They admitted that the Iranians had been killed in the storming of the consulate building by "rogue" troops, and that the latter would be arrested and punished.[35] They allowed an Iranian plane to collect the corpses.

The nationwide mourning in Iran was followed by the government announcing military maneuvers involving 200,000 troops near the Afghan border. There was much sound and fury. In the end, though, Iran's leaders refrained from invading the Taliban territory, partly because they felt that a war with the Taliban could get transmuted into a Shiite-Sunni conflict in the region with unforeseen consequences, and partly because an attack by a foreign country would rally Afghans behind the Taliban regime. Nonetheless, Iran's saber-rattling won plaudits in all Central Asian capitals, including Tashkent. They felt reassured that Iran, with its military hardened by its eight-year war with Iraq, was the most effective regional power to confront the Taliban militarily, if need be.

Preeminent among those who argued successfully against military action was President Khatami, a reformist politician who was by temperament moderate and open-minded. It was during his presidency that Iran cooperated with Armenia to reconstruct old Armenian churches, including the seventh-century St. Thaddeus Church in northwest Iran. The project was completed in 2000, on the eve of the celebration of the 1,700th year of the Armenians' conversion to Christianity in 2001, to be marked by a special Armenian cultural week in Tehran.[36]

It was also in 2000 that Khatami had a meeting with Chief Rabbi Yousef Hamadani Cohen. Three years later, Khatami became the first Iranian president to visit a synagogue in Tehran to confer with Cohen and Maurice Motamed, the parliamentary representative of an estimated 35,000-strong Jewish community—which had its own Persian language publication, *Ofogh-e Bina* (*Distant Horizon*), and maintained the Central Library of the Jewish Associations.

Khatami's actions were in stark contrast to the bigoted, intolerant policies of the Taliban, who regarded even Shiites as virtual heretics. So, as before, Tehran continued its war by proxy with the Taliban by increasing its arms supplies to the anti-Taliban Northern Alliance, led by Ahmad Shah Masoud, an ethnic Tajik. But, the cash, fuel, military equipment, technical assistance, and military advisers that the Taliban received from Pakistan far exceeded the military aid that the Northern Alliance was getting from Iran and Russia. The Taliban continued its offensives. Its capture of Taloqan, where Masoud had his headquarters, in September 2000 came as a blow to Tehran as well as Moscow and Dushanbe.

Iran rushed weapons to the Northern Alliance, now based in Dushanbe. It turned a blind eye as National Security Agency teams and CIA operatives arrived to assist Masoud. The first-ever visit to Dushanbe by U.S. CENTCOM's combatant commander, General Tommy Franks, in the spring of 2001 gave Iran an inkling of the hardening stance of President George W. Bush's administration against the Taliban.

Six months later, a rare thaw would ensue between Iran and America due to a dramatic and unexpected event—aerial attacks on New York and metropolitan Washington on September 11.

Iran's leaders were quick to condemn the attacks and called on the international community to "take measures to eradicate such crimes." Supreme Leader Ayatollah Ali Khamanei decided to deliver the sermon at the Friday prayer congregation in Tehran. "Mass killing is a catastrophe wherever it happens and whoever the perpetrators," he said. "It is condemned without distinction."[37]

Spurning Bush's call to the Iranian government to join in the anti-terror campaign led by the United States, Iran favored action against the Taliban under the United Nations aegis. On the eve of America's military campaign against the Taliban on October 7, Bush sent a confidential memorandum to Iran through the Swiss embassy assuring it that the Pentagon would not use Iranian air space. The next day, Iran replied that it would rescue any U.S. personnel in distress in its territory, thus implying its de facto membership of the coalition. That day, the Bush administration petitioned a federal judge to throw out a $10 billion suit against Iran by the 1979 American hostages.

It later transpired that Iran had allowed 165,000 tons of U.S. food aid for the Afghan people to be unloaded at an Iranian airport and shipped through their territory into Afghanistan.[38] Moreover, Tehran clandestinely shared its intelligence on the Taliban and Osama bin Laden with Washington. It also instructed the Tajik warlord Ismail Khan, based in the eastern Iranian city of Mashhad, to coordinate his attack on western Afghanistan with the Pentagon—which he did.

The spontaneous jubilation of Kabulis that followed the overnight departure of the Taliban from Kabul on November 12 to 13 highlighted the unpopularity of the oppressive Taliban regime, a point repeatedly reiterated since 1997 by Iran. In December 2001, Iran's Foreign Minister Kamal Kharrazi worked actively with U.S. diplomats at a conference near Bonn to install Hamid Karzai as the leader of the post-Taliban, interim government of Afghanisntan. Tehran awaited a quid pro quo from Washington—a thawing of relations as starters.

Instead, Iran's leaders heard their country described as a member of Bush's "axis of evil"—along with Iraq and North Korea—in his State of the Union address to the U.S. Congress on January 29, 2002. "Our second goal is to prevent regimes that sponsor terror from threatening America or our friends and allies with weapons of mass destruction . . . North Korea is a regime arming with missiles and weapons of mass destruction, while starving its citizens. Iran aggressively pursues these weapons and exports terror . . . Iraq continues to flaunt its hostility toward America and to support terror . . . States like these, and their terrorist allies, constitute an axis of evil, arming to threaten the peace of the world."[39] This shocked the Iranian leaders.

However, Bush's demonizing of Iran had no direct impact on the latter's diplomatic standing in Central Asia. With the danger of Taliban-dominated Afghanistan eliminated, normalcy returned to Tajikistan. In 2003, Iran funded the construction of a 4.5-mile-long tunnel under the Anzab Pass in Tajikistan to the tune of three-quarters of the $120 million cost. Completed in 2006, it provided a year-round link between the republic's north and south, a boon to the economy for which Tajik President Imamali Rahmanov thanked Iran profusely.[40]

CENTRAL ASIA, BUSINESS AS USUAL

Whatever commercial limitations Tehran had experienced in the Muslim-majority ex-Soviet republics due to Washington's policy so far were confined to Azerbaijan's hydrocarbon industry, and these preceded Bush's presidency.

Continuing their previous policy, both Kazakhstan and Turkmenistan kept expanding their trading links with Iran. Astana increased the size of its swaps with Tehran. In 2002, when the output of the China Petroleum National Corporation-led consortium in Kazakhstan rose to almost half of the national figure of 550,000 barrels per day, it started to ship some of its Kazakh oil by tankers in the Caspian to refineries in northern Iran. In return, the National Iranian Oil Company dispatched an equivalent amount to China by sea, thus giving China, Kazakhstan, and Iran a common economic interest.[41]

In the cultural field, in early 2006, Muhammad Khatami—chairman of the Center of International Relations in Tehran, and former president of Iran—drew a parallel between his Dialogue of Civilizations project and Kazkah President Nursultan Nazarbayev's initiative of the Congress of Leaders of World Religions. "It is logical that a dialogue between religions takes place in Kazakhstan where people of different ethnic groups and religions live and work peacefully," said Khatami.[42]

But the main emphasis remained on trade and transport infrastructure. During his trip to Tehran to attend the Second Summit of Caspian Sea Littoral States in October 2007, Nazarbayev had a meeting with Supreme Leader Ayatollah Ali Khamanei, a rare honor for a visiting dignitary. He anticipated a five-fold increase in the Kazakh-Iran trade, including exports of Kazakh food grains to Iran, from the current $2 billion, by 2015.[43] This upbeat forecast was due the agreement that Nazarbayev signed with his Iranian and Turkmen counterparts to build a 650-kilometer (400-mile) north-south railroad from Uzen (Kazakhstan) to Gorgan (Iran) via Bereket (Turkmenistan). This would provide Kazakhstan with direct access to the Persian Gulf ports. The initial transport of 3.5 million tons of cargo in the first year of the new rail link's operation was expected to rise to an eventual 10 million tons.

For Turkmen President Gurbanguly Berdymukhammedov, this was his second visit to Tehran. Within four months of taking office as president, he had flown to the Iranian capital to reiterate his predecessor's policy of strenghtening ties with Iran. His hosts had noted approvingly that his first foreign trip was to Saudi Arabia to do a short hajj pilgrimage to stress his piety.

By now Karimov had discarded his ideological hostility towards Iran and adopted a pragmatic approach. The jump in the cargo that Uzbekistan transported by the Iranian rail—from 34,000 tons in 1996 to 750,000 tons in 2003—partly explained his moderating stance towards Tehran.[44] During his visit to Iran in June 2004, he signed several cooperation agreements. A further push to close Tashkent-Tehran ties came in the wake of the Andijan massacre in May 2005, which severely strained Uzbekistan's relations with the West, particularly the United States. The Uzbek media began to print and broadcast more reports and comments on Iran than before—and in a positive fashion. For instance, on February 14, 2006, the Uzbek state radio broadcast led with an interview with Ibrahim Normatov, a Tashkent-based political commentator, who argued that Iran had the legal right to develop its nuclear program.[45]

Part of Karimov's reason for softening the policy on Iran stemmed from the thumping success of the Justice and Development (AK) Party in the Turkish parliament in November 2002, an unmistakable sign of the importance of Islam among Turks. That landmark event—followed a month later by an agreement on educational cooperation, involving shared curriculums and exchange students between Turkey and Iran—was welcomed in Tehran.

Strong trade relations that had developed between the Islamic Republic and Turkey during the Iran-Iraq war in the 1980s continued, despite basic irreconcilable differences in their constitutions. Iran was one of the seven countries invited by Necmettin Erbakan, the Islamist prime minister of Turkey, to form the D8 group of Muslim nations to form an Islamic Common Market in 1996. Nothing came of it, as Erbakan was eased out of office the next year. Yet, between 2002 and 2005, the two-way trade between Iran and Turkey jumped from 1.2 billion to $4 billion.

Unlike Erbakan, Erdogan was set to serve the full four-year term. While showing no sign of loosening or terminating the military cooperation agreements that the preceding governments, influenced strongly by the military, had signed with Israel, he did not shy away from criticizing Israel when he deemed it pertinent—a stance welcomed by Tehran. He described the assassination of Shaikh Ahmad Yassin, leader of the Palestinian Hamas organization, in March 2004 as an act of "state terrorism." Protesting against the building of the wall in the West Bank by Israel, he briefly recalled Turkey's ambassador to Israel. Hence, when Ergodan chaired the Islamic Conference Organization (ICO) in Istanbul in June, thanks to the backing he received from Saudi Arabia and Iran, he had his nominee, Ekmeleddin Ihsanoglu, a Turkish academic, appointed the ICO's secretary-general.

Little wonder that, during his visit to Tehran in July, Erdogan was accorded the rare privilege of a meeting with Khamanei. Erdogan signed a security cooperation agreement with Iran, which involved inter alia "a joint fight against terrorism." This stemmed from a reconsideration of Turkey's relations with Iran, as well as the Arab Middle East. Professor Ahmet Davutoglu —adviser to Erdogan and to then Foreign Minister Abdullah Gül—who visualized the world as composed of cultural blocs, provided insight. He argued that, for Turkey to remain powerful, it must utilize the "strategic depth" of its neighborhood, and cultivate stronger links with those Muslim neighbors to whom it is related culturally. Accepting this approach to regional policy, Erdogan's government forged cordial relations not only with Iran, but also with Syria.[47]

Just a week before the Turkish general election on July 22, 2007, Iran's petroleum minister Kazem Vaziri-Hamaneh and Turkey's energy minister Hilmi Guler signed a memorandum of understanding (MoU) under which Turkmen and Iranian gas would be exported to Europe through Turkey, and Turkey would develop three later phases of Iran's giant South Pars gas field on the basis of Tehran's buyback scheme.[48] A columnist in the *Zaman*, an Islamic daily, described the MoU as Turkey's "dream come true." By contrast, the document drew a quick condemnation from the U.S. State Department, reminding Ankara of the trade sanctions that existed against Iran.

Like Erbakan before him, Erdogan rebuffed Washington. But unlike Erbakan, he did so publicly and scathingly, well aware of the impending election and that 81 percent of Turkish voters disapproved of the Bush administration's foreign policies, with only 7 percent approving it.

Iran welcomed Erdogan's victory in the parliamentary poll, followed by the elevation of Abdullah Gül to the presidency of Turkey. These developments augured well for cordial relations between the two republics, which until a decade earlier had been presented as antithetical.

SUMMARY AND CONCLUSIONS

TURKEY AND IRAN EXISTED AS DISTINCT ENTITIES LONG BEFORE THE inception of the Central Asian republics. Their histories have been molded by religion, relations between state and mosque, secularism, nationalism, Islamic fundamentalism, Westernization, modernization, capitalist development, and moderate Islamism.

As for Central Asia, the preeminent dynamics of the constituent republics' histories have been Tsarist imperialism, territorial loyalty, Islam, pan-Turkism, the Bolshevik Revolution, Marxism-Leninism, the highly centralized Communist Party, Stalin's theory of nations, socialist development in economics and culture (including scientific atheism), the Stalinist purges, the Great Patriotic War, de-Stalinization, glasnost and perestroika, the Soviet bloc's defeat in the Cold War, ethnic nationalism, religious revival, radical Islam, the market economy, and multiparty politics.

Overall, the region's history can be divided into three distinct phases: the Tsarist era, the building of a Marxist socialist state and society, and the post-Soviet period. Of the many non-Slav regions that became part of the Tsarist Empire, and later of the Soviet Union, Central Asia underwent the most turbulent experiences during the past century. These include the delineation of several republics based on ethnicity; the formalization of several spoken vernaculars into written languages, using first Roman and then Cyrillic scripts; a thorough transformation of property rights; an almost complete abrogation of traditional religion and places of worship; and the creation of a highly centralized political party imbued with Marxism-Leninism as interpreted by the latest party leader—followed by the arduous task of nation-building, while transforming a command economy under one-party rule into a market economy in a (seemingly) multiparty system.

UNDER JOSEPH STALIN

Joseph Stalin, an ethnic Georgian, constructed his theory of nations based on Vladimir Lenin's thesis on nationalism. Since nationalism was a response to the national-social oppression caused by the emergence of early capitalism, argued Lenin, it was bound to disappear in the course of building socialism, which would foster proletarian internationalism. For the present, however, as a practical politician, Lenin recognized the specific nationalisms that had arisen in the wake of Tsarist expansion, and supported the right to national self-determination vis-à-vis the Great Russian imperialism. He later extended that concept to include "the right to free secession."

According to Stalin, a nation was a stable and historically developed community based on a common language, a unified territory, a shared economic life, and a common culture. This definition was at the root of the national delimitations that occurred in the Soviet Union from 1924 to 1925, and in 1929 and 1936. As a result, Tsarist-era Turkistan was divided into the Kazakh Soviet Socialist Republic (SSR), the Kyrgyz SSR, the Tajik SSR, the Turkmen SSR, and the Uzbek SSR. Each of these republics had its own language, written first in the Roman script, and then in Cyrillic. In 1938, Moscow decided to make Russian compulsory in all non-Russian schools in the Union. The switchover of the Central Asian languages from Roman to Cyrillic that followed came at a time when major road and rail projects in the region had been accomplished, enabling Moscow to tighten further its control over Central Asia.

Determined to eradicate feudalism and bourgeois nationalism as a prelude to building socialism, Stalin trained his revolutionary guns at religion, the religious establishment, and kulaks (rich farmers). Since Communists viewed Islam as an integral part of a feudal order resting on the troika of the landlord, the mullah, and the rich trader—and since the Sharia impinged on every facet of life, individual and social, viewed the state and mosque as two sides of the same coin, and considered the right to private property sacrosanct—Communists conducted periodic campaigns against Islam (as well as Christianity and Judaism).

They derided religious superstitions and listed the following customs associated with Islam as archaic: polygamy, bride purchase, child marriage, the veil for women, the segregation of sexes in public places, circumcision of male children, fasting during Ramadan, and self-flagellation by Shias during the Ashura ceremonies. They labeled Islam conservative because it sanctioned discrimination against women and enjoined excessive reverence for male elders. Finally, argued Bolsheviks, Islam's insistence on dividing the world between believers and nonbelievers ruled out fraternization among different peoples of the Soviet Union as equals—thus hindering the creation of the New Socialist Person, who would transcend his or her religious, ethnic, and racial background to build a socialist order.

The ruling party and state coordinated anti-Islamic education and propaganda with literacy drives and reorganized popular socio-economic activities. They focused on winning a few converts to scientific atheism in each village, with a view to using them as models of rationalism and modern thinking. These efforts went hand in hand with steps to weaken and destroy the extensive religious networks of mosques and theological institutions, and their financial support—the religious trust properties, which were nationalized. (In Turkey, Mustafa Kemal Ataturk followed a similar path, except that there were no parallel literacy campaigns and no ideological ballast of historical materialism or scientific atheism; it had more to do with destroying the possibility that the Sultan-Caliph would return on the backs of revived Islamic institutions and clerics.)

As in Turkey, the proscription of the Arabic script in the Soviet Union in 1929 struck at the root of Islamic scriptures and commentaries, making the surviving clergy totally dependent on the religious material that the Soviet authorities deemed fit to be published in the Cyrillic or Roman script. During the second phase of the anti-religious campaign in the early 1930s, the Union of Atheists transformed the places of worship into museums, places of entertainment, or factories, and encouraged Muslim women to burn their veils in public, which they did in the thousands.

Eager to crush the power and influence of kulaks, as well as tribal and clan chiefs and village elders, in the rural Soviet Union, where a majority of the people lived, Stalin introduced compulsory collectivization of farms in 1930. Collectivization proved particularly traumatic for the nomads of Kazakhstan, Kyrgyzstan, and Uzbekistan who made their living from cattle breeding. The resulting migration of whole clans to neighboring countries reduced Kazakhs and Kyrgyzes into minorities in the republics named after them.

As Central Asia largely lacked the engine of the Bolshevik Revolution—the industrial working class—locals were underrepresented among the ranks and officials of the republican Communist parties. Therefore, the task of destroying feudalism in production and social relations fell disproportionately to the ethnic Russians in the party.

Moscow overcame the opposition of local kulaks, peasants, and livestock breeders by combining force, large-scale deportations, and propaganda with the dispatch of Slav-dominated Communist Party contingents from the European sector to Central Asia to furnish the newly established collective farms with manpower and technical and managerial skills.

In due course, collective farms called *kolkhozes*, possessing land and farm machinery, and managing schools, clubs, libraries, cinemas, and agro-based industries, engendered their own milieu. Under the supervision of the local Communist Party's central committee, they enjoyed substantial freedom. Since a typical collective farm in Central Asia was established around a long-established village, it drew extended families and even whole clans, thus grafting feudal social relations onto socialist production relations, engendering distortions. This was particularly true of the cotton-growing areas of Uzbekistan, which became a major source of supply of the highly valued commodity in the Soviet Union.

Unsurprisingly, as the most populous and strategic republic in Central Asia, Uzbekistan emerged as one of the important centers of the "nationalist conspiracy" during the Stalinist purges of 1937 to 1938. The party and government positions of the purged leaders went to younger cadres whose lives had been molded totally by the Bolshevik order. The disappearance of rural property in the wake of the nationalization of land, water, and forests, followed by collectivization, destroyed the power and influence of the traditional elite, and created opportunities for young party activists imbued with Marxism-Leninism.

As Stalin became obsessed with creating a highly centralized Soviet Union, party and government leaders increasingly ignored local traditions and interests, thus deviating from one of the principal Leninist guidelines on nationalities. They thus inadvertently sowed the seeds of future disintegration.

Unquestioned loyalty to Moscow from republican capitals became highly prized; and the Russian party members domiciled in a Central Asian republic, being immune to local influences, rose fast in the republic's hierarchy, thus creating (unexpressed) disaffection among native party ranks.

The fast-rising literacy rate and the practice of mentioning nationality on a citizen's identity card created greater ethnic-linguistic awareness among the numerous nationalities in the region and elsewhere than ever before. This would prove to be a lasting legacy.

The Great Patriotic War, which began with Germany's invasion of the Soviet Union in mid-1941, resulted in untold human suffering and material destruction of the Soviet Union. But it also allowed the regime to engender symbiosis between patriotism and socialism, thereby enabling the

Bolshevik Revolution to be absorbed into the popular psyche. Noting the Russian Soviet Federation's geographical and demographic preponderance in the Union, Stalin revived Russian nationalism to mobilize the people to resist the mighty invader. He even co-opted the Russian Orthodox Church for this purpose, permitting its followers to elect a new synod and patriarch in 1943.

Stalin performed a similar about-face with respect to the Islamic leadership. The result was the establishment of the Official Islamic Administration in October 1943, operating through regional Muslim Spiritual Directorates, including the one in Tashkent for the Muslims of Middle Asia and Kazakhstan. Having uprooted the powerful Islamic tree, Stalin could now afford to allow a sapling to grow under strictly controlled conditions. Overall, though, this concordat between mosque and state had a healing effect in the Central Asian republics.

The region's Muslim citizens supported the war effort to the hilt. The uninterrupted operation of the Ashgabat railway and the Caspian port of Krasnovodsk (now Turkmenbashi)—connecting the southern fronts and the Trans-Caucasian republics with Central Russia under German occupation—during the winter of 1941 to 1942 enabled the Soviets to expel the Germans from the Volga region and the Caucasian foothills, and break the German siege of Volgograd (Stalingrad). The Muslim region of Baku produced more than two-thirds of the Soviet oil output.

The Kremlin transferred 270 factories from the frontline zones in the European sector to Kazakhstan, Kyrgyzstan, and Uzbekistan, and set up new plants in these republics. The war created unprecedented job opportunities for women, thus furthering their emancipation. It brought together numerous nationalities living in the Union republics. Working with Russian troops, hundreds of thousands of Central Asians improved their Russian. All of this reinforced the political-economic unity of the Soviet Union. The victory in 1945 was the zenith of the Soviet system under Stalin.

Citizens had been exposed to political education, and party cadres had been trained both ideologically (to engender unity between the Russian core and the non-Slavic periphery) and professionally (to perform managerial and executive jobs). A new generation of Soviet-educated, war-hardened cadres had begun to climb the hierarchical ladder in the Central Asian republics. As before, to prove their loyalty to Moscow, they initiated purges in 1951 to 1952—under the guise of eradicating "local favoritism," "bourgeois nationalism," and "archaic [i.e., Islamic] customs"—which were far less severe than those in 1937 to 1938.

By the time of Stalin's death in March 1953, the Communist state had, on its own, recovered war losses and achieved growth rates comparable with those of West Germany and Japan.

The Post-Stalin Era

Once Nikita Khrushchev had emerged as the leader of the Soviet Union, he unveiled an ambitious plan to make the Union self-sufficient in food grains, meat, cotton, and tobacco by the early 1980s. This was to be achieved by transforming underused land in the Urals, the Volga region, North Caucasus, southern Siberia, and Kazakhstan into fertile agricultural fields, with the latter two areas contributing the most.

Khrushchev also began quietly removing diehard Stalinists from power. He used the first post-Stalin Communist Party of the Soviet Union (CPSU) congress in February 1956 to mount a wholesale attack on Stalin. He denounced Stalin for trampling upon socialist legality, fostering a personality cult, and committing gross violations of basic Leninist principles in his nationalities policy by banishing entire ethnic groups to the far corners of the Soviet Union on the unsubstantiated grounds of being pro-German during the Great Patriotic War.[i]

In his report on domestic developments to the CPSU congress in 1961, Khrushchev declared that the Soviet Union had entered "mature socialism." During this phase of socialism, the dialectics of national relations would follow the line of "blooming, rapprochement, and amalgamation": the twin processes of blooming (i.e., the fullest realization of each Soviet nation) and rapprochement (i.e., the coming together of nations through cross-fertilization and the sharing of a common socialist economy and social formations) resulting in rapid progress towards ultimate amalgamation.

His successor, Leonid Brezhnev, was not so sanguine. He declared that Khrushchev's scenario of the merger of all Soviet nations was too idealistic, and would have to await the global triumph of socialism over capitalism. At the CPSU congress in 1966, therefore, he announced that the party would continue to show "solicitude" for the interests and characteristics of each of the 123 nationalities in the Soviet Union.

Likewise, on the "religious question," Brezhnev ended the excesses of Khrushchev's anti-religious propaganda from 1955 to 1959. He placated the Official Islamic Administration by allowing the restoration of religious monuments. The reconstruction of all the mosques destroyed by the 1966 earthquake in Tashkent showed his policy at work. Allowing the Muslim

Spiritual Directorate in Tashkent to publish a magazine in Uzbek, Arabic, Persian, English, and French was a further example of the new policy.

In 1970, Ziauddin Babakhan, the Tashkent-based mufti, convened an international Islamic conference in the Uzbek capital, the first such assembly in Russian or Soviet history. Mullahs justified their cooperation with the Soviet state by arguing that Marxism-Leninism was primarily concerned with managing the economy and administration, whereas Islam dealt with spiritual and ethical matters.

Officially registered clerics now dealt with a new generation of Central Asians. Reared on Soviet education and the welfare state, which guaranteed the basic needs of food and housing and provided free social services, it possessed the kind of confidence that had eluded the previous generation. Many young Central Asian intellectuals tried to rediscover their national-cultural origins. Since these were intertwined with Islamic heritage, their quest led them to Islam. But their interest in religion could not be properly satisfied by the registered clerics working under government supervision. This led to the growth of unregistered clerics, collectively called "unofficial" or "parallel" Islam. Their existence was soon to be acknowledged by officials of the Union of Atheists and others.

By 1973, Brezhnev had lost his impetus for reforming the system to which he had committed himself in 1966. Instead, he had become obsessed with achieving production targets. Also, the expensive arms race with the West distorted the Soviet economy, sucking up a hefty 25 percent of the GDP on defense and defense-related industries, as well as the major part of the first-rate scientific and intellectual talent.

The sole ruling party arrogated greater powers to itself and fostered a ruling elite: it cosseted itself with ever-rising privileges, distancing itself further from ordinary citizens and party members. This demoralized workers and peasants, many of whom lost their motivation for hard work. Attitudes towards public property—which was all that existed—deteriorated. Many employees took to pilfering from their workplaces while managers resorted to underhanded practices to procure raw or intermediate materials and other needs to meet their production targets. In agriculture, the practice of doctoring output figures, especially of cotton, took root. Graft and corruption thrived. So, too, did the mafia—men in sharp suits who, for a price, got things done in a highly bureaucratic setup.

The parallel economy thrived to the detriment of its legitimate counterpart. By the late 1970s, the system was in deep trouble and needed drastic reform by a vibrant leadership. But by then Brezhnev was gravely ill, and totally dependent on the information and advice he received from his close aides. Being sycophantic, they humored him instead of telling him the truth about the fast deteriorating situation. Despite his failing faculties, he hung onto the supreme power until his death in November 1982.

His successor, Yuri Andropov, launched a campaign to improve labor discipline and productivity, and to eliminate corruption. With graft being more common in Central Asia, especially in Uzbekistan, than elsewhere, the anti-corruption drive had more impact on this region than others. But it made headway in Uzbekistan only after Sharaf Rashidov, the long-serving party leader, had died in October 1983. The charges against him and his aides included not merely widespread bribery and nepotism, but also large-scale embezzlement of funds, stemming from fraudulent cotton output figures, and general economic mismanagement. As Uzbekistan produced nearly two-thirds of Soviet cotton, this was a serious matter. But before Andropov could stamp his imprint on the administration, he died in early 1984. Konstantin Chernenko, his successor, was by all accounts a failure. Luckily for the Soviet Union, he only lasted about a year.

Mikhail Gorbachev, the youngest leader of the Soviet Union, was determined to put things right. Within a year of assuming the supreme office, he had launched glasnost and perestroika. These were well-meaning steps, but Gorbachev, a leader cast in the CPSU mold, had not thought through the consequences of his actions. He failed to realize the basic contradiction in his strategy: democracy *and* centralized power as embodied by the CPSU. Indeed, he counted on using the CPSU to usher in a democratic setup! He never seriously considered allowing a multi-party system—either by letting the monolithic CPSU break up into three parties embodying the existing conservative, radical, and centrist trends within the CPSU, or allowing genuine non-Communist groupings to emerge and grow.

When the dictatorial state and party loosened their iron grip, the long-suppressed popular feelings and views exploded, pushing to the fore not only the economic problems stemming from decades of highly centralized planning, including party and governmental corruption, but also the unresolved or partially resolved problems of interethnic relations.

In Central Asia, the "national question" manifested itself in different forms: (a) relations between Slavs and non-Slavs, most prominently in Kazakhstan; (b) relations between ethnic groups with different religious backgrounds, e.g., Kazakhs and Russians in Kazakhstan; and (c) relations between ethnic groups sharing the same religious background, e.g., Uzbeks and Tajiks in Uzbekistan.

To stress a dramatic break with the past, Gorbachev started to get rid of old party stalwarts in the politburos of the CPSU and the republican parties. In December 1986, he replaced Dinmukhamed Kunayev as first secretary of the Communist Party of Kazakhstan with an ethnic Russian, Gennadi Kolbin, a minor party functionary. Gorbachev thus, inadvertently or otherwise, sharpened the contradiction that had existed all along between the center (Moscow) and the periphery (represented by the capitals of the republics), and reinforced Kazakh nationalism even within the Kazakh members of the Communist Party of Kazakhstan. Making matters worse, the authorities dismissed the young protesters as hooligans and extremists, and used police force to disperse the pro-Kunayev demonstrators, causing up to twenty deaths.

Republican and central Communist leaders showed similar insensitivity toward Uzbeks on the issue of corruption. Inamjan Usmankhojayev, who succeeded Rashidov, never let past an opportunity to lambaste his predecessor, only to find himself arrested for corruption, found guilty, and convicted. The conclusions of a thorough investigation into corrupt practices in Uzbekistan, published in 1987, discovered a loss to the public exchequer of $2 billion for inflated cotton production figures over a quarter century, the fraud involving over 2,600 officials in Uzbekistan and Moscow, including a son-in-law of Brezhnev.

Instead of restoring popular faith in the system now purportedly cleansed of corrupt elements, the odious scandal and the subsequent party and governmental purges left the populace confused and cynical, with their trust in the system at an all-time low. Ethnic Uzbeks felt offended by the way officials and the media in Moscow began to treat the "Uzbek Affair" and corruption as two sides of the same coin. This feeling became transmuted into a resolve to resist Moscow, creating a milieu favorable to the emergence of opposition groups, nationalist and Islamist.

As home to two-thirds of the 230 working mosques in Central Asia in the mid-1980s, Uzbekistan was the most important Soviet republic in terms of Islam. Developments in this field were therefore of great interest to both the republican and central leaders. The party hierarchy's hard line on participation in Islamic rituals collapsed when, during the run-up to the millennium celebrations in 1988, the Russian Orthodox Church was accorded an honored place in the Russian Soviet Federation. The Soviet media waxed eloquent on the inextricable bond between the Russian Church and culture, and the significance of religion in the history of Russia.

Communist leaders were alarmed by the findings of the survey of

Tashkent University undergraduates with a Muslim background in 1987. It showed 60 percent describing themselves as "Muslim" and only 7 percent as "atheist." A 1979 Soviet survey of "formerly Muslim peoples" had shown only 30 percent calling themselves "believers" and 50 percent as "unbelievers." Unlike the believers in the Tashkent University sample, those in the earlier survey had been mainly rural, old, and semiliterate.

Several factors explained the change. First, the relaxed atmosphere created by perestroika and glasnost made people less afraid of expressing their true feelings than before. Second, the events in Iran and Afghanistan made Islam a living socio-political ideology rather than a fossilized creed of feudal times, as Soviet ideologues portrayed it. Third, in the absence of knowledge of any other non-Marxist creed, people with a Muslim background fell back on Islam as an all-embracing savior. It helped them to counter the influence of the Slavic Big Brother, and assisted them in reasserting their own ethnic-cultural identity—which, stretching back many centuries, stood apart from Christianity and Europe.

New mosques built with private contributions began opening every week, and enrollment in existing theological colleges soared. So long as the Central Asian republics were part of the Soviet Union, opposition national-ist parties frequently used Islam and Islamic symbols to rally support. But once these republics became independent states in the aftermath of the collapse of the Communist Party, the situation changed somewhat.

INDEPENDENT CENTRAL ASIAN REPUBLICS

The collapse of Marxism-Leninism as the state ideology in Central Asian republics opened up opportunities for other ideologies to fill the vacuum. As the victor in the Cold War, the capitalist democracy of the Western alliance led by Washington seemed to be the prime candidate. But there was a practical problem. Neither the politicians nor the public in these countries had previous experience of multi-party democracy or private enterprise. That ruled out a wholesale adoption of the Western mode of government.

However, faced with the sole superpower, America, insisting on commit-ment to democracy as a preamble to formal diplomatic relations with it—and therefore access to sorely needed assistance from the International Monetary Fund and the World Bank—Central Asian leaders expressed faith, at least rhetorically, in a multi-party system and a market economy. By so doing, they inadvertently made redundant the establishment of a party genuinely advocating free enterprise and liberal democracy.

So it was left to nationalism or Islam to fill satisfactorily the ideo-logical vacuum. Each came in two varieties: ethnic nationalism per se, or within the overall context of pan-Turkism; and Islam as a font of ethics and spirituality, and part of Central Asian culture, or as a socio-political ideology, informing and guiding society and government at large—i.e., Islamic fundamentalism.

Whereas there was no dispute between the ruling parties—the renamed Communist Party (now called the People's Democratic Party, PDP), the Socialist Party, or even the Democratic Party—and the opposition about reviving Islam as a faith, differences arose on promoting Islam as an official ideology. There were no limitations on religious activity by citizens, and no barriers to the expansion of mosques and theological institutions. The gov-ernments unhesitatingly declared two Islamic *eids* as public holidays. They allowed state-run radio and television channels to transmit Islamic pro-grams. The presidents made a point of undertaking umra, a short hajj to Mecca, during their trips to Saudi Arabia. President Islam Karimov of Uzbekistan took his oath of office on the Quran, and took to prefacing his public speeches with "*Bismallah al Rahman al Rahim* (In the name of God, the Merciful and the Compassionate)." But Karimov and all others Central Asian presidents were determined to maintain a strict division between reli-gion and government.

On the other hand, the Islamic Renaissance Party—established in 1990 as an all-Union organization to secure the same religious rights for Muslims as enjoyed by Christians—turned radical. Accorded a legal status in Tajikistan in September 1992 after popular agitation, the IRP aimed to establish an Islamic state, but only through the ballot. Operating clandestinely in Uzbekistan, it had the same objective there.

As sovereign, independent states, Uzbekistan, Tajikistan, and Kyrgyzstan were free to conduct their affairs as their leaders saw fit. But, since they contained parts of the fertile, populous Fergana Valley, a traditional strong-hold of Islam, their leaders could not devise and implement policies towards Islamists in a sealed fashion. Indeed, at crucial points during the 1992 to 1997 civil war in Tajikistan, the Karimov government intervened against the Islamist forces first covertly and then overtly. On the other side, the fighters of the Islamic Movement of Uzbekistan, operating from Tajikistan, attacked targets in Kyrgyzstan as part of diversionary tactics to supply small arms to their cohorts in Uzbekistan.

In Uzbekistan's secular arena, ethnic nationalism was appropriated by Birlik and Erk opposition parties before independence. With Birlik denied the status of a recognized political party, the role of fostering Uzbek nationalism fell to Erk. It emphasized its nationalist, anti-Communist credentials by adopting the flag of the Kokand Autonomous Government of 1917 to 1918. With no immediate chance of gaining power, Erk could afford to be ultra-nationalist, thus preempting any lurch towards nationalism that the ruling People's Democratic Party found expeditious. On the other hand, with non-Uzbeks forming a third of the republic's population, any party propounding militant nationalism was unlikely to win power through the ballot box.

The existence of recognized and unrecognized Islamic and nationalist organizations in Uzbekistan reduced the ruling PDP's chance of adopting a coherent ideology. Since the PDP did not believe in wholesale privatization of the economy, as had happened in Russia under President Boris Yeltsin, there was no question of it embracing the IMF prescriptions, or granting meaningful freedoms to voters. In desperation, therefore, it fell back on such slogans as "discipline and order" and "the urgent task of nation-building."

In Turkmenistan, the governing Democratic Party (the renamed Communist Party) led by President Saparmurat Niyazov tried to turn its commitment to raise living standards into some sort of ideology, and imposed a virtual ban on oppositional activities until economic prosperity had been achieved. Given the natural gas riches of the republic, this was expected to take a decade. But nothing changed by the end of the 1990s—except that Niyazov acquired lifetime presidency.

The one Central Asian state where ethnic arithmetic precluded any prospect of local nationalism holding sway was Kazakhstan. The impact of a large body of Slav settlers there was reinforced by the long, unguarded Kazakh-Russian border. President Nursultan Nazarbayev understood this; and so, too, did the drafters of the new constitution. It required a registered public association to be open to every and any citizen, irrespective of his or her ethnic origins, mother tongue, or "attitudes towards religion" (which included being irreligious or atheistic). And by letting any citizen who was "fluent in Kazakh" become president, the 1993 constitution held out the possibility of an ethnic Slav winning the supreme office—a setback for militant Kazakh nationalists.

Militant ethnic nationalism was not the only ideology to fail in the region. Militant Islam allied with anti-Communist democratic forces also failed to overthrow neo-Communists in Tajikistan, despite a long civil war which claimed an estimated 60,000 to 100,000 mainly civilian lives. It ended in July 1997 with a compromise.

The Tajik civil war inducted not only Uzbekistan, Afghanistan, and

Russia, but also Iran. Peace came only when each of them realized that it was in its own interest to end the conflict that peace came. It was the Taliban's stunning military advance in Afghanistan in 1996 to 1997 that focused the minds of the Uzbek, Russian, and Iranian leaders. Karimov concluded that neo-Communist Rahman Nabiyev was incapable of bringing all of Tajikistan under his control. Both Moscow and Tehran were keen to block the Taliban's progress by arming the anti-Taliban forces in northern and western Afghanistan, and wanted a peaceful Tajikistan to be able to do so. Ultimately, therefore, geopolitics trumped ideology.

The Pentagon's strikes at the military training camps in Taliban-controlled Afghanistan in August 1998, in retaliation for Al Qaeda's bombing of the American embassies in East Africa, heralded America's overt involvement in the region's conflicts.

Until then, Washington had combined its push for political and economic liberalization in Central Asia with promoting the cause of American oil companies in the hydrocarbon industries of Kazakhstan and Turkmenistan. International financial aid to a republic was proportional to the degree of its liberalization of the local economy and politics. In this regard, Kyrgyzstan under President Askar Akayev was ahead of others.

Since the constitution of every regional republic specified the election of the chief executive with a limit of two terms of office, each of four or five years, the document acquired an aura of democracy. As for checks and balances, the division of power between the executive president and the parliament became a running point of contention; the president would try to weaken the legislature by turning it into a bicameral chamber, with the upper house containing many members appointed by the president. The election commissions, appointed by the president, often behaved like political bodies. The supreme courts, where they existed, went along with the executive president, occasionally showing independence, as in Kyrgyzstan.

There, with his supreme authority assured for five more years after the 1995 poll, and buttressed by the IMF largesse that followed, Akayev joined the ranks of his Central Asian counterparts—noted for monopolizing power, enriching themselves and their families, and suppressing opposition. And when his most formidable opponent, Felix Kulov, was disqualified from contesting the presidential election in 2000 for failing to pass the Kyrgyz language test, Akayev romped home again.

Following the 9/11 attacks, Akayev became the only Central Asian leader to give U.S.-led coalition forces unrestricted overflight rights for combat, humanitarian, and search-and-rescue missions from the Manas base near the capital. Then, to please Moscow, which had offered generous financial aid to Kyrgyzstan during the hazardous economic transition in the early 1990s, Akayev allowed Russia to set up a military base at Kant near Bishkek.

Intent on hanging onto power, Akayev rigged the parliamentary poll in late February 2005—ensuring inter alia the election of his son and daughter—to such an extent that a widespread protest ensued. It escalated until Akayev and his family fled on March 24, first to Kazakhstan and then to Moscow. This dramatic episode, unique in Central Asia, became known as the Tulip Revolution, following the success of other peaceful popular demonstrations in Ukraine and Georgia.

Akayev pointed an accusatory finger at the Bush administration, claiming that it had financed the opposition to punish him for tightening links with Moscow. He criticized Western NGOs, particularly Freedom House, for promoting Western-style democracy in Kyrgyzstan with no regard to the country's history and culture. His statement chimed with Karimov, who had been making the same argument for much longer. Akayev's downfall alarmed him.

So, when a group of armed men raided a jail in Andijan in mid-May, releasing several hundred inmates (including businessmen accused of belonging to an banned Islamist organization), occupied the regional administrative office, and called for Karimov's resignation, the president panicked. His troops mowed down 400 to 600 unarmed civilians, including women and children, in order to disperse thousands of locals who had gathered in the main city square to vent their anger at rampant corruption and high unemployment.

Such brutality elicited widespread condemnation in the West. The Bush administration called for an international investigation, to no avail. Whereas the State Department advocated severance of all relations with Uzbekistan, the Defense Department favored assessing each U.S. assistance program individually. The Pentagon wanted to retain its troops and warplanes at the Karshi-Khanabad base leased to it by Karimov on the eve of its campaign against the Taliban. Livid at the condemnation of his government by politicians, the media, and NGOs in America, Karimov gave the Pentagon six months to leave the base.

Thus ended a fifteen-year flirtation between Karimov and the White House. After a decade of unexciting relations, a thaw ensued when, following the September 11, 2001, attacks, President George W. Bush described his "war on terror" as a battle between good and evil. That was exactly what Karimov had been saying for many years in his relentless campaign against radical Islamists—referring to all those Uzbek men who sported beards and Uzbek women who covered their hair with hijabs.

Uzbek-American relations reached a high point when Karimov and Bush signed a "Declaration on the Strategic Partnership and Cooperation Framework" in Washington in March 2002. Covering political, security, economic, humanitarian, and legal cooperation between the two countries, it required Uzbekistan to "further intensify the democratic transformation of its society politically and economically." While the U.S. aid to Uzbekistan grew many fold, the Karimov government's progress towards democratic reform remained tardy. Indeed, the case of two Islamist prisoners, tortured to death by boiling water, that leaked in August 2002 illustrated regression. And a judicial system that routinely relied on confessions by the suspects, often obtained by torture, remained in place.

Karimov backed Bush's invasion of Iraq in March 2003 since the underlying rationale was the alleged link between Iraqi President Saddam Hussein and Al Qaeda leader Osama bin Laden, but refrained from committing combat troops for the war. The Uzbek leader was focused on hosting the annual general meeting of the London-based European Bank for Reconstruction and Development in Tashkent in early May. That would secure his republic a high profile in the international arena, he hoped.

Unluckily for Karimov, both Clare Short, British secretary of state for Overseas Development, and Jean Lemierre, French president of the EBRD, condemned his government for failing to keep its promise to advance democracy and human rights. For Karimov, to be given a dressing-down by foreign dignitaries before millions of his citizens on live television was a deeply humiliating experience. Among those who saw him go ashen-faced, cover his ears, and close his eyes was Kazakh President Nazarbayev.

What was remarkable about Nazarbayev was that all along Washington had treated him differently from other Central Asian leaders. Initially, this was because Kazakhstan was the only Central Asian republic where Soviet nuclear weapons and missiles were deployed. Later, its hydrocarbon reserves made it attractive to U.S. oil companies. The Chevron-led consortium, TengizChevroil, became the first foreign firm to secure contracts for exploration and extraction of Kazakh oil and gas. This went down badly with the Kremlin, which wanted Nazarbayev to give priority to the Russian energy companies. He resisted its demand.

The consequent tension between the two countries got transmuted into strained relations between Kazakhs and Slavs in the republic. Nazarbayev chose to accelerate the Kazakhization which had been in process since 1989. He capped this policy by manipulating the 1994 parliamentary poll so that minority Kazakhs ended up with three-fifths of the seats. The disheartened Slav settlers came to accept stoically their secondary position. This in turn deprived the Kazakh nationalist opposition parties of any chance to grow. To weaken them further, Nazarbayev got parliamentary approval to move the capital from Almaty to Astana, located in a region with a 58 percent Slav population, thereby highlighting his determination to retain the Slav-majority areas within Kazakhstan.

Part of the reason for building the republic's new capital from scratch was that Nazarbayev wanted to enlarge the concept of private property in a society that had only known state property. Overall, his efforts to transform a command economy into a market economy ranked higher than those of Karimov. The Uzbek president refused to privatize land on the ground that it would pauperize a large section of society, and that, in the absence of official agricultural guidance, Uzbekistan would cease to be one of the leading cotton producers in the world.

However, Nazarbayev concurred with Karimov and other Central Asian presidents that, after seven decades of authoritarian rule in Kazakhstan, transition to democracy would be difficult, and that Western views of democracy needed amending in the Asian context.[2] Unsurprisingly, Nazarbayev followed the example of Turkmen President Niyazov—the most authoritarian of them all, and whose personality cult dwarfed Stalin's—to use a referendum to extend his first tenure of office beyond 1995. In fact, he went further. Instead of a sole reference to the deferment of the presidential poll to 2000, the ballot also included the right to private property and Kazakh as the official language—and required a collective "yes" or "no."

Continuing the practices of the Soviet era, election officials routinely announced incredibly high voter turnouts in Kazakhstan—and elsewhere in the region, except Kyrgyzstan, where over 90 percent of voters unfailingly favored the incumbent. After defecting from the Kazakh government, Rakhat Aliyev, a son-in-law of the president, disclosed the details of how Nazarbayev maintained his authoritarian rule through media control, police action, and rigged elections. The regional governors competed with one another to get the highest percentage of votes for Nazarbayev by stuffing the ballot boxes with fake ballots.[3]

None of this mattered to the Russian or Chinese governments, both of which were interested in Kazakhstan's oil and gas—especially fast-industrializing China, which shared a long border with Kazakhstan. This provided Nazarbayev a degree of latitude no other Central Asian leader enjoyed. It also afforded him and his close aides plenty of scope for corruption. Illegitimate gains accrued from kickbacks on contracts awarded for exploration and the sale of oil. The considerable differences between local and international prices for petroleum, and the shipment of crude oil passing through one or more intermediaries on its way to a refinery, created opportunities to add several dollars to the price of an oil barrel at each transfer.

When a corruption scandal in the Kazakh oil industry was exposed in 2003, the chief conduit at its center turned out to be an American, James Giffen. Though a grand jury in New York indicted him in April 2004 for violating the 1974 Foreign Corrupt Practices Act, the progress of the case was stymied by the U.S. government's refusal to release certain documents demanded by the defense lawyers, who argued that Giffen was working in cahoots with top U.S. officials to further America's interests.

The ample gas reserves in Turkmenistan provided President Niyazov a chance to fill his pockets, and he grabbed it. He did not use intermediaries, but reportedly finalized kickbacks on hydrocarbon and other deals in face-to-face meetings with the prospective contractors. His grip on the government, parliament, and the media was so strong that he indulged his most fanciful ideas—particularly after made president for life in 2000. These included renaming the months after Turkmen heroes and his mother; requiring civil servants, teachers, and doctors to pass a test on his book, *Ruhnama*; banning makeup for television newsreaders; and dismissing all health visitors, nurses, midwives, and orderlies, and replacing them with untrained military conscripts.

Confident of his total control of state and society, and keenly aware of the hydrocarbon reserves in his republic and the deep-rooted aversion that Sunni Turkmen felt towards Shiites, Niyazov ignored Washington's warnings of the dangers of close ties with the Islamic Republic of Iran. He paid frequent visits to Tehran to sign various cooperation agreements, and readily joined the Caspian Sea Cooperation Council proposed by Iran. His single most important decision was to link up the Central Asian railroad system, inherited from the Soviet era, with Iran's. With that link in place in 1996, all Central Asian republics secured access to Iran's warm-water ports in the Persian Gulf. It was their shortest route to international markets.

Iran's calculation that the economic interdependence generated by the new rail link would soften the attitude of even the most secular Central Asian leaders towards it came to pass. Noting the twenty-fold increase in the

Uzbek cargo transported by the Iranian railway to the Persian Gulf, Karimov visited Tehran in mid-2004 to sign a clutch of cooperation agreements.

The commissioning of the Korpeje-Kord-Kui pipeline to carry Turkmen gas to Iran in 1997 proved mutually beneficial. It saved Tehran the expense of extending its domestic pipeline to a remote northeastern corner, while providing the Niyazov government with an additional export outlet. That broke the monopoly that Gazprom—the Russian behemoth owning the gas pipelines in Russia—had enjoyed in transporting Turkmen gas to foreign destinations. So, tightening economic links with Iran enabled Niyazov to lessen Turkmenistan's dependence on Moscow, whose continued Big Brotherly attitude irked Central Asian leaders.

Yet such were the compulsions of history, geography, and economics that none of these presidents could set themselves completely free from the embrace of Mother Russia. True. Every now and then, a Central Asian leader struck a defiant pose only to realize that he could not sustain it for long. Indeed, as Russian President Vladimir Putin started transforming Russia's political system into a "managed democracy" during his second term of office from 2004 to 2008)—marginalizing the opposition, gaining almost full control over the electronic media, virtually renationalizing energy and other important industries—the authoritarian and proto-authoritarian rulers of Central Asia began to feel at home once more at the Kremlin.

After all, under Niyazov, Turkmenistan remained stuck in one-party rule. Other Central Asian leaders distorted the multi-party system to make sure their grip on power never slackened. Uzbekistan saw the rise of different political parties, all of them sponsored by Karimov and swearing their loyalty to him. He then went on to get himself sponsored by a different party as its presidential nominee. In the marginally freer environment of Kazakhstan, wrangling over how to divide the material benefits of political power led to divisions within the elite, leading to the rise of weak opposition parties. In Kyrgyzstan, politics remained personal; political parties centered around strong personalities with minimal ideological differences. In Tajikistan, even though the Islamic Renaissance Party, the oldest opposition faction in the region with an ideology of its own, was a shadow of its former self. The secular government of Imamali Rahmanov tried to stigmatize it by associating it with the radical, extra-parliamentary Hizb ur-Tahrir.

At the same time, the United States lost its initial enthusiasm for promoting democracy and human rights. Having realized that it had done poorly in its contest with Moscow and Beijing for influence and access to the region's hydrocarbons, it settled for less ambitious aims, such as improving commerce and gaining cooperation in countering the narcotics trade and terrorism. The Bush administration justified this shift in policy under the rubric of pragmatism.

Ironically, this same rationale had led Iran to mend its relations with the neighboring Soviet Union in its dying days. The demise of communism Iran and Russia to forge strong links. As the 1990s progressed, both came to share a common aim: to ensure the United States did not become an important player in Central Asia. The Pentagon's leasing of military bases in Uzbekistan, Kyrgyzstan, and Tajikistan in the wake of 9/11 caused anxiety in Tehran. Its leaders could only hope that this was a temporary arrangement meant to last until the overthrow of the Taliban in Afghanistan. But when the American military presence in the region continued after the fall of the Taliban, the Iranian government became concerned. Its break came when, for reasons unrelated to Iran, Karimov ended the Pentagon's lease of Karshi-Khanabad base in 2005.

On the broader front of ideological rivalry between Iran's theocratic system and Turkey's secular constitution, Iran made a substantial gain when Necmettin Erbakan, an Islamist leader, headed a coalition government in Turkey in 1996. Among other things, it undermined Washington's insistent argument that Central Asian leaders faced a stark choice between following the example of secular, democratic, pro-Western Turkey or fanatical, theocratic, anti-Western Iran. With the democratic system in Turkey putting an Islamist in power, the Americans could no longer present a Manichean scenario to Central Asians.

Erbakan's premiership was also a setback for the Turkish media, dominated by secularists, who, within months of the Soviet breakup, had trumpeted that Turkey had won the race for influence in the region, leaving Iran behind, sulking. Swept away by the euphoria they felt at the birth of four independent countries of Turkic origin, the Turkish media overlooked the fact that Tehran had focused on exploiting its geopolitical advantages due to its strategic location, and its shorelines not only along the Persian Gulf and the Arabian Sea, but also the Caspian Sea. It wanted to encourage its newly acquired Muslim neighbors to integrate their economies with its own, especially in the transport and communications spheres, rather than urge them to govern society according to the Sharia.

Part of the reason why the United States went into overdrive in its campaign against Islamic influence in Central Asia was that it had come to believe its own Cold War propaganda. Following the Soviet military intervention in Afghanistan in 1979, the United States (in conjunction with

Saudi Arabia and Egypt) had mounted a broadcasting campaign to increase Islamic consciousness in Central Asia, and ally it with local nationalism to undermine the Moscow-directed Soviet system. Washington's policymakers had failed to note that, as a Shiite country with a Shiite system of religious organization and jurisprudence, Iran could only have limited impact on the Muslim citizens of Central Asia, who belonged to the Hanafi code of Sunni Islam—as did the Turks in Turkey.

Over the past several decades, Islam has recovered the place in society it had lost under the militant secularism of Mustafa Kemal Ataturk, who died in 1938. The signs of Islamization have been unmistakable. As early as 1981, during the rule of the military junta, Professor Serif Mardin forecast that if "parliamentary institutions are placed back in operation, then an Islamic revival would take the form of a slow infiltration of Islamic world-views in Turkish society without much change in the legal system and in the present legal implementation of secularism."[4] Twenty-one years later, Mardin's prediction became a fact with the overwhelming victory of the Justice and Development (AK) Party. That electoral success brought the governments in Ankara and Tehran closer than ever before.

The political future of Central Asia will basically revolve around what happens in Uzbekistan. There is ample evidence that attachment to Islam remains strong among a majority of Uzbeks. Such too was the case with the rural Turks of Anatolia during the semi-dictatorial rule of Mustafa Kemal Ataturk. It was almost two decades after Ataturk's death that the Islamic inclination of the majority impacted on national politics. And, despite periodic bans and suppression of the Islamic forces by the ultra-secular generals, moderate Islamists won power by ballot in 2002, and continue to hold it. The possibility of a similar development in Uzbekistan in the future cannot be ruled out. Indeed, accommodating the pro-Islamist views of the Uzbek masses will become a prerequisite to stabilizing the state. And just as the United States has come to accept the popularly elected moderate Islamists in Ankara, actively seeking full membership in the European Union, perhaps Russia will do the same in the event that pragmatic Islamists win power in Tashkent through comparatively free and fair elections in the future.

EPILOGUE

To meet EU standards of freedom of expression and gender equality, in February 2008 Turkish Prime Minister Recep Tayyip of the Justice and Development party (known as AKP for the initials of its Turkish name) urged Turkey's parliament to insert "freedom of dress in education" in the constitution. It did so by 411 votes to 103. That allowed women in universities to wear a head scarf.

Challenging the law, the chief prosecutor took the case to the Constitutional Court, a secularist bastion. He argued that the AKP aimed to achieve "a model of society which takes religion as its reference." The government's counsel reasoned that prohibiting scarf in universities infringed women's rights, and that all Turks, irrespective of their attire or religious belief, should be able to attend university.

In June, by nine votes to two the judges ruled that the amendment under review infringed the constitution's secularist principles.

Many AKP deputies protested the judiciary's usurping of the parliament's legislative powers. Erdogan opposed the move to override the Court's verdict with a parliamentary vote: "We have to take Turkey out of a 'clash of powers' environment."[1]

Erdogan was aware that the Court had before it a weightier case—against the AKP—since March. In his indictment, the chief prosecutor alleged that the AKP had become "a hub of anti-secular activities," citing the scarf issue and the party's attempts to reverse restrictions on Islamic education. He recommended outlawing the AKP and banning 71 leaders, including Erdogan and President Abdullah Gul, from politics for five years.

The government argued that allowing head scarf meant expanding freedom and was part of Turkey's EU membership bid, and that the case against the AKP violated the rights to free speech and free elections.

In mid-April, Jose Barrosso, president of the European Commission, said that the case against the AKP "could have major impact in the way Turkey is seen by EU nations," and wondered whether it should continue its membership bid. His intervention was condemned by Turkish secularists who opposed the government's move to amend Article 301 of the Criminal Code. It made "insulting Turkishness" a criminal offense and had been used to prosecute sixty writers and journalists. The amended version referred to "insulting the Turkish nation," and required the Justice Minister's permission to open a case. The amended article became law on May 8, a red-letter day in Turkey's history.

Another historic decision came on July 30, 2008—by a razor thin margin. Six of the 11 judges voted for outlawing the AKP, but the law required a minimum of seven. Instead, the Court decided to halve the party's state funding for the next general election. It issued a warning that the AKP was steering the country in a direction that was "too Islamic."

There was collective sigh of relief not only in Ankara but also Brussels, Washington and other Western capitals. Outlawing a party that had won two general elections overwhelmingly and was actively pursing EU membership would have created a deep crisis in Turkey and the region.

There was enough in the court verdict to let secularists claim victory too. They declared that the AKP was now "on probation."

"If the AKP was a river that has over-flown its banks, the court has set up embankments, forcing it back into its bed," said Soner Cagaptay, a fellow at the Washington Institute for Near East Policy. "It has not put a dam in front of it."[2]

While the Turkish public was gripped by the AKP issue, another drama began unfolding with left-of-center newsweekly *Nokta* revealing in mid-2007 that retired general Sener Eruygur played a key role in two aborted coup attempts in 2004. The first attempt, codenamed "Blonde Girl," was for military intervention to over throw the AKP government. It was overruled by the then chief of general staff. The second, codenamed "Moonlight," was devised to generate public opinion for a coup by creating terror and chaos. Eruygur and Hursit Tolon, another retired general, approached the media tycoons for help, but in vain.

Next came another plan with the plotters belonging to an illegal ultra-nationalist network called Ergenkon.[3] It had a similar agenda as "Moonlight."

The case against Ergenkon activists started in June 2007 with the discovery of a cache of weapons and explosives in the home of an ultra-nationalist retired military officer. The Ergenkon was accused of a series of murderous blasts, a grenade attack on the leftist newspaper, Cumhuriyet, and the murder of Armenian journalist, Hrant Dink.

By early 2009, a series of police swoops led to 200 arrests, including retired generals, serving military and police officers, journalists and lawyers. The arrest of serving army officers led to tension between Erdogan and the chief of general staff, Gen. Ilker Basbug. The government disclaimed political motives, stressing that it lacked the authority to institute investigation. The trial of 86 suspects continued.

The ongoing Ergenkon saga gave credence to those who like Belma Akcura, an investigative journalist and author of *Deep State* , believed that a powerful grouping of military and civilian bureaucrats and mafia was hell bent on forestalling the arrival of full democracy in Turkey.[4]

This gave pause to Central Asian leaders who, intent on spinning out of Russia's orbit in the immediate aftermath of the Soviet Union's disintegration, had found the Turkish model of democracy attractive. Since then, however, they had groped their way back to Mother Russia, and adopted the ways of the "managed democracy" perfected by President Vladimir Putin.

To their relief, when caught between its self-appointed mission of spreading democracy, minted in Washington, and winning the endless war on terror by fair means or foul, the Bush administration had opted for the latter.

That was why after condemning the May 2005 Andijan massacre and losing the lease on the Uzbek airbase at Karshi-Khanabad, Washington lost its passion for criticizing abuses of human rights, and sought reconciliation with Tashkent. It came—courtesy the German foreign minister, Frank Walter Steinmeier. He worked hard to ease the EU sanctions against Uzbekistan in lieu of Uzbek President Islam Karimov letting Germany keep its troops in Termez along the Afghan border. Karimov, committed to the extermination of jihadists in Afghanistan, granted the troops of America and other NATO members limited access to the German base. He also permitted NATO the use of Uzbek railroad to ferry supplies to Afghanistan.

Next door, in Turkmenistan, following the policies of the late Saparmurat Niyazov, President Gurbanguli Berdymukhamedov allowed passage of American warplanes through the Turkmen airspace on their way to Afghanistan. But he reverted to the traditional names for the months, and allowed foreign operas to perform. Though he abolished the 2,507-strong People's Council, and increased the size and powers of the elected parliament, the poll in December 2008 saw the old pattern repeated. All 288 candidates for the 125 seats belonged to the ruling Democratic Party of Turkmenistan.

Like Karimov, Berdymukhamedov too gravitated toward the Kremlin, strengthening commercial ties with Gazprom, the natural gas behemoth, which signed up a majority of the republic's gas output.

Lacking hydrocarbons, Kyrgyzstan remained poor. The leasing of the Manas air base to the Pentagon by President Askar Akayev had brought only a paltry $2 million a year rent to the public treasury. After Akayev's overthrow in March 2005, President Kurmanbek Bakiyev demanded a rent of $200 million. He settled for $63 million rent and a further $87 million in supplementary aid.

The global credit crunch sent Bakiyev begging for money to the Kremlin in February 2009. President Dmitry Medvedev wrote off debt of $180 million, and provided an emergency loan of $300 million, with a promise of $1.7 billion investment in the Kyrgyz hydro-electric sector over the next decade. The payback was ending the Pentagon's lease of the Manas air base.

Arguing that the American mission in Afghanistan had outlasted its original objectives, and that NATO strikes in Afghanistan were causing unacceptable rise in civilian casualties, Bakiyev started the process which would see the Americans pack their bags from Manas by August 2009.

Handling 15,000 military personnel and 500 tons of cargo a month, Manas was a crucial hub for the Pentagon's campaign in Afghanistan. The air tankers stationed there kept the warplanes flying in Afghanistan.[5] Its loss came at a time when the supply route from Pakistan through the Khyber Pass was being attacked by the resurgent Taliban.

This was Russia's way of getting its back on Washington for Bush's insistence on setting up parts of the U.S. anti-missile defense in eastern Europe. It was a clear signal to America and the rest of the world that Russia was back in the saddle as the Big Brother of Central Asia.

NOTES

INTRODUCTION

1. The logo of a snake coiled around a glass adopted by pharmacists internationally originates with Avicenna prescribing serpent's poison as medicine.

2. Cited in Giles Whittell, *Central Asia: The Practical Handbook* (London: Cadogan Books/Old Saybrook, CT: Globe Pequot Press, 1993), 260.

3. *Yurt* in Turkish means "homeland."

4. http://www.advantour.com/uzbekistan/culture/weaving.htm.

5. In 1886, Tsar Alexander III (1881–94) renamed the enlarged Turkistan as Turkistan Territory. Later, the Turkistan Territory would be subdivided into Syr Darya, Semirechie, Fergana, and Samarkand provinces, with the khanates of Bukhara and Khiva left as autonomous units dependent on Russia.

6. By so doing, the British made China an immediate neighbor of Afghanistan.

7. Monica Whitlock, *Land Beyond the River: The Untold Story of Central Asia* (New York: Thomas Dunne Books, 2002), 20.

8. See pp. 188.

9. Monica Whitlock, *Land Beyond the River*, 19.

10. Ibid., 67.

11. Even in present-day Tashkent, milch cows appear in family courtyards or on the verges of the road.

12. Arthur J. Arberry, *The Koran Interpreted* (Oxford and New York: Oxford University Press, 1964), 355–56.

13. Vasiliy V. Barthold, *Istoriya Kulaturnoy Zhizni Turkestan* (*History of the Civilization of Turkestan*) (Leningrad: Leningrad Institute Zhivykh Vostochnykh Iazykov, 1927), 78.

14. This meant one mosque for every 700 Muslims compared to one church for every 11,000 Christians. V. Monteil, *Les Musulmans Soviétiques* (Paris, 1982), 21.

15. By 1916, there were 5,000 reformed schools in the Muslim-populated areas of the Tsarist Empire.

16. Being illiterate, the predominantly Muslim population of Central Asia remained uninformed even of such momentous events outside the region as the abolition of the caliphate in Turkey in 1924.

17. In 1912, the Russian Social Democratic Labor Party, formed in 1899 in Minsk, split into the Russian Social Democratic Labor Party (Bolsheviks) and the Social Democratic Labor Party (Mensheviks).

18. Hence the Great October Revolution came to be celebrated on November 7 in the Soviet Union.

19. Muslim peasants and workers, mainly in the construction and leather industries, organized under the Unions of the Toiling Muslims, had backed the Soviets in Tashkent, Samarkand, and the Fergana Valley, leading to the creation of the Soviet of Muslims Workers' and Soldiers' Deputies. See Alexander G. Park, *Bolshevism in Turkestan 1917–1927* (New York: Columbia University Press, 1957), 19.

20. Though the term *Sart* meant "trader," it was used to describe all those settled in valleys and oases.

21. V. I. Lenin, *Collected Works, Vol. 6* (Moscow: Progress Publishers, 1962), 213.

22. Georgy I. Safarov, *The Colonial Revolution (The Case for Turkestan)* (Oxford: Society for Central Asian Studies, 1985), 121–22.

23. The Commissariat of Nationalities consisted of eight sections, including one for Muslims.

24. Until the mid-1920s, the Bolsheviks continued the Tsarist practice of calling Kazakh "Kyrgyz" and Kyrgyz "Kara-Kyrgyz."

25. Geoffrey Wheeler, *The Modern History of Soviet Central Asia* (London: Weidenfeld & Nicolson, 1964), 135.

26. Cited in Alexander G. Park, *Bolshevism in Turkestan*, 77, 81.

27. Adrienne Lynn Edgar, *Tribal Nation: The Making of Soviet Turkmenistan* (Princeton, NJ, and Oxford: Princeton University Press, 2004), 53.

28. The Pamir region gained formal autonomy in 1925 as the Gorno Badakhshan Autonomous Province.

29. V. I. Lenin, *Collected Works, Vol. 26* (Moscow: Progress Publishers, 1965), 175.

30. J. V. Stalin, *Collected Works, Volume 2* (Moscow: Progress Publishers, 1946), 296. (Among others, pan-Turkists found this definition deficient as it did not take into account the reality of a single nation living in different territories.)

31. Teresa Rakowska-Harmstone, *Russia and Nationalism in Central Asia: The Case of Tadzhikistan* (Baltimore, MD, and London: Johns Hopkins University Press, 1970), 34.

32. Alexander G. Park, *Bolshevism in Turkestan*, 247. (Judged by the Stalinist criteria of a nation, only a small proportion of the nationalities qualified as nations.)

33. Alexandre A. Benningsen and Marie Broxup, *The Islamic Threat to the Soviet State* (London and Canberra: Croom Helm, 1983), 48.

34. What sustained this anomaly was the fact that 72 percent of the party members in 1922 were Russians then forming 53 percent of the Soviet Union's population.

35. Teresa Rakowska-Harmstone, *The Islamic Threat*, 40. (The jobs of the purged Tajik officials often went to the newly arrived party activists from Russia.)

36. Bohdan Nahaylo and Victor Swoboda, *Soviet Disunion: A History of the Nationalities Problem in the USSR* (London: Hamish Hamilton Ltd., 1990), 67.

37. Walter Kolarz, *Russia and Her Colonies* (New York: Frederick A. Praeger, 1952), 14.

38. Geoffrey Wheeler, *Modern History*, 168.

39. *Constitution of the Tajik Soviet Socialist Republic of 1 March 1937* (New York: American-Russian Institute, 1950), 21.

40. Monica Whitlock, *Land Beyond the River*, p. 72.

41. Shirin Akiner, *Islamic Peoples of the Soviet Union* (London and Boston: Kegan Paul International, 1983), 296, 309; and Frank Lorimer, *The Population of the Soviet Union* (Geneva: League of Nations, 1946), 199.

42. Monica Whitlock, *Land Beyond the River*, 103.

43. *Middle East International*, August 26, 1994: 20.

44. Christopher Robbins, *In Search of Kazakhstan: The Land That Disappeared* (London: Profile Books, 2007), 33–34.

45. Alexandre A. Benningsen and Marie Broxup, *Islamic Threat*, 48.

46. Donald S. Carlisle, "Power and Politics in Soviet Uzbekistan from Stalin to Gorbachev" in William Ferman, ed., *Soviet Central Asia: The Failed Transformation*, Boulder, CO, and Oxford: Westview Press, 1992), 99.

47. *Great Soviet Encyclopedia*, Vol. 1 (New York: Macmillan/London: Collier Macmillan, 1973), 557.

48. Ibid., Vol. 11, p. 511; Vol. 12, p. 487; Vol. 25, p. 292; and Vol. 26, p. 660.

49 Colin Thubron, *The Lost Heart of Asia* (London: Heinemann, 1994), 11.

CHAPTER 1: TURKEY

1. Cited in James Pettifer, *The Turkish Labyrinth* (London: Penguin Books, 1998) 5.

2. John Freely, *Istanbul: The Imperial City* (London: Penguin Books, 1998), 302.

3. Nicole and Hugh Pope, *Turkey Unveiled: Ataturk and After* (London: John Murray, 1997/New York: Overlook Press, 2000), 242.

4. Dilip Hiro, *The Essential Middle East: A Comprehensive Guide* (New York: Carroll & Graf, 2003), 51.

5. Ibid., 294.

6. After the defeat of the Ottoman Empire in 1918, Enver Pasha ended up as the commander of the Basmachi rebels in Central Asia. See earlier, p. 42.

7. Cited in Edward Mortimer, *Faith and Power: The Politics of Islam* (London: Faber & Faber, 1982), 135.

8. Ibid., 137.

9. Cited in Hugh Pope, *Sons of Conquerors: The Rise of the Turkic World* (New York, Woodstock, and London: Overlook Duckworth, 2005), 93.

10. Cited in James Pettifer, *Turkish Labyrinth*, 62.

11. Serif Mardin, "Religion and Politics in Modern Turkey" in James P. Piscatori, ed., *Islam in the Political Process* (Cambridge and New York: Cambridge University Press, 1982), 156–57.

12. Cited by Feroz Ahmad, "The Islamic Assertion in Turkey: Pressures and State Response," paper at the First International Seminar, Institute of Arab Studies, June 5–6, 1981.

13. Serif Mardin in James P. Piscatori, *Islam*, 154.

14. Cited in Hugh Pope, *Sons of Conquerors*, 278.

15. Demirel was initially reluctant to resign, but felt that if he stepped down the military might desist from disbanding parliament, allowing democracy to survive, a vain hope. Nicole and Hugh Pope, *Turkey Unveiled*, 106.

16. Cited in *The Middle East*, May 1978: 10.

17. Serif Mardin in James P. Piscatori, *Islam*, 153.

18. Cited in Nicole and Hugh Pope, *Turkey Unveiled*, 68.

19. *The Middle East*, November 1980: 25.

20. Cited in Nicole and Hugh Pope, *Turkey Unveiled*, 141.

21. While Islamist and leftist activities ceased in Turkey, they continued in West Germany, home to more than one million Turkish "guest workers."

22. *Middle East International*, April 29, 1994: 17.

23. *The Times*, January 29, 1982.

24. *The Nation* (New York), June 28, 1986: 882, 883.

25. Ibid., 883.

26. *Inquiry* (Istanbul), February 1986: 30; and *The Nation*, June 28, 1986: 883.

27. Cited in *Middle East International*, April 29, 1994: 17.

28. *The Middle East*, March 1990: 8; and *Financial Times*, May 20, 1991.

29. *Financial Times*, May 20, 1991; and *Turkish Daily News*, April 9, 1992. (In Europe, there were large Turkish communities in Germany and France.)

30. *Financial Times*, May 20, 1991.

31. Also gone were the penal code's Article 141 outlawing the organizations that aimed to establish the domination of one social class (used successfully against Marxist groups), and Article 142 pertaining to undermining "national morale."

32. Interview in Ankara, May 1992.

33. Cited in Hugh Pope, *Sons of Conquerors*, 132.*

34. *Middle East International*, February 21, 1992: 13.

35. Tiziano Terzani, *Goodnight, Mister Lenin: A Journey Through the End of the Soviet Empire* (London: Picador, 1994), 289, 290.*

36. *Turkish Daily News*, April 9, 1992; and interviews in Almaty and Ashgabat in October 1992. (This was a modest beginning of a much more ambitious project.)

37. Tiziano Terzani, *Goodnight, Mister Lenin*, 290.

38. Martha Brill Olcott, *Central Asia's Second Chance* (Washington, DC: Carnegie Endowment for International Peace, 2005), 74.

39. Interview in Ankara, May 1992.

40. Cited in *Middle East International*, May 15, 1992: 12.

41. In the end, nothing came of it because Azerbaijan did not ask for such a pact.

42. Cited in Hugh Pope, *Sons of Conquerors*, 277.

43. Interview on September 15, 1994.

44. Cited in Nicole and High Pope, *Turkey Unveiled*, 334.

45. *Middle East International*, October 7, 1994: 15; and May 26, 1995: 13.

46. Rosie Ayliffe, Marc Dubin, and John Gawthrop, *The Rough Guide to Turkey* (London: Penguin Books, 2000), 597.

47. July 5, 1997: 12.

48. Interview in Ankara, May 1992.

49. *Middle East International*, July 19, 1996: 4.

50. The sanctions menu included the U.S. federal government banning purchases from the banned entity; prohibiting the sanctioned entity from acting as a primary dealer of U.S.

Treasury Bonds; and a denial of licenses for the export of controlled technology to the sanctioned entity. Dilip Hiro, *Neighbors, Not Friends: Iraq and Iran after the Gulf Wars* (London and New York: Routledge, 2001), 220.

51. Dilip Hiro, *Blood of the Earth: The Global Battle for Vanishing Oil Resources* (New York: Nation Books, 2007/London: Politico's Publishing, 2008), p. 247.

52. See Dilip Hiro, *The Essential Middle East*, 286.

53. Cited in Hugh Pope, *Sons of Conquerors*, 254.

54. Cited in *Observer Review*, May 20, 2007: 4. (The Turkish foreign ministry lodged a protest with the Iranian government.)

55. *Middle East International*, March 7, 1997: 12; and April 4, 1997: 14.

56. *Middle East International*, May 14, 2004: 22–23.

57. When confronted with this information published later, the police chief replied that he did nothing more insidious than safeguard democracy. *Middle East International*, July 11, 1997: 13.

58. Cited in *Middle East International*, July 11, 1997: 18.

59. A year later, Erbakan would figure in an alleged plot to overthrow the government of Uzbekistan by virtue of handing over cash to Muhammad Salih, a secular Uzbek opposition leader, in exile in Istanbul.

60. In July 2000, the Court of Appeals upheld the sentence of one year for seventy-four-year-old Erbakan for violating Article 312 of the penal code by "provoking hatred by displaying racial and religious discrimination" in his campaign speech in 1994.

61. In local elections, women with headscarves were elected and served as councilors.

62. *Middle East International*, March 23, 2001: 17–18.

63. Ibid., May 19, 2000: 18.

64. Nazli Ilicak did not wear a headscarf herself; and as a columnist, she had exposed several cases of corruption.

65. Cited in *Middle East International*, August 31, 2001: 19–20.

66. Halil Akinci, "Turkey's Relations with Central Asian Countries," *United Service Institution Journal*, New Delhi, October–December 2006: 536.

67. A recently released tape showed that in 1992 Erdogan welcomed the founding of the Emirate of Afghanistan. When called before the State Security Court in Ankara, he admitted that his comments had been "harsh" but they were in accord with the circumstances of that time and that his "style had changed in the past ten years."

68. Cited in *Middle East International*, November 8, 2002: 4–5.

69. Tens of thousands of Turks demonstrated outside the parliament to express their opposition.

70. *Middle East International*, June 13, 2003: 21–22.

71. Cited in *Middle East International*, June 27, 2003: 18–19.

72. At one point, 170 writers and intellectuals were in jail under Article 8, and a further 5,500 were on trial.

73. *Middle East International*, June 25, 2004: 9.

74. Ibid., July 9, 2004: 10. With its compulsory draft of eighteen months for all Turkish males, the Turkish military's strength of 500,000 was second only to the Pentagon's.

75. Altogether, thirty-nine articles limited freedom of expression, though only thirteen were commonly used.

76. After a lengthy court case, which drew international attention, the charge against Orhan Pamuk was dropped.

77. Martha Brill Olcott, *Central Asia's Second Chance*, 201; and Halil Akinci, "Turkey's Relations," 532.

78. *New York Times*, May 30, 2007.

79. Ibid., February 11, 2008.

80. Foreign investment in Turkey soared to $50 billion in three years.

81. *New York Times*, May 30, 2007.

82. In the Kurdish region, twenty-three Kurds contesting as independents, not subject to the 10 percent threshold, won.

83. *New York Times*, July 18 and August 29, 2007.

84. *International Herald Tribune*, January 30, 2008.

85. Reuters, August 14 and August 21, 2007.

86. However, many university rectors decided not to act according to the latest amendment until they received government instructions on its implementation.

87. *Guardian*, April 1, 2008.

CHAPTER 2: UZBEKISTAN

1. As such, Uzbekistan remained well ahead of its cotton-growing neighbors—Kazakhstan and Turkmenistan.

2. In the autumn of 1992, whereas Russians were only 10 percent of the population of Uzbekistan, they accounted for 35 to 40 percent of Tashkent's 2 million residents. Interviews in Tashkent, September 1992.

3. See Introduction.

4. Bohdan Nahaylo and Victor Swoboda, *Soviet Disunion*, 159.

5. Cited in H. Alleg, *Etoile Rouge et Croissant Vert* (Paris, 1983), 231.

6. As for Iran, it had started Islamic radio broadcasts in March 1979.

7. It had thirty-two members from each of the fifteen constituent republics.

8. *Pravda Vostoka (Truth of the East)*, January 31, 1986.

9. *Die Presse* (Vienna), September 1, 1986; and *Independent Magazine*, October 5, 1991: 24.

10. *Far Eastern Economic Review*, November 26, 1992: 40.

11. Donald S. Carlisle, "Power and Politics" in William Ferman, ed., *Soviet Central Asia*, 116.

12. *Literaturnaya Gazeta*, May 20, 1986.

13. *Pravda Vostoka*, August 12, 1987. (It transpired that Mikhail Gorbachev was baptized secretly by his grandparents. *Guardian G2 Magazine*, March 20, 2008: 3.)

14. Cited in Bohdan Nahaylo and Victor Swoboda, *Soviet Disunion*, 248.

15. Cited in Amir Taheri, *Crescent in a Red Sky: The Future of Islam in the Soviet Union* (London: Hutchinson, 1989), 141.

16. Natalya Kuchmi died in Tashkent in 2008 at the age of seventy-one.* When that union dissolved, Karimov married Tatyana Akbarovna, a part-Tartar, part-Belorussian economist.

17. Cited in *Independent*, October 2, 1991; and *Independent Magazine*, October 5, 1991: 28.

18. A public movement, political or otherwise, concerned itself with one or more general issues—environment, language, soldiers' welfare, etc.—whereas a political party was required to have an overall program for society covering its various facets.

19. Bohdan Nahaylo and Victor Swoboda, *Soviet Disunion*, 137.

20. *Pravda Vostoka*, December 7, 1989. (Italics in the original.)

21. James Critchlow, *Nationalism in Uzbekistan: A Soviet Republic's Road to Sovereignty* (Boulder, CO, and Oxford: Westview Press, 1992), 63, 64, 66.

22. Interview in Tashkent, September 1992.

23. *Pravda Vostoka*, November 29, 1990.

24. *Independent*, September 18, 1991.

25. Cited in *Independent Magazine*, October 5, 1991: 24–25.

26. In late November 1991, the Electoral Commission required the opposition groups to submit 100,000 voter signatures for their respective candidates within three days to qualify for the contest. Birlik managed this, but by the time its representatives reached the Electoral Commission's office on the afternoon of the deadline, a Friday, they found it closed. (Interviews in Tashkent, September 1992.)

27. Interview with Muhammad Salih in Tashkent, September 1992.

28. I. A. Karimov, *Uzbekistan: Its Own Road to Renewal and Progress* (in Russian) (Tashkent: Izdatyelsto Uzbekistan, 1992), 50.

29. Interview in September 1992.

30. Interview in Tashkent, September 1992.

31. Cited in Ahmed Rashid, *Jihad: The Rise of Militant Islam in Central Asia* (New Haven, CT, and London: Yale University Press, 2002), 139.

32. Interviews in Namangan, November 1992.

33. *Foreign Broadcast Information Service*, March 24, 1992.

34. *Central Asia Monitor*, No. 4, 1992: 27. (The situation deteriorated steadily so that in July the Erk decided to suspend its publication. Interview with Muhammad Salih, September 1992.)

35. I. A. Karimov, *Uzbekistan*, 39, 48, 49.

36. Ibid., 26.

37. Ibid., 27, 40, 43.

38. Ibid., 10.

39. Yet five years would pass before Karimov would let Saudi Arabia open its embassy in Tashkent because the Saudi kingdom was the home of the radical, puritanical Wahhabi subsect of Islam.

40. I. A. Karimov, *Uzbekistan*, 31.

41. *Far Eastern Economic Review*, November 19, 1992: 23.

42. Interviews in Namangan, November 1992.

43. *Slovo Kyrgyzstan (Word of Kyrgyzstan)*, October 10, 1992.

44. See further, Chapter 6.

45. According to a senior U.S. diplomat in Tashkent, while the Islamist forces were not currently strong in Uzbekistan, they could rapidly become so due to the existing infrastructure of mosques and religious organizations. Interview in Tashkent, September 1992.

46. Interviews in Tashkent, September 1992; and *Great Soviet Encyclopedia Annual*, 1990: 175.

47. *Independent*, January 2, 1993.

4. Interview in Tashkent, September 1992.

49. During his working life, Mikhail Gerasimov (1907–70) reconstructed the heads of more than 200 personalities, including Ivan the Terrible, Fredrick Schiller, and several relatives of Timur. He and his team later dismissed the widely believed story among locals that violation of the great warrior's grave would lead to a disaster. Soon after the violation occurred came Adolf Hitler's invasion of the Soviet Union on June 22, 1941.

50. Cited in Justin Marozzi, *Tamerlane: Sword of Islam, Conqueror the World* (New York: Harper Perennial, 2005), 313.

51. Dilip Hiro, *War without End: The Rise of Islamist Terrorism and Global Response* (London and New York: Routledge, 2002), 298.

52. Cited in Monica Whitlock, *Land Beyond the River*, 198.

53. http://uzbekistan.neweurasia.net/2006/11/20/interviews-with-russians-in-uzbekistan/

54. During the civil war in the Soviet Union, Maqsudi's affluent great-grandparents fled the country and arrived in New Jersey after a stint as factory owners in Kabul. In the aftermath of Uzbekistan's independence, diaspora Uzbeks from Afghanistan, Saudi Arabia, and Turkey visited their homeland to renew their long-lost contacts.

55. Inter Press Service, October 7, 1998; *New York Times*, June 16, 2008.

56. Cited in Monica Whitlock, *Land Beyond the River*, 201.

57. "Zokirjon Umarov [a latter-day oligarch, who served as deputy chief of the Soviet KGB in Afghanistan in the 1980s] told me that Karimov's personal fortune came chiefly from 10 percent of the production of the Murantau mine, which he had been taking for more than a decade. He took his cut as ingots, flown to Rothschild's bank in Switzerland." Craig Murray, *Murder in Samarkand: A British Ambassador's Controversial Defiance of Tyranny in the War on Terror* (London: Mainstream Publishing, 2007), 157.

58. Monica Whitlock, *Land Beyond the River*, 198.

59. Ibid., 203.

60. Cited in *Middle East International*, July 17, 1998: 18.

61. Inter Press Service, October 7, 1998.

62. *Washington Post*, October 15, 2001.

63. *Asia Times Online*, May 28, 1999. (The Pentagon sent eleven drones into Afghanistan in September and October 2000.)

64. *Voice of America*, October 6, 2000.

65. Radio Free Europe/Radio Liberty, May 27, 1998.

66. Cited in Inter Press Service, May 7, 1998.

67. BBC News, May 19 and June 1, 1998.

68. Inter Press Service, September 11, 1998.

69. Monica Whitlock, *Land Beyond the River*, 257.

70. Ibid., 83.

71. Ibid., 243.

72. Cited in Craig Murray, op. cit., p. 132.

73. Later, when expelled by Turkey at Uzbekistan's behest, Muhammad Salih would gain political asylum in Norway.

74. Monica Whitlock, op. cit., pp. 247-48.

75. Ibid., p. 252. This was only one of such trials in train, with lesser ones being heard in the lower courts of Tashkent, the Fergana Valley, and Khorezm. In one case, the suspects were accused of conspiring to blow up the Chirvak dam above Tashkent and flood the capital with the aim of "attempting to establish an Islamic state." In another instance, after reading his confession, a young suspect shouted, "Everything I just told you is a lie! They held a gas mask over my face for ten days until I agreed to say it." Ibid., pp. 254 and 255.

76. Ahmed Rashid, *Jihad: The Rise of Militant Islam in Central Asia*, Yale University Press, New Haven, CT, and London, 2002, p. 125.

77. Associated Press, January 10, 2000; Reuters, January 11, 2000.

78. *Jihad*, p. 170.

79. Dilip Hiro, *War without End*, p. 319.

80. Agence France Presse, March 13, 2002. For full text of the Declaration, visit www.state/gov/r/pa/prs/2002/8736pf.htm. Other allied agreements included replacement of highly enriched uranium at an Uzbek research reactor with a lower-grade variety, and U.S. Export-Import Bank credit of $55 million to small and medium-sized Uzbek businesses to buy American products.

81. See www.state/gov/r/pa/prs/2002/8736pf.htm.

82. Cited in Shahram Akbarzadeh, *Uzbekistan and the United States: Authoritarianism, Islamism and Washington's Security Agenda*, Zed Press, London and New York, 2005, p. 79.

83. *Nezavisimaya Gazeta*, October 8, 2002.

84. January 15–21, 2003.

85. The U.S. aid was spent on security, humanitarian assistance, water management, and health care reform. Some observers estimated total U.S. aid to Uzbekistan in 2002 at $500 million. *Guardian*, 18 October 18, 2003.

86. Freedom House, a non-governmental organization based in Washington, was established as a voice for freedom and democracy in 1941 by Eleanor Roosevelt, wife of the American president, and others in 1941.

87. *Murder in Samarkand*, pp. 108–110.

88. *Guardian*, May 26, 2003; and Craig Murray, *Murder in Samarkand*, p. 82. Of the 370 people arrested in Fergana, for instance, all but 30 were religious Muslims.

89. Visit http://www.thememoryhole.com/pol/us-and-uz.htm or http://en.wikipedia .org/wiki/Muzafar Avazov for the images. Later when Fatima Mukahadirova was arrested and given six years imprisonment for defaming the image of Uzbekistan, the Karimov government came under international pressure. At his press conference in Tashkent in February 2004, Donald Rumsfeld said that before his trip, "Fatima Mukahadirova, 62, who had been convicted of anti-government activities after claiming her son died while being tortured by Uzbek authorities, was released."

90. *Murder in Samarkand*, p. 111.

91. January 14, 2003.

92. Peter Hopkirk opens his book, *The Great Game: On Secret Service in High Asia*, with the description of how Charles Stoddart and Arthur Connolly were pushed down the well and then beheaded.

93. Dilip Hiro (ed.) *Babur Nama: The Journal of Emperor Babur*, Penguin Books, London, 2007, p. 200.

94. Ibid., p. 30.

95. Craig Murray, *Murder in Samarkand*, 189. (The title of this book derives from the killing of Shukrat Mirsaidov.)

96. This statement was posted on the White House website on March 26, 2003.

97. Craig Murray, *Murder in Samarkand*, 225.

98. Dilip Hiro, *Blood of the Earth*, 210.

99. *New York Times*, June 16, 2008; Hugh Pope, *Sons of Conquerors*, 303.

100. Martha Brill Olcott, *Central Asia's Second Chance*, 148.

101. *Army Times*, February 24, 2004.

102. Craig Murray, *Murder in Samarkand*, 333.

103. Ibid., 232–33.

104. April 4, 2004.

105. For Galima Bukharbayeva's testimony to the United States Commission on Security and Cooperation in Europe, visit www.opencrs.com/getfile.php?rid=61469

106. *Guardian*, July 6, 2005.

107. *Financial Times*, May 15, 2007.

108. By 2011, the Lukoil project will tie together three gas fields to produce 11 billion cubic meters a year. *New York Times*, December 14, 2007.

109. Though Karimov's extended term ended in January 2007, the electoral law required that presidential poll to be held in December. Thus, Karimov won an extension of a year.

110. Cited in , December 24, 2007. Yusuf Jumayev, a Bukhara-based poet, was arrested for displaying an anti-Karimov poster in his car.

111. See http://www.fibre2fashion.com/news/textile-news/newsdetails.aspx?news_id =31428.

CHAPTER 3:TURKMENISTAN
1. *Great Soviet Encyclopedia*, Vol. 26: 491; and *Turkmeniskaya Sotsialisticheskaya Republica*, Ashkhabad, 1984: 214.
2. Rakhim Makhtumovich Esenov, *Turkmen Soviet Socialist Republic* (Moscow: Novosti Press Agency Publishing House, 1972), 36; and *Great Soviet Encyclopedia*, Vol. 26: 492.
3. *Independent Magazine*, October 5, 1991: 27.
4. *Trud* (Labor), October 1, 1988.
5. Bally Yazkuliyev, *Turkmenia* (Moscow: Novosti Press Agency Publishing House, 1987), 28, 41.
6. Interview in October 1992.
7. The relative strengths of the important tribes in the early twentieth century were: Tekke, 39.2 percent; Yomut, 13.2 percent; Salori, 5.2 percent; and Sariki, 4.8 percent. Marat Durdyev and Shokhrat Kadyrov, *The Turkmens of the World* (Ashgabat: Kharp, 1989) 14.
8. http://www.turkmenistan-online.com/history_txt.html.
9. http://www.tcoletribalrugs.com/article35Moshkova.html.
10. Interview in October 1992.
11. This was the first and most outstanding statue of Lenin in Central Asia.
12. Later, the government would declare October 25 as the National Independence Day.
13. On the eve of James Baker's visit, the government put twenty opposition leaders under house arrest.
14. Later, senior officials of the two countries decided to cooperate on oil exploration.
15. *Turkmeniskaya Iskra* (*Spark of Turkmenistan*), February 24, 1992.
16. *Ashgabat Vecherni*, May 19, 1992.
17. *Central Asia Monitor*, No. 4, 1992:16.
18. Interview in Ashgabat, October 1992.
19. October 20, 1992. If this were so, how would someone like Jumakov explain the fact that such indigent and crisis-ridden countries like India and Bangladesh already have a multi-party system?
20. Interview in Ashgabat, October 1992.
21. Ibid.
22. Reuters, March 26, 1993.
23. Interviews in Ashgabat, October 1992.
24. Cited in *Central Asia Monitor*, No. 4, 1992: 4.
25. *Sunday Times Magazine*, December 17, 2006.
26. Martha Brill Olcott, *Central Asia's Second Chance*, 101.
27. Ibid., 101. (In the first half of 2004, Niyazov authorized $4.5 billion in foreign exchange for construction projects.)
28. http://www.saudiaramcoworld.com/issue/200601/turkmenistan.on.a.plate.htm.
29. Inter Press Service, April 17, 1994.
30. Martha Brill Olcott, *Central Asia's Second Chance*, 101.
31. *Middle East International*, May 30, 1997: 19.
32. Interview in Ashgabat, October 1992.
33. *Central Asia Monitor*, No. 3, 1992: 4–5. (The three-year plan was to reduce the troops stationed in Turkmenistan in stages, from 120,000 to 60,000, when 90 percent of them would be ethnic Turkmen and commanded by Turkmen officers. Interviews in Ashgabat, October 1992.)
34. *Middle East International*, May 30, 1997: 19.
35. Earlier, the Taliban had swept away all road blocks from Pakistan to the Afghan city of Herat, thus enabling Pakistani trucks to proceed to Turkmenistan unhindered to pick up Turkmen cotton for textile mills in Pakistan. Dilip Hiro, *War without End*, 241.
36. Inter Press Service, October 24, 1997.
37. *Middle East International*, November 21, 1997: 17.
38. In June 2001, all Internet cafés were closed down. Four years later, 36,000 Internet users amounted to 0.7 percent of the republic's population.
39. The second volume of *Ruhnama* was published three years later.
40. *Z Magazine* (Woods Hole, MA), June 2005.
41. Radio Free Europe/Radio Liberty, November 2, 2001.
42. *Asia Times*, March 9, 2002.

43. Cited in Hugh Pope, *Sons of Conquerors*, 107.

44. Muhammad Nazarov would be found guilty and sentenced to a maximum twenty years in jail.

45. Cited in *Z Magazine*, June 2005.

46. Niyazov's idea was not novel. As it was, in most of the Arab world, the secular calendar months did not carry the Christian Gregorian calendar. Indeed, the origins of the names of some months—Iyar, Nissan, Tammuz, and Elwul—lay in the Jewish calendar.

47. BBC News, December 26, 2002.

48. Ibid., January 25, 2003. The international community denounced the arrests of relatives.

49. The Turkmen government expelled the Uzbek ambassador.

50. Shikhmuradov's confession later appeared on the Gündogar website. See http://www .iran-press-service.com/articles_2003/Jan-2003/sheykhmoradov_sentenced_5103.htm; see also the Human Rights Watch, December 31, 2002, website.

51. BBC News, December 30, 2002, and January 25, 2003. Two other main conspirators were found guilty and given the maximum twenty-five years of imprisonment.

52.. This explained why Niyazov in his TV speech said, "I was not aware of anything and came to work. Then at work I was informed that there was a shoot-out going on there." BBC News, November 25, 2002.

53. See http://www.cacianalyst.org/?q=node/1239/print.

54. *New York Times*, July 5, 2007.

55. BBC News, February 25, 2004.

56. Turkmen TV First Channel, April 5, 2004, monitored by the BBC.

57. See http://www.turkmens.com/Dutar/openning.html.

58. BBC News, August 25, 2005.

59. July 5, 2007.

60. *Sunday Times Magazine*, December 17, 2006.

61. *New York Times*, July 5, 2007.

62. Ibid., January 23, 2008.

63. *International Herald Tribune*, December 21, 2007.

64. Ibid., September 26, November 14 and December 21, 2007.

65. Ibid., November 14, 2007, and December 21, 2007. With its proven gas reserves at 2,860 billion cubic meters, according to the *BP Statistical Review of World Energy*, June 2007, Turkmenistan had many suitors.

CHAPTER 4: KAŻAKHSTAN

1. Shirin Akiner, *Islamic People of the Soviet Union*, 294.

2. Martha Brill Olcott, *The Kazakhs* (Stanford, CA: Hoover Institution Press, 1987), 239.

3. In contrast, there were only 418 cooperative farms, each having about 500 households.

4. *Great Soviet Encyclopedia*, Vol. 11, Third Edition, 1976: 513.

5. Christopher Robbins, *In Search of Kazakhstan*, 191–92.

6. Cited in K. B. Beisembiev, *Ideino-politicheski Techeniia Kazakhstane*, Konta XIX-Nachala XX veka, Alma Ata, 1961: 113–14.

7. *Islam i Natsiya* (*Islam and Nation*), Moscow, 1975: 48.

8. *Islam i Obshchestvo* (*Islam and Society*), Moscow, 1978: 180–81.

9. The higher figure for the fatalities, including seven guards, was give by the *Guardian* on December 30, 1986. The statistics for the injured and the arrested were released by a Supreme Soviet committee on September 24, 1990. Interview in Almaty, October 1992.

10. Interview with Dinmuhammad Kunayev, October 1992.

11. June 7, 1988.

12. *Literaturnaya Gazeta*, May 21, 1987: 13.

13. Amir Taheri, *Crescent in the Red Sky*, 192.

14. Christopher Robbins, *In Search of Kazakhstan*, 205.

15. Gulag is the Russian acronym of *Glavnoye Upravleniye Ispravitelno-Trudovykh Lagerey i koloniy*, meaning Chief Administration of Corrective Labor Camps and Colonies.

16. Christopher Robbins, *In Search of Kazakhstan*: 253–54.

17. Ibid., 252–53.

18. Subsequently, the two leaders patched up their differences, with Nazarbayev recognizing Kunayev as an elder statesman.

19. Mukhtar Shahanov, chairman of the Presidium of the Supreme Soviet of Kazakh SSR,

About Conclusions and Recommendations Concerning the Final Assessment of Events on 17 December 1986 in Alma Ata, issued by Y. Asanbayev, president of the Supreme Soviet of Kazakh SSR, Alma Ata, September 24, 1990: 3.

20. The tablet reads: "On this square on 17 December 1986 took place an expression of the democratic will against the diktats of the command administrative system. Let the memory of this event bring forth unity of nationalities."

21. In an interview in October 1992, its editor Batirkhan Darimbetov claimed a circulation of 70,000.

22. *Far Eastern Economic Review*, August 1, 1991.

23. Cited in *Central Asia Monitor*, No. 2, 1992: 13–14.

24. Much to Washington's annoyance, Kazakhstan test-fired SS-19 intercontinental ballistic missiles on December 20, 1991. *Far Eastern Economic Review*, January 30, 1992.

25. Christopher Robbins, *In Search of Kazakhstan*, 206.

26. Interview with Saida Sultanat Ermakov, an Alash Orda leader, in Almaty, October 1992.

27. Interview with Haji Nisanbayev in Alma Ata, October 1992.

28. Christopher Robbins, *In Search of Kazakhstan*, 115–16.

29. *New York Times*, May 24, 1992; and Martha Brill Olcott, *Central Asia's Second Chance*, 71. (With six ICBM silos still to be demolished, the agreement was renewed after its expiry in December 2000.)

30. Interviews in Almaty, October 1992; and *Central Asia Monitor*, No. 6, 1992: 7.

31. *Azat*, June 16, 1992.

32. *Central Asia Monitor*, No. 4, 1992: 4; and *The Economist*, August 8, 1992: 56.

33. Interviews in Almaty, October 1992.

34. *Central Asia Newsfile*, No. 2, December 1992: 1.

35. *New York Times*, August 18, 1999.

36. *Wall Street Journal*, May 9, 1994; and *Financial Times*, June 28, 1994.

37. Significantly, this concept was incorporated in the draft of the Russian military doctrine, which stated, "It is our special mission to protect the rights and interests of Russian citizens and persons abroad connected with [Russia] ethnically and culturally." Cited in *The Middle East*, January 1994: 14.

38. Inter Press Service, March 11, 1994.

39. The Nazarbayev government named the first Turkish-Kazakh university after Yasawi.

40. http://archnet.org/library/sites/one-site.jsp?site_id=9063.

41. Martha Brill Olcott, *Central Asia's Second Chance*, 31.

42. Inter Press Service, May 1, 1995.

43. Ibid., May 1, 1995.

44. Dilip Hiro, ed., *Babur Nama: Journal of Emperor Babur* (London: Penguin Books, 2007), 3, 196.

45. Cited in Christopher Robbins, *In Search of Kazakhstan*, 13.

46. Interview in October 1992.

47. Cited in Christopher Robbins, *In Search of Kazakhstan*, 113.

48. The Chinese state trading corporation was the first foreign company to open shops in Almaty to supply consumer goods like shoes and clothes.

49. Interview in October 1992.

50. Cited in Hugh Pope, *Sons of Conquerors*, 128.

51. *Financial Times*, July 22, 1997.

52. Cited in *Middle East International*, September 12, 1997: 19.

53. There is a reference to Ahmad Yasawi's mausoleum in Dilip Hiro, ed., *Babur Nama*, 200.

54. Cited in Inter Press Service, October 7, 1998.

55. Ibid. Akezhan Kazhegeldin went on to publish a critical book, *Kazakhstan: The Right to Choose*, which led to his final rift with Nazarbayev.

56. *Middle East International*, October 10, 1997: 19–20; and Reuters, April 15, 1998.

57. Ibid.

58. The proposal of the 3,000-kilometer (1,880-mile) Kazakhstan-China pipeline costing $3.5 billion was dropped in August 1999 because the oil price fell to $12 a barrel, and it required a flow of 500,000 bpd—far more than the envisaged output of 150,000 bpd.

59. Saudi Arabia's Ghawar oil field with 87 billion barrels remains the largest in the world.

60. *The Times*, 2 April, 2001. (Large advertisements by the Kazakh government in Western newspapers mentioned an oil output of 3 million bpd by 2015, a realistic figure.)

61. Martha Brill Olcott, *Central Asia's Second Chance*, 32.

62. *New York Times*, November 7, 2006.

63. Ibid. (The case, deferred to February 2007, was postponed again.)

64. See http://enews.ferghana.ru/article.php?id=1230.

65. See http://ifn.org.uk/article.php?sid=2.

66. *New York Times*, November 7, 2006. (Transparency International ranked Kazakhstan 124th in its list of countries by corruption in 2004, with a score of 2.2 on a scale of 0–10 with 0 indicating a "highly corrupt" state.

67. Radio Free Europe/Radio Liberty, April 18, 2002.

68. Hugh Pope, *Sons of Conquerors*, 137.

69. Dilip Hiro, *Blood of the Earth*, 202.

70. Ibid., 169.

71. See http://en.wikipedia.org/wiki/Kazakhstan_presidential_election,_2005.

72. Dilip Hiro, *Blood of the Earth*, 169.

73 *New York Times*, January 15, 2008.

74. http://www.everyculture.com/Ja-Ma/Kazakhstan.html.

75. Since, in his previous top positions in the secret and financial police, Rakhat Aliyev had collected compromising evidence against the leading lights of Kazakhstan, it was doubtful the government would put him on trial even if he found himself in Astana through legal or illegal means.

76. *The Times*, June 13, 2007.

77. Ibid., July 7, 2007.

CHAPTER 5: KYRGYZSTAN

1. In 1926, a census year, Kyrgyzes formed 67 percent of the population of 990,000. But, owing to collectivization and famine during the 1930s, they constituted only 41 percent of the population of a little over 2 million in the early 1950s. Shirin Akiner, *Islamic Peoples*, 332.

2. Interview in October 1992.

3. Interview in Bishkek, October 1992.

4. Nancy Lubin, "Implications of Ethnic and Demographic Trends," in William Fierman, ed., *Soviet Central Asia*, 41.

5. *Chicago Tribune*, July 28, 2005.

6. According to an Uzbek journalist in Tashkent, Kyrgyz Interior Ministry forces, wearing red bands, went from house to house killing Uzbeks. His estimate of 5,000 Uzbek deaths was considered inflated. The actual figure was more likely less than 1,000. Cited in *Independent Magazine*, October 5, 1991: 28.

7. Interview in Bishkek, October 1992.

8. *The Economist*, October 19, 1991.

9. Interview in Bishkek, October 1992.

10. Cited in Hugh Pope, *Sons of Conquerors*, 175.

11. Azade-Ayse Rorlich, "Islam and Atheism: Dynamic Tension in Soviet Central Asia," in William Fierman, ed., *Soviet Central Asia*, 188.

12. Ibid., 192.

13. *Central Asia Monitor*, No. 4, 1991: 16.

14. *Great Soviet Encyclopedia Annual*, Moscow, 1990: 124.

15. Interviews in Bishkek, October 1992.

16. *The Economist*, October 19, 1991.

17. Interviews in Bishkek, October 1992.

18. According the Interfax agency, 89 percent voted for Askar Akayev.

19. Interview in Bishkek, October 1992.

20. Interfax, February 12, 2004.

21. Askar Sarigulov, brother of Dastan, was president of the republic's privatization committee. In May 1998, a truck carrying two tons of lethal sodium cyanide overturned and spilled its cargo into Barskoon River flowing into Issyk Kul Lake, the country's largest tourist attraction. Following the poisoning of 2,500 people, 800 were hospitalized and 4 died.

22. On the whole, the government had a near monopoly on printing and distributing newspapers and magazines, and used it to strangle independent journalism led by *Respublika* and *Moya stolitsa novost* (My Capital News).

23. January 3, 2000.

24. Cited in Inter Press Service, April 8, 1998.

25. Martha Brill Olcott, *Central Asia's Second Chance*, 112; and *Financial Times*, July 22, 2002.

26. Inter Press Service, April 8, 1998.

27. *Jihad*, 163.

28. Ahmed Rashid, *Jihad*, 163–64.

29. Ibid., 169–70.

30. Radio Free Europe/Radio Liberty, July 2, 2001.

31. *Financial Times*, July 22, 2002.

32. http://jamestown.org/edm/article.php?volume_id=414&issue_id=3947&article_id=2371714.

33. *Daily Telegraph*, October 24, 2003.

34. In the Georgian capital of Tbilisi, the opposition leader Viktor Yushchenko and his supporters marched to the parliament carrying roses symbolizing nonviolence. In Ukraine, the protesters carried orange-colored flags in their demonstrations.

35. See http://www.rferl.org/specials/kyrgyzelections/timeline2004.asp.

36. In 2006, the remittances of the Kyrgyz expatriates amounted to 28 percent of the GDP. *Observer*, December 2, 2007.

37. See http://www.jamestown.org/edm/article.php?article_id=2369644.

38. Erica Marat, *The Tulip Revolution: Kyrgyzstan One Year After* (Washington, DC: The Jamestown Foundation, 2006), 16, 131.

39. Ibid., 21, 131.

40. *New York Times*, March 30, 2005. (During the previous three years, independent newspapers were driven to bankruptcy; several critical journalists were harassed, with one found dead in mysterious circumstances; and an independent media center in Osh was vandalized.)

41. Erica Marat, *Tulip Revolution*, 39.

42. Interfax, February 18, 2006.

CHAPTER 6: TAJIKISTAN

1. Teresa Rakowska-Harmstone, *Russia and Nationalism*, 57, 58.

2. Dilip Hiro, *Between Marx and Muhammad: The Changing Face of Central Asia* (London and New York: HarperCollins, 1994), 194.

3. Dilip Hiro, *Holy Wars: The Rise of Islamic Fundamentalism* (New York: Routledge, 1989), 256; and Alexandre Benningsen and Marie Broxup, *The Islamic Threat*, 113.

4. Dilip Hiro, *Holy Wars*, 257.

5. Cited in Monica Whitlock, *Land Beyond the River*, 88.

6. Amir Taheri, *Crescent in a Red Sky*, 197.

7. *Central Asian Newsletter*, May 1988: 14.

8. *Observer*, May 15, 1988.

9. Shirin Akiner, *Islamic Peoples*, 308.

10. *The Economist*, September 21, 1991.

11. *Central Asia Monitor*, No. 1, 1992, 17.

12. http://www.rkac.com/people/rudaki.htm.

13. Cited in Monica Whitlock, *Land Beyond the River*, 148.

14. *Central Asia Monitor*, No. 1, 1992: 10.

15. *Far Eastern Economic Review*, January 9, 1992: 18.

16. The regional parliament acted on a petition, calling for the political-administrative upgrading of the territory, signed by 15,000 supporters of Lal-e Badakhshan, a party formed in 1989.

17. *Moscow News*, No. 20, 1992.

18. *Turkish Daily News*, September 2, 1992.

19. *Central Asia Monitor*, No. 5, 1992: 5.

20. Ibid., October 9, 1992: 5.

21. *Middle East International*, October 9, 1992: 15.

22. Monica Whitlock, *Land Beyond the River*, 169–70.

23. Other, minor sources of arms supplies were the Caucasus, with shipments sent across the Caspian Sea, and Iranian air-drops.

24. *Pravda*, October 10, 1992.

25. *Central Asia Monitor*, No. 5, 1992: 6.

26. Ibid., 9.

27. Cited in *Independent*, June 27, 1992.

28. *Central Asia and Caucasus in World Affairs Newsletter*, No. 4, February 28, 1993: 4.

29. Tajikistan Radio, October 31, 1992, cited in the *Middle East International*, November 6, 1992: 15.

30. Rahman Nabiyev died on April 10, 1993.

31. *Guardian*, December 10, 1992; and *Observer*, January 3, 1993.

32. *Central Asia and Caucasus in World Affairs Newsletter*, No. 4, February 28, 1993: 10–ll.

33. BBC World Service Radio, June 10, 1993; and *Central Asia Monitor*, No. 1, 1993: 7.

34. *Central Asia Newsfile*, No. 5, March 1993: 2.

35. Cited in *Observer*, August 22, 1993. Yeltsin's statement was apparently based on the bilateral security and military cooperation treaty that Russia and Tajikistan signed in June 1993.

36. Cited in *Middle East International*, August 6, 1993.

37. Inter Press Service, November 25, 1996.

38. Ibid., November 25, 1996.

39. Martha Brill Olcott, *Central Asia's Second Chance*, 44–45.

40. Dilip Hiro, *War without End*, 291.

41. See http://www.rferl.org/specials/tajikelections/timeline1994.asp

42. *Wall Street Journal Europe*, May 28, 1995.

43. Soon after, Rahmanov undertook the hajj pilgrimage to Mecca, the last Central Asian leader to do so.

44. Martha Brill Olcott, *Central Asia's Second Chance*, 45.

45. *Middle East International*, March 27, 1998: 18–20.

46. On November 25, 1998, the Tajik government televised confessions by captured Uzbek rebels that they had been trained in Uzbekistan. *Middle East International*, December 25, 1998: 19.

47. Ahmed Rashid, *Jihad*, 112–13. (About 200,000 men from Tajikistan left annually to work in Russia. Ibid., 107.)

48. Radio Free Europe/Radio Liberty, February 28, 2000.

49. For details, see Chapters 2 and 5.

50. Dilip Hiro, *War without End*, 274.

51. In November 2007, 3.5 sominis = 1 U.S. dollar.

52. In 2007, fifty-five-year-old Shamsuddin Shamsuddinov died in a prison on the outskirts of Dushanbe in suspicious circumstances.

53. Radio Free Europe/Radio Liberty, June 23 and 24, 2003.

54. Ibid., July 20, 2004.

55. *Eurasia Daily Monitor*, October 20, 2004.

56. EurasiaNet.org, July 28, 2005.

57. But during the next four years poverty declined only by 8 percent.

58. http://www.europeanforum.net/country/tajikistan_update.

59. Martha Brill Olcott, *Central Asia's Second Chance*, 114.

60. The reason for building this factory in Tajikistan in 1975 was the availability of cheap electricity, as aluminum smelters consume large amounts of electricity. See http://www.nationsencyclopedia.com/Asia-and-Oceania/Tajikistan-INDUSTRY .html.

61. IFES, *Public Opinion in Tajikistan 2004*, November 2004, www.ifes.org.

62. BBC News, March 27, 2007.

63. EurasiaNet.org, April 29.

64. http://www.europeanforum.net/country/tajikistan_update.

65. Martha Brill Olcott, Central Asia's Second Chance, 114.

66. *Nations in Transit—Tajikistan (2006)* (Washington, DC: Freedom House, 2006).

67. *Eurasia Insight*, July 28, 2005.

68. BBC News, March 24, 2007; and *Eurasia Insight*, April 10, 2007.

69. Radio Free Europe/Radio Liberty, September 8, 2007.

70. Ibid., September 8, 2007.

71. EurasiaNet.org, November 15, 2007.

CHAPTER 7: IRAN

1. The Twelver Shiite Imams are: Ali, Hassan, Hussein, Zain al Abidin, Muhammad al Baqir, Jaafar al Sadiq, Musa al Kazem, Ali al Rida/Reza, Muhammad al Taqi Javad, Ali al Naqi, Hassan al Askari, and Muhammad al Qasim. The last, the infant son of the eleventh imam, is believed to have gone into occultation in Samarra, Iraq, in 873 AD.

2. The Sunni hierarchy has a different terminology: starting with *maulavi* (learned man), and rising to *qadi/qazi* (religious judge), *mufti* (one who delivers fatwas, religious decrees), *mufti-al azam* (grand mufti), *shailh al Islam* (wise man of Islam), *mujtahid* (who is equivalent of ayatollah), and *mahdi* (one who is guided by Allah).

3. Nikki R. Keddie, *Roots of Revolution: An Interpretive History of Modern Iran* (New Haven, CT, and London: Yale University Press, 1981), 111.

4. Cited in *Sunday Times*, April 3, 1980.

5. See http://en.wikipedia.org/wiki/Persian_Jews.

6. *Constitution of the Islamic Republic of Iran*, trans. Hamid Algar (Berkeley, CA: Mizan Press, 1980) 29–30.

7. Ibid., 30.

8. Ibid., 60.

9. Some Islamic scholars dispute the interpretation that the term "adornment" (*zinah*) covers all parts of the body, except hands, feet, and perhaps the face. Another passage in the Quran calls on the believing women "to draw their cloaks (*jalabiyah*) tightly around them when they go abroad so that they may be recognized."

10. *Sunday Times*, April 11, 1982.

11. *The Middle East*, February 1982: 30.

12. Ervand Abrahamian, *Iran between Two Revolutions* (Princeton, NJ: Princeton University Press, 1982), 433; and *Sunday Times*, April 4, 1982.

13. Dilip Hiro, *Islamic Fundamentalism* (London: Paladin Books, 1988); and *Holy Wars*, 202–03.

14. *Constitution of the Islamic Republic of Iran* (trans. Hamid Algar), 30.

15. Islamic Republic News Agency (IRNA), November 2, 1983.

16. *Daily Telegraph*, March 22, 1980.

17. *Events* (London), October 6, 1979: 21.

18. *Report of the Central Committee of the CPSU to the XXVI Congress of the Communist Party of the Soviet Union, 23 February 1981* (Moscow: Novosti Press Agency, 1981) 23.

19. *Guardian*, April 26, 1984.

20. Cited in *The Middle East*, April 1989: 12.

21. Ahmed Rashid, *Jihad*, 219.

22. In addition, Iran had common fluvial borders with Kazakhstan and Russia in the Caspian Sea.

23. Cited in *Financial Times*, June 23, 1992.

24. Inter Press Service, August 22, 1994.

25. Interview in Ashgabat, October 1992.

26. *Central Asian and Caucasus in World Affairs Newsletter*, No. 3, January 11, 1993: 3.

27. Cited in *Financial Times*, June 23, 1992. (The total estimated population of the expanded ECO was 280 million, including 24 million non-Muslims.)

28. *Central Asia Newsfile*, No. 2, December 1992: 7; and No. 3, January 1993: 3.

29. Cited in *Financial Times*, June 23, 1992.

30. *Far Eastern Economic Review*, October 15, 1992: 22.

31. Dilip Hiro, *Neighbors, Not Friends*, 220–21.

32. Ibid., 240.

33. Inter Press Service, May 7, 1998.

34. Ibid., August 31, 1998.

35. It transpired later that the rogue soldiers were to be punished not for killing the Iranian diplomats and a journalist, but for destroying evidence of Iran's interference in Afghanistan's internal affairs.

36. http://www.panarmenian.net/news/eng/?nid=8048.

37. *International Herald Tribune*, September 13 and 17, 2001; and *Washington Post*, September 25, 2001.

38. See Dilip Hiro, *War without End*, 459.

39. See http://www.whitehouse.gov/news/2002/01/20020129-11.html.

40. http://www.redorbit.com/news/business/590618/tajik_leader_speaks_at_tunnel_launch_with_iranian_counterpart/index.html.

41. Dilip Hiro, *Blood of the Earth*, 202.

42. See www.kz-today.kz/index.php?uin=1133434981.

43. See http://www.kazind.com/newsarchives/newsvol120.htm#3.

44. See http://2004.press-service.uz/eng/vizits_eng/ve17062003.htm.

45. Radio Free Europe/Radio Liberty, February 21, 2006.
46. http://www.nationalreview.com/rubin/rubin200408100834.asp.
47. New Republic Online, September 8, 2004.
48. http://www.todayszaman.com/tz-web/yazarDetay.do?haberno=117083.

SUMMARY AND CONCLUSIONS
1. Among those who had suffered this fate were the Inguish, Crimean Tartars, Khemshins (Armenian Muslims), Kurds, and Meskhetian Turks (Georgian Muslims).
2. Inter Press Service, May 1, 1995.
3. This practice was commonplace in other Central Asian republics as well.
4. Serif Mardin, "Religion and Politics in Modern Turkey" in James P. Piscatori, ed., *Islam in the Political Process*, 157.

EPILOGUE
1. Robert Tait, "Turkish PM fights for survival with plea for Islamists and secular judges to avoid clash," *Guardian*, June 11, 2008.
2. Sabrina Tavernise and Sebnem Arsu, "Turkish court ruling ends political deadlock," *New York Times*, August 1, 2008.
3. Ergenkon is a Central Asian Turkic legend with an ultra-nationalist content.
4. Nicholas Birch, "Two Turkish generals held over plot to kill Nobel laureate," *Independent*, July 2, 2008.
5. http://www.stripes.com/article.asp?section=104&article=60560

SELECT BIBLIOGRAPHY

AKBARZADEH, SHAHRAM. *Uzbekistan and the United States: Authoritarianism, Islamism and Washington's Security Agenda*. London and New York: Zed Press, 2005.

AKINER, SHIRIN. *Islamic Peoples of the Soviet Union*. London and Boston: Kegan Paul International, 1983.

BENNINGSEN, ALEXANDRE A., AND MARIE BROXUP. *The Islamic Threat to the Soviet State*. London and Canberra: *Croom* Helm, 1983.

CRAWSHAW, STEVE. *Goodbye to the USSR: The Collapse of Soviet Power*. London: Bloomsbury, 1992.

CRITCHLOW, JAMES. *Nationalism in Uzbekistan: A Soviet Republic's Road to Sovereignty*. Boulder, CO, and Oxford: Westview Press, 1992.

CUMMINGS, SALLY N. *Kazakhstan: Power and the Elite*. London and New York: I. B. Tauris, 2005.

EDGAR, ADRIENNE LYNN. *Tribal Nation: The Making of Soviet Turkmenistan*. Princeton, NJ, and Oxford: Princeton University Press, 2004.

FIERMAN, WILLIAM, ED. *Soviet Central Asia: The Failed Transformation*. Boulder, CO, and Oxford: Westview Press, 1992.

FREELY, JOHN. *Istanbul: The Imperial City*. London: Penguin Books, 1998.

GORBACHEV, MIKHAIL. *Perestroika: New Thinking for Our Country and the World*. London: Fontana, 1988.

HIRO, DILIP. *Iran Under the Ayatollahs*. London and Boston: Routledge and Kegan Paul, 1985.

———. *Between Marx and Muhammad: The Changing Face of Central Asia*. London and New York: HarperCollins, 1994.

———. *War without End: The Rise of Islamist Terrorism and Global Response*. London and New York: Routledge, 2002.

———, ed. *Babur Nama: Journal of Emperor Babur*. London: Penguin Books, 2007.

———. *Blood of the Earth: The Global Battle for Vanishing Oil Resources*. New York: Nation Books, 2007/London: Politico's Publishing, 2008.

HOPKIRK, PETER. *The Great Game: On Secret Service in High Asia*. Oxford and New York: Oxford University Press, 1991.

KARIMOV, I. A. *Uzbekistan: Its Own Road to Renewal and Progress* (in Russian). Tashkent: Izdatyelsto Uzbekistan, 1992.

KAZHEGELDIN, AKEZHAN. *Kazakhstan: Entering the Future*. London and New York: I. B. Tauris, 1998.

KEDDIE, NIKKI R. *Roots of Revolution: an Interpretative History of Modern Iran*. New Haven, CT, and London: Yale University Press, 1981.

KOLARZ, WALTER. *Russia and Her Colonies*. New York: Frederick A. Praeger, 1952.

MARAT, ERICA. *The Tulip Revolution: Kyrgyzstan One Year After*. Washington, DC: The Jamestown Foundation, 2006.

MORTIMER, EDWARD. *Faith and Power: The Politics of Islam*. London: Faber & Faber/Rhinehart, NY: Holt, 1982

MURRAY, CRAIG. *Murder in Samarkand: A British Ambassador's Controversial Defiance of Tyranny in the War on Terror*. London: Mainstream Publishing, 2007.

NAHAYLO, BOHDAN, AND VICTOR SWOBODA. *Soviet Disunion: A History of the Nationalities Problem in the USSR*. London: Hamish Hamilton, 1990.

OLCOTT, MARTHA BRILL. *The Kazakhs*. Stanford, CA: Hoover Institution Press, 1987.

———. *Central Asia's Second Chance*. Washington, DC: Carnegie Endowment for International Peace, 2005.

PARK, ALEXANDER G. *Bolshevism in Turkestan 1917–1927*. New York: Columbia University Press, 1957.

PETTIFER, JAMES. *The Turkish Labyrinth*. London: Penguin Books, 1998.

PISCATORI, JAMES P., ED. *Islam in the Political Process*. Cambridge and New York: Cambridge University Press, 1982.

POPE, HUGH. *Sons of Conquerors: The Rise of the Turkic World*. New York, Woodstock, and London: Overlook Duckworth, 2005.

POPE, NICOLE AND HUGH. *Turkey Unveiled: Ataturk and After*. London: John Murray, 1997/New York: Overlook Press, 2000.

RAKOWSKA-HARMSTONE, TERESA. *Russia and Nationalism in Central Asia: The Case of Tadzhikistan*. Baltimore, MD, and London: Johns Hopkins University Press, 1970.

RASHID, AHMED. *Jihad: The Rise of Militant Islam in Central Asia*. New Haven, CT, and London: Yale University Press, 2002.

ROBBINS, CHRISTOPHER. *In Search of Kazakhstan: The Land That Disappeared*. London: Profile Books, 2007.

SAFAROV, GEORGY I. *The Colonial Revolution (The Case for Turkestan)*. Oxford: Society for Central Asian Studies, 1985.

TAHERI, AMIR. *Crescent in a Red Sky: The Future of Islam in the Soviet Union*. London: Hutchinson, 1989.

TERZANI, TIZIANO. *Goodnight, Mister Lenin: A Journey Through the End of the Soviet Empire*. London: Picador, 1994.

THUBRON, COLIN. *The Lost Heart of Asia*. London: Heinemann, 1994.

WHEELER, GEOFFREY. *The Modern History of Soviet Central Asia*. London: Weidenfeld & Nicolson, 1964.

WHITLOCK, MONICA. *Land beyond the River: The Untold Story of Central Asia*. New York: Thomas Dunne Books, 2002.

WHITTELL, GILES. *Central Asia: The Practical Handbook*. London: Cadogan Books/ Old Saybrook, CT: The Globe Pequot Press, 1993.

YAZKULLYEV, BALLY. *Turkmenia*. Moscow: Novosti Press Publishing House, 1987.

INDEX

PENGUIN CRIME FICTION

DEAD BIRDS

John Milne, once a policeman himself, won England's prestigious John Llewellyn Rhys Prize for a previous novel, *Out of the Blue*. Born in London in 1952, he now lives in Bath. His second Jimmy Jenner Mystery, *The Moody Man*, is available from Viking.

DEAD BIRDS

A Jimmy Jenner Mystery

JOHN MILNE

PENGUIN BOOKS

PENGUIN BOOKS
Published by the Penguin Group
Viking Penguin Inc., 40 West 23rd Street,
New York, New York 10010, U.S.A.
Penguin Books Ltd, 27 Wrights Lane, London W8 5TZ, England
Penguin Books Australia Ltd, Ringwood,
Victoria, Australia
Penguin Books Canada Limited, 2801 John Street,
Markham, Ontario, Canada L3R 1B4
Penguin Books (N.Z.) Ltd, 182–190 Wairau Road,
Auckland 10, New Zealand

Penguin Books Ltd, Registered Offices: Harmondsworth,
Middlesex, England

First published in Great Britain by Hamish Hamilton Ltd 1986
First published in the United States of America by
Viking Penguin Inc. 1987
Published in Penguin Books 1988

LIBRARY OF CONGRESS CATALOGING IN PUBLICATION DATA
Milne, John.
Dead birds: a Jimmy Jenner mystery / John Milne.
p.   cm.
ISBN 0 14 00.9704 X
I. Title.
PR6063.I3787D4   1988
823'.914—dc19   87-20714
CIP

Printed in the United States of America by
Offset Paperback Mfrs., Inc., Dallas, Pennsylvania
Set in Times Roman

To Pierre Hodgson and
Virginia Bonham Carter,
who both encouraged me
when I first began to write

Preface

Sometimes I have this nightmare, only it doesn't go away because it's true.

I'm sitting in the wheelman's chair of a small boat, the kind of fishing boat that's built for pleasure-fishing, not work. It's a modern, white-painted boat and there's a blue canvas canopy over my head. The canvas stretches over all the stern part of my boat. It looks like a rich, blue-shaded sky. A sky that protects, not burns. Not like the one outside. The sun in the real sky outside is fierce, even though it's well after noon. Outside the canopy is brilliant white light from the afternoon sky. Outside the canopy is white-painted decking reflecting the light.

I shift out of the wheelman's chair and squeeze my eyes up so I can look along the decking. I can see a seagull. The seagull is my friend.

We're on the Mediterranean Sea, about twenty miles south of Málaga; I don't exactly know where and it doesn't matter much. I can't be bothered to work out where I am. Twenty miles off Málaga will do. I reckon we should have another three hours before we reach our destination. By then it'll be dark. I'm very tired for no real reason and finding it hard to concentrate, so I decide to tell the seagull a little about myself.

'I'm going to tell you about myself, Mr Seagull, whether you're talking to me or not. I'm going to tell you a little of my story.'

The seagull didn't move. He didn't leap up and down and applaud me or anything . . . well, I didn't expect him to. He said nothing. I said nothing for a long time after that too. The only sounds were of the engines throbbing and the splash of the swell against our bows. Sometimes a glass bottle rolled back and forth in the cabin. I could hear the hollow sound. The bottle never seemed to roll in time with the boat's motions.

I tied up the wheel with rope, so that I shouldn't have to steer, and turned my attention to the seagull again. I said, 'My story's a detective story. I never dreamed how I'd get it, just like I never dreamed how I'd become a detective.'

I stared at the seagull. I waited, unreasonably, for a response. I got none. Maybe I was mistaken. Maybe he wasn't my friend. Suddenly I wanted to walk up the narrow gangway and kick the seagull over the side. I couldn't manage it, though, and I couldn't reach him from the steering-well.

'I always wanted to be a detective. When I was at school I dreamed of being a detective. When I left school I became a policeman. First a cadet, then a constable. Always wanting to be a detective. That was me . . . always wanting to be a detective.'

I rubbed my face and thought of my early days as a copper. All 'where's your road fund licence, sir?' and seeing old ladies across the road. To become a detective in the real world you needed an alarmingly high arrest-rate on real criminals or you needed to look like a prospect to your governor. I had had no chance on either count. The seagull didn't know that. I didn't tell him either. There's no point in making excuses to a seagull.

'I transferred to the West End of London. I thought it'd be more exciting. In the West End there's vice and drugs and all sorts of big-time thievery. There's embassies and royals and I suppose I thought, "If this isn't a bit more exciting I'll knock the whole business on the head." That's what I thought. If I didn't get any joy in the West End I'd give up wanting to be a detective and I'd give up being a copper. I'd become a television repair man or something. That was a laugh.'

We were both quiet for a long time. No one laughed. I said, 'I had a career in the West End, okay. I'll tell you.'

Again I was silent, again the bird made no comment. I told him anyway.

2

'My brief and spectacular career as a copper in the West End lasted three days only. My companion, my shower-round during these three days was a youngster, a flash-Harry called Willy. What a big head he was!

' "I can't show you who the villains are, James," he said, "because they could all be villains. That's how this place is. Don't think just because some Henry's in a Roller he's not a prospect . . . he may well be. Same goes for the old IC3s . . . just because a bloke's a darkie it doesn't mean he's necessarily a prospect round here. He might be a senior diplomat. He could be anyone. It'll work out well if you don't pull any diplomats on sus or something." '

'I said I knew.

' "You don't know," he said. "This isn't Romford." He took off his helmet, wiped his forefinger along his brow, looked at the sweat on his finger, then waved the hand at the street. He said no more on the subject of geography, just marched off and began talking to a copper in a flat hat at the corner of the street.

' "This is big Andy, Diplomatic Protection. Andrew Tyson . . . James Jenner." '

'Big Andy nodded. He was built like a barn door and you could see his gun, even under his loose-fitting tunic. Willy said, "Andy here is charged with making sure the bloody Ay-rabs don't wander up and down Regent Street, shooting each other. As they are wont to do, I might warn you. Andy's specific job is. . . ." '

I broke off. I'm not such a barmy as to go round explaining myself to seagulls. I just needed to talk. I was tired. The image of Andrew Tyson, the Diplomatic Protection Group policeman I'd met all those years ago in Regent Street, stayed with me. I leaned back in the wheelman's chair and closed my eyes. I'd only met him for a few minutes but his face had stayed with me. The sun beat down on my boat's canopy and I was thousands of miles and some ten years away from it but still that man's image was in my mind. I was so tired. I slept in the chair and I dreamed of Tyson's face and Willy's tough guy talk. I dreamed of Regent Street. Regent Street is my nightmare.

*

3

I awoke with a jolt. I'd only meant to doze, to 'rest my eyes'. I must have slept for some time though. The sun was descending in the west. By luck – or someone else's good seamanship – I hadn't bumped into any other boats. The sea had become heavy while I'd dozed and it was the force of the bows smacking into one of these waves which had woken me. My neck hurt and I was shivering. I couldn't go into the cabin for a sweater. I sat back in the wheelman's chair and thought about Regent Street and Willy and all that stuff again. I'd gone to sleep thinking of it and I'd woken thinking of it.

I was thinking of Andrew Tyson's face, then I was thinking about a grey BMW with a couple of fellows sitting in it. They didn't look like tourists. Tyson saw the car as I did. The passenger jumped out and did a runner, I could see the driver leaning forward under the dash. I could see a wire in his hand, too. The man I was chasing turned suddenly and faced me. I stopped dead. He held a pistol in his hand. Suddenly I went deaf and did a somersault all at once. I never saw my Arab again. I found out later he'd gone through a shop window. Just as I found out later Big Andy had gone through some railings. I was on the floor. Bits of BMW, Willy and Arab-two rained all around me. I turned and saw the smouldering bottom panel of the BMW. Its tyres were on fire. A big black column of smoke was going into the air.

Women began to scream, a man came running. He shouted. 'This one's hurt, this one's hurt!' and I thought, 'Poor bastard, who's that?'

The man shouted, 'Oh, he's lost his foot. Oh God, he's lost his foot.'

I tried to stand and help but I fell over immediately. It was me who'd lost the foot. I kept blacking out but I remember the man crying and saying I was going to die and whispering Catholic prayers to me. I remember twisting my head and looking at the burning car.

Newly woken, shivering and tired, I rubbed my face on my coat and wondered which BMW image I'd really woken with, the grey car or the smouldering wreck. There was no way of knowing. Five minutes out of a dream and it seems impossible to grasp it at all. The story in Regent Street was true, though. My true story. Not a dream at all. It was a memory.

That's my story. It's my true story and that's how I told it to a dead seagull lying on the decking of my borrowed fishing-boat. The bird was on its side on the decking and blood had run from its head, smearing red-brown on the brilliant white decking. Talking to a dead bird is crazy, but I don't think I was that afternoon. Just tired and lonely and tense.

The heavy seas broke over our bows a little now. Spume and salt-spray flew past the sides of the hull. One wave washed the seagull over the side. So much for telling stories to dead birds. The sun was dropping quickly, like a piece of red steel from a forge, liquid and angry. The white glare of the sea around me had transformed to orange and red fragments, the sun's rays shattered between the black shadows of the waves. I switched the marine radio on and clicked from channel to channel, searching for an English voice; I mean an *English*-English voice, not just the language. Somewhere out there would be an English voice.

I untied the rope from the steering wheel, turned up the motors a little and peered into the setting sun for some sign of land. The hint of a shoreline came as darkness fell, then electric lights showed, became bolder and bolder and I left off the navigation lights and let the boat bob towards the shore. I picked up the microphone to the marine radio, clicked over to coastguard calling frequency and said, 'This is A-Alpha A-Alpha C-Charlie Eight, fishing vessel from Málaga. Are you receiving me? Over.'

No reply.

'This is A-Alpha A-Alpha C-Charlie Eight, fishing vessel from Málaga. Are you receiving me, coastguard? Over.'

Still no reply. I tried several more times but all I got for an answer was a squawk from the loudspeaker. I clicked the send button again and shouted into the mike, 'This is A-Alpha A-Alpha C-Charlie Eight, fishing vessel. Are you receiving me, coastguard? Over!'

No reply. I was close enough to the electric strip to see the navigation lights of a fast-moving craft separating from

5

it. I was about eight miles from the shore then, I guessed. I had only the strip of electric light with which to guide the guess. No moon had risen and I seemed suddenly surrounded by inky darkness. I guessed the fast-moving craft was a coastguard craft and that it was about four miles from the shore and the same again from me. Sometimes its lights would merge with those on the shoreline and I'd think it wasn't there, but then I'd see the navigation lights again. I decided to let the craft come close before I would switch my lights on. In case it wasn't coming for me.

The lights kept coming and I kept chugging towards the shore. I cut the engines and turned my lights on. My fishing boat bobbed around in the waves as if it was a dinghy. I could see the outline of the approach craft now. It was a big, fast military boat. It looked to be travelling three times as fast as my fishing boat ever could and it was coming straight for me. I sat in the wheelman's chair and shivered against the cold and waited. I didn't have to wait long.

1

It started in London, as things do. I was working for myself as a private detective and enquiry agent. I had a writ to deliver for a woman on her ex-husband. I think it was about money, I'm not sure. I didn't care and I didn't read the writ or even bother to ask the solicitor who gave me the job what it was for. They're usually for money owed or children sought. My part in the business was to make sure I had the right guy, slap the writ on him, pick up my pay cheque and be prepared to stand in court to swear that I'd done just that. In fact I never swear in court, I always affirm . . . it comes to the same.

The serving of such a writ should be a routine matter, can even be done by post in more usual circumstances. These were not usual circumstances. The man I was delivering the writ to was a boxer called Tommy Lynch . . . or as the writ had it 'Thomas Edward Charles Lynch'. He was a little cockney lad and he boxed as little cockney lads do, with fire and gusto and not a little street sense. What made him different to the others was that he was a world championship prospect, the first for many years at his weight, and I was given the writ to serve just a day before his world title eliminator fight with a man called Diaz.

I took the writ to Tommy's home. He wasn't there. His girlfriend said he wasn't there, he wasn't coming back and she didn't know where he could be found.

'He trained in Yorkshire for the last fight,' she said.

'All of it or any particular part?'

She frowned and said, 'Or was it Scotland?' She meant it, too.

I tried his manager's office. The manager was called George Duncan and he had a gym in Smithfield and an office there. I phoned the office and they said they were setting up a special press bureau for the Lynch/Diaz fight.

'I'm not a pressman.' I said.

'All Lynch enquiries will be dealt with there. Mr Duncan says this fight mustn't disturb the other boxers. I'll give you the number.'

'I said I'm not a. . . .'

But she read me the number and gave me the address anyway and then put the phone down. I should have just such a middle-aged female dragon working for me, overseeing the credentials of every nutter who comes knocking on my door. I should be so lucky. I went to the place in Shoreditch where the office was supposed to be, but I met with another stone-walling secretary. She was younger than the one I'd met on the phone, about twenty-five with hennaed hair and a smocked dress but she wasn't as much of a drip as she looked and she gave me the class 'A' runaround. No, I could not have the address of Mr Lynch's training ground; no, she could not even tell me whether it was in Scotland, Ireland, Wales or England. Is it in America? I asked. She looked sternly over a pair of glasses big enough to grow cucumbers under and said she wasn't prepared to give any indication.

'Where's Mr Duncan, then?' I asked.

'I can't say.'

'What *can* you say?' I said.

'Here.' She gave me a sheet with Press release splashed in red across the top. 'I can tell you any of that.'

'Thanks. Thanks a lot.'

I went and sat in my car. After twenty minutes or so a green Jaguar XJ6 pulled up. I'd seen George Duncan a few times before – I used to use a gym he owned – and I recognised him as he got out. He was a big, grey-haired man in a blue chalk-stripe suit. He was aged about fifty with big, floppy jowls, grey eyes and burst red blood vessels on the upper part of his cheeks and the end of his nose. He had a cigar like a log and as he left the car he tapped the ash from his cigar into the gutter, as if he didn't care to have the Jag filled with cigar ash. The driver of the Jag was obviously a minder as well as a driver. Six feet two, about seventeen stone with a suit he seemed to be bursting out of and a big red neck that really did burst out of the suit to support his bullet head and ugly face. I recognised him, too. Harry Whitlock, former British heavyweight prospect. Hard as nails and always led with his chin. He had looked good until he'd met the champion, Bugner, back in the mid-seventies and Bugner had had a big enough punch to hit him right on the chin and draw the curtains on Harry Whitlock's short career as a British title prospect. Driving cars was what Harry had been reduced to . . . so much for the big time.

Duncan was in the office for ten minutes, then he and Harry came out to the Jag and set off north. I followed.

Seven a.m. the next morning found me parked in a layby in Chigwell. There are some big houses in Chigwell and Lynch was in one of them, about fifty yards from my layby. I'd followed George Duncan and Harry Whitlock here the day before from Shoreditch. I had tailed them carefully but I needn't have bothered. Harry Whitlock was no better as a minder than he was as a boxer. His driving was a bit irregular, too, swerving between the kerb and the white line. Duncan would've been better off if Harry had only been charged with polishing the Jag. It had a nice coat of polish.

Today was the day of the big fight. It was a grey May day and I sat in the layby sipping Thermos tea and waiting for something to happen. Rain splashed around me and I kept the windows nearly closed. I had a *Daily Mail* on my lap, a newspaper I don't often buy, but they'd just done a piece on me and the journalist said it would be in today. It was. Under the headline 'HOPALONG COPALONG' and the byline 'By Eric Brand' it said, '*James Jenner is a retired policeman running a private detection business. Nothing wrong with that . . . except Jenner has only one foot and is deaf in one ear, the result of the horrific injuries inflicted on him in the Regent Street Embassy Bombing. After seven years as one of our boys in blue and a further two recovering from his injuries it looked like Jenner's cherished ambition, to be a detective, had slipped from his grasp. I can reveal now, though, that not only has Jenner established his own detective agency, but his super-sleuth skills were responsible for the return of Nati Saud, a distant member of the Saudi royal family and the girl at the centre of the "Drugs in Rolls Royce scandal" . . .'*

And so it went on. There was a picture of me, too, looking as gormless as only newspaper photographs could make a man look. The technique is to get five hundred quid's worth of Minolta or Nikon, put a wide-angle lens on it, shove it into the face of some hapless interviewee and take a picture a two-year-old shaking with ague could have got from a Box Brownie. The article stank; well, they all do. I'd been forced into it by Brand, the journalist, simply because I *had* to explain what he already knew.

The girl had done a runner from her family in London. The little I know about Saudi families makes that reasonable. What no one could have considered reasonable was the information, given to me by the police when I became involved, that the girl had a drug problem and had been using the family's diplomatic corps Roller to import the stuff. Import, I should add, in quantities large enough to supply a small town. Hence the family row, hence the girl doing a runner. She was pretty easy to find, but finding her was a diplomatic problem . . . she was a diplomat's daughter, the father was important somehow to us, no one wanted to drag them through the legal system. The answer for the drug squad, who'd located the girl, was to get her father to hire a private detective to 'find' her, then have the private detective advise the girl and her father that they'd be better off in Riyadh than Reading, and wouldn't they like to take the Roller for one last drive to Heathrow?

All that meant using a private detective the police involved in the case could trust. After all, not only did they not want a Saudi in a British prison, they also didn't want anyone to know that that was the way things were. Since several of the coppers in the case knew me and knew I could be trusted to keep my mouth shut I was 'volunteered'. It all went as sweet as a nut. I went to Keighley (that's right, *Keighley*), 'found' the girl, flushed the suspicious white powder down the loo, drove her back to London. The family headed off to Heathrow. I was given a pat on the back and a fat fee by the father, and for all I know the girl was buried alive in the Arabian sands. She was a nasty piece of work and I really didn't care.

Then Brand turned up. He's a freelancer, a pasty-faced little Fleet Street porker, with washed-out blue eyes, a permanently half-shaven chin and a greasy headful of sandy hair. He was making a living in Fleet Street on the strength of his wits and his contacts. His wits were no good. His contacts were formidable. Eventually he broke the 'Princess and Drugs' scandal (though the girl was not a princess), then started pressuring me for an angle. I blanked him, but he must have had a contact either in the drugs squad or Whitehall, because he had the story better than I did. After four weeks of fobbing him off I'd given him the highly edited version that was in the *Daily Mail*: that I'd found the girl at her father's request, that I knew nothing about the alleged existence of a bag of cocaine, that I'd driven her back to London and passed her on to Daddy and they'd paid me off and headed for Saudi. As Brand had put it, *'This brave young man had been duped into becoming an agent for a foreign power while our own police had been left completely in the dark. Jenner was blameless in the affair, of course, while a spokesman from Scotland Yard told me, "We have no information on this matter, and so I can't comment."* '

In other words a politician, a diplomat, a senior policeman, the Customs and Excise service, maybe even the Saudis themselves, someone was settling a score through Brand. I suppose I should have been grateful to come out of it with two grand and not completely stinking as far as my name went. Brand certainly considered I owed him a favour . . . but then *he* would. I felt as if no copper would ever trust me again.

Trying to look on the bright side, I supposed that the *Mail* article would drum up some work. It doesn't hurt to have your name in the papers. But then you always know the kind of work you'd get from that sort of publicity would all be rubbish. I've had it all before, scrawly written letters with, 'Dear Mr Jenner Esq. I no you are a good detective and wonder if you wood be so kind as to help find my beloved Tiddles, who I have lost by leveing the back door a jar last week. We have serched high and low for him and are gettin desperate. Enclosed I have put five pounds as a fee. Plese rite and tell me if there is change . . . yrs kindest, Dorothy Perkins (ps I am a poor old lady of 75).'

I know *all* about newspaper publicity. It costs me a fortune in stamps to send their wrinkled-up fivers back. I folded the paper angrily and slapped the steering wheel with it. A headline on the back page said, '*Will Lynch do it again?*' Good question. Diaz obviously thought Lynch would not. I stared down the rainy road for what seemed like a week but was in fact forty minutes, then a green Jaguar nosed out of the hedgerow and was quickly over-taken by a very small man wearing a grey tracksuit with the hood up. The Jag crawled along the kerb following the little man. I reached into the dash for the writ. When he passed me I'd jump out, whack it on his chest and bobs-your-uncle, mission achieved. All I needed was the writ. My hand flapped around in the empty dashbox, then I had a sparklingly clear vision of the writ, all safe and sound and snuggled up tight against my mantlepiece clock – at home. So much for organisation. Maybe I should employ Harry Whitlock as my secretary. He couldn't be worse at it than me.

I walked along the road. I expected they'd be gone for half an hour or so; I mean, anything less is hardly worth putting your togs on for.

I thought I'd mooch around, find out if this was where Lynch was living permanently. I stood at the edge of the road in the gap in the hedge, looking at a big nineteen-thirties house. I didn't move forward because I didn't get a chance. Tommy Lynch was back as soon as he'd gone, almost; running right up to me. A fine drizzle brushed his face, and close-to I could see that his hood was a towel tucked into his running suit. Fine droplets of water hung on his clothes. He ran on the spot, legs lifting, hips swinging, fists punching the air before him in short, sharp jabs. The Jag's horn sounded and we both moved out of the way to let it in. I started to step back onto the slick grey tarmac of the street but Harry Whitlock leaped out and grabbed me.

'Hang on, you,' he said under his breath. With his big fist grabbing my collar I never even thought of doing anything else.

George Duncan meanwhile climbed out of the car and threw his arms around the boxer. Cigar ash fell onto the tracksuit, darkened as it met the water. Duncan said, 'A hot shower and a rest for you, my son, then down to the weigh-in. Don't drink nothing.'

Tommy Lynch stood still, shoulders hunched a little. George hugged him again and said, '*Enjoy* yourself, son. It's your day. Try to enjoy it. Let it sink in.'

Duncan leaned in the car, reached for a towel and gave it to Lynch.

'You're gonna do it, Tommy. All the way. You're gonna do it, you know that.'

Tommy said nothing. He wiped his face with the towel, still jogging lightly. They went in, crunching the gravel of the drive underfoot. Harry banged my shoulder. It felt like the nudge you'd get from a bus.

'What's your game? Spying?'

I pulled at my tie and said fiercely, 'I *beg* your pardon, my man? I'm house hunting . . . I was sent here by the estate agents.'

'What estate agents?' His brow curled up like a lettuce leaf. I could almost hear his brain ticking under the crew-cut hair.

'Regis Partners. This is Cholmondeley Street, isn't it?'

He pushed me roughly. I didn't take it so well because of my bad leg. I nearly fell.

'Hey. Don't cut up rough because a chap's come to look at a house,' I said.

'*House!*' spat Harry. 'You press boys make me sick. I can smell you a mile off. Get out of here and don't come back.'

He's a very big man and just because he couldn't turn Joe Bugner over didn't mean he couldn't eat me alive. I got out of there and I didn't come back. Just as he asked.

By eleven thirty the same morning I was outside a big new sports hall in Shoreditch. I was using my office landlord's car, a Toyota with rust latticing the wings and doors. I'd changed my clothes, too, from a cheap suit and a plain tie to a windcheater and golfer's slacks. I always reckon people don't see you as well if you've changed your clothes. That's my theory. Above the sports hall door was a painted canvas sign hung on red ropes 'Lynch v. Diaz here tonite'. A gaggle of pressmen were waiting in the entrance hall, a couple of BBC outside broadcast lorries were blocking-up the car park. I parked the Toyota next to the BBC, then I went over to the foyer of the sports hall, flashed my 'disabled' bus pass at the uniformed council official there, dragged a notebook from my pocket and joined the gaggle of pressmen.

Diaz turned up a few minutes later. He was a good-looking boy in the way that Latins often are: jet-black hair, olive skin and dark brown eyes, sad eyes. They went in. Lynch came, bouncing out of Duncan's car and minded by Duncan himself and a couple of big fellows I hadn't seen before. Harry stood by the car. All the pressmen yelled questions at once. Outside two old ladies were standing by Duncan's car. They yelled loudest of all, so their voices followed through the open doors. Duncan held an impromptu press conference in the foyer while Lynch went inside to strip off. Still the old ladies' voices came over loudest.

'It's 'im, innit? I said to her it's 'im. I said to Elsie "ain't that 'im?" and it *was* 'im.'

The other one yelled at Harry.

'It *was* him, wasn't it?'

Harry muttered something and began wiping the car with a chamois leather. George Duncan carried on his press conference, raising his voice to compete with the old ladies.

'I bet you're a boxer, too,' yelled one of the old ladies.

Harry looked grim and nodded. The woman was small and grey-faced and stunted. She wore a coat thirty years out of date. All she'd have needed was a flower-pot hat to make her into a pre-war Hoxton cleaning-lady. The shoulders of her coat were faded a lighter shade of dun than the rest.

'I was,' said Harry, as she repeated her question. I could see Duncan glancing out towards him. Harry took the hint and got in the Jag, prepared to drive away. The woman in the dun coat called after him, 'Who d'you fancy tonight, then?'

The pressmen all burst out laughing.

One said, 'She must be a spy for Harry Carpenter.'

She looked in at us and laughed, her false teeth clacking. 'Who are you backin', mate?' she called at us.

The journalist who'd spoken shouted, 'It's not a bleeding horse race, missus.'

Her friend took her arm. They looked like a couple of witches.

'Who?' she insisted.

George Duncan held his arms above his head. '*Tommy Lynch!*' he yelled. All the pressmen laughed again. '*Tommy Lynch! Tommy Lynch!*'

We began to move into the sports hall. Cameramen checked their cameras. A young man was balancing above his head some Heath Robinson device with an intense white light in a box and a lot of tissue paper stuck around it. The old women tried to come in too, but the uniformed man wouldn't let them.

' 'asn't it got a bar?' the one in the dun coat said.

'Not for you,' said the official.

'Rude git!' she yelled into his face, but he still wouldn't let them in.

The weighing-in was in a room off the main hall. It wasn't a very big room and didn't seem to be ventilated at all, but it was packed with pressmen, officials, managers, aides, fighters and me. Flashguns fired all the time. Tommy Lynch and Diaz squared up for the cameras. The Panamanian had a beetle brow and thick lips. He spoke almost no English, and when he tried to speak it came out comic-book English. He had a Spanish interpreter with him but no one could understand what the interpreter was saying. The interpreter understood the questions but the pressmen didn't understand the answers. He was like a one-way valve for language. It went in but it didn't come out. The reporters gave up and spent all their time talking to Tommy.

'Is it true you'll go for the world after this, Tommy?'

'Are you feeling good, Tommy?'

15

'Hold your fist up, will you, Tommy?'
'Are you going to beat him, Tommy?'
'Which round, Tommy?'
'Square up to him again, will you?'

Lynch smiled politely and answered all their questions and complied with all their requests except the last because the Panamanian had gone. I wandered out into the auditorium and there he was, arguing furiously with his interpreter in Spanish. His English manager sat beside them and stared at the ceiling. The gaggle of pressmen rushed over and the argument got even louder. TV technicians were setting up. They tested their lights for a second. The Panamanian was under the lights screaming at his interpreter. The English manager was sitting now with his head in his hands. George Duncan came out the side room with his arms around Tommy's shoulders. The aides followed them, turning every now and then to shoo a reporter who'd come over.

'Enough now . . . you'll see it all this evening.'

The English manager looked across at Duncan, who waved his cigar in reply. He said to Tommy, 'Look at this. Look at it all. It's your doing.' He waved his hand at the hall, the rows of seats, the ring. 'All this is yours. *You* can fill it. *I* can't and I'm sure that bloody dago can't. *You* can drag people away from their TVs. The next fight will be America, then you'll bring the championship back to the Albert Hall and take the Frenchman on there . . . eh? They'll come for *you*, Tommy. They love *you*.'

Tommy said nothing. I approached them. One of the aides jumped forward and said, 'No press now, I'm afraid. You've had your chance, watch the fight tonight.'

I ignored him and pulled the writ from my pocket and slapped it on Lynch's bare chest.

'Are you Thomas Edward Charles Lynch?'

'Yes,' said Lynch. The aide grabbed me, the same one who'd tried to shoo me off. His grip was in the same class as Harry Whitlock's. I managed to keep the writ held out, though.

'Then I serve you with this writ on behalf of the Sheriff of the High Court.'

He took the piece of paper.

'What's all this about?' he said. 'Let him go.'

'I don't know, sir', I said. 'Would you sign me a receipt?'

Lynch looked at me for a long time, then signalled to the aides with the flat of his hand. He said to Duncan, 'Wait here,' and crooked his finger at me. I followed him.

In the dressing room we were alone. There were dozens of lockers along the walls and a massage table in the middle of the room. Cool white light filtered through a fanlight.

'My wife thinks I've got a load of dough,' he said, and heaved himself up to sit on the massage table. 'But I'm skint, see. She thinks I'm going to America and not coming back . . . but I will. I'll pay her out.'

'I don't know anything about it,' I said. I held out my receipt, 'But if you'd be kind enough. . . .'

'Course,' he said. Close to, Tommy Lynch seemed very gentle. He was a small, almost frail man with short black curly hair and a handsome, unmarked face. 'Got a pen?'

I gave him the receipt and my biro.

'You're Jenner,' he said as he signed. 'I remember you. I thought I recognised you outside the house this morning.'

I nodded and took the pen and paper from him. A man stuck his head round the door.

'Give us a few minutes, Bill,' Lynch said, then to me, apologetically. 'It's my brother. He worries.' He wiped his face with a towel and stood. 'I remembered you from the newspaper stories a few years ago, I was only a kid but I remembered it. It made me want to become a copper.'

'Why didn't you?'

He laughed and held his hand flat and horizontal about four inches above his head.

'That's why.' We both laughed. 'Can't you say anything to my wife?' he said. 'I'm not going to dump her and the kids with no money . . . but I've got to earn some.'

'I don't even know your wife', I said. 'I got that from a solicitor.'

'Couldn't I hire you to talk her round?' he said. 'You could talk her round, I'm sure.'

'Sorry.' I walked towards the door.

He went to a locker.

'Here. Do you like the fight game?'

'It's okay,' I said.

'Come and cheer me.' said Tommy, 'I could use some good luck from you. I'm sorry it's only for a single seat.'

'You don't need good luck.' I held the ticket in my hand. It was printed *Row B seat 4* and had a big £75 stamped across the wavy lines that were on it to stop counterfeiting.

'This is worth a fortune.' I said.

'I could use the luck.' He slapped me on the back and led me to the door.

I said. 'You don't need luck.' But he shook his head and held his hand out.

'Nobody turns good luck down, Jimmy. Have a nice time this evening. and say hello to that stinking wife of mine.'

Then the grey door closed on him.

2

The fight was top billing, starting at ten. I took a taxi because there was no chance of parking, and I arranged to be picked up at eleven fifteen.

The seat Lynch had given me was in the second row, right behind some radio and TV commentators' tables. I was among the press boys again – I felt as if I was getting used to it. Instead of the empty, echoing hall of the morning there was a full house, passing hip-flasks and beer cans between themselves. The rough boys at the back were chanting.

'Here we go here we go here we go, here we go here we go here we go-o.'

The TV lights made a stark and blinding space, an arena where the contest should be acted out. The lights looked natural, part of a pre-ordained way the thing should be. Behind the lights would be millions of television viewers. I saw it but I couldn't believe it.

The Panamanian, Diaz, came on to cheering, whistling and jeering, all at once. He seemed to flinch even from the cheers. He came into the ring in a cold sweat, danced a few steps but he never looked convincing. He looked as if his feet would go at the first punch. He was like a jumpy amateur.

'HERE WE GO, here we go, here we go here we go here we go-o, here we go here we go here we go, here we go-oh, here we go,' sang the crowd. The Panamanian kept his hooded dressing gown on and stared at his feet.

A fanfare introduced Tommy. Four burly men in dinner suits surrounded him, marched him to the ring. Tommy kept his head down, avoided everyone's eyes. His gloved hands were on the shoulders of the dinner-suited man before him. Tommy's trainer and his second followed behind the group of five, wearing blue silk shirts with *Tommy 'Banger' Lynch* emblazoned on the back. They looked like the tail of a comet, a flash of light in the darkness.

'Here we *go*,' sang the crowd.

The fanfare went on, then a recording of 'Rule Britannia', which the crowd sang along with, la-ing most of the words.

'Ladies and gennermen, innerducing a worl title e-limi-nater, on my lef, inner blue corner . . . Tommy "Banger" Lynch.'

The crowd around me went wild. Tommy held his arms up, still careful to look at no one. He danced around the ring. The Panamanian's introduction was lost in the cheering for Tommy, but he danced around and held his arms up anyway, for the sake of form.

The fight lasted two rounds. If the Panamanian hadn't been so brave it wouldn't have gone outside the first. He took a big right from Tommy halfway through the first. It caught him on the jaw, he ran backwards into the ropes, then bounced off to meet a straight left. His nose broke. Blood poured onto Tommy's shoulder and chest.

The crowd bayed for more. A radio commentator in the seat in front of me was screaming above the noise, 'Some-one's cut, someone's cut . . . I think it may be Lynch. He's ab-so-lutely *covered* in blood. He steps back . . . no, it's Diaz, cut on the face is it? . . . and this-is-war, *out*-and-*out*-war. These two men are really going hell for leather.'

They stood toe to toe, swapping punches. Diaz knew he'd never go twelve rounds so he tried to punch it out with Lynch there and then. Tommy Lynch was the bigger puncher. He hit Diaz two more big punches to the body, on the lower ribcage. The Panamanian's arm dropped. Then Tommy hit him in the head again. Diaz reeled. An arc of blood sprayed the canvas, the ringside seats. Diaz's eyes rolled, his legs buckled. The bell went.

His corner cleaned him up, but twenty seconds of the next round was enough for the referee. He led Diaz to his corner. The Panamanian spat his gumshield out and swore in Spanish, he waved his arms furiously.

'Is okay!' he yelled. 'Is *okay!*' Blood bubbled across his nose and mouth. 'Is okay . . . I go!' He looked round frantically for his translator. Diaz's brow furrowed and his big lips twisted and he began to howl in anguish at being beaten. He put his arms around the Board of Control doctor and blubbered tears and snot and blood onto the man's dinner suit.

Across the ring, Tommy's seconds were sponging him off. Reporters scrambled into the ring. The bouncers pushed over-excited supporters back from the ropes.

'And will he go for the world, Mr Duncan . . . *George Duncan!* BBC here. Will you be fixing a fight in New York or London next?'

Tommy's seconds rubbed him down with towels. He was sweating like a racehorse, all over. One second knelt and rubbed his legs. Reporters mobbed him. A TV camera was pushed into his face.

'How does it feel, Tommy?' a reporter asked. I squeezed into the aisle and George Duncan was standing there with the BBC reporter. The reporter said, 'And surely the world next, George?' George Duncan took a pull at his big cigar and said, 'We'll have to see.'

He looked across at Tommy and seemed satisfied. Tommy was enjoying it at last and Duncan had a world title challenger on his hands. That's how it looked to me in the aisle, anyway. Later in the street it looked different. But then that *was* different.

3

Everyone expected Tommy 'Banger' Lynch to beat Diaz.
I'd seen Lynch fight a few times on the TV and I've never
seen a more obvious prospect than him. What took everyone
by surprise was the speed of the victory. It took me by
surprise. I limped up the gangway towards the exit as the
fight finished, then flashed my 'disabled' bus pass again to
gain entrance to the bar. I don't know how well it works
on buses – I've never used it – but the old 'disabled' bus
pass gets you past all kinds of officials.

The bar was empty. For tonight it was doubling as an
entertainment area for the booze firm that was sponsoring
the fight. One corner was partitioned off for press telephones and a nice young girl from BT dressed like an airline
hostess was giving instructions on how to use a phone to
some drunken lout from Grub Street. I ordered a couple of
beers and took them into a corner and settled in a big chair.
I ordered two beers because I didn't want to queue for a
second, and when the mob hit the bar five minutes later I
was congratulating myself on my foresight. I sat back and
drank my beers while less prudent souls were forced to
queue.

I was outside waiting for my cab at eleven. I could hear car
doors slamming and the metallic clunks of the TV boys
clearing up. Every now and then a yell would carry across
to me. The weather was warming up; it wasn't raining any
more and the night had become muggy and thick, like the
tropics. The TV technicians' yells cut through the air with

a blunt edge, and the sounds of cars starting were half-muffled and distant. My street was deserted. I could hear some drunks singing a couple of streets away, 'Here we go, here we go here we go . . . well we *done* it, didn't we, eh?'

Thinking back on Diaz's nervous face I began to wonder if they actually *had* done it. Lynch was just the channel for their desire. I checked my watch. Eleven-oh-five. There was plenty of time for the cab to come yet. Then a big car engine came, smooth and burbling. It stopped a hundred yards or so from me. Two men tipped out and scrambled across the pavement, arguing furiously and sometimes squaring up to each other. One was a big man wearing a suit, the other was a little slim fellow in casual clothes. They swung round and round in the yellow street light and swore loudly at each other. Then the driver got out, too, and a young woman who even at that distance was well-dressed and handsome and carried herself well. The shifting attitude of the yellow street light as she followed the men along the pavement shaded her face, but I recognised the driver. It was big Harry Whitlock, and then I could hear the voice of the little man.

'No . . . No! . . . I'm not interested . . . Stuff "up west". Stuff the press . . . no!'

Tommy Lynch was having his second fight of the night. This time it was with George Duncan. I could hear Duncan's voice too, fierce and low.

'No!' cried Tommy again. 'Our contract finished tonight and you're not coming to America with me . . . you're greedy, George Duncan. You want too much.'

A white Rover cruised slowly past me. There were four men in it and they were big enough to fill the car up as if it would burst.

'You want me to provide for you as if you were my father or something. You think I should foot the bill for your lifestyle . . . well I won't. Find someone else. You make me sick.'

The Rover stopped by them. Three men got out.

Duncan didn't appear to see them. He took a swing at Tommy. He couldn't have been surprised to miss. Then Duncan turned on one of the three men and fell on him, arms flailing, mouth spitting abuse. The man hit him hard

23

in the face. Harry stepped forward but there were still the other two and they were both as big as himself. Duncan was on the floor. Harry did nothing.

A car stopped by me.

'Mr Jenner for Stoke Newington?'

I nodded.

'That's me, sport. Sit tight a minute and put your meter on.'

Duncan got up and threw himself at the man again and the man hit him hard again. I heard a definite 'smack' as the fist connected, then another as Duncan fell to his knees and the man hit him again.

'Stone me!' said my cabbie. 'I'd better radio for the coppers.'

'Leave it,' I said. I couldn't see how having the police there would help Tommy Lynch, tonight of all nights. And whatever was happening to Duncan he seemed to be bringing on himself. The cabbie picked up his radio mike but I said, 'Leave it,' again and he did.

Tommy Lynch climbed in the Rover with the other men and they drove away.

George Duncan lay on the floor, sobbing. Harry, his minder, sat back in their Jag. I asked my cabbie to drive slowly past. When we reached them George Duncan was on his feet and the woman was slapping him hard, slowly, first one side of the face then the other. I asked my cabbie to stop, then I pulled down my window. The woman was slapping George and yelling at him at the same time.

'You (slap) stupid big pig (slap). You've ballsed it up once and (slap) for all (slap) now. You stinking (slap). . . .' A lighter one. She'd seen us and turned. I couldn't see her face still. She wore a forties-style outfit with a wasp waist and a broad-brimmed hat.

'What are you staring at?' she called across to me.

'Nothing,' I said from the safety and darkness of the cab. 'You okay?'

'Of course I am, you stupid swine. Sod off.'

Charming. They looked like they'd live through it, so I asked the cab driver to go on. It was a funny way to celebrate a big fight win, that's for sure, but then it wasn't any of my business and I put the affair out of my mind.

4

'My name's Jenner. James Jenner. I'm a detective.'

I went through my teens practising speeches, entrances like that. I could picture myself wearing a gabby mack and a pork-pie hat.

'Detective Inspector Jenner, Flying Squad. Keep your hand away from that gun, Smithers.'

The reality was different. As soon as I joined I was identified as the sort of material that's good for thirty years of School Crossing Patrol, wearing a big hat and doling out informal 'evenin' all'-type salutes from the peak of my helmet. Maybe they were right. Maybe that was all I was good for, after all, someone has to be good for it. We can't all be in charge, and most of us aren't even able to be little actors in a great big drama. We're the audience. Take a seat.

If the scheme for life had worked I would eventually have saved enough money for a semi in the suburbs and a Ford Escort to go with it. If I could only have passed the Sergeant's Examination I could have swapped the Ford Escort for a Vauxhall Cavalier. It's not much of an ambition but it was the game-plan I was offered. I even began to believe in it. I had a girlfriend, a WPC called Judy. Nowadays Judy's in the Criminal Intelligence Section in New Scotland Yard. Then she was a WPC whose main job was wiping the noses of lost kids and being present when male policemen interviewed women prisoners. Now she's a star, but then she was my little fiancée and she was all in favour both of the semi and the Ford Escort. We wanted to be man and wife. She's gone off the idea since; well, so have I. She reckons she can't stand being part of an alliterative marriage – Jimmy and Judy Jenner. I looked 'alliterative' up. She reads too many books.

There's always the chance that she'd prefer a man who's complete, who has all his parts still. I have no evidence to offer on this one and Judy has never been anything other than kind to me about the results of my 'incident'.

That happened a long time ago now, and Judy has always been very helpful. Very soothing. It took two-and-a-half years before I was in any shape to do anything. I have a false leg from just below my right knee and have to use a stick if I'm going to walk for more than a couple of minutes and stay comfortable. Judy, who was by that time a Sergeant, stayed very close, still talking about marriage and all that. I didn't want to marry, of course. They kept slicing lumps off my leg because it never worked for months and months, right up until six months, I suppose, before I went down to Roehampton and got my plastic one. I was still nervous they'd call me back and operate again . . . I know it's unreasonable but they'd done it three times and I just thought they might do it a fourth. Sometimes I felt like a ham on a slicing machine. I felt it would never end. I could imagine Judy getting just a head on a plate, like Salome. I'd be great at foreplay but things would peter out pretty quickly from there on in. Not much use as a husband.

When I said I was going to leave the job she backed off, as if I was leaving a close family. In a way I was. NSY had offered me a post in the Commissioner's Office, on the end of a phone. It was more than they had to do, I wasn't fit for duty, but I didn't want the job. I still had a little bit of that teenage ambition left in me, and I thought the promotion prospects of a one-legged telephone answerer in New Scotland Yard were even worse than for a well-meaning but stupid beat-plodder in Romford. I had a bit of dough, insurance pay-outs, Criminal Injuries Compensation, all that, so I didn't have to worry about getting it wrong. I would never starve. Anyway I told Judy I was leaving and she stopped mentioning the marriage. Just as well, really.

I was encouraged in my decision by a certain Detective Inspector of my acquaintance, a man called Denis O'Keefe.

O'Keefe is about six years off retiring, and is hell-bent on feathering his nest in Southend first. I suppose he's so active now because he knows no one'll ever put him in a position of trust again. He'd be right, too. O'Keefe is a clever dick and nasty with it. He's mobbed-up, though, with every insurance assessor in London. He's also mobbed-up with every villain. He's a very important contact for the tyro private detective to have . . . and that's what I'd decided to be. If the State wouldn't have me as a secret squirrel, I'd make myself one. I rented a room and called myself 'Jenner's', as if I were 'Pinkerton's'.

Even before I'd left the job, O'Keefe had arranged, for me to organise a payout to recover some gear for an insurance company. He would cop ten per cent, of course. So would I. I did it, the day after I put my papers in to leave. I hobbled down to a railway arch in Coldblow Lane, Bermondsey, and swapped a big packet of money for a medium-sized packet of gold trinkets. Bermondsey isn't my manor and I was a bit nervous. I mean I could hardly have run from trouble with my stick, could I? It earned O'Keefe and me £1600 each in the process; his unofficial, like. I put mine in the restoration fund of a Catholic church in the Old Kent Road. It's more than I can bear to see a church in need of re-pointing and I got a warm glow from the thought of all the bricklayers and roofers people like me can take off the dole by a small gesture. I believe O'Keefe spent his on sending a maiden aunt to Lourdes to get her cystitis cured.

I kept up my contact with O'Keefe after I left the job. Discreetly of course. I did quite a few little jobs for him and with him, the sort of thing it's not illegal for me to do but it would be indisciplined for him to do. He could get on a fizzer for it, but as a civilian, I couldn't.

I found my own work as well, made my own contacts. Most of my work is brain, not brawn. Cunning brain, too . . . you don't need a university degree to do it. I flatter myself I have a cunning brain. I'm nobody's idea of an intellectual.

I've found people. People that have gone missing from

their families. I don't do any debt collecting. I'll never be that hard up. I went into an insurance broker's and worked out a scam one of their branch managers had going on cash premiums. I liked doing that one. I worked out where a load of cakes were going for a bakery (all, I swear *all* of their delivery drivers were at it with their branch managers). The drivers would take, say, nine trays of bath buns into a shop and bring three out again. Very nice. Since the bakery couldn't sack all its drivers and all its managers they simply sent them all nasty letters and paid me a twelve-hundred-quid fee. When I pointed out they were employing criminals they sent me a cheque for another eight hundred with a note '*re. underpayment of fee, please sign receipt and return*'. I sent them a bill for three hundred quid VAT and they paid that too. So much for the murky waters of industrial relations. I found husbands who'd done runners leaving the wife and kids with the bills – it's surprising how many of these there are. I've served writs for solicitors, recovered 'tom' – booty, jewellery-style – for insurance companies, accompanied the son of a rich man to school in Dorset (the boy was under no threat, he just wouldn't go to school and his old man couldn't be bothered to take him), sat up all night looking after a load of designer clobber in Oxford Street . . . in fact I've done everything the ace private eye of my dreams should do except two. I've never been asked to offer physical protection to anyone and I've never been asked to uncover some dastardly murder. The first is easily explained . . . no one wants an enforcer who's only got one leg and a walking stick. The second only happens when people like me are played by people like Elliott Gould on the movie screen, or James Garner on the TV. You'd have to be an American to even think of it. English coppers, should they get a whiff of cadavers and dirty deeds, throw everybody who's in the slightest bit connected with the matter into the chokee until they've sorted out what's what. This is the voice of experience speaking. More than once I served the unfortunate suspects their breakfast. *Habeas corpus?* Do hop off, John. You watch too much telly. Eat your bacon and try to relax.

No one wants an enforcer with one leg . . . that's what I said. Well, you never know.

28

I've got an office in Canning Town, above a newsagent's, confectioner's, stationer's, small post-office and we-sell-anything shop run by Mr Chardray, a mate of mine. I've known Chardray since our days in Romford. He's a proper English Indian, comes to work in a tie and dons a brown dust-jacket to serve in. His nephew runs the shop in Romford now.

I haven't been busy lately, and though I've got my own front door old Chardray (he's particular about how you spell it) notices everything.

'Busy?' He came out of his door and watched me as I fumbled with the key to mine. He knew I wasn't busy. He knew I hadn't been busy for weeks. That's how my game seems to go . . . all rush rush rush, then quiet for a couple of months.

'I'm all right. You?' I said. I wasn't all right. I'd been knocking back gin and Italian vermouth with some mates in Hackney. Now, at four o'clock, I was just about all in. I've got an old horsehair sofa in my office. It would do me a treat. I've got some gin and a telly, too.

'I'm all right. You had a visitor.' He smiled. He loves to be one in front all the time.

I opened the door and looked onto the mat. There was an envelope.

'He left a note,' Chardray called.

'Thanks. Thanks for telling me.'

'I recognised him from the old days.'

'Good. Indian, is he?'

Chardray laughed and tidied the papers on the stand beside his front door. Week-old, yellowing *Guardians* were shuffled to the top, a new City Prices *Standard* went into pole position, at eye-level.

'No. I recognise him from the Romford days. You knew him then, I'm sure . . . *I* did, but I can't put his name on him.'

I looked at the envelope. I didn't recognise the writing. Chardray was still hanging around. I said, 'Nor can I', went upstairs, threw the papers off my desk and poured a gin. I don't like gin. I was introduced to it by a lady whose husband I was supposed to be finding. She got me drunk on gin and then I behaved in a thoroughly unprofessional way with her, so much so that I sub-contracted the finding of the husband and concentrated my own resources on comforting the client. *That* worked so well the husband came round and said if I wasn't a cripple he'd beat my head in, but for now just a sock on the jaw would do. She was as pleased as hell to get the husband back, I got two hundred quid, a sore jaw and the remains of a gin bottle. I have a *taste* for the stuff, but I don't *like* it. It makes my jaw sore.

The note in the envelope read '*Urgent I speak with you soonest. Would you please ring my hotel a.s.a.p. George Duncan*. It was written on paper headed 'Hotel Bonaventura, Knightsbridge'.

It was ten days since the fight in Shoreditch. Tommy Lynch had been in the papers both for the prospect of a world title fight and for the fact that he'd gone over to the managership of Lenny Grant, a retired boxer in his mid-thirties. Judging by the photographs I'd seen in the papers of Grant with his new signing, Grant was the man I'd seen thumping George Duncan outside the boxing hall in Shoreditch. So the fight game was getting a little rough. I rang Duncan anyway, though if he was looking for protection he was on to the wrong man.

'James! Good to hear from you, James! God when I came to that fly-blown dump in Canning Town I thought I must've been in the wrong place. It was only the sign and that darkie from the shop that convinced me you were the James Jenner I used to know in Romford. How've you been doing?'

'I'm fine. I'm doing fine.'

'Listen. I should have recognised you when you came out to that place in Chigwell, but you know how it is . . . I was busy and I had a lot on my mind.'

'That's okay. No reason why you should've.'

'Good . . . good. I always knew you were the kind of fellow who could take it okay. I knew you wouldn't hold a grudge just because I never recognised you.'

'Right. We've got that clear . . . well, what can I do for you?'

'It was my wife that recognised you, and she'd never met you,' he went on. 'She saw your picture in the paper and

she said, "That's the chap who served the writ on Tommy"
. . . that's what she said and my God she was right. The
Daily Mail, it was.'

'I know.'

'Well of course I should've recognised you from the very
beginning, I know. Have you changed your hair?'

'No.'

'Well, I just don't know what it was, but I couldn't see
you for the young man who used to come to the old gym
in Romford until . . . until. . . .'

'Yeah yeah. I've got it. What can I do for you?'

'Well, Jimmy old friend. When I realised who you were
I realised that you were just the man to do a job of work
for me in your new trade. I realised I could trust you and
I could talk to you honestly . . . know what I mean?'

'Go on.'

'That's all. Let me talk to you, Jimmy.'

'What about?'

'I've got a proposition I'd like to put to you. I'd like you
to do a piece of work for me. All very simple stuff, but a
bit private.'

'What is it?'

'It's a bit private, like I said. Could you come down here
for an hour and have a drink?'

'When?'

'Now?'

'It's rush hour, Mr Duncan. I won't be able to park my
car there. I have to use my car. Can't we make it nine
o'clock?'

'Nine's fine. Look forward to seeing you then. *Bye.*'

He put the phone down. I drank my gin and went down
the creaky wooden stairs to the street-door. Traffic roared
past. I fumbled the keys again. Chardray was positioned by
the papers again. The *Guardian* was on the move again,
back to the centre of the stack. Maybe he was expecting an
SDP voter to pass.

'I just can't place him,' Chardray said.

'Who?' I hung my stick round my neck while I buttoned
my coat. Even during May I feel the cold nowadays. I don't
know why. My central heating bill's a cricket score.

'Your visitor. I just couldn't place his face from my

31

memory. But I know who he is, somehow. Didn't it say on the message?'

Nosy swine. I just turned my back on him and walked away. I knew it would drive him crazy for days.

I've got a couple of lads that do odd jobs for me. One's called Gary or Gal for short, the other Zorba. Zorba's a miserable, stunted, ex-pat Greek. I think he may be a Cypriot. I don't know whether he picked up his nickname because he's the absolute A1 opposite of the Anthony Quinn character in the movie or because his real name is just a load of consonants jumbled up. That's how Greek names all look to me. For whatever reason he's come by the name, Zorba is Zorba. Five feet six and two-twenty pounds of unrestrained out-and-out nastiness. He's so swarthy the hair seems to grow straight out of his collar, as if it's bursting to get somewhere. His eyes are so shifty they've turned into permanent slits, no eyeball revealed, between his stubbly chubby cheek and his hairy chubby brow. I'm glad he's on my side, because, as my grandad would say, he'd skin a turd for a tanner.

I use Zorba to look after me if I've got a dodgy bit of work going on. If I had to do that payout in Coldblow Lane nowadays I'd have Zorba backing me up. I'm getting too old for nervous afternoons and evenings, and I've always been nervous of dark places.

I had to walk a bit to find Zorba. He's not the kind of bloke you open up the phone book at 'Z' for and give a bell . . . he's dodgy. First of all you have to find Gal. And finding Gal means walking. I worked my way up the coffee bars, greasy spoons and various dives of Barking Road. No Gal. I took a cab (my leg was giving me gyp) to Roman Road, Bow, had a pie-and-mash and jellied eels because I can't walk past one, then found my boy Gary in the first amusement arcade I came to. He's a big skinny kid; nineteen, faded denims, on the dole, mucky brown hair and a washed-out face. He carries a scruffed-up copy of the *New Musical Express* permanently in the back pocket of his jeans, and as often as not he's wearing a faded denim Bob Dylan pillbox cap. I told him once and he said, 'Bob who?'

That's how life goes forward, by leaps and amnesia. Gal knows everyone who's anyone in the . . . shall we say the seedy end of London life? He knows all the deals that are doing and all the dealers that are doing them. He has also sworn to defend the world against Pacman, or whatever the latest Japanese electronic invasion is called. When I found him he was bending over an electronic screen, green flashes racing past his ears, his body jerking spasmodically. His back twitched all the time. I only recognised him because of the *NME* sticking out of his pocket. I snapped the main electric switch to the machine with my walking stick, then held my hands up as he turned angrily.

'*What* the . . . oh, hello Jimmy.'

'Where's Zorba?'

'I dunno. He was drinking down the road until an hour ago . . . I don't know where he might have gone since then.'

I drew him outside to the street.

'I want you two to do a little job for me. Discreet enquiries about a man called Duncan, George Duncan. He's a boxing manager. Here's the key to my office. I should be back by eleven, say. Get all you can, then dump your body on my sofa and wait there till I come. Wait till half eleven.'

'Zorba too?'

'No. Only one of you need come. But I want all the dirt on him, anything and everything . . . and Gal.'

'What?'

'I've marked the gin. Bring your own booze.'

5

I took a cab across to Knightsbridge. I'm lazy about driving. All the way across the cabbie treated me to his family history. A very interesting family they were too, *if* you were a family member. His uncle had the Burma Star and his Dad had been to Germany. Well, not *to* it so much as *over* it. In a Lancaster. He'd got a sister who'd married a wally, his own wife was an 'absolute dear, a darling' and he'd got a two-year old son. He got all that out between Cambridge Heath Road and Knightsbridge. If I'd been going to Heathrow I've no doubt he'd have told me when his mother lost her cherry and he'd have been recommending psycho-analysts to me.

The Hotel Bonaventura was between Knightsbridge and the Brompton Road. It had obviously been a family house once, perhaps before the war. Now it was shabby. The building had suffered generations of kids doing *Europe on Six Dollars a Day* or whatever the lastest incarnation of that book is. Outside there was a bunch of North American girls and boys helping each other strap on rucksacks and an angry coach driver trying to gee them all up.

I went inside and stopped one of the preppy North American kids.

'Where's reception?'

He laughed and went on. There was no reception. I yelled up the stairs, 'Duncan, hey! George Duncan.'

'Hello. Wait!' echoed back.

Right place, anyway. I waited. Kids smiled, stared or frowned at me, as it took their fancy. Then George came down the stairs wearing a blue chalk-stripe suit, a grey fedora hat and a bowtie.

'I've got to stay here on the quiet,' he confided. 'I don't want no one to know where I am.'

We wandered down to a pub in Knightsbridge, looking like George Melly and Hopalong Cassidy. The idea that no one would notice us, that we'd be here on the quiet, was a non-starter.

He took the hat off, grinned, drank half an enormous measure of scotch and sat at a table out of the crowd before he apologised.

'I expect you're thinking it's not my thing, eh? I expect you're wondering why's a big fight manager like me staying in a dump like that, eh?'

He sucked at a flame through an enormous cigar.

'I didn't think about it really. I suppose you have a reason,' I said. Of course I was wondering.

'I'm trying to fix up a fight . . . no no. I can't say *what* fight. Just a fight. It's got to be *well* on the quiet, so I've got the geezer from stateside visiting here rather than somewhere that could be staked out by a load of mateys from the press. Know what I mean?'

'Uhuh.' I nodded. George fluttered his eyelashes, sucked his cigar and picked at some fluff on his lapel.

'I need some looking after . . . no, no,' he held his hand up, 'not heavy minding. Gawd knows I've got enough hooligans if I just want someone on the door. More?'

I said yes, he went to the bar and refilled our glasses. I tapped my walking stick on the floor. It had better not be heavy minding. George eased himself back into the seat and went on.

'I've had some threats. I can't go into them, and there's no good asking me who from because I don't know. Some fruity-pie shot a twelve-bore into my front door the other day, I've had a lot of nasty phone calls. All that sort of thing.'

'Letters?'

'One. I've got one. What it's all about doesn't concern you.' He pulled a big handkerchief from his pocket and mopped his brow. 'Well, it's all about a fighter. Let's just say that. The point is that I'm well tied up over the next couple of weeks and I want someone to look after my missus.'

'How "look after"?'

'She don't know it's going on. I can lay on no end of brawny yobbos to take care of her, but I want someone with a little savvy. Whoever's having a go at me is doing just that, having a go at *me*. She's under no threat and I don't expect she will be . . . I just want someone to be an eyes and ears for me, make sure she doesn't walk into any stupid trouble.'

'Who's threatening you?' I asked.

'Not your business. I pay a ton a day and you make sure my missus doesn't fall under any buses, that sort of thing, for the next two weeks. Then I'll have finished all my deals and all that crap and I'll take back responsibility.' He put an envelope on the table. 'There's the first two days' worth. You shape out how I think you will and I'll be able to pay you a bonus, three days' pay, say, at the end. That'll mean seventeen hundred greenies for swanning round in my Jag for a fortnight. Not bad work, eh?' He pushed the money towards me. 'My address is in there. It's in Saffron Walden. Get the train up tomorrow, then a cab from the station. I'll pick up the expenses. I've got a chauffeur, Harry . . . do you know him?'

I shook my head.

'I think he was around the gym in Romford when you were. He's a good bloke but thick as a plank. No use for this at all. I've sent him on holiday, and you're his replacement for the holiday . . . that's what she thinks.'

'Why not tell her the truth?' I asked.

He shook his big, silvery-haired head.

'It'll get her all lathered-up. She'll stick to me like a limpet and I don't need that now. I can't do with having me missus cracking up right at the moment. Know what I mean?'

'No,' I said. I didn't, either. The woman I'd seen slapping him around in Shoreditch didn't look like she'd stick like a limpet to anything except herself.

He pushed the money again.

'Count it. Take the job. Turn up at my drum in Saffron in one day's time. What d'yer say?'

'What time?'

'Same as now. Get there for eight or nine. You get the train up from Liverpool Street. Leave your car in London because I think you'll finish with us in London. It'll save you coming back out to fetch your motor.'

'Your car an auto?' I slapped my leg.

'Yeah. I already thought about that.'

I stood up. He leaned forward and shook my hand. I couldn't believe him: chalk-stripe suit, big yellow bowtie (*lemon* yellow at that), comes in wearing a fedora and then goes to a quiet corner of the pub 'so we won't be noticed'.

'Deal?'

'I'd prefer to know what you're worried about. It's hard to see it coming if you don't know what you're looking for.'

He ignored me.

'Deal?'

'Call my office in the morning and I'll let you know.'

I went outside. It was a stormy, muggy night. All wrong for May. I walked as far as Hyde Park Corner, then went down to the tube. A man was drunk, sick-drunk on the stairs. He was on his knees and wobbling about. I would have picked him up if I could have. I was frightened he'd fall down the steps and split his skull. If I tried to pick him up we'd both go down the stairs head first, I knew that for sure, so I had to leave him.

I'm a strange man to hire for muscle, for protection. *I* wouldn't hire me as a minder . . . why should Duncan want to? As the train came in I heard a wail from the drunk on the stairs, then a dull thud. Either the muggers or the forces of gravity had got him. Whichever, he was beyond my help. The doors shushed open and I stepped aboard.

6

I was surprised to find myself at the Lynch-Diaz fight in Shoreditch again. They weren't in the ring. Two soppy-joes were beating each other's heads in for a warm-up. I could feel it and smell it and hear it, and even though it was all wrong it was exactly as it should be, with all the sweat and leather in glorious three-D before my very eyes. I was in the front row and the two soppy-joes were trying to kill each other above my very head. The timekeeper's table was just along from me a way and he rang the bell and the joes kept fighting and he rang the bell more and they still kept fighting and he was ringing and ringing and ringing.

Then I was sitting up, sweating in my bedclothes. On the floor there was a trail of abandoned female underwear, plus the wrapper for a new pair of tights, plus the normal debris Judy leaves as she gets up late for work . . . one shoe, a hairbrush, a crumpled skirt she'd stepped out of last night. Last night! I didn't even remember her coming, didn't even know she was here. The bell kept ringing. I yelled, 'All right!' and strapped up my leg before pulling my dressing gown on and staggering down the corridor to the door.

'Gal. What are you . . . oh, last night, eh?'

'You should open a window,' he said. 'Also you shouldn't get up so late. It's after ten. You'll waste your life.'

'I had a few bevvys in Soho, then I . . . er. . . .'

'Forgot,' Gary said. 'You forgot your ace assistant was waiting faithfully in your office, all primed up with info just as you asked. You meanwhile. . . .'

'Was being a bar prop in Greek Street. I know. What did you get?'

'What's it worth?'

I struggled with an expresso machine, a very expensive birthday present from Judy. I can't work it though. I spilled ground coffee all over the worktop, then gave up and put a kettle on.

'Tea do? Good. Don't muck about, Gal. How am I supposed to know what it's worth before you've told me?'

'It's good. Very good.'

I went to the living room and fetched my wallet. Pulled out two fivers and put them on the table. With no coffee in it and no hint from me that it should the coffee machine started pouring out steam. Why do machines feel entitled to be so unreasonable? I switched it off and pushed the fivers at the kid.

'Come on, Gal. I haven't got all morning.'

'Okay.' He took his cap off and sat up straight. 'George Duncan had a boxer called Lynch, Tommy Lynch. Tommy Lynch left him, you must have seen all that in the paper.'

I shook my head.

'I didn't see it in the paper. I was *there*. Tell me something I don't know, Gal.'

'And Lynch went to a geezer called Grant, Leonard Grant. He's an up and coming manager . . . *as* they say in the papers you don't read.' He paused and smiled. Gal was pleased with himself. 'And Grant is a front man – and *only* a front man – for a mob of villains led by a guy called Wilkins. Very nasty piece of work, Wilkins. It seems Duncan and Grant had a barney in the street on account of Duncan not being entirely over the moon about his man being poached just when he's ready to go for a big one.'

'I know . . .' I said.

'Don't tell me,' he broke in, 'you were there when the barney took place. Why ask me to find out things you already know?'

'Because I'm an organiser, Gal, and you're an operative. You do what you're good at and let me do the thinking. Tell me what else you've got.'

'All right.' He stood and poured boiling water over the tea bags in our mugs, then swizzled the bags around with the wrong end of a fork. 'I don't suppose it matters. I only wore me feet out, lied me head off and almost got a kicking getting this information for you. Why should it worry me you can't be bothered to open the paper and find out the basics of who's who and what's what in the fight game?' He gave me a mug of tea. 'I'll give it to you from the top. . . .'

'Don't bother. I've got it. Where did you go other than the public library?'

'Ha ha.' He slurped at his tea, set the mug on the table and leaned back in his chair. 'You don't want to know the rest, then.' A pause. 'I thought you would. People have been leaving Duncan in droves, and word is that Grant is using the Wilkins muscle to fix venues and contracts if not actual fights. George Duncan is up against it. Rumour has it he's getting out of the fight game altogether . . . either that or the game's getting out of him, since he don't have no boxers.'

'What else do you have on him?'

'Lot of rubbish. He's on his third marriage. A South African bird called Alison. Pretty tasty by all accounts. He's got a flat in the Barbican and a house in Cambridgeshire. He lives well, plenty of dough. He's reckoned to be mouthy but not much bottle . . . oh, and he's disappeared for the last week. No one's seen him or his wife. A guy that knows his chauffeur reckons he's pissed off to some little hotel to do some deal. If he's going to run up against Wilkins' lot his best deal would be if he got himself measured up for a cheap wooden overcoat.'

I laughed so much that tea ran up my nose. Wooden overcoat! This boy, when he isn't playing Pacman, watches nineteen-forties gangster movies. I could imagine him lying on my horsehair sofa thinking that one up.

'Wasser matter?' Gal pouted.

'Nothing. Remind me not to let you make the tea any more. What did Zorba get?'

'Nothing. I couldn't find him. I brought your car round. The keys were on the desk.'

'Cheers. Where does Wilkins run out of?'

'Walthamstow.'

I pushed him another fiver.

'Not bad for one evening, eh? I've done well, I mean . . . only for a couple of hours' work. I don't s'pose you want to make a small contrib to the time I wasted in your office, eh?'

'No,' I said, 'but I won't charge you rent either, nor for the cup of tea I've just donated. I won't deduct anything for telling me he had a house in Cambridgeshire when it's in Essex, either, dummy.'

Gal was hurt he'd got that wrong. He's half-man, half-boy still. Sometimes hard and clever, sometimes very vulnerable. I like him. If I really liked him, I'd buy him a cheap home computer and then he could save his money in the arcades. But then he'd never see daylight, never meet anyone and never be any use to me. He'd never make any vitamin D, either . . . or is it vitamin E? Who cares, unless you're short of it? That's true for everything. It's too early in the morning for philosophy, I thought, and took my tea back to bed.

I have one of those funny phone-answering things, a tape machine in the office and then I have a little gadget I keep in my pocket so that I can 'collect important messages *all* over the world'. I don't know about all over the world, but sometimes it works around London and sometimes it don't.

'*You are through to Jenner's. James Jenner speaking. If you'd like to leave a message wait till the tone, then leave your name, number and message if you wish and I'll get back to you as soon as I can.*'

Beep.

'Hullo, Sjimmy. Zorba here. I'm no goina be round for a few days, so I'll be here in touch as soon as I can.'

Beep.

'O'Keefe here. I'd like you to phone me on my home number as soon as.'

Beep.

Beep.

'James. It's Judy. Where the hell are you? It's ten thirty and you were going to meet me here at nine thirty. *Here*, in case you've forgotten, is The Marquess of Anglesey, Bow Street. Do you remember where Bow Street is? I'm stuck here with a couple of lemons from the Serious Crimes Squad and if you don't come and rescue me soon I'm going to be *really* angry.'

Beep.

'Duncan here. I take it you're not in your office yet. I'll call back later, Jimmy.'

Beep.

Beep.

There followed half a dozen beeps, then a long, rambling message from a guy I'd found his wife for. He'd gone off the beam, I don't know why she wanted him back. I suppose she loves him or something. He's small, in his thirties, balding and he smokes so much he smells of it all the time. He smells terrible. I read a survey once that said that women who smoke too much conceive less than women who don't smoke. The reporter suggested nicotine as the cause. But it's not true. They don't conceive because they smell bad and then no one wants to sleep with them. Sleeping with someone is a vital part in the conception process, *I* know. I think that woman must have really loved her nutty husband, who was called Bernard something. I forget the whole name. As soon as I hear Bernard's voice on my telephone I put my right ear to the phone. My right ear doesn't work very well.

I called Judy and arranged to take her out to lunch. I also asked what the name Wilkins from Walthamstow meant to her. Then I called Duncan's hotel in Knightsbridge and told him I'd see him in Saffron Waldon that evening. Then I went back into the kitchen to do battle with the expresso machine. I'm not being beaten by a mere lump of metal . . . oh no.

'What's wrong with your hand?' Judy said. We were in a big boozer in Horseferry Road.

'I scalded it. It's nothing.'

'Looks sore.'

'It's okay. Come here.' I put my arm round her. She's lovely. Good skin, better figure and wide blue eyes, pools of cobalt. There, I'm a poet, too. She's so clever it makes me weep. Top ten in her Sergeant's Exam, looks like she's passed her Inspector's, too. She's a uniformed officer, though she works in Criminal Intelligence. Her thing is computers. Sometimes she brings home great piles of green-lined computer paper, all gobbledegook to me but she understands it. I don't know what she's doing with me . . . I've told her too: 'You should find some brilliant young barrister and marry him.' Then she gets angry.

Judy was wearing a nondescript beige mackintosh. It more or less covered the uniform underneath. I pulled at her collar and apologised about last night.

'Good Jimmy,' she sipped her orange juice. 'I'm glad you remember where you were getting drunk. It's a good thing not to lose control completely. For myself, I ended up being bored to death by a couple of louts all evening, then I had to fight one off all the way home in the taxi while his mate sat in the other seat, laughing. I had a really good time.'

'I'm sorry. I did come all this way to apologise.'

She shook her head, then brought her lips to my ear and said, 'No you didn't. You came all this way to find out about Albert Wilkins, you bastard. Don't lie to me.'

She kissed my ear. I felt like fainting. I've known her for years and years and it always drives me mad when she kisses my ear. Who cares about Wilkins?

'I've got my car outside,' I said. 'We could go off.'

'I've got fifteen minutes of lunch left. Time for another orange juice and a walk back.'

We walked close to each other on the way back. I like that. I like it when it's rainy and you can smell her perfume and she's close but not close. I like walking with her, nearly touching.

'Albert Wilkins,' she said, 'was born in Leytonstone in 1928. He's the son of a labourer, one of seven children. Here's a photograph of him. Don't look at it now, but tear it up and throw it away when you have looked at it. It's one of ours, taken on obbo. Wilkins has only two bits of form; one, believe it or not, for handling forged petrol coupons. That was in 1947. The other is for GBH in 1958.'

'What GBH?'

'He cut a bloke's ear off outside a dance hall in front of witnesses.'

'Charming.'

'He did time for that. He was nicked for attempted

murder in 1960 too, but that didn't stick. Something to do with the witnesses to the 1958 case all falling down stairs once a month while Wilkins was doing his bird for the GBH. The word got round, I suppose.'

It wasn't raining yet but it looked like it would. The sky hung dark and heavy over Victoria Street. Buses passed, lamps aglow. The traffic lights seemed unnaturally bright. Above us, in the New Scotland Yard building, neon lamps flickered on. I tucked the hooked part of my walking stick into my rainmac pocket, then took her in my arms.

'Thanks,' I said. 'I don't like to ask.' I kissed her. She smiled.

'It's okay. The things I've told you are matters of public record. You could have spent days finding them out, but it's not breaking any rules to tell you about it. It's a bit of a cheek to kiss your lover outside your boss's office, I think.'

I let her go and took my walking stick out of my pocket again.

'But ten floors below,' I said.

'Okay. Ten floors below. Jim, it definitely would be against the rules to tell you that Wilkins has run his own organisation for the past twenty years and that he's very high on the league table of target criminals. A lot of people inside that building are absolutely dying to get his scalp on their belt. Well, that's the sort of thing I wouldn't tell you.'

The rain started. Dollops of water splattered on the pavement. There was a flash in the distance, miles away, and a low rumble. The rain audibly splashed around us. I pulled a floppy, showerproof canvas trilby from my pocket and belted my mackintosh. Judy put up her umbrella and we crossed the road together. We parted in the entrance hall of NSY. The guard on the door recognised me and nodded. I think it's the stick as much as anything. I nodded back.

'What wouldn't you tell *me*?' Judy asked.

'I'm going away, probably for a few days. I've got a client who feels he's under threat from Wilkins, or at least from one of his drones, a man called Grant. Lenny Grant. That dodgy bugger Denis O'Keefe wants to get hold of me. I don't want to see him. I've decided I don't need him any more.'

'Good move.'

'Thanks. A solicitor in Clapton, Menke, is having trouble getting the money to pay me out of one of his clients. That's his story, anyway. Apart from that my entire life is hunky-dory and there's nothing I wouldn't tell you.'

'He's not asking you to offer physical protection, this client?'

'No. Don't be silly. I'll phone you at your flat when I get back.'

'Do,' she said and touched my lapel. We didn't kiss goodbye. It's not the sort of place you do.

7

I drove straight from NSY to Saffron Walden. I wasn't having any of that 'just get the train' nonsense from Duncan. I wanted to give his place a good look over and I wanted to be able to put his money through his letter-box and buzz off home under my own steam if I felt like it. All the way there I listened to a radio phone-in about when the Task Force was going to kick the Argies out of Port Stanley. I'd only heard of the Falklands a couple of months ago. Now it looked like people would die for it. I hoped not. I certainly wouldn't have volunteered to face any guns I didn't have to and I could do without losing any legs I didn't have to lose. I wished I could've told those boys that.

If I'd had the sense I'd have put Duncan's money through his letter-box there and then. I already knew he was lying to me. His wife, who he'd reckoned had recognised me in the paper, had never clapped eyes on me before. She hadn't been in the hall in Shoreditch when I went for the weigh-in before Lynch's fight, later in the street she hadn't seen me any better than I'd seen her, and she hadn't been George Duncan's wife when I used to use his gym in Romford all those years ago . . . no, I didn't believe a word of that. All the buddy-buddy crap from Duncan himself was hard to take, too. I mean, he'd owned the gym, I'd worked out in it. So had a couple of hundred other fellows in the course of a week. Duncan didn't know me from Adam. He'd seen my face in the papers – *maybe*, as an outside chance – and he'd seen me for two minutes maximum when I'd tried to serve the writ on his fighter. Someone may have reminded him that I'd used his gym in Romford, and he'd needed a private detective and just lit upon me because I'd come to his attention. As for Alison Duncan needing protection . . . that was a joke, as far as I could see.

My trouble is I've got an over-developed sense of humour. Also, it beat finding lost spouses and serving writs. Unwittingly, George Duncan had offered me a piece of real detective work, and I was hooked. The way things worked out later, I came to wish I hadn't been. Curiosity killed the catfish.

I'd never been to Saffron Walden before. It's not very remarkable. It's just about commutable from London, full of picture-postcard Essex houses, all coloured plasterwork, pargeting and revealed oak beams. It's the kind of place that makes me sick. Like Disneyland . . . though I haven't been to Disneyland. Chocolate-box-top England. Syrupy.

I put my car in the station car park at Audley End. That's where you go for Saffron Walden on the train. Then I pulled my gumboots on – not as easy as it sounds – and took a cab into town.

We went past a big house, no doubt the home of the Duke of Audley or some such robber baron made good. The cab driver pointed it out; very proud, as if he lived there.

He dropped me off in the main street. It's a pretty rich street, plenty of Range Rovers and all that stuff. Lots of middle-aged women in Home Counties uniform, pleated blue skirts and fluffy dogs. If Saffron Walden has any council estates they're well tucked away.

I bought a map of the area, located Duncan's house on it, then took a taxi to a road I reckoned was two fields away. The rain had started to fall pretty heavily here, too, and the cabbie clearly thought I was barmy for getting out of his car in a deserted country lane in the middle of a storm. I waited till he'd rounded a bend and then struck up the bank into a field. The field was full of green stuff and mud. The mud I recognised but the green stuff has to be in a sealed plastic Sainsbury's bag and clearly marked 'Broccoli' or 'Brussels Sprouts' or 'Bobby Beans' before I know what it is. I plodded through the green stuff and the rain fell on me and the mud stuck to my gumboots.

I got to a ditch and a hedge about a hundred yards from Duncan's house. I had to lie on the bank of the ditch, rain or no rain. I'd overestimated my walking ability – or underestimated the fact that ten minutes' downpour can turn a dry field into a quagmire. I was all in. I lay there with the rain splashing on my face for some minutes. The ditch smelled terrible. My back was soaked by the grass on the bank, my front by the rain. My hair was getting wet from rain soaking through the showerproof material of my hat. I turned over and watched the house through a hole in the hedge. I could see Duncan moving around inside. All the lights were on and I could see him moving back and forth in front of the window. If he was scared he wasn't acting like it. The house was lonely and exposed, a big red-brick job from the middle of the nineteenth century. There were a couple of outbuildings and I saw him go out to them once, scurrying with a coat thrown over his shoulders and a hat on his head. He didn't see me. He wasn't looking.

I didn't see his wife. I only saw George moving around and some laundry van delivering. The wife didn't even go out to that. Maybe they *were* scared. There was no wall around or in front of the house and you could see into it for miles around. The rain kept falling and I was tired and wet and cold now, cold as if I were catching a chill. It wasn't the weather. George Duncan made himself a cup of tea and settled down in his chintzy sitting room with a newspaper. Lucky old George. A rabbit sat on the lawn and stared at me. I left care of George to the rabbit and walked back into town. It's a long walk. It's even further to the station, which is where my dry clothes were in a bag in the boot of my car. What would the cab drivers of England do without me? I wondered.

By eight o'clock I was in a comfortable chair in a pub. I could still hear rain outside and I was reading previews of cricket matches from the morning's *Times*. I had three large scotches inside me, a fourth on the table in front of me, dry clothes on my back and a cab on the way to pick me up. It beat lying in a field. There's something nice about reading journalism when you've got the drop on the journalist, like

48

knowing the matches he'd previewed couldn't be played and hadn't been.

'Taxi for you sir,' called the barman. The driver was the same one who'd driven me out to my rendezvous with the rabbit, but if he recognised me he said nothing. I made him carry my bag. I don't tip for nothing.

8

'*Jimmy! Jimmy!* Come in, Jimmy.' George Duncan greeted me as if I were a long-lost brother and the suitcase at my side were full of pound notes instead of shirts, socks and underpants. 'Alison, c'm 'ere. This is the guy I was telling you about. Harry's short-term replacement.' His accent hovered in mid-Atlantic. I wondered which side it would land.

A woman came down the stairs. Mid-to-late twenties, blonde but natural – not-too-blonde. Beautifully dressed in an emerald green long thing, all off the shoulder and clinging where it should. She looked a cracker. I was in love until she opened her mouth.

'*So* pleased to meet you, Mr Jimmy. My husband has told me much about you.' She was reciting lines she'd learned and she wasn't very good at it. I took the hand she offered. It was cold and damp. She was apprehensive, I could see that from her face. I didn't know what of; not the threats against Duncan. He'd said he hadn't told her.

'*Jenner*,' I said. 'Jimmy, or more precisely James, is my first name.'

'Oh.' She let her hand drop. 'How stoopid of me, Mr Jenner. I'm so sorry.'

It was me. *I* was making her nervous. She turned half away. She had her hair up, pinned loosely behind her head, and as she turned she showed a long, cool, naked neck, downy and handsome. I smiled to let her know she wasn't 'stoopid' but she wouldn't look into my face.

'Why don't you run upstairs and fix your bag or something while I give Jimmy a drink and have a chat with him?'

50

She went up. Slim ankles slid in and out of a vent at the back of the green clingy dress. Looking after Mrs Duncan would be the nicest job I ever had – as long as she didn't open her mouth again. No . . . who cares? For a hundred quid a day I'd even listen to the mouth.

Duncan steered me into a study off the hall. It was lined with photographs of boxers and books about boxers. There was a big mahogany desk with a leather inlay. On top of the desk was a tray with a whisky bottle and glasses.

'I'll only give you a small one. You won't be staying long, I'm afraid. Your first job is to take Mrs Duncan back to London tonight. See her to our flat, but you can just leave her there and go back in the morning.' He handed me a huge glass with a very lonely bead of whisky in the bottom.

'Ice?'

'No. I don't want to smother it.' I put my hand over the top of my glass. He didn't even laugh.

'Trouble?' I said.

'Nothing to concern you.'

I drank my whisky before it evaporated.

'Nothing to do with your "dispute"?' I asked.

He sat in a mock-antique captain's chair on the other side of the desk, rocked back in it and took a good gulp of his whisky.

'I told you all I'm telling you. I'm paying you good money to make sure my wife's okay. Don't fill your head with a load of stuff that's not your business.'

'I need to know what's going on, though,' I said. I sat on the edge of the desk. He frowned. This obviously wasn't a desk that was sat on a lot. 'For instance, is your wife going to a party?'

'Party?' He frowned again. He was not a pretty man and his muscles must've been practising that frown for well over forty years. It made him look like he'd been eating a lemon when the elephant sat on his face. 'Oh . . . you mean the dress.'

I nodded. I could've been rude and sarcastic but he was paying for the interview. I'm only ever rude and sarcastic for free.

'She likes to dress up when she's meeting people,' he said.

'Who's she meeting?'

He stood, drained the glass and set it on the leather. I noticed there was a space on the wall, pride of place in the middle of the photographs. I'd have laid a pound to a penny that's where Tommy Lynch's photograph had been until recently.

'*You*, dummy. Come on, I'll show you the car.'

We went back into the hallway. Alison Duncan was heaving a large suitcase down the stairs. She was wearing a three-quarter length pale blue rainmac over the emerald green evening dress. Some of her hair had fallen down from the clasp behind her head.

'Will this do?' she called down. She meant the mac, I guessed. George Duncan looked at her for a second.

'You'll do.'

'I've got another bag upstairs,' she said.

George waved his hand magnanimously.

'Plenty of time, doll. Bring them out in your own time.'

He opened the door and pointed at a shed.

'The car's over there. Have you driven a Jag before?'

I nodded that I had. I wondered why he hadn't put the mortise lock on if he was so frightened. The door was held by a rim latch alone.

George Duncan showed me all the controls of the Jaguar as if it were Concorde 002. He insisted. By the time he'd finished his wife had dragged the bags down and across the yard to our shed. George lifted them easily and dumped them in the boot. He said goodbye to her and pulled the shed doors wide to let me get the car out. I flicked the headlamp switch and the beams fell on old rusted farm implements, a hayrake, a pitchfork and some big metal flail thing that goes on the back of tractors. Alison Duncan sat in the front passenger seat and I nodded at the rusty farm gear.

'I didn't realise this was a whole farm you had here.'

'Oh it's not, Mr Jenner.'

I nodded again.

'What's all that stuff for then?'

She stared through the windscreen, blinking.

'What stuff?'

She sounded like a speak-your-weight machine. I backed

52

the car out. I hung around so he could come over and say goodbye properly to her. He never did though. Now it was time to go, Duncan seemed nervous and anxious to get on. He never even waved goodbye to her. He just stood in front of his house, watching in the rain till we turned the first bend and we lost sight of him. Mrs Duncan didn't look back, either. I thought perhaps they'd rowed before I got there. What was it to do with me, eh? Duncan was right – it was no concern of mine. The fact that she was nervous, didn't want to speak, had no South African accent and sat next to the hired hand in the front of the car; all this was no concern of mine also. Nothing was my concern. A man has an ugly villain making threats against him – and, I presume, his wife – he has bird-shot fired at his door, a threatening letter delivered to his house, and then he hires a crippled detective to protect his wife; a wife who's a rotten actress and has clearly never been chauffeured around before, a wife who's supposed to come from Cape Town but whose accent wandered between Stafford and South London. It stank.

We'd been set up, I was sure. I drove north to Cambridge. Even Alison knew we weren't in London.

'This isn't London,' she said.

'I'm missing the motorway,' I said. 'I saw a sign in Saffron saying the motorway was closed.'

'I didn't see a sign.'

'Don't worry, Mrs Duncan. I saw it.'

She leaned forward and switched the radio on, pushing the buttons until she got some pop music. What sounded like a cat being strangled swore everlasting love and loyalty to his Ramona, then plucked his guitar with his brothers. A husky, late-night lady DJ assured us she was filling in for someone else. I knew how she felt. I took the road for Baldock and London. I kept looking in the rear-view mirror for car headlamps. It was rainy and night-time, though. What should I expect to see but headlamps in my rear-view mirror? I saw hundreds. By the time I was on the A1 all the headlamps were keeping pace with me. That's the point of a motorway. Things are never the way they're made out in films. My back was soaked with sweat from fear, my hands gripped the wheel too hard, I flinched every time a car moving too fast went past. I was dying for a pee but I wasn't stopping the car in the service area. Who wants to die in South Mimms? It's not very prepossessing. They don't put that in the films, either.

We reached the Barbican around midnight. It's surprising how empty the streets of the City can be. The rain had stopped at last. The water squelched between the big tyres of the Jag and the tarmac. We drove down Chiswell Street, then under the arch and down Aldersgate Street. We went round and round the Barbican, with her peering out of the window.

'Haven't you lived here long?' I said.

'Oh, ages. I just get confused by it all. I always get confused.' She said all this without looking at me.

We found her block. A copper showed us, one of those pantomime City of London coppers with a big hat, rolled up rain-cape and a red-and-white duty-band on his arm like nothing had changed in the City of London police for fifty years. Like they'll never be short of time to give you directions. I followed his directions, with the woman I was now convinced was not Mrs Duncan avoiding my eyes and not speaking and me trying to drive and follow the street signs all at the same time. When we got there I locked her in the car, walked upstairs and had a good poke around the flat and the landing outside. It was an expensive flat, expensive to rent and expensively furnished. All brash and bad taste but very clean and very tidy and smelling of lavender polish. There were more pictures of boxers on the wall and another gap where I suppose Tommy Lynch had rested till recently. He must feel like Stalin's ghost. I sat on the sofa and listened to the silence. Nothing. A tap was dripping in the bathroom. I went out on the balcony. All clear, no muggers or murderers or bashers-up on the balcony. So far so good. A hundred feet below me I could see the shape of the Jaguar. I'd left the sidelights on. I knew the woman would be sitting in there waiting for me. I wondered what would be going through her mind . . . did she know Duncan had set the two of us up? I doubted it. Had he? I thought so. Should I tell her? I supposed I should. I didn't know. I went inside, poured myself a big measure of Duncan's whisky and went to the fridge for ginger ale and ice. I went back onto the balcony and drank the whisky from Duncan's big expensive tumbler. I looked at his big expensive living room through the french windows. I turned and looked over London. Yellow strips of street-lighting ran towards me. Some lights were on in an office block in Wood Street. I could see matchstick figures moving about in it. I looked down at Duncan's expensive car again, drank my whisky and then threw his expensive cut-glass whisky tumbler over the top of the balcony. I heard it tinkle as it hit the ground, but by that time I was inside again and on my way to the lift.

'Where have *you* been?' 'Mrs Duncan' had decided to go on the attack.

'Get out,' I said. 'Is the stuff in the bags yours or hers?'

'I don't know. . . .'

'Cut that rubbish out. I'm not in the mood.' I went to the boot and pulled the bags out. I nearly fell over. '*Are these yours?*'

'I'm sorry, I don't know what you mean.'

She was either very stupid or Duncan had promised her something.

'Look, whoever-you-are. I think Duncan's been having me on. Either he's been having you on too, or you're in it with him. What's it to be?'

She hung her head and looked at the bags and said again, 'I don't know what you mean.'

'Suit yourself,' I said. 'The lift's over there. I've been upstairs and there are no bogey men. I won't offer to carry your bags,' I picked up my stick from where it had been lying, against the side of the Jaguar. 'You can see why.'

'I don't think my husband's going to be very pleased about this,' she said. I couldn't see her face properly in the gloom. I wanted to help her but I needed a shove, some push towards it. I thought if Duncan was using us as targets for Wilkins then 'Mrs Duncan' would be able to use any help she could get. The best help I could give her would be to put her in a taxi back to wherever she come from. She picked up the bags.

'I don't know your husband, Missus. But I think you may be right. Why don't you go home?'

But she carried the bags over to the lift. It took her several goes. She had to keep stopping because the bags were too heavy. I locked up Duncan's car and took her the car keys.

'You'll need these, too,' I said.

The lift door was open. I took a long look at her face in the light of the lift compartment. I smelled her perfume, looked into her eyes. They were brown and soft and stupid, like a milch cow. I had a nasty feeling that's what she was to Duncan, and it's what I was meant to be. I turned and walked away as quick as I could.

I walked to Finsbury Circus, went in and sat on a bench for half an hour. I was really angry with Duncan. I could hear some tramps drinking and arguing on the other side of the little park. A copper came and threw them out. I left before he came over to me. I splashed through the puddles to Liverpool Street Station, bought a coffee and drank it watching trains that didn't move. A policeman was moving people on here too, but I obviously looked like a bona fide traveller because he ignored me. Other bona fide travellers embraced over the ticket gates, holding each other desperately, kissing passionately. A loud but muffled announcement came over the public address. A black man passed me pushing a broom and a pile of rubbish. He waited patiently for me to lift my legs without asking me to do it. I ignored him and after a while he went away, still pushing the rubbish. I couldn't go home. I'd presumed I was staying in Saffron Walden and left my flat keys in the car. Judy had a set, but I didn't feel like waking her at one a.m. to ask for my flat keys. I went to a phone and called Zorba's number. No answer. He could've put me up. I rang Gal.

'Were you already awake?' I said.

'Yeah. It's okay.'

'Have you got a motor?'

'Me brother's.'

'Come and pick us up in Liverpool Street, will you, Gal? And bring my office key too.'

'Whereabouts?'

'In front of Bishopsgate nick.'

9

Canning Town had been washed clean by the rain. As clean as it was ever going to be, anyway. Gary drove me there in his brother's Rover three-and-a-half litre. I don't believe a kid like Gal could be insured to drive it. Come to that, I'd be surprised if his brother's insured to drive it.

I felt better with Gal. Being with Duncan and the woman had left a nasty taste in my mouth. I washed it away with two cans of Special Brew Gal had in the back of the car and a take-away doner kebab we picked up in Whitechapel. The nice thing about doner is that if you have enough raw onion and chilli sauce on it you never know what harm it's doing you. Wash it down with two cans of Special Brew and you'd think nothing could do you any harm. That's how I felt when Gary dropped me off. I gave him some of Duncan's money, told him to go to Audley End and get my car in the morning and to dump the stolen Rover now and walk home so he didn't get arrested.

'What stolen Rover?' He grinned.

'Just dump it, Gal, and give me the office keys.'

He gave me the keys and drove away like a man possessed. One day the police'll catch him. I could see one of their Transits from my doorstep, cruising slowly on the Canning Town flyover. I went upstairs, noticed that Gal had brought his own wax crayon for the gin bottle last night, pulled an old army blanket from a cupboard and curled up on the sofa. I felt dead. I'd picked some letters up on the way in. They could wait. I just needed to sleep. I slept in my jacket and trousers under the old army blanket and I went off as if I'd been drugged.

I woke at dawn, whenever that is. I don't see it often. Maybe the chilli woke me, maybe sleeping in an unfamiliar place (for sleeping), or maybe it was the sun. There wasn't much traffic on the flyover so it was pretty early, I knew. I made some Camp coffee in a cup and opened my letters. They were all rubbish, including a request from the solicitor, Menke, that I find the disappeared owner of the house a client of his wanted to buy. Menke's jobs were money for old rope as long as you didn't ever expect to *get* the money. I wrote 'no' on the bottom of the letter he'd sent me, then sealed the envelope with sticky tape and wrote 'return to sender, not known at this address' on the front and drew an arrow pointing to Menke's address on the back. I don't mind earning easy money but I like to get paid for what I do.

I phoned directory enquiries for Duncan's number. I thought I'd give him a good morning call, some obscene message like what he could do with his rotten job. He wasn't in the book. Then I rang Zorba's flat again. No Zorba. How come I'd woken at dawn for the first time in my life and no one wanted to be awake with me? I rang Gal's flat and his young lady answered and said she didn't know where he was, she thought he was with me, and did I know what the time was? I said no and hung up. I played my tape machine.

'*You are through to Jenner's. James Jenner speaking. If you'd like to leave a message wait till the tone, then leave your name, number and message if you wish and I'll get back to you as soon as I can.*'

Beep.

'Where've you been, Jimmy? Didn't you get my message? I've been looking all over town for you, but I can't find you. I've been looking all over for your crazy Greek pal, too. Phone me at home, whenever. Any time.'

O'Keefe again. He's persistent. I wondered what he wanted with Zorba. Even if I were in a mood to talk to O'Keefe, which I wasn't, I couldn't help him find Zorba. I didn't know where he'd gone, either. All I'd had was the tape message: 'Hullo, Sjimmy, Zorba here. I'm no goina be round for a few days.' If O'Keefe wanted him, Zorba had better make it a few months.

I lay back on the sofa. I could feel a lump by my spine.

I pulled the blanket over my head. I remember thinking I should get the sofa restuffed if I was going to keep using it as a bed, then I was asleep.

I woke up when the door caved in. It only came part the way at first and then a big meaty fist came through the smashed panel and turned the key on my side of the mortise lock. What seemed to be ten but were in fact three men burst into the room. They were ugly and large and unshaven and they looked angry. They were also carrying pistols and the pistols were pointing at me.

'Hi,' I said.

'Shuddup,' said the one in the middle. He was over six feet and as wide as he was tall. He holstered his pistol under his arm and it was then I knew they were policemen, not maniacs in the service of Duncan or Wilkins. The policeman in the middle advanced on me while his fellows covered him. Maybe they'd been told I had a sten gun built into my leg.

'Hands in the air,' said the one who'd advanced on me. He was a dark-haired fellow with a bushy beard and gleaming brown eyes; deep brown, almost black. I held my hands up. Who wouldn't, having been asked so nicely at the point of two guns? He pulled me upright.

'We haven't been introduced,' I said.

'Shuddup,' he said again. 'Lie face first on the floor.'

My office is just that, an office. It has two chairs, a sofa, a desk, a built-in cupboard, two filing cabinets, a telephone, an answering machine, a desk lamp and me in it, as a rule. I can easily accommodate one other person in it, two extra's a squeeze and three a definite crush. All that's presuming no one tries to lie down. We compromised on the matter by having me lie on the stairs. They handcuffed me behind my back and then searched me. The big bearded fellow stopped when he got to my leg and said, 'What's this?' meaning the harness for the false part. I'm afraid I lied and told him it was something I'm sure my mother would be shocked to discover I even knew such a word for. Maybe she wouldn't. I had noticed a marked absence of Judge's Rules, even *Christie versus Leachinsky* and all that in these boys' techniques, but when I pointed it out to the bearded guy he kicked me in the side. I can take a hint. Meanwhile the other two detectives were ripping my office apart. Through the doorway it looked like a snowstorm, only made of paper. Glass broke, drawers slammed.

'Just tell me what you want,' I said, 'I'll bring it to you.'

The bearded man came down to me again.

'Okay, okay . . . I'll shut up. Stop kicking me,' I said. But he kicked me again anyway. I had the distinct impression that the three detectives had taken against me. I'd been in on arrests and searches before, but I don't think I'd ever seen it done so roughly, or unfeelingly. I didn't stay to see the end of the search. Two uniform men came and half-pulled, half-carried me down the stairs. I said I needed my stick but they wouldn't speak, and then when I got to the street they were surprised by my wobbly walk. I'd have been okay if the big ape hadn't kicked me in the side. The uniform men stuffed me in the back of a traffic car – strawberry stripe, blue light, the lot – then they sat either side of me. There was a sergeant in the driver's seat. I didn't say anything more, my brain had woken up by now. I didn't know what they were all so upset about but I'd worked out they'd tell me sooner or later. I could wait, at least till my hands went numb. Then I'd have to say something.

The sergeant put the blue light and the two-tones on and we drove down to the Blackwall Tunnel Approach, then along the motorway to Hackney and finally Shoreditch via Old Ford, Old Ford Road, Cambridge Heath Road and the Old Bethnal Green Road. I guessed the time for about ten a.m.. The traffic was heavy. The driver didn't rush. Wherever we were going didn't need the fire brigade. We just kept the horns on and drove at a regular pace, he didn't make the tyres screech. We crossed Hackney Road and went into a maze of little streets, then stopped next to a railway arch.

They pulled me out of the car. The sun was warming up. Little white clouds moved slowly across the sky. The railway arch looked dark and uninviting, and there was red-and-white tape across the road to stop people straying into the arch. At the far end I could hear a generator going and an arc lamp cast a little pool of light on two men bending over a bundle. Out of the other side of the arch I could see a group of people milling around and more of the red-and-white tape. The people were lit by daylight there. Then I could see cars and vans and I could hear police radios. A middle-aged man separated from the crowd and ducked under the tape at the far end of the arch. He walked towards me.

'All right, sergeant. Thanks very much. Can you release the cuffs and come down here with us, please?' It was framed as a question but it was an order. The sergeant called one of the uniform boys over from their Rover to uncuff me. I took a long look at the middle-aged man. He was about fifty, dressed in a smart but not flashy blue suit. Neat tie, neat haircut, sharp blue eyes, almost white hair. His face had that repose, that confident look of a man used to giving orders and having people follow them. I thought he's the sort of man who'd never yell, and that would make him all the more dangerous and difficult. The uniform policeman released the cuffs and the detective held up the tape for me to bend under.

'I can't,' I said. 'My leg.' I could, but I wanted to give nothing away. I didn't even want to bend under a tape. 'I can't walk far. They wouldn't let me bring my stick.'

The detective unpeeled the tape from the two-sided sticky stuff holding it to the wall.

'I'm Chief Superintendent Maher. You are Mr Jenner. Sergeant, would you be so kind as to let this gentleman lean on your arm? He's disabled.'

We walked through the arch to the arc lamp like this. When we got there the Chief Superintendent waved the two men away from the bundle, then indicated I should draw near and keep out of the cast of the light. A train went over. The arch shook. Maher waited until the rumbling had quite died away and then said, 'You used to be a policeman, I believe, Mr Jenner.'

I wanted to say, 'I've got a police pension, a Commendation from the Commissioner himself and the Queen's Police Medal, now what's the idea of having me roughed up?' It came out as a silent nod.

'Well?' he said. 'I'm right in that presumption, yes?'

'Yes.'

'I wonder if you'd give me the benefit, then, Mr Jenner, of your considered opinion about this.'

He leaned over the bundle. It was covered by a plastic sheet, dull, green plastic the colour of shooting boots. Maher pulled the sheet back. Under it was a bundle of clothes. Some of the clothes had arms and legs pointing out of them. Some of the clothes were a pale blue ladies' rainmac. The others were a green emerald evening dress. It was a long dress but it was all twisted up around the shins of the body inside it. I could see a little vent at the front that was originally meant to be at the back and let the slim ankles slide in and out as the lady wearer walked upstairs.

'It's a body,' I said.

Maher nodded.

'Good, good.' He held me by the lapel and dragged my face down close to the body. 'Dead, you think, eh?'

'Huh.' I nodded.

He pulled me down closer yet, leading me sideways so as not to lose the light from the arc lamp.

'And what do you make of this?'

I was inches away from the head of the corpse. It wasn't like a head I'd ever seen. There was no skin from the mandible up to the crown of the cranium. No scalp, no hair, no flesh on the cheeks and there appeared to be no tongue within them. Several teeth appeared to have been torn out, but most were there. The eyes had gone, too. So had the ears.

'It's had the flesh stripped off,' I said.

'Good. What else do you see?' said Maher. He whispered the words close by my side. His face was near to mine, his hot breath on my cheek. Another train went over.

I waited until it had gone this time and then I said, 'There's no blood. It didn't happen here.'

'Good. Good.' He let me go and I wavered for a second, about to topple into the corpse, my face into its 'face'. The uniformed sergeant pulled me back. I breathed heavily. I was sweating.

'You could've been a detective,' said Maher. 'Anything else you want to tell me? No little bells being rung?'

'No.'

Maher wiped his brow with his palm, then turned his hand to the light so he could see what had come off.

'It could be quite a long journey you and I are setting out on, Mr Jenner, I can see.'

I shrugged. He said, 'Would you take this gentleman down to Peter Street, sergeant?' The sergeant took me back to the Rover. I could see flashguns going off under the arch, official photographers, not press, I knew. I wanted my walking stick and a cup of coffee and a roll. I wanted a newspaper to read while I sorted my thoughts out. Most of all I wanted to get out of the Rover and walk away. They handcuffed me again, only this time with my hands in front of my body. It's against regulations (Force Orders, policemen call them) to handcuff a man behind his back. The two uniformed constables piled in on either side of me and the sergeant drove us away from the arch.

10

They kept me in for twenty-four hours. It seemed like a month. During the day nobody spoke to me hardly. They noted who I was, took my tie, belt and shoelaces away, then took me down to a cell. When I asked for something to read, a pink-faced young constable brought me a week-old copy of the *Guardian*. I don't even like fresh copies of the *Guardian*, but I took it anyway. They gave me three meals I'd have had to have been starving to eat. I ate the supper because I was starving by then and I drank some watery cocoa at about ten. I remembered that when I was a probationer a fat desk sergeant locked us new boys in a cell, one to a cell, for about an hour one night. He said it was to make sure we knew how it felt. It was a fine idea but I could have told him now that it doesn't compare to when someone locks the door and means it. I didn't like that night locked in. I still had ground-in ink on my skin from where they'd taken my dabs during the afternoon. I lay all night in the brightly lit cell looking at my dirty fingers, then reading every page of the newspaper, then looking at my fingers, then reading every page of the newspaper. I finally fell asleep around dawn and was immediately awoken by another pink-faced young constable and offered two slices of old, unsmoked bacon with the rind on and a half-cooked, still-watery egg. I gave it back but drank the tea that came with it. The young constable took the stuff away and came back with my shoelaces and belt. Not my tie, though, and not my jacket.

'I hope you've got my jacket hung up neat somewhere,

constable. It's a very important jacket. Very good-quality stuff.'

He stood in the doorway and swung the keys on the big gaoler's ring but he said nothing.

'I don't know why you took my shoelaces, anyway. I mean, I'd understand it if a man could commit suicide by hanging from his wrist or his ankle but he can't. It absolutely *has* to be the neck, and unless you pick up a man in mountaineering boots there just ain't enough material in a shoelace to go round even *my* neck. Know what I mean?'

He still wouldn't talk. We walked along the corridor to a door then through the door and into a little yard.

'Exercise,' he said.

I heard someone locking the door behind us. I said, 'Walking stick, Tonto.'

But he just turned and began to pace the little yard. Above us a patch of morning blue sky stared down. The young constable walked round the little yard, about ten paces in each direction, as if to show me how it was done. I hobbled along behind him. After ten minutes of this the door to the yard opened and a nose peeped out.

'Bring him in.'

It's very strange to be talked about in the third person while you're there. Only parents and schoolteachers do it, hospital consultants with their students, lawyers in court. That more or less exhausts the list. Now I have to add policemen, though I was a policeman for years and never noticed.

I was taken in, through the charge room and upstairs to the CID offices. I was shoved into a room there full of typewriters, phones and desks. That's all – no people. Chief Superintendent Maher followed me in and then came a young detective I'd never seen before, with mid-brown hair, a five-ten, inconspicuous young man; more or less the perfect detective, I should think. He had a plain, ordinary face with mid-brown eyes and the most ordinary mouth I'd ever seen. A lip on the top and one on the bottom. He didn't even have a broken nose. If I had seen him five minutes later in the street I'd never have noticed him.

'Sit down, please,' said Maher. 'This is Detective Sergeant

Robson. He'll make notes.' The door opened again. 'Not now!' called Maher. And it closed.

I sat.

'Give me your version of it, Mr Jenner.'

'Of what?' If they hadn't taken me into the detention cell or an interview room it must mean the place is full of 'suspects'.

Maher sighed. He looked at the plain-faced detective who sighed too. I sighed . . . why not?

'Let's go from Tuesday. Where were you on Tuesday?'

'On Tuesday I was in Essex. On Wednesday I was beaten up by men in your employ, then shown a body and brought here. This is Thursday. I've been here continuously over Wednesday and Thursday.'

'Fill it out.'

'No . . . you.'

Maher sighed again and sat in a chair by my side, very close. He looked in front of himself while he spoke and at first he was wringing his hands, as if he was very agitated. He soon calmed down, though.

'Mr Jenner. You are something of a hero to the Metropolitan Police, to the public at large and, most importantly, to the press. I don't know why you did it but you left the job and you've spent the years since consorting with the scum of the earth, muggers, pimps. . . .'

'Coppers, lawyers?' I offered. He ignored me.

'Every type of social undesirable. You were seen in the company of a woman. Her husband claims he employed you to protect her. You do not appear to have made a very good job of the protecting. She is dead. When I look at the hire car her husband had, I find your dabs all over it. When I go to her flat, I find your dabs all over it. Did you kill her?'

'No.'

'Make a note of that, Sergeant Robson.' Robson made a note. Maher turned and clapped his hand on my shoulder. '*Now* fill it out. Tell me why I shouldn't believe this man's wife was killed by you.'

I shook my head.

'Why should *I* kill her?'

'Tell me,' he said, 'tell me.'

I gave Maher the story of my couple of days in the employ of George Duncan, how he'd contacted me, how he'd asked me round to the Bonaventura. I didn't tell him about my recce in Saffron Walden. I told him about meeting 'Mrs Duncan' and how I'd been led to believe she would be South African.

'She wasn't,' I said.

'How do you know?'

'Her accent. It was all wrong. It wandered.'

'She'd lived here a long time,' Maher said. 'She was even born here.'

'She'd have had to have spent her life on the M1 motorway to get *her* accent.'

He smiled to show he had a sense of humour. I went on.

'I'd seen her before, anyway, after the Lynch fight in Shoreditch.'

'Yes?' He sat forward. I had him hooked. This was something new.

'I delivered a writ on Tommy Lynch the morning of the fight. We got chatting, very friendly like, and he ended up giving me a ticket. Afterwards I waited outside for a cab. Duncan and Lynch argued. A car full of heavies drove up and took Lynch away, then Duncan's wife started yelling at him and whacking him round the head.'

'Did you get a good look at her?'

'No. It was dark and I was some distance away.'

'Did you hear her speak clearly? You're the only one who's mentioned a South African accent.'

I shook my head.

'No. The bit about the accent was supposition. She was yelling and you know how it distorts someone's voice.' I cracked my knuckles and leaned back in my chair. 'I don't have any evidence that the woman I picked up at George Duncan's house wasn't his wife. . . . I just felt it. She was the right shape for the woman I saw outside the boxing hall, she was the right age too, I guess. The accent bit I just don't know about. It just *felt* wrong, you know? It just felt like a set-up.'

'You're claiming that the woman you picked up from Duncan's house wasn't his wife?' Maher said.

I nodded.

'Yes.'

'And you don't have any evidence to offer. It was just a feeling.'

'Yes.'

'And you're claiming that you thought the whole thing was some sort of set-up, and that you didn't like the look of it so you got out . . . am I right?'

'That's what I thought. I still do.'

'If you were right and this woman wasn't Duncan's wife, didn't it occur to you you were putting her in danger?'

A phone rang. D. S. Robson picked it up and said, 'No.'

I said no too. I said I'd made her a perfectly good offer of an 'out' and she'd chosen not to take it. What could I do? Move in with her?

'As a matter of fact,' I said, 'I don't even know that that cadaver you showed me *was* even the woman I dropped off. She was wearing a similar dress and coat, but I guess you could get those anywhere. Maybe there were three women. Or maybe it was her. I don't know. I just had a gut feeling.'

Maher didn't look very sympathetic to my 'gut feeling'.

'It was her. We printed her, of course. Her dabs were in the car, plus yours and Duncan's and a couple of thousand others. We're working our way through the others. For now all we have is you and Duncan.'

'What about him?'

'He spent that night at the house of a close friend in Saffron Walden. He went over there after you and his wife left, drank rather more than was good for him and stayed the night.'

'Maybe the friend was lying,' I said.

Maher shook his head and stood up. 'Coffee,' he said to the DS, who duly left. 'The friend is the head of a Regional Crime Squad. I don't think he's lying. He's been in the job for twenty-seven years and he's never been caught lying. I don't see why he should now and I'm going ahead on that basis. You might be, though, Jenner. Someone might have got at you to take the Duncan woman somewhere quiet and do her in. The characters who took Duncan's boxer away, for example. Maybe they got you to do it. Maybe they only got you to deliver the woman . . . I don't know. You look like a good suspect and all you're giving me by way of alibi or excuse is some nonsense about the body not being Mrs Duncan. You're the only person who thinks that.' He sighed. He didn't believe I'd killed her. He was just trying the story on me.

Suddenly Maher said, 'Do you know who drove Lynch away that night?'

'I think it could have been a bloke called Grant, a rival manager.'

'And he never hired you to kill the woman?' There was a twinkle in his eye as he spoke. He was asking the question for the sake of form, I knew. He was asking so he could write, 'I asked Jenner. . . .'

'And why should I do it?' I said.

'Money?'

I shook my head. Robson brought the coffee back. It was good coffee, not the stuff they gave me downstairs. In the cells they give you the cheapest instant brown stuff they can lay hands on. I drank the coffee and asked for another. Robson scowled but Maher sent him off for it.

'You'll find a cheque book in my belongings downstairs. Prepare a letter of authorisation and I'll sign it and you can find out for yourself how my bank account is. I don't need money and I don't need to kill for it.'

He nodded. 'I'll do that.'

'You do. I'll sign.'

'Something else?'

'What? *I* had no reason to kill her. I've never killed anybody and I don't have any reason to start now. You find someone who did have a reason and there's your killer. But it ain't me.'

Maher took my arm and pulled me towards the window. Outside ordinary people rushed past on their daily business. Lucky them.

'What do you see?' he asked. It was obviously a favourite trick of his.

I said, 'I don't know.' I was tired of the trick. Maher pulled my arm more and held me close to himself and to the window.

'I see people,' he said. 'Hundreds of people. Bus-loads of people. Pavements full of people, shops full of people. I see people walking and people waiting. People standing . . .

look, I even see one sitting.' He pointed to a child who'd obviously gone off this walking lark and sat on the pavement's edge, refusing all exhortations from his mother to abandon his kerb and come home. 'What do *you* see, Jimmy Jenner? Tell me what you see.' He let me go. I pulled back the anti-blast net to see better.

'I see people too,' I said.

'But what's the difference between those people and you, Jimmy Jenner?'

I stared a little longer. Robson came back and put a fresh cup of coffee on the window-sill between us. Maher put his hand on the cup.

'Answer me.'

'They're out there and I'm in here.'

He pursed his lips.

'Not bad. Not bad, Sergeant Robson, eh?'

'Not bad, sir.'

'We think that's quite a good answer. What other differences, Jimmy Jenner?'

I was really fed up by now, I said, 'They've all got two legs and I've got one.'

Maher nodded, letting his brow touch the window where I'd pulled the net back. A film of grease stayed on the glass. I looked closely at his face. He was tired, he seemed to have aged ten years since our meeting in the street yesterday. We were getting on towards lunch on Thursday and I'd have been willing to bet this man had hardly slept since early Wednesday. Whenever they'd found the corpse.

'Shall I tell you what I see, Jimmy Jenner?'

I didn't answer. He said, 'I see hundreds of people who *weren't* the last person to be seen with Mrs Duncan. I see hundreds of people who *weren't* hired to look after her. That's what I see. That's why they're out there and you're in here.'

'Do you believe I killed her?'

'No. Though I'm willing to have it proved to me. You're our only real suspect. You know how it is.'

I took Maher's hand off my coffee and lifted the cup to my lips. It was nearly cold but I drank it anyway.

'I know you've got nothing on me. I haven't gone in for all that "Where's my lawyer" caper up till now because I thought you'd ignore it, but I have to say now I've heard it that you don't appear to have a whole lot of stuff to hold me on. I'd like you to charge me with her murder or let me go because I'm getting a bit fed-up in the glossy green steel barred paradise I have for a home at the moment. I want out.'

Maher nodded. 'I'll let you out.' He opened the door.

'I'd like you to call off your hounds, too. I'd like you to tell your colleagues on this investigation that you don't believe I did it. I don't want to be followed round London by coachloads of flatfeet. It'll ruin my business. I don't want any early-morning alarm calls like yesterday's.'

He smiled.

'Come with me and I'll do it now. I'm sorry about yesterday. The men who came weren't from here. They just got the message you were a murder suspect, then they went to get you with the kind of firmness a murder suspect might need. As for your business,' he held his hands out, palms up, 'I couldn't harm that the way you have. I don't suppose there'll be much call for your services once the word gets around that your clients' wives die. Come this way, anyway.'

I followed him along a corridor. We went into a large room through a door marked 'Incident Room'. There were telephones, typewriters and *people* in this one. It was crowded and noisy and busy. The noises subsided as people saw Maher. He held his arms up for silence, like a football star.

'For those who aren't familiar with him, this is Mister James Jenner, formerly of the Metropolitan Police. I'm sure you will remember the unfortunate series of events that overtook him a few years ago in the West End. Some of you probably know he's been mixed up in this business we have to hand, and he's anxious that you should all know I don't believe he murdered the Duncan woman.'

People nodded and carried on working. I had to admire him, it was much better than showing my photograph round 'this is one of our suspects, keep your eye on him'. They'd never forget me now. Maher bent into a cupboard and came out with my walking stick and a set of keys. My flat keys.

'We borrowed these from a young lady friend of yours so you could get home okay. You can pick up the rest of your property at the desk. Show Mr Jenner out, will you, sergeant?'

The sergeant touched my elbow. I moved away. My attention was fixed on a poster-sized photograph on the far side of the room.

'Who's that?'

'Alison Duncan.'

'No it's not,' I said. 'That's not the woman that I brought to London. That's someone else completely.'

The room stopped again. Men and women looked at me. A young WDC speaking into a phone dropped her voice to a whisper.

'It *looks* like her but it's someone else. Definitely. That's not the woman I dropped off at the Barbican,' I said.

Maher walked me downstairs himself.

'Photographs make a difference,' he said. 'You may have trouble just with the photograph. It wouldn't be the first time a man or woman didn't look like his or her photograph.'

'It's not her.'

'Who is it then?' he asked.

'That's your job.'

He waited while the desk sergeant counted out my belongings from a plastic bag and I signed for them. He looked over my shoulder while I loaded my pockets with the kind of rubbish you need in your pockets. Then he opened the frosted glass door and led me to the street door.

'Goodbye,' said Maher, ' . . . by the way, a youngster was picked up yesterday in a stolen Rover. Barking police reckon there are three sets of dabs inside it. One's the kid's. One of the others appears to match the owner. They reckon the third matches the ones we took off you.'

'Oh yes.'

'That's right. I told them they were wrong. They must have been. What do you think?'

I pretended to consider it.

'Looks like a mistake to me.'

'Mm. That's what I told them.'

'Good. What happened to the kid?'

'What kid?'

'The one in the car.'

'I should think he's on remand in Ashford. Why do you want to know? I could find out for you if you'd like to step back in.'

I shook my head and walked away quickly. 'It's okay, don't worry!' I called over my shoulder. 'I don't care!'

There's a word for people like Detective Chief Superintendent Maher. Let's see if I can think of it. . . .

11

When Maher let me go I wandered the streets aimlessly for
a while. I wanted to think. I stopped and looked in the shop
windows, any windows. Travel shops, re-upholsterers, a
railway modelling centre (as it proclaimed itself). I wanted
to look at anything, hear the traffic around me, let the light
fall on me. If you're like that after twenty-four hours, God
knows that you'd be like after twenty years. I wondered if
you'd get used to confinement. There's no reason why you
should. I meandered along for half an hour. Fat black ladies
pushed past me with their shopping, pretty girls stared at
clothes in shops, or told each other jokes or lit cigarettes,
workmen paused to let me and my stick past. When I got
tired I hopped on a bus (haha). I left it in Islington, on
Upper Street. I knew I was being followed. I expected it.
As I pushed my way along the lower deck of the bus to get
off I saw a big, black-haired and black-bearded man stuff
his face into the women's page of the *Guardian*. I'd never
seen such an obvious *Daily Express* reader in my life. It was
the copper who'd kicked me all round my office yesterday.
'Right,' I thought, 'I'll have you.' I'd lose him. There's a
cinema that does matinees in Upper Street. It'd be just the
job. They've got a lav with two doors. He'd never know.
Then he'd have to go back and tell Maher he'd lost me.

That was the plan.

I walked along the kerbside, looking for a place to cross.
The traffic was heavy and there was dust and noise in the
air. I turned and saw the black-bearded man about twenty
yards behind me. He made no attempt to conceal himself.
I saw the plain-faced DS Robson too. He looked surprised

that I saw him, then he followed my gaze to the bearded man and looked even more surprised. Robson opened his mouth to say something but was pushed to one side by the bearded man, who ran at me, grabbed me and began to shove me in the back of a Ford Cortina that had stopped by my side. He was much too big for me to resist, you need a lot of strength and a lot of balance before you start to take on a man that big. I managed to get the handle of my walking stick into his crutch, though, and I gave it a good shove. He yelled but kept shoving me into the Cortina. The stick broke as he knelt on it. Then we were accelerating away with the rear door swinging and Robson clutching at it. The bearded man pushed him away, closed the door and then turned back to me. I butted him very hard between the eyes. He put his hands to his face and when he took them away the hands and his beard were full of blood.

'Bravo, Jimmy my son!' cried the driver. 'Nobody's drawn blood on that big ape for years. Bravo!'

He slowed the car, turned left into the City Road and turned his head half-sideways.

'Brian Borden, James Jenner . . . I believe you two have met but never been introduced.'

'Denis', I said, 'this is not very funny. This is the second time Lizzie Borden here has attacked me in two days. One more time and I'm going to get *really* angry.'

'He's sorry about yesterday, aren't you, Brian?'

Brian Borden said, 'Yuff,' through his bloody hands.

'Is he sure?' I said.

Brian's black eyes glared at me over the tops of his fingertips.

'Well?' said Denis O'Keefe.

'Yuff,' said Brian. 'Ayer thorry.'

I could have asked him to kiss me better (one of the places he'd kicked me was my bum) but I thought I wouldn't push it too far . . . today.

'Brian knew you were my friend but he thought he'd better act as if he didn't yesterday morning.'

'Perhaps you'd ask him not to be so convincing next time, Denis.'

He laughed and drove us down to Old Street, then through Clerkenwell. At Lamb's Conduit Denis got out.

'My friend and I are going to have lunch, Brian. You drive this back and I'll see you in the office later.'

Brian nodded. I shook my head.

'I'm not going anywhere, Denis. You wait here, Brian and me are just going round the block.'

'Why?'

'We're only running down to Bloomsbury Way. Brian's offered to buy another stick for me, to replace the one he's just broken.'

Denis O'Keefe thought that was very funny. Brian Borden didn't. He bought the stick, though.

Denis O'Keefe looks more like a gangster than a copper. He wears flashy, smooth-cut suits, he appears to have his hair cut three times a week, he wears a gold ring with a large diamond in it on his left little finger and he always has a silk tie on. He's not a handsome man but he makes what he thinks is the 'best of himself'. Brian Borden dropped me off outside Holborn Police Station and Denis was on the far side of the road. He looked older than when I'd last seen him, some six months before. Maybe he'd put on weight or something. He had fine, crinkly brown hair that he fiddled around the front of his head to hide his receding hairline and he had calm, sure brown eyes that made you trust him more than his clothes or his manner would suggest you should; more than prudence would normally allow anyone to trust a Detective Inspector of the Metropolitan Police that everyone *knew* was bent. I suppose I had trusted him in the past because I knew what form his bentness took – he liked money too much. With other people it might be power or promotion or choirboys or all three. I'd trusted Denis in the past because I'd known what he was. Also because he'd given me a lot of introductions in the insurance and security worlds. I'd stopped trusting him some time ago because he was about to retire on twenty-five years' service and he seemed to be getting a bit frantic and a bit chancy in his rush to put his 'nest egg' together. I didn't want to take part in any chancy deals.

He took my arm and we walked south, down Red Lion Street and into a pub. The pub was full of lawyers and nineteenth-century frosted glass. I couldn't say which century the lawyers were from. There didn't appear to be any policemen.

'The best place to talk business, James, is surrounded by lawyers. They don't want to know. They don't want to get involved, so they don't overhear. What'll you have to drink?'

'Orange.'

He raised an eyebrow but ordered me the orange. He had a glass of something clear with lemon in it. I didn't catch what but if I know Denis it was 'slimline' something or other because he's always worrying about his weight. If you own as many clothes as Denis does growing out of them could be a financial disaster.

'What were the amateur dramatics in aid of?' I said.

'Maher had a man following you. I didn't want him to notice us meeting.'

'*Denis!*'

He patted my hand and shoved my glass of orange into it.

'Don't worry, they won't trace us through the motor. I've fixed that.'

'How?'

'Er . . . we borrowed it from a police station yard.'

'Your police station?'

'No. Don't *worry*. You worry too much.'

I shook my head.

'I'm not worried. I'm not drinking any more bloody orange juice with you either. You're crackers.'

I went outside. The air was fresh and warm and really summery. A line of office workers had formed outside a sandwich shop. A traffic warden was arguing with a cab driver. This was a normal world, the one we all know about. There were no bodies with their heads stripped of flesh here, no nights in the cells, no DCS Maher, no Brian Borden and DS Robson. No dawn raids. There were no Denis O'Keefes here, either.

'Come on, James. Let's take a walk.'

'I'm not walking anywhere with you, Denis.'

We walked south towards Holborn.

'I was disappointed you didn't ring me. You should get

77

that machine of yours fixed. It's no good if you don't get anyone's messages.'

'I get all the messages I want. I'm not walking with you, Denis, and I'm not talking to you either.'

We continued south to Lincoln's Inn Fields, through Great Turnstile and into the calm of the park on the Fields. Old buildings looked down on old trees which in turn looked down on old men sitting on benches and making a plastic cupful of tea last for hours. O'Keefe and I found a bench of our own. It faced the tennis courts and pretty young girls bobbed about in front of us wearing miniature dresses and waving racquets. There are worse places to sit.

'I'll tell you straight,' said Denis.

'It would be the first time ever.'

'Come *on*. Stop talking tough and listen to what I have to say. I need desperately to find your pal, Zorba.'

'Why?'

Denis rubbed his face with his hands, nodded appreciatively at a failed overhead shot which left a tennis player upside-down against the wire netting.

'He was doing a job for me. A payout. The payout seems never to have got made and now I can't find your Greek pal nor the insurance company's money.'

'How much?' I asked.

'Quite a lot.'

'How much?'

'Er . . . my bit of it was three-five.'

'And Zorba's?'

'Five hundred.'

'So he was carrying forty thousand?'

O'Keefe nodded.

'I know it wasn't a very shrewd move but I had to get it done quick and you seemed to have lost interest in it. I thought we'd known him for long enough.'

'What you should have done, Denis, was paid him out properly or just given him a tenner. For two grand he wouldn't have looked and for ten quid he wouldn't have bothered. For five hundred it's worth having a peek . . . it doesn't matter, anyway. I'm sure we've seen the last of him. His wife took their kids off home a couple of months ago because they'd fallen out. No doubt he's popped off there

78

with your forty grand to buy a big house and keep all seven of them in comfort and style for the rest of their naturals. You've been stuffed, Denis.'

He shook his head again, stood up and walked around in a little agitated circle. He wasn't even noticing the girl tennis players now, though he wasn't so distracted by his problem as to forget to smooth down his jacket and make sure there was the right amount of shirt cuff sticking out.

'More than you think. I was on a cert for a consultancy place with this firm when I finished in the job. That's gone down the tube.' He sat next to me again. 'Find him for me, Jimmy. I'll pay you, I'll cover your expenses too but find him and get the dough back, otherwise my name'll be mud.'

'Have you got forty grand?'

'No. They'd never be able to sue me for it anyway. . . .'

'But they could get you dismissed from the job, eh? And that'll put the kibosh on your pension and any chance of you getting another job. And you might go inside for it . . . right?'

'Yes.'

'I wish I could help, Denis. I like you in a funny way.' I stood. 'I can't though. I'm up to my ears with your mate Maher. I don't even know where to begin with Zorba. I don't know his proper name. All I've got is his phone number and the address of the council flat where he lives. I'll give you those.'

'Done it. Been all round there. Tried his mates, too, but they just clam up when they see me. I look too much like the copper. You don't, though, Jimmy. Have a go for me . . . see what you can find for me.'

He swallowed and walked away.

'Hang on,' I called. 'I can't go that fast.' He waited till I caught him up. 'I'll do what I can. Let's go and have our drink, Denis . . . and let's have a proper one. There's something I want from you in return; several things, in fact.'

I had several drinks with Denis while I explained to him what I wanted. Then I went via Liverpool Street to Audley End to pick up my car. I didn't chance my luck by driving over to look at Duncan's place . . . there would be nothing to see, anyway. Any leverage I'd get on him I wouldn't get face to face. I drove straight home. At that time I was living in a flat in Stoke Newington. It was a purpose-built block from the nineteen-sixties with a car park in front of it. As I leaned under the bonnet of my old Humber auto (to disconnect the ignition – I'd had to 'steal' it at Audley End because Gal had my car keys and he was still in the nick) I saw a young man in casual clothes across the road kicking the tyres of his Ford. The tyres looked okay to me and they seemed to have his entire attention. So much for undercover surveillance.

I went upstairs. The German lady who lives next door with her teenage son said there were some men in my flat yesterday and that when the son went to find out who they were they were very rude to him. I thought, 'I bet they were', but I said, 'I'm sorry to hear that and would you please thank your son for his diligence,' or some such rubbish. A visit was exactly what I'd expected. I went in, picked my way through the mess – though to be fair I'd seen worse messes – and lifted the phone. Two clicks and a dialling tone.

'Hullo, Mr Maher. Jimmy Jenner here, reporting in. How are you doing? Any news? I hope you'll get back to me.'

The dailling tone went on. I put the phone down, poured myself a glass of whisky and sat on top of a load of broken-spined paperbacks that had taken up residence on the settee. I had to think.

I had to think that either George Duncan had had his 'wife' killed or that Lenny Grant and Wilkins had had it done. None of the three had any particular gripe against me, so they hadn't done it to fix me. They'd done it to fix the woman or each other. If they'd done it to fix the woman the body wouldn't have been found . . . she'd be off Shoe-buryness wearing what my boy Gal would describe with loving care as a 'cement overcoat'. I could hear him say it. No. Whoever had caused that mess under the railway arch had done it so the mess would be found . . . and the only reason for that would be so that it put the frighteners on someone. Why else? – so someone could get something out of possession of a corpse, maybe. Like an insurance claim, or property, or both.

I went downstairs and walked a couple of streets to a phone box. I wanted one of those blue pay-phone affairs, so I didn't get any pips. The undercover man with the Ford did the best he could, following me fifty yards behind and staring at hedges.

I phoned Judy first at work.

'How are you? I've been worried,' she said as soon as she heard my voice.

'I'm okay. I took it you knew where I was.'

'Yes. We have to talk, James.'

'I know. I'm going to stay with my auntie in Southend. You know where it is. Come down for the weekend.'

'Thanks.'

'Come alone, Judy.'

'I will. . . . . Jimmy. . . . .'

'Yes.'

'Oh . . . nothing. Take care.'

She is never going to get to the top of her particular tree like that. She should have just made out she didn't know me. I rang Peter Street nick.

'Hopkins here, from the *Argus*,' I said. 'Is Chief Superintendent Maher there still?'

'He's in conference, sir,' said the boy on the desk, 'can I help?'

It's gratifying when people show initiative.

'Yes, you may be able to. When he briefed me earlier I wrote down some wretched scrawl for the name of the Home Office doctor who's doing the post mortem.'

'*Done*, Mr Hopkins. He's done it. His name is Sir Mark White . . . okay?'

'Thanks a lot, constable. It's stupid of me.'

'We're here to help, sir,' he said cheerily. I couldn't believe he was serious. I rang Shoreditch Mortuary and got an assistant clerical officer.

'Detective Sergeant Robson here, Peter Street CID,' I said, 'look, I've got a nearly unreadable copy of Sir Mark White's p.m. report here, and I can't raise his secretary on the blower. What *exactly* is the knife used on the Duncan woman?'

'A flat-bladed knife, sergeant. Something like a carving knife only with a point on it.'

'And the cause of death was?'

'A thirty-two calibre pistol shot in the chest. Lodged in the right atrium.'

'Thanks.'

I put the phone down. My babysitter was tying his shoe-laces. By the amount of times he swapped legs I reckon he'd done them good and tight – all three. I didn't ask the mortuary desk for the time of death because it didn't matter. There were a lot of other questions I wanted to ask him but one of the things I had asked O'Keefe for was a copy of the report. It would all be there. If I were just to be patient for a few days I'd have all my answers about the demise of Mrs Duncan. Except who did it, of course. Maybe I'd even get that.

Something else I'd asked O'Keefe for was waiting for me when I got home. The phone was ringing. I opened the door quickly and rushed to it. I hate that minute when you're jiggling your key in the lock and knowing, absolutely *knowing* that it's going to stop ringing by the time you reach it. This time I knew wrong.

'Watcher cock, I've been bailed.'

'Good. I can't talk now, I'm in a rush, Gal. Meet me in the old place at eight, eh?'

'Okay, what's the time now?'

'Ah . . . I don't know. I haven't got a watch and the clock's in the kitchen. It's about four, I think. What's the time, constable?'

'Constable?' said Gal.

'Yeah. Don't forget my car keys.'

'Haven't you got any spares?'

'Zorba's got them. He's got my spare flat keys too. As a matter of fact Zorba seems to have everything at the moment.'

'Oh . . . oh. Oh! *Constable* . . . *I* get it. Meet me in the *old* place. *Yeah*.'

'Bye, Gary.'

Perhaps I won't buy him the home computer. I padded round the flat picking up torn books and papers and stuffing them in a black plastic bag. I don't like a lot of my books anyway. Perhaps I should get the CID to pay me a visit more often. I shoved the drawers back in my tallboy. It's the only decent piece of furniture I have and I wished they hadn't treated it so rough. Then I got fed up with the whole business and left the drawers as they were, half-open, half-closed, and went to shave and shower and change.

By five I was chugging up Leytonstone High Road looking for the Canary Club. I had a whole convoy of coppers in tow, the Ford and a Bedford van that I could see. They obviously thought I knew something. I thought I knew something too, I just didn't know what it was. All the facts of a particular case are always there, it's just a question of seeing them and then putting them in the right order. What I knew for sure was that *I* hadn't done it. I don't know how Maher and his boys felt about that, so my list of suspects was minus one compared with theirs. I also had no idea of any other extra suspects they had, no extra information. All I had was Wilkins, Grant, Duncan and me. I was on my way to see Wilkins.

The Canary Club was above a bookshop. It wasn't the kind of bookshop you'd find in competition with W. H. Smith. There was a plastic fly-curtain on the bookshop door and a fat guy dressed-up-to-look-tough to catch any flies the curtain didn't. The Canary Club was entered through a mock-Georgian door at the side of the bookshop. The door had one of those 'speak-here' boxes, a brass spy-hole and peeling yacht varnish. I can never work the 'speak-here' boxes. You push the button and the box squawks and you lean over to talk to it and a buzzer goes in the door and by the time you've pushed the door it stops going. Then you push the button again and talk over the top of the squawk and you step back in frustration and the buzzer in the door goes while you're stepping back so you miss it again. Then you push the button again and the squawk says 'stop messing around with the button' and you say 'sorry, it's Jenner, can't you just open the door?' and then you're not sure whether you should be pushing the buzzer to speak or not so you push it anyway and hold it there. Eventually they come down and let you in. People always come down and let you in in the end so I don't know why they didn't just stick with the old system of having a doorbell and their own eyes, ears and legs.

There was a plastic multi-coloured fly-curtain behind this door too, but the man who let me in wasn't just a fat guy dressed up to look tough. He was small and wiry. He had dark eyes and a pinched mouth, a turtle-neck shirt and a dark blazer. He searched me in the little space behind the fly-screen and he laughed when he found my leg.

'What's that?' he said.

'It's my leg.'

He laughed again and led me upstairs.

Wilkins was holding court in a back room of the club. The front of the club was opening soon and a smooth, oily-looking young man was polishing glasses. He let us past his bar counter to a rear door which led into the back room with Wilkins on a sofa and a racing print above his head and two men and two women in there with him. There were two lamps on a sideboard – that's all the light there was. Wilkins stood and waved the four out of the room, then motioned that I should sit on the sofa.

'It's a little low for me,' I said. 'My leg.'

'He's got a false leg, Wilkie,' said the little fellow.

Wilkins laughed. It was a sharp laugh and not the sort you were expected to join in with. You were expected to smile politely and shyly for the big man's joke.

'A policeman with one leg,' he laughed. 'Now I've heard everything.' He gurgled the words out between laughs. It sounded like a crow being strangled. He pointed at a tall stool. 'Sit on that then.'

'I'm not a policeman,' I said, 'I'm a private detective.'

'I thought they only had those in America now that you can get divorced so easily here. What keeps you in work?'

'Insurance claims, mostly. A little company theft, a little company fraud. A few missing persons.'

'He works for insurance companies,' he said to the little fellow. 'And the Salvation Army.' They both laughed this time. Suddenly Wilkins grew serious. He pointed at my leg.

'Take it off,' he said, 'and Charlie'll take it outside. I don't want to find out you've got an electronic leg with a *real* copper on the other end of it.'

Wilkins and Charlie were almost crying, the whole thing

seemed so funny to them. Just when they'd both subsided to chuckles again he poked little Charlie in the ribs and said, 'I can't do business with a man who's got a bugged leg.' And they both started all over again, slapping their thighs with their palms and dabbing at their eyes with paper tissues from a box on a coffee table in front of his sofa.

'We don't get many people around here as funny as you, Jenner.'

The barman put his head in from next door.

'Bring us a drink. Bring us all a drink, Bill. Charlie and me're having a drink with a one-legged tough guy.'

Bill brought two drinks, ice cold beers for Wilkins and me. Little Charlie had nothing – a thimbleful would have got him drunk. The beers were foreign lagers and beads of water dripped down the sides of the bottle as the barman poured them. Wilkins shoved a lot of used glasses to the end of the coffee table.

'Put 'em on here Bill.'

Bill brought the drinks from the sideboard to the coffee table.

'Clear up later. I want to talk to this one-legged tough guy.' He laughed again. 'Pull back the curtains on your way out. I want to get a good long look at him.'

The barman pulled back some mock-velvet curtains that ran all along one wall of the room. Light flooded in, rushed round the room like a happy child, touching things, examining the dust, passing the used and greasy glasses on the coffee table, then brushing Wilkins' face. He looked heavy, thick-jowled. He was close-shaven and his hair was cut short; black, spiky hair that had clearly been dyed to keep it black. The face was sad. Wilkins had thick lips and washed-out grey eyes; busby black-dyed eyebrows above the eyes, red lines of burst capillaries on the fat cheeks below the eyes. He wore a mohair suit with a broad chequerboard design on the cloth, one soft grey square laid on another, all the grey squares darkening then lightening, shimmering as he leaned forward to pick up his beer.

'Why do you need me, Jenner?'

'Sorry?'

'Why d'you come here?'

'You know about George Duncan's wife?'

He nodded.

'Terrible business. My heart goes out to him . . . what about it?'

'I've just spent two days in the chokee. The police seem to think I had something to do with it.'

'*No.*'

'I'm afraid so.'

He smiled into his beer.

'And you claim you didn't.'

'No. Not quite that. I had plenty to do with it. I was hired by Duncan to look after her and as far as the whole world is concerned I ballsed-up. As far as the police are concerned that's the very least I have done.'

'What else do they think you've done?'

'Well . . . they know I can't account for myself for the night it happened. They're not pushing me on that one yet but they've given me warning they will. Duncan's flat is full of my fingerprints, his car is full of my fingerprints and his wife is dead. I was the last person to see her. Nobody else is tied to her at that time.'

Wilkins waved at the little fellow, Charlie, to fetch more beer.

'Yeah, yeah, yeah . . . got the story. Don't give me the television series. Tell me what you want.'

'Okay,' I said. I drew in my breath. '*I* didn't kill her. Perhaps you know who did. But it wasn't me. If the police know now that it wasn't me they're not saying so in public – but they will have to soon. And then everyone's going to go round looking for who else might have done it. And they're going to be looking at her husband, Duncan, and Lenny Grant. In this case "Lenny Grant" means you.'

The new beers came. I hadn't drunk half of the first. Wilkins poured his greedily into the glass. The foam ran over the top.

'Specially imported,' he said. 'I can't drink English beer.'

'Word is, Mr Wilkins, that Lenny Grant is only fronting a gym and a licence for you. Word is he gets venues stitched up easier than any man who ever lived, know what I mean? The word I have is that he has access to your muscle.'

'I haven't got any muscle. I'm a businessman.'

I poured some beer into my glass and swirled it around to make some of the fizz go out.

'I really don't have a tape recorder in my leg.' I tapped the shin with my empty beer bottle 'Hollow . . . see? You don't have to make out to be related to the Archbishop of Canterbury to me . . . you don't even have to make out you only own a dry-cleaning business and a porn shop. I don't care. But let me put something to you.'

'Okay, put something to me.' He leaned over near my leg and yelled, 'But that don't mean nothing you've said up till now is true, *right*? And it's not a porn shop. It's a marital aids centre which deals with a growing social need in our society!' He addressed all this to my knee, then sat up again and started chuckling.

I said, 'Alison Duncan is reckoned to be murdered. I'm first on the list but I don't fit for lots of reasons. They'll have to find somebody else. Next on the list is George Duncan, but by all accounts he's playing the part of the widower very nicely. He has a cast-iron alibi for the time when his cuddles is getting her chips . . . right?'

'Go on.'

'And all his carpets have shrunk on account of all the crying and upset poor old George is going through. Next on the list is your friend Leonard Grant, who had a big ruck with George Duncan in the street. Public knowledge. Not-so-public knowledge is the fact that there's a big hole in the front door of Duncan's house where someone shot it with a twelve-bore. Not-so-public knowledge is the fact that he reckons he's had threatening messages of a more explicit kind, like phone calls and a letter telling him to lay off Tommy Lynch.'

'Lynch?'

'A boxer. Don't play dumb.'

He smiled. It wasn't a very friendly smile.

'A boxer you've taken away from Duncan. A boxer who'll have to pay a bit to get the last fight option off Duncan.'

'Balls! Seven thousand quid, the last one's worth on his contract with Duncan. That's pin money compared with what the fight'll gross. We've already paid Duncan his seven thousand quid.'

'Are you receiving me loud and clear?' I tapped my leg

again. I looked Wilkins in the eye. 'Are you sure he's cashed his cheque? Are you sure he's got it? My guess is that he hasn't, and that when the police get fed up with tagging me they're going to try to do it to you. They'll pick up Grant and ask him about the phone calls and the shot-gun blast and the letter. They'll want to know where he was the night Mrs Duncan was murdered and he'd better come up with somewhere better than me, because *he*'s no holder of the Queen's Police Medal. Then they'll show him the contract, which I didn't know the details of until just now but sounds a beaut, and say that he was leaning on Duncan and when Duncan didn't give Lenny Grant did Mrs Duncan in in a very nasty way. The way the story goes after that depends on you, I should think, and your relationship with Lenny Grant. If he loves you and enjoys working for you he'll say "I don't know any Wilkins". Then they'll throw him in the deepest cell in England on his own for a fortnight while they turn you and your entire business upside down. Then they'll drag him out again and ask whether he arranged to have Alison Duncan killed or you did. Again it all depends on your relationship with him. . . .'

'This fairy story is boring. I never killed this woman. I've heard of Duncan but I never even knew he had a wife till today. I'll pay him his seven grand. For all I know I already have. The police won't have anything on me because I didn't do anything. Neither did Len.'

'Well, *somebody* did. It wasn't Santa Claus. And while our friends in the Metropolitan Police are looking for that somebody, business is going to go slack for some people. Some people's faces are going to be in the papers. Some third party is going to get his manager's licence revoked. Somebody's hard-fought-for-and-gained world title prospect fighter is going to go off the boil and all the millions and millions of US dollars that could go with him are going to go off the boil. I think that when the police get fed up with me and start on Lenny Grant you're going to be in a whole pile of trouble, no matter what way they read it.'

'Lenny's all right. He was in here with me and a few others the night that woman was killed.'

'Mr Wilkins.' I stood up. '*That* is not an alibi.'

'So what should I do?'

'What should you do? You should listen. You should pay attention to me, then you do what I ask you and I'll do something for you.'

Wilkins stood and pulled his suit straight.

'Show Mister Jenner downstairs, Charlie. He's finished his beer.'

'I haven't,' I said.

'Show him down.'

Charlie took hold of my elbow. I let my beer fall on him, brushed him aside and pointed at the window.

'Down there you'll see a Ford Cortina and further down the road a Bedford van. They're babysitting you, Wilkins.'

'They're always babysitting me. It doesn't mean anything. I'm a legit businessman. I pay my taxes. Someone in the local nick's just got a down on me because I did bird when I was a kid.'

He smiled, waved little Charlie away from my side. I said, 'Those aren't from your local nick and you know it. At the moment they've got a dead woman, a grieving husband with a watertight alibi, me, Lenny Grant and you. I didn't do it and I don't think the police will believe I did it. George Duncan is tucked up tight with a copper who says he was with him, you reckon you never did it and I haven't spoken to your man Grant yet but you reckon he didn't do it too. You two are the best candidates the police will have.'

'Sit down, Jenner. Finish your drink.'

We all three sat.

'It could have been an outsider, some nutter,' Wilkins said.

I shook my head.

'No. It's too much effort to go to. The body was really cut up bad. No one would do that unless it was for a reason.'

'A nutter might.'

'Okay, one might. How'd she get from the Barbican to a railway arch in Shoreditch? If she went out to get fags she wouldn't need to go that far.'

'Maybe someone took her there. Maybe it's some sort of ritual killing . . . how the hell do I know? I'm not a copper. What else could it be if you didn't do it and I didn't do it and Lenny never? Maybe he's fell behind with his freemason's subscription and that's their debt collection department making an example of him . . . maybe anything. It's probably a random killing.' He gulped at his beer, signalled Charlie for another then said, 'London's full of nutters and criminal types and all that. Maybe she was killed by a jealous lover.'

'The police will think you did it,' I said. 'They always go for the best prospect and you're it, you and Grant. You had a reason, you've got a rotten alibi and you're quite capable of doing it. All they'll need is one concrete bit of evidence and you'll go in the nick so fast your feet won't touch the ground.'

'Maybe. But they won't find any evidence because I didn't do anything. Nor did Lenny.'

'That won't stop them finding some,' I said. He nodded slowly, squeezing his fat cheeks with his hands so that they nearly reached his eyebrows, then mopping his forehead with the sleeve of his grey suit. I said, 'When I first came in you asked why I needed you. Well I don't. You need me.'

'No I don't. I haven't done nothing.'

'Famous last words, Mister Wilkins. As it happens, I know they're true.'

'How?'

'For several reasons. Some of them I won't go into now. The main one is that I don't see what you have to gain from it. You already had his business.' I held my hand up. 'Okay, okay . . . Lenny Grant did. It doesn't matter. Either way, I don't see why you'd want to put the squeeze on him *if* you were in the squeeze-putting business. There's no profit in it. There's even less profit in killing someone. I'm not sure the police will see it that way, though. They'll just think of you as a good prospect and then they'll go round looking for the evidence. I've no doubt they'll find *something*: a few little things, you getting yourself alibi-ed by known criminal types so it won't stand up in court. . . .'

'. . . *I didn't know I'd need a bloody alibi!*' he yelled. 'If I did I would've been having dinner with a copper or something too . . . a lawyer at least. The first I heard about this is someone phones me this morning.'

He was angry now, pacing the little room. He looked as if he would start throwing things.

'I believe you,' I said.

'Who asked you round here anyway? I haven't done nothing.'

'I believe you. I believe there may be someone else involved here.'

'Who?'

I shrugged. 'Duncan?'

Wilkins went to the wall and leaned his head against it. I went and stood by him.

'Duncan,' he repeated after me. 'Duncan.'

'Or someone doing it for him . . . any idea who that could be?'

'No. George Duncan, eh? What for, insurance money?'

'That's how I see it. I haven't any evidence yet. But I'll find some.'

'What do you want from me?' He turned suddenly and looked into my face.

'Someone did a house in Onslow Gardens, South Ken. Got a lot of gear, two hundred grand's worth of insurance at least, but it's unfenceable. It was someone local to here, I know, because a local copper organised an insurance pay-out. Trouble is, the guy he sent with the money didn't get there. No one knows where he's gone. No one knows where the money's gone either. The copper is understandably getting a little concerned.'

'And?'

'We'd like the gear or the money back. Also the messenger. I believe the copper would prefer the gear to the money. Keeps his street credibility up, know what I mean?'

'Okay. I'll see what I can do.' He waved at Charlie who went outside. Whether for more beer or to make a phone call I never found out. Wilkins sat again.

'What am I getting out of this, Jenner?'

'A cloud of dust,' I said, 'a big one in front of you while I go round leading the men with the big hats towards the real killer. If I keep pointing out that George Duncan may have done it, maybe they'll lay off you and Grant a bit. Maybe you'll still have the fight business. Maybe you won't have to sit on your hands in Brixton nick while they turn you inside out.'

He just turned his back on me, sunk his head down and

began drinking beer again. When I went through to the bar Charlie was nowhere to be seen. Perhaps he was hiding under a table. He wouldn't even have to bend down to do it. It was a bit strange the bar-room was empty, though. Even the oily barman had gone. All there was left was the atmosphere and the furnishings. The atmosphere was stale, old beer, cigarettes and a lavatory smell. The furnishings were nicotine-stained, tacky, well-worn but not too old. The formica had split along the edge of the bar. I don't know what Wilkins spent his money on other than beer, but it certainly wasn't on the trappings of a rich man's life. Apart from a mohair suit and a door entry-phone he seemed to spend his life in slightly more seedy circumstances than me. And that was saying something.

I went downstairs. The door was swinging wide. A light breeze rustled the multi-coloured plastic fly curtain. I pushed the curtain aside and stepped forward. A big hand gripped my throat and I found myself looking at a gun. I made a note to break this new habit as soon as I could.

'Not him. Leave him go.'

The gun dropped, the hand released my throat ever so slowly. I gulped and wiped the tears from my eyes, then stepped fully onto the pavement to find myself confronted by Detective Chief Superintendent Maher.

'Hullo, Jenner. What are you up to, a bit of private enterprise?' He was cocky, dead pleased with himself.

'Someone's got to prove to you I didn't kill that girl,' I said. 'I had ideas that I might as well make a start . . . know what I mean?'

He smiled and took my arm, leading me away from the door and signalling a posse of plainclothes-men up the stairs to Wilkins' drinking club. Wilkins would certainly be in for a surprise when he stepped out for his next beer. I wondered whether he'd get the throat-and-gun treatment too. It concentrates the mind wonderfully.

'How are you, James?'

The street was full of policemen. The staff of the porn shop were all lying on the pavement, including the fat one from behind the porn shop's fly-curtain. He was wearing a red and gold striped shirt and looked like nothing so much as an abandoned sofa at the kerbside. Charlie, Wilkins' miniature minder, and Bill the oily barman were there too, both face down, both handcuffed.

'Is this a raid of some sort?' I asked. Maher was leading me away from the Canary Club's door, away from the porn shop. No doubt he had minions who'd deal with all that. We walked past the prostrate bodies on the pavement. It made me feel like the Pope. Maher held onto my arm, spoke softly to me.

'What did you want from friend Wilkins?'

'I just wanted to know what the score was. I felt pressured by you lot. I wanted to know a bit about him, where he was the night she was killed.'

He nodded thoughtfully and let go of my arm. We walked through the heavy traffic in the High Road, till we were through the little crowd that had gathered around the Canary Club and could look at the incident as outsiders.

It was Thursday. I'd met Duncan in the Bonaventura on Monday. A lot had happened in between. I'd met Maher on Wednesday. Now he was treating me like an old friend, like some old drinking pal he'd tripped over someplace he didn't expect to find him. He waved his hand at the crowd surrounding the Canary Club.

'Ghouls. They want to see blood. They want to see some big criminal. A murderer, eh, Jimmy?'

I didn't answer.

'So, while you were playing private eye, we've got our man. That's what police work is all about, Jimmy. What did you do exactly while you were in the job? Uniform, wasn't it? Unit beat, all that stuff.'

He paused and leaned back against a wall. Maher was enjoying himself. He was telling the long-lost drinking pal about all the things he'd done while he was drunk, all the indiscretions, all the slobbered sentences. Maher would have total recall, of course. He's the type who never gets drunk.

I didn't answer his questions. I didn't want to play his game. A few feet in front of us a truck stopped, waiting to let the traffic in from a side road. The driver looked at the scene outside the Canary Club, then looked at me and laughed and touched his head, as if to say 'stupid'. He leaned forward and let his handbrake off. There was a screech and a puff of air.

'We got our man by detection. First of all we found the gun in the Grand Union Canal,' Maher said.

'The right gun?'

'Looks like it. It's a .32. Preliminary tests say it's our gun. Then the gun appears to have been used in the Manor House bullion job back in 1980. A Hampshire copper went down to Albany Prison and put this to someone – I can't say who of course – who's doing bird for the bullion job.'

I nodded. Of course he couldn't say who. He couldn't say any of it. Why was he doing it? To score a cheap point over me? Didn't seem likely. Maher went on. 'The lag coughed immediately; after all, he's already in custody and a gun he's connected with is used in a murder. He obviously doesn't want to get tangled with it.'

'Good alibi,' I said. He didn't even laugh.

'What the lag coughed was the name of a man, shall we say a third party, he'd passed the gun to. We picked up this third party even before we released you.'

'How long have you had the gun then?'

'Since the morning of the murder; or rather, since the morning we found the corpse. Now, the third party is very frightened, says he's going to cop for it and all that, know what I mean?'

I didn't but I didn't say so. Across the road the crowd was parting to let police vans through. A couple of uniform men were staring at us. A detective, was it Robson? waved at us. The evening sun made the walls of Leytonstone glow yellow and warm. Drivers shielded their eyes. The whole lower deck of a passing bus seemed to burst into laughter spontaneously. I presumed the conductor had been making jokes, but still a busful of laughing Londoners is a strange sight. Maher turned away from the waving detective and watched his own shadow on the sunny yellow wall.

'Well, what good's it getting a man to cop for illegal possession when you've a stiff on your hands. James? No use at all. We stuck him in the cooler for twenty-four hours and he comes out saying a name. The name he's frightened of. The name he'd cop an illegal possession of firearms plea for. Guess what name?'

'Don't tell me – Wilkins.'

Maher nodded at the wall. He said without looking at me, 'You should have stayed in the job, you know. You're good at this.'

'Ha *ha*. Thank you, Mister Maher. I think there are a couple of holes in your story. First of all Wilkins has an alibi.'

'Not one that'll stand up in court.'

'The second is that he has no motive.'

'Oh, come on, James. He's been crowding Duncan out of the fight game for a couple of years.'

'*Grant* has.'

'Grant. Wilkins. It doesn't matter at that point. You know that.'

'I know it,' I said, 'but it doesn't work as a motive. It's useless. He'd already taken Duncan's stuff over – why threaten him? Why kill his *wife* of all people? I'm sorry, Mr Maher. It won't wash. If you've arrested him on that I don't expect your file to get past the Director of Public Prosecutions. Any good defence lawyer would take it to pieces . . . for a start, how did you find the gun?'

'Anonymous tip.' He shrugged.

'It sounds dodgier by the minute.'

He turned and looked into my eyes. His eyes were grey and clear and cool. He wasn't the sort of man to get panicked into showing his hand like that, either for fear or to boast. There had to be something else. Maher provided it.

'Before Alison Duncan was Alison Duncan she was Alison Clark, without an 'e', of Cape Town, South Africa. She came to England and lived here for two years before she met and married Duncan.'

'And?'

'*And* during those two years she appears to have had no visible means of support.'

'On the game?'

'No. Not prostitution. She was supported by *someone*. Didn't you wonder about Wilkins only pressurising Duncan? No other fight managers have been squeezed by him.'

'I'm not an expert at the fight game,' I said. 'I'll take your word for it.'

'*Thanks*, James. Now, Leonard Grant's gymnasium only started in business two years ago . . . *two* years. Getting it now?'

'You're saying she was Wilkins' bird before she upped sticks and married dear-old-nearly-legit George Duncan.'

'Yes. There's your real motive, I'd have to say.'

'And what about Duncan going skint? Has he a lot of insurance on his wife? Could he have arranged it?' I said.

'He could. But the case for him isn't as good as the case for Wilkins. With Wilkins I've got motive, opportunity and strong evidence connecting him to the murder weapon. A witness. It would be impossible not to prefer him and his poxy drinking-club alibi as a candidate for arrest when you put him up against George Duncan with his policeman friend as an alibi, his lack of a criminal record and his "all I've done wrong is gone skint . . . since when's that a crime?" I'd be laughed out of court. On the evidence I've got Wilkins is my man. The DPP's office would insist *I'd* have to insist.'

'And his scalp is a nice one to have hanging on your belt next time the Commissioner asks you over for tea and cucumber sandwiches, is that it?'

Robson was waving more urgently from across the road now, yelling something too. Maher waved back. He acted as if he hadn't even heard me.

'You've got a car here, haven't you, James? I must go.'

'Hang on. Has the gun got Wilkins' dabs on it?'

'No. There are none on it at all.'

'And how much insurance does Duncan have?'

'Going on for three hundred grand. It's not unusual in his business, and it costs the same to insure a man and wife as it does the man alone, normally. There's nothing dodgy about the amount of it. It wasn't even taken out recently, nor all at the same time. I don't think that would be an angle. If I were to look somewhere other than Wilkins I wouldn't look in that direction.'

'Where would you look?'

He lit a cigarette, blew the smoke away from me, then looked at his hands. There was nicotine on his fingers.

'I mustn't do this, you know. It's killing me.' He waved the cigarette. 'I don't know where else I'd look. I suppose

I'd think the case against Wilkins will be open and shut. I wouldn't look anywhere. I'd end up charging Wilkins and being congratulated for it.'

'I think that stinks. Why are you telling me all this?'

He puffed unhappily at the cigarette again and said, 'Because I think it stinks too.'

He went to walk away, then came back after a few paces.

'Uh . . . I don't think my sergeant's that chuffed about the way you parted company with him earlier. I don't think he's pleased at all. I don't think he'd be thrilled to find out you were using his name over the phone to Shoreditch Mortuary, either, James.'

'Me?' I said, all innocence and hands open.

'You. How else could you know she was shot with a pistol? You didn't question it when I told you and the press don't have it yet. Only someone who phoned the mortuary clerk and asked questions making out to be a policeman would know that. It's a crime to impersonate a policeman, James.'

'Hm,' I said. 'It wasn't me. I haven't got a helmet any more.'

'Good. You could also ask your pal O'Keefe to be a bit more subtle than taking a copy of the post-mortem report off a desk in the CID room and making a photocopy. Tell him he's not bloody invisible.'

I laughed.

'You can tell him that.'

Maher shook his head and dogged his filter tip. He'd only taken half a dozen puffs.

'As long as the copy is back on my desk first thing Monday I won't say anything to him. Bye now. I must rush.'

He sounded like a schoolmaster with a class to take. As he crossed back over to Robson he looked like a schoolmaster too, only the class was murder and the students were grown-up men and women.

12

I met Gal in front of the 'old place' as promised at eight. The 'old place' is the Arabian, a boozer on the corner of Cambridge Heath Road and Bishop's Way. It's the 'old place' because my first office was round the corner from it. Gal was leaning on the wall outside when I drove up, hands in pockets, faded-blue-denim, everything. He pushed himself off the wall without taking his hands out of his pockets. I asked him to drive. It wouldn't have surprised me if he'd done that with his hands in his pockets, too.

'That was a manky trick with the Rover, wasn't it?'

He didn't answer.

'Do you know where I've been all day?'

He nodded.

'I know where you've been the last couple of days. Same place as me.' He laughed. 'I'm sorry, Jim, but it's a good laugh us being in nick at the same time.'

'Hysterical. And don't pick me up in any more nicked motors, kid. My credit with the coppers can't stand it.'

We were driving along Hackney Road, towards Old Street.

'Where are we going?'

'To eat first. I was being followed, and I thought I might have to ask you to lose them for me, but they've gone away now.'

'I thought you'd gone off my way of losing tails?'

He was right. Gal was the best loser-of-tails in the business, if there's such a business, but his method is a bit of a strain on the old ticker. Last time he did it for me I was looking for a villain. I only wanted to serve a divorce writ.

Unfortunately some other villains in a Ford Granada wanted him too, and they followed me around like an ambulance waiting for an accident to happen. The accident was going to happen when I (that is, when *they*) found villain number one. I didn't want to serve the writ on a stiff so in all innocence I asked Gal to lose these four mateys in the Granada. I thought he could rush down a side street and turn his lights off, something like that. It would work a treat, I thought. I thought wrong. He did it a couple of times but the Granada stuck with us. Gary decided something a bit more drastic was called for. He drove us all the way to Mortlake, to a level-crossing he knew. Then he waited till the gates were dropping and slammed the old motor through like some sort of demented version of Evil Knievel. I went to sleep for months after with the image of the front of a suburban train etched on my mind. I woke up every morning cut in three. We lost the villains following us. I served the writ for the divorce, which the lady wife got. The husband got ten years in Chelmsford Gaol, but that wasn't just for being a bad husband. The level-crossing keeper got a nervous twitch. I swore I'd never again use Gal as a tail-loser or getaway driver unless it was essential that I lose the tail or get away. My constitution wouldn't stand it.

We drove to Westbourne Grove. I'd had enough of the East End and anyway you have to go to West London if you want to eat half decently. There are a few places in the West End but I didn't fancy them, and there are one or two in the East End but I didn't want to go bumping into any more coppers, guns, villains or what have you. I wanted a big curry and some lager, all that nonsense. I wanted some company that wasn't going to bash me up, point guns at me or put me in a cell. We went to Khan's: a big queue, polite service and good food. I felt as if I'd joined the human race again. Gal sat pushing okra around with his fork and complaining about 'spices'.

'I can't think they're no good for you. They go through me like a dose of salts,' he said. He ate it though, and I told him about my time in the nick and about the dead woman. I told him Wilkins had been arrested for it too.

'Don't surprise me.' He shook his head to emphasise it.

'He's a very dirty specimen. He's got lots of people frightened of him.'

The fans sliced slowly through the thick air above our heads. Plates clattered in some outside room. The waiters glided past, grinning and chattering to each other. They looked happy. People at the tables around us chattered too. They looked happy. Through the plate-glass windows. I could see cars passing, no doubt full of happy, chatting people. I thought of the woman I'd driven from Saffron Walden. Gal was right, of course. Lots of people were frightened of Wilkins and his reputation. That's why he looked such a good prospect for the police. The closer they got to him, the less likely they were to let go. That was even true for Maher. The pressure would be on him not to let go. Wilkins would be a big fish to have on a hook.

I lost my appetite all of a sudden. I paid up and we pushed our way back through the crowd to the street and our car. The weather was breaking, going back to the usual cold way May presents itself. There was quite a breeze out in Westbourne Grove. I still kept all the windows down as Gal drove us down the Euston Road, then over Pentonville Hill. The traffic was heavy again, even though it must have been after ten. People edged their cars forward, creaking their brakes and losing their tempers. Gal hummed to himself and tapped his fingers on the dash. Fumes blew through the open windows. 'You're not saying much. You haven't said why the cops stopped following you,' he said.

'They obviously think Wilkins is their man. They've got him tucked up tight.'

Gal swore and waved his fist at a dark man driving an Alfa with foreign plates. He knows rude signs in all European languages, does Gal. He turned to me again.

'You don't think so though, do you?'

'Drop it for now, Gal,' I said. 'I hope we're going to see something of my Greek friend soon. You worry about turning him up.'

'Are you sure Wilkins won't think you brought the old bill down on him?'

'I'm sure. Leave it. What I want you to do is find Zorba. That's enough for you to think about.'

Gal dropped me and the car both in Stoke Newington,

then set off for the bus. I washed, poured a big scotch, settled in front of a horror movie on the telly and watched all of thirty seconds of it before I was asleep in the chair. Then the phone rang. That's the way it always happens.

13

I let the phone ring. I didn't want to talk to anyone. I got up and took my untouched whisky into the kitchen. I was still picking my way over cushion covers and books and papers from when the flat had been searched by the police. I knew it wasn't Judy ringing me so I just let the phone ring on. Judy was the only person I wanted to be disturbed for and we have a strict rule that we don't phone each other at home late at night without a very good reason. That way we never find out things about each other we'd rather not know. The phone stopped. If it was Judy she'd give it a couple of minutes then ring again.

I left the whisky on the side and made some cocoa. My kitchen has two stools, a breakfast bar, a fridge, a cooker and two eye-level cupboards. It's so small that if two people go in together getting them out is a surgical matter. It's great if the other person's a girl but if it's a fat man . . . forget it. I crammed myself into this little space and looked down at the street. The window-blind was up and the street looked friendly. There was no Bedford van, no Ford Cortina, none of Wilkins' boys that I could see, just a stepped image of my naked torso reflected in the double glazing. I pulled the blind on that. The phone rang again.

'Hullo.' Pips sounded. A coinbox.

'Jenner?'

'Go on.'

'The matter you discussed with a certain party this evening is solved. You should go to your office.'

It was Wilkins' one-man-submarine, Charlie. I wondered how he reached the phone . . . on a milk crate?

'I thought you went for a ride with the men in blue, Charlie.'

'Not me. It was all a big mistake. I was there for less than an hour when my boss's lawyer got me out.'

'And Wilkins?'

'Not so simple. Someone's stitched him up good and tight. The promise you were made has been kept. Bill and me are both out and rooting for him. We thought you would be rooting for him too.'

'Drop dead, Charlie. I'm tired. Some of us are human. Some of us have to sleep.'

'I think you should go to your office, Jenner. You will need to keep your side of things.'

'Do I look like a fairy godmother?'

'No. I think you should go to your office and I think you should make every effort to help. We would remember it in a very friendly way if you helped.'

'Drop dead.'

I put the phone down, then climbed around the debris of my flat looking for a clean shirt. The ones from my chest of drawers were more crumpled than the one I'd been wearing, but they smelled better. I put on a crumpled shirt, a crumpled rainmac and then I limped my crumpled limp down to my car. Some fairy godmother. Long John Silver was more like it. I bet the little fellow thought of that, too. He didn't say it of course. He wanted something from me.

It was about twelve when I reached Chardray's shop. The door to my office was slightly ajar. I could see that without getting out of the car. Drizzle fell, gathered on my wind-screen. I drove on and stopped at a phone box. I rang my number. The tape machine answered. I felt in my pocket for my bleeper. The playback tape only had messages from Bernie-the-barmy-husband. I didn't know what I was going to do about him. If I got the number changed he'd find that. Barmies can be cunning in their obsessive little way. I thought I'd probably write to the wife and ask her, since I'd been kind enough to find her ever-loving Bernie-the-barmy, wouldn't she put a little time into dissuading him from phoning me twice a day; I mean half my phone calls are from Bernie-the-barmy. It's getting beyond a joke.

I drove the car back past Chardray's again, parked a hundred yards away and hurried through the drizzle. I gave my door a good wallop with my walking stick, then leaned back tight on the dirty damp concrete wall until a man blundered downstairs. I didn't stop him politely to ask why he was there, was he waiting for me to open up in the morning or something. No. All my politeness was worn out. For all I knew he might have a gun too, like everyone else I seemed to meet nowadays. Maybe he'd be a judo expert and I'd need the aid of a little surprise.

As I heard that man blundering down the darkened stairs I decided to play it dirty. As he came through the doorway I hit him clean in the mouth with the handle of my stick. I heard a nasty crack and it wasn't the stick that got broke. He pitched forward and I heaved it back and gave him a mighty whack on the back of the head too. It is in the hope of such instantaneous retribution for burglars and muggers that Tory ladies live, it is for this kind of justice that they whip themselves into a frenzy at Brighton conferences, peeing on the seats and shrinking the covers. If the hang-'em and fling-'em law-and-order types had been there they'd have loved me. I'd have got a bar to my medal. Unfortunately there was no one to see me do it. The other slight fly in the ointment was the fact that the 'mugger' squirming about on the floor minus his front teeth and in need of a stitched scalp was none other than Bernie-the-barmy-husband. I expected at least a little remonstration from him . . . I mean, he's only slightly barmy. He's enough cogs to know when he's being walloped and whether he's done anything to deserve that treatment.

Bernie said nothing. First of all he sat up and spat into his cupped hands. Under the yellow street lamps it looked like he was spitting black.

'You'll get wet,' I said.

Bernie just pointed up the stairs.

'You'd better get up. It's raining, Bernie.' I was wondering whether you could get caps done overnight, like a tyre change or something. I bet there's an all-night dentist in Earl's Court. I bet he's above an all-night doner-kebab house and I bet he spells it 'All Nite Dentistry. Get Your Caries Clobbered'. I bet he charges two hundred greenies to have it done *per tooth*, too. Oh God, I thought. There's going to be hell to pay when Bernard's ever-loving wifey-poos sees him. She'll sue me, and she'll be right to sue me and what's more she'll win. It was a disappointing thought. No bar to my medal.

'Uh,' said Bernie, pointing up the stairs. 'Uh uh.'

I went upstairs. The stair light was broken, the inner door to my office was open. I pushed it wide. My office has no curtains. Yellow streetlight fell across the room, across the desk. The yellow light fell on my chair and on the man in it. I switched the electric lamp on. He moaned.

'Zorba,' I said. I moved quickly across to him. He looked like he'd fallen off a bus. Face first. His features were bloody and swollen, his lips had ballooned up.

'Sorry,' he whispered through them. 'Sorry, Sjimmy.' His eyes closed for a second and he breathed a long sigh and I thought, 'Not another, I can't stand someone else dying on me', but he opened his eyes and he wasn't dead or anything like it, just all beaten up. He looked at the ceiling, and then at the walls. 'I retire,' he said. 'I no play this bishnesh any more.' He closed his eyes again. The effect of talking had exhausted him.

'I'll get an ambulance,' I said.

He kept his eyes closed but shook his head.

'No. I'm gonna be a decorator. You be my first case.' He raised his left hand weakly and waved at the walls. 'This place a mess, Sjimmy. I decorate for you.'

'Okay. You decorate. I'll hire you. Consider yourself hired. Now I'll get the ambulance.'

Zorba raised himself from the chair as well as he could. He grabbed me with the left hand. I looked down, then I realised it had to be the left hand. His right hand was flat on my desk. The fingers were spread wide. The flesh on Zorba's hand looked a little blue. And there was a nail running through the fleshy part of the palm, under his thumb. The nail had been driven into my desk top.

He said, 'No ambulance.'

I nodded. 'I'll be back.'

I went downstairs and started hammering on Chardray's

door. He has a little flat at the back of his shop. I hammered and I rang the bell and then I hammered and I rang the bell and I shouted all sorts of rude and vile language that doesn't normally come into my vocabulary. Chardray came down looking all sleepy and asking if I knew it was half-twelve.

'Give me a hammer,' I said.

'A hammer? Why do you want a hammer at this time? Are you gone mad, James? Are you drunk? I have to be up in four hours and you're asking me to fetch you one hammer. Do you want nails too?'

He fetched a nail, to go with the hammer. Then he went inside and bolted the door good and proper and gave me to understand that I shouldn't do it ever again. I threw the nail in the gutter. Bernie-the-barmy had gone. That was one blessing. I went upstairs and fetched the biggest book I could find, then I lay the book next to Zorba's hand, hooked the claw through the nail and pulled, using the book and the hammer head as a fulcrum. I did it quickly. There was no point in hanging about. The nail hadn't hurt him half as much as the beating. I yanked it out and he didn't say a word, just tightened the lids of his closed eyes a little, winced a little.

'Sorry,' he said again.

I tried to lift him. I couldn't do it.

'How do you feel?' I said. It was a stupid question. He smiled. Even that seemed to hurt him. I touched his face. His beard was like a cheese-grater. It's like that every time he leaves off shaving for half an hour.

'I'll get Gal.'

I phoned Gary at home. He didn't complain when I asked him to come out. Gal didn't even complain when I told him not to get in any illegal motors.

'Get a cab,' I said.

'I haven't got any dough . . . what's the time?'

'Quarter to one. Just get one. I'll pay.'

I gave Zorba some gin. I'm sure it's not what you're supposed to give people in his position but I didn't have anything else. He sat back in the chair and sipped the gin and told me what had happened. As I'd figured from what O'Keefe had told me, Zorba hadn't been able to resist a peek in the brown paper bag he'd been given, and when he'd peeked he hadn't been able to resist the packets of used fivers and tenners he'd found inside. It was silly of O'Keefe to trust him with that much money. He'd carried money before but that was when he was doing it for me. Zorba and me are friends . . . so with me it was a question of trust. When O'Keefe dealt with him directly, Zorba felt under no such obligation.

It was partly my fault. I'd cut O'Keefe out when I'd decided not to work with him any more and I should've known he'd try a bit of private enterprise with Gal or Zorba. The trouble was, when Zorba had found out how much money he was carrying, he'd simply taken it straight down the Bank of Nicosia, swapped it for a money draft and sent the draft to his wife with a note saying, 'All is forgiven. Buy a house. I'm following soon.' Or whatever the Greek equivalent is.

Zorba's big mistake was that he didn't take himself with the money. Nobody could've done anything about it. O'Keefe would never have found him. The insurance company O'Keefe had been negotiating for could only have made a fuss about O'Keefe, not about Zorba. He could have spent the rest of his days in peace on some Cypriot balcony, shading his delicate features from the summer heat and quaffing vast amounts of ouzo while he watched his children grow.

I suppose that was his plan in the end, anyway. But he decided first of all to stay around London, 'tidying my affair' as he put it. Tidying his affair took a vital few days, and by that time little Charlie was telling the sellers that, money or no money, they had to get whatever they were selling back to me. Mr Wilkins had said so and Mr Wilkins' word was, in the sellers' world, law.

'How did they find you?'

'They hold blowlamp to my cousin,' he muttered and shook his head slowly. These guys showed a certain style. Their interrogation technique left the likes of O'Keefe and myself asleep at the starting gate. Neither of us had been to the school of blowtorch confessions. O'Keefe had tried to find Zorba and failed, Gal had tried to find him and failed and I've little doubt that if I'd tried I'd have failed too. That's where madmen score . . . they do madder things than the rest of us, things we wouldn't imagine doing.

I poured Zorba some more gin, then went and sat on the stairs. I knew he couldn't answer a load of questions and I felt angry and hurt that someone would treat him so badly, no matter what he'd done. I sat on the stairs and looked down to the doorway, then through the doorway and into the street. The rain kept falling and sometimes a car would pass. I went upstairs again and said, 'Couldn't you get the money back to them? Couldn't you have handed over the cash anyway?'

He shook his head.

'My wife and kids have it.'

I said, 'Damn you,' under my breath and he smiled a little, then Gal came and carted him down to my car. Zorba told us to bring the bag, too, from under my desk. The bag was an old cardboard suitcase with unlikely stickers on the outside (Port Said, Piraeus and New York I saw. There were others) and something more substantial than a spare shirt on the inside. It was because they'd been forced to return the bag the thieves had nailed Zorba to my desk. We drove him down to Bart's Hospital, which has a night casualty ward and is far enough away from Canning Town as to make us feel a little more comfortable about my local police. Gal took him in. I sat in the car and watched. They looked like a couple of drunks staggering across West Smithfield. I turned the radio on and listened to a late-night smooth talker while I waited for Gal. I could hear the articulated meat lorries running up their refrigerator engines. I could see the lights under the market building. I could hear the yells of the night workers, 'All right, all right, back a bit . . . woah!' I left the car and went to a phone box.

'Hullo.'

O'Keefe sounded drowsy, but he'd picked the phone up on the first ring.

'You can stop worrying,' I said. 'I've got something for you.'

He was awake immediately.

'Got it with you?'

'In my car. Can we talk?'

He was silent for a second. I could imagine him looking at the sleeping woman by his side.

'I'll go down to the kitchen.' He put the phone down. I read the names in the phone box. Vera: big, black and willing. Elaine: all requirements catered to. Anne: bottom marks for naughty boys. All the names were followed by phone numbers, all were written in laundry marker. The man from British Telecom with the scrubbing brush was fighting an uphill battle. I wondered if the sleeping woman O'Keefe had just left was really so naïve. Did she think she was married to an upright citizen, a guardian of law, order and morality, or did she think Denis was a bit of a yob . . . did she know where the money for the house in Thorpe Bay and the three weeks a year in Ibiza came from? Not off a copper's salary.

'Go on then,' came O'Keefe's voice again.

'I'm outside Bart's,' I said. 'Zorba's in it. I've got your gear because Wilkins told whoever it was to cough up.'

'*I* told them too. They wouldn't, though,' he said. '*I* told them I'd send them down for five years each. It didn't seem to worry them.'

'Well, Denis, I suppose they knew you weren't serious . . . after all, they could blow the gaff on you. That's one thing. The other is that you don't have the powers of persuasion Wilkins has. Little Charlie probably said, "Give Denis the gear or I'm going to cut your toes off . . . slowly". I can imagine it, Denis, can't you?'

'Mm.'

'Anyway they got the gear back to me and they found Zorba.'

'How'd they find him? I've been looking for a week.'

'They have the same advantage over you in the persuasion stakes as Wilkins does. That's how. They nearly killed Zorba.'

'Serves the little slag right.'

'Maybe. What are you going to do about them?'

'We'll see.'

'We'll certainly see, Denis. I want a lot of returns on this favour. Know what I mean?'

He didn't answer.

'I'll see you tomorrow night, Denis.'

I could see Gary skipping over the road. O'Keefe still didn't answer so I put the phone down.

'They're keeping him in,' Gal said as we climbed in the car. 'I'm sorry I was a long time. The night clerk got all stroppy when I told him I didn't know where it had happened and I'd found him on the roadside. He got particularly upset when I told him my name was Samuel A. Ritan. It took a while to convince him. He was all for calling the cops.'

I drove round the one-way system in Smithfield.

'There's Duncan's gym,' said Gal, pointing to a Victorian boozer. I stopped. I could just make out the shadows of the equipment in the upper rooms, through the uncurtained windows. Behind us the market men had started work with a vengeance. I left the car and walked back to Grand Avenue, then walked through the painted-iron and glass splendour of the meat market. I don't know what I expected to see. There was sawdust on the floor and men in blood-stained white coats pushed past me. I looked at a lamb, all strung up and hanging from a rail by its hind legs. The salesman ignored me, I obviously didn't look right for a wholesale buyer. I turned and looked from the market back towards George Duncan's gym. I could see straight up to the windows of his gym from here. Another porter pushed past with fresh blood on his coat. He was pushing a big tub full of pigs' heads. Pigs' eyes, past pain now, stared through their blond lashes at me. Some of the blood on the porter's coat had caught my hand as he'd pushed past. I stood under a neon lamp and looked closely at my hand. Blood never seems real. Blood never seems like blood. I thought of the body we'd seen in Shoreditch and a shiver ran down my spine. I went back into the darkness to my car. Gal had re-tuned the radio to a French pop-music station. He was drinking Coke and smoking a cigarette. Gal stood for life and light. Blood and meat meant death and darkness.

I opened the car door. The courtesy light came on. Gal smiled and swigged his Coke. I felt like putting my arms round him but he wouldn't have understood. Instead I said, 'Drive us home, Gal.' And walked round to the passenger side of the car. Gal slid behind the wheel of the car and engaged 'drive'. As we reached the end of Carthusian Street a couple of big red Salvage Corps machines came racing round the corner. Their blue lights were on but the sirens weren't sounding. In the cab we could see the officer pulling on his fireman's jacket: then they were past, all polished paint work headlamps and sliding tyres on the wet street.

'I wouldn't mind driving one of them,' said Gal. ''s a fair old job.'

We crossed the bright lights of Aldersgate Street, then plunged into the darkness of Fann Street and he said it again and I said, angrily and unreasonably, 'Just shut up and drive us home.'

He turned the radio up and did just that.

14

My auntie used to have a pub in Hadleigh. When I first knew Judy and we were young and innocent we used to go and stay with her for the weekend. It was a nice, unspoilt pub where you could get arrowroot biscuits and a game of darts. Locals would chat politely if you wanted to chat and leave you alone if you wanted to be left alone. On summer Sunday afternoons you could walk down to the castle, which was built for King John or someone and is in such an advanced state of disrepair he wouldn't even be able to raise a mortgage on it nowadays. Judy and I would stand in the ruins of the old castle and look down on the flatlands on the banks of the Thames. Trains would rumble along a track below us, the light would be courtesy of John Constable, with tall black and white cotton wool clouds towering over the Isle of Grain and shafts of sunlight breaking through to us. Judy and I would make big plans for a future that isn't here now and even back then we must've known would never be here. That's half the fun of planning the future . . . unless you're the most boring man on earth it's *never* going to work.

On Friday evening I was driving along the A13 in heavy traffic. Dirt and drizzle lifted off the tarmac before me, making little greasy smuts on the windscreen that the wipers wouldn't shift. By the time I reached Pitsea the rain had stopped and the roads were dry. By the time I reached Hadleigh I was positively bathed in evening sunshine and all the commuters had turned off for someplace else. How kind.

My auntie has long since gone to the great saloon bar in the sky, where there are not only 'afters' but 'befores' (or maybe there are no licensing laws at all), the 'special' is never off, the barman always turns up for work on time and the landlady (i.e. auntie) has a tap of draught champagne conveniently situated next to a tall barstool she favours. I only hope the Guinness in the saloon bar in the sky is good enough for my dad (her brother) to be standing near her tall barstool somewhere reading a celestial *Sporting Life*, backing nags with an endless supply of white fivers and arguing with his mates whether or not B. J. T. Bosanquet really invented the googly. He always swore it was a sporting Abo that invented the googly and he'd read it in a book. He also swore that my auntie's Guinness came up too cold. The idea of the Guinness argument creating (another) rift which would this time last for all eternity is more than I can bear. The Abo would be less of a problem.

The pub's still there and Judy's Metro was in the car park. I went inside and thought I'd got it all wrong at first. It seems as soon as auntie died the brewers sent in a team of interior designers who'd come up with a foolproof plan to make money: '. . . all we need is a leatherette and velour version of Santa's Grotto. They haven't got one of them in Hadleigh.' They certainly have now. The interior walls of auntie's pub had gone. The floor had been raised (or was it the ceiling lowered?) and everything coloured womb-red. The space between the floor and the ceiling was filled with throbbing music and flashing lights.

Judy was at the bar drinking a salad.

'Hullo,' she yelled. 'Pimms?'

'Light and bitter,' I said, shaking my head.

We were the only people in the room apart from the bar staff. It's the kind of pub people don't go to till late. If I'd known in advance I would've been a month late, or a year late, or even never come. By a complicated series of hand gestures the barmaid and I exchanged the information that I wanted a light and bitter and no, I couldn't have one. Would I like a Schlitz instead?

'A *what*?'

'*Schlitz!*'

Time was that the only schlitz girls Hadleigh had were in their schkirtz. I had a Schlitz, then swapped lip-reading lessons with Judy for half an hour.

'*I wanted to meet here because I was being followed,*' I shouted.

'*Oh yes?*'

'*But now I'm not.*'

'*Oh yes?*'

'*No. Did you bring a bag?*'

'*Yes.*' She sipped her fruit salad.

I sipped my Schlitz. I swear I did it. I sipped my Schlitz then I slurped my Schlitz then I swallowed my Schlitz. A certain Stevie Wonder boomed advice on life into my ears and for the first time since one didn't work properly I gave thanks for that fact. Judy insisted I have another beer and I said no but she didn't hear, then we had another of those '*Had a good day at the office?*', 'It's about quarter past seven', '*I didn't ask for the time*', 'What?', '*What?*' conversations. I staggered outside with my head reeling and my eyes seeing everything a green tint. I supervised Judy humping my overnight bag and Zorba's/O'Keefe's cardboard suitcase into the boot of her Metro, then we locked my car good and proper and left it in the pub car park for the weekend while Judy drove us down to Thorpe Bay.

'I'm a bit tired,' I said.

'I'm not surprised.' She drove smoothly and unfussedly. She was always in the right gear and she did all that stuff about never crossing your hands on the steering wheel they teach you at the Police Driving School. I never got the hang of it while I was there – at least not enough to be trusted with more than a Panda car. If you want to drive a big Rover with a red stripe down the side you must *never* cross your hands. You must also remember all the rules in the police driving manual, be able to give a commentary on traffic hazards as you approach them and *never ever* bump into anything while you're driving. I failed on all counts.

Judy drove us beautifully into Southend and then I took over and used my special expertise to find a quiet pub, somewhere to park and a table in the corner where we couldn't be overheard.

'You should have told me what you were going to do,' she said. 'When you saw me outside Scotland Yard you should've told me.'

'I did,' I said. 'I was asked to look after George Duncan's wife and that's what I went off to do. It only became complicated afterwards.'

Judy frowned. She frowns well, even if I say so myself. I kissed her and she frowned more.

'Well it's all over now, Jimmy, and I'm pleased. You can just imagine how I felt when I found out you were in a cell in Peter Street. I never want to go through that again.'

'Nor do I,' I said.

'I felt so helpless.'

'So did I.'

Judy sipped her drink, rum and Coke. I had chosen a pub that didn't do any salad drinks or thumping music. I'm getting too old for that.

'Still it's over now,' she said again.

'You already said that.'

'But you didn't agree. Don't you agree?'

I didn't say anything. It would only lead to an argument.

'Don't you agree?' she insisted. She was getting that 'you'd better agree' look women sometimes go in for.

'No I don't. I don't believe they've got the right man. I don't even believe the woman I took there was George Duncan's wife. That's how I feel about it. The way I feel is that it isn't finished with me and I haven't finished with it . . . all right?'

But it wasn't all right, and she let me know it.

The idea was that we would stay a couple of days with the O'Keefes. The idea was that we'd go there after dinner on Friday night and stay till Sunday afternoon. Mary O'Keefe is a dun-coloured little woman who stays in the posh house in Thorpe Bay and feeds the kids three times a day and gets them off to school in her Ford Escort bang on time. She makes sure Denis has an endless supply of ironed shirts while he makes sure she has an endless supply of money which she doesn't appear either to notice or use. Judy and me had been there before and Mary O'Keefe had immediately bagged her as a fellow female, leading into the kitchen for a fluffy-slippered ladies' meeting, a recipe-swapping session. Judy would rather die than buy fluffy slippers and her idea of a recipe is 1) drive to Chinese takeaway, 2) order food, 3) collect food and pay, 4) drive home, 5) eat it. She thinks brownies and flapjacks is a game described in *Scouting for Boys*.

Denis and Mary O'Keefe live on Dunbarton Avenue, Thorpe Bay. It must be the suburban street that out-suburbans all others. There are neat clipped hedges, new double-glazed windows, mock-Georgian doors and bumper-to-bumper Granada Ghias all the way along it. Denis told me once that, when his girls were tiny, he'd had a deputation of middle-aged male neighbours at his door complaining about them peeing in the gutter. That's Thorpe Bay. Nowadays the O'Keefe daughters are neo-pubescents and don't admit to peeing anywhere, ever. They stay in their rooms and listen to pop music while their father rolls his eyes downstairs. The next deputation will be teenage boys.

Judy and me arrived in an icy silence. The girls were in bed and Denis offered me a scotch and the women sherry. Judy didn't even snap at that. She didn't want to hear what Denis had found out and she didn't want to stay in the same room while I listened. Judy went happily into the kitchen to experience the delights of a small glass of sherry and a private viewing of the O'Keefe's new Siemens dishwasher.

Denis threw me the copy of the p-m report.

'Where's the gear?' he said.

'In that cardboard suitcase you took up to our room.'

I read the report while Denis went upstairs and checked the suitcase, then hid it somewhere. I could hear muffled banging about under the roof. The p-m report wasn't very interesting. Female, late twenties, cause of death bullet wound to heart, time of death between midnight and six a.m. (don't stick your neck out, Sir Mark–*I* left her after midnight and she was found not long after six). Under 'Other Comments' he'd written, '*Scars on arm consistent with healed puncture marks. The marks are of a type that would be caused by the misuse of a hypodermic syringe, though there is no evidence of drug abuse present in the corpse. It would not be unreasonable to infer the subject may be a cured drug abuser of some description.*' There was an empty line and then he'd written, '*The subject had seen a pregnancy through to full term within the last five years.*'

Denis came down and gave me another whisky. Sir Mark had bravely hazarded a guess that the missing flesh on the face had been 'cut off with some sharp object, perhaps a butcher's knife'. He noted there were fresh wounds in the gums where the teeth (and he gave the teeth numbers) had been torn out. He wrote that there were marks on the remaining teeth which indicated a pair of pliers may have been used. A hurriedly handwritten addition to the typewritten text said: '*In response to your telephone enquiry I can't as yet be positive that the wounds to the face, eyes, teeth and scalp took place after death, though that would at the moment seem likely. You will appreciate this is a preliminary report and . . .*' then it drifted off into bureaucrat-ese and was signed '*Squiggle-squiggle-squiggle*' and then a load of letters to prove he was a medical doctor. Just the unreadable signature would have been enough.

There were some more papers with the report. There was a telex to Officer-in-Charge, CID Cape Town asking for any criminal, medical or dental record available for one Alison May Clark, giving her date of birth as February 3rd 1954, place of birth London, England, a note of the parental address in Cape Town, S.A. and a brief outline of the case in the guarded way that coppers outline things (I don't know for sure the sun'll come up tomorrow, though of course it has come up every morning since the start of time so it *may* do). There was a photostat of the dabs taken off the corpse which I presume would have been transmitted to the South African coppers under separate cover from the telex. They have a special machine that does it at New Scotland Yard. There were some witness statements, including a long and detailed description of me by the cabbie who'd picked me up twice in Saffron Walden. It was a pretty accurate description, too, and gave the lie to the idea that people don't see you . . . they just don't say anything. So *English*, that.

'Well,' said Denis, 'enough?'

I slapped the papers with my hand.

'I thought you'd only taken a copy of the p-m report?'

Denis nodded and put his glass on top of a little coaster-shaped lace mat on the coffee table. Everywhere was polished. I could even smell the stuff, smell the lavender they put in it.

'I did,' Denis said. 'Then I had a phone call from DCS Maher's assistant, a Sergeant Robson . . . know him?'

He smiled. So did I.

'A little,' I said, 'Brian Borden's the authority on Maher's assistants. What about it?'

'He was asking me over to see Maher. He said Maher would like some help from me on the Duncan case. He said Maher thought I might have some inside knowledge of the Wilkins organisation . . . what d'yer reckon to that, eh? I said I had a full case-load and he'd better get Maher to speak to my gov'nor about it.'

'And?'

'And quarter of an hour later I was zooming down to join the Murder Squad. On loan. I went and saw Maher and said that I didn't know anything about the "organisation" that wasn't on collators' files in our nick or CIS at the Yard. Then Maher says yeah but he'd like me to lend my mind to it and my guv'nor's agreed so would I mind just doing that? Then he told me to go and see the SOCO and get clued-in from them and he gave me a great stack of statements and stuff to read. He said take it home for the weekend and he said I'd find the top half-dozen – which is the stuff you've got there – the most interesting. Then he asked me a load of questions about you . . . I got the impression, James, that he expected me to see you and he expected, even *wanted* me to show you that stuff.'

He played with his diamond ring, twisting it round and round his finger. I said, 'What did the Scenes of Crime people tell you?'

'Was I right about Maher?' he insisted.

'Yes,' I said. He fetched the whisky and poured us both some. Even the bottle had been polished by his obsessive little Mary. I picked up my glass. I could see clear grease marks where my fingers had been. I saw Denis wiping his glass absently with his handkerchief. He looked through the amber liquid at me. 'I don't think Wilkins did it,' I said. 'Maher has his doubts, too.'

Denis kept squinting through his glass. 'That's hot,' he

118

said. I could hear his girls arguing upstairs. Mary yelled politely at them that they should go to sleep, then came in to us and pulled the curtains and switched the lamps on. I noticed she touched the curtains lightly as she moved away from them, neatening their hang, evening out the puckers. Judy stayed firmly in the kitchen. I knew she'd be in a hell of a temper, biting her knuckles and learning about strong-flour and cream-cleansers and spray-on-oven-degreasers.

When Denis' wife had gone I said again, 'What did the SOCOs tell you?'

'Nothing. The prints in the Saffron Walden house fit the ones on the body. The prints in the hired Jag fit the ones on the body, the prints in the Barbican flat fit the ones on the body. Boring, isn't it? The only others we could find belong to you and Duncan. Not Wilkins, not Lenny Grant . . . no others.'

'None?' I sat up.

'None. No postman, no gas man, no electricity-board man. None. It seems that Alison Duncan was house-proud.' He waved at the room. 'People *are*, you know.'

The smell of lavender. The polished glass in my hand. A cut glass tumbler with whisky in it. I remembered the scene in Duncan's flat. I remembered the girl not knowing exactly where her own flat was supposed to be. If you wanted to kill someone you'd wipe your fingerprints off, everyone who's ever watched TV knows that. That would mean wiping the surface clean. It would mean wiping *all* the finger-prints off if the scene of the crime was your own home.

'Has everywhere been printed?' I said. 'All over the flat, all over the house in Saffron?'

He nodded. Of course it had. The Scenes of Crime people would go over it with a fine-tooth comb.

'I don't believe it was her, Denis. I don't believe it was his wife.'

'I know. Maher told me you didn't.'

'I think it was a stooge,' I said.

'Then who murdered her and why?'

'The Duncans. For the insurance money. It's obvious.'

'It may be to you, Jimmy, but it's Wilkins that is going to be obvious to everyone else. If you wanted to prove it was someone other than Alison Duncan you'd have to come up with concrete evidence that the body is someone else or you'd have to come up with the real Alison Duncan. One or the other. If Alison Duncan still exists who's in the mortuary? If Alison Duncan still exists then where is *she*? If George Duncan was after getting hold of their insurance money how's he going to share it with his 'dead' wife, and since George was tucked up tight when it happened who *did* do it?'

'I don't know. Have you had an answer from South Africa?'

'Yes. A nice one. Although Mrs Duncan had no parents living she'd a brother called David Clark who's alive and well and living in Cape Town . . . and he's got more form than the Derby winner. Her father had too, but since he's been dead for ten years we can hardly put this down to him.'

'What about medical records and dental records?'

'Unfortunately the doctor who dealt with her had a fire in his office a couple of weeks ago. Very unfortunate, that. He did say that she hadn't had a pregnancy to his knowledge, but that didn't mean she hadn't had a pregnancy. Same goes for the drugs thing. He knew nothing about it, but he says that's probably a habit she'd picked up in Europe, anyway. There's no trace of any dental records as yet.'

'What about immigration?'

'*What* immigration? She's *British*. She comes and goes here as she pleases.'

'And South African immigration?'

He shook his head again.

'She was a kid when she went there. They don't print kids going in. There's no reason. She never committed any crimes either here or there. None we know of. All the evidence is in those houses and in that hired Jag. Both you and Duncan identified the body.'

'Well, he would!' I stood. I felt angry. 'Let me spell out to you what I think, Denis. I think the girl whose body is in the mortuary was duped into being Mrs Duncan for a night. I don't know *how* but I think she was. I think the real Mrs Duncan has hopped off somewhere to lie low while Georgy boy collects the insurance money. She's got this tied up tighter than a duck's backside. I think the flat and the house were cleaned up so that only the new girl's dabs and mine and George's would be in them. Do you see what I'm saying? I think the murderer is the person you think is the victim. Got it? Why on earth else should someone cut off the face on that body?'

'Evidence?' said Denis.

He can be very annoying.

'I haven't got any evidence unless you count a body with a missing face.

'Exactly. Sit down, you'll wake the girls. *Think* about it, Jimmy. Even the missing face isn't evidence. It's exactly what you'd do to terrorise someone.'

I sat on his big velour sofa. The wife popped in again, I presume to find out why I was shouting.

'Having a good time, boys?' she said.

'Fine,' I said.

'Everything all right? Denis has got some beers in the cellar, haven't you, Denis? Why don't you boys try that? I think it's going to be better for you than nasty whisky all evening.'

Denis, to my surprise, dutifully went off to fetch a pack of four fizzy light ales.

'Everything all right?' said Mary when he'd gone.

'Okay. Are you *girls* having a good time?' I said as loudly ι·· I could and as sarcastically as I dared.

'Oh *wonderful*,' she said and clasped her hands together and meant it. 'I get *so* few visitors connected with Denis's work . . . he says he likes to keep it out of the home and I respect that.'

Denis came back. She gave us fresh glasses and took the whisky ones away, smiling at me with her dun-coloured eyes under her dun-coloured soft-set hairdo.

When she'd gone I said, 'If Maher were to broaden his investigation a little he might think along the lines of the body being some poor stooge that would stand for Alison Duncan. He might think the murderer is a murderess. He might want to run those dabs off the cadaver through CRO and he might want to circulate all missing persons agencies with a description of the woman I brought to London . . . who is *not* the woman in the picture they're using in the incident room. He could try drug agencies with the description . . . I mean, if she was some sort of user she'd have to pay somehow. That normally means crime. If there was no crime she'd be registered on a scheme. At least that. Often they're registered and committing crime. There must be a note on her *somewhere*.'

Denis shook his head.

'Done it. He's done all of it. The prints aren't on CRO, but neither were Alison Duncan's. That's a blank – it's a minus to your theory. The description you gave is being circulated now, but Maher says it doesn't differ any from the description of Alison Duncan. Come in on Monday and we'll try a photofit.'

'And what about women of that description who've disappeared?'

'In the last week only two. It's neither of them . . . one's been found and the other has a record and her prints don't fit. In the last month there's probably a dozen who'd fit the description . . . but don't forget if your theory is right they've probably picked someone who's got no ties to anyone.'

'Like who?'

He shrugged and pulled the ring on another can.

I said, 'Like who?' again.

'A whore. A dropout. Something like that. Didn't she talk to you?'

'She talked. But she didn't tell me her prices or something, you know. She might have been, I suppose. I don't know. What about this pregnancy angle?'

'Jimmy, do you know how many women have had babies in Britain and South Africa in the past five years?'

'Okay. Quite a few. What do you think, Denis?'

'I think you're wrong. Wilkins did it. I think it was horrific because it was meant to be. That was his style. He reckoned he'd get away with it because he didn't have to worry about the gun. First of all we wouldn't find it and then we wouldn't tie it to him. Well, we did both and he's well strapped and I'm pleased. We've got him at last.'

Denis's attitude was realistic and mine wasn't, of course. The 'girls' came back in and we played Monopoly till well after midnight, all the time with Judy avoiding talking to me as much as she could so that we built up into one of those huge cold rows that nobody can remember how they started but are ugly enough to hurt everybody. Denis affected to ignore it and his wife bought Mayfair and Park Lane and squealed and squealed when everybody landed on them one after the other and wouldn't let any of us go to bed till she'd won.

I could've sworn she was playing footsie with me under the table . . . at least, something kept rubbing my leg and when I looked up Judy was staring fiercely at her metallic top hat while Denis was counting his money. Mary, meanwhile, smiled and said, 'Your turn.'

Maybe there's more to Mrs Dowdy Thorpe Bay than meets the eye. I certainly hope so . . . for Denis's sake.

15

We lay awake all night, Judy and me. It's quite a trick to spend five hours in a double bed and never touch. We managed it. After an eternity of lying on my back and staring at the ceiling I felt it must be dawn, so I went and pulled the curtains and looked down at the dark garden, then all around the dark sky. Not a speck of light. I went and sat on the edge of the bed and then Judy rose too, and we dressed together without speaking and without putting the light on. We went out and I left Denis's front door on the latch. There are enough police patrols in Thorpe Bay to protect him in the small hours, I thought. Anyway, the idea he might be burgled amused me.

Judy and me walked down to the front, side by side and still not talking. There was a purple slash across the sky to the east, and a reflection of it in the sea. The houses were black and the road grey. We walked along the promenade, which is merely a seaside road, nothing special, then we stepped down onto the mudflats and began to walk out towards the sea. The purple slash had changed into the edge of a sun now and it rose in a grey sheet of a sky and was striped by black bands of low cloud. We walked through millions of grey worm casts, splashed through tiny flat rivulets of steely sea water and all the time the sun rose slowly and we said nothing. I stopped and rested on a wall which was covered with seaweed. I turned and could see early morning cars moving along the road at the sea's edge — or now the mud's edge. Their lights were on still, even though the dawn had come. I could smell salt in the air and had that metallic, early morning taste in my mouth that comes from seeing a dawn without sleeping first. I had a slight ache in the pit of my stomach and the feeling of my brain being dull and slow. The light fell on us and a sea breeze touched us and the dark bedroom of an hour ago seemed like an eternity away, seemed like someone else. Judy leaned against me and squeezed my arm. Her eyes were closed and there was a slight sheen of light off her smooth pale skin, a faint halo shining through her blond hair.

'I'm sorry I was angry, Jimmy,' she said. 'I was scared for you, and then angry because everyone at work knew about it and you'd embarrassed me. All those stupid things.'

She still hadn't opened her eyes.

I said, 'I know.'

I had no idea what it was supposed to mean. I had to say something. I wasn't thinking of her by now. I was thinking about George Duncan. Why hadn't he told me his Jag was hired? I couldn't think that one out. Perhaps he'd thought it didn't matter. Perhaps it *didn't*. If the flat in the Barbican and the house at Saffron were okay from the point of view of having prints that matched the body, what *wasn't*? Where would I get a load of prints that belonged to someone else? How would I match them to a real Alison Duncan? Where would I find her? It made my head spin just to think about it all.

Past Judy's face I could see two men, hundreds of yards out on the mudflats, digging for bait. They were the shadows of men, not real men. They were matchstick men drawn on a silver grey board. One matchstick man stood and eased his back.

Judy said, 'And so I think it's getting between us. And I think we have to come to some sort of decision. Either we give up our jobs and try something else . . . and probably marry, too . . . or we admit that this thing of ours is coming to an end and we have to part company. That's what I think, Jimmy.'

She opened her eyes and followed my gaze to the bait-diggers.

'You're saying you want to split?' I said.

'*No!* I'm offering to go into an alliterative marriage. I'm saying that I'm willing to put my ticket in on Monday and follow you to the ends of the earth . . . but not if you keep up this private detective fantasy. I'll give it up and you'll give this up too.'

'What'll we do?' I said.

'We're not short of cash between us. We'll sit by a beach in a tumbledown shack and dig worms out of the sand. We'll do anything. Run a pub.'

'I couldn't carry crates.'

'Then I will. Maybe we'll go abroad.'

'There aren't any pubs abroad.'

'Not both!' She laughed. The laugh flew across the mudflats and the bait-diggers stopped and looked towards us. They looked like grave-diggers, suddenly. A shiver ran down my spine. I touched Judy's cheek, for safety and for good luck.

'Sounds good to me, kid,' I said.

We embraced.

'You have three months' notice to work, though, eh?' I said.

She nodded but said nothing.

'Well I'm going to try to sort out this mess in three months. Okay?'

Judy shook her head angrily and walked away, back towards the coast road and reality. A lorry growled over there and clunked its gears. Lights were on in some of the houses overlooking the sea. The real world wanted us back.

Denis was frying bacon when we arrived. Mary and their children were still in bed. A man on the radio was discussing with himself the prospects for a good summer's cricket.

'I've made bacon sandwiches for all of us,' he said. 'And I've got champagne in the fridge for a champagne breakfast.'

'What for?' said Judy suspiciously. Maybe she thought Denis had a mental hook-up with me and knew all about what she'd said on the beach.

'Because your boyfriend here saved my bloody neck this week and I want to celebrate with him, that's why.'

We could hear the girls moving around upstairs.

'What did he do?' Judy said, then immediately, 'No, don't answer. If it's to do with you, Denis, I don't want to know.'

Denis laughed.

Judy laughed too, then she said, 'We don't eat bacon.'

Then we all laughed and we told Denis we'd decided to go into the marriage stakes and we all laughed again and he said, 'Well, drink the bloody champagne!'

So we all drank the bloody champagne, even Mary and her daughters Sharon and Cheryl drank bloody champagne, even if it was only a sip for the girls with their mother frowning. Everyone giggled a lot and had a bloody good champagne time, and though we were all doing it for different reasons the good time lasted right through too many bacon sandwiches and a whole lot of cornflakes with yoghurt on top till I went and spoiled it by asking Denis could he get me introduced to the security characters in a couple of the insurance companies that were due to pay out Duncan and also could he discover for me whether Duncan had any car registered to him at DVLC Swansea.

'Any?'

'Absolutely *any*,' I said.

Then I asked couldn't you get fingerprints off paper with some funny trick with powdered graphite the SOCOs had developed and Denis said he thought you could and he'd find out more. Then Judy threw a moody and insisted we had to go home and then Mary O'Keefe threw a moody about that because she'd gone and bought half a cow or something to roast for lunch. Denis took the future bridegroom to his potting shed to explain the facts of life and also plan a campaign for the next seven days. Mary and Judy stayed indoors and I was pleased to see someone else getting the icy silence treatment.

So much for Southend. After picking up my car we diverted and drove home on the more northerly A127. Getting the car meant taking us to auntie's pub again, and I really didn't feel like it. Change is not made without inconvenience, even from worse to better, and auntie's boozer certainly hadn't got any better. As we left auntie's pub's car park I realised I was gritting my teeth so hard it hurt. And I realised I'd been doing it for quite a while.

16

When I got back to London it seemed dirty, dirtier than usual, and I was tired of it. Any normal man would have taken up Judy's offer like a shot. A normal man would be off planning the wedding and choosing curtains for the new home, wherever that would be. Instead I devoted myself to the task of proving the Metropolitan Police wrong; I devoted myself to freeing a known criminal and gangster from prison on the premise that he was falsely charged, and proving that a dead woman was not dead at all but lurked somewhere in the streets of London, ready to make off with her 'widower' and their ill-gotten cash.

I spent Sunday straightening out my office and my flat. They both looked like a whirlwind had been through them. Though the police are happy to wreck your premises in the course of searching them, they have no real interest in providing a team of cleaning ladies and re-packers to put the joint back into some sort of state.

Judy had agreed that I needed to put things straight, though she made me promise to do it in harness with Maher and O'Keefe and not to take any risks or get involved with Wilkins or any characters like that. When her three months' notice were up we'd pack our bags into a VW camper and spend the rest of the summer finding somewhere sunny where we could put down roots as a married couple. I promised readily, and I kept my promise all through Sunday while I was cleaning my flat, then through most of Sunday evening while I cleaned up my office. It was about nine p.m. my promise went down the tube. I had Chardray upstairs with me, drinking gin. I was explaining that I was getting out of the detective fantasy and getting into the marriage one. He sat on my lumpy sofa and said he thought marriage was a very good idea, which was big of him considering he was losing a regularly-paying tenant and that the reasons we were drinking gin in *my* office was that his wife didn't allow alcohol of any description into their house.

'Is she strict Muslim?' I asked.

He raised his hands and laughed.

'Good heavens no! We're all Christians in my family. No, my wife is just being a strict female . . . I got drunk many years ago and she swore the stuff must never enter the house again.'

'But marriage is good for me?' I said.

Chardray nodded.

'Your Judy is a different cup of tea.'

He giggled at his own joke. There was a light tap at the door and it swung open. Chardray excused himself and little Charlie came in, hiking himself up onto my sofa.

'Hello.'

'Hello, Charlie. What do you want?'

'Uh. . . .' He squeezed his little face with his hands, then dragged them down so that his lower lip pulled clear of his yellow teeth and pink gums for a second. 'There was a misunderstanding here the other day. When I gave orders for you to have that clobber returned I didn't say anything specific about what should happen to your . . . your pal.'

'Zorba?'

'That's right. It was a mistake on my part and I apologise for making it.'

'Don't apologise to me,' I said, 'it wasn't me that ended up nailed to this desk.' I put my finger where the hole in the wood was. Little Charlie inspected the hole, then arched his eyebrows by way of another apology.

'Animals,' he said. He pulled a wad from his jacket and threw it on top of the desk.

'Mr Wilkins, as you know, has been falsely accused. He would like to hire your services to get to the bottom of the matter, since he does not believe the police officers involved will give him a fair crack. He thinks they would like to see him in stir no matter what happens, and that this would be a . . .'

'Shut up, Charlie,' I said. 'I'll get to the bottom of this but it won't be for you or Wilkins. As far as I'm concerned Wilkins could stay in prison for a thousand years. I just want to nail the people that did it.'

'Good.' He leaned back to the sofa. 'Any ideas? Someone who knows him well is stitching the man right up.'

'I've got ideas.' I poured myself another gin and was careful not to offer him one. I picked his wad off my desk and threw it into his lap. 'And they're *my* ideas,' I said loudly. 'They're not for sale to creeps like you.'

He smiled and stuffed the wad back into his jacket. I heard a deep throated cough on my stairs.

'Just my driver,' Charlie said. 'Relax, Alf. Wait down in the motor for me,' he called.

There was the sound of heavy feet descending, then a slam of the outer door.

'Try one of your ideas for who this person might be on me,' Charlie said.

'How about Alison Clark . . . didn't she live with Wilkins?'

Charlie laughed a little strangled laugh, pulled some cigarettes out of his pocket and lit one. He blew smoke through his nostrils, looking like a tiny dragon, laughed again and said, 'No one's going to kill herself just to get at Mr Wilkins. *No one* is that mad.'

I said nothing. Charlie looked at me for a long time.

'Well,' I said, 'you probably know that the shooter was used in a bullion job and that the coppers have drawn a good line on the gun from the robbery to Wilkins.'

'Huh,' he snorted. I gave him the gin. I decided I wanted to pump him a little.

'It's a good line,' I said. 'Good evidence. So I have to presume that Wilkins was once in possession of this shooter. Then his ex-girlfriend is found shot with it. Either Wilkins shot her or someone close to him got the gun away from him knowing that it would frame him . . . who could that be?'

He shook his head.

'Not you, Charlie?' I said.

He laughed. It was an ugly laugh but he was confident.

'Not me. You can take that for granted.'

'Who then?'

He blew smoke through his nostrils again, then hopped down from my sofa and went over to the window. He let the roller blind loose so that it smacked up against itself and the springs rattled. We both watched the lights of cars passing over Canning Town flyover for a while, then Charlie said, 'There's no one close enough who'd have anything to gain by it. There are lots of people who'd do it, given a chance, but none close enough to do it.'

I smiled.

'Except Alison Clark,' I said. 'She could have done it . . . are you with me now?'

Charlie went to the desk, snapped his head back and threw the gin down his throat.

'I'm with you,' he said. 'What about fingerprints and all that? Don't the coppers go into all that?'

'Is it possible about the gun?' I insisted.

He nodded.

'She could have come by that gun, yes . . . she could have known where it was. I'll find out for sure. Er . . . about the Greek. . . .'

'Yes?'

He wrung his hands like a moneylender.

'I've got them round the corner in a car. We've got a hammer and nails down there too, if it'd make you feel any better about being on our side.'

The only reason I didn't bellow, rush at him, pick him up and throw him bodily down the stairs was that I'm not physically capable of it, even with a little worm like Charlie.

'Go away, Charlie, and take your disgusting little mind with you. Let your victims go and tell them they owe me one.'

He shrugged and opened the door.

'I don't suppose your Greek mate would see it like that. He'd probably want to get them back for what they done to him.'

'You're wrong,' I said. 'Zorba's a Christian through and through. He wouldn't *dream* of nailing them too.' Not half he wouldn't. He'd fry them as well.

'You'll keep us in touch with developments, though?'

'Go away, Charlie. Don't call me any more.'

He paused and looked up the stairs at me.
'Go away, Charlie,' I repeated.
He went away.

17

At seven on Monday I was back at Smithfield. The side entrance of the Dog and Duck was thoroughly bolted and barred and George Duncan's gym above looked deserted. If it was still operating as a gym it should have been full of sweating men by seven a.m. I wasn't very surprised to see it empty.

I walked back into the market. Carcasses hung all around me. Piles of cow flesh were being counted by men in white coats and white straw trilbies. A well-dressed young man rolled up the sleeve of his suit jacket, then poked around the innards of a turkey. When he pulled his hand out again the remains of giblets adhered to his fingers. He shook his head and wiped his hand.

I walked out to the front of the market. To the place where Wallace was executed heaven knows how many years before, and where now cars were queuing to enter the underground car park.

In front of one building stood a line of butchers, facing the street. Half a dozen men. They wore chain mail on one arm and hand. In the other hand they carried sharp, pointed knives about a foot long. Before each man hung a sharpening iron, and right along the row of men, at waist height, was a zinc or dull steel counter about three feet deep. The men worked quickly and smoothly. From behind themselves they picked up a pig's head, cut the ears off (one wipe of the knife on the sharpening iron), cut the cheeks out (another wipe of the knife on the sharpening iron) then the tongue and snout, freeing the flesh with the sharp points of the knife. By the time they'd finished there was a pile of pig flesh ready to swipe into the huge grey bucket behind them and a pink clean skull ready to throw into a grey bin by each man's side. I watched them for a while. One man broke off to greet a girl, an office worker. She was pretty and well-dressed and leaned towards him in an exaggerated way, so as not to brush the bloody apron as she kissed him. The man smiled. He was big and brawny with a freckled, shapeless face and receding ginger hair. He held out a brain-spattered arm to take a polystyrene cup from the girl, then waved her a cheery goodbye as she trotted away. I went over.

'Hello.'

'Can I help you?' he said.

'Maybe. I suppose a lot of people watch you here.'

He nodded and sipped his coffee.

I said, 'Is there anywhere else it's done like this, just facing the street?'

The flabby-faced ginger man shook his head.

'I wouldn't know,' he said. 'This is the only place it's done hereabouts.'

'Buy you another coffee?'

He eyed me suspiciously.

'You a copper?'

'Sort of. I'm a detective. The coffee?'

He muttered no, put his polystyrene cup down and slapped his mailed hand against the other.

'Are the knives special?' I said.

'What do you think?'

I sighed. I was going to get no joy here, I could see.

'Where can you get them?'

'Long Lane . . . what's all this about?'

'Just a few questions. I won't keep you long. Listen, do you remember being watched by a blonde . . . late twenties, very attractive, about five-eight or a bit taller and a little under nine stone? She was probably expensively dressed.'

'No.'

I barred his way back to the counter.

'Will you just think about it?'

He pushed me with a bloody hand.

'If you're a detective where's your warrant card? I don't think you're a detective at all. You're just a chancer . . .

we get all kinds of loonies here, but they normally come after the pubs shut at lunchtime. You're the exception. Now sling your hook, exception.'

'I'm a private detective,' I said, 'and a lot depends on whether you. . . .'

The butcher laughed out loud.

'A *private* detective, eh? Pull the other one, John.'

All his colleagues stopped butchering pigs' heads and laughed too, waggling their knives in their hands as they laughed. A man in a white coat and a straw trilby hat looked out of a door behind the men and scowled, calling, 'Now now, let's be having you.'

I limped off, followed by their jeers. The white-coated man came right out onto the pavement and watched me out of sight, legs apart, hands bunched into fists and the fists leant firmly on his hips. Behind me I could hear the butchers calling.

'Oy-oy-oy! He's a dee-tect-tive!'

Not all my investigations are unalloyed successes.

I went back to Duncan's gym. The locks were undone and I went upstairs, hoping I might find him there. I didn't know what I'd say to him, but I'd have to confront him at some stage. The stairs smelled dank and were dark. I pushed the door open. The equipment lay around, dusty and unused. It doesn't take long for decay to set in. A couple of weeks ago the room would have been bustling at this time in the morning. I'd never been there but I'd been in other gyms and I could imagine it. Now the room looked as if nothing had happened there *ever*. It was eerie. I went through the room to the offices and pushed the frosted glass door of the back office wide with my stick.

A little black man sat behind a desk. I imagine the desk had been Duncan's. There were photos all round it like the photos I'd seen in Duncan's house in Essex. The black man had his feet on the desk and a whisky bottle in his hand.

'Who are you?' he said.

'I was just about to ask the same question.'

'My name's Leary. Named after the great man.'

'Jimmy Jenner. Named after my dad. D'you work here?'

'Another copper?'

I shook my head.

'Does he owe you money?' asked Leary. He was a neat, handsome man, very poorly dressed. He had slivers of grey in his jet-black woolly hair and fine, even creases around his eyes and mouth. He could have been aged anywhere between thirty-five and sixty, but I guessed he was in the middle of that range somewhere and had just stayed good-looking as he'd become middle-aged.

'No. Not money. How about you?'

Leary tipped the whisky bottle over a glass and held the neck up to me enquiringly.

'No thanks. It's before eight, you know,' I said, then again, 'How about you?'

Leary giggled. The sound echoed round the dusty office and raced round the gym outside, sounding flat and nasty before it came back to me. When I had spoken, my own voice had had the same quality, I'd noticed. I turned and looked back through the doors. Rays of sunlight filtering through the dust in the room outside. In George Duncan's gym the edge seemed to go off things. There was no brightness, no clarity . . . just slowly settling dust.

'I'm the cleaner,' Leary said.

'Does he owe you money?'

He poured himself another scotch and giggled again.

'Yeah. I'm two weeks' wages out. I'm drinking one of them in the boss's whisky right now.' He held the bottle up again. 'Want a day's pay?'

'No thanks. He was mean with you, eh?'

'He was mean with everyone. He was always mean but when that bitch came along he was meaner and she put him up to it.'

'You didn't like her, Leary?'

'She was a bitch. Nothing but the best for them, everybody else gets to eat dust. Even Tommy Lynch she treated like a bum. I was here. I saw it all. You can believe me.'

He slung back the scotch and poured himself another.

'She was a bitch, okay. She was even having George on . . . playing the field. I saw it all. Nobody notices the cleaner, you know? But I was there, even if I was just a nobody. She used to get all the young black boxer boys to squire her round town, and all the rest of it. She was dirty, I'm telling you. She banged like a lavatory door . . . and about as often.'

'Did Duncan know all this?'

He shrugged and sank deeper into his chair. I noticed a hole in the sole of one of his shoes as he crossed one foot over the other on the desk. His right leg, the one that ended up underneath, stayed perfectly still throughout. Leary leaned forward and looked closely into his glass. Then glared at me.

'Who *are* you?'

'Jimmy Jenner, just like I said.'

'Oh yeah . . . that's right. You was a copper once, weren't you?'

He smiled. He wasn't as drunk as he looked.

'That's right,' I said, 'I was.'

'I thought so. I remember faces well and I read the papers a lot. Well, I don't know what you want it for and if anyone asks me I'll swear I never said it, but that girl was the bird of a real villain called Wilkins before he got onto her evil ways and slung her out. Know what I mean?'

'I know.'

'And then she landed on her feet okay when she got tied up with ol' Georgy Porgy here, because he couldn't believe an attractive young bird wanted him and he went all gooey over her and ended up marrying her. I'm glad she's dead; I know you shouldn't speak evil of them but I'm glad she is. He was a mean payer but okay as a bloke before she turned up and then she turned him mean both ways. I hated her.'

He poured another scotch. He'd be a stretcher case by lunchtime if he kept it up.

'She was even going with that other boxing bloke.'

'Which?'

'Grant. Lenny Grant. Young Tommy Lynch told one of the other fighters in the locker room. I was there but they never took no notice of me. Tommy said to the other guy, "I saw her ladyship and Lenny Grant canoodling in a restaurant up west the other night . . . what d'yer think of that?" and they both laughed. It was common knowledge.'

I only didn't whistle because I forced myself not to. Here

was a reason for George to bump his wife off. Here was a big problem for my substitute theory. Here was plenty. It confused me.

'What do you want from me, Leary?'

He smiled.

'How about a week's wages?'

'How much is that?'

'A score.'

I put two ten-pound notes on the desk. Did Duncan really only pay twenty pounds per week?

'How do you manage?' I said. 'How do you pay your rent and eat?'

Leary eased his legs off the table. He stood, heavily favouring the right, which was the one with no hole in the shoe.

'I used to be a sailor,' he said, 'many years ago. Then I had an accident and lost my leg, so I've got the old green card and a disability pension.'

I laughed loud and long. We both walked our funny walks through the gymnasium. I was still laughing. I didn't care about any dusty rooms or bad magic and I didn't think any more about there being no edge on things. Leary just made me laugh.

'Listen,' I said, 'where's Long Lane?'

'Two streets over, Jimmy Jenner. I'll see you.'

'You may do that, Leary. You may.'

And I went downstairs chuckling still. I could hear drunken Leary laughing upstairs, too.

18

That Monday was a busy day for me. By nine thirty I was in Denis O'Keefe's temporary office with the Murder Squad. The operation had been wound down to about half its original size, which wasn't very surprising. There wasn't an infinity of leads and once the original workload of statement-taking was over the job was one of perseverance rather than manpower. It's no good keeping a load of men and women locked up somewhere making passes at each other when they could go back on the street and do a job of work.

I kept the knife I bought in Long Lane hidden till Denis and me were alone together. Denis blanched when I threw it on his desk.

'What's that for?'

'Try it on your forensic people for a comparison with the cuts on that cadaver.'

He picked it up as if it was explosive, between finger and thumb.

'Where d'you get it, Jimmy?'

'From a shop. It's a representative of the genus 'butcher's knife'. As far as I know it's done nothing so far in its life except be wrapped in waxed paper.'

Denis took the knife out of the paper and found a minion to charge with the task of getting it to the forensic lab without chopping any fingers off. Then we settled down with a DC I'd never met before (and whose breath smelled so bad I hope we never meet again) to make up one of those daft identikit pictures that look at once like no member of the human race and all of them – insofar as all members of the human race have eyes and ears and stuff like that. Usually.

It took all morning and about a hundred cups of coffee. We ended up with a picture that, given the circumstances, wasn't unlike the girl I'd driven from Saffron to London. The DC and Denis went out and left me with the identikit for ten minutes and by the time they came back (with yet another cup of coffee each and one for me, too) I'd convinced myself that we'd made a fair likeness.

'What do you think, Denis?'

He shook his head.

'It's the same girl.'

'Nah.' I was sure.

Denis threw a snapshot of Alison Duncan on the desktop. It was a small version of the big picture I'd seen with Maher in the incident room.

'It's the same girl,' he repeated.

I shook my head. The DC with the smelly breath picked up the photograph and my identikit job, looking from one to the other.

'No doubt about it,' he said. 'It's the same girl.'

I slammed my fist on the desk. 'It's not.'

The DC left and Denis came over all fatherly and arm-round-the-shoulders.

'I've got us a lunch-date,' he said. 'You'll enjoy it. It'll do you good.'

'I want to go to Smithfield first and I want you to come with me.'

'We'll be late for the lunch.'

'Phone them, Denis. Display some of that charm of yours. Tell them you hate soup. Anything.'

He shook his head but he phoned our lunch-date anyway. I slipped the snapshot of Alison and the identikit picture into a brown envelope old smelly-breath had left for that purpose, then we went in search of Brian Borden, who was providing the wheels.

By twelve forty-five we were in Smithfield again and I was asking the butcher to look at my pictures. The butcher said something very rude. Brian Borden didn't take kindly to it, and he seemed to think it was a matter of honour not to show the man his warrant card. As if anyone should doubt Brian's word! I was a bit apprehensive about getting heavy with all these wicked-looking knives lying around but Brian would have none of it. He grabbed ginger-bonce's apron and shirt front all in one hand and said, 'We're in a bit of a hurry. Would you please co-operate,' or words to that effect. When the butcher didn't look lively Brian screwed the apron and shirt front up in his hand like you would a paper hanky . . . only the butcher was still inside this paper hanky. His face went red and his freckles stayed the same colour, a sort of ginger brown. He looked as if he had some horrible disease.

'Give me the picture,' said Brian. I gave it to him.

'Do you recognise this person?'

The butcher nodded. Brian let him go. He showed the picture to the other butchers. One other man recognised the photograph of Alison, too. He said. 'She came here and watched us work one day. She asked if she could have a go but old misery-boots in the office was around so I couldn't let her. She was very attractive, though. You'd remember her.'

'Good,' smiled Brian. The man seemed visibly relieved he'd been spared the same treatment as Ginger.

'How about this one?' I pulled my identikit effort from the big brown envelope.

'It's the same girl, sir,' said Ginger. He let the corners of his mouth rise into a smile, then stopped it as he caught Brian Borden's mad eyes.

'Sure?' I said.

He nodded.

'Positive . . . would you gentleman like a nice bit of pork to take away? I'm sure I can fix it with our tally clerk if you want.'

One look along the bloodstained metal counter, one glance at the contents of the grey buckets, convinced the other two they didn't want any free pork, thanks all the same. For myself, I'd come to a decision on the matter before eight o'clock that morning. I was a vegetarian. All I needed was a green 2CV, a shapeless jumper and a 'Nuclear

Power No Thanks' sticker and I could get into just about any party I fancied in Hackney or Islington. Lucky me.

The next stop was carried out with a little less tension on all sides, which was a relief to me at least. We went to the butcher's sundries suppliers where I'd bought my knife. The man there was very polite and very helpful. He just gave all the wrong answers.

'Hello, sir. Anything wrong?'

'No,' I said, 'everything's fine.'

The counter assistant was a narrow, dark-suited man with a dark face and deep-set eyes. He had features about as long as an undertaker's and a nose as sharp as one of his knives. I pulled my photograph out.

'These men are police officers,' I said, 'and we'd like you to take a look at this.'

He picked the picture up.

'Oh *yes* . . . that's poor Mrs Duncan. Her husband is a boxing manager.' He looked at me quickly. 'Is this anything to do with her . . . ?'

'Yes, it's to do with her death. Did she ever buy a knife like the one I bought this morning?'

He pursed his lips.

'I couldn't say, sir. She bought lots of butchery equipment here for her kitchen. We sell the very highest quality. . . .'

'I'm sure you do,' I said, 'but that *particular* knife?'

The same pursing of the lips. If he'd breathed in deeply through his nose he would have got a lungful of his own lip.

'Maybe. I can't say.'

'Don't you keep records?' I said. 'It's important.'

'Not that sort of record, sir, no.'

'Recognise her?'

I'd pulled the identikit picture out too. He smiled.

'It's the same lady, sir.'

'Are you sure? *Look*.'

The counter assistant looked closely at the picture, though I had the impression he did it just to placate me.

'Definite. It's the same lady.'

142

19

Our lunch-date had waited for us, which considering who
they were was a big deal. We left Brian Borden and the
wheels in Smithfield. Denis wanted him to take statements
from the counter assistant and the two butchers who'd
recognised Alison Duncan. As we walked back to St Bartho-
lomew's Hospital to find a cab I saw a small, perky looking
female traffic warden putting a parking ticket on Brian's
official Ford Cortina. There'd be some fun when he found
that.

We took a cab to the city, then went half a mile in the
air to the most luxurious office I've ever been in. We were
greeted by two silver haired men in grey suits called Tinner
and Lockwood. I never did work out which was which. They
were officials of the London and Home Counties General
Mutual Insurance Company, which is enough name for three
ordinary organisations. Lockwood and Tinner worked in an
office which had leather everything, deep-pile carpets and
wall-to-wall pretty girl assistants. Panoramic windows
looked out over London, and the glass was darkened a little
so that nobody got sunstroke or tired eyes or anything. The
place was full of phones that rang with a muted, polite
burbling sound and they never rang more than once before
a pretty girl reached out and answered in hushed tones,
'Mister Tinner's office' or 'Mister Lockwood's office',
depending which phone she was answering.

Lockwood or Tinner poured us a couple of drinks while
I peered out of one of the windows. It was a long way down.
The office seemed like it was the centre of England, at least
of London. All roads led to it. Red buses chugged along

the streets towards us with the sole purpose of depositing more workers at the foot of the marbled building.

'Good view, eh?' said one of our hosts.

'It's okay.'

He was a blue-eyed dream of a man who would be everybody's perfect Grandaddy at the weekend when he wore his yellow cardy with the leather buttons. I looked across at his companion. The man was a clone of my one.

'Shall we go in?' said my companion. We went through satin-polished oak doors and sat at a table groaning under the weight of a lunch big enough for fifty. Just the four of us ate.

'Denis tells us you're an investigator,' said my companion. I said 'yes' . . . I mean what else is there to call it? The man went on, talking in hushed and reverential tones about the London and the Home Counties General Mutual Insurance Company. Another pretty girl drifted in and out with dishes, empty or full depending on which way she was going. She managed to clear away plenty of unused knives and forks too. I looked over at Denis. Either Tinner or Lockwood was talking to him in reverential tones too, just like my one, and Denis was leaning forward and hanging on the man's every word. It made me sick just to watch him crawling to these creeps.

Suddenly I heard my man saying, 'Directly and through subsidiaries we're exposed to the tune of a hundred and seventy-five.'

'A hundred and seventy-five whats?' I said.

His blue lips tightened and a crumb of cottage cheese stuck to them. A silver-grey eyebrow arched.

'Thousand, Mr Jenner. Directly and through subsidiaries we're exposed in the Duncan affair to the tune of a hundred and seventy-five thousand pounds. Denis says you have a theory on the matter that might save us all of that money. I can assure you we'd be very grateful if you could help us save the money. I'm sure other insurers will feel the same way. We appear to be about a month from having to. . . .'

'Shell out?' I offered. 'Why worry? A hundred and seventy-five grand must be peanuts to an organisation like this.'

He shook his head. The crumb of cottage cheese fell to

his deeply cleft chin while he dabbed at the lip where it had been with a linen napkin. I wanted to laugh at him but I couldn't let myself – yet. I wanted to know what he wanted.

'I wouldn't put it like that. We will always pay a legitimate claim. As for the money . . . well, it is a small sum compared with the assets of this organisation. But it wouldn't be a small sum if you save it for us. We'd be *very* grateful. We have shareholders, you know, and they expect us to be frugal with their money and only meet proper claims.'

Just then a pretty waitress cruised in and offered him two bottles of wine that were nearly as old as she was. He didn't even blink.

'We have a lot of work we could offer a trustworthy investigator here, Mister Jenner,' he said.

I shook my head.

'You've got the wrong man. I'm getting out. This is Jenner's last case.'

The blue lips went into a line again and the eyebrow arched again and this time the cottage cheese dropped to his stiff collar. I smiled politely and said, 'You've got lunch on your collar, mate.'

I enjoyed that.

In the lift going down to the street Denis sighed and loosened his collar. 'Well, I've got it but it's no damn thanks to you. . . . "You've got lunch on your collar, mate" indeed. I'm going to have to spend my life working with these blokes, Jim. You should try to be a bit fairer to me if no one else.'

He brandished an envelope very much like the one I was holding.

'So what's that?'

'It's the Duncans' proposal form. And I've got a finger-print officer going there this afternoon to take the dabs of anyone who might have handled it.'

'And then?'

'And then they'll give the proposal form the alcohol and powdered graphite and abracadabras and whatever else they do to them and see what's what by way of prints on the form. And then they'll see if there's a set of female prints that don't fit. And if there is *then* your theory becomes something resembling a runner.'

My stomach settled and the doors opened silently. More light softened by bronze-tinted glass flooded around us and an ancient job's-worth in a commissionaire's uniform took our lapel pins off us and made us sign out.

The street was noisy and boisterous and welcoming and I was glad to be in it: fumes, dust, dirt and all.

'Being a detective means doing lots of long, slow, tedious work,' said Denis. 'You have to engage your brain and those of everyone around you. You have to be intelligent and scientific, all at once.'

He paused to burp, then asked, 'How does your first taster of real detective work feel, then?'

I looked closely into his face to make sure he meant it, then walked away without another word.

20

I spent the afternoon in the bath at home. About four Gal rang and said he was just about to put Zorba on a plane for Cyprus. Zorba was getting out. Who could blame him? He'd got away with a little nest egg and a few contusions. Getting out while he was in front made sense. I could hear all the ding-dong-paging-Mr-Slobberchops-from-Air-France-flight-201 announcements in the background and Zorba came on the line to mutter a fond farewell, hampered only by the fact that his face was still swollen up and his jaw wired so he couldn't actually *say* anything. I said, 'Goodbye, Zorba, hope it works out, give my love to your wife,' and he said, 'Ugh.' I wasn't too upset because it resembled many of our conversations. I said a lot and he said ugh.

About half-four Maher phoned to say that the knife I'd brought in was a 'close mechanical fit' for the weapon that had inflicted the wounds on the body they'd found under the arch. That's forensic-speak for 'the same article'.

'Thanks a lot, James. I'm not sure where it gets us but that's a good piece of detective work by you,' he said.

'What about the stuff O'Keefe brought in?'

'That'll take a couple of days. Come and have a chat with me tomorrow.'

'Okay.'

I made a big pot of tea and tipped it into a Thermos. I wanted to spend an evening thinking and I didn't want to spend it getting up and down to deal with kettles. Then I put on some cotton pyjamas and a terry dressing gown, went into the living room and tipped a huge jigsaw on the table there. The box said it was a view of Hamburg. It could have been anywhere as far as I could see. I suppose I didn't care.

About seven Judy rang.

'Are you busy?'

'A bit. Why?'

'I just wanted to talk, Jimmy, that's all. I've put my papers in and arranged terminal leave – sounds horrible, doesn't it? – and I have to work another five weeks. Then we're fancy free.'

'Great,' I said.

'And I've got the forms.'

'What forms?'

'For the registry office. We said yesterday I'd get them. Are you okay?'

'I'm okay, Judy. I'm a bit preoccupied. That's all.'

'With Duncan?'

'Yes.'

I stared at a jigsaw piece that looked like a crane, only I couldn't work out which way up it should be. What good's a jigsaw you can't do?

'Will it be all done by the time we're ready to pack up and go?'

I crushed the cardboard jigsaw piece in my hand. I could hear that old guardedness in her voice. Then I knew why we'd never done this before. Judy was protecting herself from me.

'Judy, we'll leave as soon as things are ready whether I've finished with this thing or not.'

'Good. Bye, Jimmy.'

'Bye.'

I straightened the jigsaw piece out, then turned the crane round and round in my hand. It still wouldn't go anywhere. If what Leary the cleaner had told me was true George Duncan would have a good motive for killing his wife apart from collecting on the insurance. In fact anyone who had ever met her seemed to have a good motive for killing her. Maybe it was true the way Duncan told it and he hadn't had anything to do with the business. Maybe that was true, but if it was I couldn't account for his strange behaviour in hiring me to protect her and I couldn't account for the weird way they behaved together when he was sending her off.

148

Also George had a really good motive – he needed the money. The only thing he didn't have was opportunity. Grant, as far as I knew, had an opportunity and I suppose what Leary told me just might have given him a jealousy motive. I wrote a note to myself to check Grant's whereabouts for the night of the murder. His motive didn't look half as strong as George Duncan's though.

I put two bits of sky in my puzzle, then the crane went in. Then I put another bit of sky and looked round for another bit of crane. Outside some kids were arguing shrilly about the ownership of something. A bike, a cart, a pair of roller skates . . . something.

Why cut the face off if not to fool people as to who the body was? It didn't make sense. There were missing pieces.

I rang Denis.

'Hello, prima donna.'

'Don't be like that. How would *you* feel if I lectured *you*?'

He didn't answer.

'Denis,' I went on. 'Did you do that DVLC check to see if Duncan owned any cars?'

'Yes. Nothing there, I'm afraid. He does own a Jag just like the one you drove, but it was nicked a couple of months back. It doesn't have any bearing on this business at all.

'Jim? . . . Jimmy?' Denis called. My throat tightened.

'Has it been found?'

'No. Why?'

'Because I want a fingerprint from an Alison Duncan who isn't in the mortuary, and I want to confirm it. If I can get a fingerprint from the insurance proposal form and a matching one from somewhere on George Duncan's Jag I've got her.'

'No, James, you haven't got her. You've got a very circumstantial case for the person who signed the insurance form being in George Duncan's motor at some stage. But you won't have another Alison Duncan if such a person exists, until you've got her in your hand or until you can give the body we have a different identity. I'll put the Jag in the Police Gazette as a 'special notice' and we'll hope to turn it up. I'll gee up the forensic lot about the magic they're working on the insurance form, too.'

'I suppose that if I got the fingerprints, even if we didn't have her in custody, your pals Tinner and Lockwood would be saved a payout?'

'I should think that's very likely, Jimmy. You'd be likely to make quite a big of dough.'

'I've already got quite a bit of dough, Denis.'

'Oh yeah.'

I gave up drinking tea and I gave up playing jigsaws. I sat on the sofa drinking scotch and watching people being horrid to each other on TV. It's all they ever seem to do on TV. I couldn't work out where Lenny Grant fitted, if at all.

I rang Lenny Grant's office next morning at nine.

'He can't speak with you, sir. He's in Florida.'

'Give me the number.'

I rang Florida. Eventually I got a tired voice on the end of a hotel switchboard.

'Grant, please,' I said. 'I don't know the room.'

'Hold, please.'

A few seconds later he was on the line. He had a voice that had been trained out of being a cockney, though he still had plenty of cockney inflections. His voice was deep and confident-sounding.

'Grant.'

'Hallo, Mr Grant. My name's Jenner. You don't know me but I know one of your fighters. Tommy Lynch.'

'Yes?'

'Well, I have to talk to you, Mr Grant.'

'Talk.'

'I'd rather not do it over the phone.'

'I'm here for another five weeks, Jenner. Why don't you come round?'

'I'm in England,' I said, 'so coming round won't work, I'm afraid.'

'Then it'll have to be the phone. What about Lynch?'

I cleared my throat.

'Nothing about Lynch. I just said that I knew him by way of introduction. I'm a private detective, Mr Grant, and I was hired to look after a young woman you may know, a woman called Alison May Clark.'

'Don't give me the runaround, Jenner. It's very early here.' He groaned. 'Four thirty a.m. my clock says.'

'Okay. I'll give it to you straight. Alison Clark's married name was Alison Duncan, and I have reason to believe you had an intimate relationship with her before she died. I want to talk to you about that relationship.'

'Not on the phone, you don't. See me when I come back to England.' He hung up. I rang the hotel in Florida again.

'Grant, please.'

'I'm sorry, that line's busy. Would you like to hold?'

'No. Do you know where he's calling?'

'I'm sorry, sir. That's private information. Would you like to hold?'

This time *I* hung up.

21

Grant checked out. The knowledge that he would be covered settled upon me like a great weight even as I did the checking. He'd spent the night 'Alison' was murdered with some immaculately respectable friends . . . in fact the dodgiest thing about the whole business was the way everyone (except Wilkins and myself, of course) had a watertight alibi. As far as I was concerned that meant Wilkins was the only one who definitely hadn't done it – apart from me. Unfortunately the DPP didn't agree and when the file went over to the legal boys Wilkins' arraignment was a foregone conclusion. He was left to rot in Brixton Gaol while the legal people got their act together. Alison's body was interred at Kensal Green cemetery, having had all the possible evidence extracted from it and having been released by the coroner. The murder squad was reduced to DS Robson and some uniformed constable while the rest of the circus moved on to a series of race attacks in Camden. *Camden*, for heaven's sake . . . I mean, who's an indigenous Camdener? The race attacks culminated in a murder, all the murder experts went to Camden and the trail on Alison May Duncan's murder went cold.

I shouldn't have been surprised and I shouldn't have been angry but I was both. The days slipped past, became weeks. After Maher did a lot of arm-twisting some Deputy-type character went round to the hotel Grant was staying in in Miami, Fla. and established that the number Lenny Grant had called directly after I called him was his mother's house in Welling, South London. Needless to say, the mother was a little old lady who knew nothing about anything.

I sold my flat and moved in with Judy. We were going to keep her place on as a base after we were married, though the plan was we should buy a VW camper and spend the late summer and autumn wandering around Europe looking for somewhere warm and pleasant to settle. Judy's flat was a sort of backstop, in case all else failed. I gave up the office with Chardray and devoted myself more or less full-time to playing pool with Gal. Then he got a job in a bakery and I was back on the science-fiction novels and jigsaws. I bought a lot of maps and felt like I'd learned them off by heart. Sometimes I played with the idea of having a verbal 'showdown at the okay corral' with George Duncan but I never did it. Denis thought he'd talked me out of it but really I didn't need much talking. There's no point in big dramatic arguments unless you can win them, and I suppose I still dreamed of a day when Maher would slip the cuffs on dear old George.

They did find 'foreign' fingerprints underneath Alison's signature on their joint insurance proposal form, but on its own it didn't count for much. Several other documents were scrutinised but they didn't give up any secrets. No more leads came from South Africa. No women of the right type were reported missing since the night of the murder. George Duncan's stolen Jaguar stayed stolen. Eventually the insurance companies paid him out and he put his big house in Saffron on the market. Robson had his phone tapped and had him followed for a few days at my insistence but we drew a blank. He even had the South African coppers turn over Alison's brother, David, but there was no sign of her there, either. Eventually everyone except me became convinced that Alison May Duncan (née Clark) was in a hole in Kensal Green, albeit minus her mush.

It was the first week of August before we had a break, and even then we had to make it. Duncan's car was dragged out of five fathoms of Loch Rannoch. We were lucky – it was the shallowest part of the Loch. The car had been used months before in a bank hold-up in Glasgow and was carrying false plates. The Scottish police traced it through the engine number, giving the lie to the idea that they're all gamekeepers and traffic wardens. Maher took me up to see it in a boatshed. The car was a mess.

'There's the end of the line for your theory, James,' Maher said.

He was right, too. What wasn't mud was rotten. What wasn't rotten was rusty. It was difficult to believe a car could get into such a state in three months.

'No fingerprints?' I asked hopefully.

Maher shook his head.

'Nothing.'

'Who else has seen it?' I said.

'No one. Just a load of Jock coppers.' He squinted at me. 'Do you have an idea?'

'I was wondering just how quiet we could keep it,' I said.

Outside the rain was belting down, a typical Scottish summer's afternoon. We stood with the boatman, getting soaked while he locked up good and proper, then Maher gave him thirty quid to buy an even better lock for his shed on condition that he kept his mouth shut about the car for a couple of days. Rainwater streamed down our faces as we swore the boatman to silence. He bit his lip and glared at Maher's three damp tenners in his palm for an age before agreeing. Maybe Scottish tenners look different. I've never seen one so I wouldn't know.

'I've never been here before,' I said, trying to be friendly. 'Lovely looking place. Pity about the rain.'

We were squelching back to our car. The boatman said, 'It keeps the midges down.'

We cooked up a good plot driving back to London. The plan was to drop hints at people George Duncan knew. The hints would be to the effect that we'd matched a print from the Jag with a print from their insurance application form. Harry Whitlock would do. Robson was given the job of pulling him in.

Coincidentally, the night Robson collared Harry Whitlock was the night of Tommy Lynch's World Championship fight in Miami. There were plenty of interviews with him and

Lenny Grant; plenty of pictures in newspapers and on telly. The fight was on the box live. Maher and me sat in the CID room at Peter Street nick, watching a portable telly while we waited. Lynch got slaughtered. We did a little better.

'Just a few questions, Harry. I think you know Mr Jenner here.'

Harry nodded. His brow was furrowed, his bottom lip stuck out. Harry was telling the world he was unhappy.

'I will help in any way that I am able,' he said in a manner which gave me to believe he had been practising it for half an hour. 'But you must understand, sir, that I know very little about this sad affair. Mister Duncan has left the fight game and I am no longer in his employ.'

'Okay, Harry. Cut the speech,' said Maher. 'I have to ask you a few personal questions about your ex-boss.'

Harry stared at the window before him. Maher presumed that meant he would answer and went on.

'It's to do with the Jaguar car he had stolen . . . you remember that?'

Harry nodded. He remembered the stolen Jaguar.

'Well, we've found it.'

'Good,' said Harry. 'Mister Duncan will be *well* pleased.' Maher smiled.

'But I have a problem with it, Harry. You see, the Jag is covered in a woman's fingerprints. The fingerprints are the same as those we took off an insurance proposal form. They're the same as some prints we took off the inside of the lift to their flat in the Barbican.'

Harry concentrated. The brow and the jutting lower lip nearly met. Harry Whitlock concentrating was a pitiful sight.

'Ye-es.'

'Here's my problem, Harry. It would be reasonable to presume that the fingerprints of the woman who'd had her hands all over George Duncan's car and had put her fingerprints all over their insurance proposal form and had ridden in the lift to their flat was none other than Mrs Alison Duncan. That would be reasonable don't you think?'

'Yes.' Harry was sure about that one.

'But Harry, the prints are *not* those of the woman six feet under in Kensal Green . . . cop my drift? The woman pushing up daisies does not appear to be his wife. I need

155

to know from you whether Duncan had any . . . er, any extra-*marital* relationships.' I do believe Maher was embarrassed.

Harry looked blank.

'Birds. Did he have any birds, Harry?' I said. Maher smiled at me in an indulgent way, but I got the hint. Don't interfere.

'No. He never had no birds. He was always very faithful.'

They went on like this for a while, till DCS Maher had the idea firmly planted in Harry's little mind that we had good forensic evidence that the dead woman wasn't Alison. Then Maher let him go. We didn't think Harry was in on it. We just wanted the message got to Duncan.

'Will you have him followed?' I asked.

'No.' Maher's eyes were gleaming. 'I don't need to. I've got some men on observation outside Duncan's house with cameras. I've got his and Harry's phones both tapped. All we have to do is relax. Would you like to have supper with me?'

'Why not?' I said. Why not indeed . . . we had something to celebrate – nearly. We'd sold thick Harry Whitlock a load of lies . . . clever us.

The next day the papers were full of Tommy Lynch's battered face. He'd been outclassed and outpunched by his American opponent. Tommy said, 'I'll be back,' but according to a little paragraph at the bottom of a story in the *Sun* Lenny Grant wouldn't. He was retiring from the fight game. Wouldn't it be nice to retire before you're forty? I had to laugh at myself, because that's exactly what Judy and me were about to do . . . retire to the sun. I lay abed with Judy reading the papers and feeling clever.

My phone went at eleven.

'Mister Jenner?'

'Yes.'

'Detective Sergeant Robson here. Mister Maher asked me to call you. We have a problem. Duncan's dead.'

'Where's Maher?' I said.

'The Barbican.'

'I'll see him there.'

George Duncan had been waiting outside his bank at nine thirty. He'd emptied his accounts, insurance money, money from the sale of the house in Saffron Walden, the lot. Over four hundred thousand. He'd been covered by police all the way, photographed at every stage. Then he went home, still covered every step of the way by police. No one could work out how he'd managed to shoot himself and no one heard it, but he'd done it. The money had disappeared too.

'The phone?' I asked Maher.

He nodded. A Scenes of Crime Officer was flashing camera lights over the body. The balcony leading into Duncan's house had been taped off, even some parts of the flat were taped off.

'The money?' I asked.

Maher raised an eyebrow. His face was as grey as his hair, pasty. Like a dirty sheet.

'No money anywhere. Harry phoned him from a box ten minutes after he left us last night.'

'Was it Harry?'

'No. He's too dim to be anything other than innocent.' He walked out onto the balcony. I followed. We stood on the spot where I'd thrown Duncan's cut-glass tumbler from all those weeks before. It seemed like a lifetime ago. It was several. 'I'd better come up with a good explanation of this, James,' Maher said.

Well, we didn't think up anything there and then. But I remembered the retiring Lenny Grant in Florida. And I told Maher about my conversation with Leary in Duncan's gym. I can't say he was very happy about me holding out on him, and he simply refused to follow the logic of my argument about how knowing there was another motive for murder would have made him go cold on my substitute woman theory once and for all. He left in bad humour and he wouldn't speak to me, but he had Denis O'Keefe call me in the next day.

22

My new wife wasn't too pleased about me disappearing up
to Scotland with Maher. She didn't like me closeting myself
with Maher when I should have been closeting myself with
her. She was *most* displeased about me being involved with
the events around George Duncan's death. But she took
Denis's phone call the worst of the lot. He rang at a quarter
past four.

That's quarter past four in the a.m.

'Huh,' Judy said when the phone rang. She said 'huh'
when she answered it, too. Then she said, 'No.'

Then she said, 'No.' Again.

Then there was a silence. Then she said, 'Denis, you pig,
I've been married for less than a week. Now get off my
sodding phone and leave my husband alone.'

Then she put the phone down. When it rang again I
answered.

'Thank God it's you. I was getting my head bitten off
there,' Denis said. 'Present yourself in Peter Street nick, as
soon as. We've got something to show you, my son.'

Peter Street police station smelled of old cabbage and was
full of the sound of billiard cues and the World Service
Radio. Neon lights flickered in the public areas. That's how
police stations always are at night. Denis was waiting behind
the desk for me. He looked like the cat that had got the
cream.

'Come in . . . come in.'

I followed him up two flights of stairs and along a corridor

158

painted the vilest green imaginable. Then we went into a darkened room. I could make out the shapes of half a dozen men in chairs.

'Take a seat, James,' came Maher's voice. 'Look at this.'

A beam split the darkness. A bright, blue-white light that burned straight into my eyes. I walked towards it, stumbled against a chair and then turned to look at the wall behind me.

'It's a photo taken by one of our obbo blokes outside the Barbican,' said Maher.

The photograph was of the back of a delivery girl. It was a black-and-white photograph, but from the tone of it the delivery girl seemed to be wearing a green-nylon shopgirl's smock and a green pillbox hat to go with it. She was carrying a large bunch of flowers.

There was a mechanical clatter, then darkness, then a picture of the girl from the front. Her face was a little smudged, but she was young – under thirty – slim, and looked as if she might be attractive once the features were focussed.

'This is the same girl leaving, James. It's the best picture we've got.'

'And?' I said.

'My men spent yesterday afternoon and evening interviewing every person in those flats, establishing exactly who went in and out.'

The mechanical clatter again, and we were back with the first picture.

'No one had any flowers delivered. No one mentioned any flower girl. I sent them back to drag everyone out of bed and ask again . . . but the same. No flowers. Then we turned the rubbish chutes out. You might smell some of my colleagues here.'

There was a polite giggle from Maher's underlings. The boss had made a joke.

'And we found a large bunch of flowers and a cushion with a bullet hole in it.'

Again the mechanical clatter, again the second photo.

'I may be wrong, James, but I think we're looking at a photograph of Alison May Duncan. George is dead, the money's gone, the little bird has flown the nest. I've warned the ports and airports. We'll pick her up.'

'And Wilkins?' I said.

Maher's voice was closer to me now, and I turned and made out his figure in the darkness.

'We'll have him released in a couple of days. Maybe even today. We'll get her, James.'

Then they applauded me and all told me what a loss I'd been to the service. All this was with the lights on. There was hardly a dry eye in the house. Then everyone slapped my back and told me how pleased they were I'd persisted. Then they all assured me they'd catch her.

They didn't, of course.

The last I saw of Alison May Duncan (née Clark) was the headstone above her grave in Kensal Green. She was a lovely girl. I wondered who the hell she was, how they'd ensnared her. I wondered where the real Alison had killed her. And the post-mortem report . . . somewhere should be a young child who was missing her. *Why* did no one miss her?

We went to Kensal Green on what was my way out of London for the last time. I'd sworn privately to myself that I'd never come back. Judy thought it was stupid and morbid to want to go and visit this grave with the wrong body in it, but she didn't resist when I made a fuss about it. She held my arm as we walked down the long tarmacadamed path to the graveside through the thousands of other graves, and she even let me use her handkerchief when we got there. It was a sunny day. I couldn't even pass off my emotions as rain on my face or something. I just had to stand over this grave with the wrong name on it and wonder and regret my own thickheadedness that night in May.

Well, that's how it was that day I left London. We drove back across town and I made a point of going via Archway, which was out of our way. I wanted to say goodbye. I stopped the VW under Suicide Bridge, as the locals call it, and looked over the dusty city. It looked mean and dirty and ugly and I was glad I wouldn't go there any more. That's how I felt.

23

'Today is the first of August 1985. Our travels have made us a little wiser but I think that maybe there's more than one type of wise.'

I wrote this in a little journal I keep by my bed. The journal's secret not because I keep it secret but because my wife Judy doesn't pry. I wrote these facts in the journal while sitting on a chair on my balcony drinking beer. It's seven a.m. and I shouldn't be drinking beer. My beer is cold. So's my chair. The sun doesn't hit the balcony until noon because there's an old building opposite that must have been all kinds of things in its time but now is a café and the café has a tall stuccoed front which hides my balcony from morning sunlight, just as the café is in its turn hidden from morning sunlight by a garage behind, and just as my house and bar hide the house behind me from morning sunlight. The sun arrives at noon and by half-twelve everyone wishes it didn't come till three or four in the p.m. But for the morning we all resent the fact that our balconies are looked out over by the next house.

I sit on my balcony and write. Above me, on the lush green hill that overlooks our town, I can see the baking white concrete walls of the rich villas that rich Englishmen and Germans live in. I should write 'rich English and German criminals', for our little town has its share of spectacular north European bankrupts and similar. They live within their white concrete walls and only deign to speak to you over their wallmounted loudspeakers—'Hello, hello, who's calling?'—so that you have to stand in the sun with your straw hat on your head and sweat trickling down your shirt and just wait like the pleb you are until the great man within slips out of his clear-blue-water swimming pool and waves at the maid to let you in. I go to a lot of these houses because I have cooled English beer in the cellar of my bar, Worthington 'E' and Guinness and Bass and several others, and when the guy who normally delivers to the white concrete houses for me gets a breakdown in his van or his mother gets sick or he needs to go to a soccer match or a bullfight, I go. I don't like doing the deliveries because the people in the white concrete houses up the hill treat you as if you're a night-soil carrier or something, just because they've got enormous houses and servants and sun-tanned floozies and Mercedes air-conditioned cars while you, of course, only have a beat-up SEAT and you're delivering their beer. I'd prefer to have my Spanish delivery man go and face all that. That's the economic bargain, that's what it does to you. It gives you the ability to make someone else do the dirty job.

I sit on my balcony and nod my head because I'm tired, and I write in my book when I'm not nodding. Long blue shadows are cast on the roofs around me, then red splashes of pantiles run up the sides of gables. The walls exposed to the sun are an angry, stark white.

I hear a voice singing softly. Below me in the street a kid in a waiter's uniform is wiping marbled table tops. It's him singing some ghastly Spanish pop song. Inside the café early morning workers are taking breakfast in the yellow of the electric-lit room. Sometimes I can hear their voices raised. I'll never speak Spanish well enough, though, to latch onto their conversations.

I could hear the buzz of a Japanese motor-cycle back in the town somewhere and the burble of the BBC World Service coming from my bedroom, two doors away from this balcony.

I was thinking about my wife, Judy. She's coming here from England today. She doesn't like to fly so she gets the ferry to Santander, then drives. I was thinking that she'd be waking up now in some roadside hotel. When we go away together we make a real trip, finding special places to stay and planning sights to visit. Doing it alone, though, she'll just drive as straight as a die across Spain, through the green and mountainous Basque country, then across the plains of Old Castile, always heading south. If she'd put her foot down she'd have made Madrid last night and stayed there.

We live in Cristo de Limpias, a small town on the southeast coast. If there weren't two headlands in between you'd be able to see Málaga ten miles or so to the north. I don't know why you'd want to see Málaga and neither does anyone else in Cristo, but if you did you'd have to go into the headland flattening business. Due south is the way Judy's heading, or as near due south as dammit. And it's one full day's drive from Madrid.

I was thinking Judy would be getting up about now and having some rock hard cylinder of Spanish bread offered to her for breakfast. She'd wash and go down to our Citroën. She'd throw her bag in the back and wipe the dust off the windscreen. With any luck she'd think about me a little.

I should leave her a note but I just don't know what to say. What should I say? I don't know.

24

I've been here in Cristo de Limpias since 1983. I run a bar. The bar's halfway to running me, really. In the two-and-a-bit years I've been here I've gone back to England only twice. I haven't made that many trips in Spain, even. How did I come here? Partly by coincidence, partly by choice.

Judy and me left London in the late summer of 1982. I was mentally exhausted by the Duncan case, far more than I ever thought while I was in London. It was only after a few weeks pottering round France in our VW camper that I started to relax a bit, and it was then I realised what a strain the whole business had been. I blamed myself. I believed that I'd been stupid when I'd parted company with that poor girl in the Barbican. I had *known* something was wrong. I knew from the first moment Duncan asked me to come and see him. I knew from the first time I clapped eyes on that girl in his house in Saffron Walden. I abandoned her because I'd thought she was working some scam with George Duncan and I didn't want to get involved. I never for a moment thought that *she* could be the scam. I never thought people would coldly and brutally kill a young woman just to make some money. *Who* would think that? Maybe some clever people would but I didn't, and I felt stupid and guilty as hell because I hadn't.

The woman, Alison Duncan, never turned up. I had told Maher that I had information (via Tommy Lynch and Leary) she had some sort of involvement with Lenny Grant. The way I saw it, she'd wound George up into believing they could work a number on the insurance, then when we'd dropped word through Harry that we knew what his little game was George must have panicked and phoned her. Alison had gone to the flat in her flower-girl outfit (knowing it would be watched) and shot him. That way she wouldn't have to share the money and she'd be rid of a man she must have considered a ball-and-chain. The way they'd behaved when I'd seen them in the street after the Lynch fight, I had the impression she didn't care much for old George. But then nobody did. He wasn't much of a man. Alison had shot him and wrapped his hand round the gun in a crude attempt to imitate suicide. It never works . . . the finger-prints end up all wrong; the burn marks, if they are present at all, are never in the right place. It simply never works. I suppose Alison would expect the cops to find the whole business an enigma, something they'd never solve. Police-men aren't generally great believers in coincidences and enigmas, though, and I think even if we'd never got that smudgy photograph of her leaving the building the file would have stayed open. Two enigmatic murders in one family are two more than the likes of Maher are able to leave go of lightly. The same must be true of me, in the light of events since then.

Tommy Lynch retired, I know, to a pub in the home counties. All boxers do that, then they get incredibly fat and no one can believe they ever punched their way out of a paper bag. Tommy could've gone on, fighting less good opponents for smaller purses, being interviewed by local radio breakfast programmes instead of Harry Carpenter for *Sportsnight*. He chose not to, and I think he made the right decision. Maher went and interviewed him about the Lenny Grant/Alison Duncan angle Leary had handed to me that morning in Duncan's dusty, abandoned gym. Tommy said it was true okay, and they should talk to Grant about it. The problem was, where was Grant?

He'd gone to ground in the States after leaving the fight game. There had always been something dodgy about Grant, he was always such an *elusive* figure. Always just off-stage, always the man whose name kept coming up. And yet he was the one with a completely clean record. I'd never met the man but I knew instinctively that there was something very wrong, perhaps that he was the one pulling strings on Alison. Anyway, the Yank coppers managed to follow Lenny Grant's trail of credit card purchases across the United States, then the last anyone saw of him was a suit bought in Las Vegas. The bill for a blue summer-weight men's suit, Maher told me, was the last worldly sighting of one Leonard Grant, wanted for questioning by the British police in the matter of two murders. My feeling was that when they found him Alison May Duncan wouldn't be far away . . . and Grant had to turn up sometime. He had to earn a living. We all do. George's insurance money never would go far, even if Lenny Grant had part of it. No, I was convinced Lenny would turn up. The surprise was *where* he surfaced.

New Year's Day 1983 was when we got a break.

Judy and me were staying in an hotel near Barcelona. You can't spend the winter in a motor-caravan, not even in Spain, and we discovered that if you could put up with being surrounded by 1910 to 1925-vintage English men and women, you could get a real deal on staying in what would be a fairly expensive tourist hotel during the summer. So we checked into the Tiempo, a concrete and glass joint ten miles north of Barcelona city. We were on the fifth floor with a concrete balcony overlooking a concrete plaza. After the concrete plaza was a concrete pavement and a concrete road, then sand, then the sea. Raw-boned old men played canasta with fat ladies for hour after hour in the hotel's painted lounge. The most it could lead to was a walk on one of the concrete strips outside, yet the old men and old women flirted remorselessly.

We stayed in our room and plotted which bar we would buy. We planned trips up and down the Spanish coast, visiting properties, judging and weighing prices and facilities. By Christmas we were ready to move on to a little place near Rosas.

On New Year's Day Denis phoned. After passing over the season's greetings and a lot of gossip he said, 'I bumped into your pal Detective Chief Superintendent Maher the other day. He still hasn't given up on that Duncan business, you know.'

'It doesn't surprise me,' I said.

'That's right, Jimmy, that's what I told him. I said, "It won't surprise old Jimmy you're still looking." '

'Well, Denis, you were right,' I said. 'It doesn't surprise me he's still looking for Grant.'

'No, no,' said Denis. 'You've got the wrong end of the stick. He's *found* Grant. Had a good old chat with him. He says Grant seems as clean as a whistle . . . very open, willing to admit he'd had an affair with that bird, Alison. Says he didn't have nothing to do with any murders, though, and he hasn't seen Alison since the night her stand-in was bumped off. Nor for several weeks before that. Maher is still looking for Alison Duncan.'

I lay on my bed and watched storm clouds rolling across the Mediterranean. From a few doors away I could hear the raucous cackle of a couple of old women sharing a joke. Judy was in the bathroom, I could hear the occasional light splash from her bathwater. My hand tensed upon the old-fashioned candlewick bedspread the Spanish hotel supplied.

'Did Maher seem convinced . . . just like that?' I asked.

'Well, he *said* he was, Jimmy. But he said you'd be interested, and to be sure to tell you all of it. It seems like Grant's a building project manager for some American company. He gave the hint that the project was run by the legit end of dirty money.'

'What sort of dirty money, Denis?'

'Yanks' dirty money. I suppose Maher was saying it was crime money . . . you know what he's like, Jimmy. Twenty minutes with Maher and you come out wondering if he's actually said anything at all. You know?'

I knew okay. Maher never said anything without having four other things in his mind as he said it.

'So what did Grant say that convinced Maher?'

'Well, I asked him that question too. He said, "Nothing much." . . . What do you make of the man?'

'He's devious.'

Judy came out of the bathroom. Getting a suntan during the summer had done her lovely legs no harm at all. I wanted the conversation to finish. I had other things in mind.

'He's devious, all right. Anyway, he said to tell you that Grant was a building project manager for a place called the

167

Juli Complex, a load of time-share villas in some dump down in the south of Spain.'

'*Where?*'

'The south of Spain. Aren't you near there? Maher says the fellow's living in a place called Cristo de Limpias and it's near Málaga and you're especially to know that he hasn't got any girlfriend. That's what Maher said.'

Judy sat beside me on the candlewick, dripping beads of bathwater and dabbing herself with a towel. I made her say 'hullo' to Denis, then when he'd rung off she said, 'What's all that about?'

'He was wishing me Happy New Year,' I said. 'Didn't he wish you?'

'He wished me,' she said. 'What else?'

'Oh, and he said Maher had had a few breaks looking for Lenny Grant.'

'And what's that to do with us? . . . move up a bit.'

'Oh nothing . . .' I said. 'It's nothing.'

'Good.'

We kissed. I said, 'Do you want to go way down south and check it out there? Málaga, that way.'

'No. I would like to buy the place in Rosas we saw.'

'Let's check Málaga. It's only a day's drive each way. Let's check it. We haven't been down there.'

'No.'

She pushed me back on the bed. Who was I to resist? Málaga could wait.

25

We spent a week in Málaga on that first occasion. Judy thought we were looking round the seaside villages in the area, *I* was trying to find a way of having a look at Lenny Grant without him having a look at me. I'd had his address from Denis on a second phone call – Maher *really* wanted me to find him – but the problem was Grant's villa was in an exposed position high above the town while the Juli Complex he was meant to be managing was still at the concrete-mixer-and-artist's-impression stage. The only way I could go there without being noticed would be to deliver a load of reinforcing rods. What's the Spanish for 'reinforcing rod'? I didn't have any fears about being spotted on the street by Grant, I'd put on twenty pounds, grown a beard and looked tanned enough to pass for a Spaniard. But I wanted to have a look at him. Really, I'd have liked to observe him for some length of time. I was convinced the woman had to be around somewhere.

Judy, who didn't even know Denis and myself had spoken about the place, came up with the answer.

'I might have found somewhere,' she said. We were eating lunch.

'What somewhere?'

'You know that little place we were in yesterday, Cristo de Limpias? Well, there's a bar there owned by an Englishman. Daniel . . . Daniel . . . oh I can't remember. Anyway Martínez says he's sure this man would sell out. . . .' She paused to crunch at some green salad. 'If he was given the right offer. Martínez says he's fed up with it.'

'Martínez?'

'No.' She laughed. 'This Daniel person. Martínez says Cristo de whatsisname is on the verge of being built up and there's always call for an English bar in a place like that. It could be a good one.'

'Mm.'

'Let's just go there and have a drink,' said Judy. 'Let's go this evening.'

I wiped my mouth with a table-napkin. Suddenly my appetite had gone. I looked through the plate-glass window of the restaurant. A boy was revving a scooter at the kerb-side. One of the waiters went out to remonstrate with him. Great columns of cloud swirled around the sky above us.

Judy said, 'I think we shouldn't keep taking wine with the lunch. You're getting fat, Jimmy.'

'Of course,' I said. I poured myself another glass of wine and drank it anyway. I pulled at my beard, stared at the table . . . did anything rather than look at her for a few seconds. When I did look there was an amused light in her blue eyes. She arched an eyebrow.

'Out with it.'

'I've got something to tell you,' I said. 'Something rather important.'

I won't say she took it well. I won't even say she took it calmly. The meal didn't last much longer, but in the time it did last I think the waiters must have learned enough colloquial English to hold their own on the terraces of Millwall Football Club. Judy was not amused. At first she believed I'd only brought her to Spain because I'd thought I might find Alison there. Then when I finally convinced her I'd only found out from Denis a few days ago that Grant was in Cristo she was all for flying to London and 'having it out' with Maher, the source of the information.

It's a long way from Málaga to Barcelona. We made the entire journey in silence. We spent the next few days in our concrete hotel in silence too. I was reduced to attending the tea-dances with the ancient nut-brown Britons (thank God I can't dance) and watching imported videos. As far as my wife was concerned I was in the doghouse.

At the end of the second week in January she finally spoke.

'I've been on the phone to Martínez,' she said. 'I've asked him to make an offer on Bill's Bar.'

'What's Bill's Bar?'

'Don't come the old soldier, Jimmy. Bill's Bar is the one in Cristo de Limpias, you bastard.'

'I thought his name was Daniel,' I said.

'Would you expect the Marquess of Anglesey to be pulling pints in all the pubs with his name?'

I didn't answer. Some days later she made it clear that I was expected to follow up the Alison May Duncan thing one last time and forget it. I didn't know really if Judy had changed her mind because I needed to lay this ghost or if it was because she'd been a policewoman for so long. I never had the nerve to ask, not then nor since. It would be pushing my luck a bit too far. She did say once that she thought Bill's Bar was a very good commercial proposition in an area which was being developed and she didn't see why she should miss out on that because of some crackpot idea I had. 'You're not the Lone Ranger, you know, Jimmy,' she said, which was true. I don't know about the 'commercial proposition' business, though. It sounded like she was looking for a way to let me off the hook. I never asked so I never found out. Marriages are full of things like that.

26

I've never needed to change my name or conceal myself.
With the peculiar logic common in Spain the owner of Bill's
Bar is generally referred to as Bill. Grant didn't use the bar
much – he came in once or twice – and I had no fear of
being recognised. I'd never met him in England and anyway
my appearance had changed considerably since I'd left. The
only thing to connect 'Bill' with Jimmy Jenner was the limp.
Lots of men have limps. I just settled down and went about
my business in the little town. In another part of town Grant
went about his. When the Juli Complex was built he began
to supervise work on some similar place ten miles away. He
kept his house in Cristo, though.

Months went past, then a Christmas, then another Christmas. I'd obviously got it wrong about Mister Grant. He
was obviously legit. I met him in the usual course of things;
we were, after all, English residents in a small town and I
did, after all, sell him his wholesale English beer for his
villa. Judy and I just ran our lives and ran our bar and
didn't let ourselves be worried by the reason we'd first come
here. We treated it as a mistake . . . what the hell. People
settle in places for all sorts of reasons. I was just the guy
who runs Bill's Bar. Even Judy called me Bill in the bar.

Our lives were *orderly*.

It was nearly two months ago I spotted Grant with the
girl. He has a convertible VW Golf and I saw them driving
through town. Grant waved 'hullo'. I waved back. The girl
next to him was a dark, dark brunette, almost black-haired.
As far as I could see her sitting in the car she had a good
figure. She was wearing a black cotton dress and it showed

her tan to good effect. Her skin was lightly oiled, I saw. She had a red scarf over her shoulders and she was holding it against the wind with her fingertips. As they passed I caught a glint of sunshine from her dark glasses, a flash of a smile aimed at Grant and then they were past me. I pushed through the tourist crowds till I reached the harbour. The Golf was parked there. Grant and his girlfriend in black were taking a table under the sunshade of the most expensive restaurant in Cristo. Blue shade dappled them. The waiter gave them a smarmy smile and bowed. The table had imported English roses on it, blood red and intense against the brilliant white of the starched table cloth. I stepped back into a grocer's doorway and watched them for ten minutes or so. I would have stayed longer but my leg began to hurt. I walked back to my bar and phoned Maher's office. He wasn't there but I spoke to his sergeant (a new one – Robson is now an Inspector).

'My name's Jenner. James Jenner. I want Mister Maher to send me a photograph of a woman called Alison May Clark. He has the address.'

The sergeant had never heard of me and I had to give him the message several times to make sure he'd got it right. I'd made the call from our living room above the bar. Downstairs I could hear the hubbub of my countrymen getting drunk. The day was as hot as hell. Sweat drenched my clothes. I leaned against the wall and felt the cold return of my shirt-back as it pressed against my skin. I felt slightly sick. Judy wasn't around and I wished she was. My heart was beating fast, my forehead was cold and clammy. I went downstairs and pushed myself to the bar. I wanted to drink to obliterate my feelings. I drank but it didn't work. I drank way into the evening when the barman decided enough was enough, even if I was the boss, and he phoned Judy in her friend's house in Málaga and she came home and they both carried me upstairs.

The woman was Alison May Duncan (née Clark) okay. There was no mistaking her from the photograph once it came, dyed hair or no dyed hair, phony American accent or no phony American accent. It was Alison. Grant even brought her to my bar a few times. I stood arm's length away from her and poured them both brandies. I wasn't afraid of being found out. I was Bill MacDonald of Bill's Bar. As far as everyone in Cristo was concerned I was a nice young Englishman with a limp who'd done well in business and come to Spain to half-retire and run a little bar for fun and profit. My wife was just a wife – nearly invisible to outsiders. She was just a young woman with good legs she browned on the balcony above our bar late in the afternoons. If the Spaniards thought of me at all it was as 'the man of the woman with the legs'. So Lenny Grant brought Alison into the bar and introduced me to her as 'Bill' and her to me as 'Susan'. Judy didn't associate Grant's girlfriend with Alison and I didn't encourage her to . . . after all this was two years later and the woman with Grant was a brunette called Susan. I didn't let anyone apart from Maher know of my interest in the woman.

I was biding my time. I wanted her and Lenny Grant. I wanted them for personal reasons. For the poor stupid girl I'd let down. I wanted them for my own pride. I wanted them for justice . . . that's the word. Justice.

At first my plan had been to sit on them until the Spaniards changed their extradition laws. The Spanish would have to before they could join the EEC. The plan was that when the Spanish changed the law I'd pop back to London and lay an information with Maher. It was important not to lay the information too early because the birds would get wind of it and fly . . . to Brazil or Peru or somewhere.

That was the first plan. Then Maher phoned and said he had it from a source in the Home Office that the 'fugitive' legislation in Spain wasn't going to be retrospective.

'He's not sure,' said Maher, 'but that's what he's heard.'

Well, I decided not to take a chance. I began to plan a fishing trip.

27

I have a friend called Jesus.

Don't we all.

My one, though, is called Jesús María (fifteen other saints'
names) Muela and is a used car dealer in Málaga. I suppose
the used car business is doing well in Málaga, because Jesus
has an American car with air-conditioning, a big house
also with air-conditioning on the green hill above Cristo de
Limpias and a fishing boat with no air-conditioning but a
pair of Perkins diesels, a marine radio, a cassette player, a
lavatory and three bunks. It's a pleasure fishing boat and
he keeps it in the marina, not all scruffed up on the beach
like real fishermen would. Real fishermen wouldn't have
the bunks or the stereo cassette player either. Jesús likes
his home comforts.

Jesús is a friend to me indeed. He lets me use his boat
to fish with. I know damn all about fishing but I like driving
his boat, so I take it out 'fishing' whenever I can get someone
to go with me. I need a companion because I find it hard
to get around the boat quickly. When I found out how the
governments of Britain and Spain were letting me down I
planned my fishing trip. I bought a map of the whole coast
down to Gib. It looks like it's two hours with the twin
Perkins running flat out. Then I waited till my delivery boy
was off sick next (it happens about twice a week) and casu-
ally dropped a line at Len Grant.

'Here's your Bass. It's cans this time . . . yeah, I'm sorry
but the supplier says there's trouble getting the bottled stuff
down here. He says we should live in Barcelona . . . ha ha
ha. Good joke, eh? By the way, I've got the loan of a little

fishing boat, how about a trip out next week with your good lady and mine? The tuna will have started running.'

I wouldn't know a tuna from a mackerel. Jesús wouldn't know either from a '77 Buick, and he *owns* the fishing boat. I do know that when the tuna come into the Med they come through the Straits of Gibraltar, I mean how else would they do it, via Suez? I reckoned I could con my passengers into letting me float them south in a boat with a couple of fishing rods in their hands. I would then go to the head (I know all the technical terms . . . it's a lavvy on a boat) and come out with a gun and a phrase something like, 'Okay sweetheart, now you get yours. Shaddup and drive this bus to Gib.' American accent non-compulsory.

First of all I sent Judy to London. That wasn't difficult. Her mother is old and broken-down and I know Judy feels guilty about making her sister take all the responsibility. The sister has a life to lead as well. I'm normally pretty negative about Judy disappearing to her mother's house for weeks on end. When I suggested it this time she leaped at the idea.

The next problem was what to do about a boat-hand. At first I thought of asking José, my useless noisy cleaner for my bar. He spent all the time he was in the bar tippling my brandy and boasting about the old days when he'd been a fisherman. I'd no doubt he could handle the boat, but it wasn't fair to let him put himself in danger without volunteering for it. And since I couldn't tell him the story, he couldn't volunteer. Also, I thought the Spanish government wouldn't take too kindly to him abducting foreigners. No, the problem was to find someone who'd do for the job but also it had to be someone who stood to gain from the job. Maher would be perfect, but I couldn't see the Commissioner's Office being very enthusiastic about one of their Detective Chief Superintendents going in for a touch of DIY extradition. That would be taking the spirit of private enterprise a little too far. I couldn't even *tell* Maher, for to tell him would be to compromise him. If I were to be able to pull this trick off, I'd need someone . . . but who?

The day after Judy set out to drive to London I flew there from Málaga. It doesn't take long. I was back the next morning.

28

The first place I went to in London was Northcliffe House, the offices of the *Daily Mail*. The big city was dusty and noisy and confusing, even though I'd once felt it was my own. On this visit I felt like a hick. Red buses boomed past me. Taxis whirled at junctions and raced off in the direction they'd come from. People pushed past me, rude, hurried. The ticket man at the tube station affected not to understand what I was asking for. Eventually I emerged at Chancery Lane Station and made my way down to the *Daily Mail* building feeling like a nervous foreigner.

'He doesn't work for us,' said the polite young man who saw me – even getting as far as him was a triumph of persistence – 'he's a freelancer. He doesn't work for anyone on a regular basis. He just comes up with his own stories.'

'Can't you give me his number? He knows me . . . he's written a couple of pieces on me.'

'I'm sorry.' The young journalist was dressed very formally, the way people would have dressed for his job in the nineteen-fifties. He pulled at the neat knot of his neat red tie and said, 'I'm sorry,' again.

'I've come all the way from Spain,' I said. 'I've come especially to see him and give him a story.'

'Wouldn't one of our staffers do if you just want to sell a story?'

I shook my head.

'Well, I can't help you, Mister . . . Mister. . . .'

'Jenner. I told the bloke in the commissionaire's outfit.'

The neatly dressed young man walked me down to the

door. His adam's apple bobbed as he walked, as if gravity had some effect on it.

'If you'll leave your number I'll have him call if he contacts us,' he said. It was by way of a consolation. I could see now, in the foyer, that they must get nutters in there all day every day asking for someone to sell a scoop to. Who could blame him for rejecting me?

'I haven't booked into an hotel yet,' I said. 'Here's my number in Spain. If he comes give it to him, would you?' He smiled like a young father confessor doling out indulgences, then handed me over to the commissionaire.

I walked a couple of blocks, then headed north to Holborn again, then north again through Gray's Inn. I went into the library in Theobalds Road and began looking through the Brands in the phone book. It was hopeless. Then I picked up the Yellow Pages. There it was . . . *Brand, E. F., Freelance Journalist*. Address and phone number. I went down to the entrance of the library. A young woman was arguing with a porter about whether she was entitled to leave her pram there. I pushed past them and called Brand on the public phone. He answered first time it rang.

My other visit in London was to Leytonstone. I went to see Wilkins. I got little Charlie. He greeted me like a long-lost brother.

'Jimmy, oh Jimmy. It's good to see you. Well, we were only talking about you a few days ago, weren't we, boys?'

Two men I'd never seen before nodded agreement. We were in Wilkins' shabby plush room behind the bar of the Canary Club. Little Charlie indicated the door and the two men headed for it.

'Beer, Jimmy?'

I shook my head.

'Where's Wilkins?' I said.

'Semi-retired. I'm looking after the front-of-shop part of Mr Wilkins' business operations for him now. Any favours he owes you, consider I owe you.'

'Okay. It's a bit difficult.' I hesitated. Little Charlie hoisted himself onto the sofa and made himself comfortable.

179

I went on, 'I need a shooter. You know I'm running a club near Málaga now?'

He nodded. Well, I'd promoted my bar to a club . . . what was it to him?

'I have a problem with some heavy old villains moving in on me.' I said. 'So I want to keep a shooter, a pistol, in the place. I don't want anyone shooting at me and me trying to beat them off with a load of bread . . . you know? Even Spanish bread, Charlie. In the ordinary way a bar or club owner would approach the cops for a licence and then go and buy a gun. But I'm a foreigner. It's not allowed.'

He screwed up his tiny face, staring at me.

'If I could come by such an item, how would you get it into Spain?'

'Break it down and put it in my false leg,' I said. 'If I went back by ferry to France and then by train I won't have to go through any of those screening devices they have in airports.'

He thought for a while longer and then stood.

'Have a chair,' he said. 'I've got to make a phone call and there's no way I could do it from here. . . . Er, Jimmy?'

'Yes?'

'You won't be reckless with a shooter if I get you one, will you?'

I shook my head.

'Scout's honour, Charlie.'

'Okay. Shout outside if you want a beer or a sandwich or anything. I'm off for about twenty minutes, okay?'

I waited. He was back in ten.

'I've got a geezer coming down from Gerona to give you one. It's a bit old fashioned, a Smith and Wesson. The sort the army used to have. Ever shot one?'

'Yes. I've shot one.'

'Right. Well this guy's doing me a favour. You don't need to pay him for the shooter but it wouldn't hurt anyone if you gave him a good drink for his trouble. He's driving halfway across Spain, he says.'

'Down it.'

'Yeah. That's right. Down it. Did you get your beer? Come on out to the bar then . . . you know Mr Wilkins is going to be *so* choked he's missed you.'

I think if he'd been big enough he would've put his arm round my shoulders. As it was Charlie had to content himself with holding the door open with an excess of politeness.

29

I'm on my balcony, trying to compose some note for my wife. I know I won't do it.

It's 7.30 a.m. now. I can hear José crashing about downstairs. Every morning he wakes Judy and me while he breaks the glasses he's supposed to be cleaning and shovels the dirt around from the centre of the bar to less obvious corners. I've never had the heart to sack him. Whenever he cleans Judy and me just lie up here giggling while he crashes around, then he stops and we know he's drinking the cheap brandy I leave out specially rather than have him going behind the counter and beating up my Rémy Martin. I sat on my chair on the balcony thinking of the day ahead and thinking of all the things I should write to my wife. Then there was a banging on the shuttered door and an Englishman yelling.

'Jenner . . . hey! Jenner.'

I looked over the balcony and could see Brand standing in front of my shutters, hammering his bare fist on the door part of the shutters. I heard José go and open it.

'I want to speak to Mister Jenner,' Brand said. 'He's expecting me.'

'We no open now. Lunchertime, efen-ing only opening this bar. You go there to café. Good café.'

'I want to speak to Mister Jenner,' Brand repeated patiently.

'No. No Jenner.'

Leaning over the railings I could see José's hand outside the shutter. The finger was waggling back and forth, metronome-style, to emphasise the 'no'.

'You go over there.' The hand pointed at the café.

'Let him in!' I yelled. I finished my beer. Beer for break-fast. It was cold, blond Spanish beer and the bottle dribbled it onto my journal. I went downstairs and told José to pull up all the shutters, then to take off home. Brand slid onto a barstool and I pulled the cap off a beer for him. A couple of flies circled lazily over the counter. José heaved the shutters half-up, then eyed the bottle of cheap brandy. I threw him the Rémy Martin and said, 'Go home to your wife. I'll see you tomorrow.'

I didn't believe I would though.

Brand smiled.

'An old friend?' he said. It was a stupid question and I ignored it. Brand was nervous. I'd kept him hanging around my bar for three days. When I'd phoned him in London I'd told him he was on to a scoop. A real one. I'd told him Alison May Clark was not dead and buried in Kensal Green but alive and well and living in Málaga. I'd lied about where she was (I mean Málaga versus Cristo) because I hadn't wanted him ferreting around Cristo on his own account.

I didn't like Brand but I could use him. He was a small, tubby Englishman with balding sandy hair and – since he'd been in Spain – a peeling red face. He'd decided when he'd come out that the designer-jeans-and-cheesecloth-shirt was not for him. He was right. He'd have looked like a sweaty cheddar cheese on a denim plinth. Brand went instead for the colonial Africa look: jackets from Alkit with padded triangles clipped in the shoulders, white cotton trousers, heavy, English-leather Jesus-boots. He looked as if he was into Evelyn Waugh in a big way. He stuck out in Cristo like a sore thumb, and I only hoped Lenny and Alison hadn't seen him in my bar.

'Have a beer, Eric. You and me should start the day by drinking some beer. This is going to be a very unconventional day. I'm going fishing. We're going fishing. We're going to be fishers of men.'

Brand grinned and drank his second beer. Shafts of light fell through the half-raised shutters. The area around our feet was flooded with light, but from the waist up we were striped men of darkness.

'Thanks, Jenner.'

A trickle of sweat ran down his brow. I could see dampness under the arms of his linen jacket. Sweat adhered to his peeling, unshaven cheeks, then slipped slowly on to his cracked-skin thick lips.

'Today the story happens for you, Eric. Today you have included yourself on a scoop. A real one.'

He nodded. He was pleased. This was why he'd come.

'Good. What's the plan?'

I slapped his shoulder. 'Drink your beer, kid. Leave the planning to me.'

He swigged the beer and stared at me. I must have looked mad.

'Whereabouts in Málaga are they?' he said.

'Nowhere . . . you're sweating. Are you hot?'

Brand nodded that he was hot. I don't think it was the heat which made him sweat, though. I think it was that he was near the lode. He wanted it. He was compulsive, like an old lady on the machines in Las Vegas.

Past Brand, in the street, I saw a kid walk by with his mongrel. Or rather I saw the mongrel and I saw the kid's skinny legs. I walked over to the shuttered door and pushed it wide. I wanted some air. The street was white, then heavy dark shadows fell where the buildings sheltered each other. I was in shadow, brilliantly lit after the darkness of my bar, but still in shadow. The kid with the dog turned and waved but I didn't recognise him. He was standing in the white light by then and I couldn't see him properly. Sweat trickled down my neck, down my back. I could taste the salt on my upper lip. And the day had only just begun. Some men smoked cigarettes down at the corner. Wisps of smoke lifted above them, fat old palms surrounded them, like a crowd. A blue-white sky beat down on us. A couple of black birds strutted up the road, then flapped away as a dusty car passed.

I turned to look across to the café. The waiter nodded to me and I nodded back. A tall man splashed olive oil along a loaf and held it up to eat. He was deep in the darkness of the café and I could only see his head and torso. His face was olive-coloured and pain-featured. All the men in the bar were workers who were breaking-off for breakfast. The tourists came at lunchtime. Since my bar was an English

184

bar I never bothered to open before lunch. The English spent better but they didn't get up in the morning to do it. Right at that moment I felt very warm towards the Spaniards.

I went back in and said to Brand, 'If you want coffee we'll have to go across the way.' I was half hoping he'd say 'yes.'

'I'm okay,' he replied.

'I've got a coffee machine but it takes twenty minutes to start up, so I'm not starting it just for us.'

He didn't answer. I leaned under the bar counter and came up with a plastic bag.

'What do you make of these?' I said.

He smacked his lips and stared at the counter.

'Army issue Smith and Wesson pistol, a bit on the veteran side of vintage. The other one's a sawn-off twelve-bore. Yes?'

He looked tense. I hadn't mentioned guns before. I hadn't even told him exactly *how* Alison Clark and Len Grant were going to be arrested. Brand thought he was just here to watch and then he could sell his world exclusive to the highest bidder. The guns changed all that. He laughed a cracked laugh.

'I thought you'd become just a bar-owner now. What d'you need all the ironmongery for?'

'To go fishing with,' I said. I stood behind the counter with my hand on the guns. 'Don't worry, I'm not going to shoot you.'

Brand made his cracked laugh again.

'So what's it all about? I thought you said they were going to be arrested. Where? What do the guns have to do with it?' he said.

'The police will do the arresting in Gibraltar. The guns are to go fishing with. I'm going fishing and you're coming along to steer the boat.'

Brand smacked his lips and shook his head over his drink. I said nothing. I rang an English number from a wall-phone behind the bar. There was no answer. I rang another.

'Denis? Hi. It's Jimmy here. Listen, Denis, I need you to do something. I want you to wait till about one o'clock your time, that's two ours. Then I want you to give my pal

185

Maher a ring and tell him he needs to have someone
standing by at Gibraltar quayside for a fishing boat registered A-alpha A-alpha C-charlie-eight from Málaga, Spain.
Tell him it'll have Alison Duncan, Lenny Grant, a journalist
called Brand and me on board. No, Brand's just coming for
the ride and the story. He's nothing to do with the other
two. I don't think Maher will be very surprised when you
call him . . . and Denis! Don't call him any earlier, please.
Think of this as the last instalment of the favour I did you
over the Zorba business.'

Brand put his beer down when I rang off. He closed his
eyes and said, 'Are you serious?' Then opened them and
stared at me while I put the guns back in the plastic bag
and back under the counter. I didn't answer him.

'How do you know I won't tell the Spaniards?' he said.
'How do you know I don't have enough of a story already
anyway?'

'I don't,' I said. 'But this is a real cracker, a real scoop.
And I think you're not able to pass it up. I reckon you'll
want to be on the quay in Gib making notes and snapping
away with your Kodak Instamatic. I don't think any
journalist could turn it down.'

'Say we're caught?'

'So what? I'm the one with the guns, I'm the one
abducting them. You're just a third party. All you have to
do is keep your nerve and steer the boat.'

He sighed. He put his beer glass on my counter and I
topped another bottle for him. He poured it, sighed and
said, 'You're right. I'll do it. You knew I would, eh? Is that
why you asked me out here? A staffer couldn't take a chance
on being caught, eh?'

I didn't answer. He knew that was why. He looked at his
hands and then at me.

'What makes you think I'll keep my nerve?'

I tapped the counter above the guns.

'These. You let me down and I'll shoot you before I shoot
them. You'll be more frightened of me than them. I've got
the guns.'

Brand eased himself off his stool.

'I think I believe you,' he said. He was right to believe
me. By that stage I'd have done anything rather than give

186

up my targets. I was using Brand because I needed a crewman. It was the only way I could think of finding someone who had as much to gain as me by transporting Alison and Lenny. I reckoned his greed for a story that was a real winner would lead him to do almost anything. It was a gamble bringing him in but one I had to take.

30

I went down to the marina at eleven. Row on row of expensive marine hardware seemed to be used only as lilos for pretty girls. 'Here's a daybed, darling. It only cost two hundred and fifty thousand quid and takes four men to run it.' Jesús's boat was down with the more modest ones, though even the modest ones have more in common with a floating motorhome than a trawler. I threw my bag on the deck, then eased myself down off the floating wooden pier. Anyone else would've jumped. I can't. The boat's handrail was burning hot, it stung my fingers. The sky above was clear and the sun was approaching its noon position . . . right over the top of my neck. In half an hour the girls lying on the expensive boats would have to go in or be fried.

I pulled open the door to the saloon. A wave of hot air burst out, beating my face. My shirt was wet with sweat. I could feel salt on my lips. Inside even the soft furnishings were hot to touch. The varnish on the wood felt sticky; maybe it was my imagination. Maybe it was my hand that was sticky. I opened up the hatch to the Perkins, checked their oil, ran my hand along the tappet covers . . . I don't know why. I just needed to touch them. I'd checked the oil only last night. I tucked the sawn-off behind the fire extinguisher, in a corner behind where the hatch opened. A quick look round would never find it, but anything more than that would. Then I went up to the lavatory and stuck the Smith and Wesson under the little wash basin with some gaffer tape. It wasn't very secure and if the sea got rough someone would find themselves with a shooter between their feet while they were having a pony. I didn't expect to be at sea for long enough to let things get rough, weatherwise.

I went back into the little saloon and lay on one of Jesús's bunks. The heat was stifling. I dozed a while. Then I heard someone on deck.

'Jimmy. Hey, Jimmy.'

It was Brand. He sat in the wheelman's chair and oozed sweat and fear.

'You okay?' I said.

He nodded.

'I'm okay. I've brought a friend.' He pulled a bottle of scotch from his bag. 'Want some?'

I said, 'Yes', took the bottle from him and threw it in the drink. He looked as if he was about to cry.

'I'll buy you another in Gibraltar. Have you checked out of your hotel?'

'Yes.'

'Paid?'

'It was a package. I told you. The bloke in the hotel thought I was mad. Haven't you even got some beer?'

'No. There's a kettle down there.' I pointed with my thumb at the saloon. 'Make us some tea.'

'Tea?'

'That's right, *tea*. Then familiarise yourself with the boat. Then come back up here and help me cast off.'

'What about our passengers?' He scratched absently at some peeling skin on his arm.

'We're picking them up at the end of the mole. On the way I have to pick up fuel. I have a gun behind the fire extinguisher in the engine compartment and another taped under the handbasin down there . . . if you should need them.'

Brand's piggy blue eyes narrowed.

'You don't want me to handle a gun, do you? I've never done it.'

'No I don't. I want you to know where they are. Then I want you to put the kettle on. Then I want you to come up here and help me put the sun-canopy up before we catch fire or melt, then I want you to cast off the ropes that are tying us to that wooden pier. Got it?'

Brand went below. I turned the key next to the steering

189

wheel so that the plugs would warm in the Perkins, then after a few seconds I turned the key right round so that it spun the self-starter. The engines whined but didn't catch. I left it.

Brand came up and began to pull at one end of the canopy. The blue canvas was bleached by the sun, the metal stays had been pitted by salt, then painted. We heaved at the canopy until it covered the entire after-part of the boat. Then I went and turned the engine key again.

'Trouble?' said Brand.

'No trouble.'

The engines whirred when I turned the key to 'start', then they caught. I revved them for a few seconds, then let the roar die to a throaty burbling sound. Blue diesel smoke drifted lazily across the marina. White light glinted on the little wavelets, then on to my eyes. It was like looking into a glistening white kaleidoscope. Black silhouette figures moved among the tied-up boats. Brand let the ropes go, then jumped back aboard and I gunned the engines and headed for the service pier.

Lenny Grant and Alison Duncan were waiting on the end of the mole, as we had arranged. Alison was wearing a white linen 'sackdress', dark glasses and a white hat tied down with a scarf. Her dyed dark hair peeped from under the hat and scarf. Her lips were full and strong, with red lipstick. I couldn't see her eyes. Grant was sitting on a wicker hamper. He was wearing a short sleeve blue Breton fisherman's shirt and crisp white trousers. He looked as if Harrods or Simpsons had kitted him out for fishing. I never knew Grant in London. I only spoke to him on the phone in Florida the once. Though he was in his late thirties he was tall and dark and well muscled. He looked ten years younger. I don't know how he was in his London days, but the man I picked up on the mole didn't look like a former boxing manager, not if boxing managers were like George Duncan. Leonard Grant looked like he was a retired male model. He had a good tan and a strong jawline and an easy, graceful way of moving. He stood from the hamper and waved to us. I waved back and drew the boat alongside.

Ve bobbed a little in the swell. Grant handed the hamper
ɔ Brand.

'Okay?' He grinned. 'Be careful with that. It has our
upper in it.'

Brand helped Alison onto the boat. He stared at her so
much I was sure he'd give the game away.

'Be careful with her, too,' Grant said, and leaped aboard.
Ie was very jolly and helped Brand take the hamper down
ɔ the saloon.

'No Judy?' Alison said.

'No.' I shook my head and opened up the engines to take
is clear of the concrete mole and into open sea. 'She had
ɔ go to England for a couple of days.'

'Oh.'

'She'll be there tonight when we get back, I should think.'

Alison nodded. She sat back and clasped her hands on
ɪer lap. I looked at them and thought about the girl under
ɪe arch in Shoreditch. These were the hands that had done
ɪ, I was sure. I'd looked at her hands like that sometimes
n my bar. Grant and Brand came out to the deck area
ɪgain, both carrying bottles of beer and tipping them up to
ɪrink.

'I told him you didn't want any,' said Brand.

'Okay.'

'Where's the fishing gear?' said Grant.

'Down the side of the boat in that long box. I can't get
t out on my own. . . . I have a bad leg. You know.'

He nodded. A pleasant breeze was running against us
ɪnd we were having to lift our voices a little to speak clearly.
ʃhe canvas of the deck canopy flapped above my head.
ɪpray bounced over the bows.

'I'm going out until we get in the stream, about fifteen
miles,' I called. 'Then we'll get the canopy rolled back and
ɡet the fishing gear out. We'll turn towards the Straits and
ɪoll upstream for a couple of hours, then downstream until
ve get back to our starting point. That's what the guy who
ɔwns the boat told me to do. He knows all about fish.'

ɪrant nodded agreement, then he climbed forward and
ɪeaned over the bow.

'How long?' he called back.

I turned the boat into the swell and set the engines a little faster.

'Three hours this direction. We'll start trolling before four. Then a couple of hours upstream, one back. That's three clear hours fishing. You see the basket of mackerel? That's our bait. We should be all over fishing by seven thirty, then I reckon three hours back to Cristo maximum . . . more like two running with this swell. Should get back for ten.' The finest sea spray flew around Grant's body and he waved and grinned again to show he'd heard.

Oh God, I thought. I hope he doesn't know about fishing because I don't and Jesús was no good to me on that score at all. He just offered me the use of as many Abba tapes as I wanted and kept bothering me about was I bringing a girl. I bought the mackerel from a fishing smack on the way out to the mole. The fishermen nearly burst a gut laughing when I said 'Tonno' for the fish we wanted. How long are you staying out there for? they asked, with tears streaming down from their eyes and all their backs red-raw and sore because of all the slapping that had been going on. 'A few hours,' I'd said, and they'd all laughed as if they couldn't bear it, the Englishman was so stupid, and one called out 'Six weeks is more like it,' and they all laughed again. They sold me the mackerel and they took my money anyway, with that special Spanish philanthropy they often reserve for foreigners . . . especially Englishmen.

Alison settled down to stare at her nails and be beautiful in one of the fishing chairs. I gave Brand the wheel because I thought it would keep him out of trouble, then I went down and lay on a bunk which was both too short and too narrow for me. I wanted to relax. After half an hour Alison came down and sat on the bunk opposite. She took her scarf and hat and sunglasses off and shook her head so that her hair swung. I could have gone to the lav and pulled the gun then but I wanted to be out of Spanish waters first.

'Well, Bill,' she said, 'how are you?'

'Not bad,' I said. I was lying on my back as best I could, holding a pulp novel above my head as if I were reading it.

'What took our Judy to England?'

'Family stuff, you know. It's boring. Have you been to England, Susan?'

She shook her head.

'I met Len when he was working back home . . . in the States, I mean. And I guess I just,' she laughed nervously, 'well, you know . . . fell in love. So I followed him here.'

'What a nice story,' I said.

She smiled appreciatively. Her American accent was fake, of course, but then so many Americans give themselves fake English accents that she was just bad enough to be accepted by anyone who didn't know. I knew. I hated her. I thought about the guns again. Alison ran her hands down her shins, then caught me watching her.

'Like them?' she said.

I nodded.

'Lenny says they're my best asset. What do you think?' She turned herself a little one way, then a little the other, showing me both profiles.

'I like your face,' I said. 'I've always thought your face is your best asset, Susan. A woman's face is her fortune. Where would she be without it?'

'Where indeed?' she said, and smiled. The hamper was between us, facing her. She flapped the lid open and began to rummage inside.

'Glass of wine? Sandwich? I think Lenny's even put some real caviar in here . . . *doesn't* he know how to live?'

I looked forward. Facing the bow the cabin had two oblong windows made of thick glass. They were screwed into place like portholes, with big brass clips holding them down. I could see Len Grant through one window, at least I could see his feet. I could see the basket of mackerel-bait through the other window. A seagull landed on the basket's edge and peered into it. Suddenly the bird flopped forward into the basket. Len leaned down and grinned at us through the glass. He pulled the dead bird out of the basket and held it against the window. The head had been smashed with a bullet through the eye. The bird's blood smeared the glass. I could see Len was holding a stubby revolver in his other hand. He dropped the bird and slapped his hand against the glass to steady himself. He grinned again and mouthed some words, waving the little gun.

I turned and looked at Alison. She had leaned back from

193

the hamper and was holding a sandwich in one hand and
the brother of Grant's revolver in the other.

'I think he's asking you to put your hands up, Jimmy
Jenner,' she said. She bit into her sandwich slowly and
voluptuously. Alison had all the time in the world. I was
struck by that thought, and the image of my time running
out. I'd misjudged them.

'Why?' I said.

'Oh . . . I think he'd like you to do it for lots of reasons.'
She brushed a crumb from her lips with the mouth of her
gun-barrel. 'But you can put them down. I don't like a lot
of drama. Just tell me where your gun is, Jimmy, and that'll
be enough for me.'

The American accent had gone completely.

She shook her head slowly and sighed. The bright light
from the oblong windows fell across her face, first one side
then the other. She fired the pistol into my leg. I cried out
and lay back on the bunk.

'Give me your gun or I'll fire it into your real leg,' she
said.

'It's tucked behind the fire-extinguisher just in that hatch.
I'll fetch it if you want.'

She waved the nose of the little gun.

'You sit right where you are. I just wanted to know where
it is.'

I sat right where I was. The room stank from the
explosion. I tried to move my ankle a little but it stayed
stuck.

'You've shot it through the bloody joint,' I said. I was
raising my voice, I knew. I'd been deafened by the pistol
shot.

'Bring him out!' Grant yelled.

I climbed the three steps to the deck with difficulty, drag-
ging my false leg like a pirate with one of those stiff wooden
things they wear in pantomimes. Grant was at the wheel.
He swung the boat from south south east to due east.

'Where are we going?' I said. 'Libya?'

'*We're* going back to Spain,' said Alison. '*You* and your
boat are going to sink, way out there at sea.'

'Doesn't that leave a little problem about getting back?'

'Not for us.' Alison said. 'We're being met. You'll have to make your own arrangements.'

Brand was standing in the doorway where Grant had shoved him. His eyes widened in horror.

'You're going to make us swim?'

Alison shook her head.

'No. Of course not. Someone might find you. We're going to shoot you and sink your boat. We'll weight your bodies down, of course.' There was a kindly edge to her voice.

Brand's eyes got even wider. His face twisted, whether in anger or horror I'll never know. He began to lift his hands and take a step forward. Grant shot him twice, once in the chest, once in the head. A big weal of torn flesh appeared, red and glistening above Brand's eye and along his temple. White bone showed through the red tear for a second. Brand clutched his hands to the hole in his shirt front. It was a little hole and it didn't bleed much.

'My God,' he said slowly. 'My God. I'm shot.'

He lifted one hand away from the hole and looked at the smear of his own blood on his palm before using the hand to steady himself on the door jamb.

'I'm shot,' he said again. 'They've bloody shot me.'

He raised his eyes accusingly to mine, then Grant shot him again, high up on the sternum, and this time he did give out a little bow-tie of splashed blood onto his shirt before toppling heavily back into the little cabin. The door swung back and forth, banging lightly on its brass catch with each wave, before one heavier wave made it snap shut on Brand's body.

An hour later we were still heading due east. I was at the wheel. Grant was sitting on the bow drinking from a green glass beer bottle and sweating in the sun. Every now and then he looked out through a pair of binoculars. Alison sat in one of the fishing chairs covering me with a gun.

'Doesn't your hand get tired?'

'You'd better hope it doesn't, Jimmy Jenner, because when I get too tired to hold the gun on you I'll shoot you.'

I looked round at her. She had the sunglasses on again and she looked as if she would shoot me. She was going to eventually, anyway. Her sunglasses were the deepest black. I couldn't see Alison's eyes behind them. I could only see the reflection of the horizon, a flash of sunlight as her head from time to time moved. Waves ran against the dark glass but didn't break. Then my bearded face appeared, and she was about to speak but checked herself.

'How did you recognise me?' I said. 'I've never advertised who I am in Cristo. We'd never even met.'

She shook her head slowly and pointed the gun at me.

'Look where you're going, Jenner. I don't want to bump into anything.'

I looked forward. Apart from the bow, Grant and the horizon there was nothing to see. I kept staring forward though. I didn't want to give her an excuse to shoot me. She'd be doing that soon enough.

Suddenly I was aware of Alison close by my side, almost as an animal presence. She spoke softly.

'George was going broke. That . . . well, Wilkins was driving him out of the business. It was Wilkins' revenge for George taking me. Ha! *Taking* me. I *ran* to him. How could I live with a pig like Wilkins?'

I didn't answer. The steady throb of the diesels ran through us, the sea thudded on the hull. The sun burned my eyes. My head was on the throttles. She was quiet for a long time, then she said, 'We decided one of us had to die, then we could claim the insurance. George had a lot of money for insurance . . . you know about all that of course. What you don't know is that we scoured England for a detective as stupid as you. Then I remembered reading a piece in a newspaper about a bloke with one arm and one leg or something who reckoned he was a detective. When I looked it up I came up with you . . . then George remembered he'd already known you.'

'I've got both arms,' I said, still looking forward. She was touching my shoulder now, and the gun was digging into my side; not hard, just enough to remind me it was there.

'Yes, you have. Well you turned out a bit cleverer than George and I thought, Jenner. Not *much* cleverer, but enough to be a nuisance.'

'But how did you know it was me in Cristo?'

'I *recognised* you. That very first day I saw you here in

196

Cristo, hiding in the shop door while Lenny and I were having lunch . . . what do you think you are, invisible? I thought it was you the minute I saw you. Lenny phoned your wholesaler to check. He asked when Mister Jenner's order was due. The clerk said Mister Jenner's order would be along as usual, but if he wanted to make a supplementary he'd take it now. Simple. One Englishman speaking bad Spanish sounds the same as another.'

I nodded. The wholesaler had my real name because I always paid by cheque. Grant was leaning over the bow now. I didn't know why, then I heard him retch.

'Your friend's not all that well,' I said.

Alison leaned on me, her cotton-covered breast touching my bare arm, her face close to mine, her gun sticking into my ribs. She said nothing. I could see nothing except the reflection of my own face in her glasses. I saw myself reflected in her. I shivered.

'Who was the girl I drove from Saffron to London?' The words stuck in my throat. I leaned away from her so I was against the safety rail. I could see Lenny-the-bad-sailor chundering over the bow and every now and then a waft of it would come back on the spray. Alison leaned close again and stuck the gun in my ribs again, so hard this time it hurt. She held her face up to mine as if she would be kissed.

'Don't think of jumping overboard, Jenner. I would just as well shoot you in the water as on the boat. I don't care.'

'What about our bodies?' I said. 'Won't you have some explaining to do?'

She laughed. I could feel her breath on my face as she did it. Her spit landed on my lips.

'We're not going back. You two and your boat are going down and you're never going to be found.'

'Don't tell me,' I said, 'someone's waiting ahead with another boat . . . your brother?'

She laughed again.

'A *fast* boat.' She smiled a red-lipsticked smile and ran her tongue over her pearly teeth. 'And yes you're right, my brother's waiting for us.'

'And we get to die, just like before with the girl. Where *was* she from?'

'She was just some prossie. George found her at Kings

197

Cross. Gave her a story about standing-in as his wife for a couple of days as part of a con he was working. He gave her a few quid.'

'A few quid?'

'A hundred.'

The boat pitched forward and Lenny retched.

'Is that all she was worth? What am *I* worth?'

'A lot of trouble, that's what you're worth. Why all the fuss about some bloody prossie? Did she do a trick for you, Jenner? Is that it?'

This time she stuck the gun even harder into my ribs and leaned up and kissed me on the lips. I wanted to slap her, to spit in her face.

'Did you get the idea for the face job in Smithfield?' I said against her mouth. She kissed me hard again and said, 'How clever you are. How very clever.' She stepped back. 'You've got it all worked out. I killed George too. I hadn't left England at all before then. I didn't for months even after I shot him. Then I went out to Baltimore and set up with Lenny and my brother, but Lenny had to come here. Some very important people he was involved with in America thought he should come. So he came and I've waited till now. I wasn't sure at all about coming back to Europe. . . . Things were pretty good for me as they were.' She laughed again. 'Did you know *he* never knew who you were at all?' she added as an afterthought. 'And all the time you were waiting for me.'

'Not quite. I didn't know you'd turn up. You didn't *need* Lenny. You had George's money, right?'

'*My* money. *I* died for it. What would a good looking woman like me be doing squandering over three hundred thousand on *him*? No, once he told me Harry had phoned to say the police thought he was up to something with me I thought, 'George, my love, you are just going to *have* to go'.

'The suicide wasn't very convincing.'

'I was improvising.' She held the gun up to my head. 'Boom! Like that I went, then I wrapped his hand round the gun. It was the best I could do. He had all the money ready. He thought I was going to run away with him. The suicide was crude but it didn't matter. No one was looking

198

for George's dead wife except you because you were the only one who knew the girl I dumped in Shoreditch wasn't me. We always knew the person we chose for that part might catch on but we reckoned if we used a really rotten, stupid, useless detective it wouldn't matter. No one would take any notice of him.'

Grant retched again, then yelled, 'Boat!' gagging as he did. Alison said, 'So far I've been right,' then turned to look at the boat. 'It's him okay!' she said. 'Looks like the end of the line for you, Jenner.'

She held up the gun and kept it on me for a long time. I could see her finger moving on the trigger. I could hear Lenny retching in the bow. The boat he'd seen was a couple of miles in front of us.

'What will you do about *him*? I said. 'What'll happen when you need to unload him?'

She smiled.

'Why do you think we're all out here?' She said. 'We've realised all our assets, Lenny and me, ready to skip once we'd disposed of you. I don't want to skip with Lenny, though. I've found a nice fellow in Baltimore. An Italian. He'll suit me fine. I thought you and Lenny could die in a shoot-out . . . isn't that a good one?'

'I suppose it is. When will he find out?'

She squeezed the trigger lightly again and said 'Boom!', then she let the gun drop a little.

'He'll find out soon enough.'

She was right. The other boat was coming up fast. Its engines had been started and it was running straight towards us. It was a pleasure fishing boat like ours, only bigger. I could see the dark figure of a man at the wheel as the boat approached. A little closer yet and I could see he was wearing a dark, peaked cap, dark glasses and denim clothes. He swung his boat so that it came to rest beam-on about a hundred yards ahead. Alison stepped back from me and grinned. I knew if I was to try anything it would have to be now. My mouth was dry and my stomach was churning. Alison waved at the dark figure in the other boat and he waved back.

'Come *on*,' she said. 'Get a move on, Jenner.'

I saw a figure move behind the one at the wheel of the

other boat. I couldn't see Grant but I could hear him. I knew that I had to move now but I had no idea what I should do. Alison was too far away for me to jump her. She'd shoot me first. We came closer yet to the other boat. She took her eye off me a second and waved at it again. There was a flash behind the man at the wheel and Alison staggered backwards. She hit the bulkhead and dropped her gun. I bent over her and picked it up. Her neck had been torn open. Blood seeped into the sackdress. Her eyes were open and she was conscious. Air bubbled the tear in her neck every time she breathed. There was a film of sweat on her brow.

I stood up with the gun and shut off the engines. Lenny turned and began to advance. He clearly hadn't heard the shot or seen the flash from the other boat. I pointed my gun at him.

'Stand off, mate. And I bet I'm a better shot than you.'

He kept his gun on me. The other boat approached.

'Jenner! You all right?' a voice called. I didn't recognise it. 'Jenner!'

'Drop the gun now, Lenny,' I said. 'Don't be a hero. You haven't killed anyone.'

Lenny dropped the gun. It slid off the deck and into the sea.

'I'm okay!' I shouted. 'Who are you?'

The boat drew alongside. The man in the denim and the dark glasses threw a rope over. A very small man took his place at the wheel and the man in denim jumped over to me once we'd drawn the boats close together.

Wilkins.

'Is she dead?' he said.

'Not yet.'

He went over and kicked Alison.

'Cow. She soon will be. I won't waste another bullet on her. I'll have him and we'll be on our way.'

I sat heavily in the wheelman's chair.

'Hang on.' I said, 'What are *you* doing here?'

'I wanted that cow more than you did, Jenner. She set me up. And you can't go wandering round London asking for bent shooters without anyone asking themselves "What does he want that for?" With you there could only be one real answer, I reckoned, so little Charlie and me came out here.' Alison groaned and Wilkins scowled. Lenny was sitting on the roof of the cabin, gazing at us in open-mouthed astonishment. Wilkins talked about his trip to Cristo. He was chuckling all the time except when Alison groaned. Then he looked angry. Eventually she groaned one time too many for him and he pulled a little revolver from his pocket and leaned over her and shot her in the head. The bullet went in the middle of the brow and fragments from the back of her skull ricocheted around the steering well like pieces of shrapnel. She didn't lie still though. Her legs and arms flapped on and on, like newly-landed fish. Wilkins had to talk with the soft sound of the flaps and thuds Alison's body made on the deck.

'We followed her brother down to the Marina early this morning, but he spotted us so we had to grab him. He told us about the meeting out here. They'd had you taped for ages, Jimmy. This fishing trip you planned was a godsend. You walked into it.'

Lenny shook his head. He didn't moan or cry or retch or anything now though and I didn't blame him. Wilkins wasn't going to waste much time on them.

'Got a beer, Charlie?' he yelled. Charlie lobbed a can over. 'Open it for us,' said Wilkins. I did and got soaked in foamy beer. He thought it was hilarious.

'Why did the brother tell you?' I asked. 'Why not keep his mouth shut?'

'He did at first. We encouraged him to open it. Now let's get down to business. My plan is we shoot this slag and sink the boat. Then you come back with us and say the boat sank somewhere else. That way everybody's happy . . . eh?'

I shook my head. 'Wait a minute,' I said. I went below and brought up my guns.

'Get in the cabin,' I called to Grant. He climbed past us without a word and went below. I locked the cabin door on him.

'I'm taking him back.'

Wilkins shook his head now and he wasn't laughing any more.

'No.'

'You'll have to shoot me as well, because I have a gun

201

and I don't intend to see you shoot him and do nothing,' I said. 'If you kill him you'll have to kill me.'

'How do you know I won't?'

I threw the sawn-off and the Smith and Wesson over the side. I pushed Alison's revolver into Wilkins' fat stomach.

'Because I like and trust you,' I said. 'Because you've saved my life. Because I'm going to keep your name out of any reports of what's happened here. Grant won't say anything because life in an English prison wouldn't be too good for him if he did, I guess. *I* won't say anything. All you've done here is to shoot a woman who was about to shoot me. I'm willing to say I had a struggle and overcame her. Don't you think that's better?'

He took my wrist and pulled my gun out of his fat stomach. Wilkins' grey eyes glared at me. His face darkened. I thought he would shoot me and then go on for Grant. I was sure he would. We'd just watched him murder Alison. Wilkins raised his gun to my face and then turned away quickly. He climbed back into his own boat.

'Can you hear me, Grant?' he called.

A muffled 'yes' came from the cabin.

'You do exactly what this man says. Any messing about and I'll be back for you. And I won't bring a shooter. I won't need one.'

I freed the line and little Charlie gunned the big motors. The sea churned behind them.

'No one owes any favours now, Jenner,' Wilkins called. 'We're all square. You just remember that.'

When they'd gone Grant carried Brand's body from the cabin. 'How do you know I won't tell?' he said. 'I saw what he did to her and the cops'll love it. I'll tell all right.'

'You won't have to,' I said. 'I will.' I locked him in the cabin again.

I eased the engines up and set the course to a few degrees west of south west, which I reckoned would take us to Gibraltar. Then I sat back in the wheelman's chair and shivered, even though the sun was high in the sky. I was still shivering when I reached the Rock.